RICHARD A. YATES
British Columbia Institute of Technology

TERESA BEREZNICKI-KOROL
Northern Alberta Institute of Technology

TREVOR CLARKE
Northern Alberta Institute of Technology

YO-BTE-786

Business Law
in Canada

ALBERTA VERSION

FIFTH EDITION

Prentice Hall Canada Inc., Scarborough, Ontario

Canadian Cataloguing in Publication Data

Yates, Richard
        Business law in Canada

Alberta version.

ISBN 0-13-082448-8

1. Commercial law — Canada. I. Bereznicki-Korol, Teresa, 1957– .
II. Clarke, Trevor, 1952– . III. Title.

KE919.Y376 1999   346.7107   C98-931279-8
KF889.3.Y372 1999

Prentice-Hall, Inc., Upper Saddle River, New Jersey
Prentice-Hall International (UK) Limited, London
Prentice-Hall of Australia, Pty. Limited, Sydney
Prentice-Hall Hispanoamericana, S.A., Mexico City
Prentice-Hall of India Private Limited, New Delhi
Prentice-Hall of Japan, Inc., Tokyo
Simon & Schuster Southeast Asia Private Limited, Singapore
Editora Prentice-Hall do Brasil, Ltda., Rio de Janeiro

ISBN 0-13-082448-8

Publisher: Patrick Ferrier
Acquisitions Editor: Mike Ryan
Developmental Editor: Amber Wallace
Senior Marketing Manager: Ann Byford
Production Editor: Nicole Mellow
Copy Editor: Allyson Latta
Production Coordinator: Jane Schell
Permissions/Photo Research: Susan Wallace-Cox
Cover Design: Mary Opper/Monica Kompter
Cover Image: Dan Paul
Page Layout: Steve Eby

   3 4 5   HP   03 02 01 00

Printed and bound in the United States.

BRIEF TABLE OF CONTENTS

Preface   x

PART 1
Introduction   1

CHAPTER 1
Introduction to the Legal System   2

PART 2
The Fundamentals   81

CHAPTER 2
The Law of Torts   82

CHAPTER 3
Formation of Contracts   124

CHAPTER 4
Formation of Contracts
(continued)   150

CHAPTER 5
Factors Affecting the Contractual
Relationship   175

CHAPTER 6
The End of the Contractual
Relationship   204

PART 3
Commercial Transactions   233

CHAPTER 7
Sales and Consumer Protection   234

CHAPTER 8
Priority of Creditors   270

CHAPTER 9
Negotiable Instruments   305

PART 4
Employment and Agency   339

CHAPTER 10
Employment   340

CHAPTER 11
Agency   381

PART 5
Business Organizations   407

CHAPTER 12
Sole Proprietorship and
Partnership   408

CHAPTER 13
Corporations   429

PART 6
Property   473

CHAPTER 14
Personal and Intellectual Property
and Insurance   474

CHAPTER 15
Real Property   511

PART 7
Dealing with Government   547

CHAPTER 16
Environmental Law and the Regulation
of Canadian Business   548

APPENDIX: CASE STUDIES

INDEX

TABLE OF CONTENTS

Preface   x

PART 1
Introduction   1

CHAPTER 1
Introduction to the Legal System   2

What Is Law?   2
  Philosophical Basis of Law   2
  From Theory to Practice   3
  A Workable Definition   4
Origins of the Law   4
  Civil Law   5
  Common Law   5
Sources of Law   7
  Common Law   7
  Equity   8
  Statutes   9
Canada's Constitution and the Charter of Rights
and Freedoms   10
  Confederation   10
  Constitution and Division of Powers   11
  Statutes   15
  Protection of Rights and Freedoms   17
  The Canadian Bill of Rights   17
  Human Rights Legislation   18
  Charter of Rights and Freedoms   22
  Charter Provisions   26
  The Importance of the Changes   29
The Courts and Procedures Before Them   30
  The Process of Civil Litigation   34
  Procedure Before Alberta's Provincial Court,
  Civil Division   36
  Procedure Before Alberta's Court of Queen's
  Bench   39
  The Trial   41
  Judgment and Its Enforcement   41
  Judicial Remedies Before Judgment
  (in Alberta)   45

Limitation Periods   46
  Alternatives to Court Action   47
Summary   49
Questions   49
Cases   51
Legislation   52
Weblinks   53
References for Part 1   54
Appendix 1-1   55
Appendix 1-2   58
Appendix 1-3   68
Appendix 1-4   72
Video Case   80   **CBC**

PART 2
The Fundamentals   81

CHAPTER 2
The Law of Torts   82

Introduction   83
Development of Tort Law   83
Intentional Torts   85
  Assault and Battery   85
  Trespass to Land   87
  False Imprisonment   89
  Private Nuisance   91
  Defamation   92
Negligence   96
  The Reasonable Person Test   97
  Determining the Existence of a Duty   98
  Standard of Conduct   101
  Res Ipsa Loquitur   102
  Special Situations   103
  Negligent Misstatement and the Liability of
  Professionals   107
  Experts and Children   109
  Material Loss   111
  Causation   111
  Defenses   112

Strict Liability 115
Other Business Torts 117
Summary 118
Questions 119
Cases 120
Legislation 122
Weblinks 122

CHAPTER 3
Formation of Contracts 124

The Contractual Relationship 125
Ingredients of a Contract 125
Terms and Definitions 125
Consensus 127
Offer 128
Acceptance 134
Consideration 139
Adequacy of Consideration 141
Existing Duty 141
Past Consideration 142
Paying Less to Satisfy a Debt 142
Settlement Out of Court 143
Illegal Consideration 143
Request for Services 143
Promissory Estoppel 144
Sealed Documents 145
Summary 145
Questions 146
Cases 147
Weblinks 149

CHAPTER 4
Formation of Contracts (continued) 150

Capacity 151
Infants 151
Insanity and Drunkenness 155
Native Indians 157
Corporations 157
Aliens 158
Married Women 158
Unions 158

Bankrupts 159
Legality 159
Illegal Contracts 159
Contracts Against Public Policy 160
Intention 163
Form of the Contract 165
Statute of Frauds 166
Summary 171
Questions 171
Cases 172
Legislation 174
Weblinks 174

CHAPTER 5
Factors Affecting the Contractual Relationship 175

Mistake 176
Shared Mistake 177
Misunderstanding 178
One-Sided Mistake 179
Rules of Interpretation 181
Misrepresentation 183
Allegation of Fact 184
Silence or Non-disclosure 185
False Statement 185
Statement Must Be Inducement 186
As a Term of the Contract 186
Innocent Misrepresentation 186
Fraudulent Misrepresentation 187
Negligent Misrepresentation 188
Duress and Undue Influence 189
Duress 189
Undue Influence 190
Unconscionable Transactions 191
Privity of Contract and Assignment 193
Privity 193
Exceptions—Apparent and Real 193
Assignment 195
Negotiable Instruments 199
Summary 199
Questions 200
Cases 201
Weblinks 203

CHAPTER 6
The End of the Contractual Relationship 204

Performance 205
    Substantial Performance 205
    Tender of Performance 205
    Independent Obligations 207
Breach 208
    Conditions and Warranties 208
    Exemption Clauses 209
    Fundamental Breach 210
    Repudiation 212
Discharge by Agreement 213
    Contractual Terms 215
Frustration 216
    Circumstances Not Constituting Frustration 218
    Effect of Frustration 219
    Legislation 219
Remedies for Breach of Contract 220
    Rescission and Rectification 220
    Remedies Provided in Contract 221
    Damages 222
    Limitations on Recoverable Damages 223
    Equitable Remedies 224
Summary 227
Questions 227
Cases 229
Legislation 231
Weblinks 231
References for Part 2 231
Video Case 232 **CBC**

PART 3
Commercial Transactions 233

CHAPTER 7
Sales and Consumer Protection 234

The Sale of Goods 235
    The *Sale of Goods Act* 235
    Title and Risk 238
    Rights and Obligations of the Parties 242
    Title 243

Description 244
    Fitness and Quality 245
    Sample 246
    Other Implied Terms 247
    Remedies on Default 247
Consumer Protection Legislation 249
    Responsibility for Goods Sold 251
    Unacceptable Business Practices 254
    Control of Specific Businesses 257
    Loan Transactions 258
    Debt Collection Processes 259
    Consumer Service Bodies 260
    Federal Legislation 261
Summary 264
Questions 265
Cases 266
Legislation 268
Weblinks 269

CHAPTER 8
Priority of Creditors 270

Methods of Securing Debt 271
    Personal Property 272
    Legislation 274
    Floating Charges 282
    Bulk Sales 283
    Other Legislation 284
Guarantees 285
    Rights and Obligations of the Parties 286
Builders' Liens 287
Bankruptcy 292
    Priority Among Creditors 295
Summary 298
Questions 299
Cases 300
Legislation 302
Weblinks 303
Appendix 8-1 304

CHAPTER 9
Negotiable Instruments 305

Negotiability 307
    Essential Characteristics 307

Historical Context 308
Types of Negotiable Instruments 309
    Bills of Exchange 309
    Cheques 311
    Promissory Notes 313
Negotiation 314
    Requirements for Negotiability 315
Rights and Obligations of the Parties 318
    Holder in Due Course 318
    Other Holders 323
    Payees 325
    Endorsers 325
    The Drawee 327
Consumer Bills and Notes 328
Letters of Credit 329
Summary 332
Questions 332
Cases 334
Legislation 336
Weblinks 336
References for Part 3 336
Video Case 337 CBC

PART 4
Employment and Agency 339

CHAPTER 10
Employment 340

What Is Employment? 341
The Law of Master and Servant 344
    Termination 345
    Liability of Employer 351
    Legislation 352
    Other Legislation 362
Collective Bargaining 362
    Organization of Employees 364
    Bargaining 367
    Contract Terms 369
    Strikes and Lockouts 370
    Picketing 371
    Public Sector and Essential Services 373
    Union Organization 374
Summary 374

Questions 375
Cases 376
Legislation 379
Weblinks 379

CHAPTER 11
Agency 381

The Agency Relationship 382
    Formation by Contract 382
    Formation Without a Contract 383
Authority of Agents 383
    Actual Authority 384
    Apparent Authority 384
    Ratification 386
    Agency by Necessity 387
The Rights and Responsibilities of the Parties 388
    The Agent's Duties 388
    Duties of Principal 393
    Undisclosed Principals 393
    The Third Party 396
    Liability for Agent's Tortious Conduct 397
    Termination of Agency 398
    Enduring Powers of Attorney 399
    Specialized Agency Relationships 400
Summary 401
Questions 401
Cases 402
Legislation 404
Weblinks 405
References for Part 4 405
Video Case 406 CBC

PART 5
Business Organizations 407

CHAPTER 12
Sole Proprietorship and Partnership 408

Types of Business Organization 409
The Sole Proprietorship 409
    Government Regulations 409
Partnership 411
    Legislation 411

Creation of the Partnership   411
The Partner as an Agent   415
Vicarious Liability   416
Unlimited Liability   416
Registration   417
Rights and Obligations of the Parties   418
Advantages of Partnership   419
Dissolution of a Partnership   420
Distribution of Assets and Liabilities   421
Limited Partnerships   422
Summary   424
Questions   424
Cases   425
Legislation   428
Weblinks   428

CHAPTER 13
Corporations   429

The Process of Incorporation   430
Other Incorporated Bodies   432
Separate Legal Entity   432
Capacity   435
The Role of Agents   435
Funding   436
Par-Value Versus No-Par-Value Shares   436
Special Rights and Restrictions   437
Borrowing   438
Non-Distributing and Distributing
Corporations   439
Corporate Officers   440
Directors (Managers)   440
Officers and Senior Executives   444
Shareholders   446
Pros and Cons of Incorporation   451
Advantages   451
Disadvantages   454
Termination of the Corporation   455
Summary   456
Questions   457
Cases   458
Legislation   460
Weblinks   460
References for Part 5   461
Appendix 13-1   462
Video Case   472   CBC

PART 6
Property   473

CHAPTER 14
Personal and Intellectual Property
and Insurance   474

Introduction   475
Personal Property   476
Bailment   477
Intellectual Property   481
Copyright   482
Patents   487
Trademarks   489
Industrial Designs   492
Confidential Information   492
Insurance   497
Property Insurance   498
Business Interruption Insurance   499
Life and Health Insurance   499
Liability Insurance   500
Insurable Interest   500
Other Features   501
Bonding   505
Summary   506
Questions   506
Cases   507
Legislation   509
Weblinks   510

CHAPTER 15
Real Property   511

Legal Interests in Land   512
Real Property   512
Interest in Land   514
Lesser Interests in Land   516
Tenancy in Common and Joint Tenancy   519
Other Interests in Land   519
Transfer and Registration of Interest in
Land   520
Condominium Legislation   521
The Landlord/Tenant Relationship   522
Leasehold Estates   522
Types of Tenancies   524
Rights and Obligations of the Parties   525

Remedies 528
Residential Tenancies 530
Mortgages 533
Mortgages at Common Law 533
Remedies Upon Default 536
Summary 541
Questions 541
Cases 542
Legislation 544
Weblinks 545
References for Part 6 545
Video Case 546 **CBC**

PART 7
Dealing with Government 547

CHAPTER 16
Environmental Law and the
Regulation of Canadian Business 548

Regulatory Role of Government 549
The Protection of the Environment 550
Common Law 550
Statutory Law 551

Administrative Law 560
Challenging Government Regulations 561
The Authority of the Decision Maker 561
Statutory Interpretation 562
Rules of Natural Justice 564
Judicial Review 568
Methods of Judicial Review 570
Privative Clauses 573
Other Remedies 575
Summary 576
Questions 577
Cases 577
Legislation 580
Weblinks 581
References for Part 7 581
Video Case 582 **CBC**

APPENDIX: CASE STUDIES

TABLE OF STATUTES

TABLE OF CASES

INDEX

PREFACE

PREFACE TO THE ALBERTA VERSION

Earlier editions of *Business Law in Canada* were designed for a national audience; consequently, reference to provincial variations and specific provincial statutes was generally not possible. Much of business law, however, falls within the jurisdiction of the provincial governments. An Alberta-specific text can thus proceed beyond general principles of law and describe the case law and particular statutory provisions that regulate business in this province. The aim of the *Alberta Version* is to focus on how the law *works* in Alberta.

Throughout the text, case decisions arising from Alberta's courts have been inserted.

Chapter 1 has been significantly expanded. Alberta's human rights legislation is examined in some detail and excerpts from the Act are appended. A major addition is in the area of civil procedure. Students are guided, step-by-step, and shown how to sue in the Provincial Court, Civil Division. Samples of forms used to commence a suit and forms used to enforce a judgment are included. An overview of civil procedure before the superior trial court (the Court of Queen's Bench) is also presented.

Additions to Chapter 2 include specific references to statutes such as the *Defamation Act* and *Innkeepers Act* of Alberta. The unique treatment of trespassers under the *Occupiers' Liability Act* is explained. Recent case law impacting professional liability is described.

The law of contracts does not differ significantly from province to province. Most of the changes to Chapters 3–6 therefore involve references to specific provincial legislation or to court decisions involving the interpretation of Alberta law.

Chapter 7 deals with the law relating to sales and consumer protection. The relevant sections of the Alberta *Sale of Goods Act* (and other related legislation) are cited, as are cases relating to that legislation. The law of consumer protection is very province specific, so the *Alberta Version* of the text contains significant revisions, based upon the relevant legislation (and proposed legislation).

Many of the topics dealing with the priority of creditors fall within the jurisdiction of provincial governments. Chapter 8 therefore emphasizes significant Alberta legislation, such as the *Personal Property Security Act*, the *Civil Enforcement Act*, the *Guarantees Acknowledgment Act*, and the *Builders' Lien Act*. The law of negotiable instruments, on the other hand, is a federal matter. Accordingly, there are very few changes to Chapter 9 in the *Alberta Version*.

Part 4, dealing with Employment and Agency law, has been expanded through an examination of Alberta's *Employment Standards Code, Labour Relations Code,* and the *Human Rights, Citizenship and Multiculturalism Act*. The rights of workers and obligations of employers are thus detailed.

Part 5 deals with the different forms of business organizations. The amendments to Chapter 12 (Sole Proprietorship and Partnership) involve references to the appropriate Alberta legislation, such as the *Partnership Act*. Chapter 13

(Corporations) has, however, been significantly revised such that the focus is on the Alberta *Business Corporations Act* and all related provincial legislation. The articles of incorporation approach has been emphasized. Forms used to incorporate a business in Alberta have been included as an appendix to the chapter.

Chapter 14 deals largely with areas regulated by the federal government. Changes are largely restricted to the area of insurance law. Cases examining the consequences of misrepresentation by the insured are described together with the specific provisions of the *Insurance Act*.

Real property law varies significantly from province to province. Alberta's Torrens system of land identification and the Land Titles System are both examined. Tenancy law, as shaped by the *Residential Tenancies Act*, and the specific rights and obligations of landlords and tenants are described. Alberta's mortgage and foreclosure law is unique; the protections enjoyed by mortgagors in this province are illuminated.

Finally, in Chapter 16, how judicial review operates in Alberta is described. Also, the *Environmental Protection and Enhancement Act* is reviewed. The procedures followed to secure approvals are detailed.

We trust that students shall find the *Alberta Version* to be more specific than texts written for a national audience. We have striven to develop a text that illustrates how the law works in Alberta, and that clarifies the rights and obligations of parties doing business in this province.

Acknowledgments

We wish to thank all those who have made sacrifices to enable us to develop this *Alberta Version*, especially our colleagues at NAIT and our families. We thank our Dean, Terry Cooke, for having faith in us and providing us with this opportunity. We are deeply indebted to Kelley Tees, a former student, whose dedication, ambitious efforts, and sense of humour encouraged and enabled us to complete this *Alberta Version* in the tight time constraints we faced. We would also like to thank our reviewers for their comments: Jasmine Sihra, Grande Prairie Regional College; Karen J. Reschke, Grant MacEwen Community College; and Mitchell Wise, Southern Alberta Institute of Technology.

Teresa Bereznicki-Korol, BA, LLB
Trevor Clarke, BSc, MBA, LLB

The Northern Alberta Institute Of Technology School Of Business

THE NORTHERN ALBERTA
INSTITUTE OF TECHNOLOGY

The School of Business at The Northern Alberta Institute of Technology offers six distinct diploma programs and one certificate program preparing students for careers in various aspects of the business enterprise. The types of businesses served are vast and varied—from the world of banking and high finance to customer service. The school provides students with the flexibility to complete their studies in both full-time and part-time formats and in both of Canada's official languages. The four flagship programs of Accounting, Finance, Marketing, and Management use a common first-year course package followed by a second year of required core courses with electives in specialty areas. The school has strong linkages to professional associations and articulation agreements with several universities for post-diploma degree study.

PREFACE TO THE FIFTH EDITION

Business Law in Canada was originally designed to meet the needs of a one-term business law course when two-term courses were the norm. Since then the one-term course has become standard. Over the years I have tried not only to keep pace with changes in the law and developments in the legal system but also to respond to the changing role of law courses in business schools as well. This new edition reflects those concerns.

Changes To The Fifth Edition

The text has been divided into sections comprising related topics to increase the flexibility of the book and facilitate dealing with subjects in different ways. Part 1, Introduction, provides an introduction to the legal system. Chapters 2 to 6 are grouped in Part 2, The Fundamentals, and should be studied together and in order. The other sections can be covered in whatever order the instructor feels is best for the class. The chapter dealing with negotiable instruments (formerly Chapter 13) has become Chapter 9 in Part 3, Commercial Transactions, and this has resulted in corresponding changes in the numbering of subsequent chapters. Variation within the sections is more difficult, although some chapters may be deleted if desired. Chapter 16 could be dealt with after Chapter 1. While it may not be possible to cover all 16 chapters during a term, the total number of chapters has been retained in order to allow the instructor to give a course a particular slant or orientation. What is needed in a business law course for accountants is a little different than in a course for students in marketing, real estate or banking. It is expected that some chapters will be skipped, such as those relating to property, negotiable instruments or dealing with government agencies. But it is better for an instructor to choose to delete material rather than have to find additional materials for a text that is not comprehensive enough.

Instructors have indicated that the case summaries introducing each chapter are valuable, so I have added more of them to illustrate legal problems and set the tone for the discussion. The issues that had been included at the end of each chapter have been eliminated from this edition. Those who still wish to make use of them can find them in the *Instructor's Resource Manual.* The practice of identifying points in the text that correspond to cases discussed in the companion *Business Law in Canada Casebook* prepared by D'Anne Davis has been continued by printing the icon (shown in the margin here) at the appropriate location.

Many areas of the text have been expanded, clarified or modified. Additions or expansions have been made in areas such as human rights, especially in the field of employment; negligence and professional liability; letters of credit in negotiable instruments; and the liability of directors, officers and promoters of corporations. Topics such as mistake, privity, fundamental breach of contract, personal property security legislation, and bailment have been simplified and clarified. The discussion of environmental law has been updated, as has the discussion of intellectual property (which now includes a brief examination of some of the problems associated with the Internet).

Another very significant addition is an Appendix consisting of a series of business-oriented legal problems that can be used in a case study format. I have spent a considerable amount of time in recent years examining how to better integrate the study of business law into the business school curriculum. I have found that a consideration of how business people deal with their legal problems is an important area that is normally not covered in business law texts. These cases are designed to provide exercises for students that raise both legal and business issues that must be dealt with together. A link is thus provided between the examination of legal issues and principles and a general business education. I hope that their inclusion will enhance student presentations and stimulate others to develop more case studies of a similar nature.

My examination of what should be covered in a business law course and how it ought to be taught culminated in a report I wrote for my colleagues. I have included a version of that report in the *Instructor's Resource Manual.* I hope it may be useful and stimulate further discussion.

I am gratified at the reception *Business Law in Canada* has received over the years, and have tried to limit changes to those that contribute to the usefulness of the text or are a needed response to a changing legal environment. The following pedagogical elements have been added to the fitth edition:

- *Case Synopses.* These brief summaries of cases, which have been highlighted throughout each chapter, are intended to support the legal rule, principle or concept being discussed.

- *Weblinks.* Addresses for helpful Internet sites can be found at the end of each chapter in the Weblinks section.

- *References.* Additional business law resources are listed at the end of each Part.

- *Full-color photographs.* Throughout each chapter, key concepts and applications are illustrated with full-color photographs.

- *CBC Video Cases.* Eight end-of-Part video cases, based on episodes of the CBC series *Venture, The National,* and *Undercurrents,* illustrate key concepts in the book using real-world examples.

Finally, I would like to remind all those who use this text that it is designed as a tool for learning business law and not as an authoritative source for legal advice. When faced with a specific legal problem the reader is advised to seek the assistance of a lawyer.

Supplements

Business Law in Canada, Fifth Edition, is accompanied by a complete supplements package:

- *Instructor's Resource Manual with Video Guide* (013-080882-2). This contains summaries of each chapter, answers to the questions found at the end of each chapter, solutions to the cases and their full citations, issues from the fourth edition, and notes to assist in the use of both the Case Studies in the appendix and the CBC Video Cases. Also included is the report of my research into the teaching of business law in the U.S. and Canada.

- *Test Item File* (013-080886-5). This contains over 1600 multiple choice, true/false, and short essay questions. Each question is rated by level of difficulty and includes a text page reference. It is available in both printed and electronic format.

- *Prentice Hall Custom Test* (013-080889-X). This merges the *Test Item File* with a powerful software package in the Windows platform. With the *Custom Test*'s user-friendly, test-creating abilities, you can create tailor-made, error-free tests quickly and easily. The *Custom Test* allows you to create an exam, administer it traditionally or online, and evaluate and track students' results—all with the click of a mouse.

- *Transparency Resource Package* (013-080891-1). Over 250 transparency masters highlighting key concepts featured in the text are available in printed format and electronically in PowerPoint 4.0.

- *Prentice Hall Canada/CBC Video Library.* Prentice Hall Canada and the CBC have worked together to bring you eight segments from the CBC series *Venture, The National,* and *Undercurrents.* Designed specifically to complement the text, this case collection is an excellent tool for bringing students in contact with the world outside the classroom. These programs have extremely high production values and have been chosen to relate directly to chapter content. Contact your Prentice Hall Canada sales representative for details.

- *Student Study Guide and Workbook* (013-080884-9). This provides an overview of each chapter, including review questions with answers and where to find the answers in the text. It also contains a glossary of legal terms and guidelines for conducting legal research and briefing a law report.

- *Companion Website.* For a multitude of practice questions, key terms and concepts, Weblinks to related sites, Newsgroups, CBC video updates, a syllabus builder and more, check out the *Business Law in Canada*, fifth edition, Companion Website at **www.prenticehall.ca/yates**.

Also Available:
- *Business Law in Canada Casebook* by D'Anne Davis (013-080597-1).

Acknowledgments

I wish to thank all those who have contributed suggestions for this new edition, especially my colleagues at BCIT and Simon Fraser University. I would also like to thank the instructors who have patiently reviewed the text, including Douglas H. Beatty, Lambton College; Teresa Bereznicki-Korol, NAIT; Douglas J. Clarke, Ryerson Polytechnical University; William A. Fitzgerald, Mohawk College; Lloyd Phillipps, Niagara College; Brian Shaughnessy, Humber College; Greg Sheehan, Sheridan College; Gerry Stephenson, Okanagan University College; and Paul Tambeau, Conestoga College; and the staff at Prentice Hall Canada, particularly Amber Wallace and the copy editor, Rodney Rawlings, whose encouragement and patience helped immensely in getting the work of revision done.

Dedication

I would like to dedicate this edition to my wife, Ruth. Without her support, encouragement and contribution to the creation and development of this book and its supplements, they simply would not have come to be.

Richard A. Yates, LLB, MBA

Introduction

The study of business law involves the examination of duties and obligations associated with specialized legal relationships as well as the rights and duties created by various types of commercial transactions. Before we can look at those specialized areas it is necessary to understand the legal system, its institutions and the principles upon which those specialized transactions and relationships are based. This section is devoted to an examination of those fundamentals. Chapter 1 examines the sources of our law, the Canadian constitutional structure, including the *Charter of Rights and Freedoms*, human rights legislation, and the court structure and processes.

Photo by Tom Hanson/Canapress.

Introduction to the Legal System

OBJECTIVES OF THE CHAPTER

- To develop a workable definition of the term "law"

- To distinguish between common law and civil law

- To outline Canadian constitutional history and the workings of the parliamentary system

- To describe the court system in place in Canada today

- To explain the litigation process and consider various alternatives to it

- To examine the *Charter of Rights and Freedoms* and its impact on the Canadian legal system

SECTION I

We live in a complex world in which our success depends largely on how effectively we interact with one another. An understanding of the legal concepts and principles that govern personal and commercial relationships is essential for orderly progress in our society.

WHAT IS LAW?

Most of us readily recognize the rules and regulations that are considered law, but it is difficult to establish a satisfactory, all-inclusive definition. Philosophers have been trying for centuries to determine just what is meant by law, and their theories have had an ongoing effect on the development of our legal system.

Philosophical Basis of Law

In ancient times, the prevalent moral code determined whether any given rule was a law or not. Thus, a mad king's order that all children under the age of three be put to death would not be considered law since carrying out the order would be immoral. The legal philosophy that supports this interpretation of rules is called **natural law theory**, and reflects the quality and nature of individual rules. The problem with this approach was that it depended on the moral code established by the dominant religious body of the time.[1] When reform movements took exception to established codes, governing institutions could not tolerate the conflicting ideas of what constituted right and wrong behaviour.

Legal positivism, which eventually overshadowed natural law theory, examined the status rather than the quality of the rule and recognized a rule as a law only if the person or body enacting it had the authority to do so. Legal positivists recognize as valid law the rules laid down by even a mad king and are bound by them.

A more practical approach, called **legal realism**, developed in the United States from the teachings of Oliver Wendell Holmes. In this system, a rule is only recognized as a law when the courts are willing to enforce it. It makes no difference whether the rule is moral or who passed it; if the courts will enforce it, it is a law. These three philosophies define law in terms of what is morally justifiable, who makes the law or whether the law is enforced. There are many other approaches to legal philosophy, each with a different definition of law. This brief discussion simply illustrates why it is so difficult to give a concise, simple and workable definition of law.

No wholly satisfactory definition of law

From Theory to Practice

To understand the problems involved in applying these ideas, it is worthwhile considering the dilemma facing the German courts and the war crimes tribunals, set up by the victorious Allies, at the end of World War II. Both the German courts and the Allied tribunals had to deal with people who had committed unjust acts that were not contrary to Nazi law. The Third Reich was a lawfully constituted government, Hitler came to power legally, and the changes made to the German Constitution were properly passed. The legal realists had to acknowledge that the laws passed in Nazi Germany were real laws in that the courts enforced them. The legal positivists had a similar problem since an authorized body passed the laws. Only the largely abandoned natural law theory provided a philosophical basis for the trial of war criminals. The judges at the Nuremberg war trials found that the acts for which the defendants were being tried were so despicable and so terrible that no rules or no amount of authority could justify them. The acts were wrong by their very nature. More significantly for our discussion, after the war the German court system convicted people who had committed unjust acts during the Nazi regime on the same philosophical basis. When the defendants argued that they had only done what was legal and permitted under Nazi law, the court's response was that their acts were "contrary to the sound conscience and sense of justice of all decent human beings" and therefore unlawful.[2] One suspects that the courts merely searched for a philosophical basis to support what they had decided to do in any case.

These examples are not presented to support the validity of the natural law theory, but rather to demonstrate that there is no simple answer to the question of what law is. Knowing that various theories have contributed to the development of our legal system helps us to appreciate the complexities involved in the administration of that system.

Problems applying theory

1. Oliver Wendell Holmes, "The Path of the Law," *Harvard Law Review* (1897) p. 457.

2. H.L.A. Hart, "Positivism and the Separation of Law and Morals," *Harvard Law Review* (1958) p. 593.

A Workable Definition

For our study of law at this introductory level, it is helpful to be able to use a simplified definition of law. **Law is the body of rules which can be enforced by the courts or by other government agencies**. We are exposed to many rules in our daily activities. Courtesy demands that we do not interrupt when someone else is speaking. Social convention determines that it is improper to enter a restaurant while shirtless or shoeless. Private clubs usually have rules or bylaws governing procedures for meetings. Universities and colleges often establish rules of conduct for their students and faculty. None of these rules falls into our definition of law because the courts cannot enforce them. But when there is a disagreement over who is responsible for an accident, a question of whether a crime has been committed or a difference about the interpretation of the terms of a contract or a will, the participants may find themselves before a judge. Rules which can be enforced by the courts govern these situations; thus they are laws within the definition presented here.

A person dealing with government agencies such as labour relations boards, the Workers' Compensation Board, or city and municipal councils must recognize that these bodies are able to try matters in dispute before them, and render decisions that affect the rights of the parties. The rules enforced by these bodies are also laws within this definition. The unique problems associated with government agencies and regulatory bodies will be discussed in the last chapter of this text.

While defining law as enforceable rules has practical value for our study, this simple definition does not suggest what is just or moral. People must decide for themselves what rules they will obey. Many choose to live by a personal code of conduct, which involves adherence to even more stringent rules than those set out as law, while others choose to disregard even these minimum requirements. Some think that moral values have no place in the business world, but in fact the opposite is true. There is now an expectation of high ethical standards in business activities and it is hoped that those who study law especially will appreciate and adhere to those higher standards. We must at least understand that whether we are motivated by conscience, religion, avarice or moral indifference, serious consequences may follow from disobedience to the body of rules called law.

Law consists of rules with different functions. **Substantive law** deals with rules that govern behaviour and set limits on conduct. The provisions against stealing and killing are examples of such law. **Procedural law** deals with the rules that set out how we enforce those rights and obligations. The rule that we must initiate an action by a Civil Claim or Statement of Claim and that we have a limited time within which we must start such an action are examples. **Public law** involves rules affecting our relationship with government including criminal law and the body of regulatory law relating to government agencies. **Private law** deals with the rules that affect our relations with each other. While the material in this text concentrates on substantive and private law matters as they relate to business, reference will be made to public law as it relates to the government regulation of business. Procedural law will be briefly dealt with in this chapter under the heading of civil litigation.

→ ORIGINS OF THE LAW

Nine of the ten Canadian provinces have adopted the common law system developed over the last thousand years in England. Québec's legal system is based on the

Québec

French Civil Code. Although this text focuses on common law, understanding it may be assisted by briefly examining the basic differences between the two systems.

Civil Law

Modern **civil law** traces its origins to the Emperor Justinian who had Roman law codified for use throughout the Roman Empire. This codification was adopted and formed the foundation of the legal system in place in continental Europe through to modern times. Its most significant modification occurred early in the nineteenth century when Napoleon revised and recodified it. The Napoleonic Code was eventually adopted throughout Europe and the French colonies. Today, variations of the Civil Code are used in all of continental Europe, South America, most of Africa and many other parts of the world including Québec, Scotland and Louisiana. The most important feature of French civil law is its central code, a list of rules stated as broad principles of law. Under this system, people wanting to know their legal rights or obligations refer to the civil code. For example, if a person were to suffer injury in Québec because of the careless acts of an employee delivering fuel oil, the victim would turn to the Québec *Civil Code* to determine his or her rights. Articles 1457 and 1463 of the most recent *Code* state the following:

Civil Code used throughout world

> 1457. Every person has a duty to abide by the rules of conduct which lie upon him, according to the circumstances, usage or law, so as not to cause injury to another. Where he is endowed with reason and fails in this duty, he is responsible for any injury he causes to another person and is liable to reparation for the injury, whether it be bodily, moral or material in nature.

He is also liable, in certain cases, to reparation for injury caused to another by the act or fault of another person acting on his behalf.

> 1463. The principal is liable to reparation for injury caused by the fault of his agents and servants in the performance of their duties; nevertheless, he retains his recourses against them.

Québec courts rely on the *Code* for guidance and solutions. Civil law judges are influenced by decisions made in other cases and lawyers will take great pains to point out what other judges have done in similar situations, but the key to understanding the civil code system is to recognize that ultimately the *Code* determines the principle to be applied. While the decisions of other judges and the opinions expressed by learned people discoursing on the law can be very persuasive, they do not constitute binding precedents in a civil law jurisdiction. A new Québec *Civil Code* has been developed and came into effect January 1, 1994. It is estimated that one-quarter of the 1994 code is new law, making its introduction a very significant event in the evolution of the law of Québec.

Civil Code provides predictability

There are many important differences between the civil law and the principles of common law. In this text we have limited the discussion to the common law, and, while there are many similarities, care should be taken not to assume the same principles apply to Québec.

Common Law

As Roman civil law was taking hold in Europe, relations between the existing English and French kingdoms were frequently strained. It has been suggested that this

Common law grew from
struggle for power

strain is the reason England maintained its unique **common law** system of justice rather than adopting the more widely accepted Roman civil law. The Norman conquest of England in 1066 is considered a significant event in the development of English common law, not because of any great changes brought about in the legal system at that time but because of the centralization of power that took place under King William.

The development of the English legal system was further affected by the ongoing struggle for power between the king and the nobility and between later kings and Parliament. William the Conqueror was a strong king who had no difficulty controlling the nobles whom he had brought with him to England. Rather than giving them land outright, he restricted them to merely holding it under the very precise terms of the feudal system. William was followed by several weak kings who lost much of this power. Stronger kings who followed in turn set out to regain control and influence.

One of the great rulers of this succession was Henry II. Before his rule, people with disputes had to go to local lords, barons or sheriffs whose concepts of justice were often arbitrary and capricious. These courts often resorted to barbaric practices such as trial by battle or ordeal.

In trial by battle, the litigants or their chosen champions participated in armed combat. The theory was that God would ensure that the survivor of the conflict would be the one in the right. Trial by ordeal involved a test such as being forced to hold a red hot iron bar. If the bandaged wound festered after a week, it was assumed that the person was in the wrong. If the wound was clean, God was presumed to be protecting that person and the truth of his or her statements was verified.

Henry II establishes courts

King Henry was responsible for establishing travelling courts which provided a more acceptable method of resolving disputes between citizens of the kingdom. His royal judges were less likely to be biased, incompetent or corrupt, and their judgments were more reasonable and predictable. The more just Henry and those who followed made the courts, the more popular they became and eventually the courts of the nobles fell into disuse. The royal courts did not impose any particular set of laws. Their purpose was to administer justice, but justice was defined in terms of what the local population considered to be just and fair. Rather than imposing rules created by the king or his advisers, the travelling courts simply discovered the laws that were already in place in the form of local customs or traditions of the communities they visited. The judges also began to look to each other for rules to apply when faced with new situations.

Stare Decisis.

Judges follow each others'
decisions

Gradually, a system of justice developed in which the judges followed each other's decisions. This process is called *stare decisis*, or following precedent. Another factor that affected the development of *stare decisis* was the creation of appeal courts. Although appeal courts as such are a relatively modern development, the rudiments of an appeal structure existed during the early phases of the development of common law. When a decision made by a lower court judge was overturned on appeal, the reason for the reversal was stated and made available to the rest of the legal community and the lower court judge was declared to be in error. To avoid this kind of embarrassment, judges would simply follow the principles laid down by the appeal court. Eventually, the practice of following precedent became institutionalized. The most significant feature of our legal system today is that the decision of a judge at one level is binding on all other judges in that system who function in a court of equal or lower rank, providing facts in the two cases are similar. Strictly speaking, a judge is not bound to follow decisions made by other judges in a court at the same level in that province. However, the practical effect is the same since these judges must follow their colleagues' decisions, "in the absence of strong reason to the contrary."[3]

Thus today, a judge considering a case in the Court of Queen's Bench for Alberta would be required to follow a similar decision laid down in the Court of Appeal for Alberta or the Supreme Court of Canada, but would not have to follow a decision involving an identical case from the Court of Appeal for Manitoba. Such a decision would be merely persuasive since it came from a different jurisdiction. Because the Supreme Court of Canada is the highest court in the land, its decisions are binding on all Canadian courts.

The role *stare decisis* plays in the English common law system is similar to the role the civil code plays in the French system. It allows the parties to predict the outcome of any litigation and thus avoid going to court. However, a significant disadvantage of following precedent is that a judge must follow another judge's decision even though social attitudes may have changed. The system is anchored to the past and bound to it with only limited capacity to adapt and change to meet the needs of modern circumstances. A judge will often be confronted with several conflicting precedents presented by opposing legal representatives to support their arguments. The judge's job is to analyze the facts in the precedent cases and compare them to the case at hand. Since no two cases are ever exactly alike, this gives the judge some flexibility in deciding whether or not to apply a particular precedent. Judges often try to avoid applying precedent decisions to cases in which they feel such a finding would be unjust. A judge will usually be able to find essential differences between the two cases if he or she does not want to apply the precedent. This process is referred to as distinguishing the facts of opposing precedents.

Stare decisis provides predictability

Results in an inflexible system

→ SOURCES OF LAW

Common Law

At an early stage in the development of common law, three great courts, the **court of common pleas**, the **court of king's bench** and the **exchequer court**, referred to collectively as the common law courts, were created. The rules developed in the courts were called "the common law" because the judges, at least in theory, did not create law but merely discovered it in the customs and traditions of the people to whom it was to be applied. However, the foundation for a complete legal system could not be supplied by local custom and tradition alone, so common law judges borrowed legal principles from many different sources. Roman civil law gave us our concepts of property and possessions. Canon or church law contributed law in relation to families and estates. Another important European system that had an impact on the common law was called the law merchant. Trading between nations was performed by merchants who were members of guilds (similar to modern trade unions or professional organizations) which developed their own rules to deal with disputes between members. As the strength of the guilds declined, common law judges found themselves dealing increasingly with disputes between merchants. The law merchant was then adopted as part of the English common law and it included laws relating to negotiable instruments such as cheques and promissory notes.

Customs and traditions major source of common law

Roman Law

Canon Law

Law merchant

3. Rex Ex Rec. *McWilliam v. Morris* [1942] O.W.N. 449 High Court of Justice.

Equity

Common law courts had some serious limitations. Parties seeking justice before them found it difficult to obtain fair and proper redress for the grievances they had suffered. Because of the rigidity of the process, the inflexibility of the rules applied and the limited scope of the remedies available, people often went directly to the king for satisfaction and relief. The burden of this process made it necessary for the king to delegate the responsibility to the chancellor who in turn appointed several vice-chancellors. This body eventually became known as the **Court of Chancery**, sometimes referred to as the Court of Equity. It dealt with matters that for various reasons could not be handled adequately or fairly by the common law courts.

The Court of Chancery did not hear appeals from the common law courts; rather, it provided an alternative place to go. If people seeking relief knew that the common law courts could provide no remedy or that the remedy was inadequate, they would go to the Court of Chancery instead. The advantage of the Court of Chancery was that it was not hampered by the great body of formal and technical rules that was the heritage of the common law courts. Initially, at least, the chancery judges did not have to follow precedent, nor were they restricted by rigid procedures; rather, they decided a case on its merit or by what was morally fair or just.

The system of law developed by the courts of chancery became known as the **law of equity**. The most significant asset of equity was also one of its greatest drawbacks. Each decision of the courts of chancery appeared arbitrary; there was no uniformity within the system and it was difficult to predict the outcome of a given case. The common law judges resented the fact that the judges in the courts of chancery could ignore the great body of law that had been developed and could arbitrarily follow their own consciences. Inevitably, conflict arose. Although a truce was reached during the reign of James I, the friction was only completely eliminated when the courts were amalgamated by the *Judicature Acts* of 1873–75. Part of the resolution of this dispute was that whenever the principles of equity and common law conflicted, equity would prevail. Another outcome of the friction between the common law judges and chancery judges was that the courts of chancery adopted many of the formal rules of common law courts including the following of precedent. Eventually, courts of chancery became as formal and rigid as the common law courts.

The rules of equity were designed to meet the objectives of fairness and justice, but as society's concept of right and wrong has changed, the principles of equity have been unable to make corresponding changes. Today, equitable principles must be viewed as a body of rules developed by the courts of chancery which may or may not be consistent with today's concepts of right and wrong. When modern judges are asked to apply equitable principles, they are not being asked to be fair and just but to apply the rules developed by the chancery court. It is hoped, however, that the application of equitable principles will accomplish that objective. Equity serves as a supplement to rather than a replacement of the common law. The courts of chancery have been instrumental in developing such new principles in law as the trust (in which one party holds property for another) and have also provided several alternative remedies, such as injunction and specific performance, which we will examine later in this text.

As part of the general reform movement in English law in the nineteenth century, the common law courts, the courts of chancery and several minor English judicial bodies were abolished and replaced by a single system of courts, divided into

TABLE 1-1   Sources of Law in Canada

Branch of Goverment	Legislative	Executive	Judicial
Who fills these positions?	Federally: Parliament	Prime Minister and Cabinet Ministers together with each department's civil servants/ bureaucrats	Judges appointed by the various provinces and federally appointed justices
	Provincially: Legislative Assemblies	Premier and the Cabinet together with each department's civil servants/ bureaucrats	
Type of Law Made	Statute law (legislation)	Subordinate legislation • regulations made by order-in-council or as authorized by legislation • bylaws made by municipal governments	Case Law
Example	(Federal) • Immigration Act • Employment Insurance Act • Criminal Code (Provincial) • Workers' Compensation Act • Highway Traffic Act • Business Corporations Act	(Federal) Federal Court Immigration Rules (Provincial) Worker's Compensation Regulation	The decision of the Supreme Court of Canada in R. v. Keegstra The decision of the Alberta Court of Queen's Bench in Vriend v. Alberta

several trial divisions and a separate appellate court.[4] The common law Canadian provinces also adopted this system. The separate bodies of law created by the common law and chancery courts, however, remain distinct to this day and a judge may be asked to apply common law principles in one case and equitable principles in another. Of course, judges must always be alert to the fact that any applicable parliamentary statute will override both.

Statutes

In many situations, justice was not available to litigants in either the common law or chancery courts and the parties had to turn to yet another source for satisfaction. The English Civil War of the seventeenth century firmly established the principle that Parliament rather than the king was supreme and from that time, Parliament handled any major modification to the law. Parliamentary enactments are referred to as statutes and take precedence over judge-made law whether based on common law or equity.

When we speak of the government, we must differentiate between the legislative, the judicial and the executive branch. Parliament legislates or creates the law, the judicial branch is the court system, and the executive branch and its agencies implement that law. Organizations such as the RCMP, Human Resources

Statutes and regulations override judge-made law

4. Judicature Acts (1873–75) 31 Geo. III.

Development Canada (formerly the Unemployment Insurance Commission), the military, and the Workers' Compensation Board are all part of the executive branch of government. Most of these bodies have been given the power by statute to create subordinate legislation called **regulations** by which they accomplish the goals of the act and enforce its terms as well as regulate themselves. Therefore, when legislation is considered as a source of law, regulations passed by government agencies must be included. In the same way, municipal bylaws have the authority of the statute under which they were passed.

SECTION II

CANADA'S CONSTITUTION AND THE CHARTER OF RIGHTS AND FREEDOMS

Confederation

Canada came into existence in 1867 with the formation of a federation of Upper Canada, Lower Canada, Nova Scotia and New Brunswick. Other provinces followed, with Newfoundland being the most recent to join Confederation. Every jurisdiction except Québec adopted the English common law system before joining Confederation. Québec elected to retain the use of the French Civil Code system for matters falling within provincial jurisdiction.

BNA Act created Canada and divided powers

Confederation was accomplished when the British Parliament passed the *British North America Act*, now renamed the *Constitution Act (1867)*. The *Act*'s primary significance is that it created the Dominion of Canada and determined the functions and powers of the provincial and federal levels of government. Most of the basic rights and protections established under the American Constitution are not present in the *Constitution Act (1867)*. The preamble to the *Act* says Canada has a constitution "similar in principle to that of the United Kingdom." That is, we claim as part of our constitution all of the great constitutional institutions of the United Kingdom such as the *Magna Carta* and the English *Bill of Rights*. Also included are such unwritten conventions as the **rule of law** which recognizes that, although Parliament is supreme and can create any law considered appropriate, until it does so, citizens are protected from the arbitrary actions of government. The rule of law will be discussed more extensively in the last chapter of this text. In addition, our constitution includes those acts passed by both the British and Canadian Parliaments

More to Canadian Constitution than BNA Act

subsequent to the *Constitution Act (1867)* that have status beyond mere statutes, such as the *Statute of Westminster (1931)* and the *Constitution Act (1982)* which includes the *Charter of Rights and Freedoms*. In fact, the *Constitution Act (1982)* sets out a list of enactments that have constitutional status, including the 1870 *Rupert's Land and Northwest Territory Order*, pursuant to which the Hudson's Bay Company surrendered its land to the new Dominion. The *Constitution Act (1871)* gave Parliament the legislative authority to create new provinces, which later was used to create the provinces of Alberta and Saskatchewan pursuant to the *Alberta Act (1905)* and the *Saskatchewan Act (1905)*. Numerous statutes are thus one component of Canada's Constitution. Judicial decisions on constitutional issues and unwritten conventions also dictate how government is to function in Canada.

Constitution and Division of Powers

U.T.U. v. Central Western Railway[5]

The railway in question was built in 1911, consisting of over 1930 kilometres of track entirely within the province of Alberta, and its purpose was to collect grain from local farmers. It was operated by the CNR until they made application to abandon it in the 1980s. Permission to do so was refused and instead they sold the line to Central Western Railway Company in 1986. Prior to that date the line was operated simply as a part of the overall CNR operation. After that date the line was separated by 10 centimetre gap from the CNR tracks, and when the CNR delivered empty grain cars to that section a gap connection device was installed, the cars were transferred to Central Western lines and the device was removed. The cars were then taken by Central Western locomotives to the various grain elevators, filled and returned to the CNR.

There was no doubt that the railway, while part of the CNR system, fell under federal jurisdiction and federal laws, including the *Canada Labour Code.* A number of unions were involved with the CNR employees and the *Canada Labour Code* provided that when a business was sold, the employees involved had "successor rights," meaning that a new owner would be bound by the same collective agreement that was in place with the old owner. In this case the Supreme Court of Canada had to decide whether that federal legislation with its successor rights still applied or whether this was now subject to provincial law. While Section 92(10) of the *Constitution Act (1867)* declares that local works and undertakings are under the provincial power, it also sets out a number of exceptions including interconnecting railways with other provinces.

> 10. Local Works and Undertakings other than such as are of the following Classes:
>
> *(a)* Lines of Steam or other Ships, Railways, Canals, Telegraphs, and other Works and Undertakings connecting the Province with any other or others of the Provinces, or extending beyond the Limits of the Province;

The problem is that while this line used to interconnect with the rest of the CNR, it no longer does; and for this reason the Supreme Court found that the line was no longer under federal jurisdiction, that the successor provision of the *Canada Labour Code* did not apply to this sale, and that now provincial labour legislation would apply to those working for this railway.

This division of powers accomplished by Sections 91 and 92 of the *Constitution Act (1867)* has proved very important in the development of Canada as a nation and until the recent entrenchment of the *Charter* was the main consideration of courts when faced with constitutional questions.

In Canada, as in Britain, Parliament is supreme and traditionally has had the power to make laws that cannot be overruled by any other body, although the *Charter of Rights and Freedoms* and the *Constitution Act (1867)* place some limitations on this supremacy. This supremacy must be contrasted to the state of affairs in the American

Constitution Act (1867) and *Charter* limit power of federal and provincial governments

5. 76 D.L.R. (4th) 1 (Supreme Court of Canada).

system, where a painstakingly established system of checks and balances ensures that no government institution has absolute power. In England and Canada, parliamentary bodies until recently had the power to pass any form of legislation, subject only to the realities of the political system in which they functioned. Unlike the United Kingdom, though, Canada has a federal form of government with 11 different legislative bodies, each claiming the supreme powers of Parliament. The powers of the federal government are set out in Section 91 of the *Constitution Act (1867)*, and those of the provincial governments in Section 92 (see Appendix 1-1). The federal government has power over such matters as banking, printing currency, the postal service, criminal law (although not its enforcement) and the appointment of judges in the higher-level provincial and federal courts. The provinces have jurisdiction over such matters as hospitals, education, the administration of the courts and commercial activities carried on at the provincial level. Under the Peace, Order, and Good Government clause in the introduction to Section 91, the federal government has residual power to make law with respect to things not listed in the *Constitution Act (1867)*, such as broadcasting and air transportation. The provinces under Section 92(16) are given broad power to make law with respect to all matters of a local or private nature.

Constitution Act (1867) divides powers between federal and provincial governments

It is important to note that these areas of jurisdiction cover the nature of the legislation that can be passed, rather than the individuals or things that can be affected. Thus, while the federal government has the power to pass legislation dealing with banks, it can deal not only with the banks themselves but with anything to do with the banking process, including interest rates, the amounts that must be kept on deposit and how those deposits can be invested. Similarly, the federal government can enact legislation dealing with all aspects of criminal law or the military and the provinces have been given power to enact legislation dealing with anything to do with education.

Sections 91 and 92 deal with types of legislation not things

On occasion, one level of government passes legislation that may infringe on the powers of another. For example, municipal governments have tried to control prostitution or pornography using their zoning or licensing power when, in fact, these matters are controlled by criminal law, a federal area. To keep prostitutes out of the west end of Vancouver, the city used its zoning power to prohibit that activity. The courts struck down this bylaw stating that it was an attempt to pass criminal law since it was designed to control moral conduct. This type of legislation

SECTION 91 GIVES AIR TRANSPORTATION TO FEDS

Air-Dale Ltd. is a provincial Crown corporation wholly owned by the Ontario government and provides regular air services for them. Employees of Air-Dale, including pilots, were seeking certification as a bargaining agent for all employees in dealing with the company, and they made application to the Ontario Public Service Relations Tribunal for such certification. The Tribunal refused their application, saying that they had no jurisdiction, even though there was no federal legislation in the area. This application was brought to the Ontario Court to review the refusal. The Court agreed with the Tribunal that air transportation falls under federal jurisdiction, and that labour relations is an important aspect of such a business and therefore also falls under that jurisdiction. The Tribunal did not have the authority to grant certification in such circumstances. The federal authority derives from the "Peace, order, and good government clause" of Section 91.

O.P.S.E.U. v. Air-Dale Ltd., 111 D.L.R. (4th) 163 (Ontario Court [General Division], Divisional Court)

CITY CAN'T CONTROL CRIME

In this case the City of Calgary passed a bylaw prohibiting people from being on the street for the purposes of prostitution. This bylaw could not be taken to be for the purpose of controlling the street, but rather was clearly an attempt to control or punish prostitutes. In pith and substance the bylaw dealt with criminal law and therefore fell exclusively within the federal jurisdiction. This bylaw was declared *ultra vires* and thus void, and the appellant was acquitted.

R. v. Westendorp (1983) 1 S.C.R. 43 (Supreme Court of Canada)

is called colourable legislation, and the court simply looks at what the governing body is really trying to do as opposed to what it claims to be doing and asks whether or not it has that power.

The powers of the federal and provincial governments can overlap considerably. For example, the Alberta government passed legislation prohibiting the production and sale of the hallucinogenic drug LSD shortly after it came on the market. This legislation was valid under the province's public health power. Subsequently, the federal government passed similar legislation under its criminal law power which was also valid. When overlap does take place, the principle of **paramountcy** requires that the federal legislation be operative and that the provincial legislation go into abeyance and no longer apply. If the overlap between provincial and federal legislation is merely incidental, both are valid and both are operative. An individual must obey both by adhering to the higher standard, whether provincial or federal. It is only when the laws are such that only one can be obeyed that a true conflict exists. The doctrine of paramountcy requires that the federal legislation be obeyed in such circumstances.

When provincial and federal law conflict, follow federal

Since neither the federal nor the provincial levels of government are considered inferior legislative bodies, both are supreme parliaments in their assigned areas. Over the years, for various reasons, these bodies have sometimes found it necessary to transfer the power given to them to the other level of government. However, direct delegation between the federal and provincial governments is prohibited. For example, during the 1930s depression it became clear that a national system of unemployment insurance was needed. The provinces, which have jurisdiction in this area, attempted to delegate their power to the federal government. The court held

WHEN STATUTES IN CONFLICT, OBEY FEDERAL

In this case the husband and wife were divorced and the division of family assets was being dealt with under the *Family Relations Act* of British Columbia. The husband owned land within an Indian reserve and the wife sought for a declaration under the *Family Relations Act* for an interest in that land. The federal *Indian Act* provides specifically that land held by Natives on a reserve could not be transferred, nor could there be an agreement to transfer any right of possession of those lands without the approval of the Minister. But under the *Family Relations Act* the court controls who can have access to and possession of that land. The court held that to allow the B.C. *Family Relations Act* to empower the wife to have a claim against that asset would be inconsistent with the provisions of the *Indian Act*. There was a true conflict between the two acts, and as a result the principle of paramountcy which gives priority to the *Indian Act* prevails and the wife does not have a claim to this property.

Derrickson v. Derrickson, 9 D.L.R. (4th) 204 (British Columbia Court of Appeal)

STATUTES MAY NOT CONFLICT

Ripplinger operated an art gallery that did not provide wheelchair access. He acquired the building next door, made renovations and still did not provide this access. Ryan, who used a wheelchair, made a complaint to the Saskatchewan Human Rights Tribunal. They found Ripplinger in violation of the *Human Rights Code*. This was appealed and reversed at trial on the basis that the *Uniform Building Accessibility and Standards Act* does not require such accessibility.

When this decision was itself appealed, the Court of Appeal held that the duty to accommodate established in the *Code* of Saskatchewan and this *Act* were not in conflict. The *Human Rights Code* merely created a higher standard that had to be adhered to. There was a duty to accommodate.

Ripplinger v. Ryan, 131 D.L.R. (4th) 697 (Saskatchewan Court of Appeal)

that they could not do so as it was an "abdication" of the "exclusive powers" given to the provinces under the *Constitution Act (1867)*. To make unemployment insurance an area of federal responsibility, the British parliament needed to amend the constitution. This amendment is now incorporated in Section 91, Subsection 2A of the *Constitution Act (1867)*.

Direct delegation prohibited

Although direct delegation is prohibited, it is possible for the federal and provincial governments to delegate their powers to inferior bodies such as boards and individual civil servants; in fact, this is usually the only way that governmental bodies can conduct their business. It is also possible for the federal government to delegate its power in a particular area to a provincial board or a provincial civil servant. Similarly, a province can give power to federal boards, since these are also inferior bodies. In this way governments overcome the prohibition against delegation.

Another means used to circumvent the constitutional rigidity created by the 1867 division of powers are federal and provincial government agreements to share powers. These agreements may consist of transfer payment schemes, or conditional grants, under which the transfer of funds from the federal government is tied to conditions as to how the money is to be spent. Through such schemes, the federal government can exercise some say as to how a provincial government operates programs that fall under the province's constitutional area of control. The federal government may set certain national standards to which the funding is tied and in this fashion ensure that all Canadians have access to similar levels of service.

Transfer payment schemes are evident in the areas of health, social programs and education. One hundred thirty years ago, government spending on these services was minuscule. Now, these areas may account for two-thirds of all government spending. The provinces, with their restricted taxing powers, would have difficulty providing these services without federal funding.

OTTAWA CLASHING WITH ALBERTA

The Battle over Health Care Funding

Most Canadian social programs rely on federal funding. In the area of medicare, the federal government set the basic principles for eligibility for funding. The five basic criteria—universality, portability, accessibility, comprehensiveness and public administration—are set out in the *Canada Health Act*.[6]

6. *Canada Health Act*, R.S.C. 1985 c. C-6.

This cost-sharing plan worked well until federal budgets repeatedly went into deficits in the mid-1970s. The federal government's response was to squeeze (reduce) transfer payments. As the federal government reduced its share of funding from the 50/50 split, the provinces struggled with how to do more with less. They also wanted to decide for themselves what services medicare should cover.

These tensions erupted into a federal/provincial battle in Alberta in October 1995. The provincial government, promoting various cost-cutting measures, downsizing and privatization, allowed extra billing by semiprivate health clinics. The federal government claimed this move violated the principles of universality and accessibility under the *Canada Health Act.* It withheld transfer payments of $422 000 per month as a result. Alberta's taxpayers were not pleased that this battle, resolved in May 1996, cost them over $3.5 million in lost transfer payments. On the other hand, critics question whether Ottawa should be setting the standards for health care while *cutting* health transfer payments to the provinces.

Statutes

Legislation is introduced to the parliamentary process in the form of a **bill** which goes through a sequence of introduction, debate, modification and approval referred to as first, second and third readings. When it is finally enacted it has the status of a statute (although it may be referred to as a bill or an act). Such a statute does not have the status of law until it receives the approval (signature) of the Governor General at the federal level or the Lieutenant Governor in the provinces, a process referred to as receiving royal assent. They are the Queen's representatives in Canada and can sign on behalf of the Crown. Because the Queen is merely a figurehead in Canada, her representatives sign as they are directed by the government in power and so such a signing is essentially a formality. The government may use this requirement to delay the coming into effect of legislation and so care should be taken when examining an act to make sure that it has received royal assent. The statute itself may have provisions for different parts of it to come into force at different times. There are many examples of whole acts or portions of them that look like normal statutes but have no legal effect for these reasons.

Statutes must receive royal assent

The Government of Canada publishes a compilation of these statutes annually; they can be found in most libraries under *Statutes of Canada.* The federal government summarized and published all current statutes in the *Revised Statutes of Canada* in 1985, cited as *R.S.C.* (1985), and so it is not necessary to go back any earlier than this compilation to find current legislation. Indexes and guides are provided to assist in the process of finding the federal statutes and subsequent amendments.

Federal and provincial statutes published and summarized

Similarly, each province annually publishes the statutes passed by its legislative assembly. Each province also provides a compilation of all current legislation in the form of revised statutes. Unfortunately, there is no uniformity in the timing of the revisions, and each province has revised and summarized its statutes in a different year.

Alberta's statutes were last summarized in 1980. The bound volumes of the *Revised Statutes of Alberta* (1980), as updated by the bound annual volumes of the *Statutes of Alberta,* are the official proclamations of the law. In Alberta, one can also refer to the unofficial, consolidated statutes. This ongoing service updates statutes

TRADITIONAL PASSAGE OF BILLS*

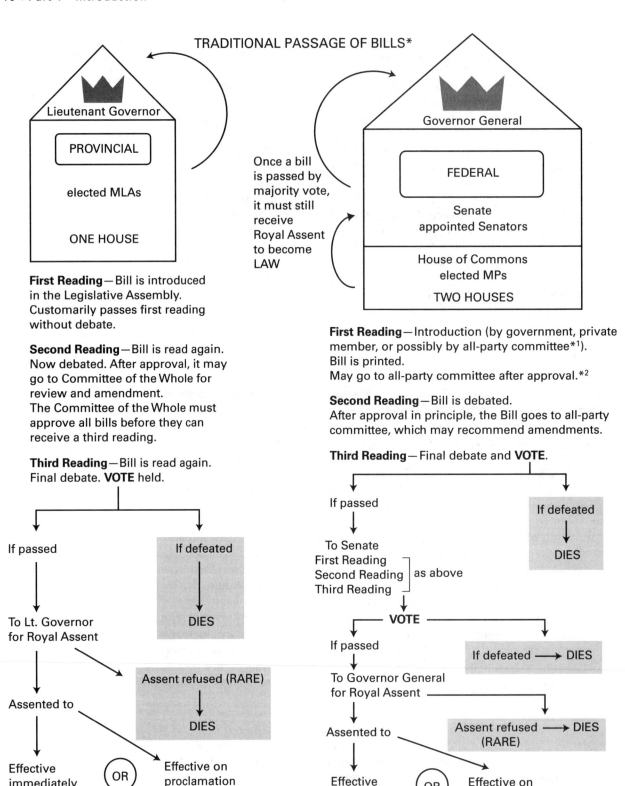

Lieutenant Governor

PROVINCIAL

elected MLAs

ONE HOUSE

Once a bill is passed by majority vote, it must still receive Royal Assent to become LAW

Governor General

FEDERAL

Senate
appointed Senators

House of Commons
elected MPs

TWO HOUSES

First Reading—Bill is introduced in the Legislative Assembly. Customarily passes first reading without debate.

Second Reading—Bill is read again. Now debated. After approval, it may go to Committee of the Whole for review and amendment.
The Committee of the Whole must approve all bills before they can receive a third reading.

Third Reading—Bill is read again. Final debate. **VOTE** held.

First Reading—Introduction (by government, private member, or possibly by all-party committee*[1]).
Bill is printed.
May go to all-party committee after approval.*[2]

Second Reading—Bill is debated.
After approval in principle, the Bill goes to all-party committee, which may recommend amendments.

Third Reading—Final debate and **VOTE**.

If passed

To Lt. Governor
for Royal Assent

Assented to

Effective immediately   OR   Effective on proclamation

If defeated

DIES

Assent refused (RARE)

DIES

If passed

To Senate
First Reading
Second Reading   as above
Third Reading

VOTE

If passed

To Governor General
for Royal Assent

Assented to

Effective immediately   OR   Effective on proclamation

If defeated

DIES

If defeated ⟶ DIES

Assent refused ⟶ DIES
(RARE)

*The Federal Government now allows for two variations from the "traditional" passage of bills. *[1] A motion may be tabled for a Committee to prepare and introduce a bill. *[2] Bills may now be referred to Committee BEFORE second reading. In any event, a bill only goes to Committee ONCE.

as they are amended and is available in a loose-leaf format. Queen's Printer has also made statutes available on CD-ROM, and they can be viewed on the Internet at a fee. (See the weblink for Queen's Printer listed at the end of this chapter.)

As indicated above, statutes often empower government agencies to create further rules to carry out their functions. As long as these regulations meet the terms of the statute, they have the effect of law. They are also published and are available to the public as regulations of Canada or the respective provinces. Cities and municipal areas pass bylaws under their statutory authority in the same way and these too are published and made available by those jurisdictions.

It must be remembered that the effect of such statutes (passed within the power of the respective governments as set out in the *Constitution Act [1867]* and other constitutional provisions) overrides any previous law in place, whether judge-made law (common law or equity) or prior legislation.

A trial judge required to deal with a statute must first determine what it means. This task is not always simple, since the legislation is not usually drafted by someone who knows all of the situations in which it will be applied or who understands all of the legal implications of the wording. The judge must then determine whether or not, under the *Constitution Act (1867)* and other constitutional provisions, the legislative body that passed the statute in question had the power to do so. If the Alberta government passed a statute making it a crime to perform an abortion it would be declared *ultra vires* (beyond the power of the body that passed it), because the power to enact criminal laws under Section 91, Subsection 27 of the *Constitution Act (1867)* is given exclusively to the federal government. When a judge interprets and applies a statute, that decision becomes a precedent and henceforth the statute must be interpreted in the same way by courts lower in the provincial or federal court hierarchy. Thus, we are back into the system of judge-made law and stare decisis.

Judges interpret and apply statutes

Decisions create precedent

Protection of Rights and Freedoms

In the preamble of the *Constitution Act (1867)*, it states that Canada will have "a Constitution similar in principle to that of the United Kingdom." The courts have interpreted that phrase as importing into Canada the unwritten conventions and traditions of government developed in Great Britain over the centuries. Thus Canada inherited the British tradition of protecting human rights and individual freedoms as founded in the common law and supported by its culture and practice.

In the aftermath of World War II, concern arose over the adequacy of entrusting protection of personal rights and freedoms to the common law. Two streams of legislation developed, one dealing with protecting human rights against abuses by the government, the second aimed at protecting individuals against discrimination and intolerance by society.

The Canadian Bill of Rights

It is important to understand that the basic human rights protections set out in ordinary statutes passed by the federal or provincial governments may not protect people from abuses by government. Because Canada adopted the English method of government, which is based on the supremacy of parliament, the provincial and federal governments were free to interfere at will with civil rights through legislation. One need look no further than the way the Japanese Canadians were treated during World War II to conclude that it could be dangerous for Canadians to leave the protection of their basic rights to the political process.

The first attempt at limiting the federal government's power to pass legislation changing basic human rights was the passage of the *Canadian Bill of Rights* (passed in 1960).[7] Because it was not entrenched in the Constitution, the courts viewed the *Bill of Rights* as just another statute that could be repealed, amended or simply overridden by any subsequent federal statute. Furthermore, the courts, when asked to apply the *Bill of Rights*, approached its provisions in the same narrow, restrictive way that they did any other legislation, thus significantly limiting its scope and effect. For example, when subsequently passed federal legislation was found to be in conflict with the provisions of the *Bill of Rights*, instead of applying the *Bill* and limiting the operation of the new statute, the courts would take the new legislation to override the old, and disregard the provisions of the *Bill* in those areas where they were in conflict. This, of course, effectively defeated the purpose of the *Canadian Bill of Rights*, and while it is still considered law in Canada, its effectiveness is extremely limited. Something more was needed.

Human Rights Legislation

The human rights statutes passed prior to 1980 were merely statutes; they could be repealed, amended or overruled by the legislative bodies that had passed them when that course of action became politically expedient.

It was also necessary to protect individuals against discrimination and intolerance by society. World War II made awareness of these problems more widespread, and steps were taken to address the rights of individuals and minority groups. Initially these statutes were designed to stop discrimination in specific service areas such as hotels and restaurants. In 1944 Ontario passed the *Racial Discrimination Act*, and other provinces followed with similar statutes shortly thereafter.

In the 1960s and 1970s these acts were expanded. Today, the federal government and all provinces have specific statutes designed to protect individuals against human rights violations in all areas of public activity and, to some extent, in private relationships as well.

Central Okanagan School District No. 23 v. Renaud[8]

Mr. Renaud worked as a custodian in an elementary school in British Columbia. The school gymnasium was rented out to a community group on Friday evenings. This necessitated the presence of a custodian for emergency and security purposes. Mr. Renaud was required to work a 3:00 p.m. to 11:00 p.m. shift Monday through Friday. This shift was incorporated into the collective agreement with the union. Mr. Renaud was a Seventh Day Adventist and an important tenet of that religion is that their members refrain from working from sundown Friday to sundown Saturday. This created a conflict between Mr. Renaud's religious beliefs and the work schedule set out in the collective agreement. The school district made considerable effort to accommodate Mr. Renaud to overcome this difficulty and they eventually agreed that the best solution was for him to work a Sunday to Thursday afternoon shift. This modification was not recognized within the terms of the collective agreement and so needed a special agreement with the union to implement, which it refused to make, with the result that Mr. Renaud's employment was terminated because he would not work on Friday evening.

7. *Canadian Bill of Rights*, S.C. 1960 c. 44.
8. 56 B.C.L.R. (2nd) 126.

Mr. Renaud filed a complaint under the B.C. *Human Rights Act* against the employer and the union claiming discrimination in employment. The B.C. Human Rights Council found that this was an example of adverse effect discrimination, since the terms of the collective agreement between the union and the employer had the effect of discriminating against Mr. Renaud because of his religious beliefs. There is an obligation on the employer to make a reasonable effort to avoid such discrimination even if it means overriding the provisions of the collective agreement. The matter eventually was heard by the Supreme Court of Canada, which supported the Council. In this case the union had not only participated with the employer in setting up a schedule which discriminated against Mr. Renaud, but also interfered with the reasonable efforts of the employer to make alternative arrangements that would accommodate his religious beliefs. This case illustrates the operation of human rights legislation, the role of the various commissions in place to enforce those rights and the relation of the courts to that process. Similar legislation creates a duty to accommodate disabled and handicapped workers as well.

In 1996, Alberta's government amended the 1970 *Individual's Rights Protection Act* and renamed it the *Human Rights, Citizenship & Multiculturalism Act*.[9] This *Act* promotes equality in the workplace, protects equal access to tenancies, public facilities and services, and prohibits discriminatory notices and signs. The Act prohibits discrimination but only upon the following grounds: race, religious beliefs, colour, gender, physical disability, mental disability, ancestry, place of origin, marital status, source of income, family status and, to some extent, age (defined as 18 years and older).

The federal government has similar legislation, entitled the *Canadian Human Rights Act*.[10] It governs abuses in areas controlled by federal legislation, such as the broadcast and telecommunication industries, whereas the provincial Acts impact areas controlled by provincial legislation.

The federal *Act* now also protects against discrimination upon the grounds of sexual orientation and criminal conviction; Alberta's legislation does not go so far (but see the discussion of the *Vriend* case below as to how the *Act* has been interpreted by the Supreme Court of Canada). Even in those provinces where discrimination based on sexual orientation is prohibited, it is still not clear whether the protection given to same-sex relationships will go as far as that extended to traditional marriages.

Recently, privacy and harassment have become areas of particular focus. Harassment is usually thought of in terms of sexual harassment, a form of gender discrimination. But now, a growing concern is about people using positions of authority to pressure, force or otherwise interfere with the rights of the individuals over whom they have power. Another new development is the concern about effective discrimination in the workplace or where public services are provided. Human rights tribunals have imposed a duty to take reasonable steps to accommodate the person who is discriminated against. Usually the discrimination is based on a physical or mental disability, but in the *Renaud* case described above, it was because of his religious beliefs. Perhaps the most significant area affected by human rights legislation is the field of employment. This will be dealt with as a specific topic in Chapter 10.

9. *Human Rights, Citizenship & Multiculturalism Act*, R.S.A. (1980) c. H-11.7.

10. *Canadian Human Rights Act*, R.S.C. 1985 c. H-6.

Both federal and provincial governments have set up special human rights tribunals authorized to hear complaints of human rights violations, to investigate, and where appropriate, to impose significant sanctions and remedies. An issue that has arisen since the adoption of the *Charter of Rights and Freedoms* is whether these human rights acts go far enough. Where protection against discrimination on the basis of sexual orientation has been left out of human rights legislation, the courts[11] including the Supreme Court of Canada[12] have shown a willingness to imply the existence of this protection. The principle applied is that under the *Charter of Rights and Freedoms:* every individual is entitled to the "equal protection and equal benefit of the law"[13] and so such rights ought to have been included. By such decisions the courts are, in effect, rewriting statutes. The issue of whether "judicial legislating" is proper under Canada's Constitution has been debated publicly by both politicians and judiciary.

Is human rights legislation under-inclusive if it prohibits discrimination upon certain grounds (e.g., race) but not others (e.g., sexual orientation)? Does it violate the guarantee of equality rights found in section 15 of the *Charter*? Should some groups be protected from discrimination but not others? Are governments now required to extend protection to all groups equally? Such were the issues raised in the *Haig*[14] and *Vriend*[15] cases.

Mr. Haig and Mr. Birch were members of the Canadian Armed Forces. When Mr. Birch informed his supervisor that he was a homosexual, he was told that the policy directive regarding homosexuals would apply to him. He would no longer qualify for further promotions or further military training. Dismayed by this overt discrimination on the part of his employer, Birch tried to take the matter before the Canadian Human Rights Commission. (The federal legislation applied because the employment fell within an undertaking regulated by the federal government.) Birch was informed that the CHRC had no jurisdiction to hear the complaint as discrimination based on sexual orientation was not prohibited by the Act. The applicant then challenged the legislation itself, arguing that the *Canadian Human Rights Act* was under-inclusive since it failed to protect an identifiable group (homosexuals) against discrimination in the workplace. The Court agreed with the claimant's position and initially stayed its decision for 6 months to give Parliament a chance to readdress the issue. On appeal, the court chose to read in a declaration that the *Canadian Human Rights Act* be interpreted as though it contained sexual discrimination as a prohibited ground of discrimination. Parliament responded by enacting Bill C-33. Section 3 of the amended *Act* now prohibits discrimination upon several grounds including sexual orientation.

In Alberta, Mr. Vriend was fired by his employer, King's College (a Christian college), after admitting his homosexuality to the college's president. Like Birch and Haig, Vriend tried to have his dismissal reviewed by the appropriate human rights commission. It dismissed the complaint, raising lack of jurisdiction as the reason; the Alberta human rights legislation does not prohibit discrimination based on sexual orientation. Vriend launched a *Charter* challenge, arguing that the *Individual's Rights Protection Act (IRPA)* failed to provide him with equal benefits or equal protection under the law as required by Section 15 of the *Charter*. The Alberta Court of Queen's Bench agreed that the provincial legislation was under-inclusive. Instead of striking down the *IRPA* (as permitted by section 52 of the Constitution), Madam

---

11. *Vriend v. Alberta* (1994) 152 A.R. 1 (Alta. Q.B.), (1996) 181 A.R. 16 (Alta. C.A.), (2 April 1998), 25285 (S.C.C.).

12. *Haig v. Canada* (1993) 2 S.C.R. 995 (S.C.C.).

13. *Constitution Act, 1982,* being Schedule B to the *Canada Act, 1987,* (U.K.), 1982, c. 11.

14. *Haig v. Canada* (1993) 2 S.C.R. 995 (S.C.C.).

15. *Vriend v. Alberta* (1994) 152 A.R. 1 (Alta. Q.B.), (1996) 181 A.R. 16 (Alta. C.A.), (2 April 1998), 25285 (S.C.C.).

Justice Anne Russell opted to read the *Act* as if sexual orientation was included as a prohibited ground for discrimination. The Province appealed and the Alberta Court of Appeal (in a split decision) allowed (granted) the appeal, stating that the lower Court ought not to have engaged in "judicial legislating." The matter was appealed to the Supreme Court of Canada where it was argued in late 1997.

In April 1998, the Supreme Court delivered its decision. All nine of the Supreme Court justices (with the Albertan, Mr. Justice Major, dissenting in part) declared the legislation invalid. Specific sections were found to violate section 15 of the *Charter* and these violations could not be saved or justified under section 1 of the *Charter*. The Court decided to read in sexual orientation as a prohibited ground. It was on this point that Mr. Justice Major disagreed. He quoted from an earlier Supreme Court decision, *Hunter v. Southam Inc.* (1984) 2 S.C.R. 145 @ 169:

> "While the courts are guardians of the Constitution and of individual's rights under it, it is the legislature's responsibility to enact legislation that embodies appropriate safeguards to comply with the Constitution's requirements. It should not fall to the courts to fill in the details that will render legislative lacunae constitutional."

Major, J. stated that "except in the clearest of cases courts should not dictate how underinclusive legislation must be amended.... Deference and respect for the role of the legislature come into play in determining how unconstitutional legislation will be amended where various means are available." Major, J. would leave this decision to the legislature, namely, whether to include sexual orientation in the human rights legislation, or use the notwithstanding clause to override section 15 of the *Charter*, or repeal the human rights legislation altogether and leave a vacuum in the area.

Given the apparent legislative opposition to including sexual orientation in the *IRPA*, Major, J. concluded it was inappropriate to read in sexual orientation as a prohibited ground. And so Mr. Justice Major would have declared those sections dealing with employment (sections 7(1), 8(1), and 10) invalid, but would suspend the declaration for one year, to give the Government of Alberta time to choose the path it would follow.

The majority, on the other hand, found that the preamble and sections 2(1), 3, 4, 7(1), 8(1), 10, and 16(1) of the *IRPA* infringed section 15(1) of the *Charter*. As a remedy, the Court concluded that reading sexual orientation into the impugned provisions of the *IRPA* was the most appropriate way of remedying the underinclusiveness. The Court states that one of the court's objectives was to respect the role of the legislature. The Court thus examined the purpose of the *IRPA*, which was to recognize and protect the inherent dignity and inalienable rights of Albertans. It decided that in light of the *Act's* preamble, if the legislature had the choice of having no human rights statute or having one that extended protection to homosexuals, the latter option would be chosen.

It is important to note that the Court did not deal with the substantive issue of whether King's College had the right to fire Vriend because of his sexual orientation. The decision simply says that Vriend should have been able to complain to the Human Rights Commission if he believed that he had been discriminated against because of his sexual orientation. It is possible, for example, that King's College may have been allowed to discriminate against Vriend because of his sexual orientation, on the basis that sexual orientation in such circumstances is a bona fide occupational qualification (pursuant to Section 7 of the *IRPA*).

These cases are interesting because they raise the issue of how far the Courts can go in shaping the law. Can Courts merely interpret statutes and enforce them, or does the *Constitution Act (1982)* now empower them to effectively rewrite any legislation which in their opinion violates *Charter* rights?

Charter of Rights and Freedoms

The human rights statutes passed prior to 1980 were merely statutes; they could be repealed, amended or overruled by the legislative bodies that had passed them when that course of action became politically expedient. They did not protect individuals' fundamental freedoms or other rights against violations by the government itself. A constitutional guarantee of these basic rights and freedoms arose in 1982. After a series of constitutional conferences, the *Constitution Act (1982)*[16] was simultaneously enacted in Canada and England. In England, it was contained in a statute called the *Canada Act.*[17] These enactments made a very significant addition to the Canadian Constitution in the form of the Canadian *Charter of Rights and Freedoms.*

Peterborough (City) v. Ramsden[18]

It may seem strange for the Supreme Court of Canada to become involved in something as trivial as posting notices on hydro poles, but the principle involved is very important under the Canadian *Charter of Rights and Freedoms.* In this case Mr. Ramsden was a member of a rock band, and in order to promote upcoming performances, he attached several posters to various hydro poles around the city of Peterborough. There was a bylaw in effect in Peterborough making it an offense to attach any bills, posters or other forms of advertising to poles, trees or other such devices on any public property in the city. He was charged with committing a violation of this bylaw. He did it again and was charged a second time. He disputed the charge and after various appeals the matter was brought before the Supreme Court of Canada. The case is important because he argued that the bylaw in question was unconstitutional, interfering with his freedom of expression as protected under the Canadian *Charter of Rights and Freedoms* Section 2(b).

Freedom of expression

The Supreme Court had to consider two questions: first, whether the bylaw prohibiting posting the bills and advertisements was in violation of the freedom of expression provision of the *Charter,* and second, whether it was a reasonable interference under Section 1 of the *Charter.* The court held that posting notices clearly conveyed information and was often used for political and cultural purposes and so the bylaw was in contravention of the freedom of expression protection set out in the *Charter.* The city argued, however, that even so it was a reasonable interference since it was intended to stop litter and visual blight. Section 1 of the *Charter* provides an effective limitation on the provisions of the *Charter* if the act that violates the *Charter* is reasonable. The court said that although the objective of the bylaw was reasonable, it went too far in prohibiting such posting on all public property in the city, and was therefore unconstitutional.

This case illustrates not only how the courts protect fundamental rights and freedoms, but also how Section 1 of the *Charter* can be an important limitation on them. The case is interesting in that it shows us how something that may seem completely trivial can have important consequences when looked at from a broader perspective.

16. *Constitution Act, 1982,* being Schedule B to the *Canada Act, 1987,* (U.K.), 1982, c. 11.

17. *Canada Act, 1987,* (U.K.), 1982, c. 11.

18. 106 D.L.R. 233 (S.C.C.).

The effect of including the *Charter of Rights and Freedoms* in our Constitution is twofold. First, neither the federal government nor the provinces have the power to modify or otherwise interfere with the basic rights set out in the *Charter* except through constitutional amendment. Thus, the provisions are said to be entrenched in the Constitution and became, as declared in Section 52 of the *Constitution Act (1982),* "the supreme law of Canada." The section goes on to state "any law that is inconsistent with the provisions of the Constitution is, to the extent of that inconsistency, of no force or effect." Because the *Charter* is included in the *Constitution Act (1982)* it is also part of the Constitution. Second, the burden of protecting those rights has shifted from the politicians to the judges. Now, an individual who feels that his or her rights have been interfered with by legislation or other forms of government action can seek redress in the courts, relying on the provisions of the *Charter of Rights and Freedoms.* Hence, the doctrine of parliamentary supremacy has been modified, the courts now being able to check the power of Parliament and the legislatures in those areas covered by the *Charter,* moving us closer to the "checks and balances" system found in the United States.

Canada gains control of its Constitution.

Canapress photo.

Burden of protecting rights now on the courts

Limitations.

There are three important limitations on the entrenchment of these basic rights. Section 1 of the *Charter of Rights and Freedoms* allows "reasonable limits" on those rights and freedoms that are "demonstrably justified in a free and democratic society." This gives the courts the power to interpret the provisions of the *Charter* so as to avoid an unreasonable result. (Some of the provisions of the *Charter,* if applied literally, could create chaos in our society.) The rights and freedoms set out in the *Charter* are, therefore, not absolute. The *Charter* guarantees freedom of expression but there would be little dispute that libel, slander or hardcore pornography must be controlled. Section 1 of the *Charter* is also used to impose reasonable limits on the rights of prisoners, and the requirement of invoking special powers in times of emergency such as war (*Emergencies Act*). But the interests of the public must be weighed before applying Section 1, and that is why it was not applied in the Ramsden case used to open this section. In contrast, section 1 did operate to justify limiting freedom of expression in the Keegstra case.

Government cannot interfere with basic rights and freedoms except:

PROHIBITION OF HATE PROPAGANDA JUSTIFIED

James Keegstra, an Alberta high-school teacher, was charged under section 319(2) of the *Criminal Code* with wilfully promoting hatred against an identifiable group by communicating anti-Semitic statements to his students. Before the trial was heard, Keegstra challenged the validity of the charge, arguing that section 319(2) violated his freedom of expression. That challenge was dismissed. Keegstra was tried and convicted. On the appeal, however, Keegstra successfully argued that section 319(2) of the Code violated his freedom of expression, and further, that section 319(3)(a) infringed his presumption of innocence. Section 319(3)(a) affords a defence of "truth" to the wilful promotion of hatred, but only where the accused proves the truth of the communicated statements on a balance of probabilities. Keegstra argued that this reverse onus, requiring him to prove the truth of the statements, violated his presumption of innocence.

The matter was appealed to the Supreme Court of Canada.[19] Where the Supreme Court and the Alberta Court of Appeal differed, however, was in their assessments as to whether these infringements were justifiable under section 1 of the *Charter*. Contrary to the Court of Appeal, the Supreme Court of Canada declared them to be constitutional. The objective of preventing the harm caused by hate propaganda was found to be of sufficient importance to warrant overriding a constitutional freedom. Further, the Supreme Court of Canada determined that there was minimal impairment to the presumption of innocence caused by section 319(3)(a), which, in light of the object of preventing the harm caused by hate propaganda, was justifiable.

• If legislature so declares

The second limitation is contained in Section 33 which allows each of the provinces and the federal government to override the basic rights contained in Section 2 and Sections 7–15 of the *Charter* simply by stating that the new legislation "operates notwithstanding" the specific provision of the *Charter* that would otherwise make the new legislation inoperative. These sections include such provisions as freedom of conscience and religion, of thought and belief, of opinion and expression, and of assembly and association; the right of life, liberty, and security of person; security against unreasonable search and seizure, arbitrary imprisonment and detention; the right not to be discriminated against on the basis of sex, age, religion, race or colour; and the guarantee of equality before the law.

It would appear that Section 33 weakens the *Charter of Rights and Freedoms* considerably. Supremacy of Parliament appears to have been restored at least in relation to those sections, and the reliance again switched to the politicians to protect basic rights and freedoms. It was originally hoped that most provinces would not find it politically expedient to override the *Charter*, and as a result would refrain from doing so. This hope has proved unfounded, and Québec, for example, has shown little hesitation in using the section to pass language legislation restricting the use of English on business signs in that province. This would clearly violate the *Charter* without the use of this section. Governments best be wary of using the notwithstanding clause in a callous fashion. Whereas the use of the notwithstanding clause to preserve usage of the French language in Quebec was generally politically acceptable, Alberta's proposed use of section 33 for economic reasons was a political disaster. When the Klein government proposed using the notwithstanding clause in legislation designed to put a cap on the amount recoverable by litigants suing the Provincial Government, the outcry was immediate and loud. Within a day, the proposed bill was dropped. (The proposed bill would have limited claims of persons sterilized under Alberta's *Sterilization Act*[20] to $150 000 per claimant.)

The notwithstanding clause does not apply to any of the other sections, such as those guaranteeing the right to vote, to elect members to Parliament and legislative assemblies, to enter and leave Canada or to use both official languages. In addition,

19. *R. v. Keegstra* (1990) 3 S.C.R. 697 (S.C.C.).
20. *Sterilization Act*, R.S.A. (1970) c. 341 (repealed).

the rights of Native Indians and the rights guaranteed to both sexes cannot be overridden by the federal or provincial governments by the application of the "notwithstanding" qualification in Section 33. A "sunset clause" is applied to the operation of section 33. If the "notwithstanding clause" is invoked, it must be reenacted by that legislative body every five years. This forces a reexamination of the decision to override the *Charter* which will likely involve different legislators who may not be as willing to pay the political cost of using the "notwithstanding clause."

The third limitation is the restriction of the operation of the *Charter* to government and government-related activities. Section 32(1)a declares that the *Charter* applies only to matters falling within the authority of "the Parliament and government of Canada" and the territories, and Section 32(1)b "to the legislature and government of each province." A serious problem facing the courts is determining just where government stops and government institutions acting in a private capacity start. Are government institutions such as schools and hospitals, and Crown corporations such as the CBC affected? While there are still many questions, it does seem clear that when such institutions are acting as an arm of government the *Charter* applies. Certainly the *Charter* applies to the legislation creating them and to the services provided directly by government departments, including the police and military. When government agencies act in their private capacity, employee relations for example, the appropriate federal or provincial human rights legislation applies and such legislation must in turn comply with the provisions of the *Charter*. If a section of a statute is in conflict with the provisions of the *Charter*, the offending section will be void or an appropriate section will be added. This was the case with the *Canadian Human Rights Act* which did not contain a provision prohibiting discrimination on the basis of sexual orientation. While the *Charter* directly affects an individual's relationship with government it only indirectly affects the relationships between individuals and between individuals and private institutions. It is also important to remember that the provisions of the *Charter* apply not only to the regulations and enactments of these government bodies and institutions, but also to the conduct of government officials employed by them. These officials derive their authority from provincial or federal enactments. If they are

Charter restricted to government-related activities

CHARTER RESTRICTS STATUTE

Twelve-year-old Justine Blainey wanted to play amateur hockey but was not allowed to because of rules which only allowed boys to play in the league. Justine's mother made a complaint to the Ontario Human Rights Commission, which refused to hear her. The Ontario *Human Rights Code* specifically prohibits discrimination on the basis of sex, but Section 19.2 of that *Code* states that discrimination on the basis of sex from participation or membership in athletic organizations and events is exempted and does not constitute discrimination. The matter went to the Ontario Court of Appeal, which decided that though the matter was private and the *Charter* protections did not directly apply, the *Code*'s Section 19.2 was inconsistent with the *Charter* provisions prohibiting sex discrimination. The court also found that it was not saved by Section 1 of the *Charter* because the exclusion of girls was not reasonable in a free and democratic society and that even if it was, it went too far, in effect putting up a sign for such events saying, "No Females Allowed." The offending section of the *Code* was declared void; but other sections in the *Code* protected Justine so she was allowed to play. The *Charter* therefore protected these private rights in an indirect way.

Re Blainey and Ontario Hockey Association et al., 26 D.L.R. (4th) 728 (Ontario Court of Appeal)

acting in a way that violates the provisions of the *Charter*, either they are not acting within their authority or their action itself is in violation of the *Charter*. In either case, such offending conduct can be challenged under the *Charter*.

Charter Provisions

Types of rights protected under *Charter*

A brief summary of the types of rights and freedoms Canadians now enjoy because of the *Charter of Rights and Freedoms* follows. (The complete *Charter* is set out in Appendix 1-2 at the end of this chapter.) The *Charter* sets out several rights which are available in some cases to citizens of Canada and, in other cases, to everyone in the nation. The extent of the rights and freedoms set out in the *Charter*, their meaning and the limitations on those rights are still being defined by the litigation that is taking place in our courts. Recourse is available in the courts if the declared rights set out in the *Charter* are interfered with by legislation, regulations, laws or the acts of public servants. The courts have been empowered under Section 24 of the *Charter* to "provide such remedies as the court considers appropriate and just in the circumstances." These powers are in addition to the inherent power of the court when faced with offending legislation or conduct by government officials, to declare that the offending legislation or conduct will be of no effect, and will have no impact on the person complaining. This provision allows the courts to award damages, injunctions and other remedies when otherwise they would have had no power to do so. Section 24 also gives a judge the power in a criminal matter to exclude evidence that has been obtained in a way that violates an accused's *Charter* rights if its admission "would bring the administration of justice into disrepute."

Personal Freedoms.

Freedom of belief, expression, press

Section 2 of the *Charter* declares certain underlying, fundamental freedoms available to everyone in Canada. These are freedom of conscience and religion and of belief, opinion and expression, all of which relate to our right to believe in whatever we wish, to express that belief and carry on activities associated with it free from interference. The *Lord's Day Act* imposed the Christian observance of no work on Sunday on others. It was overturned by the Supreme Court of Canada because it violated this section.[21] The restrictions that have been imposed on such expression and activities come about mainly when the practice of an individual or group interferes with the rights and freedoms of others.

Freedom of the press and freedom of expression are considered extremely important for preserving the democratic nature of Canada, and our courts are very careful to uphold these rights. Still, there are many limitations on them, such as the laws of defamation and obscenity. Although a free press is also considered vital to a democratic society, it appears that the Supreme Court will not significantly reduce the impact of the law of defamation as it applies to the media. Similarly, the right to peaceful assembly and freedom of association have been limited when riots may occur or in the field of employment when employer rights are interfered with by inappropriate trade union activity. Note that the rights set out in Section 2 can be overridden by a declaration of the "notwithstanding clause" (Section 33).

Democratic Rights.

Right to vote and hold office

Sections 3, 4 and 5 protect our right to vote and to be elected to the House of Commons or the provincial legislative assemblies. It is likely that these rights were

---

21. *R. v. 3M Drug Mart Ltd.* [1985] 3 W.W.R. 481 (S.C.C.).

protected in the past by constitutional convention, but now they are enshrined in the *Charter*. Section 4 ensures that there will be an election at least every five years except in times of war, and Section 5 requires that the elected body be called into session at least once every 12 months. Reasonable limitation can be put on this right to vote, restricting those under age and most likely the mentally incompetent, but the abuses of the past, where racial groups such as the Chinese were denied the vote, are now prohibited. The government in power still has the right to decide when to call an election within that five-year period and also whether to call the session into sitting more often than the "once every 12 months" minimum. The government also has the power to determine what that session will consist of, which also gives some potential for abuse. These sections cannot be overridden by the "notwithstanding clause."

Mobility Rights.

This section ensures that Canadians can travel and live anywhere within the geographic limitations of Canada as well as enter and leave the country at will. It also ensures that all Canadians have the right to earn a livelihood in any part of Canada. But again these assurances are qualified. Programs that are of general application in a province or region can be valid even though they appear to interfere with these rights. In the field of employment, for instance, provincial licensing and educational requirements may prevent people trained and licensed in other parts of the country from carrying on their chosen profession. Section 6(4) specifically allows for programs that are designed to better the condition of those "who are socially or economically disadvantaged" even when those programs interfere with the mobility rights of other Canadians who might want to take advantage of the programs but are prohibited from doing so.

Right to enter and leave Canada, and work and live anywhere in Canada

Legal Rights.

The rights listed under this heading are intended to protect individuals from unreasonable interference from the government or its agents, to assure that when there is interference it is done according to the rules of natural justice, and to ensure that any punishment is not excessive or unreasonable. Section 7 lays down that we have the right to life, liberty, and the security of person and the right not to have these rights taken away except in accordance with the "principles of fundamental justice." A 1972 judgment by Fateauex J. summarized what is meant by these basic rules of procedural fairness. He said "The tribunal which adjudicates upon his rights must act fairly, in good faith without bias and in a judicial temper, and must give him [her] the opportunity adequately to state his [her] case."

Rights to life, liberty and security; fair trial and punishment

A significant omission in the *Charter* is the right to property. There is no protection of a right to property provided for in this part or anywhere else in the *Charter*.

Subsequent sections under this heading prohibit such activities as unreasonable search and seizure and arbitrary imprisonment and provide for the right to be informed of the reason for an arrest, the right to retain counsel, the right to be tried within a reasonable time, the presumption of innocence, the right not to be tried twice for the same offense and the right not to be subjected to any cruel or unusual punishment. The common theme here is to protect people from abusive, arbitrary or unequal application of police and prosecutorial power. Not only is the individual protected in the event of such an abuse, but the provisions also serve to discourage the police and prosecutors from acting outside of the law. The powers given to the courts, especially under Section 24(2) discussed above, further help to persuade the law enforcement community to act properly by allowing the court to exclude evidence obtained in violation of these provisions where not to do so "would bring the administration of justice into disrepute." These basic legal rights can be overridden by the invocation of the "notwithstanding clause."

Equality Rights.

Discrimination prohibited

The equality rights set out in Section 15 of the *Charter* prohibit discrimination in the application of the law on the basis of sex, religion, race, age or national origin and ensure that all people in Canada have the same claim to the protection and benefits of the law. This means that the various provisions of the federal and provincial laws must be applied equally to all, and that anytime a distinction is made in any provincial or federal law or by a government official on the basis of one of these categories, it can be challenged as unconstitutional. Even where the discrimination relates to a category not listed, there is a general prohibition against such discrimination and so victims will be protected. Thus, even though Section 15 makes no reference to sexual preference the courts have had no difficulty in concluding that a denial of benefits because of sexual preference to same-sex couples is prohibited. It is important to note that Section 15(2) provides for affirmative action programs. When a provision is intentionally introduced that has the effect of discriminating against one group of people, it may still be allowed if its purpose is to correct an imbalance that has occurred through discrimination in the past. Thus the government may intentionally set out to hire women or specific ethnic minorities in order to get a better balance in the civil service. This is permissible even though it will have the effect of preventing people of other groups such as Caucasian men from having an equal opportunity to obtain those same jobs. Universities will often have similar programs to encourage minorities to enter faculties or professions if they were not equally represented in the past to correct such an imbalance. These basic equality rights can also be overridden by the operation of the "notwithstanding clause."

In addition to the provisions set out in Section 15, there are other provisions in the *Charter* setting out equality rights. Section 28 guarantees that the provisions of the *Charter* apply equally to males and females. Section 35 states that the *Charter* in no way affects the aboriginal and treaty rights of the Native Indians of Canada. Although this last provision may have the effect of preserving inequality rather than eliminating it, the object of this section was to ensure that during the process of treaty negotiations and land claims disputes between provincial governments and the native population of Canada, nothing in the *Charter* would interfere with the special status rights associated with that group. Section 33 cannot be used to affect the gender equality rights or the protection given to the position of the aboriginal people of Canada.

Language Rights.

French and English language rights guaranteed

The part of the *Charter* headed "Official Languages of Canada" outlined in Sections 16 to 22 ensures that French and English have equal status and the rights of minorities to use those languages are protected. Of the Canadian provinces only New Brunswick is officially bilingual, and so Section 16 of the *Charter* declares that English and French are the official languages of Canada (federally) and New Brunswick. All federal government activities, including court proceedings, publications and other services where numbers warrant must be available in both official languages. Similar rights are established for New Brunswick. Note that some language rights are set out in the *Constitution Act (1867)*; for example, Section 3 requires that Québec provide court services in English as well as French. The *Constitution Act (1867)* also requires that Manitoba provide many government services in both English and French although this was ignored for many years.

Minority language educational rights are outlined in Section 23 and guaranteed for the citizens of Canada ensuring that those whose first language is English or French who received their primary education in English or French, or have had one of their children educated in English or French, have the right to have their other children educated in that language. People who are immigrants to Canada have no such rights no matter what their native language may be. Note that the right to be educated in English or French only applies where community numbers warrant the expense of setting up such a program. Language rights and minority language educational rights cannot be overridden by Section 33 of the *Charter* (the "notwithstanding clause").

Section 52.

The *Constitution Act (1982)* makes other important changes to Canada's constitution. In addition to declaring that the Constitution is the "supreme law of Canada" Section 52 also sets out all the statutes that have constitutional status in an attached schedule. Important amendments are also made to the *Constitution Act (1867)* creating Section 92A which expands the power of the provinces to make law with respect to nonrenewable natural resources including the generation of electric power and forestry resources. (See Parts VI and VII of the *Constitution Act (1982)* in Appendix 1-2.)

The Importance of the Changes

The significance of these 1982 additions to the Canadian Constitution cannot be overemphasized. The *Charter of Rights and Freedoms* will shape the development of Canadian law over the next century. Canadian courts had adopted the position that their function was to apply the law as it existed. If the law needed to be changed, the judiciary left the job to Parliament and the legislative assemblies. It is likely that one of the significant changes which will take place in our legal system as a result of the enactment of the *Charter* is that the courts will play a more active role and create new law through their interpretation and application of the provisions of the *Charter*. The broad, generalized nature of *Charter* provisions contributes to this more expansive role of the courts. Statutes have traditionally been interpreted in a very narrow way and because of this they are always very carefully and precisely worded. But the *Charter* provisions are generalizations and so the courts must take these broad statements and fill in the gaps, thus making new law.

Charter leads to a more active court

The *Constitution Act (1982)* also eliminated the requirement that any major change involving Canada's constitution had to be made by an act of the Parliament of Great Britain. Because the original *BNA Act* was an act of the British Parliament, any changes to it had to be made by that body. When the provinces and the federal government agreed on a formula for amending the Constitution, the British Parliament passed the *Canada Act* making Canada completely independent of Britain. Québec, however, did not assent to this document. Since then, another important agreement, known as the Meech Lake Accord, was drawn up which attempted to change this amending formula. The Accord did not receive the required unanimous approval by the provinces within the specified time limit. Its

British power eliminated

Meech Lake Accord

failure and the failure of the subsequent Charlottetown Accord which went to a national referendum has created a constitutional crisis in Canada with Québec refusing to participate in any interprovincial negotiations or meetings. Québec continues to seek independence from Canada and took the question of sovereignty to a provincial referendum in 1996 which failed by only a one percent margin. Discussions regarding granting Québec special status in Canada have occasioned much debate and dissension within the federation.

But Queen remains monarch

It should be emphasized that although Canada's ties to the British Parliament have been severed, our relationship with the monarch remains. The Queen remains the Queen of Canada, just as she is the Queen of England, Australia, New Zealand and other independent nations.

SECTION III

THE COURTS AND PROCEDURES BEFORE THEM

Trials opened to public, with exceptions

As a general rule, Canadian courts are open to the public. The principle is that justice must not only be done but must be seen to be done; no matter how prominent the citizen and no matter how scandalous the action, the procedures are open and available to the public and the press. There are, however, important exceptions to this rule. When juveniles are involved or when the information coming out at a trial may be prejudicial to the security of the nation, the courts will hold in camera hearings which are closed to the public.

The hearing or trial must be fair. The parties to the action must have notice of the matters in dispute and an opportunity to present their side of the case. The actual procedure involved is discussed in this chapter. The courts in Canada preside over criminal prosecutions or adjudicate in civil disputes. While civil matters are the major concern of this text and criminal law is only incidentally discussed, it should be noted that there are some important differences between civil and criminal actions. In civil actions, two private persons use the court as a referee to adjudicate a dispute and the judge, or in some cases judge and jury, choose between the two positions put before them. The decision will be made in favour of the side advocating the more probable position. The judge in such circumstances is said to be deciding the matter on the balance of probabilities.

Both criminal and civil function

Criminal prosecutions are quite different. When a crime has been committed, the offense is against the state, and victims of the crime are merely witnesses at the trial. The government pursues the matter and prosecutes the action through a Crown prosecutor. The person charged is called the accused. Since the action is taken by the government (the Crown) against the accused, such cases are cited as, for example, "R v. Jones" (the R stands for either *rex* or *regina* depending on whether a king or queen is enthroned at the time of the prosecution). While a civil dispute is decided on the balance of probabilities, in a criminal prosecution the judge (or judge and jury) must be convinced beyond a reasonable doubt of the guilt of the accused. This is a much more stringent test in that even when it is likely or probable that the accused committed the crime, the charge must be dismissed if there is any reasonable doubt about guilt. Criminal law is restricted to the matters found in the *Criminal Code* as well as certain drug control legislation and a few other areas under federal control which have been characterized as criminal matters by the courts. There is a much broader area

Civil test—balance of probabilities

Criminal test—beyond reasonable doubt

of law in which people can be subject to fines and imprisonment, but does not qualify as criminal law. These are regulatory offenses sometimes referred to as quasi-criminal matters and include areas such as environmental, fishing, and employment offenses, as well as the whole area of offenses created under provincial jurisdiction such as motor vehicle regulations, and hunting violations. Only the federal government has the power to make criminal law and although people may be punished by fine and sometimes even imprisonment for violations of these provincial offenses, the violations do not qualify as criminal acts. People charged under these provisions usually go through a process similar to a summary conviction offense under the *Criminal Code*.

Trial Court.

It is before this court that the disputing parties first appear and testify, witnesses give evidence, the lawyers make arguments, and a decision is reached. When both a judge and a jury are present, the judge makes findings of law and the jury makes findings of fact. When the judge is acting alone, which is much more common, the judge decides both matters of fact and matters of law. Matters of fact are those regarding the details of an event. For example, was Erasmus at the corner of Portage and Main in the city of Winnipeg at 7:00 a.m. on March 5, 1989? Did a portion of the building owned by Bereznicki fall on Erasmus? Was he paralyzed as a result of his injury? Was Bereznicki aware of the danger? Had he taken steps to correct it? Questions of law, on the other hand, concern the rules or laws that are to be applied in the situation. For example, was Bereznicki obliged to keep the outside of his building in good repair? How would the obligation be affected if Bereznicki was unaware of the danger?

Appeal Courts.

If one of the parties is dissatisfied with the decision or an error in procedure is identified, the decision may be appealed.

Questions of law only can be appealed

The court exercising an appellate jurisdiction does not hold a new trial. Rather than have all the witnesses and the parties testify again, the appeal court will read the record made in the trial court and deal with the specific objections to the trial judge's decision raised by the lawyers in submissions presented to the court before the actual hearing. Usually only the lawyers appear in court to make their arguments, normally to a panel made up of three or more judges. As a general rule, an appeal is limited to questions of law, not questions of fact.

It is felt that the individuals best qualified to determine questions of fact are the judge or jury who hear all the evidence presented by witnesses at the trial. They are the ones who have seen the parties and the witnesses. They have seen the body language and the other subtle things that play such a crucial role in persuading one person to believe another. Therefore, a claim that a lower court judge made a mistake must be based on questions of law in order to be considered by an appeal court. In fact many of the decisions of appeal courts are ones of mixed law and fact where the rules that are applied are inseparably connected to the facts that are found. Whether a person lived up to the standard of a reasonable person in a given situation would be an example of such a question of mixed law and fact.

The Courts of the Provinces.

The nature and structure of these courts vary from province to province, but there are essentially three levels. At the lowest level are the **Provincial Courts** (called by various titles across Canada), with a criminal jurisdiction over the less serious criminal matters assigned to magistrates and judges under the *Criminal Code* of Canada.

TABLE 1-2　Trial Courts and Appeal Courts Contrasted

Appeal Courts
- presided over by a panel of judges
- "Leave" or permission to appeal may first be required
- one judge presides or a judge with a jury
- usually consider questions of law or mixed law and fact
- do not hear testimony of witnesses, but have the transcript from the trial to review

Appeals

Appeals are heard by the "higher" Appeal Court

Trial Courts
- one judge presides or a judge with a jury
- witnesses testify, exhibits are entered, findings of fact are made
- lawyers submit legal arguments as to what the law is
- judge determines questions of law, applies that law to the facts, and renders the Court's decision

Sometimes as a separate body but usually as a division of the Provincial Courts, most jurisdictions also have small claims courts and family courts. Some provinces maintain separate youth courts. These deal with offenses under the *Young Offenders Act*.[22] In Canada youth offenders ages 12 to 18 are subject to the same *Criminal Code* provisions as adults, but are subject to a different level of punishment and so the role of youth courts is very important. Small claims courts deal with civil matters that involve relatively small amounts of money, usually no more than $10 000.

The Provincial Court Act[23] of Alberta creates a Provincial Court with four divisions: Criminal, Civil (small claims), Family and Youth. As prescribed by the *Criminal Code*, those accused facing criminal charges are initially brought before the Provincial Court, Criminal Division, to enter a plea and make an election as to mode of trial. Even if a trial before the higher trial court (the Court of Queen's Bench) is elected, some of the evidence will be brought forward in Provincial Court at the preliminary inquiry. Accordingly, the Criminal Division is very busy and is a most significant court of criminal jurisdiction. The Traffic Division is a further subdivision of Criminal Division, handling a variety of motor vehicle infractions.

The Family Division has jurisdiction to handle custody issues that arise once the parents have separated. Enforcement of maintenance or alimony can be dealt with here, but note that the Court has no jurisdiction to issue divorces. The *Divorce Act*[24] requires parties to apply to the Court of Queen's Bench if seeking a divorce.

The Youth Division has jurisdiction to handle two types of actions: offenses under the *Young Offenders Act*, and dealing with "children in need of protection" under the *Child Welfare Act*.

The Civil Division has jurisdiction to handle small claims actions, for debt or damages, where the amount claimed does not exceed $7500. The monetary limit can be increased by regulation to $10 000, but when the government will do so is uncertain. (The monetary limit was increased from $4000 to $7500 on October 1, 1997.)

22. R.S.C. 1985 c. Y-1.

23. *Provincial Court Act,* R.S.A. (1980) c. P-20 s. 36.

24. *Divorce Act,* R.S.C. 1985 (2nd Supp) c. 3, as amended.

Section 36(1), which sets the monetary jurisdiction of the court, uses conjunctive wording. It has been argued successfully that a plaintiff should thus be entitled to claim up to $4000 (now $7500) in damages as well as another $4000 (now $7500) in debt as a result.[25] A plaintiff could have a total potential claim of $15 000 under the current wording of the Act and regulations. Certain civil matters lie outside the Court's jurisdiction, including matters involving ownership of land, matters involving wills, tort actions for false imprisonment, defamation and malicious prosecution, and matters involving governments.[26]

The second-highest level of court is variously referred to as the Supreme Court, High Court, the Superior Court of Justice, the General Division, the Superior Court, or, in the case of Alberta, the Court of Queen's Bench. Those variations exist because under the *Constitution Act* (1867), Section 92(14), the power has been given to the provinces to determine the structure of their court systems. The Court of Queen's Bench, Alberta's superior trial court, has unlimited monetary jurisdiction in civil matters and deals with serious criminal matters. Some provinces have also retained specialized courts, referred to as surrogate or probate courts, dealing with the administration of wills and estates. The Surrogate Court of Alberta, a subdivision of the Court of Queen's Bench, is an example.

The highest level court in each province is the Court of Appeal. This court's function is to hear appeals from the other courts of the province. It must hear an appeal before a matter can go to the Supreme Court of Canada. Superior court judges and judges of the Court of Appeal are appointed by the federal government from a list of candidates supplied by the provinces.

Federal Courts.

There are two courts that have jurisdiction in all of Canada. The first is the Supreme Court of Canada, which is the highest court in the land and has a strictly appellate function as far as private citizens are concerned. There are nine judges chosen from throughout Canada, and typically three or five of them will hear an appeal. There is no longer an automatic right of appeal to the Supreme Court of Canada; leave must be obtained and this will usually only be granted if the case has some national significance. Decisions of the Supreme Court are binding on all courts in Canada. It hears criminal and civil cases and is sometimes asked to rule directly on constitutional disputes involving federal and provincial governments.

Supreme Court of Canada

The Federal Court of Canada serves a function similar to that of a provincial superior court. It has a Trial and an Appellate Division. The Trial Division hears disputes that fall within the federal sphere of power such as those concerning copyrights and patents, federal boards and commissions, federal lands or money, and federal government contracts. The Appellate Division hears appeals from the Trial Division. An appeal from the Appeal Division will go directly to the Supreme Court of Canada. Both divisions of the Federal Court can hear appeals from decisions of federal regulatory bodies and administrative tribunals such as Human Resources Development Canada (formerly known as the Unemployment Insurance Commission).

The Tax Court of Canada is another very specialized court, which was established in 1983 to hear exclusively disputes concerning federal tax matters. This body hears appeals from assessment decisions made by various federal agencies enforcing taxation statutes. Recently the Auditor General of Canada has recommended that the Federal Court and the Tax Court be merged.

25. *Parris v. Reber* (1994) 168 A.R. 79 (Prov. Ct.).

26. *Provincial Court Act*, R.S.A. (1980) c. P-20 s. 37.

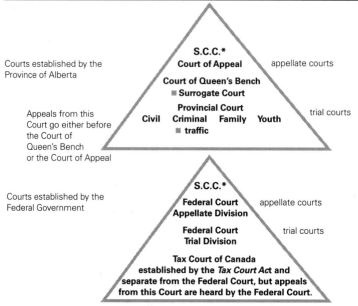

TABLE 1-3 Paths of Appeal

Courts established by the Province of Alberta

S.C.C.*
Court of Appeal — appellate courts
Court of Queen's Bench
■ **Surrogate Court**
Provincial Court
Civil   Criminal   Family   Youth — trial courts
■ **traffic**

Appeals from this Court go either before the Court of Queen's Bench or the Court of Appeal

Courts established by the Federal Government

S.C.C.*
Federal Court Appellate Division — appellate courts
Federal Court Trial Division — trial courts
Tax Court of Canada established by the *Tax Court Act* and separate from the Federal Court, but appeals from this Court are heard by the Federal Court.

*Note: The Supreme Court of Canada is constituted in accordance with the Constitution of Canada and the *Supreme Court Act*. It is Canada's final court.

Government tribunals are not courts

In addition to the courts discussed above, there are bodies called administrative tribunals that may look and act like courts, but are not courts in fact. Administrative tribunals are part of the executive branch of government at the federal, provincial and municipal level and they, along with all government bureaucrats, are empowered to make decisions which affect our lives, and must exercise those powers within very restricted boundaries. Government decision makers within their areas can be every bit as important as are courts, and so it is important to be aware that these bodies are not courts and we all have certain rights when we are affected by their decisions. These rights will be discussed in the last chapter of this book

The Process of Civil Litigation

Consumer Glass Co. Ltd. v. Foundation Company of Canada Ltd.[27]

In 1963, Foundation, a contractor and engineering company, designed and built a building (a wareshed) for Consumer Glass. There were no problems with the building and no indication of any difficulty until the roof collapsed suddenly in 1981. Consumer Glass sued Foundation for negligence in the way they built the building or its design. But the builder claimed that the action should have been brought in contract, and that under the provisions of the *Limitation Act*, the action had to be brought within six years of the breach, that is, when the faulty work or design was done in 1963. The *Limitation Act* sets time limits within which various kinds of actions must be brought and failure to do so means that the action cannot be pursued.

Timely start to action necessary

27. 20 D.L.R. (4th) 126 (Ont. C.A.).

The problems that the Ontario Court of Appeal had to resolve were (1) whether the action should be based on negligence—a tort action, a topic which will be covered in Chapter 2—or as a breach of contract and (2) whether the limitation period started running in 1963 when the work was done or in 1981 when the damage occurred.

The Court of Appeal, after examining several important precedents, decided that when a person was suing because of failure to live up to a duty to be careful, that person was free to sue for the tort of negligence even though the relationship that gave rise to that duty was based on a contract between the parties. After the court decided that Consumer Glass could sue in negligence it looked at when the limitation period should start to run. The justices considered several important precedents, but in effect they found that it would be silly if the victim of such negligence was barred from suing before he knew of the damage. Dubin J.A. reflected on "the injustice of a law which statute-bars a claim before the plaintiff is even aware of its existence." And then he said that this would be equally unjust in contract law or negligence.

This case is raised here to illustrate how important it is to start the process of suing properly. Not only do you have to sue for the right thing, in this case negligence or breach of contract, but you have to do so in a timely manner. Failure to sue within the time limits set out in a limitation act can bar an action from proceeding.

Most of this text deals with matters of substantive law, that is, law that summarizes rights and obligations of the "thou shalt" or "thou shalt not" variety, rather than procedural law which deals with the process by which we enforce those rights and obligations. But it is important to be familiar with the procedures involved in bringing a dispute to trial, if only to understand the function of lawyers and the reasons for the expense and delays involved. Before a decision is made to sue someone, all avenues for settling the dispute outside of court ought to be exhausted. Alternative methods for resolving legal disputes have been developed including negotiation, mediation and arbitration, and often the court requires the disputing parties to have tried these dispute resolution mechanisms before a trial procedure will be instigated.[28] The litigation procedures may vary somewhat from province to province, but they are substantially the same in all common law jurisdictions and they apply to most superior courts. The procedure set out below is taken from the system used in Alberta.

Should try to settle dispute

Some variations from province to province

The first step in a legal suit is to determine which court should hear the action. The jurisdiction of a court can be a very difficult question, but generally the plaintiff or person bringing the action can choose a court in the area where the defendant resides or in the area where the matter complained about arose. If a traffic accident happened in Alberta between a driver from B.C. and one from Ontario, the Ontario driver would have to sue in B.C. or Alberta. Once the province has been chosen, the plaintiff must then choose the court. In a civil action this is either the small claims court or the superior court of the province. The Provincial Court, Civil Division (small claims court), has a monetary limit of up to $7500, but cases involving more can be tried in small claims if the plaintiff waives any claims to a higher amount by filing a form called an Abandonment. Although it is simpler and less expensive to bring an action in small claims court, one disadvantage from a plaintiff's point of view is that the court is restricted in the costs it can award. Costs incurred for representation by a lawyer usually cannot be recovered unless the action is brought at a superior court level. On the other hand, the procedure followed before the small claims court has been significantly streamlined. It is designed to enable ordinary people to present their legal problems without the need to hire a lawyer. Hiring a lawyer, or asking a friend to assist in Court as your agent, or handling the action yourself, are all options.

Procedure Before Alberta's Provincial Court, Civil Division

Preliminary Matters. Before suing, one may send a **written demand** to the opposite party, requiring payment by a certain date in the hope that litigation can be avoided. If the opposite party fails to satisfy the claim, then one may have to resort to litigation.

There are time limits. The *Limitation of Actions Act*[29] generally requires tort actions (e.g., seeking compensation for damage) to be commenced within two years of the injury. For debt claims and other contractual claims, the action must be commenced within six years from the time the debt began or the contract was breached. There are, however, many exceptions to the above rules. To sue one's own insurance company for failure to pay under the policy, the time limit is one year. This is a complex area and one should consult a lawyer if there is any doubt as to which limitation period affects the case.

Is it worth suing? Two other considerations are the costs of suing (time and money) as well as the probability of recovery. There are filing fees imposed when one files the Civil Claim ($25) and services fees and possible witness fees to consider. The amount of time spent picking up forms, filing pleadings, and serving documents, and the time spent on the trial itself should be viewed as "investments" for one cannot sue for wages lost while attending to these procedural matters. Second, if the proposed defendant is without assets and unemployed, recovery of any judgment is likely to be drawn out, time consuming and questionable. (The judgment is valid for 10 years, so if the defendant's future holds promise, it may still be worthwhile to sue.)

A third consideration is whether one has sufficient evidence to support the claim. Do documents exist or are witnesses available to corroborate the claim?

Who to sue? The party commencing the action (the one with the complaint) is the **plaintiff**, the one defending the action is the **defendant**. One or more parties can be named as co-defendants. Full names of individuals and the correct name of any business entity sued must be ascertained, for suing the wrong person can cause one to lose the suit. To determine the exact name of any incorporated business ("Limited" or "Incorporated" or "Corporation" is the last word in its name) a *companies search* is conducted through an Alberta Registries agent. Partnerships and sole proprietorships are unincorporated so one must include both the owners' names and the business name on the Civil Claim. One may be able to determine who owns such businesses by doing a trade name search through Alberta Registries.

"Pleadings" or documents used. The pleading used to commence the action is the Civil Claim. This fill-in-the-blanks form is available from the Clerk of the Provincial Court, Civil Division. It must be completed disclosing the following:
- the plaintiff's and defendants' names, addresses and phone numbers;
- the amount one is asking for (the claim);
- details as to when and where the problem occurred; and
- the reasons one is suing. (See the Civil Claim and other documents in Appendix 1-4.)

29. *Limitation of Actions Act,* R.S.A. (1980) c. L-15.

One copy of the Civil Claim is filed with the Court (for a fee) and the plaintiff must then **serve** both the **Civil Claim** and a blank **Dispute Note** upon all defendants.

Service of documents involves giving documents to another by one of the authorized methods. Service can be attended to any day of the week. Whoever serves the documents (the plaintiff or someone on her behalf) will then be required to swear an **Affidavit of Service** proving service. The affidavit is provided on the back of the blue copy of the Civil Claim. There, the authorized methods of service are set out (see Appendix 1-4). They include service of the Civil Claim and blank Dispute Note on a person by

- giving the pleadings to the person;
- leaving the pleadings at that person's usual residence with someone apparently 16 years of age or older;
- mailing the pleadings by double registered mail and establishing receipt by attaching the Acknowledgment of Receipt card and postal registration receipt to the Affidavit.

Authorized methods of service upon a corporation or partnership are also described in the Affidavit of Service. If unable to effect service by one of these methods one can contact the Civil Division office for instructions as to how to secure a Court order authorizing service by some other method (substitutional service).

Defendant's Options. The defendant has four options. One is to ignore the claim and lose the lawsuit. Unless the defendant acts within 20 days of receipt of the Civil Claim, the plaintiff can apply for and secure a default judgment.

A second option is to negotiate a settlement with the plaintiff. Such a compromise saves both parties the time and expense involved in going to court. If an agreement is reached, the defendant should require the plaintiff to notify the Civil Division of the settlement and file a Notice of Withdrawal.

A third option is to pay the claim and costs directly to the plaintiff or into court. The defendant should obtain a receipt. A court appearance will now not be necessary.

The last option is for the defendant to defend the action. To do so, the Dispute Note must be delivered personally or by mail to the Civil Division Clerk's office within 20 days of being served with the Civil Claim (30 days if served outside Alberta). The Clerk of the Court will set a trial date and notify all parties by mail after receiving a valid Dispute Note.

The defendant may include in the Dispute Note any denials, defences, versions of fact and any claims against the plaintiff. Claims brought against the plaintiff (counterclaims) will be looked at by the judge simultaneously with the plaintiff's claim at the trial.

Compulsory Mediation. Pursuant to the Mediation Rules of the Provincial Court–Civil Division, which are an Appendix to the *Provincial Court Act*, the Court, or a "mediation co-ordinator" (of the office of the Clerk of the Court), may refer any action for mediation, at any time after a Dispute Note is filed. Unless a party applies to the Court for an order exempting him from mediation, a trial date will not be set unless a notice of completion of mediation is obtained. If a party fails to attend a scheduled mediation session, his pleadings may be struck out by the Court, unless there was a reasonable excuse for the non-attendance. Furthermore, the Court may order the non-attending party to pay costs of $50 to the other parties. The Mediation Rules only apply if the chief judge of the relevant court has so determined.[30]

---

30. *Provincial Court Act,* R.S.A. (1980) c. P-20.

Default judgment. If the claim is not settled or paid, or if a Dispute Note is not filed in time, the plaintiff can obtain judgment against the defendant without having a trial. Once the time for defending expires, the Clerk will enter a Default Judgment, upon the plaintiff's request and upon proof of service of the Civil Claim and Dispute Note. A Certificate of Judgment is mailed to all parties. However, if the plaintiff has sued for a sum that is not the result of an agreement with the defendant (such as compensation for injuries suffered), the plaintiff must still go before a judge as a hearing is needed to determine compensation.

Preparing for Trial. The parties must prove, through personal, first-hand evidence, their version of the facts. To ensure that witnesses appear at the trial, a **Notice to Attend** should be served on each one. These notices are court orders requiring attendance; disobeying one is against the law.

The documents used in court should be originals. If entering copies as exhibits, the person who made the copy should be in court to verify the copy. Similarly with photographs, the photographer must testify as to when the photographs were taken.

The Trial. Judges of the Provincial Court are addressed as **Your Honour.** To show respect, everyone must rise when the judge enters or leaves the courtroom. When the judge calls a case forward, the parties should rise and identify themselves. Witnesses will likely be asked to leave the courtroom until it is their turn to testify. The plaintiff bears the onus of proof (she must prove her case on a balance of probabilities) and so the plaintiff calls her witnesses to testify first.

Each witness may be subjected to three types of questioning. The party calling the witness conducts a **direct examination** of the witness. Leading questions (questions that, in effect, paint a picture of the facts) are not allowed. The purpose of direct examination is to prompt an answer while allowing the witness to describe what they know about the matter.

The opposite party is then entitled to **cross-examine** the witness. The purpose of cross-examination is to bring out inconsistencies or perhaps cast doubt on the witness's testimony. During the questioning, leading questions are permitted. Cross-examination is not required.

To counter or clarify statements made during cross-examination, the party who first called the witness may conduct a **re-examination**. No new facts may be brought out at this time. Again, such questioning is optional.

Once all of the evidence is admitted, be it the testimony of witnesses or the submission of physical evidence or exhibits, the parties are each given the opportunity to briefly summarize their positions and suggest how the evidence supports their claims. This last step is called the **summation**. Thereafter, the judge may either deliver his judgment from the bench immediately or may reserve the decision to a later date.

Enforcement of Judgment. After the trial decision is made, the parties will be sent a Certificate of Judgment. The successful party (**judgment creditor**) now bears the task of collecting the judgment. Not all judgment debtors pay up voluntarily or promptly. The procedures for enforcing the judgment through seizure or garnishment are described below.

The party who loses the suit has two alternatives: to pay the amount ordered (although some debtors try to avoid this obligation), or to appeal the judge's decision. If the first option is taken, the debtor should ensure that he receives a receipt.

To commence an appeal, one must act quickly. The Notice of Appeal must be filed within 30 days with the Provincial Court that rendered the judgment. A transcript of the evidence must be ordered and paid for. Also, the Notice of Appeal must be served on the other parties. Within 37 days after judgment, the Affidavit of Service of the Notice of Appeal and the Notice itself must be filed with the Court of Queen's Bench, which is where the appeal will be heard. Within the next six months, the transcript from the trial must be filed at the Court of Queen's Bench. Only then may one contact the Court of Queen's Bench to set a date for the appeal. Pending the outcome of the appeal, one can seek a stay of proceedings so that enforcement of the judgment is postponed until the appeal is resolved.

The foregoing describes the streamlined procedures before the Provincial Court, Civil Division. The **Rules of Court**, consisting of approximately 800 rules, determine the procedure to be followed before the superior trial court, the Court of Queen's Bench. Because of the complexity of the process and the greater amount of the claim, it is advisable to retain a lawyer to conduct such litigation.

Procedure before Alberta's Court of Queen's Bench

An action in a superior trial court is commenced by the plaintiff's lawyer by drawing up a **Statement of Claim**, paying a fee, having the documents officially authorized (issued) by a court clerk, and then serving them on the defendant. There are other methods of initiating a court action depending on the nature of the dispute and the remedies sought. Divorce actions, for example, are commenced by filing a Petition. Commencement of actions by filing a Statement of Claim is most common. This pleading contains the names of the parties and their addresses as well as those of the plaintiff's lawyer. The Statement of Claim sets out in detail the plaintiff's dispute with the defendant and notifies the defendant of the nature of the claim. The Statement of Claim must be filed with the court clerk and sent to the other party. After receiving the Statement of Claim, the defendant is obligated to file a **Statement of Defence** in which he provides answers to the claims of the plaintiff. This must be done within 15 days or the plaintiff may have the defendant noted in default and seek a Default Judgment.

If the defendant feels not only that he has a good defence but also that he was in fact the victim, he can attach to the Statement of Defence a **Counterclaim**. This initiates a claim against the plaintiff and is treated as a Statement of Claim by the defendant. It should be noted that the exchange of these documents is not the process of arguing and justifying the two positions; rather, the parties are merely stating the positions that give rise to the dispute between them. If one of the parties feels that the documents don't make her position completely clear, further documents may pass between them, replying to statements and/or demanding more information.

Once the pleadings (Statements of Claim and Defence, etc.) have been closed, the parties have the right in many jurisdictions to initiate the process of discovery. Discovery may be divided into two different parts:

1. **Discovery of documents.** The lawyers of the parties have the right to arrange for the inspection of any document in the possession of the other party that may be used in trial as evidence.

2. **Examination for discovery.** The parties and their lawyers meet before a court reporter, and under oath are asked detailed questions about the problem to be tried.

The parties are required to answer these questions fully and truthfully. Anything that is said is recorded and may be used later at the trial. Note that this process of examination for discovery generally applies only to the parties to the action, not to witnesses. When corporations are involved, a representative is examined who has personal knowledge of the matter. Once the discovery process has been completed, either party can arrange a time for trial with the trial coordinator and give notice to the other party. A pre-trial conference between the lawyers and a judge may be held to determine whether there is a triable issue and if it is possible to resolve the matter. Pre-trial conferences are required for trials before civil juries and trials set for three days or longer duration, amongst others. All of these procedures are designed to provide as much information as possible to the parties before trial and encourage the parties to settle their dispute. In fact, most private disputes are settled between the parties during this pre-trial process.

Payment into court

Other tools available to parties before a trial are payment into court and filing an offer of judgment. A defendant being sued for damages may admit liability but think that the amount being demanded by the plaintiff is too high. When Resnick, for example, fails to perform the terms of his contract with Wong, he may freely admit his liability and be willing to pay $15 000 but balk at Wong's claim for $25 000 damages. Resnick can either deposit $15 000 with the court and notify Wong of the payment or serve an offer of judgment upon the plaintiff specifying the terms upon which the defendant is willing to settle the claim. Wong can either take the money (or accept the offer), thus ending the action, or ignore the payment and proceed to trial in hopes of getting the additional $10 000. But in doing so she takes the risk of losing not only the $15 000 but also the award for costs which would have covered her court and legal fees. In making a decision on the case, the judge is unaware of the payment or offer and if the judgment is for less than the amount offered by the defendant, the plaintiff will not be compensated for any of the costs incurred after the offer was filed or payment was made. The plaintiff had an opportunity to accept a fair settlement and any costs incurred after the failure to do so must be borne by her. If the amount awarded is more than the amount offered, the defendant's offer obviously wasn't fair and the plaintiff will be able to claim compensation for any costs that have been incurred. This encourages the defendant to make a fair offer of payment and the plaintiff to accept it and not risk unrecoverable expenses. This, then, is a mechanism designed to persuade the parties to settle the matter before trial.

Offer to settle

In Alberta a related provision exists for the plaintiff to file an offer to settle which has a similar effect. If the plaintiff sues for $25 000 but is willing to settle for $15 000, he can make the offer and file it with the court and notify the defendant. If the defendant refuses to accept the offer and insists on a trial, he runs the risk of the judgment being for more than the offer to settle. If this happens, the defendant will be required to pay double the plaintiff's costs incurred after the offer to settle was made. If the judgment is less than what was offered, of course, the defendant will only have to pay the costs of the plaintiff in the normal way.

If at this stage the dispute between the parties is still not settled, the next step is to go to trial. This is the part of the civil procedure that is open to the public and readers are urged to attend both civil and criminal actions at a local courthouse to see the justice system in action.

While it is obvious that the purpose of this long, involved and expensive pre-trial process is to encourage the parties to reach a settlement, thus avoiding a trial, it is also clear that the process results in frustrating delay for the parties. For this reason various provinces have initiated reforms to streamline litigation, especially when lower amounts are involved. For example, in B.C. the option of a summary proceeding is available in a supreme court action in personal injury cases where in-

stead of holding a trial with witnesses and testimony, the matter is decided on affidavit evidence. This same objective has motivated Alberta to expand the monetary
limits of its small claims court where the procedures have been dramatically simplified, thus reducing the unreasonable delay and costs associated with litigation.

The Trial

The trial usually proceeds in the following manner. As before the small claims
court, the plaintiff's case and witnesses are presented first. The plaintiff's lawyer
will assist witnesses in their testimony by asking specific questions, but the types of
questions which can be asked are very restricted. The plaintiff's lawyer is prohibited
from asking leading questions in which the answer is suggested, e.g., "You were
there on Saturday, weren't you?" When the plaintiff's lawyer completes this direct
examination of the witness, the defendant's lawyer is given the opportunity to
cross-examine the witness. In cross-examination, the defense lawyer is permitted
more latitude in the type of questions asked and is also permitted to ask leading questions. When the opposing lawyer feels that the lawyer questioning the witness is
abusing the process by asking prohibited questions, he or she will object to the
question and the judge will rule on the objection and decide whether to permit
the question or order the lawyer to withdraw it. The rules governing the type of
testimony that can be obtained from witnesses and all other types of evidence to be
submitted at a trial are referred to as the rules of evidence. (These rules are very complex and beyond the scope of this text.) If something new arises from the cross-
examination, the plaintiff's lawyer can then reexamine witnesses on those matters.
After both sides have finished calling witnesses, the plaintiff's lawyer and then the
defendant's lawyer are allowed to summarize the evidence and make arguments to
the court. Again, if anything new comes up the other party is given a chance to respond to it.

Judgment and Its Enforcement

If a jury is involved, which is not very common in civil cases, the judge will then
make a submission and give instructions to the jury. The jury then retires to consider
the case and returns to announce its decision to the judge. The function of the
jury in such cases is to decide questions of fact; the judge decides the questions of
law. If the matter is being heard by a judge alone, the judge retires after hearing the
arguments of the lawyers, and returns when ready to give a decision. In the case of
a superior court trial, it is more common for the judge to hand down a judgment
in writing some time later. The judge will include reasons for the decision as part
of the judgment. These reasons can form the basis for an appeal as discussed above.

Jury trials

The process of initiating an action to sue someone is usually very expensive,
and creditors may decide to write off a debt rather than incur this expense. In
most provinces the cost of court services is minimal, but the cost of hiring a lawyer
is often prohibitive. This is one of the reasons small claims courts have been introduced in most common law jurisdictions. In small claims courts, the presence of
a lawyer is the exception rather than the rule. But even when the plaintiff's complaint
qualifies as a small claims action, unless the plaintiff is willing to appear personally, the services of a lawyer or some agent must be obtained. Although the parties have the right to represent themselves, lawyers are generally the rule in
higher-level courts.

*Obtaining judgments can be
a costly process*

The plaintiff has to pay for the lawyer even when the suit is successful. If the amount of the claim is large enough to qualify for superior court, the successful claimant will obtain judgment from the defendant for the amount owed and for costs as well. This means that the defendant will be required to compensate the successful plaintiff for a portion of the legal expenses. A variety of factors can be considered in calculating the amount of costs to be awarded. Several tariffs or categories of costs exists. Party-party costs are those usually awarded in an action to the victorious party; solicitor-client costs are those normally charged to the lawyer's own client and are generally higher than party-party costs, and the actual costs paid may be higher still. As a general rule, the plaintiff will face some legal expenses even when successful and there is always the risk of losing and having to bear all the costs.

Remedies.

Damages and other remedies

One of the things that must be decided when a civil suit is begun is determining what the plaintiff will ask the court to do. The most common remedy requested in a court action is monetary payment in the form of **damages**. Usually such damages are designed to compensate the victim for any loss suffered but in some circumstances may take other forms. **Punitive** or **exemplary damages** are intended not to compensate the victim, but to punish the wrongdoer and may result in a windfall for the victim. Only in very serious cases will punitive damages be awarded. Some Canadian companies have discovered to their regret that juries in the United States are not as reluctant to award huge damage awards. The Loewen Group of Funeral Homes faced a jury award of $500 000 000 in a civil action in Mississippi where the company was found liable for a breach of contract in the $8 000 000 purchase of a local funeral home operation. In some circumstances it is also possible to obtain an **accounting** which results in any profits wrongfully obtained by the wrongdoer paid over to the victim. When money has been incorrectly paid over to the defendant the court can order that those funds be **restored** to the rightful owner.

The court also has the power to order that continuing wrongful conduct be stopped, or some existing wrong be corrected by ordering an **injunction.** The court may compel proper performance of a legal obligation by **specific performance**. In some situations it may be appropriate for the courts to simply make a **declaration** as to the law and the legal rights of the parties.

There are other unique remedies usually associated with specific situations that are not mentioned here, but by far the most common remedy asked for in the courts is monetary payment or damages. The following discussion assumes that the remedy sought is payment of a judgment for damages. The key thing to remember in all of this discussion, however, is the adage that you cannot get blood out of a stone.

Enforcement.

A judgment does not ensure payment

Even when the process is complied with and judgment obtained, there is no guarantee that the amount awarded will be paid. The judgment normally eliminates any dispute over the liability of the defendant, but the plaintiff must take further steps to enforce that judgment if the defendant still refuses to pay. If the defendant is unable to pay, it is referred to as a dry judgment. Thus, a plaintiff who has apparently been successful may still be required to bear his or her own costs because of the inability of the defendant to satisfy the judgment. It may also happen that although the defendant has no assets to satisfy the judgment at the time, the prospects for being able to do so in the future are brighter. In this event, it may be wise for the plaintiff to proceed to judgment in order to enforce it some time in the future. Such a judgment remains enforceable for a considerable period of time. In Alberta, judgments are valid for 10 years and may be renewed for an additional 10 years on application to the Court of Queen's Bench. The plaintiff must take into consideration all of these factors as well as the risk of losing the action when deciding to proceed with a civil action against a defendant.

Imprisonment of the Debtor.

In the past, failure to pay debts frequently resulted in imprisonment. Such a drastic course of action is rarely taken now and the use of imprisonment in matters of debt has been severely restricted. An order for imprisonment can only be obtained when the debtor has been ordered by the court to pay the judgment and refuses to do so (as opposed to being unable to pay) or when the debtor attempts to avoid payment through fraud or by leaving the jurisdiction. But in these circumstances, the punishment is for being contemptuous of the court's authority rather than failing to honour a debt.

Imprisonment of debtor only for contempt of court

Enforcing Judgment.

Once judgment has been obtained, most provinces, including Alberta, provide for a further hearing, usually referred to as an examination in aid of execution, to determine which of the defendant's assets are available to satisfy the judgment. In this process, the creditor is able to question the debtor—who is under oath—about his or her wealth, assets, employment, bank accounts, safety deposit boxes and so on. The creditor can also ask about any property transfers in which the debtor may have been involved. At the conclusion of the process, the creditor is in a more knowledgeable position and is better able to instruct seizure of a particular property or garnishee any funds owing, such as wages, bank accounts, and rental or mortgage payments.

Hearing to aid execution

Collecting a Judgment in Alberta.

Before one can proceed with either garnishment or seizure, the judgment (be it from Provincial Court or the Court of Queen's Bench) must be filed with the Clerk of the Court of Queen's Bench. A **Writ of Enforcement** must then be prepared and filed first with the Clerk of the Court of Queen's Bench and then registered with the Personal Property Registry (PPR). The creditor is now entitled to enforce collection and to share in money paid pursuant to the garnishment or seizure proceedings undertaken by other **enforcement creditors** (persons owed money under a judgment against that debtor).

The Writ of Enforcement (Writ) must be completed accurately because once issued, most corrections cannot be made except by court order. (See Writ of Enforcement in Appendix 1-4.) The Writ discloses the Court location and file number, the full names of the debtor and creditor, the date and amount of the judgment, any post-judgment interest that has accrued, the taxed costs and the current amount owing. Writs **authorize** enforcement proceedings in accordance with the *Civil Enforcement Act*.[31] It is advisable to register a copy of the Writ against the debtor at the Land Titles Office in Calgary and/or Edmonton, depending on where the debtor's land is situated. The debtor may then have to satisfy the writ and have it removed if he wishes to transfer the title or grant a mortgage.

---

31. *Civil Enforcement Act,* S.A. (1994) c. C-10.5.

A Writ expires every two years. It is the creditor's responsibility to register a **Status Report** at PPR every two years to avoid expiry and keep the Writ active. A Status Report must also be registered following any receipt of payment by the creditor from the debtor. Whenever enforcement proceedings are utilized, collection is made on behalf of all enforcement creditors.

Any monies collected as a result of enforcement proceedings are paid out as follows: first to pay the costs of seizure/garnishment; second, to the instructing creditor the next $2000 (unless prior claims/statutory claims are asserted); and third, the remaining funds are distributed on a **pro-rata** (ratable) basis among all enforcement creditors. Any excess goes to the debtor.

Prior claims may be asserted by secured creditors. When a security is involved, that is, when the debtor has given the creditor an interest in some property to ensure repayment of the debt, the priority of the creditor is restricted to the specific goods used as security. A creditor who has been given a mortgage secured by a particular asset is likely to assert a priority (first claim) to the proceeds of sale of that asset. Legislation may also create other priorities amongst creditors. The *Workers' Compensation Act*, for example, creates a statutory preference in favour of the Workers' Compensation Board that has priority over writs, judgments, debts, liens, charges and securities other than claims for wages asserted by employees.[32] It is only after these claims have been satisfied that the writ holders who are **unsecured creditors** will be entitled to share in the remaining funds. Real property (land and buildings) can be seized to satisfy a judgment, but a court order authorizing sale must be secured. Often registering the judgment against the property is enough to pressure the debtor to pay, for then the debtor can no longer freely deal with (sell, mortgage, etc.) the land.

Seizure of Property.

This execution process involves seizure and eventual sale of the debtor's property to satisfy the judgment. The Sheriff no longer attends to seizures as this service was privatized pursuant to the *Civil Enforcement Act*.[33] In Alberta, one instructs a Civil Enforcement Agency to seize the property of the debtor, and, unless the debtor pays the debt in the meantime, to sell the seized property and divide the proceeds amongst the creditors. Civil Enforcement Agencies typically require a deposit for seizure costs and fees.

When seizing the debtor's assets, the bailiff will serve a Notice of Seizure of Personal Property and Notice of Objection to Seizure of Personal Property upon the debtor (see Appendix 1-4). The debtor has 15 days to object to the seizure. If the Notice of Objection is served by the debtor upon the agency in time, sale of the seized goods is prevented unless the creditor obtains a court order authorizing sale.

Rather than taking the goods into storage and incurring storage fees during the 15-day waiting period, the bailiff may agree to leave the assets in the possession of the debtor or some other party upon a Bailee's Undertaking. The one given possession (the bailee) promises to keep the goods and deliver them to the Agency when instructed to do so. It is an offence, punishable under the *Criminal Code*, to fail to deliver up the goods.

Certain kinds of property cannot be seized by a Civil Enforcement Bailiff. The *Civil Enforcement Regulations* set out these exemptions. Furniture, clothing and

---

32. *Workers' Compensation Act,* S.A. (1981) c. W-16 s. 126, as amended.

33. *Civil Enforcement Act,* S.A. (1994) c. C-10.5.

motor vehicles under a certain value cannot be seized. It would not serve society to permit seizure of everything, leaving the debtor destitute and penniless.

Garnishment.

If the judgment is executed by seizing a bank account, wages or other outstanding claim, the process is called garnishment, which is sometimes referred to as the **attachment of debt**. Garnishment is much like an interception where the creditor tries to intercept or catch the monies before they get into the hands of the debtor. Accordingly, one must serve a Garnishee Summons upon a third party (called the **Garnishee**) who owes money to the debtor, and attach or claim that money before it is paid over to the debtor.

The Garnishee Summons is addressed to the Garnishee and directs that the money be paid into court rather than to the debtor. The Garnishee Summons is in effect for one year from the date of issuance, except where a bank account is garnished. Then it is effective for only 60 days. It attaches (is effective against) money owed at the time the Garnishee Summons is served as well as future obligations arising during the currency of the document. A Garnishee Summons can also be renewed over and over again.

In addition to completing the Garnishee Summons, the attached Affidavit in Support of Garnishee Summons must be sworn. The deponent is prompted to swear that a judgment has been obtained against this debtor, a Writ has been registered at the Personal Property Registry, the proposed Garnishee is within Alberta, and the deponent believes that monies are or may be payable by the Garnishee to the debtor.

If employment earnings are being garnished, the debtor is entitled to some exemptions. The amount exempted varies according to the number of dependants the debtor has as well as the size of the debtor's earnings. A certain amount must remain with the debtor for survival. (The exemptions formula is spelled out on the third page of the Garnishee Summons.)

The creditor must serve three copies of the Garnishee Summons on the Garnishee. The Garnishee in turn is to serve one copy on the debtor, then complete the Certificate of Service. Next the Garnishee is to forward the money and above Certificate to the Clerk of the Court of Queen's Bench. The Clerk will notify the creditor if funds are paid in. Only the Clerk may distribute garnishee monies.

Note that the creditor can conduct garnishment proceedings without being required to hire a Civil Enforcement Agency or lawyer. Forms can be purchased from Queen's Printer, bookstores and most stationery stores. A copy of the Garnishee Summons is attached (see Appendix 1-4).

Judicial Remedies Before Judgment (in Alberta)

Although most methods of execution require first the obtaining of a judgment, there are some judicial remedies available to the creditor even before that judgment is obtained. Alberta's *Civil Enforcement Act* enables a claimant to apply for an attachment order where the claimant has commenced or is about to commence an action in Alberta or has commenced an action before a foreign tribunal. If the claimant satisfies the court that it is reasonably likely that its claim will be established, and there are reasonable grounds to believe that the defendant is selling, encumbrancing or otherwise dealing with his property in a manner detrimental to the

Prejudgment remedies limited

claimant, then the Court may grant an attachment order. That order may do any of the following: prohibit any dealing (selling, mortgaging, etc.) with the defendant's nonexempt assets, authorize the clerk to issue a garnishee summons, require the defendant to deliver possession or control of her nonexempt assets to the person named in the order, amongst other such directions. Simply put, the attachment order enables both seizure and garnishment to be conducted before a judgment is obtained.

An application for an attachment order may be made **ex parte**, meaning the defendant need not be notified and the application can proceed in her absence. Orders obtained on an ex parte basis expire after 21 days unless the Court orders a later expiry date. Typically, the issue of who is actually entitled to the property attached by attachment orders is determined at or after the trial, but if the Court is convinced that it is necessary or prudent to sell the property, an order for sale may be made before the claim itself is established at a trial.

The process of collection and enforcement of judgment as described here may appear cumbersome. The process can be expensive and may not be justifiable economically considering the amount of the debt and the likelihood of recovery. Note that when an agreement providing that specific property be used as security is involved, that agreement will usually also provide that in the event of a failure to pay, the property can be seized without recourse to the courts. Such agreements are valid although the creditor's rights may be severely restricted by legislation, especially when personal property is involved. Another factor which can affect the debtor's obligation to pay is the process of bankruptcy. Both of these topics will be discussed in Chapter 8.

Limitation Periods

If court action could be initiated for an indefinite period after the act complained of had taken place, this could leave potential defendants in a state of uncertainty for the rest of their lives. In addition, prolonged delay in bringing an action can make it much more difficult to arrive at a fair outcome: witnesses become unavailable, memories dim and documents get lost or destroyed. For this reason all provinces have introduced legislation requiring that legal proceedings commence within a relatively short period of time. Usually such legislation is referred to as a statute of limitations. In Alberta, for example, a person who is owed money from a simple sale of goods transaction and wishes to sue for the debt, must bring an action against the debtor within six years of the failure to pay the debt. An action is initiated by filing a statement of claim with the appropriate court and serving it upon the defendant(s). Failing to fulfill that step within the limitation period will result in the plaintiff being barred from pursuing the action. This time limitation will vary according to the nature of the complaint involved and may be embodied in several different statutes in a province. Whether this limitation period had expired was the problem facing the court in the *Consumer Glass* case used at the beginning of this section.

With the expiry of the limitation period and the threat of court action removed, the potential defendant is not likely to settle out of court and the plaintiff is left with no recourse. For this reason it is important for a person involved in a potential lawsuit to get the advice of a lawyer as quickly as possible. Once the matter is put into the lawyer's hands, the responsibility to act within the limitation period rests on the lawyer. Failure to commence the action within the time limit specified can result in the lawyer being sued for negligence and the client can claim what would

Expiration of limitation period prohibits suing

have been awarded had the action proceeded as it should have. Limitation periods vary not only with the nature of the action but also from province to province.

Alberta's *Limitation of Actions Act* [34] establishes two major limitation periods: six years to sue for breach of contract, two years to sue in tort running from the date of injury. Sometimes the breach or the injury is not apparent for several years. Should a litigant be barred from suing even before he discovers that he has a cause to sue? To cure this, the courts developed a discoverability rule, namely that the limitation period would not start to run until the injury or breach became reasonably discoverable. In 1996, a controversial *Limitations Act* [35] was passed (but had not yet been proclaimed as of the publishing of this text). This *Act* would reduce the limitation period to two years for all actions (based on contract or tort), the time to run from the date of discovery, but the *Act* also imposed a 10-year maximum time limit running from the date of actual injury or the date the contract was breached or discharged.

Alternatives to Court Action

In recent times there has been an upsurge of interest in alternatives to court action for solving disputes between parties. In family matters, it is becoming more common to involve mediators to help the parties come to an out-of-court settlement. Mediation involves the selection of an outside person usually chosen by the parties to listen to their problems and help settle their differences. By listening to both sides and facilitating the negotiation process, the mediator helps the parties to reach an agreement or suggests possible resolutions to their dispute. Professional mediators are very skilled, and while they cannot impose a decision on the parties, they can reduce the adversarial atmosphere which predominates in a courtroom and enhance the possibility of an amicable agreement. The use of professional mediators has for years been an option in labour disputes and the process has been institutionalized in that field. Mediation is also becoming more common in business areas where ongoing contractual relationships are involved. Because in the end the parties reach their own agreement, a continuing relationship is encouraged, whereas the court litigation process usually destroys any goodwill the parties may have had.

Mediation

Another alternative to court action is arbitration, wherein the disputing parties agree to select an independent person or panel to make a decision and agree that the decision will be binding on them. Although the arbitrator may try to facilitate the parties reaching agreement and encourage settlement, this is more like a court where the arbitrator's major function is to listen to evidence, hear the arguments of both sides and make a decision in the matter that is binding on both parties. Unlike a court, however, the arbitration process can be much more informal and is not burdened by the complex rules that govern the field of civil litigation. Arbitration has been used for collective bargaining when there are disputes over the meaning of contracts already in place. It has the advantage of allowing the parties to get the perspective of an independent person who has expertise in the area in dispute and understands the needs and practices of the industry involved. The fact that the parties have agreed to arbitration and chosen the arbitrator also contributes to the likelihood that they will be much more satisfied with the result even if they lose.

Arbitration

ADR

Arbitration and mediation typically are much cheaper and result in a faster, more satisfactory and confidential resolution of the dispute. Thus ADR (alternative dispute resolution) has become a very important alternative to expensive and time-

34. *Limitation of Action Act,* R.S.A. (1980) c. L-15.

35. *Limitations Act,* S.A. (1996) c. L-15.1.

consuming court action and many provinces have encouraged the development of professional ADR specialists. Many business contracts now include provisions which require disputes arising under them to be submitted to arbitration rather than the courts. This is becoming a common practice in such fields as the construction industry, international trade and commerce, and insurance. Banks are using mediation and arbitration in disputes with their clients. And in the field of human rights complaints mediation is being used extensively. The courts are encouraging mediation and in Alberta, judges are now participating in judicial mediation and mini-trials.

The mini-trial is a recent experiment in Alberta. Litigants may opt to present agreed facts to a judge of the Court of Queen's Bench and have the Court deliver a non-binding opinion at the end of the day. This process is entirely voluntary. Parties submit an agreed Statement of Facts; no formal evidence is adduced at the trial. Counsel argue the law and present summations. Finally, the judge renders a decision but it is **not binding**. Time and costs are saved, but this method can only work with the cooperation of all involved and a general willingness to get the dispute resolved and move on.

A second new process is judicial mediation or judicial dispute resolution (J.D.R.). This process is also completely voluntary. The judge acts as a facilitator. Although counsel may present briefs, the judge does not make a decision. Only the parties themselves can reach a settlement; the judge's opinion is merely persuasive. There is no assurance that the time invested in a mini-trial or in judicial mediation will resolve the dispute. If the parties remain entrenched in their own positions, a trial may still be necessary.

Advantages and disadvantages of ADR

Alternative dispute resolution has the advantage of being a cheaper and quicker method of resolving conflict and as a result there is considerably less stress on the parties. But there are some disadvantages to ADR and not all disputes should be handled in this way. The process requires as a rule that the two parties be in roughly equal bargaining positions. It is not uncommon in situations such as family breakdown for one of the parties to attempt to overpower and take advantage of the other. In such cases it is important that a lawyer acting for the vulnerable party review the proposed agreement before it is finalized, because even a mediator or arbitrator cannot always be relied on to assure that a balance is struck in such situations—though part of the skills brought by them is the ability to identify such imbalances and overcome them.

It is also necessary that both parties want to reach an agreement for ADR to be effective. Both mediation and arbitration can be abused when one of the parties is seeking an advantage by delaying the process and introduces procedural obstructions to that end. As a rule the best situations for the involvement of the ADR process is when the relationships are likely to continue and it is important to retain goodwill between the parties.

SUMMARY

There are many different definitions of law, but a simple and useable one is, "that body of rules that can be enforced by the courts or other government agencies." Québec uses a legal system based on the French Civil Code; the other provinces base theirs on the English common law. Our common law system comprises common law and equity (based on decided cases), and statutes, which, because of parliamentary supremacy, override common law and equity when they are properly passed.

The *Constitution Act (1867)*, formerly called the *British North America Act*, created Canada from several British colonies and divided powers between the federal and provincial levels of government. In 1982, the last ties between the British and Canadian parliaments were severed with the passage of the *Constitution Act (1982)* which also contained the *Charter of Rights and Freedoms*. Supremacy of parliament is limited by the requirements of the *Constitution Act (1867)* and the *Charter of Rights and Freedoms*. The meaning of an ambiguous statute is determined by the court using certain rules of interpretation. The *Charter* limits the power of government at all levels and protects personal freedoms, democratic, mobility, legal and equality rights as well as language rights. These rights are qualified by Section 1 of the *Charter*, which allows reasonable exceptions, and Section 33, which allows both federal and provincial governments to opt out of the operation of several important sections. The federal government and each of the provinces have also passed human rights legislation aimed at prohibiting discriminatory practices and encouraging equality of treatment in certain specified fields of activity.

The court systems of the provinces vary but most have a lower-level trial court, an upper-level trial court, and an appeal court. The Supreme Court of Canada is the highest court in Canada and the Federal Court and Federal Court of Appeal have been established to hear matters within the jurisdiction of the federal government. There are also many administrative tribunals created within various government departments to deal with disputes arising within them. The lengthy civil litigation process is designed to give both parties as much information as possible and to encourage settlement before trial. Once a judgment has been obtained it can be enforced through the seizure of property and garnishing wages and bank accounts. Today alternatives to the litigation process in the form of mediation and arbitration are becoming more popular. Recently ADR has been more frequently adopted as a cheaper, faster and more effective alternative to court action.

QUESTIONS

1. Why is it difficult to come up with a satisfactory definition of law?

2. Where do we look to predict the outcome of a legal dispute

    a. in a common law system?

    b. in a civil law system?

3. Explain how the use of previous decisions differs in civil law and common law jurisdictions.

4. Describe what is meant by the following statement: "Common law judges did not make the law, they found it."

5. Explain the advantages and the disadvantages of the system of *stare decisis*.

6. Explain which disadvantages in the common law system led to the development of the law of equity.

7. Explain what was accomplished by the *Judicature Acts* of 1873–75.

8. Explain what is meant by the phrase "the supremacy of parliament."

9. Explain what effect a properly passed statute will have on inconsistent judge-made law (cases).

10. Explain how a parliamentary bill becomes law.

11. Using the principles of *stare decisis*, explain how judges determine whether or not they are bound by another judge's decision in a similar case.

12. What is included in Canada's constitution?

13. Explain why the Canadian Bill of Rights was of only limited effectiveness?

14. Explain how the *Constitution Act (1982)*, including the *Charter of Rights and Freedoms*, affects the doctrine of supremacy of parliament?

15. Explain how the provisions of the provincial human rights codes differ in their application from the *Charter of Rights and Freedoms*.

16. Give examples of democratic rights, mobility rights, legal rights and equality rights as protected under the *Charter*. Give examples of three other types of rights protected under the *Charter*.

17. What is the effect of Sections 91 and 92 of the *British North America Act*, also known as the *Constitution Act (1867)*?

18. How did the *Constitution Act (1867)* limit the power of the federal and provincial governments? How is it possible, given that division of powers, to have identical provisions in both federal and provincial legislation and have both valid? Explain what is meant by the doctrine of paramountcy. When does the doctrine apply?

19. Describe the limitations on the federal or provincial governments' power to delegate their authority to make laws.

20. Distinguish between questions of law and questions of fact and explain why this distinction is significant.

21. Distinguish between administrative tribunals and courts and explain why this distinction is significant.

22. How does the discovery process take place and what is its significance in civil litigation?

23. Explain how a payment into court can affect the judgment award made by the court to the plaintiff.

24. Why might a creditor be reluctant to sue a debtor even when he or she can be sure of successfully obtaining a judgment? What advantage might there be to obtaining a dry judgment?

25. Distinguish between the various remedies available to a successful plaintiff in a civil action.

26. Under what circumstances can a debtor be imprisoned in Canada today?

27. Explain what an examination in aid of execution is and describe its value in the execution process.

28. How can a judgment be enforced against a debtor who is trying to avoid payment?

29. Explain the value of an injunction as a prejudgment remedy. Discuss other prejudgment remedies available to aid in the collection of debt.

30. What is a limitation period and what effect can it have on the right of parties to litigate a matter in dispute?

31. Explain why ADR is becoming much more popular today as an alternative to court action.

....

CASES

1. Re The Queen in Right of British Columbia and Van Gool et al.

Mr. Van Gool owned property in Surrey, a municipality outside Vancouver, on which he operated an airfield for ultralight planes. His property was in an area designated as an agricultural zone in Surrey which prevented the use of the property as an airfield except for his own personal use. Since Van Gool rented space out to others, he was in violation of that bylaw. He was also without a permit, license or other accreditation or certificate from the federal government to operate an airfield. The problem here is whether or not the municipal bylaw applies and whether he can be found in violation of it, considering the constitutional division of powers and the jurisdiction of the federal government over aeronautics. Discuss. Would your answer be different if the bylaw in question simply listed what the property could be used for and did not list an airfield? (See *Venchiarutti v. Longhurst*.)

2. B. (R.) v. Children's Aid Society of Metropolitan Toronto

In this case the parents were Jehovah's Witnesses and when their child was born prematurely with several physical ailments, they resisted the recommendations of the doctors to use blood transfusions. An application was made to a provincial court judge to make the child a ward of the court. This was done and the transfusion was administered. The parents objected to this as an interference with their *Charter* rights. Discuss what sections of the charter they might use in these circumstances as well as the arguments that can be put forward to support the position of the authorities and the likely outcome. Discuss the operation of the *Charter* in these circumstances and whether the transfusion administered to the child violated these basic rights and freedoms.

3. Dartmouth/Halifax County Regional Housing Authority v. Sparks

According to the *Residential Tenancy Act* in place in Nova Scotia, residents who have been renting premises for over five years have security of tenure, which means that they can only be given notice to leave if they are in violation of their obligations under the lease. The *Act*, however, specifically excludes people who are living in public housing, and Mrs. Sparks, a single mother with two children, had been living in the public housing for ten years when she was given one month's notice to leave. She claimed that the *Residential Tenancy Act* provision which makes an exception in the case of public housing discriminated against her. Mrs. Sparks was a black woman and she argued that because many of the people in public housing were black women on social assistance, they were, as a group, being discriminated against by this provision. What do you think?

4. Roberts v. Ontario

The Ministry of Health in Ontario started a program to assist disabled children by providing them with various types of devices. That program was gradually expanded to provide services to other disabled people. Part of this service was to assist in providing vision aids for the blind. In 1986 Mr. Roberts, who was legally blind, applied for financial assistance to purchase such a vision aid and was turned down. The reasons given was that he was 71 years of age and too old. Mr. Roberts purchased the device himself and filed a complaint under the *Human Rights Code* of Ontario. Explain the likely outcome of that complaint.

5. Toronto Blue Jays Baseball Club v. Tri-Tickets Inc.

Tri-Tickets Incorporated and Ticket Time Inc. bought tickets to Toronto Blue Jays baseball games and resold them at a premium to various customers. The terms of the contract under which these tickets were purchased stated that the tickets could not be resold, and this was clearly indicated on the back of the ticket. The Toronto Blue Jays brought this action against the defendants for breach of contract. Explain the appropriate remedies in these circumstances and whether or not they would be granted by the courts.

....

LEGISLATION

Alberta
Civil Enforcement Act, S.A. (1994) c. C-10.5
Court of Appeal Act, R.S.A. (1980) c. C-28
Court of Queen's Bench Act, R.S.A. (1980) c. C-29
Human Rights, Citizenship and Multiculturalism Act, R.S.A. (1980) c. H-11.7
Judicature Act, R.S.A. (1980) c. J-1
Limitations Act, S.A. (1996) c. L-15.1 (not proclaimed at date of publication)
Limitation of Actions Act, R.S.A. (1980) c. L-15
Provincial Court Act, R.S.A. (1980) c. P-20
Provincial Court Judges Act, S.A. (1981) c. P-20.1

Federal
Canadian Charter of Rights and Freedoms, R.S.C. (1985) Appendix II
Constitution Act, R.S.C. (1985) Appendix II
Federal Court Act, R.S.C. (1985) c. F-7
Supreme Court Act, R.S.C. (1985) c. S-26

WEBLINKS

General

The following sites on the World Wide Web (WWW) provide links to information in the area of business law and are relevant to all chapters. Sites listed subsequently have been chosen for specific chapter topics.

Access to Justice Network
www.acjnet.org/
WWW access to legislation, people and organizations, publications, databases, and discussion forums on justice and legal issues.

Alberta Community Development: Human Rights, Citizenship and Multiculturalism
www.gov.ab.ca/~mcd/citizen/hr/hr.htm

Alberta Queen's Printer
www.gov.ab.ca/qp/index.html

Canadian Legal Information Centre
www.wwlia.org/ca-home.htm
A Canadian non-profit corporation based in Victoria, British Columbia, making legal information available to everyone 24 hours a day.

The Canadian Legal Network—Canlaw.com
www.canlaw.net/canlaw/
Provides Canadian lawyers with Internet access to their peers, legal resources and research, and provides the general public with Internet access to the Canadian legal community.

Canadian Legal Resources: A Guide to the Internet
www.fis.utoronto.ca/~schweyer/canleg.htm
Annotated resource guide to Canadian legal and law-related sites currently available on the Internet.

Canadian Legal Resources on the WWW
www.mbnet.mb.ca/~psim/can_law.html
A list of resources on Canadian law and government maintained by Peter Sim, Barrister and Solicitor, Winnipeg.

Virtual Canadian Law Library
www.droit.umontreal.ca/doc/biblio/en/index.html
Canadian legal documents on-line.

Osgoode Hall Law School—Canada Law: A URLs Court of Legal Links
www.yorku.ca/faculty/osgoode/uc.htm

Hieros Gamos—Law and Government
www.hg.org/
Comprehensive law and government site with over 20 000 original pages, more than 70 000 links, and information on over 6000 legal organizations.

Canada: Ministry of Justice
canada.justice.gc.ca/

Canadian Bar Association
www.algonquinc.on.ca/cba/engmenu.html

Specific to Chapter 1

Roman Law: Homepage
www.jura.uni-sb.de/Rechtsgeschichte/Ius.Romanum/english.html

Canadian Law: A History
www.wwlia.org/cahist.htm

BNA Act text
www.nlc-bnc.ca/confed/constitu/ca_1867.htm

Canadian Constitution
canada.justice.gc.ca/cgi-bin/folioisa.dll/const_e.nfo/

Charter of Rights and Freedoms
www.solon.org/Constitutions/Canada/English/ca_1982.html

Canada: Supreme Court of Canada
www.scc-csc.gc.ca/

REFERENCES FOR PART 1

Banfield, Jane, ed. *Readings in Law and Society*, 6th ed. Toronto: Captus Press, 1995.

Magnet, Joseph E. *Constitutional Law of Canada*, 2nd ed. Toronto: Carswell, 1985.

Morton, F. L., ed. *Law, Politics and the Judicial Process in Canada.* Calgary: University of Calgary Press, 1987.

Smyth, J. E., D. A. Soberman, and A. J. Easson. *The Law and Business Administration in Canada.* 8th ed. Toronto: Prentice Hall Canada, 1998.

The *Constitution Act (1867)* (formerly the *British North America Act)* Sections 91 and 92*

APPENDIX 1-1

VI.—Distribution of Legislative Powers

Powers of the Parliament

Legislative authority of
Parliament of Canada

91. It shall be lawful for the Queen, by and with the Advice and Consent of the Senate and House of Commons, to make Laws for the Peace, Order, and Good Government of Canada, in relation to all Matters not coming within the Classes of Subjects by this Act assigned exclusively to the Legislatures of the Provinces; and for greater Certainty, but not so as to restrict the Generality of the foregoing Terms of this Section, it is hereby declared that (notwithstanding anything in this Act) the exclusive Legislative Authority of the Parliament of Canada extends to all Matters coming within the Classes of Subjects next herein-after enumerated; that is to say,

1. The amendment from time to time of the Constitution of Canada, except as regards matters coming within the classes of subjects by this Act assigned exclusively to the Legislatures of the provinces, or as regards rights or privileges by this or any other Constitutional Act granted or secured to the Legislature or the Government of a province, or to any class of persons with respect to schools or as regards the use of the English or the French language or as regards the requirements that there shall be a session of the Parliament of Canada at least once each year, and that no House of Commons shall continue for more than five years from the day of the return of the Writs for choosing the House: provided, however, that a House of Commons may in time of real or apprehended war, invasion or insurrection be continued by the Parliament of Canada if such continuation is not opposed by the votes of more than one-third of the members of such House. (39)

1A. The Public Debt and Property. (40)
  2. The Regulation of Trade and Commerce.
2A. Unemployment insurance. (41)
  3. The raising of Money by any Mode or System of Taxation.
  4. The borrowing of Money on the Public Credit.
  5. Postal Service.
  6. The Census and Statistics.
  7. Militia, Military and Naval Service, and Defence.
  8. The fixing of and providing for the Salaries and Allowances of Civil and other Officers of the Government of Canada.
  9. Beacons, Buoys, Lighthouses, and Sable Island.
10. Navigation and Shipping.
11. Quarantine and the Establishment and Maintenance of Marine Hospitals.
12. Sea Coast and Inland Fisheries.

* Reproduced by permission of the Minister of Supply and Services Canada.

13. Ferries between a Province and any British or Foreign Country or between Two Provinces.
14. Currency and Coinage.
15. Banking, Incorporation of Banks, and the Issue of Paper Money.
16. Savings Banks.
17. Weights and Measures.
18. Bills of Exchange and Promissory Notes.
19. Interest.
20. Legal Tender.
21. Bankruptcy and Insolvency.
22. Patents of Invention and Discovery.
23. Copyrights.
24. Indians, and Lands reserved for the Indians.
25. Naturalization and Aliens.
26. Marriage and Divorce.
27. The Criminal Law, except the Constitution of Courts of Criminal Jurisdiction, but including the Procedure in Criminal Matters.
28. The Establishment, Maintenance, and Management of Penitentiaries.
29. Such Classes of Subjects as are expressly excepted in the Enumeration of the Classes of Subjects by this Act assigned exclusively to the Legislatures of the Provinces.

And any Matter coming within any of the Classes of Subjects enumerated in this Section shall not be deemed to come within the Class of Matters of a local or private Nature comprised in the Enumeration of the Classes of Subjects by this Act assigned exclusively to the Legislatures of the Provinces.

Exclusive Powers of Provincial Legislatures

92. In each Province the Legislature may exclusively make Laws in relation to Matters coming within the Classes of Subject next herein-after enumerated; that is to say,

Subjects of exclusive province legislation

1. The Amendment from Time to Time, notwithstanding anything in this Act, of the Constitution of the Province, except as regards the Office of Lieutenant Governor.
2. Direct Taxation within the Province in order to the raising of a Revenue for Provincial Purposes.
3. The borrowing of Money on the sole Credit of the Province.
4. The Establishment and Tenure of Provincial Offices and the Appointment and Payment of Provincial Officers.
5. The Management and Sale of the Public Lands belonging to the Province and of the Timber and Wood thereon.
6. The Establishment, Maintenance, and Management of Public and Reformatory Prisons in and for the Province.
7. The Establishment, Maintenance, and Management of Hospitals, Asylums, Charities, and Eleemosynary Institutions in and for the Province, other than Marine Hospitals.
8. Municipal Institutions in the Province.
9. Shop, Saloon, Tavern, Auctioneer, and other Licences in order to the raising of a Revenue for Provincial, Local, or Municipal Purposes.
10. Local Works and Undertakings other than such as are of the following Classes:

(a) Lines of Steam or other Ships, Railways, Canals, Telegraphs, and other Works and Undertakings connecting the Province with any other or others of the Provinces, or extending beyond the Limits of the Province;

(b) Lines of Steam Ships between the Province and any British or Foreign Country;

(c) Such Works as, although wholly situate within the Province, are before or after their Execution declared by the Parliament of Canada to be for the general Advantage of Canada or for the Advantage of Two or more of the Provinces.

11. The Incorporation of Companies with Provincial Objects.

12. The Solemnization of Marriage in the Province.

13. Property and Civil Rights in the Province.

14. The Administration of Justice in the Province, including the Constitution, Maintenance, and Organization of Provincial Courts, both of Civil and of Criminal Jurisdiction, and including Procedure in Civil Matters in those Courts.

15. The Imposition of Punishment by Fine, Penalty, or Imprisonment for enforcing any Law of the Province made in relation to any Matter coming within any of the Classes of Subjects enumerated in this Section.

16. Generally all Matters of a merely local or private Nature in the Province.

The *Constitution Act (1982)*, including Part I: *Charter of Rights and Freedoms*, and Parts V–VII. Also: *An Act Respecting Constitutional Amendments**

Constitution Act, 1982

Part 1: Canadian Charter of Rights and Freedoms

Whereas Canada is founded upon principles that recognize the supremacy of God and the rule of Law:

Guarantee of Rights and Freedoms

Rights and freedoms in Canada

1. The *Canadian Charter of Rights and Freedoms* guarantees the rights and freedoms set out in it subject only to such reasonable limits prescribed by law as can be demonstrably justified in a free and democratic society.

Fundamental Freedoms

Fundamental freedoms

2. Everyone has the following fundamental freedoms:
  (*a*) freedom of conscience and religion;
  (*b*) freedom of thought, belief, opinion and expression, including freedom of the press and other media of communications;
  (*c*) freedom of peaceful assembly; and
  (*d*) freedom of association

Democratic Rights

Democratic rights of citizens

3. Every citizen of Canada has the right to vote in an election of members of the House of Commons or of a legislative assembly and to be qualified for membership therein.

Maximum duration of legislative bodies

4. (1) No House of Commons and no legislative assembly shall continue for longer than five years from the date fixed for the return of the writs at a general election of its members.

Continuation in special circumstances

(2) In time of real or apprehended war, invasion or insurrection, a House of Commons may be continued by Parliament and a legislative assembly may be continued by the legislature beyond five years if such continuation is not opposed by the votes of more than one-third of the members of the House of Commons or the legislative assembly, as the case may be.

Annual sitting of legislative bodies

5. There shall be a sitting of Parliament and of each legislature at least once every twelve months.

*Reproduced by permission of the Minister of Supply and Services Canada.

Mobility Rights

6. (1) Every citizen of Canada has the right to enter, remain in and leave Canada.

(2) Every citizen of Canada and every person who has the status of a permanent resident of Canada has the right

    (a) to move to and take up residence in any province; and

    (b) to pursue the gaining of a livelihood in any province.

(3) The rights specified in subsection (2) are subject to

    (a) any laws or practices of general application in force in a province other than those that discriminate among persons primarily on the basis of province of present or previous residence; and

    (b) any laws providing for reasonable residency requirements as a qualification for the receipt of publicly provided social services.

(4) Subsections (2) and (3) do not preclude any law, program or activity that has as its object the amelioration in a province of conditions of individuals in that province who are socially or economically disadvantaged if the rate of employment in that province is below the rate of employment in Canada.

Mobility of citizens

Rights to move and gain livelihood

Limitation

Affirmative action programs

Legal Rights

7. Everyone has the right to life, liberty and security of the person and the right not to be deprived thereof except in accordance with the principles of fundamental justice.

8. Everyone has the right to be secure against unreasonable search or seizure.

9. Everyone has the right not to be arbitrarily detained or imprisoned.

10. Everyone has the right on arrest or detention

    (a) to be informed promptly of the reasons therefor;

    (b) to retain and instruct counsel without delay and to be informed of that right; and

    (c) to have the validity of the detention determined by way of *habeas corpus* and to be released if the detention is not lawful.

11. Any person charged with an offence has the right

    (a) to be informed without unreasonable delay of the specific offence;

    (b) to be tried within a reasonable time;

    (c) not to be compelled to be a witness in proceedings against that person in respect of the offence;

    (d) to be presumed innocent until proven guilty according to law in a fair and public hearing by an independent and impartial tribunal;

    (e) not to be denied reasonable bail without just cause;

    (f) except in the case of an offence under military law tried before a military tribunal, to the benefit of trial by jury where the maximum punishment for the offence is imprisonment for five years or a more severe punishment;

    (g) not to be found guilty on account of any act or omission unless, at the time of the act or omission, it constituted an offence under Canadian or international law or was criminal according to the general principles or law recognized by the community of nations;

Life, liberty and security of person

Search or seizure

Detention or imprisonment

Arrest or detention

Proceedings in criminal and penal matters

(h) if finally acquitted of the offence, not to be tried for it again and, if finally found guilty and punished for the offence, not to be tried or punished for it again; and

(i) if found guilty of the offence and if the punishment for the offence has been varied between the time of commission and the time of sentencing, to the benefit of the lesser punishment.

Treatment or punishment

12. Everyone has the right not to be subjected to any cruel and unusual treatment or punishment.

Self-incrimination

13. A witness who testifies in any proceedings has the right not to have any incriminating evidence so given used to incriminate that witness in any other proceedings, except in a prosecution for perjury or for the giving of contradictory evidence.

Interpreter

14. A party or witness in any proceedings who does not understand or speak the language in which the proceedings are conducted or who is deaf has the right to the assistance of an interpreter.

Equality Rights

Equality before and under law and equal protection and benefit of law

15. (1) Every individual is equal before and under the law and has the right to the equal protection and equal benefit of the law without discrimination and, in particular, without discrimination based on race, national or ethnic origin, colour, religion, sex, age or mental or physical disability.

Affirmative action programs

(2) Subsection (1) does not preclude any law, program or activity that has as its object the amelioration of conditions of disadvantaged individuals or groups including those that are disadvantaged because of race, national or ethnic origin, colour, religion, sex, age or mental or physical disability.

Official Languages of Canada

Official languages of Canada

16. (1) English and French are the official languages of Canada and have equality of status and equal rights and privileges as to their use in all institutions of the Parliament and government of Canada.

Official languages of New Brunswick

(2) English and French are the official languages of New Brunswick and have equality of status and equal rights and privileges as to their use in all institutions of the legislature and government of New Brunswick.

Advancement of status and use

(3) Nothing in this Charter limits the authority of Parliament or a legislature to advance the equality of status or use of English and French.

English and French linguistic communities in New Brunswick

16.1 (1) The English linguistic community and the French linguistic community in New Brunswick have equality of status and equal rights and privileges, including the right to distinct educational institutions and such distinct cultural institutions as are necessary for the preservation and promotion of those communities.

Role of the legislature and government of New Brunswick

(2) The role of the legislature and government of New Brunswick to preserve and promote the status, rights and privileges referred to in subsection (1) is affirmed.

Proceedings of Parliament

17. (1) Everyone has the right to use English or French in any debates and other proceedings of Parliament.

Proceedings of New Brunswick legislature

(2) Everyone has the right to use English and French in any debates and other proceedings of the legislature of New Brunswick.

Parliamentary statutes and records

18. (1) The statutes, records and journals of Parliament shall be printed and published in English and French and both language versions are equally authoritative.

New Brunswick statutes and records

(2) The statutes, records and journals of the legislature of New Brunswick shall be printed and published in English and French and both language versions are equally authoritative.

19. (1) Either English or French may be used by any person in, or in any pleading in or process issuing from, any court established by Parliament.

Proceedings in courts established by Parliament

(2) Either English or French may be used by any person in, or in any pleading in or process issuing from, any court in New Brunswick.

Proceedings in New Brunswick courts

20. (1) Any member of the public in Canada has the right to communicate with, and to receive available services from, any head or central office of an institution of the Parliament or government of Canada in English or French, and has the same right with respect to any such institution where

Communications by public with federal institutions

　(*a*) there is a significant demand for communications with and services from that office in such language; or

　(*b*) due to the nature of the office, it is reasonable that communications with services from that office be available in both English and French.

(2) Any member of the public in New Brunswick has the right to communicate with, and to receive available services from, any office of an institution of the legislature or government of New Brunswick in English or French.

Communications by public with New Brunswick institutions

21. Nothing in sections 16 to 20 abrogates or derogates from any right, privilege or obligation with respect to the English and French languages, or either of them, that exists or is continued by virtue of any other provision of the Constitution of Canada.

Continuation of existing constitutional provisions

22. Nothing in sections 16 to 20 abrogates or derogates from any legal or customary right or privilege acquired or enjoyed either before or after the coming into force of this Charter with respect to any language that is not French or English.

Rights and privileges preserved

Minority Language Educational Rights

23. (1) Citizens of Canada

Language of instruction

　(*a*) whose first language learned and still understood is that of the English and French linguistic minority population of the province in which they reside, or

　(*b*) who have received their primary school instruction in Canada in English or French and reside in a province where the language in which they received that instruction is the language of the English or French linguistic minority population of the province, have the right to have their children receive primary and secondary school instruction in that language in that province.

(2) Citizens of Canada of whom any child has received or is receiving primary or secondary school instruction in English or French in Canada, have the right to have all their children receive primary and secondary school instruction in the same language.

Continuity of language instruction

(3) The right of citizens of Canada under subsections (1) and (2) to have their children receive primary and secondary school instruction in the language of the English or French linguistic minority population of a province

Application where numbers warrant

　(*a*) applies wherever in the province the number of children of citizens who have such a right is sufficient to warrant the provision to them out of public funds of minority language instruction; and

　(*b*) includes, where the number of those children so warrants, the right to have them receive that instruction in minority language educational facilities provided out of public funds.

Enforcement

24. (1) Anyone whose right or freedoms, as guaranteed by this Charter, have been infringed or denied may apply to a court of competent jurisdiction to obtain such remedy as the court considers appropriate and just in the circumstances.

Enforcement of guaranteed rights and freedoms

Exclusion of evidence bringing administration of justice into disrepute

(2) Where, in proceedings under subsection (1), a court concludes that evidence was obtained in a manner that infringed or denied any rights or freedoms guaranteed by this Charter, the evidence shall be excluded if it is established that, having regard to all the circumstances, the admission of it in the proceedings would bring the administration of justice into disrepute.

General

Aboriginal rights and freedoms not affected by *Charter*

25. The guarantee in this Charter of certain rights and freedoms shall not be construed so as to abrogate or derogate from any aboriginal, treaty or other rights and freedoms that pertain to the aboriginal peoples of Canada including
  (a) any rights or freedoms that have been recognized by the Royal Proclamation of October 7, 1763; and
  (b) any rights or freedoms that may be acquired by the aboriginal peoples of Canada by way of land claims settlement.

Other rights and freedoms not affected by *Charter*

26. The guarantee in this Charter of certain rights and freedoms shall not be construed as denying the existence of any other rights or freedoms that exist in Canada.

Multicultural heritage

27. This Charter shall be interpreted in a manner consistent with the preservation and enhancement of the multicultural heritage of Canadians.

Rights guaranteed equally to both sexes

28. Notwithstanding anything in this Charter, the rights and freedoms referred to in it are guaranteed equally to male and female persons.

Rights respecting certain schools preserved

29. Nothing in this Charter abrogates or derogates from any rights or privileges guaranteed by or under the Constitution of Canada in respect of denominational, separate or dissentient schools.

Applications to territories and territorial authorities

30. A reference in this Charter to a province or to the legislative assembly or legislature of a province shall be deemed to include a reference to the Yukon Territory and Northwest Territories, or to the appropriate legislative authority thereof, as the case may be.

Legislative powers not extended

31. Nothing in this Charter extends the legislative powers of any body or authority.

Application of Charter

Application of *Charter*

32. (1) This Charter applies
  (a) to the Parliament and government of Canada in respect of all matters within the authority of Parliament including all matters relating to the Yukon Territory and Northwest Territories; and
  (b) to the legislature and government of each province in respect of all matters within the authority of the legislature of each province.

Exception

(2) Notwithstanding subsection (1), section 15 shall not have effect until three years after this section comes into force.

Exception where express declaration

33. (1) Parliament or the legislature of a province may expressly declare in an Act of Parliament or of the legislature, as the case may be, that the Act or a provision thereof shall operate notwithstanding a provision included in section 2 or sections 7 to 15 of this Charter.

Operation of exception

(2) An Act or a provision of an Act in respect of which a declaration made under this section is in effect shall have such operation as it would have but for the provision of this Charter referred to in the declaration.

Five-year limitation

(3) A declaration made under subsection (1) shall cease to have effect five years after it comes into force or on such earlier date as may be specified in the declaration.

Re-enactment

(4) Parliament or the legislature of a province may re-enact a declaration made under subsection (1).

Five-year limitation

(5) Subsection (3) applies in respect of a re-enactment made under subsection (4).

Citation

34. This Part may be cited as the *Canadian Charter of Rights and Freedoms.*

Citation

Part II: Rights of the Aboriginal Peoples of Canada

35. (1) The existing aboriginal and treaty rights of the aboriginal peoples of Canada are hereby recognized and affirmed.

Recognition of existing aboriginal and treaty rights

(2) In this Act, "aboriginal peoples of Canada" includes the Indian, Inuit and Métis peoples of Canada.

Definition of "aboriginal people of Canada"

(3) For greater certainty, in subsection (1) "treaty rights" includes rights that now exist by way of land claims agreements or may be so acquired.

Land claims agreements

Part V: Procedure for Amending Constitution of Canada

38. (1) An amendment to the Constitution of Canada may be made by proclamation issued by the Governor General under the Great Seal of Canada where so authorized by

General procedure for amending Constitution of Canada

(a) resolutions of the Senate and House of Commons; and

(b) resolutions of the legislative assemblies of at least two-thirds of the provinces that have, in the aggregate, according to the then latest general census, at least fifty per cent of the population of all the provinces.

(2) An amendment made under subsection (1) that derogates from the legislative powers, the proprietary rights or any other rights or privileges of the legislature or government of a province shall require a resolution supported by a majority of the members of each of the Senate. the House of Commons and the legislative assemblies required under subsection (1).

Majority of members

(3) An amendment referred to in subsection (2) shall not have effect in a province the legislative assembly of which has expressed its dissent thereto by resolution supported by a majority of its members prior to the issue of the proclamation to which the amendment relates unless that legislative assembly, subsequently, by resolution supported by a majority of its members, revokes its dissent and authorizes the amendment.

Expression of dissent

(4) A resolution of dissent made for the purposes of subsection (3) may be revoked at any time before or after the issue of the proclamation to which it relates.

Revocation of dissent

39. (1) A proclamation shall not be issued under subsection 38(1) before the expiration of one year from the adoption of the resolution initiating the amendment procedure thereunder, unless the legislative assembly of each province has previously adopted a resolution of assent or dissent.

Restriction on proclamation

(2) A proclamation shall not be issued under subsection 38(1) after the expiration of three years from the adoption of the resolution initiating the amendment procedure thereunder.

Idem

40. Where an amendment is made under subsection 38(1) that transfers provincial legislative powers relating to education or other cultural matters from provincial legislatures to Parliament, Canada shall provide reasonable compensation to any province to which the amendment does not apply.

Compensation

41. An amendment to the Constitution of Canada in relation to the following matters may be made by proclamation issued by the Governor General under the Great Seal of Canada only where authorized by resolutions of the Senate and House of Commons and of the legislative assembly of each province:

Amendment by unanimous consent

(a) the office of the Queen. the Governor General and the Lieutenant Governor of a province;

(b) the right of a province to a number of members in the House of Commons not less than the number of Senators by which the province is entitled to be represented at the time this Part comes into force;

(c) subject to section 43, the use of the English or the French language;

(d) the composition of the Supreme Court of Canada; and

(e) an amendment to this Part.

Amendment by general procedure

42. (1) An amendment to the Constitution of Canada in relation to the following matters may be made only in accordance with subsection 38(1):

(a) the principle of proportionate representation of the provinces in the House of Commons prescribed by the Constitution of Canada;

(b) the powers of the Senate and the method of selecting Senators;

(c) the number of members by which a province is entitled to be represented in the Senate and the residence qualifications of Senators;

(d) subject to paragraph 41(d), the Supreme Court of Canada;

(e) the extension of existing provinces into the territories; and

(f) notwithstanding any other law or practice, the establishment of new provinces.

Exception

(2) Subsections 38(2) to (4) do not apply in respect of amendments in relation to matters referred to in subsection (I).

Amendment of provisions relating to some but not all provinces

43. An amendment to the Constitution of Canada in relation to any provision that applies to one or more, but not all, provinces, including

(a) any alteration to boundaries between provinces, and

(b) any amendment to any provision that relates to the use of the English or the French language within a province,

may be made by proclamation issued by the Governor General under the Great Seal of Canada only where so authorized by resolutions of the Senate and House of Commons and of the legislative assembly of each province to which the amendment applies.

Amendments by Parliament

44. Subject to sections 41 and 42, Parliament may exclusively make laws amending the Constitution of Canada in relation to the executive government of Canada or the Senate and House of Commons.

Amendments by provincial legislatures

45. Subject to section 41, the legislature of each province may exclusively make laws amending the constitution of the province.

Initiation of amendment procedures

46. (1) The procedures for amendment under sections 38, 41, 42 and 43 may be initiated either by the Senate or the House of Commons or by the legislative assembly of a province.

Revocation of authorization

(2) A resolution of assent made for the purposes of this Part may be revoked at any time before the issue of a proclamation authorized by it.

Amendments without senate resolution

47. (1) An amendment to the Constitution of Canada made by proclamation under section 38, 41, 42 or 43 may be made without a resolution of the Senate authorizing the issue of the proclamation if, within one hundred and eighty days after the adoption by the House of Commons of a resolution authorizing its issue, the Senate has not adopted such a resolution and if, at any time after the expiration of that period, the House of Commons again adopts the resolution.

Computation of period

(2) Any period when Parliament is prorogued or dissolved shall not be counted in computing the one hundred and eighty day period referred to in subsection (1).

Advice to issue proclamation

48. The Queen's Privy Council for Canada shall advise the Governor

General to issue a proclamation under this Part forthwith on the adoption of the resolutions required for an amendment made by proclamation under this Part.

49. A constitutional conference composed of the Prime Minister of Canada and the first ministers of the provinces shall be convened by the Prime Minister of Canada within fifteen years after this Part comes into force to review the provisions of this Part.

Constitutional conference

Part VI: Amendment to *The Constitution Act*, 1867

50. *The Constitution Act, 1867* (formerly named the *British North America Act, 1867*) is amended by adding thereto, immediately after section 92 thereof, the following heading and section:

Amendment to Constitution Act., 1867

"Non-Renewable Natural Resources. Forestry Resources and Electrical Energy"

92A. (1) In each province, the legislature may exclusively make laws in relation to

Laws respecting non-renewable natural resources forestry resources and electrical energy

   (a) exploration for non-renewable natural resources in the province;

   (b) development, conservation and management of non-renewable natural resources and forestry resources in the province, including laws in relation to the rate of primary production therefrom; and

   (c) development, conservation and management of sites and facilities in the province for the generation and production of electrical energy.

(2) In each province, the legislature may make laws in relation to the export from the province to another part of Canada of the primary production from non-renewable natural resources and forestry resources in the province and the production from facilities in the province for the generation of electrical energy, but such laws may not authorize or provide for discrimination in prices or in supplies exported to another part of Canada.

Export from provinces of resources

(3) Nothing in subsection (2) derogates from the authority of Parliament to enact laws in relation to the matters referred to in that subsection and, where such a law of Parliament and a law of a province conflict, the law of Parliament prevails to the extent of the conflict.

Authority of Parliament

(4) In each province, the legislature may make laws in relation to the raising of money by any mode or system of taxation in respect of

Taxation of resources

   (a) non-renewable natural resources and forestry resources in the province and the primary production therefrom, and

   (b) sites and facilities in the province for the generation of electrical energy and the production therefrom.

whether or not such production is exported in whole or in part from the province, but such laws may not authorize or provide for taxation that differentiates between production exported to another part of Canada and production not exported from the province.

(5) The expression "primary production" has the meaning assigned by the Sixth Schedule.

"Primary production"

(6) Nothing in subsections (I) to (5) derogates from any powers or rights that a legislature or government of a province had immediately before the coming into force of this section."

Existing powers or rights

Idem

51. The said *Act* is further amended by adding thereto the following Schedule:

"THE SIXTH SCHEDULE
Primary Production from Non-Renewable Natural Resources and Forestry Resources

1. For the purposes of section 92A of this Act,

    (a) production from a non-renewable natural resource is primary production therefrom if

        (i) it is in the form in which it exists upon its recovery or severance from its natural state, or

        (ii) it is a product resulting from processing or refining the resource, and is not a manufactured product or a product resulting from refining crude oil, refining upgraded heavy crude oil, refining gases or liquids derived from coal or refining a synthetic equivalent of crude oil; and

    (b) production from a forestry resource is primary production therefrom if it consists of sawlogs, poles, lumber, wood chips, sawdust or any other primary wood product, or wood pulp, and is not a product manufactured from wood."

Part VII: General

Primacy of Constitution of Canada

52. (1) The Constitution of Canada is the supreme law of Canada, and any law that is inconsistent with the provisions of the Constitution is, to the extent of the inconsistency, of no force or effect.

Constitution of Canada

(2) The Constitution of Canada includes

    (a) the Canada Act: 1982. including this Act;

    (b) the Acts and orders referred to in the schedule; and

    (c) any amendment to any Act or order referred to in paragraph (a) or (b).

Amendments to Constitution of Canada

(3) Amendments to the Constitution of Canada shall be made only in accordance with the authority contained in the Constitution of Canada.

42-43-44 Elizabeth II

Chapter 1

An Act respecting constitutional amendments

[Assented to 2nd February, 1996]

Her Majesty, by and with the advice and consent of the Senate and House of Commons of Canada, enacts as follows:

1.   (1) No Minister of the Crown shall propose a motion for a resolution to authorize an amendment to the Constitution of Canada, other than an amendment in respect of which the legislative assembly of a province may exercise a veto under section 41 or 43 of the *Constitution Act, 1982* or may express its dissent under subsection 38(3) of that *Act,* unless the amendment has first been consented to by a majority of the provinces that includes

    (a) Ontario;

    (b) Quebec;

    (c) British Columbia;

    (d) two or more of the Atlantic provinces that have, according to the then latest general census, combined populations of at least fifty per cent of the population of all the Atlantic provinces; and

    (e) two or more of the Prairie provinces that have, according to the then latest general census, combined populations of at least fifty per cent of the population of all the Prairie provinces.

(2) In this section,

"Atlantic provinces" means the provinces of Nova Scotia, New Brunswick, Prince Edward Island and Newfoundland;

"Prairie provinces" means the provinces of Manitoba, Saskatchewan and Alberta.

Definitions

"Atlantic provinces"

"Prairie provinces"

Excerpts from Alberta's *Human Rights, Citizenship and Multiculturalism Act*

Preamble

WHEREAS recognition of the inherent dignity and the equal and inalienable rights of all persons is the foundation of freedom, justice and peace in the world;

WHEREAS it is recognized in Alberta as a fundamental principle and as a matter of public policy that all persons are equal in: dignity, rights and responsibilities without regard to race, religious beliefs, colour, gender, physical disabilities, mental disability, age, ancestry, place of origin, marital status, source of income or family status;

WHEREAS multiculturalism describes the diverse racial and cultural composition of Alberta society and its importance is recognized in Alberta as a fundamental principle and a matter of public policy;

WHEREAS it is recognized in Alberta as a fundamental principle and as a matter of public policy that all Albertans should share in an awareness and appreciation of the diverse racial and cultural composition of society and that the richness of life in Alberta is enhanced by sharing that diversity;

WHEREAS it is fitting that these principles be affirmed by the Legislature of Alberta in an enactment whereby those equality rights and that diversity may be protected:

THEREFORE HER MAJESTY, by and with the advice and consent of the Legislative Assembly of Alberta, enacts as follows:

Effect of Act on provincial laws

1(1) Unless it is expressly declared by an Act of the Legislature that it operates notwithstanding this Act, every law of Alberta is inoperative to the extent that it authorizes or requires the doing of anything prohibited by this Act.

(2) In this Act, "law of Alberta" means an Act of the Legislature of Alberta enacted before or after the commencement of this Act, any order rule or regulation made thereunder, and any law in force in Alberta on January 1, 1973 that is subject to be repealed, abolished or altered by the Legislature of Alberta.

Alberta Heritage Day

1.1 In recognition of the cultural heritage of Alberta, the first Monday in August each year shall be observed as a day of public celebration and known as "Alberta Heritage Day."

Code of Conduct

Discrimination re publications, notices

2(1) No person shall publish, issue or display or cause to be published, issued or displayed before the public any statement, publication, notice, sign, symbol, emblem or other representation that

    (a) indicates discrimination or an intention to discriminate against a person or a class of persons, or

    (b) is likely to expose a person or a class of persons to hatred or contempt because of the race, religious beliefs, colour, gender, physical disability,

mental disability, age, ancestry, place of origin, marital status, source of income or family status of that person or class of persons.

(2)   Nothing in this section shall be deemed to interfere with the free expression of opinion on any subject.

(3)   Subsection (1) does not apply to

(a) the display of a notice, sign, symbol, emblem or other representation displayed to identify facilities customarily used by one gender,

(b) the display or publication by or on behalf of an organization that

(i)   is composed exclusively or primarily of persons having the same political or religious beliefs, ancestry or place of origin, and

(ii) is not operated for private profit, of a statement, publication, notice, sign, symbol, emblem or other representation indicating a purpose or membership qualification of the organization, or

(c) the display or publication of a form of application or an advertisement that may be used, circulated or published pursuant to section 8(2),

if the statement, publication, notice, sign, symbol, emblem or other representation is not derogatory, offensive or otherwise improper.

Discrimination re goods, services, accommodation, facilities

3   No person shall

(a) deny to any person or class of persons any goods, services, accommodation or facilities that are customarily available to the public, or

(b) discriminate against any person or class of persons with respect to any goods, services, accommodation or facilities that are customarily available to the public,

because of the race, religious beliefs, colour, gender, physical disability, mental disability, ancestry, place of origin, marital status, source of income or family status of that person or class of persons or of any other person or class of persons.

Discrimination re tenancy

4   No person shall

(a) deny to any person or class of persons the right to occupy as a tenant any commercial unit or self-contained dwelling unit that is advertised or otherwise in any way represented as being available for occupancy by a tenant, or

(b) discriminate against any person or class of persons with respect to any term or condition of the tenancy of any commercial unit or self-contained dwelling units,

because of the race, religious beliefs, colour, gender, physical disability, mental disability, ancestry, place of origin, marital status, source of income or family status of that person or class of persons or of any other person or class of persons.

5 Repealed 1996 c25 s7.

Equal pay

6(1) Where employees of both sexes perform the same or substantially similar work for an employer in an establishment the employer shall pay the employees at the same rate of pay.

(2) to (4) Repealed 1996 c25 s8.

(5)   No employer shall reduce the rate of pay of an employee in order to comply with this section.

(6)   When an employee is paid less than the rate of pay to which the employee is entitled under this section, the employee is entitled to recover from the employer by action the difference between the amount paid and the amount to which the employee was entitled, together with costs but

> (a) the action must be commenced within 12 months from the date on which the cause of action arose and not afterward,
>
> (b) the action applies only to the wages of an employee during the 12-month period immediately preceding the termination of the employee's services or the commencement of the action, whichever occurs first,
>
> (c) the action may not be commenced or proceeded with when the employee has made a complaint to the Commission in respect of the contravention of this section, and
>
> (d) no complaint by the employee in respect of the contravention shall be acted on by the Commission when an action has been commenced by the employee under this section.

Discrimination re employment practices

7(1) No employer shall

> (a) refuse to employ or refuse to continue to employ any person, or
>
> (b) discriminate against any person with regard to employment or any term or condition of employment,

because of the race, religious beliefs, colour, gender, physical disability, mental disability, ancestry, place of origin, marital status, family income or source of income of that person or of any other person or class of person.

(1.1), (1.2) Repealed 1990 c23 s4.

(2) Subsection (1) as it relates to age and marital status does not affect the operation of any bona fide retirement or pension plan or the terms or conditions of any bona fide group or employee insurance plan.

(3) Subsection (1) does not apply with respect to a refusal, limitation, specification or preference based on a bona fide occupational requirement.

Applications and advertisements re employment

8(1) No person shall use or circulate any form of application for employment or publish any advertisement in connection with employment or prospective employment or make any written or oral inquiry of an applicant

> (a) that expresses either directly or indirectly any limitation, specification or preference indicating discrimination on the basis of the race, religious beliefs, colour, gender, physical disability, mental disability, marital status, age, ancestry, place of origin, family status or source of income of any person, or
>
> (b) that requires an applicant to furnish any information concerning race, religious beliefs, colour, gender, physical disability, mental disability, marital status, age, ancestry, place of origin, family status or source of income.

(2) Subsection (1) does not apply with respect to a refusal, limitation, specification or preference based on a bona fide occupational requirement.

9 Repealed 1996 c25 s11.

Membership in trade union, etc.

10   No trade union, employers' organization or occupational association shall

> (a) exclude any person from membership in it,

(b) expel or suspend any member of it, or

(c) discriminate against any person or member,

because of the race, religious beliefs, colour, gender, physical disability, mental disability, marital status, age, ancestry, place of origin, family status or source of income of that person or member.

Prohibitions regarding complaints

11(1) No person shall retaliate against a person because that person

    (a) has made or attempted to make a complaint under this Act,

    (b) has given evidence or otherwise participated in or may give evidence or otherwise participate in a proceeding under this Act,

    (c) has made or is about to make a disclosure that that person may be required to make in a proceeding under this Act, or

    (d) has assisted in any way in

        (i) making or attempting to make a complaint under this Act, or

        (ii) the investigation, settlement or prosecution of a complaint under this Act.

(2) No person shall, with malicious intent, make a complaint under this Act that is frivolous or vexatious.

Reasonable and justifiable contravention

11.1   A contravention of this Act shall be deemed not to have occurred if the person who is alleged to have contravened the Act shows that the alleged contravention was reasonable and justifiable in the circumstances.

Definitions

38 (1) In this Act,

    (a)   "age" means 18 years of age or older;

    (e.01)"family status" means the status of being related to another person by blood, marriage or adoption;

    (e.02)"marital status" means the status of being married, single, widowed, divorced, separated or living with a person of the opposite sex in a conjugal relationship outside marriage;

    (i.1) "religious beliefs" includes native spirituality;

    (i.2) "source of income" means lawful source of income;

  (2) Whenever this Act protects a person from being adversely dealt with on the basis of gender, the protection includes, without limitation, protection of a female from being adversely dealt with on the basis of pregnancy.

APPENDIX 1-4 Provincial Court Forms and Civil Enforcement Forms

---

Docket No. _____

**In The Civil Division of
The Provincial Court of Alberta**

Between:

Plaintiff

and

Defendant

Civil Claim

The Plaintiff Claims from the Defendant $ _____ and costs of this action. The Claim arose at

_____ , Alberta on or about the _____ day of _____ ,19 _____ .

The reasons for the Claim are:

The Plaintiff's Mailing Address is:					
Street Address	City	Province	Postal Code	Res. Phone	Bus. Phone

The Defendant's Mailing Address is:					
Street Address	City	Province	Postal Code	Res. Phone	Bus. Phone

The Defendant's Mailing Address is:					
Street Address	City	Province	Postal Code	Res. Phone	Bus. Phone

Dated this

_____ day of _____ ,19 _____

at_____ , Alberta.

Signature of Plaintiff / Agent / Solicitor   Print Name

The Court's Address is:

I will be calling _____ witnesses.

Issued by The Provincial Court of Alberta

this _____ day of _____ ,19 _____ .

_____
Clerk of The Provincial Court

Default Judgment / Noting in Default

The Defendant _____

having been served with a Civil Claim and not having filed a Dispute Note and the time for doing so having expired,

☐ the Defendant named above is noted in default.

☐ Judgment is entered in favor of the Plaintiff for $ _____

interest of $ _____

and costs of $ _____

Entered this _____ day of _____ , 19 _____   for a total judgment of $ _____

a.m.
at _____ p.m. at _____ , Alberta.

_____
Clerk of The Provincial Court

AG 1461 Rev Apr 96

**In The Civil Division of
The Provincial Court of Alberta**

Docket No.

Between:

Plaintiff

and

Defendant

Dispute Note

1. I dispute the Plaintiff's Claim for the following reasons:

2. I Counterclaim or Claim a set-off for $ _____ , for the following reasons:

3. **My Mailing Address is:**

Street Address	City	Province	Postal Code	Res. Phone	Bus. Phone

Dated this

I will be calling _____ witnesses at the hearing of this matter.
number of

_____ day of _____ ,19 _____

at _____ , Alberta.

_____   _____
Signature of Defendant / Agent / Solicitor   Print Name

Instructions to the Defendant

*   *If you do not have a legitimate reason for disputing a claim, filing a
Dispute Note may result in increased costs to you.*

1. In paragraph 1, state clearly the reasons you are disputing the Plaintiff's Claim.
If the Plaintiff's Claim is disputed in part only, state which part is disputed.

2. In paragraph 2, if you are claiming an amount from the Plaintiff, clearly state
the amount you are claiming and the reasons.

3. In paragraph 3, give an address at which documents may be sent to you.

4. Deliver the completed Dispute Note in person or by mail to the Court address
shown on the front of the Civil Claim.

5. **Please do not send any additional material with your Dispute Note
(i.e. books, papers, etc.).**

6. After you have filed the Dispute Note, you will be notified in writing by the
Court of the time, date and place of the hearing. Bring your additional material
to court for your hearing.

For office use only

Received at _____   a.m.
p.m.

J 1924 Rev Jun 94   **It is your responsibility to notify the Court of any change of address.**

**In The Civil Division of
The Provincial Court of Alberta**

Docket No.

Affidavit of Service

Print Name and Address

I, _____

of _____

make oath and say / solemnly affirm and declare that on the _____ day of _____ , 19 _____

I served _____

Cross out which ever
are inapplicable

with a true copy of the attached Civil Claim and Dispute Note \ Order \ Notice of Application \ Notice of Assessment by:

Personal Service
on an individual

a) delivering the copies personally to the Defendant at

_____

Service by Double
Registered or Certified mail
on an individual

b) mailing the copies by double registered / certified mail to the Defendant at

_____

Attached and marked Exhibit "A" is the receipt from the Post Office and attached and marked Exhibit "B" is the acknowledgement receipt from the Defendant or a person receiving it on the Defendant's behalf.

Personal service at the most
usual residence of
individual

c) leaving the copies with _____
a resident thereof apparently 16 years of age or older at the Defendant's most usual place of residence at

_____

Personal service at
Registered office of
Corporation only

d) leaving the copies at the registered office of the above named corporation at

_____

Service by Registered mail
at Registered office of
Corporation only

e) mailing the copies by registered mail to the registered office of the above named corporation at

_____

Attached and marked Exhibit "A" is the receipt from the post office.

Personal service on
President, Head Officer,
Director, Manager, Agent or
Officer of the Corporation

f) leaving the copies with _____

a / an _____ of the above named corporation

Service on a Partnership

g) leaving the copies with _____
a partner of the above named partnership

As directed by the Court

h) _____

_____

Sworn / Affirmed before me this

_____ day of _____ , 19 _____

at _____ , Alberta.

_____
Commissioner for Oaths for Alberta

_____
Print Name and Expiry

J 1451 Rev Mar 94

FORM F

Financing Statement

Writ of Enforcement
Civil Enforcement Act

FILED

COURT LOCATION _____

COURT FILE NUMBER _____

TYPE OF JUDGMENT   CROWN ☐   **EMPLOYMENT STANDARDS** ☐   OTHER ☐

This Writ authorizes enforcement proceedings in accordance with the Civil Enforcement Act. The particulars of the Writ are as follows:

DEBTOR   INDIVIDUAL ☐ — Male   OTHER ☐   **OCCUPATION** _____

Female   **DATE OF BIRTH** _____

Business Name or Last Name	First Name	Middle Name	
Address	City	Province	Postal Code

CREDITOR   INDIVIDUAL ☐   OTHER ☐   **P.P.R. PARTY CODE** _____

Business Name or Last Name	First Name	Middle Name	
Address	City	Province	Postal Code

☐ Additional Debtors and Creditors and/or other information listed on attached addendum.

☐ If claiming priority based on an Attachment Order or partial

Date of Judgment (or date Judgment effective, if different) _____ day of _____ .

Original Judgment . . . . $ _____   This Writ is issued for the amount of the judgment plus costs and interest.

Post Judgment Interest . . . . $ _____   ISSUED this _____ day of _____

Costs . . . . $ _____

Current Amount Owing . . . . . . $ _____

CLERK OF THE COURT

SOLICITOR / AGENT   **P.P.R. PARTY CODE** _____

Name in Full

Address	City	Province	Postal Code
Area Code & Telephone Number	Fax Number	Call Box	Your Reference Number

TO REGISTER AGAINST SERIAL # GOODS AT PERSONAL PROPERTY REGISTRY, COMPLETE THE FOLLOWING:

SERIAL NUMBER (Only Applicable to serial number goods, e.g. motor vehicles.)	YEAR	MAKE AND MODEL	CATEGORY

1

Authorized Signature   **Print Name**   **Control Number**   Page   Of

Oct. 01/95

Form 5
Civil Enforcement Regulation

Civil Enforcement Agency File Number

Notice of Seizure of Personal Property

TO: _____

_____
Name and Address of Debtor

Take notice that to satisfy a claim against you for the sum **$** _____ plus costs and related Writs, if applicable.

_____

_____
Name and Address of Creditor

has caused the following personal property and personal property listed in the addendum to be seized:

Addendum attached listing additional property.　☐ Yes　☐ No

Notice of Objection applicable to this seizure.　☐ Yes　☐ No

STRIKE OUT
IF NOT
APPLICABLE

If you object to the seizure, you must deliver the attached Notice of Objection within 15 days from the date of seizure to the Civil Enforcement Agency listed below:

_____　_____

Bailiff's Signature　　　　　　　　　　Print Name

Name of Civil Enforcement Agency

Address of Civil Enforcement Agency　　　　　City

Province　　　　　Postal Code　　　　　Telephone Number　　　　　Fax Number

Oct. 01/95

Page 1 of _____

Form 6
Civil Enforcement Regulation

Civil Enforcement Agency File Number

Notice of Objection to Seizure of Personal Property

TO: _____

_____

Name, Address and Fax Number of Civil Enforcement Agency

This Notice of Objection to Seizure of Personal Property will not be accepted if a reason for the objection is not provided.

I object to the seizure of the personal property mentioned in the Notice of Seizure of Personal Property for the following reason(s):

_____

_____

_____

_____

_____

_____

_____

(IF ADDITIONAL SPACE REQUIRED, PLEASE WRITE ON REVERSE.)

IF YOU OBJECT TO THE SEIZURE OF PERSONAL PROPERTY, THIS NOTICE MUST BE DELIVERED TO THE ABOVE NOTED CIVIL ENFORCEMENT AGENCY W ITHIN 15 DAYS OF THE DATE ON WHICH THE SEIZURE DOCUMENTS WERE SERVED.

If there is no valid reason for objecting to the seizure of the personal property, the sending of this notice may result in increased costs to you.

_____   _____

THE FOLLOWING MUST BE COMPLETED:

_____   _____

Signature of Debtor   Print Name

_____   _____

Mailing Address of Debtor   City

_____   _____   _____   _____

Province   Postal Code   Telephone Number   Fax Number

Oct. 01/95

IN THE COURT OF QUEEN'S BENCH OF ALBERTA
JUDICIAL DISTRICT OF_____

BETWEEN:

CREDITOR

_____ AND _____

DEBTOR

_____
AND

_____

GARNISHEE

GARNISHEE SUMMONS

This Garnishee Summons is issued on _____

for the amount of $_____ (this amount may be adjusted from time to time)

against ☐ Employment Earnings   ☐ Deposit Accounts   ☐ Other obligations

_____

Clerk of the Court

Judgment is for Alimony or Maintenance ☐

NOTE: In the case of judgments for alimony or maintenance, where employment earnings are being garnished, the Maintenance Enforcement Act employment exemptions apply (See section 13(1) of the Maintenance Enforcement Regulation).

This summons expires:
  a)   in the case of a deposit account, **60 days from the date it was issued.**
  b)   in all other cases, one year from the date it was issued, unless renewed.

Affidavit in Support of Garnishee Summons

I, _____ of the Town / City of _____

in the Province of Alberta, make oath and say that:

1.   I am (the solicitor/agent for) the Creditor and in accordance with the judgment / Attachment Order specified in this Garnishee Summons, a Writ of Enforcement / Attachment Order has / has not been registered at the Personal Property Registry.

2.   The proposed Garnishee and the Debtor have a contract or other legal relationship under which monies are or may become due from the proposed Garnishee to the Debtor.

3.   The proposed Garnishee is within Alberta.

Sworn/Affirmed before me at

_____ .

Alberta, on _____

_____
Signature

_____
A Commissioner for Oaths in and for the Province of Alberta

_____
Print Name and Expiry Date

To the Clerk:

The Creditor has a Judgment / Attachment Order against the Debtor, and a Writ of Enforcement / Attachment Order has been registered at Personal Property Registry as

_____
PPR Registration Number

The amount specified in the Writ of Enforcement / Attachment Order is

$ _____ , of which the present

Balance owing is	$	_____
Plus related writs (as per the attached search results)	$	_____
Plus probable costs	$	_____
TOTAL	$	_____

Number　_____

IN THE COURT OF QUEEN'S BENCH OF ALBERTA

JUDICIAL DISTRICT OF

BETWEEN:

_____
　　　　　　　　　　　　　　　　Creditor

_____
Address, Telephone Number and Fax Number

AND

_____
　　　　　　　　　　　　　　　　Debtor

_____
Address, Telephone Number and Fax Number

AND

_____
　　　　　　　　　　　　　　　Garnishee

_____
Address, Telephone Number and Fax Number

Certificate of Service on the Debtor

I, _____

hereby certify that on _____ ,

I served _____ .
　　　　　　　(Name of Debtor)

☐　personally

　　or

☐　by ordinary mail

with a true copy of the Garnishee Summons pursuant to the Alberta Rules of Court and the Civil Enforcement Act.

Dated _____ .

_____
Garnishee/Creditor Signature

_____
Print Name

(If there is more than one Debtor, please complete an additional Certificate of Service for each Debtor.)

GARNISHEE SUMMONS

☐ Before Judgment ☐ After Judgment

Filed By:

_____
Name/Firm

_____
Address

_____
Telephone Number　　　　　　　　Fax Number

Class Action Lawsuits

VIDEO CASE

CBC

The courts are becoming increasingly difficult to access by ordinary citizens, particularly when their complaints are against large corporations that have unlimited wealth and power with which to defend their actions. A relatively new method of dealing with this problem has emerged in the past decade: the class action lawsuit. Class action suits are being used to help individual consumers who have similar complaints against a manufacturer of a product that has caused them injury.

The procedure requires that an individual representing a group of plaintiffs appear before a judge to apply to have an issue heard as a class action and the judge determines whether they can proceed. All the parties then share the costs of the action. There are currently upwards of 200 class action lawsuits in process in Canada. The defendants in such actions are usually large companies that have ignored or failed to remedy defects in their products or services. Large corporations have been immune from liability cases largely because the expense for an individual to undertake such a court challenge is prohibitive. And even if a complainant did sue and won, the company's payment of damages and court costs would be significantly less than that of recalling or correcting the defect. But when hundreds of people with the same complaint band together, the manufacturer of a defective product has a big problem and the class action lawsuit has provided another way to force them to deal with it. The downside, of course, is that "the price of doing business [goes] through the roof," and lawyers seem to be the group most likely to benefit from the trend. A prominent example of such a case is the women who have been injured or become ill as a result of silicone breast implants and have been parties in a class action against Dow Corning, claiming that the implants they manufactured were defective. Other such suits include owners of condominiums suing the builder for defective construction and the students of a business college claiming the college has not lived up to its claims to prepare them for the job market.

This video relates to the process of civil litigation described in Chapter 1 of the text, but it also has implications for those who have been injured by the negligent or careless conduct of others. Three Canadian provinces, Ontario, Québec and B.C., have enacted class action legislation.

Source: "Class Action," *Venture,* Show Number 617; telecast date: November 17, 1996. Running time: 5:45.

DISCUSSION QUESTIONS

1. Compare and contrast a class action to a regular lawsuit, outlining its advantages and disadvantages.
2. Examine the class action statute in place in your jurisdiction. (If there is no such statute yet, consider whether there should be.) Does the statute accomplish its purpose? Discuss any negative implications.
3. Discuss what effect class action suits might have on manufacturers and their responsibility for the products and services they provide.
4. Consider the impact of class actions on the courts and consumer prices.

PART

2

The Fundamentals

Before dealing with the specialized legal relations and transactions that are the major focus of this text, it is necessary to understand the basic concepts and principles upon which they are built. These fundamentals are covered in Chapters 2 to 6. Chapter 2 is an examination of tort law, the basis of liability imposed on professional and business people for their wrongful conduct that causes injury to others. Chapters 3 to 6 examine the law of contract including the requirements for a valid contract, problems that can arise between contracting parties, and how a contractual relationship ends. Most of the transactions and relationships discussed in the rest of the text are specialized forms of contracts with their own unique rules.

Photo by Jack
Dagley/Canapress.

The Law of Torts

2

OBJECTIVES OF THE CHAPTER

- To define torts and describe various types of tortious conduct
- To distinguish between careless and negligent conduct
- To determine whether or not a duty of care is owed
- To set out the standards of care expected
- To identify defenses to tort actions
- To indicate trends in the development of the tort of negligence
- To relate tort actions to business activities

While washing their truck at a service station, the parents of a four-year-old boy allowed him to play without supervision behind the station. Unknown to the parents, there was an open cesspool there. It was unmarked and its opening was flush with the ground. Their son fell in and although rescued became very ill, required hospitalization and suffered significant physical problems as a result of the accident. The parents brought an action against both the oil company that owned the station and the operators who leased it. The judge found that the defendants were negligent and liable under the Ontario *Occupiers' Liability Act* since they had known of the open cesspool. By doing nothing about it, they had failed to take reasonable steps to protect the little boy from its dangers.[1]

The most serious source of unexpected and unplanned for liability in business today results from the torts committed by those businesses or their employees. This tort liability may result from services including advice improperly provided, defective or dangerous products supplied, or dangerous premises as was the case in the above example. When injuries result from our negligent or willful conduct, whether it be in business or in our personal lives, under the law of torts we are liable to compensate the victims for the injuries they suffer.

1. *Vachon et al. v. Roy et al.*, Ont. Dist. Ct., Jan. 1987, 642-009.

INTRODUCTION

When people engage in commercial activities, conflicting interests or simple interactions often lead to the commission of torts. There is no wholly satisfactory definition for torts because there is considerable disagreement over whether there is one underlying principle governing all types of tortious activity or whether there are many different torts, each governed by different rules. Some general principles, however, do apply. Tort law mediates situations in which an individual's conduct interferes with another's person, property or reputation. If the interfering conduct falls below a minimum social standard and causes injury or loss, a tort has been committed and the victim has the right to sue for compensation. For this reason, torts can be defined as social wrongs other than crimes or breaches of contract. *Because the resulting court action is civil rather than criminal, such torts are usually called civil wrongs.*

A tort is a civil or social wrong

DEVELOPMENT OF TORT LAW

It is the courts that are responsible for the development of this body of law. By looking at tort law's development, one uncovers certain underlying principles. The first is **fault**. The courts were reluctant to award compensation to a victim unless the tortfeasor was shown to be at fault. The definition of fault has expanded over the years. Early on, fault could only be established if there was **intentional** or deliberate behaviour that caused injury. Damages would not be awarded if the injury was accidental; if accidentally caused, an injury would have to be borne solely by the victim. No redistribution of loss would be justifiable. Over time, fault became defined more broadly. Now one can be found at fault if one hurt another by not being careful enough, or by being **negligent**.

Another concept that has received a broader interpretation over the years is **injury**. Early tort law only recognized physical or bodily injuries as being compensable. Today, the Courts are awarding damages for economic losses as well. And if the plaintiff satisfies the Court that emotional or mental injuries have been suffered, those losses are likewise compensable.

A third development is in the area of **causation**. With this element the courts have moved in the opposite direction by narrowing when and where a defendant will be liable for injuries caused by that defendant. Whereas the direct consequences test used to be the sole criterion for determining causation (namely, that the defendant was responsible for any injuries he directly caused), now the remoteness test is often used as well. Under the remoteness test, the defendant is only responsible for injuries that were or should have been foreseeable. If too remote or unforeseeable, the injuries are not the defendant's legal responsibility. Although this aspect of tort law has been treated more restrictively recently, tort liability in general continues to expand dramatically.

Conduct so serious that it poses a threat to society generally is said to be criminal in nature. The object of the courts in dealing with criminal activity is to punish the wrongdoer, not to compensate the victim. With many crimes, the victim retains the right to sue for tort. Thus, wrongful conduct is often both a crime and a tort. Most of the torts discussed in this chapter have a *Criminal Code* counterpart. It is also important to note that prosecution for a crime whether it results in a conviction or acquittal, does not affect the plaintiff's right to sue civilly in tort. One need only think of the two cases heard in California involving the former NFL football player and Hollywood personality O.J. Simpson. Simpson was found not guilty of criminal charges for the deaths of Ronald Goldman and Nicole Brown Simpson. In a criminal case the state has the burden of proving guilt beyond a reasonable doubt. This, the prosecution failed to do. But later, at the civil trial where Goldman's family sued for damages for the tort of wrongful death, O.J. Simpson was found liable. At a civil trial the burden of proof is less onerous; the plaintiff need only prove that the defendant *probably* committed the wrong.

A tort must also be distinguished from a breach of contract. An act that breaches a contract may not be inherently wrong, but the contractual relationship makes the violation of its terms unacceptable. A tort on the other hand is inherently wrongful conduct that falls below a minimum acceptable social standard that is judicially imposed. The court determines who should bear the loss for the injuries suffered and the amount that will adequately compensate the victim.

Torts may involve intentional or inadvertent conduct

Two major categories of tortious activities will be considered in this chapter: intentional or deliberate acts, and careless or negligent acts that cause another to suffer loss or injury. One important difference between intentional torts and negligence is in the remedies that the courts are willing to grant to the injured party. When the interference has been intentional, the courts may be persuaded to grant punitive damages in addition to the more common general and special damages. Special damages are awarded to cover actual expenses and calculable losses and general damages are the estimated costs of such unmeasurable factors as pain and suffering. Punitive damages are designed to punish the wrongdoer and don't relate to the injury suffered. Occasionally where appropriate the court may also order the return of property or an injunction to stop some offending activity. Major criticism of the enormous damage awards given in the United States where personal injury is involved has led to considerable debate and call for reform in that country. The problem has been avoided in Canada to a large extent by a Supreme Court of Canada decision[2] in which the court put a cap of $100 000 on the damages that could be awarded in personal injury cases to compensate for such things as pain and suffering and loss of enjoyment of life. Because of inflation this limit today is about $250 000.

Employer can be vicariously liable for employee's tort

For businesses especially, it is important to keep the concept of **vicarious liability** in mind while studying these categories of tort. An employer can be held liable for the tortious act an employee commits during the employment. This liability is limited to torts committed while carrying out the employee's employment responsibilities. The employer will not be vicariously liable when the employee is "on a frolic of his or her own." The importance of vicarious liability in the business world cannot be overemphasized. A detailed examination of the master/servant relationship and vicarious liability can be found in Chapter 10. Several provinces have imposed vicarious liability by statute on the owners of motor vehicles, making them liable for damage and injury caused by other people whom they allow to drive their cars, whether or not they are employees, and even when such people are not acting within the scope of their employment. Note, for example, the wording of Section 181 of Alberta's *Highway Traffic Act*[3]:

When driver deemed agent of owner

> **181** In an action for the recovery of loss or damage sustained by a person by reason of a motor vehicle on a highway,

2. *Thornton v. Prince George* [1978] 2 S.C.R. 267.

3. *Highway Traffic Act*, R.S.A. (1980) c. H-7.

(a) a person driving the motor vehicle and living with and as a member of the family of the owner of it, and

(b) a person who is driving the motor vehicle and who is in possession of it with the consent, express or implied, of the owner of it,

shall be deemed to be the agent or servant of the owner of the motor vehicle and to be employed as such, and shall be deemed to be driving the motor vehicle in the course of his employment, but nothing in this section relieves any person deemed to be the agent or servant of the owner and to be driving the motor vehicle in the course of his employment from the liability for the damages.

INTENTIONAL TORTS

Assault and Battery

Malette v. Shulman[4]

Mrs. Malette was a Jehovah's Witness who was seriously injured in an automobile accident. She was brought into the emergency ward where Dr. Shulman practised as a physician. She was unconscious and in very serious condition and the doctor decided she needed a blood transfusion, but before he could administer it, a nurse going through her bag found a card which specifically stated that she was not to be given blood. The card made it clear that she wanted to obtain other forms of treatment, but under no circumstances were blood products to be administered to her in any form. Dr. Shulman, after considering the situation, decided that the transfusion was necessary to preserve her life and proceeded. While the transfusion was being administered, her daughter came in and Dr. Shulman refused to follow the instructions of the daughter to have the transfusion terminated. Mrs. Malette recovered and brought an action against Dr. Shulman for battery. In the Ontario Court of Appeal, the judge found that Dr. Shulman was motivated by the highest professional motives, that he carried out the treatment in a "confident, careful and conscientious manner," and that the treatment may well have saved Mrs. Malette's life. But the court found that despite Dr. Shulman's honest and even justifiable belief that the treatment was necessary and his good intentions, he still had committed a battery against the plaintiff and the court awarded $20 000 damages against the doctor. This amount was not trivial and was intended to show that doctors, despite the best intentions, don't have the right to interfere with people against their specific instructions. Trespass to person or battery, as we deal with it in these pages, is any interference with a person against their wishes. Normally, there would have been a right for a doctor to presume a consent on the patient's part to treatment in an emergency situation. However, such implied consent cannot be presumed in the face of a specific indication otherwise. Hence, Dr. Shulman committed a battery. We normally think of assault and battery as taking place in violent situations where people for evil motives intentionally interfere with others. This case illustrates that battery in fact is broader, and that people have the right not to have their person interfered with by others even when they are well motivated to do so.

Consent needed to avoid trespass to person

Fear of contact—assault

Actual contact—battery

Intent to harm not required

Consent is a defense

Assault and battery (or trespass to person) is intentional physical interference with another and becomes important for business people especially where they are engaged in serving the public in businesses such as retail sales, sporting events, hotels and restaurants. An action which makes a person think that he or she is about to be struck is an **assault**. If someone takes a swing and misses, points a gun or picks up a stone to threaten another person, an assault has been committed. A **battery** takes place when someone is in actual physical contact with another person. Since battery almost invariably involves an assault, the term "assault" is often used to refer to both assault and battery.

It is not necessary to show that any actual injury was suffered to be successful in an action. In the case of *Cole v. Turner*[5] the judge declared that "the least touching of another in anger is battery." Normal, unavoidable contacts we all experience in social situations such as tapping someone on the shoulder to gain attention or brushing against another person in a crowded hallway do not constitute battery. Battery involves intentional conduct by the offending party and the application of physical force to the victim. Negligence involves inadvertent conduct and will be discussed below.

In considering whether an action amounts to assault, it is not necessary for the victim to be fearful of imminent harm, only that unwelcome contact is expected. When a person threatens to kiss another, there may be no fear involved but the action may still constitute an assault. The action complained of must be a physical gesture and not only words, although words accompanying the action can turn the conduct into an assault. Conversely, a person rushing towards you might seem to be an assault were it not for the words "How nice to see you again." Thus, the words and the action must be considered together. The words accompanying the action might make an innocent action an assault or might take the threat away from a threatening gesture. It is not necessary that the person committing the assault or battery have an evil or malicious goal. A doctor, with the best of intentions, might operate to save the life of a protesting patient. Such an act, when consent is denied, may nevertheless constitute a battery.[6]

Normally, doctors escape liability for their actions when operating or otherwise treating patients through the principle of **consent**. Essentially, a person who consents, either expressly or by implication, to conduct that would otherwise constitute an assault or battery, loses the right to sue. This is the reason injured boxers cannot sue their opponents. One cannot consent to an illegal act, however; and if one of the parties to a consensual street fight is seriously injured, the other may be liable for the battery despite the consent. Sometimes the level of violence goes beyond the nature of the consent. Excessive violence in a hockey game or other sporting activity is an example and will also constitute a battery despite the consent.

The consent must be informed consent; people must know what they are consenting to. Some people for religious reasons resist medical intervention, even when it would save their lives. Refusal is their right. The doctor who persists in treating them after being told of their refusal has committed a battery and is liable to the victim. The court may award significant damages in such a case, as was the result in the *Malette* case used to open this discussion.[7]

5. *Cole v. Turner* (1705) 87 E.R. 907 (Kings Bench Div.).

6. This right may not extend to others within their care. When parents refuse treatment needed to save the lives of their children for religious reasons, the courts are often willing to interfere by taking custody of the children away from the parents and ordering treatment.

7. See also *Mulloy v. Hop Sang* (1935) 1 W.W.R. 714 (Atta. C.A.).

One way an assault can become a problem for the business person is when an uncooperative patron needs to be ejected. The general rule is that when a patron becomes a trespasser by violating the rules of the establishment, the occupier or servant of the occupier is justified in asking the patron to leave. If the patron refuses, the occupier then has the authority to use as much force as is necessary to eject the trespasser. However, if excessive force is used and the patron is injured, the operator will be held liable for those injuries.

Reasonable force permitted to eject trespasser

In the case of *Cottreau v. Rodgerson,*[8] the plaintiff was a patron in the defendant's establishment and became intoxicated. When he refused to leave, the bartender ejected him into the back lane. The bartender turned and was walking back to his establishment when he thought he saw the patron lunging toward him. The bartender turned and struck him a severe blow in the face, causing a serious injury. The plaintiff sued, claiming the bartender had used excessive force. The court held that the bartender had acted properly in asking the patron to leave, then, when his request was refused, by removing him forcibly. But the court held that even if the patron had been lunging to assault the defendant in the lane, a blow of such force was not needed to subdue the patron because of his intoxicated condition. The defendant was liable, therefore, to compensate the victim.

Self-Defense.

The law entitles people who are being attacked or think that they are about to be attacked to use as much force as is necessary to defend themselves. The test is reasonable force. When one person attacks another with a clenched fist and the person being attacked shoots the attacker with a gun, such a response is considered excessive, and the injured party has the right to sue for assault and battery. Of course, when someone with no experience in responding to violence is threatened by someone twice his or her size, the person being attacked might have difficulty in measuring exactly how much force is necessary to subdue the other party. The court will take this lack of experience into consideration in determining if the amount of force used in the response was reasonable. The test the courts use is what a reasonable person with the same skills, knowledge and background as the person being attacked would have done in the circumstances.

Reasonable force to defend permitted

It is important to note, however, that the victim can use the concept of self-defense as a defense only while being attacked. Once the danger has passed, self-defense cannot be used to support later acts of vengeance. It is not the responsibility of private citizens to punish perpetrators of tortious or criminal acts. Court action provides a substitute for personal retaliation.

Trespass to Land

Trespass to land involves someone who goes onto another person's property without having either the lawful right or the owner's permission to do so. Business people often must

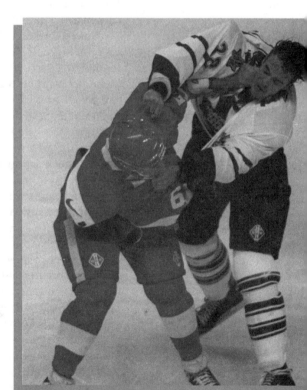

The problem of consent—just how far can you go?
Photo by Frank Gunn/Canapress.

8. *Cottreau v. Rodgerson* (1965) 53 D.L.R. (2d) 549 (Nova Scotia Supreme Court).

On land without authority

deal with individuals that they don't want on their premises and it is important to know at what stage a person become a trespasser and what can be done to remove them from the property. Some individuals have statutory authority empowering them to enter private property for specific purposes. Municipal inspectors, meter readers, police officers and other officials have the lawful right to be on private property, and cannot be charged with trespass if their purpose in being there is in keeping with their official duties. Permission to enter private property for anyone other than those legally empowered to be there may be expressed or implied. If an owner or occupier has knowledge that people have been using his or her property for some time, but has done nothing to discourage them, they may be said to have implied permission or license to be on the property and cannot successfully be sued for trespass. An implied permission to come onto property is presumed when a business is offering services to the public such as a department store or a shopping mall. People visiting these premises are not usually considered trespassers even if they do not come to shop. But unruly or disruptive patrons can be asked to leave and if they fail to do so they become trespassers. Reasonable force can be used to eject them and they can be asked not to return. It should be emphasized, however, that the reason for the exclusion or ejection must not be a violation of their civil rights under the various human rights codes of the provinces as would be the case if it was done because of racial, religious or ethnic considerations.

Trespass to land is an intentional tort to the extent that a person who is voluntarily on another's land without lawful right or permission has committed trespass. It is only necessary that the person be there of his or her own volition. A trespasser cannot avoid liability by claiming ignorance of where the property line is.

However, when a person is found on the property of another through no act of his or her own, it is not a case of trespass. In the early case of *Smith v. Stone*,[9] the defendant was carried onto private property by the violent acts of other people. The judge determined that the trespass was committed not by the defendant but by the people who carried the defendant onto the property. This case also illustrates the point that the defendant need not come onto the land to commit a trespass. It is also trespass when objects are thrown or placed on another's property. A vandal who throws a rock through a window has committed a trespass.

Trespass can be indirect

Trespass is actionable even if no injury or loss has taken place. The "mere bruising of the grass" is said to be enough to support a trespass action. In such cases, the courts are usually reluctant to award anything but nominal damages, but a trespass has been committed nonetheless. More significantly, the occupier of property has the right to use as much force as is necessary to eject a trespasser. Typically, this right means that the occupier can demand that the trespasser leave; if the trespasser refuses, the occupier then has the right to use reasonable force to eject the trespasser without being liable for assault and battery. In the case of *Cottreau v. Rodgerson* discussed above under the heading "Assault and Battery," the bartender was within his rights to eject the intoxicated patron who had become a trespasser. But the blow struck was unnecessary and this unreasonable force was actionable battery.

Trespassers who cause damage while on private property bear responsibility for any injury or loss caused, whether it was foreseeable or not. In cases where a person is suing for injuries suffered while on private property, there is only a minimal duty owed by an occupier not to injure a trespasser. In Alberta, when a person is on another's property for a criminal purpose or is a trespasser, the obligation is only not to willfully or recklessly cause that trespasser harm.

---

9. *Smith v. Stone* (1647) 82 E.R. 533 (Kings Bench Div.).

Continuing Trespass.

Continuing trespass is involved when a party puts up a building or other structure that encroaches on the property of another. The problem, especially when large commercial structures are involved, is that once the building is found to be encroaching on another's property, the costs of correcting the situation can be enormous. In the case of *Gross v. Wright*,[10] the owners of two adjoining properties agreed to establish a common wall on the property line. The wall was to be 24 inches (0.6 metres) at its base and taper as it went up. The finished wall was 12 inches on each side at the base as agreed, but as it tapered towards the top, the builder made sure that the full width of 12 inches was maintained on the property of his neighbour and that all the tapering took place on his side. The wall at the top was entirely on the property of the neighbour in violation of the agreement. When the neighbour discovered this, he took the defendant to court. The court decided that a continuing trespass was taking place and issued an injunction ordering that the continuing trespass cease. An injunction is an equitable remedy whereby the court orders that a condition or activity in violation of the law be stopped or corrected. In this case, the court suspended the operation of the injunction to give the defendant time to make adjustments so that the wall would conform to the agreement. One can readily see the kinds of problems this might cause for structures such as the multistoreyed buildings now located in most urban areas.

Injunction available to remedy continuing trespass

False Imprisonment

False imprisonment including false arrest (also a form of trespass to person) as a cause of action occurs when people are unlawfully and intentionally restrained against their will. Businesses are susceptible to this particular tort when they supply goods or services to the public. Retail stores are plagued by shoplifting and restaurants by customers who leave without paying for their meals. The problem is compounded when the establishments in question have undertrained or overzealous staff. For an imprisonment to have occurred, the restraint may take place in a prison cell or in any completely confined room. There is no imprisonment if people are barred from crossing a bridge or going down a passageway because they can go back the way they came. Nor is there imprisonment if it is possible to slip out through an unnoticed door or an open window. This does not mean that imprisoned victims have to use heroic means to obtain their freedom. It is not necessary for people confined in a ship to jump into the water to free themselves.

Restraint without lawful excuse—false imprisonment

Imprisonment may also take place when the person being imprisoned submits to another's control through recognition of authority or a threat. When a police officer, a security guard or even a store clerk orders someone to remain in a particular location and the person complies thinking there is no alternative, there has been a submission of will to the authority of the police officer and therefore imprisonment. If a person goes voluntarily with the police officer, no imprisonment has taken place, but the willingness to cooperate with the officer must be real. If the person accompanies the officer to avoid embarrassment or because of fear that refusal would result in being forced to comply, then an imprisonment may have taken place. For a person to be imprisoned, there must be a true submission of will.

Submission to authority can constitute imprisonment

The case of *Bahner v. Marwest Hotel Company Ltd., Muir et al.*[11] is typical of the kind of problems facing restaurants, hotels and retail stores. In that case, the defen-

10. *Gross v. Wright* [1923] 2 D.L.R. 171 (Supreme Court of Canada).

11. *Bahner v. Marwest Hotel Company Ltd., Muir et al.* (1969) 6 D.L.R. (3d) 322 (B.C.S.C.).

dant, a patron in a Vancouver restaurant, was unfamiliar with the provincial liquor laws when he ordered and obtained a bottle of wine at 11:30 p.m. The waiter opened the bottle and left it on the table. At a few minutes to twelve, the waiter told Bahner that he would have to drink the wine before midnight. The customer replied that he could not do that without becoming intoxicated and suggested that he take the bottle with him. The waiter said that was not permitted and Bahner refused to pay for the wine. When he got up to leave after paying for the meal but not the wine, a security guard ordered him to stay while the police were called. When the police arrived, Bahner was taken to the police station where he had to spend the night before being released. Bahner sued the restaurant for false imprisonment. At the trial, the restaurant argued that, because there were other ways out of the restaurant, the plaintiff had not been imprisoned. The court decided that this was a situation in which the customer had submitted his will to the command of the security guard so there had been an imprisonment. The judge said,

> The plaintiff, commanded by the security officer to stay and prevented by the officer from leaving by the ordinary exit, behaved with admirable restraint in making no forcible attempt to pass the security officer. After what the officer had said and done he could reasonably expect to be restrained by force if he tried to leave by any exit and he was not required to make an attempt to run away.[12]

Imprisonment is false—where no authority

There are two factors to consider when examining this kind of action. First, it must be clearly demonstrated that there was an imprisonment and, of equal importance, that such imprisonment was false or without authority. Once it had been established that there had been imprisonment, the court had to deal with the second point: whether or not the plaintiff had done something for which he could be imprisoned, that is, refusing to pay for the wine. Since the plaintiff had intended to pay for the wine when he ordered it, the only recourse left to the restaurant was to sue for breach of contract. Had the restaurant demonstrated that the customer had never had any intention of paying for the wine, that would have amounted to a crime and the imprisonment would have been justified even when made by a private citizen or security guard. In fact, the police, security guards and even the owners of property being threatened have greater powers to arrest than the ordinary citizen.

This case also illustrates the circumstances under which courts will award punitive damages. The primary object of tort law is to compensate victims of actionable wrongs for the injury or loss they suffer. When the plaintiff can show that expenses have been incurred or that specific, calculable losses, called **special damages**, have resulted, the victim will be compensated for them. When it is not possible to place an actual value on the loss, as in the case of pain and suffering, harm to reputation or future loss of earnings, the court will assess the loss and award **general damages**.

Punitive damages may be available for false imprisonment

The main object of tort law is to compensate people for wrongful injury or loss, not to punish wrongdoers. Only on rare occasions will a court order the defendant to pay damages to the plaintiff in excess of any injuries suffered. Such an award serves to punish the wrongdoer rather than compensate the victim and is referred to as **punitive damages**. In the *Bahner v. Marwest Hotel* case, the judge considered the action of the hotel employees sufficiently objectionable to award significant punitive damages in addition to the general and special damages awarded as compensation. This, like most such cases, was an instance where the legal costs

12. *Ibid.*, p. 325.

and judgment overwhelmed the few dollars that would have been lost had the employees not detained the plaintiff.

A charge of false imprisonment is a significant risk for any business involved in serving the public, including restaurants, hotels, retail stores and bars. This risk is especially strong when, either because of store policy or inexperienced staff, customers are detained whenever they are suspected of wrongdoing. The managers of many establishments which serve the public discourage their employees from apprehending shoplifters. Their reasoning is that the potential loss from goods stolen is far outweighed by the danger of losing a false imprisonment action. This is one area in which training staff to know when they can detain a person and when they cannot is a well-justified expense.

Private Nuisance

The tort of **private nuisance** is committed when a individual or business uses property in such a way that it interferes with a neighbour's use or enjoyment of his or her property. Such interference is usually ongoing and continuous. The most common complaint arises from the escape of polluting or dangerous substances such as noise, odours, smoke, water or falling debris which are usually the product of some commercial activity. If a foundry is built near a residential neighbourhood and the resulting smoke and odour make it impossible for neighbours to use their yards, they could have an action for nuisance. Similarly, when a factory emits pollutants into the air that destroy paint on neighbouring cars and buildings, those parties could also sue.

Private nuisance—use of property interferes with neighbour

There are certain limitations to this principle of law; the offending neighbour must be using the property in an unusual or unreasonable way and the problem caused must be a direct consequence of this unusual activity. A person living in an industrial section of a city cannot complain when a factory begins operating in the neighbourhood and emits noise, smoke and dust. It is also doubtful that residents of a rural area could successfully complain about the smells escaping from a neighbouring farmer's property when they are the normal odours associated with farming.

Until recently problems giving rise to complaints had to emanate from reasonably close or adjoining properties, but in the Alberta case of *Motherwell v. Motherwell*[13] the judge made a significant departure from this tradition. In this case, the defendant persistently used the telephone to harass the plaintiffs. The judge

NOISE AND FUMES ARE NUISANCE

The plaintiff operated a motel adjacent to some lands that Ontario Hydro had leased to the defendants who operated an amusement business that consisted of a racecourse for a scaled-down version of a Grand Prix racing car. The noise from the motors and screeching tires as the cars raced around the track was constant during the summer season from 11:00 a.m. until 11:00 p.m. The court found that this constituted a nuisance and so awarded damages to the plaintiff and granted an injunction. The court deemed that this was an unusual use of the property. Both the noise and the air pollution generated from the activity were out of keeping with what was normally expected from the area.

Banfai et al. v. Formula Fun Centre Inc. et al., 19 D.L.R. (4th) 683 (Ontario High Court of Justice)

---

13. *Motherwell v. Motherwell* (1977) 73 D.L.R. (3d) 62 (Alta. S.C. Ap. Div.).

determined that this was a private nuisance even though there was no adjoining property. Because the harassment interfered with the plaintiffs' enjoyment of their property, they were successful in their action.

A more recent development with private nuisance is the suggestion that a person will be found liable only when injury to the plaintiff is reasonably foreseeable, as with a negligence action. Negligence will be discussed below. Because nuisance often involves offending substances, it has become important as a tool of environmental protection. The law of the environment is one of the subjects that will be discussed in the final chapter.

Defamation

(Identity of parties withheld)[14]

The plaintiff was 18 years old, single and pregnant, living in a small town. She wanted to keep her circumstances confidential, but unfortunately she read in the local newspaper a notice which said. "Surprise, congratulations [her name] on your new coming baby." She sued the newspaper for defamation.

This case is very interesting, because it illustrates a number of points that come up in the area of defamation. The first question is whether the statement could be defamatory at all. The newspaper argued that there was nothing sinister about the notice and that any normal reader wouldn't have had any problem at all—at least one who wasn't acquainted with the plaintiff. The court found, however, that there was innuendo hidden in those words, that people aware of her special circumstances would know that the words were derogatory, and therefore, defamatory.

The newspaper then raised the defense of qualified privilege (which will be discussed below). Qualified privilege requires a duty and the newspaper claimed that they had a duty to publish the notice. The court found that the newspaper had a right to report but no obligation, and therefore no qualified privilege.

The newspaper also raised the defense of fair comment, claiming that they had a right to comment on a matter of public interest. But it wasn't a matter of public interest and in any case the newspaper couldn't show that it was an expression of their honest belief. All these factors made the notice defamatory.

However, legislation has been passed in most jurisdictions, including the province in question, reducing the damages that plaintiffs in such actions can obtain if the newspaper can show that the defamatory article was published in good faith, was done by mistake and a full apology or retraction was made. If these things can be established, damages payable are limited to special damages or out-of-pocket expenses. The plaintiff didn't claim any. The newspaper did meet these qualifications including the publication of a full and fair retraction along with an apology and therefore, the plaintiff lost because there were no special damages. This case illustrates how defamation developed and how it has been limited and modified over the years.

Defamation—detrimental statement

Defamation is a published false statement about a person which is detrimental to his or her reputation and most often affects media businesses such as radio and television. But any commercial activity can involve this kind of risk even when something as simple as a letter of reference is involved. If a statement is true, no matter

14. 97 D.L.R. (4th) 764.

how derogatory, the victim has no complaint. But one must be careful, as strictly speaking, a statement is defamatory merely if it can be shown to be detrimental to a person's reputation; the court presumes that the statement is false. Thus, once a person establishes that such a detrimental statement has been made, it is not necessary for him or her to prove that it is false as well. Of course, if the defendant demonstrates that the statement is true, this is an absolute defense to the action.[15]

When the statement complained of is untrue but not derogatory, there is no defamation. If a manager said that an employee was the hardest worker in the plant, the employee could not successfully sue for defamation even if it could be demonstrated that the statement was false.

The case of *Youssoupoff v. Metro-Goldwyn-Mayer Pictures Limited*[16] determined the test of what amounts to a defamatory statement: "Statements which are calculated to bring under hatred, ridicule or contempt ... or [a statement that] causes them to be shunned or avoided. ..." On appeal, Lord Justice Scrutton said that he preferred the test "a false statement about a man to his discredit."[17]

It is not possible to defame a dead person. The estate has no right to sue, but sometimes when a dead person is defamed it casts a shadow on the living and that disparaged living person may be able to bring a defamation action.

It should also be noted that since a company is a person in the eyes of the law, a corporation can be defamed as well. Generally, when a group is defamed, it is not actionable by any member within that group because the victim cannot prove that the remarks referred specifically to him or her; but if it is clear that every member of the group was included, then the statement is actionable by each of the individuals included. If an employee were to say that the management of a plant was ignorant and lazy, an individual manager would not likely be able to successfully sue because most people would understand this to mean "most managers." But if the worker had said that "all the managers" were ignorant and lazy, any individual could sue because they were clearly included.

Note also that it is possible to defame a product. When the CBC on their Marketplace program were critical of a particular brand of paint sold because of its mercury content, they inaccurately implied that it was the same kind of mercury as that associated with disastrous pollution problems. Colour Your World Corp. was able to successfully sue and was awarded $85 000 for their damaged reputation.[18]

To succeed in a defamation action, the plaintiff must prove that the offending statement is detrimental, that it refers to the plaintiff and that it was published. In this situation, "to publish" means that the statement had to be communicated to a third party. Publication could have occurred in a newspaper, in the broadcast media or simply by word of mouth. It is sufficient publication if just one other person hears the defamatory statement.

Statement must be published

Another important factor to consider is that statements often contain innuendo: implied or hidden meanings. A statement may appear perfectly innocent on the surface but, when combined with other information, it may take on a different meaning. This was the situation in the case used to open this discussion. To say that Mary Navarro had a baby yesterday could be an innocent remark, but if one of the hearers of that statement knows that Mary Navarro is a very religious,

Innuendo

15. *Elliott v. Freison et al.* (1984) 6 D.L.R. (4th) 338 (Ontario Court of Appeal). Affirming (1982) 136 D.L.R. (3d) 281 (Ontario High Court). Leave to Appeal to S.C.C. refused.

16. *Youssoupoff v. Metro-Goldwyn Mayer Pictures Limited* (1934) 50 T.L.R. 581.

17. *Ibid.*, p. 584.

18. *Colour Your World v. Canadian Broadcasting Corp.* (Ont. Gen. Div.) 17 O.R. (3d) 308.

unmarried 15-year-old committed to living a chaste life, the remark takes on a sinister air and might be defamatory. It is no excuse to say that the person making the statement thought it was true or did not know of the special facts that created the innuendo. Such a mistake is no defense, and the offending party can be held liable for the defamatory remark. Because of the constitutional protection of the press in the U.S., mistake is an effective defense when the media are involved. This appears not to be the case in Canada, but just how far the freedom of the press provision in Section 2(b) of the *Charter of Rights and Freedoms* will be taken is still an open question.

Mistake no excuse

Newspapers and the broadcast media often find themselves in serious difficulty because of such mistakes. In the case of *E. Hulton & Co. v. Jones*,[19] a newspaper published a fictitious story lampooning the double standards of the English upper-middle class. In the story, a man named Artemus Jones was depicted frolicking on the continent in the company of "a woman who was not his wife." It was clear that the author and publishers of the story thought they were creating entirely fictitious characters. Unfortunately for them, there really was an Artemus Jones who fit the description of the character in the story, and his friends and acquaintances thought the article was about him. He sued for defamation. Even though the author and publishers had no idea of Mr. Jones' existence, he succeeded in the action against them.

Libel and Slander.

Libel written/slander spoken

Defamation can be either **libel,** which is written defamation, or **slander**, which is spoken defamation. One important aspect of the distinction between the two lies in the area of proof. Libel is of a more enduring nature, is easier to prove and supposedly causes more harm than slander. However, with modern means of mass communication, the rationale for this distinction is beginning to break down. In fact, the distinction between libel and slander has been eliminated by legislation in Alberta. The *Defamation Act*[20] simply defines defamation as consisting of libel or slander. Accordingly, obstacles which made slander actionable only if the plaintiff could prove special damages have been swept aside in Alberta.

Defenses.

Truth is an absolute defense

Once it has been established that a defamatory statement has been made, several defenses are available to the defendant. **Truth**, sometimes called the defense of justification, is an absolute defense. But even when a statement is technically true, it can still be derogatory if it contains an innuendo or if it is capable of being interpreted as referring to another person about whom the statement is false.

Absolute privilege

The second method of defense is called **absolute privilege**. Anything discussed in certain defined situations cannot give rise to a defamation action no matter how malicious, scandalous or derogatory. Any statement made on the floor of any provincial legislative assembly or in Parliament in Ottawa as part of the proceedings of that body is immune from defamation actions; no matter how false and damaging a statement is, no matter how much malice is involved or the motivation behind it, the person being defamed cannot successfully sue. The same principle applies to testimony given in court. If a witness on the stand lies viciously about another, there can be no defamation action. The same protection is afforded communications between lawyers and their clients. Of course, other methods are used

19. *E. Hulton & Co. v. Jones* [1910] 26 T.L.R. 128 (House of Lords).
20. *Defamation Act*, R.S.A. (1980) c. D-6.

in these situations to discourage the abuse of this privilege. Legislative bodies have their own rules to control the conduct of members on the floor and the courts can charge a witness with perjury for false statements.

Another defense which is often raised and has a broad application, is **qualified privilege**. This defense can be used when a person makes a defamatory remark about another in the course of fulfilling a duty or an obligation. When there is no duty or special interest, there is no qualified privilege. For this reason the newspaper could not use this defense in the case used to open this discussion. As long as people are fulfilling their duties and their motives are sincere, with no knowledge of falsehood and without malice, they are protected and will not be held liable for losses resulting from defamatory remarks. For example, if, a supervisor thinks that a worker is stealing and reports this to the manager, the worker could not succeed in a defamation action against the supervisor even if the accusation was false. In fact, a good part of the supervisor's job is to ensure that such theft does not takes place. As long as the supervisor thinks that the accusation is true and has no other motive this defense can be used. However, a person can lose the protection of qualified privilege by making accusing statements to a larger audience to whom no responsibility is owed or to a reporter who broadcasts the information. In this example if the supervisor made his accusation in front of the whole workforce or put it in writing on a bulletin board, the defense of qualified privilege would be lost.

The final defense available in the field of defamation is the defense of **fair comment**. When someone becomes a public figure by publishing a book, producing a movie or becoming involved in politics, they create the right for people to express uncomplimentary opinions about their work or character. The evidence, such as the movie, book or voting record, must be available to the public and the comments complained of must relate to the work. Even if everyone else thinks the work is exceptionally good, it is possible for a someone such as a critic to state a negative opinion as long as that opinion is drawn from the facts available. A food critic expressing a negative opinion of a restaurant or a theatre critic attacking a play or movie are examples of fair comment. This principle also applies to all public figures, but the law does not permit abuse. If malice or another unjust motive can be demonstrated, the defense of fair comment is lost.

When dealing with the subject of defamation it must be remembered that the courts have tried to balance the democratic concepts of free speech and individuals' rights to have their prestige and reputation spared from unjustified assault. Because of this and historical anomalies in the separate development of the laws of slander and libel, these rules have become cumbersome and inefficient and many jurisdictions have passed legislation summarizing, and in many cases significantly modifying, the common law. When the defamation has been done by the media, most jurisdictions significantly reduce the damages that can be claimed if the newspaper, TV or radio station make an adequate apology soon after, as was illustrated in the discussion of the case used to open this section.

Alberta's *Defamation Act* stipulates that no action can be commenced against a newspaper or broadcaster unless the plaintiff serves notice on the defendant (within three months of learning of the defamatory publication) of his intention to bring an action. This notice must identify the defamatory material complained of. If the defendant broadcasts or publishes a retraction and apology promptly thereafter, it may be able to mitigate the damages. This opportunity to mitigate damages arises only if no malice or gross negligence was involved on the defendant's part. The defendant may further be able to restrict the plaintiff to special damages if the

Qualified privilege, requires duty

Fair comment

retraction and apology are promptly published. It must be established that the material was published in good faith, in mistake or misapprehension of the facts and that there were grounds to believe that publication was for the public benefit. Furthermore, it must also be established that the defamatory material did not impute to the plaintiff the commission of a criminal offence.

When defamation is proven, the damages can be substantial. In a defamation action the main objective of the damages awarded is not to compensate the victim, but to rehabilitate that person's reputation. For this reason the Supreme Court of Canada upheld a decision to award a government employee defamed by a church $1.6 million in damages, far in excess of the cap established in the Thornton case discussed above.[21]

NEGLIGENCE

Crocker v. Sundance Northwest Resorts Ltd.[22]

Mr. Crocker and his friend went to Sundance Resorts and one evening after a day of skiing they were at a bar, where they saw a video of an inner-tube race that was part of the activities associated with an event called the Sundance Spring Carnival. The race was run on the regular ski slopes in a section where there were "moguls" that caused the tubes and the people on them to bounce around like "rag dolls"; a videotape of the event showed the contestants "falling off these tubes, being bounced off, releasing their grip chasing after the tubes," and generally having what was described by another contestant as a "blast." The event was put on by the defendants, the operators of the ski slope.

The plaintiff, Crocker, signed up for the race, and in the process he signed, without reading, a release absolving the ski slope operators of all responsibility for any injuries he might suffer as a result of the race. Crocker and his friend, in a festive mood, went down the slope once, with only minor injury, and won their heat. By the second heat it was clear that Crocker had been drinking and the manager of the facility suggested that he not go down the hill. In fact, Crocker had not only had a couple drinks at the bar, but also had been given two large swallows of brandy by the driver of a beer van. In the next race Crocker fell off the tube and broke his neck, which rendered him a quadriplegic.

The Supreme Court had to decide whether Sundance should be responsible for Crocker's foolish conduct and if so to what extent. It had to determine just what nature of duty was owed by Sundance to Crocker and the other contestants. The court determined that a clearly dangerous competition was established for commercial gain. There was a duty of care towards visibly intoxicated participants who are obviously susceptible to more damage and more potential injury than the normal person. Sundance had an obligation to take all reasonable steps to keep Crocker from competing in his inebriated state. Although Crocker was told he should not proceed, not only did Sundance fail to prevent him from competing, but also when he dropped his inner tube they provided him with another. This clearly breached their duty of care towards Crocker and so negligence on the part of Sundance was established.

Resort must protect patron from self

21. *Hill v. Church of Scientology of Toronto* (1995) 126 D.L.R. (4th) 129 (S.C.C.).

22. (1988) 51 D.L.R. (4th) 321 (Supreme Court of Canada).

The Court then determined that Crocker had contributed to his own loss by his own negligence and under the statute in place in Ontario the court apportioned the blame assessing Crocker at 25 percent responsible, reducing the judgment accordingly.

The case not only illustrates the requirements of a duty of care and the reasonable person test in determining the nature of that duty, but also illustrates the defense of contributory negligence and voluntary assumption of risk. In this case it was argued that Crocker put himself voluntarily into a position of danger and in the process assumed the risk which would completely bar the negligence action on his part. The court pointed out that the principle of voluntarily assuming the risk has been restricted in recent times to such an extent that it has to be clear that Crocker not only assumed the physical risk but absolved Sundance of any legal responsibility for anything that happened. In fact Crocker had signed a waiver to that effect, but the court said it was meaningless since he hadn't read it.

The second general category of torts includes **negligent** or inadvertent conduct that causes injury to another person or damage or loss to property. One of the most common causes of court action is the suit for damages arising out of accidental or careless conduct. By far this is the most common tort committed by business or professional people. Careless behaviour must be unintentional and result in injury or damage to another person to qualify as negligence and to be recognized by the courts as cause for action. The court's duty is to establish the standard of care required of the defendant and whether or not that standard was met. The plaintiff must prove that a duty to be careful was owed, that there was a failure to act at the level of care required, that actual injury or loss was suffered and that the conduct complained of caused the injury.

Negligence—careless conduct causing another injury

Defendants may raise several factors in their defense. They may argue that the injury suffered was too remote from the offending conduct or that the plaintiff contributed to the injury through his or her own negligence. Defendants may also suggest that the plaintiff was ineligible for compensation as the risk of injury was voluntarily assumed.

The Reasonable Person Test

The reasonable person test helps courts establish the standard for measuring socially acceptable behaviour. The concept of the **reasonable person** is used in various ways throughout our legal system. This hypothetical character has become a point of reference to help courts make decisions without imposing rigid standards. Faced with the problem of having to decide if certain conduct is socially acceptable, the judge or members of the jury simply ask themselves, "What would a reasonably prudent person, in possession of all the facts of the case, have done in this situation?"

Reasonable person test establishes standard

A common misunderstanding is that courts using the reasonable person concept require people to live by an average standard. This is not so. Since the test asks what a reasonably prudent person would have done in the circumstances, it is measuring the conduct of a person who is being particularly careful or considerably better than average. On the other hand, the conduct is not required to be perfect since even reasonably prudent people can sometimes make mistakes. The conduct of the reasonable person falls somewhere between average and perfect.

Reasonably prudent is better than average

A good comparison is "par" in golf. A standard score, called par, is established for each of the 18 holes found on a golf course. If par for a hole is three, it does not mean that the average score for that hole is three strokes but that the average score is four or five strokes. On the other hand, three is not the best possible score. Rather, par is the score you would expect from a good golfer playing well. Similarly, the reasonable person test represents the standard of care expected from a prudent person who is being careful.

Determining the Existence of a Duty

For a litigant to sue successfully in a negligence action, it is necessary to establish that the defendant owed a duty to be careful. The court uses a variation of the reasonable person test, referred to as the **reasonable foreseeability test**, to determine whether or not such a duty exists. If it were reasonably foreseeable that the conduct complained of would cause harm to the plaintiff, a duty to be careful exists. In other words, if the likelihood of injury would have been apparent to a reasonable person had he or she considered who was put at risk by his or her conduct, then the defendant owed a duty.

Reasonable foreseeability establishes duty

The case of *Palsgraf v. Long Island Railroad Co.*[23] illustrates this point. During rush hour, a man attempted to board a train at a station in New York. Two employees of the railway company tried to help him onto the train but caused him to drop the bag he was carrying onto the tracks below. The bag contained fireworks which exploded on impact. The blast caused a heavy object mounted on the station wall several yards down the track to fall on and injure Mrs. Palsgraf, who sued the railroad company and the two employees for negligence. The court was faced with the question of whether or not the employees of the railroad company owed a duty to be careful to Mrs. Palsgraf. The court found that the railway employees owed no duty to Mrs. Palsgraf because they had no knowledge of the fireworks. They did owe a duty to be careful to the person they were assisting onto the train, and they may have failed to live up to that duty. However, Mrs. Palsgraf could not rely on the failure of that duty to support her action. The duty had to be owed directly to her and had to be based on the principle of reasonable foreseeability. Duty was not owed, because the employees could not be expected to reasonably anticipate that she was at any risk.

Knowledge of potential danger must exist

The result would probably have been different, however, if Mrs. Palsgraf had sued the passenger carrying the fireworks. Again, the court would have had to determine if he owed her a duty to be careful. The test would be the same. Would the possibility of injuring someone several metres away be apparent to a person carrying explosives? The answer would be yes, since the man ought to have known that what he was carrying was dangerous and could cause injury to those even at some distance if dropped. The court would then have to determine whether he had failed to live up to the appropriate standards.

One of the most significant cases concerning torts in this century is *Donoghue v. Stevenson*.[24] Two women went into a café where one ordered a bottle of ginger beer for her friend, Mrs. Donoghue. After consuming some of it, Mrs. Donoghue discovered part of a decomposed snail at the bottom of her bottle. She became very ill as a result of drinking the contaminated beverage. In the process of suing she discovered that she had some serious problems. She could not successfully sue the café that had supplied the ginger beer for breach of contract; she had no contract with the establishment, as her friend had made the purchase. Similarly, she could

---

23. *Palsgraf v. Long Island Railroad Co.* (1928) 248 N.Y. 339 (New York Court of Appeal).

24. *Donoghue v. Stevenson* [1932] A.C. 562 (House of Lords).

not successfully sue the café for negligence, since the ginger beer was bottled in an opaque bottle and served to her in the bottle. There was no opportunity for the café to discover a problem in the product and, therefore, no negligence on their part.

Since it was obvious that the snail had entered the bottle at the point of manufacture, the plaintiff sued the manufacturers for negligence. In their defense, the manufacturers claimed that they owed no duty to the victim, because they could not be expected to anticipate who would consume their product or anything that might happen to it in the meantime. This is not as ridiculous as it sounds because manufactured products go through several stages before reaching the consumer. At any of those stages the product could be inspected, modified or otherwise interfered with. To hold the producer responsible for damage done at any stage could place an undue hardship on manufacturers. Indeed, it was generally accepted before this case that a manufacturer had no duty to be careful to the ultimate consumer. It was also generally accepted, because of the way the law of negligence had developed, that the duty was owed only to those in the immediate vicinity. In this case, however, the plaintiff pointed out that the drink was bottled and capped with the idea that no intermediate inspection or interference would take place, and hence the bottle of ginger beer would get into the consumer's hands in the same condition in which it left the factory. In fact, the design of the product ensured this result. The House of Lords took an important step forward in the area of negligence when it decided that the manufacturers of the ginger beer did owe a duty to be careful to Mrs. Donoghue. Lord Atkin, the judge in the case, made the following classic statement when discussing how to determine to whom we owe a duty:

> The rule that you are to love your neighbour becomes in law, you must not injure your neighbour; and the lawyer's question, Who is my neighbour? receives a restricted reply. You must take reasonable care to avoid acts or omissions which you can reasonably foresee would be likely to injure your neighbour. Who, then, in law, is my neighbour? The answer seems to be— persons who are so closely and directly affected by my act that I ought reasonably to have them in contemplation as being so affected when I am directing my mind to the acts or omissions which are called in question.[25]

We owe a duty, then, to anyone we can reasonably anticipate might be harmed by our conduct. Over the years, the decision of the court in *Donoghue v. Stevenson* has had a tremendous impact on the law of negligence both in England and in Canada. But problems arose as the law of negligence was applied to new areas not previously encountered by the courts such as situations where only economic loss was suffered. In 1977, the English *Anns* case[26] further developed the *Donoghue v. Stevenson* test by establishing that when looking at new areas dealing with situations where the court has not already determined whether a duty is present, the court should go through a two-stage process in determining whether a duty to be careful existed. The first question to ask is whether there was a degree of neighbourhood or proximity between the parties such that if the person being sued had thought of it he or she would have realized that his or her actions posed a risk of danger to the other. Essentially this question restates the *Donoghue v. Stevenson* reasonable foreseeability test. The second question, however, is whether there was any reason that the duty should be not imposed, that the scope of the duty be reduced, that the class to whom the duty is owed be limited or that the damages be reduced. This question

Duty owed to anyone who could foreseeably be harmed

25. *Ibid.*, p. 580.
26. *Anns v. Merton, London Borough Council* [1977] 2 All E.R. 492 (H.L.).

allows the court to consider social policy rather than strict legal rules when looking at special situations and relationships such as when negligent words are involved and when the damage complained of is only economic loss. The principles developed in the *Anns* case have been abandoned in England but appear to be still accepted as good law in Canada (the *Hercules Managements* case).[27] Today, then, at least in this important area, the law of Canada and that of England seem to be diverging. It is enough to understand the principle that duty is established by the reasonable foreseeability test set out in *Donoghue v. Stevenson* and developed in the *Anns* case for those new situations not before dealt with by the court.

This discussion of duty should not end without observing that as a practical matter the question of whether a duty is owed seldom comes up in actual court cases. In most situations the existence of duty is obvious and not the subject of litigation unless the action involves negligent misstatement or the loss is only economic. Usually the court is dealing with physical damage or injury and is asked only to determine whether the conduct of the person being sued fell below the standard imposed by that duty or to determine what monetary compensation ought to be paid. Still, establishing a duty of care is the important first step in determining liability for negligence.

In addition to developing a general test to determine the existence of a duty to take care, *Donoghue v. Stevenson* also introduced the principle of **product liability** into English and Canadian tort law. Historically, because there were several intervening steps between the manufacturer and the ultimate consumer, it was accepted that the manufacturer owed no duty of care to the ultimate consumer. This case established, however, that if a product is designed in such a way as to get into the hands of the consumer without intervening inspection or modification, a duty of care does exist. When it can be shown that the manufacturer breached that duty through carelessness, a negligence action can be successfully brought against the manufacturer.

To sue manufacturer negligence must be established

It must be emphasized, however, that the action must be based on negligence rather than strict liability. Although the result of *Donoghue v. Stevenson* may have made it easier for the plaintiff to prove negligence in such cases, negligence must still be shown. In the United States, the courts have imposed a much greater responsibility on manufacturers by only requiring injured consumers to demonstrate that a defect in the product caused the injury. There is no need to establish negligence by demonstrating the existence of a duty or the existence of a failure to live up to a standard of care.

This strict liability approach to product liability has not yet been adopted in most provinces in Canada. In this country it is still necessary for a plaintiff to establish that the defendant was negligent. It must be emphasized, however, that liability for damage or injury caused by products is not always based on negligence. When a contract exists between the injured party and the seller and the product is defective, dangerous or otherwise causes injury or damage, that seller may be liable for a breach of the contract of sale even when there is no fault in the seller. In the case of *Donoghue v. Stevenson* had Mrs. Donoghue been the one to purchase the ginger beer instead of her friend, she could have sued the cafe for breach of contract, the product not being fit to consume. But because she was not the purchaser, she had no action against the seller. Some provinces have removed this **privity of contract** restriction in product liability cases, thus imposing a contractual duty on the manufacturer and the wholesaler as well as the seller to protect the ultimate consumer even when no fault is involved.

---

27. *Hercules Managements Ltd. v. Ernst and Young* (1997) 2 S.C.R. 165.

For a more complete discussion of such contractual product liability refer to Chapter 7 under "Consumer Protection Legislation." In addition the courts in Canada have shown a willingness to rely on the principle of *res ipsa loquitur* in product liability cases, which goes some distance in making it easier for the plaintiff to succeed in such an action. This principle is discussed below under "*Res Ipsa Loquitur.*" It should also be noted that it is becoming increasingly rare, especially when a civil jury is involved, for the manufacturer not to be found liable when its product causes injury. Whether this reflects a raising of the standard imposed, a move toward adopting strict liability, or a decision to place the liability on the party likely to have insurance remains to be seen.

Misfeasance and Nonfeasance.

The law imposes a duty on people to be careful in carrying out their activities so that they will not cause harm to others. The courts will provide a remedy in a case of **misfeasance**, that is, when a person acts in a socially undesirable way. But the courts are very reluctant to provide a remedy in a case of **nonfeasance** (when a person fails to do something) unless it can be established that a particular relationship existed, such as in the case of a swimmer and lifeguard, or a child and guardian. People who see a child drowning have no duty in tort law to rescue that child unless they happen to be lifeguards. But if a person were to initiate and then abandon a rescue attempt, it is no longer a case of nonfeasance but a case of misfeasance. The would-be rescuer would have failed to live up to a socially imposed duty and the conduct would be actionable. There are many other situations in which a person can assume an obligation or a duty where there was previously no duty. When someone attempts to repair a car, there is no duty in tort law requiring a friend to help. But if a friend does start to help, responsibility to act carefully is assumed. If lack of care results in damage to the car, the owner of the car would be able to sue for the damage caused, even though the work was performed for free.

> *Unacceptable action— misfeasance*
>
> *Failure to act—nonfeasance*

Like any other private citizen, a medical doctor has no legal obligation to render assistance at an automobile accident. On the other hand, if a doctor does start to help, he or she has an obligation to render assistance measuring up to the standard of a reasonable doctor in the circumstances. If the treatment given is lower than this high standard and further injury results, the doctor could be sued for negligence and would be liable for the resulting loss. In an attempt to alleviate such harsh consequences, some jurisdictions have introduced legislation designed to protect such rescuers from liability for injuries arising out of their rescue efforts. Alberta's *Emergency Medical Aid Act*,[28] for example, absolves those who render emergency first aid of liability for ordinary negligence, but not for gross negligence. The *Act*, however, only shields health practitioners from liability only where no fee for their services is expected or charged. Paramedics attending to patients at the scene of an accident do so for a fee, and accordingly would not be excused of liability if negligent. Without such legislation, the law would discourage people from helping because of the risks involved.

> *Usually no duty*
>
> *Doctor must give care up to a reasonable doctor's standard*

Standard of Conduct

Once it has been established that a duty is owed, the court will determine the nature and extent of that duty, that is, what standard of care the defendant in the case was required to exercise. The reasonable person test is applied in a slightly different

> *Reasonable person test determines standard of care*

---

28. *Emergency Medical Aid Act,* R.S.A. (1980) c. E-9.

context: "What would a reasonable person have done in the circumstances?" If a reasonable person would have responded in the same way the defendant did, there is no negligence. However, if a reasonable person would have been more careful, then the defendant's actions fall below the standard accepted by society and he or she would be liable for any injury or loss resulting from the conduct.

Risk of injury affects standard

The standard imposed by the court can vary depending on several different factors. The element of risk is an important consideration. A case heard in the English Court of the Exchequer in 1856 asked just how careful a person should be. In *Blyth v. Birmingham Water Works, Co.*,[29] the plaintiff's home was flooded when a water main serving a fireplug froze and burst during a severe winter cold spell. The pipe had been installed 25 years before at a level deep enough to avoid freezing under normal conditions. The plaintiff's claim was that the pipe should have been placed deeper. The court decided in favour of Birmingham Water Works because the weather that provoked the incident was the worst the city had experienced in 50 years. The court held that a reasonable person would not have incurred the significant additional expense involved in placing the pipe deeper. The standard of care was satisfied and there was no liability. The judge in the case said:

Negligence determined by what a reasonable person would do

> Negligence is the omission to do something which a reasonable man, guided upon those considerations which ordinarily regulate the conduct of human affairs, would do, or doing something which a prudent and reasonable man would not do.[30]

Risk can play a role in determining the standard of care required in other ways. A person driving a car is expected to be more careful than a person driving a wagon, not only because the risk of an accident is greater, but also because the potential for damage is greater. The greater the risk of injury, the higher the standard of care required. Similarly, the greater the potential for severe damage, the higher the standard imposed. The courts have shown that they will take into consideration the cost involved in reducing the risks and weigh them against the potential value of the loss resulting from the failure to reduce those risks. The point to remember is that a person must take steps to protect those who would be placed at unreasonable risk as a result of his or her conduct. It is reasonable to expect the areas of the Grand Canyon frequently visited by tourists to be fenced off, but it would be unreasonable to expect that a fence be placed around the whole canyon. Similarly, the courts are a lot more likely to regard the actions of the driver of a fire truck racing to a fire as reasonable than the same conduct exhibited by a person testing a new sports car.

Res Ipsa Loquitur

To establish liability in a negligent action, it is usually necessary for the plaintiff to prove not only that the injury took place and that it was caused by the defendant, but also that the defendant was "careless" in that the conduct fell below an accepted standard of care. In some situations, however, such "carelessness" is apparent from the injury.

Until recently the courts would turn to a legal doctrine known as ***res ipsa loquitur*** (the facts speak for themselves) to deal with such a situation. For example, if a piano were to fall into the street from a fourth-floor apartment, injuring a passerby, those facts by themselves seem to say more eloquently than anyone could that the

---

29. *Blyth v. Birmingham Water Works, Co.* (1856) 156 E.R. 1047 (Court of Exchequer).
30. *Ibid.*, p. 1049.

DUTY OF OCCUPIER

Mrs. Bains accompanied her friend Mrs. Hill to pick up some things from Hill's house which had been seriously damaged by a fire. The two ladies walked arm-in-arm down an icy driveway to get to the premises. They had to go back because her key didn't work. Mrs. Hill decided to go back and try it again, but this time she walked directly across the lawn while Mrs. Bains walked down the driveway. Bains slipped and fell, hurting her ankle, and brought this action against Mrs. Hill under the *Occupiers' Liability Act* for the injuries. The court held that even though Mrs. Bains was aware of the icy conditions, Hill was responsible for them and had to compensate her. Even the section of the B.C. *Act* which says that an occupier has no duty of care "in respect of risks willingly accepted as his own risks," the court held that that meant not only her own physical risk but her own legal risk as well. But Mrs. Bains would have had to have made it clear to her that she was being relieved of any legal responsibility for any injuries she, Bains, suffered as she walked down that ice-covered driveway.

Bains v. Hill, 93 D.L.R. (4th) 117 (British Columbia Court of Appeal)

people who were handling the piano were careless in the way they moved it. It would then be up to the defendant to show that they were not negligent.

The Supreme Court of Canada in *Fontaine v. B.C.* (Official Administrator) file no. 25381, has recently abolished the legal principle known as *res ipsa loquitur.* They have taken the position that rather than a principle of negligence law, this problem is better handled as an evidentiary matter. *Res ipsa loquitur* was quite restricted in its application and this change in approach gives the courts greater flexibility. Once the plaintiff has established the fact that the event took place, i.e., the piano fell, the court can take this as circumstantial evidence of the existence of negligence. In effect, the court can infer, from those proven facts, negligence on the part of the defendant. This establishes a prima facia case, meaning the plaintiff has proven their case on the face of it. The effect is to shift the burden to the defendant who then must produce evidence that they were not negligent. Without such evidence the plaintiff will win.

Res ipsa loquitur requires defendant to prove no negligence

This change in approach may make it easier to successfully pursue product liability cases in Canada. Although in the U.S. strict liability has been applied in cases dealing with defective products, in Canada it is still necessary for the plaintiff to establish negligence on the part of the manufacturer. The courts now seem to be encouraged to look at the circumstances of the injury, and if that circumstantial evidence is strong enough, to draw an inference that the manufacturer was careless. The manufacturer will have to show that they were not careless in order to avoid liability. A mouse in a bottle of beer would be enough for the court to draw an inference of negligence on the part of the defendant.

Special Situations

Although great reliance has been placed on the reasonable person test in determining negligence, there are some situations in which the court will abandon that standard. Perhaps the most visible example is the degree of care demanded from the owner or occupier of property in relationship to the people who use that property. The obligation towards people using the property lies with the occupiers, or those in possession of the property, rather than the owners. Occupiers also include those who have responsibility for and control over the condition of the premises and the activities conducted thereon. In a rental situation, the obligation to keep the

Occupiers owe special duty

property free from dangers lies with the tenant, not the landlord. If a visitor is hurt while on the premises, the tenant, not the landlord, is normally responsible although this responsibility has been extended to the landlords in several of the occupiers' liability acts discussed below. The tenant might also have some recourse against the landlord for compensation for loss suffered as a result of being sued.

Traditionally, a distinction was made between various kinds of visitors when assessing occupier liability. Invitees were on the property for some mutually beneficial business purpose, the presence of a licensee was tolerated on the property with the permission of the occupier, and trespassers were there without legal right. At common law each was owed a different level of care by the occupier of the land with the highest being owed to the invitee where the occupier was required to take reasonable steps to protect that invitee from any dangerous conditions on the property. When a licensee was involved the occupier only had to warn that licensee of any hidden dangers. The only obligation by an occupier to a trespasser was not to recklessly or willfully cause that trespasser harm. These different levels of required care created serious difficulty, especially when children were involved, and the common law proved unsatisfactory. Most provinces enacted legislation in the form of occupiers' liability acts which eliminated the distinction between invitees and licensees, imposing just one standard of care for visitors and their property on the premises of others. Alberta's legislation[31] simply imposes a duty on occupiers to take reasonable care of all **visitors** coming onto the premises. "Visitors," by definition, include people lawfully there, those permitted to be there and those whose presence has become unlawful but who are taking reasonable steps to leave.

> **5** An occupier of premises owes a duty to every visitor on his premises to take such care as in all the circumstances of the case is reasonable to see that the visitor will be reasonably safe in using the premises for the purposes for which he is invited or permitted by the occupier to be there or is permitted by law to be there.

The legislation causes occupiers to be responsible not just for the condition of the premises; occupiers are also responsible for the activities on those premises and the actions of third parties on the premises. In other words, the owner of a restaurant and bar is responsible not just for items like clearing the surrounding sidewalks of ice and snow; the owner is also responsible for ensuring that the bar doesn't get too crowded and that any inebriated customers do not cause harm to others on the premises.

Furthermore, the liability of the occupier to the visitor extends to loss or destruction of the visitor's property brought onto the occupier's premises. The occupier, however, is not liable for loss or damage to the visitor's property caused by the acts of third parties. Thus the bar owner would not be liable for the damage to a patron's clothes if, for example, the patron's jacket was torn during a fight with another customer.

In the case introducing this chapter, the garage proprietors were liable for the injuries the boy suffered because they had failed to take reasonable steps to protect him from the danger of the open cesspool, as required by the provincial act.

The duty owed to trespassers differs from province to province depending on the specific act in place. Whereas at common law, the only duty owed to trespassers is not to willfully or recklessly cause them harm, in some provinces trespassers are entitled to the same protection as anyone else on the premises. Alberta's legislation does not go so far. The common law position is essentially restated as far as adult

Invitee/licensee question may no longer be important

31. *Occupiers' Liability Act,* R.S.A. (1980) c. O-3

trespassers are concerned. But if the trespasser is a minor (under 18 years of age), then depending on the risks involved, the foreseeability of injury and the age of the minor, the duty of care owed may well equate that extended to visitors. Sections 12 and 13 of the Act provide.

12 (1)   Subject to subsection (2) and to section 13, an occupier does not owe a duty of care to a trespasser on his premises.

(2) An occupier is liable to a trespasser for damages for death of or injury to the trespasser that results from the occupier's willful or reckless conduct.

13 (1)   When an occupier knows or has reason to know

(a) that a child trespasser is on his premises, and

(b) that the condition of, or activities on, the premises create a danger of death or serious bodily harm to that child,

the occupier owes a duty to that child to take such care as in all the circumstances of the case is reasonable to see that the child will be reasonably safe from that danger.

(2) In determining whether the duty of care under subsection (1) has been discharged consideration shall be given to

(a) the age of the child,

(b) the ability of the child to appreciate the danger, and

(c) the burden on the occupier of eliminating the danger or protecting the child from the danger as compared to the risk of the danger to the child.

(3) For the purposes of subsection (1), the occupier has reason to know that a child trespasser is on his premises if he has knowledge of facts from which a reasonable man would infer that a child is present or that the presence of a child is so probable that the occupier should conduct himself on the assumption that a child is present.

An even more onerous duty is imposed on occupiers when an inn or hotel is involved. Innkeepers owe a duty to their guests to provide protection from the wrongful acts of others even when the innkeeper or servant is not at fault. This is a much higher duty than would normally exist. It is only when the damage or loss to a guest's property is caused by that guest's own negligence that the innkeeper is relieved of responsibility. Most provinces have reduced the common law liability of innkeepers through legislation, but only when the provisions of that legislation are properly followed by the innkeeper. The appropriate sections of the Alberta *Innkeepers Act* are as follows:[32]

Special duties of innkeepers

5 No innkeeper is liable to make good to any person who is not registered as an occupant of a room or rooms in his inn any loss of or injury to property brought into his inn, except

(a) when the property has been stolen, lost or injured, through the default or neglect of the innkeeper or his employee, or

(b) when the property has been deposited expressly for safe custody with the innkeeper and a check has been issued for the property.

32. *Inkeepers Act*, R.S.A. (1980) c. I-4.

7 An innkeeper is not liable to make good to his guest any loss of or injury to property brought to his inn, except

(a) when the property has been stolen, lost or injured through the wilful act, default or neglect of the innkeeper or his servants,

(b) when the property, other than a vehicle, has been expressly delivered for safe custody to the innkeeper, but the innkeeper may, if he thinks fit, require as a condition of his liability under this clause that the property be deposited in a box or other receptacle and fastened and sealed by the person depositing it, or

(c) when a vehicle has been expressly delivered into the custody of the innkeeper for storage or parking in a place specifically reserved and designated by the innkeeper for the storage or parking of vehicles, in which case the liability of the innkeeper for the vehicle and its contents is that of a bailee for reward.

Section 7(c) imposes the duty of a bailee for reward on the hotel where a car has been left in their keeping. Bailments will be discussed in Chapter 14. And Section 6 requires the posting of notice or the liability reverts to the higher common law standard.

6 Every innkeeper

(a) shall keep conspicuously posted in the office of his inn, and in every bedroom ordinarily used for the accommodation of inn guests, a printed or plainly written copy of section 7, and

(b) is entitled to the benefit of this Act only in respect of property that is brought to his inn while the copy of section 7 is posted as required by this section.

A special problem arises when alcohol is served. The courts are willing to hold commercial dispensers of alcoholic beverages at least partially responsible when a patron becomes intoxicated and is injured, as the Supreme Court of Canada made clear in the *Crocker* case used to open this section. Following this trend we can expect companies and even individual hosts to be liable when private parties or gatherings lead to similar results.[33]

Legislation.

Modification imposed by statute

Because of the concept of supremacy of parliament, all of the standards that have been developed and imposed by the courts can be and often are modified by legislation. Motor vehicle acts, innkeepers' acts and occupiers' liability acts are a few examples of legislated changes in the common law standard of care. When reading these statutes one must be careful to determine whether they really do establish a different standard of care. If the statute applies to an area in which a common law obligation of tort is already in force, such as occupiers' liability, then the existence of legislation may increase or decrease that standard. However, when a statute prohibits some conduct traditionally not considered a tort, such as racial discrimination, that legislation will not create a new type of tort action unless specifically provided for in the legislation. For this reason, whenever human rights legislation is breached, victims must rely on the enforcement provisions set out in the statutes, rather than on bringing tort actions. Many statutes, especially in consumer and environmental

---

33. *Jacobsen v. Nike Canada Ltd*, 133 D.L.R. (4th) 377 B.C.S.C.

protection areas, specifically create such a right of action for the victims. In B.C. for example, the *Privacy Act* specifically gives a right to the victim to sue in tort where a violation of specific privacy provisions has taken place.[34] A tort action for breach of privacy does not exist at common law, nor does a statutory action for breach of privacy exist in Alberta.

Tort law generally, and negligence in particular, is a system based on the imposition of liability by the assessment of fault. One person or the other bears the loss, although this loss can be shared in some circumstances (see discussion of contributory negligence below). In situations, however, where the potential of devastating loss exists, a system based on fault breaks down. Large judgments can be ruinous to the person found at fault or the victim may be left without compensation when the judgment debtor is unable to pay. This problem has become particularly pronounced when motor vehicles are involved, prompting several provinces to pass legislation requiring that all drivers have their cars insured against personal liability for accidents. Many consider compulsory insurance schemes to be only a partial measure. Several provinces, including Ontario, have instituted a *no-fault* or partial no-fault system in which all injured parties will receive some compensation for their injuries whether they are at fault for the accident or not. Ontario has recently retreated from their no-fault system, and now with some restrictions injured motorists again have the right to sue for compensation. Alberta has never adopted a no-fault system. Compulsory insurance is relied upon as the main method of distributing loss among all of the driving public. Alberta has also enabled those injured by uninsured drivers to claim against a fund created pursuant to the *Motor Vehicle Accident Claims Act.*[35]

The trend away from fault

Negligent Misstatement and the Liability of Professionals

A recent development in common law that has had a significant impact on accountants, bankers, lawyers, business consultants and other professionals giving advice has been the broadening of the law of negligence to include a right to sue for negligent words. Historically such professionals were only liable where a contractual relationship existed and there was a breach, or where fraud was involved or where some close relationship creating a fiduciary duty (a duty to act in the other's best interests) was present and that duty was breached. Otherwise professionals were only liable to strangers where some form of physical damage resulted from their conduct such as where an engineer designed a bridge that collapsed.

Courts have always been reluctant to award damages when the only injury was economic loss unaccompanied by physical injury. This was especially true when the injury was caused by negligent misstatement and no contractual duty, fiduciary duty or fraud was present. Only in the past 30 years have the courts granted compensation for this kind of loss. In 1963, England's House of Lords was faced with this question in *Hedley Byrne & Co. Ltd. v. Heller and Partners, Ltd.*[36] An advertising firm asked its bank to inquire into the financial condition of a client. The bank stated that the client was in a good financial position but disclaimed any responsibility for the statement. It turned out that the client was in very poor financial shape and, as a result, the advertising company lost a substantial amount of money. The advertising company sued the bank that had misled them. The House of Lords

Negligent words causing economic loss actionable

---

34. *Privacy Act*, R.S.B.C. (1996) c. 373 s. 1.

35. *Motor Vehicle Accident Claims Act*, R.S.A. (1980) c. M-21.

36. *Hedley Byrne v. Heller* [1963] 2 All E.R. 575 (House of Lords).

held that it was possible to award compensation for the victim of a negligent mis-statement even if there had been no contract, no fiduciary duty and no fraud. But it also concluded in this particular instance that the bank's disclaimer absolved it of any responsibility and, therefore, the bank was not liable.

Since then, in many cases the courts have held defendants liable for the losses caused by their negligent words. The Supreme Court of Canada was faced with this problem in the case of *Haig v. Bamford et al.*[37] An accounting firm negligently prepared financial statements for a company knowing that the statements would be used to encourage investors. Mr. Haig purchased a number of shares, but found the company to be considerably less profitable than the incorrect financial statements had led him to believe. As a result, he suffered a financial loss.

Here there was no direct relationship between Mr. Haig and the negligent firm. The firm was negligent in the performance of its services to the firm of which Mr. Haig was merely a potential investor. Previously, the imposition of liability depended on the negligent conduct causing physical injury or damage. Here, there was no physical contact and or loss. Mr. Haig lost money when he relied on the financial statement. This case is significant because, for the first time in Canada, liability for the tort of negligence was extended to pure economic loss caused by negligent words spoken by experts. As a result such experts find themselves responsible not only to their immediate clients, but to others who suffer loss because of their careless statements.

Negligent words may create liiability

Donoghue v. Stevenson, discussed above, established that the test for determining whether a duty of care exists in a negligence action is reasonable foreseeability. Many argue vigorously, however, that this test is much too broad for determining liability when mere words are involved and only economic damage has been suffered. In fact, the judges in *Haig* did not go so far as to adopt this test but said only that a duty of care was owed when the person making the misleading statement knew it was to be used by a limited class of people. The *Anns* case discussed above has been welcomed in Canada because it retains this general reasonable foreseeability test but provides a framework for dealing with negligent misstatement and mere economic loss on a more restrictive basis. The first question in *Anns* established duty on the basis of the injury being reasonably foreseeable, but the second question allowed for this duty to be diminished or limited where policy considerations warranted the duty to be restricted to a specific class or the damages to be reduced. In other words, the *Anns* case creates a second test to be used after the reasonable foreseeability test establishes a *prima facie* duty of care; this second test asks whether the duty of care should be set aside, restricted or negated because of policy considerations. *Haig* clearly established that we can be held liable for our careless words but there has always been a question of where to draw the line. Now there seems to be some clarification: liability will be restricted to those situations where we knew (or should have known) that our words would be relied on by an individual or by someone who was a member of a group we knew would be relying on the statement.

Duty restricted to a limited group

There are several examples of cases involving accountants or auditors preparing incorrect financial statements and being sued by third parties (investors) relying on those incorrect statements. A recent example decided by the Supreme Court of Canada has further clarified the tests to be used to establish existence of a duty of care.

This *Hercules Managements Ltd. v. Ernst & Young*[38] decision evidences a more restrictive approach. The case was brought by a group of shareholders and investors

37. *Haig v. Bamford et al.* (1976) 72 D.L.R. (3d) 68 (Supreme Court of Canada).

38. *Hercules Managements Ltd. v. Ernst & Young* (1997) 2 S.C.R. 165.

who had relied on audited financial statements in making their investment decisions. They sued the auditors for negligent misrepresentation. The Supreme Court confirmed that the *Anns* test governs negligent misrepresentation cases as it does other types of negligence cases. Using the *Anns* two-stage approach, the Court found a *prima facie* duty to exist, as the plaintiffs were reasonably foreseeable, and as reliance on the financial statements by the plaintiffs would, in the particular circumstances, also be reasonable. But when policy considerations were factored in, such as the danger of indefinite liability, the *prima facie* duty was wiped out. The Court's concern about limitless liability to an indeterminate class for an indeterminate time caused it to restrict duty of care on policy grounds. But the decision does recognize that a duty of care may exist on a "transaction specific" basis. A duty is owed to those plaintiffs who auditors know will receive and rely upon audited statements for the specific purpose or transaction for which the statements were made. Evidently, the *Hercules* decision has sharply restricted to whom professionals owe a duty of care.

In *Hercules* the Supreme Court of Canada has, therefore, further refined accountants' liability. The shareholders of a company relied on incorrect financial statements to make further investments in that company. The shareholders were clearly a group that the accountants could expect to rely on the statements and so, using *Haig*, a duty was owed. But these financial statements were prepared not to encourage further investment but to evaluate the capabilities of the management team at the shareholders' meeting. Should accountants' liability extend beyond the purpose for which the statements are prepared? Applying the *Anns* case, the Supreme Court found there was a *prima facie* duty owed by the accountants. But applying the second part of the test developed in *Anns*, the court also decided the duty of the accountants should only imposed liability for the purpose for which the financial statements were prepared, in this case to evaluate management.

Experts and Children

In the past, professionals and other experts only faced liability for shoddy work to their clients on the basis of contract law and to their colleagues and clients on the basis of a breach of a fiduciary duty. (Contract law will be covered in the following chapter and fiduciary duty will be described in the chapters devoted to business relationships.) Only experts such as architects and engineers whose services resulted in a physical structure were subject to liability if their negligence caused the structure to collapse. Today all professed experts who cause injury by their negligent misstatements may be held responsible for their words not only to their clients but to others hurt because they followed the advice. Whether the liability is for careless conduct or careless words, the standard of care imposed on professionals is very high.

Another problem in applying the reasonable person test to determine the standard of care arises when dealing with people who have special skills and abilities. Essentially, they are required to have the skills and abilities that one would expect an expert or professional to have. They are required to exercise that skill with a degree of care that would be expected from a reasonable person with the same expertise. The level of care expected from children and the mentally disabled reflects their degree of maturity or the extent of their disability.

Reasonable person in the circumstances

In assessing liability, the court determines what a reasonable person, possessed of the same skills and abilities as the defendant, would have done in the circumstances. For a doctor, the test is that of a reasonable doctor; for an accountant,

PARENTS NOT LIABLE FOR CHILDREN'S TORTS

A child was caught shoplifting in the defendant's store, and the store through their lawyers sent a letter to the child's mother demanding payment to compensate them for the losses and threatening to start a civil action against her if she didn't pay. The amount demanded was more than the amount stolen; the store justified this by suggesting that it was designed to offset the cost of security people the store was forced to employ. The mother paid the money, but after receiving legal advice she brought this small claims action, demanding return of the money. She was successful. The judge found that parents ought not to be held liable for torts of their children. Unless some personal liability on the part of the mother could be shown, such as negligence, there was no liability and no right to demand payment from her.

B. v. Arkin et al., 138 D.L.R. (4th) 309 (Manitoba Court of Queen's Bench)

a reasonable accountant; for a lawyer, a reasonable lawyer. It must be emphasized that a client or patient is not required to tolerate ineptitude on the part of professionals because of inexperience. It may be true that a doctor or mechanic in the first month of employment is more likely to make a mistake, but these people have represented themselves as proficient members of their profession and so must live up to the level of competence one would expect of a normal member of their profession functioning in a reasonably prudent manner.

In addition, simply showing the conduct complained of was common practice among professionals will not necessarily absolve the defendant of liability for negligence. The test is that of a reasonable person, not an average person. Although one hopes that the average standard of practice in the skilled professions and the practice one would expect from a reasonable person would coincide, this is not always the case. When it is obvious that the common practice is dangerous or careless, then such sloppy practice will not be tolerated. The court, in such circumstances, is not reluctant to declare that the common practice falls below the standard of a reasonable person and is therefore negligent. This principle has recently been reinforced by the Supreme Court of Canada in *Waldick v. Malcolm* where Iacobucci J., quoting Linden, states: "tort courts have not abdicated their responsibility to evaluate customs, for negligent conduct cannot be countenanced, even when a large group is continually guilty of it." In short, no amount of general community compliance will render negligent conduct "reasonable ... in all the circumstances."[39]

The *Kripps v. Touche Ross & Co.* case[40] is another relevant example. The B.C. Court of Appeal held that financial professionals cannot hide behind Generally Accepted Accounting Principles and Generally Accepted Audit Standards to protect themselves from negligence claims. Auditors cannot use these tools to shield themselves where the financial statements nevertheless misrepresent the financial position of the company audited.

One would hope, however, that such negligence in the face of common practice in a profession would only happen in extraordinary circumstances.

The opposite is true when children are involved. The courts recognize that a 13-year-old can't be expected to act to the same level of responsibility as an adult. Children are liable for their torts, but the standard required of them is the level of

39. *Waldick v. Malcolm*, 83 D.L.R. (4th) 125, S.C.C.

40. *Kripps v. Touche Ross & Co. et al.*, CA019919 B.C.C.A., April 25, 1997, *The Lawyers Weekly*, May 30, 1997.

conduct that would be expected of a reasonable child of the same age. Thus a small child playing with matches may not be liable for a resulting fire whereas a teenager doing the same thing could very likely be held responsible. At this point we usually turn our attention to the parents. Although many people don't realize it, parents are not as a general rule vicariously liable for the torts committed by their children. In the absence of a statute to the contrary, they are only liable if it can be established that they were negligent in their own right by failing to properly train, control or supervise their children.

Material Loss

In addition to establishing that the defendant owed a duty to be careful and failed to live up to that duty, the plaintiff must also show that some sort of loss to either person or property has been suffered. When a customer slips and falls on a wet floor in a store but suffers no injury, it may well be that the store has failed to live up to the required standard of care but since no damage has been done, there is no right to sue. However, if the customer breaks a leg, this would be a tangible, physical injury which would provide grounds for an action.

Damage or injury must be present

In the past, the courts refused to grant compensation if the injury suffered had only an emotional or mental impact on the victim unless it was accompanied by physical symptoms such as vomiting, miscarriage, ulcers or heart problems. Similarly, the courts traditionally refused to find liability if the only injury suffered was economic loss due to loss of income. Today, there is no question but that a victim can be compensated for economic loss, although there is still some debate on just what limits will be placed on the availability of purely economic loss. The Supreme Court of Canada in *Canadian National Railway Co. v. Norsk Pacific Steamship Co.*[41] adopted the test set out in *Anns* for pure economic loss. By this test it is necessary to establish that there is a close causal connection between the act complained of and the damage, and secondly that there is no social policy reason to deny the claim. It is the second part of the rule that gives the courts flexibility and creates some confusion. Canadian courts have also shown a willingness to compensate victims if the result of the negligent conduct is a recognizable mental disorder such as depression or schizophrenia. Canadian courts are still reluctant to give an award if only mental distress such as anger or anxiety is present.

Causation

The injury complained of must be a direct result of the careless conduct. If the operator of a motor vehicle knowingly drives at night without tail-lights, the driver can be said to be careless. However, if the vehicle is involved in a head-on collision, the driver of the other car could not rely on the first driver's failure to have tail-lights to support a negligence action. The test usually applied in such situations is called the **but for** test. The plaintiff must prove to the court's satisfaction that but for the complained-of conduct, no injury would have resulted. In this illustration, the plaintiff cannot say that but for a failure to have properly functioning tail-lights no collision would have occurred.

Conduct must be cause of injury

In the Ontario case of *Kauffman v. Toronto Transit Commission*,[42] two boys were scuffling on an escalator and bumped into a man causing him to fall against the

41. *Canadian National Railway Co. v. Norsk Pacific Steamship Co.*, (1992) 91 D.L.R. (4th) 289 (S.C.C.).
42. *Kauffman v. Toronto Transit Commission* (1959) 18 D.L.R. (2d) 204 (Ontario Court of Appeal).

plaintiff who in turn fell down and was injured. She sued the Toronto Transit Commission, claiming that they had been negligent in not supplying proper handrails. The court found that the Toronto Transit Commission had not been negligent. Mrs. Kauffman failed to prove that the lack of a handrail had anything to do with her injuries. The court was satisfied that she would have been injured no matter what handrail had been supplied. The plaintiff was unable to establish that, but for the negligent conduct of the Toronto Transit Commission, she would not have suffered an injury.

Defenses

Once the plaintiff has established that the defendant owed a duty to be careful to the plaintiff, that the defendant's conduct fell below the standard of care required in the situation and that the conduct complained of caused some injury or loss to the plaintiff, negligence is established. Still, there may be some matters the defendant can raise in defense. These are summarized below.

Remoteness.

Problem of remoteness

Clearly, when the injury complained of is a direct result of negligent conduct, there is a right to sue for negligence. Where the connection between the conduct complained of and the injury is only tenuous, the defendant may be able to avoid liability. One of the most difficult problems in the law of negligence is when the connection between the damage suffered and the conduct complained of is remote or indirect, or when the resulting injury is out of all proportion to what one would have expected. Again, it is important to realize that the decision about where to draw the line is often no more than an application of social policy. In the case of *Abbot v. Kasza*,[43] Justice Clement of the appellate court of Alberta recognized the difficulty of developing any hard and fast rules in this area.

> The common law has always recognized that causation is a concept that in the end result must be limited in its reach by a pragmatic consideration of consequences; the chain of cause and effect can be followed only to the point where the consequences of an act will be fairly accepted as attributable to that act in the context of social and economic conditions then prevailing and the reasonable expectations of members of the society in the conduct of each other.[44]

Remoteness is an issue in those unique situations we tend to regard as bizarre accidents. But when the problem does arise, the courts do little more than make policy decisions which have been variable and uneven. It was originally thought that whenever there was a direct cause-and-effect relationship between the conduct complained of and the injury, there was liability no matter how unusual that injury.[45] Subsequently, in a case referred to as *Wagon Mound #1*, which dealt with the problem of a spark from a welder's torch that fell on some floating cotton and caused a spill of oil to catch fire, the English Privy Council adopted a different test. The court decided that a defendant is liable only if the injury is reasonably foreseeable.[46] But this position caused some unacceptable results and English courts

43. *Abbott v. Kasza* (1977) 71 D.L.R. (3d) 581 (Alberta Supreme Court, Appellate Div.).

44. *Ibid.*, p. 588.

45. *Re Polemis v. Furness, Withy* [1921] 3 K.B. 560 (Court of Appeal).

46. *The Wagon Mound (No. 1)* [1961] A.C. 388.

continued to vacillate over the appropriate test to apply in this area.[47] The position in Canada is somewhat different from the present state of the law in England and is summarized by Mr. Justice Dickson in *The Queen v. Coté*.

> It is not necessary that one foresee the "precise concatenation of events"; it is enough to fix liability if one can foresee in a general way the class or character of injury which occurred.[48]

If it can be shown that the general type of injury suffered was reasonably foreseeable, that is enough to impose liability in Canadian law. It is easy to confuse this test for determining remoteness with the reasonable foreseeability test used to determine the existence of a duty in the first place. The distinction is that, when determining whether a duty exists, the court asks whether a reasonable person would have anticipated injury in any form as a consequence of the conduct. With remoteness, however, the test is whether a reasonable person would have anticipated the general nature of the injury suffered. Thus, if a person slips on an icy sidewalk, a broken bone or sprained ankle is foreseeable. But if the person slips and drops chemicals they are carrying causing serious burns, this type of injury might be seen as too remote. Although the issue of remoteness relates to the existence of a duty of care, it is dealt with here because it is conceptually easier to deal with after the basic elements of negligence have been established.

Foreseeability of type of injury sufficient

Although there is much confusion in the application of these principles, there is one area of certainty when the nature but not the extent of a personal injury was reasonably foreseeable. The rule is simply that we take our victims as we find them. If a person has a weak heart, a tendency to a particular disease or a physical condition such as having a skull as thin as an eggshell, we cannot avoid responsibility by claiming that we could not reasonably be expected to foresee the special condition. If a person experiences greater injury from our conduct than would be expected because of a unique physical condition, there is nonetheless a responsibility to compensate for all consequences of the injury. This principle is often referred to as the **thin skull rule.**

Thin skull rule

We take our victims as we find them

The defendant's act triggers it

In the case of *Smith v. Leech Brain*,[49] the defendant's employee was hurt when he was struck on the lip by a drop of molten metal. Because of a precancerous condition existing in the employee, this burn developed into cancer which eventually killed him. Although this consequence of the injury was in no way reasonably foreseeable, the employer was held liable for the death of the employee because the original accident was caused by the employer's negligence.

But we must be careful in applying the principle. If the aggravated injury was inevitable and the conduct of the defendant simply determined the timing, the defendant will not be responsible for the additional loss. If a worker has one eye and loses the other in an accident, the damage is much more devastating than the loss of a single eye. Under the thin skull rule the defendant will be responsible for the greater damages resulting from the total blindness. But if that one-eyed worker had a deteriorating condition in his remaining eye that would have eventually caused its loss, the defendant's conduct is not responsible for the worker's blindness, the deteriorating condition is and the worker will receive considerably less compensation. This has been dubbed the **crumbling skull rule** and must be used in conjunction with the thin skull rule.[50]

47. *The Wagon Mound (No. 2)* [1967] A.C. 617 (P.C.).
48. *The Queen v. Coté* (1974) 51 D.L.R. (3d) 252 (Supreme Court of Canada).
49. *Smith v. Leech Brain* [1961] 3 All E.R. 1159 (Queen's Bench Division).
50. *Athey v. Leonati* (1996) 140 D.L.R. (4th) 235.

Contributory Negligence.

When the plaintiff is partially responsible for his or her own loss, the defendant can raise this contributory negligence to reduce liability. Historically, whenever carelessness on the part of plaintiffs contributes to their injuries, they are considered authors of their own misfortune and the defendant cannot be held responsible for the injury. For example, if a driver fails to stop at a light and a second driver fails to notice the car coming into his path because he is adjusting his radio, he will not be able to recover for any injuries suffered in the accident.

Negligence of victim may reduce or eliminate award

In this case, it is clear that the second driver was being careless by not being fully aware of what was happening on the road; this conduct at least contributed to the accident and completely bars him from recovery of damages. Because this approach is rather harsh, it was somewhat modified by the **last clear chance doctrine**. This means that the person who had the last opportunity to avoid the accident is responsible for all of the loss. In the example given, the second driver could have avoided the accident if he had been paying attention. He must assume responsibility for the loss because he had the last chance to avoid the accident. This is a little fairer but also results in some unjust decisions, and legislation has been passed to alleviate this problem. The *Negligence Act* in Ontario and Albera's *Contributory Negligence Act* are typical examples.[51] The problem with the traditional common law approach of the last clear chance doctrine is that it is all or nothing. The statutes mentioned above permit the courts to apportion responsibility between the two parties and then orders that compensation be paid in proportion to that assigned responsibility. In the example above, the first driver was at fault for driving through the stoplight and the second driver contributed to the accident through lack of attention. The courts would apportion liability and require each to bear a percentage of the responsibility for the losses suffered. A recent decision of the Alberta Court of Appeal, *Wickberg v. Patterson*,[52] has cast doubt over whether the last clear chance doctrine has been eliminated in that province. Because the *Contributory Negligence Act* does not specifically abolish the doctrine, it may still be available to litigants.

Act allows apportionment of responsibility

Voluntarily Assuming the Risk.

When people voluntarily put themselves into positions where there is obviously risk of injury, the person in control of the dangerous situation may be able to avoid responsibility for injuries suffered by the volunteers. For example, if a passenger entered a motor vehicle knowing that the driver was intoxicated, he or she may be said to have voluntarily assumed the risk (*volenti non fit injuria*) and may be barred from recovery for injuries suffered in an accident caused by the intoxicated driver.

The law will not assist volunteers

But the risk must be obvious and there must be a clear indication from the conduct of the parties not only that they knew the risks and participated voluntarily, but also that they were giving up any claim against the driver if injury resulted. When a person puts himself or herself in harm's way like this, he or she is completely barred from recovering any damages.

The courts are now backing off from this all-or-nothing approach. Now, for a claim of voluntary assumption of risk to bar recovery in a negligence action, the victims must make it clear that they are assuming not only the physical risk but the legal risk as well. They must make it clear that they are absolving the other party of any responsibility for any injuries or damage that results. Because, in fact, this rarely if

But assumption of legal risk must be clear

---

51. *Negligence Act,* R.S.O. (1980) c. 315; *Contributory Negligence Act,* R.S.A. (1980) c. C-23.

52. *Wickberg v. Patterson* (1997) 145 D.L.R. (4th) 263 (Alta. C.A.).

ever happens, it is not likely today that a claim of voluntary assumption of risk will be successful. The courts now usually deal with such foolhardy behaviour under the heading of contributory negligence and this in turn permits the courts to apportion the loss between the parties—a much more satisfactory result.

As discussed above, the occupiers' liability acts in place in most provinces, in addition to imposing a duty on the occupier of property to take reasonable steps to protect people and their property on those premises, also make it clear that this liability is not imposed when the visitor is aware of the danger and uses the property anyway. Section 7 of the Alberta *Act* states:[53]

> 7 An occupier is not under an obligation to discharge the common duty of care to a visitor in respect of risks willingly accepted by the visitor as his.

This, in effect, imposes by statutory enactment the *volenti non fit injuria* principle discussed here into the field of occupiers' liability. In *Waldick v. Malcolm*[54] the Supreme Court of Canada faced the problem of deciding whether this assumption of risk took place when a person assumed the physical risk if they simply knew of the danger and participated on the property anyway or whether they had to assume the legal risk as well, making it clear that they were absolving the occupiers of any responsibility for any damage that took place. The Supreme Court in this important case made it clear that for the occupier to escape liability the Ontario statute should be interpreted as requiring the assumption of the legal risk. There must be a clear indication just as with the common law principle that there was an intention to absolve the occupier of any legal responsibility for injury or damage. Although the wording varies from statute to statute it is obvious that this approach will apply to the occupiers' liability acts of other provinces as well.[55]

When a rescuer is involved, he or she cannot be said to have voluntarily assumed the risk. The person causing the danger should have anticipated the possibility of an attempted rescue. If the rescuer is injured, the author of the danger cannot escape liability by claiming the rescuer voluntarily assumed the risk. The person who caused the danger must pay compensation to both the victim and the injured rescuer.[56] Similarly, the principle does not apply to work-related accidents even if the work being performed is inherently dangerous.

Strict Liability

There are some situations in which the standard imposed is so high that there is liability no matter how cautious or careful the person responsible has been. The case of *Rylands v. Fletcher*[57] established a rule applicable in such instances. Rylands had a reservoir built on his property but was unaware of a shaft leading to a coal mine being operated by his neighbour. The accumulated water escaped, causing damage to the plaintiff's mine. It was clear from the facts that Rylands had not been negligent, nor was there any intentional wrongdoing. Nevertheless, the court held Rylands responsible for the damage done to his neighbour's mine. The principle adopted was that if something inherently dangerous is brought onto property

Strict liability imposed when dangerous substances escape

53. *Occupiers Liability Act,* R.S.A. (1980) c. O-3.

54. *Waldick v. Malcolm* (1991) 83 D.L.R. (4th) 114 (S.C.C.).

55. *Tutinka v. Mainland Sand and Gravel Ltd.* 110 D.L.R. (4th) 182 (British Columbia Court of Appeal); *Murray v. Bitango* 135 D.L.R. (4th) 443 (Alberta Court of Appeal).

56. *Videan v. British Transport Commission* [1963] 2 All E.R. 860 (Court of Appeal).

57. *Rylands v. Fletcher* (1868) L.R. 3 H.L. 330.

STRICT LIABILITY FOR DANGEROUS SUBSTANCES

The tenant, Skrow's Produce, owned a truck that had propane tanks built into it. One of the tanks leaked when the truck was parked in front of the plaintiff's place of business during a sale. The fire department ordered evacuation of the premises until the gas dissipated, causing considerable loss of business. The plaintiffs sued under the principle of strict liability. The court agreed that storing propane on the truck was a dangerous and unusual use of property and applied the precedent from *Rylands v. Fletcher*. The court also found that the defendant had caused a nuisance and the case was actionable on that basis as well. At the time that the truck was parked alongside the store, the driver knew it was discharging propane. That made it an abnormal use.

Ira-Berg Ltd. v. Skrow's Produce (1971) Ltd., 76 D.L.R. (4th) 431 (Ontario Court, General Division)

and it escapes, the occupier is responsible for any consequence whether or not there is negligence or any other form of fault. The House of Lords supported Mr. Justice Blackburn's decision, which said,

> The true rule of law is, that the person who, for his own purposes, brings on his land and collects and keeps there anything likely to do mischief if it escapes, must keep it at his peril; and if he does not do so, is *prima facie* answerable for all the damage which is the natural consequence of its escape.[58]

This principle may at first appear redundant given the rules of nuisance discussed above. There are, however, several distinctions between the rule of *Rylands v. Fletcher* and private nuisance. Private nuisance requires interference with the plaintiffs' use and enjoyment of their property whereas with dangerous activities it is only necessary to show an escape of the dangerous substance from the land of the defendant. Thus, even a passerby could sue if injured by the escaping substance. As well, a nuisance is usually an ongoing, continuous activity whereas the rule of *Rylands v. Fletcher* can be applied even when the event complained of has happened only once. In addition, the modern position appears to be that a defendant cannot be successfully sued for private nuisance unless some injury or harm was reasonably foreseeable, whereas the rule of *Rylands v. Fletcher* is both the origin and embodiment of the concept of strict liability.

It must be noted that strict liability will not be imposed unless the use of the property is unusual. Today, electricity and plumbing are part of a normal operation of modern buildings, and damage caused by these modern conveniences will not support a claim of strict liability. To succeed in such situations, nuisance or negligence must be established.

Strict liability, that is, liability without fault, is also imposed when an employer is held liable for torts committed by employees during the course of their employment. This is referred to as vicarious liability. The employer is without fault and yet is held liable for the wrongful acts of employees. This will be covered in Chapter 10 under "Liability of Employer." When dangerous products, processes or animals are involved, the standard of care required is high because the risk of injury is great. The obligations of persons in control in such situations approach strict liability. Food handlers, for example, find themselves in this unenviable position.

Strict liability involves escape of dangerous substance

58. *Ibid.*, p. 339.

Other Business Torts

People involved in business activities can find themselves faced with tortious liability for their conduct in all of the categories of torts listed above. Businesses that deal directly with the public, especially in the service industries such as restaurants, hotels and retail merchandising, are often faced with their employees' becoming involved in altercations with customers in the course of their employment. Such altercations can result in actions against the business based on vicarious liability for assault and battery, negligence, trespass and even false imprisonment. When business premises visited by customers or the public are involved, there can be actions for negligence based on occupiers' liability.

Much more likely, however, are actions for negligence for injury or damage caused by improper performance of the service supplied or product sold. Even if only careless words are involved and the business is restricted to giving advice and opinions, there can now be liability to both clients and third parties who suffer financially from relying on those words. And if those words cause damage to someone's reputation, the business can be sued for defamation. Those providing consulting services to businesses and private individuals such as bankers, accountants, auditors, lawyers, financial advisors, engineers, and architects are only a few of the professionals who find themselves increasingly vulnerable to damage actions for both tort and breach of contract.

In addition to the categories of torts discussed in this chapter, there are other, unique ones that can be important to businesses: inducing breach of contract; deceit; conversion; passing off; and defamation with respect to a product, called injurious falsehood.

Inducing breach of contract usually involves an employer persuading an employee of another business to leave that employment and work for him or her. This practice is common when that employee has special knowledge about trade secrets or customer lists, or has a special relationship with customers enabling her to bring them with her to the new job. If she is contractually committed to stay in that position of employment for a period of time or not to disclose the secret information, she will breach that contractual obligation if she does so. For the other employer to persuade her to do so, usually with financial incentives that make it worth the risk, violates a duty not to intervene in that relationship. The new employer may face the tort action of inducing breach of contract as a result. This type of tort can also be committed when one business induces another to breach contractual relations with someone else, as when a supplier is persuaded to abandon one customer in favour of a competitor.

> Inducing breach of contract actionable

The tort of **deceit** involves the fraudulent and intentional misleading of another person, causing damage. This is a common wrong committed in business and will be dealt with in Chapter 5 under "Fraudulent Misrepresentation."

> Fraud or deceit actionable

Conversion involves one person intentionally appropriating the goods of another person for his or her own purposes. Theft of goods, in addition to being a crime, is also actionable under the tort of conversion. When someone wrongfully disposes of goods belonging to someone else, such as by selling them, there is a conversion. Conversion also takes place when a person acquires possession of goods through deceit and the goods are damaged or destroyed to the extent that they are no longer of any value to the rightful owner. The courts in such circumstances will usually award damages as a remedy, the person converting the goods in effect being forced to purchase them. The courts also have the power to order the return of the goods if that is a more appropriate remedy. Of course, any direct

> Conversion actionable

intentional interference causing damage to the goods of another is a trespass to chattels, and other remedies may be available as a result.

Passing off actionable

A **passing off** action is appropriate when a business or product is presented to the public in such a way as to lead the public to believe that the product is being provided by another. When imitation Rolex watches are sold as the real thing or when a restaurant adopts the golden arches logo leading the public to believe it is part of the McDonald's chain when it is not, the tort of passing off has been committed. This will be discussed in more detail in Chapter 14 under "Intellectual Property."

Injurious falsehood actionable

The tort of **injurious falsehood** will also be discussed under that heading. This tort takes place when one person attacks the reputation of another's product or business. When a person spreads a false rumour that the wine manufactured by a competitor is adulterated with some other substance or that his business is about to become bankrupt, she has committed an injurious falsehood. Although this tort is often called trade slander or product defamation, it must be distinguished from the tort of defamation which involves injury to the personal reputation of the injured party. Injurious falsehood deals with the reputation and value of a person's property.

SUMMARY

The law of torts protects people from intentional or unreasonable interference with their person, property or reputation. Assault and battery, trespass to land, false imprisonment and defamation are the most common examples of intentional torts. Consent or self-defense can be an adequate defense to assault and battery actions but when self-defense is used, only reasonable force can be involved. Trespass requires someone to enter directly or indirectly onto another's property without authority or permission. Trespass can take the form of a temporary intrusion, such as when someone comes onto the property or places some object onto it, or it can be a permanent intrusion, such as when a building or other structure is built on the property. For false imprisonment to be actionable the plaintiff must not only establish that there was an imprisonment, which can take a physical form with restraints or a mental form when someone submits to the authority of another, he or she must also establish that the imprisonment was done falsely, without authority. Defamation takes place when a false statement is made about a person to his or her discredit. Libel is written defamation and slander is spoken. Defenses that may be available to defamation are absolute privilege, qualified privilege, truth, and fair comment.

Negligence is the most common form of tort action today. It involves inadvertent conduct falling below an acceptable standard of behaviour. To succeed in a negligence action the plaintiff must first establish that a duty of care was owed to the plaintiff. The test of reasonable foreseeability is used to establish that such a duty of care was present. When the courts are faced with situations they have not encountered before, they will also ask if there is any social policy reason not to impose such a duty. In addition, to succeed, the plaintiff must show that the defendant's conduct fell below the level of conduct which would be expected from a reasonable person in the same circumstances, that material damage resulted from the conduct complained of, that the injury or damage was not too remote, and that the victim had not voluntarily assumed the risk. Historically, contributory negligence would also have absolved the defendant of any responsibility for the loss, but today statutes have been enacted in most jurisdictions that allow the courts to apportion the losses between the parties where contributory negligence is present. The obligations of occupiers to people using their property has been modified by statute so that today, even some trespassers can sue if injured on an occupier's premises. Inducing breach of contract, deceit, conversion, passing off and injurious falsehood are also torts of concern to business people.

QUESTIONS

1. Explain what is meant by the statement "A tort is a civil wrong."

2. How do the courts usually determine what standard people must meet to avoid being declared negligent?

3. Distinguish between an assault and a battery.

4. How do doctors avoid liability for the tort of assault and battery when operating on, or otherwise treating, patients?

5. What limitations are there on the right of self-defense when people are defending themselves against an assault?

6. Describe the situations in which battery may be justified.

7. What are the necessary elements that must be present for a person to be classified as a trespasser?

8. What may the proprietor of a business do when faced with an unruly patron?

9. Imprisonment can take the form of confinement, arrest or submission to authority. Explain.

10. What must be established to sue successfully for false imprisonment?

11. Distinguish between libel and slander and explain the significance of the distinction in Alberta.

12. Define the terms "innuendo" and "qualified privilege."

13. List and explain what a plaintiff must establish to succeed in a negligence action.

14. What remedies are available when an tort is committed intentionally that may not be available when the conduct is unintentional?

15. What test do courts use to determine whether the defendant owed a duty to be careful to the plaintiff?

16. What problem normally faced in product liability cases was overcome by the decision made in *Donoghue v. Stevenson*?

17. Distinguish between misfeasance and nonfeasance and explain the significance of the difference in tort law.

18. Explain how the test used to determine the standard of care required from professionals is different from the test used to determine the standard of care required generally.

19. Explain how the standard of care that an occupier must exercise to a person using the property has changed in recent years.

20. How does the "but for" test help to satisfy the requirements of causation?

21. Why is the case of *Hedley Byrne v. Heller* considered so important in the recent development of tort law?

22. Explain how the effect of the presence of contributory negligence has been modified in recent years.

CASES

1. Chaytor et al. v. London, New York and Paris Association of Fashion

The plaintiffs were employed by a competing department store and went to the defendant's place of business to compare prices. The defendant accused them of being spies, some angry words were exchanged, and the defendant called the store detective and told him to, "Watch these people." The defendant shouted at the plaintiffs to get out of the place and then telephoned the police. Two constables arrived shortly afterward and escorted the plaintiffs out of the store. When one of the plaintiffs started to go in another direction, the police took him by the arm and said, "You must come with us." The plaintiffs claimed they were falsely imprisoned but the police claimed they went with them voluntarily. Discuss.

2. Edwards v. Tracey's Stars Shows (Edmonton) Ltd.

In this case a man and his friend went to a nightclub for dinner and a few drinks and to see the show. Towards the end of their visit both men went to the washroom. When they returned, the plaintiff tripped over a step that protruded into the aisle from the stage, fell and was seriously injured. It is likely that had he been watching where he was going he would have seen the step and avoided it, though there was some dispute about the lighting. The judge in this case said that he was distracted by a nude dancer on the stage and that's why he fell. Explain the liability of the nightclub in these circumstances and any defenses they might have. Would your answer be different in a jurisdiction where there was no occupiers' liability act?

3. Brushett v. Cowan et al.

Mrs. Brushett was experiencing difficulty with her leg and went to see Dr. Cowan who decided to do a muscle biopsy. He had her sign a form consenting to this procedure which included the term, "I also consent to such further or alternative measures as may be found to be necessary during the course of the operation." In the process of doing the muscle biopsy the doctor noticed that there was some abnormal bone in the area and decided to do a bone biopsy at the same time. He never informed the patient of this, but did give her some crutches to use. He did not tell her not to put weight on the injured leg. One day while not using crutches, the patient did put weight on the leg and the leg broke at the site of the bone biopsy. She sued Dr. Cowan.

4. Russo v. Ontario Jockey Club

Mrs. Russo attended several racetracks in Ontario and was a very successful bettor. These racetracks were owned by the Jockey Club. One day she was approached by an officer of the Club and presented with a notice which informed her that she was required to leave and would not be permitted to come to any other racetrack owned or operated by the Jockey Club. She was given no reason for being refused entry. There was no suggestion in this case of wrongdoing, only that she was a successful bettor. She was informed that if she came back, she would be arrested and prosecuted. What grounds could the Jockey Club use to support such action and explain what arguments she might raise in her defense?

5. Kovacs v. Ontario Jockey Club

Mr. Kovacs tried to use a credit voucher that he had obtained from one racetrack at another, both owned and operated by the Ontario Jockey Club. Because of some misunderstanding, he was identified as a person who had committed a fraud on the racetrack. He was approached by two security guards and was asked to go to the office to discuss the matter. Mr. Kovacs felt that he had no choice and he accompanied them. The matter was straightened out in about 20 minutes and he went on his way. Mr. Kovacs sued for false imprisonment. What is the likely outcome?

6. Conrad v. Snair

Mr. Snow operated and owned a 10-metre sailboat which he had built by hand and which he moored along with several other boats in Echo Bay. Mr. Snair was visiting his former girlfriend who owned property in Echo Bay in his 4.6-metre Boston Whaler runabout. Snow's vessel was already in the bay when Mr. Snair arrived. Dinner was served overlooking the bay containing the various boats and later that night Mr. Snair took Ms. Conrad in the Boston Whaler over to the yacht club in the process of which he had to pass by Snow's boat. Shortly after midnight on returning from the yacht club, Mr. Snair operated his boat at high speed and collided with Snow's sailboat. Ms. Conrad suffered severe brain damage. The Canadian collision regulations require that sailboats moored in this fashion hang a white light from the mast. Mr. Snow had failed to post such a light. Several other vessels in the bay also failed to post such lights and it seemed to be the practice in that area not to bother. Ms. Conrad sued Mr. Snair as well as Mr. Snow for negligence. Explain who would be responsible for the accident.

7. Jacobsen v. Nike Canada Ltd.

Mr. Jacobsen was an employee of Nike Canada and was working for them setting up a display at a trade show in B.C. Place Stadium. Because of the nature of the job, he was required to work for a long period of time and the employer, through its representative, supplied the workers with food and considerable amounts of beer, that they were allowed to drink while on the job. At 11:30 p.m., they finished and Mr. Jacobsen along with some of the other employees went to two clubs where they consumed more beer. The plaintiff consumed about ten beers while working and more at the clubs. Driving home that night, he was involved in a serious single-vehicle accident that left him a quadriplegic. The question here is whether his employer is responsible for the injuries he suffered.

8. Van der Zalm v. Times Publishers, Bierman, McClintock and Underhill

The plaintiff was the Minister of Human Resources for the government of British Columbia and had been responsible for initiating some significant changes in the province's welfare programs. Many people in the province were very critical of what they perceived to be a restrictive and retrogressive approach to welfare. The defendants published in their newspaper a cartoon depicting the plaintiff "gleefully pulling wings from flies." The defendants claimed that since the plaintiff had carried on his duties as Cabinet minister in a way that inflicted suffering on those who could not protect themselves, their depiction of him as cruel and thoughtless was fair comment. The evidence before the court, however, indicated that the minister had carried out his duties in good faith and there was no evidence to show that he was a person of cruel or sadistic character who enjoyed inflicting suffering. The court was left with the problem of deciding whether the message contained in the cartoon was fair comment. Discuss the probable outcome.

9. Dixon v. Deacon Morgan McEwan Easson

Mr. Dixon was an investor who chose to invest $1.2 million in National Business Systems when the share price was $12.89 per share. These shares went up in price somewhat but, before he could sell, the Securities Commission suspended trading. When trading resumed the shares sold at about $3. Dixon had invested on the strength of financial statements, including one marked "Consolidated Statements of Income and Retained Earnings (Audited)" which had been audited by the defendants. In fact these statements were based on fraudulent information supplied by the management of National Business Systems to indicate annual profits of $14 million when the company had lost $33 million. There is no question but that the accounting firms involved in the audit were negligent for not detecting the inaccuracy. Mr. Dixon sued the accounting firm for negligence. Nothing on the document indicated who the auditors were and the statements had been prepared without the auditors knowing that they would be used by an investor such as Mr. Dixon. The question the court had to determine was whether the auditor owed a duty to Mr. Dixon to be careful. If the auditors had known that the statements were being prepared to attract investors, would this affect your answer?

....

LEGISLATION

Alberta

Contributory Negligence Act, R.S.A. (1980) c. C-23
Defamation Act, R.S.A. (1980) c. D-6
Emergency Medical Aid Act, R.S.A. (1980) c. E-9
Fatal Accidents Act, R.S.A. (1980) c. F-5
Innkeepers' Act, R.S.A. (1980) c. I-4
Occupiers' Liability Act, R.S.A. (1980) c. O-3
Petty Trespass Act, R.S.A. (1980) c. P-6
Tortfeasors Act, R.S.A. (1980) c. T-6
Trespass to Premises Act, R.S.A. (1997) c. T-8.5

....

WEBLINKS

Alberta *Trespass to Premises Act*
www.gov.ab.ca/qp/ascii/acts/T08P5.txt

Alberta *Defamation Act*
www.gov.ab.ca/qp/ascii/acts/D06.txt

Alberta *Occupiers' Liability Act*
www.gov.ab.ca/qp/ascii/acts/003.txt

Alberta *Tortfeasors Act*
www.gov.ab.ca/qp/ascii/acts/T06.txt

Supreme Court of Canada Rulings: *Waldick* v. *Malcolm*
**www.droit.umontreal.ca/doc/csc-scc/en/pub/1991/vol2/html/
1991scr2_0456.html**

Alberta Contributory *Negligence Act*
www.gov.ab.ca/qp/ascii/acts/c23.txt

Formation of Contracts

OBJECTIVES OF THE CHAPTER

- To list and describe the requirements of a valid contract

- To show the necessary conditions for an offer and an acceptance to be effective

- To explain the requirements of consideration in a contract

- To describe the principles of promissory estoppel and *quantum meruit*

- To show when a seal is required to validate a contract

Mr. and Mrs. McIntyre decided to purchase a house being offered for sale by the Pietrobons. They signed an interim agreement and paid a deposit of $10 000. The interim agreement contained a standard provision, which stated "Subject to purchaser obtaining satisfactory personal financing." The McIntyres didn't obtain financing; they didn't even try. They simply changed their minds and wanted their $10 000 deposit back. The Pietrobons would not return the money, because they claimed that the McIntyres had breached their contract and had forfeited their right to it. The McIntyres sued. The judge held that since the clause was so vague there was no agreement, and ordered the return of the money.[1] The terms of a contract must be certain and show that there is in fact agreement between the parties over what their obligations are.

While this decision may yet be challenged as an accurate summary of the law in this area, it does illustrate the need for business people working in real estate and other commercial activities to be well versed in the law and very careful when drawing up such agreements.

Commerce is based on contracts, and contracts is the subject of this and the following three chapters.

1. *McIntyre v. Pietrobon* (1987) 15 B.C.L.R. (2d) 350 (B.C.S.C.).

THE CONTRACTUAL RELATIONSHIP

A knowledge of contract law is vital to all business people because most commercial transactions have contracts at their base. A general understanding of the principles upon which contracts are made is also important to anyone who enters a store, buys a drink, purchases a postage stamp, rides a bus, invests in a car or buys a house. At the outset it is important to understand that when drawing up a contract people are creating and defining their own rules and obligations as opposed to areas of law such as torts where those rules and obligations are imposed on them. **A contract is a voluntary exchange of promises, creating obligations which, if defaulted on, can be enforced and remedied by the courts.** A contract may be written, verbal or implied. It creates a relationship in which the contracting parties establish a world of law unto themselves. The modern principles of contract law developed at a time when laissez-faire was the dominant economic principle, so the courts have adopted a hands-off approach to the contractual relationship, creating an environment often referred to as freedom of contract. Thus, for the most part, courts do not concern themselves with the social desirability or fairness of the contract but simply enforce the rights and obligations the parties have assumed in their agreement. The primary concern of the courts then is to enforce the reasonable expectations of the parties to the contract or what the parties have clearly committed to do.

Contracts may be written, verbal or implied

Ingredients of a Contract

Not all agreements are contracts. To be enforceable in our courts an agreement must meet certain basic qualifications. These are:

1. *Consensus.* Parties to a contract must reach a mutual agreement to commit themselves to a certain transaction. They are assumed to approach the agreement from equal bargaining positions, free to enter it as they choose. The process by which this agreement is reached involves an offer and an acceptance.

2. *Consideration.* There must be a commitment on the part of both parties to do something or to abstain from doing something. The consideration is the price each is willing to pay to participate in the contract.

3. *Capacity.* Parties to a contract must be legally capable of understanding and entering into the bargain. Limitations in contracting capacity have been placed on infants, insane or intoxicated persons, aliens and, in some instances, native peoples and corporations.

4. *Legality.* The object and consideration involved in the agreement must be legal and not against public policy.

5. *Intention.* Both parties must be serious when striking the bargain and both must intend that legally enforceable obligations will result from it.

6. *Writing.* Although the general rule is that an agreement reached verbally between parties is every bit as binding as a written one, legislation has been passed requiring that certain types of contracts be supported by evidence in writing before they can be enforced in the courts.

Terms and Definitions

Before addressing these elements of a contract in more detail, it is necessary to outline some basic terminology used in the discussion of contractual obligations.

Formal and Simple Contracts.

A formal contract is one that is sealed. A modern seal is usually a paper wafer affixed to a document by the party to be bound. Simple contracts, sometimes called parol contracts, may be verbal or written but are not under seal.

Express and Implied Contracts.

An express contract is one in which the parties have expressly stated their agreement either verbally or in writing. An implied contract is inferred from the conduct of the parties. When people deposit coins in vending machines, it can be inferred that they intend to create a contractual relationship and thus an implied contract is in force. Portions of an express contract may also be implied.

Valid, Void and Voidable Contracts.

A valid contract is one which is legally binding on both parties. A void contract does not qualify as a legally binding contract because of some missing ingredient. If the parties to a void contract thought they were bound and followed the agreement, the courts would try to put the parties back to their original positions. A voidable contract does exist and has legal effect, but one of the parties has the option to end the contract. This distinction between void and voidable can have important implications for outsiders to the contract who have acquired an interest in the subject matter.

Unenforceable and Illegal Contracts.

An example of an unenforceable contract is one that is required to be in writing under the *Statute of Frauds*, and is not. It may be good and valid in all other respects, but the courts will not help either party to force the other to perform such a contract. As well, if it has been performed, the courts will not help either party get out of it.

An illegal contract is one that has as its objective the performance of an unlawful act. It is void, and the parties to such an agreement cannot be required to perform it. If the contract has been performed or partially performed, the court, because of the moral taint, normally will not assist either party to undo it by returning them to their original positions as would usually be the case in a void contract. For example, when a deposit has been paid, the court will not order its return nor will it require property to be returned even when one of the parties has been enriched at the other's expense.

The status of these two types of agreement then is quite different. The unenforceable contract is valid and the illegal contract is void. The two are handled in a similar fashion by the courts; however, the courts are more sympathetic where an unenforceable contract is involved and are more likely to help the parties when disputes arise than is the case with an illegal contract.

Bilateral and Unilateral Contracts.

A bilateral contract is one in which both parties assume obligations to be performed. There is no exchange of promises in a unilateral contract. A promise is made by only one party without a corresponding commitment from the other. Only when the other party voluntarily does what has been requested does the contract come into effect. A reward is an example of a unilateral contract. It is not until the lost item is returned that the offer is accepted and the contract created.

Consensus

Dickinson v. Dodds[2]

One of the best cases to illustrate how offer and acceptance works is an old case from the latter nineteenth century. John Dodds owned a parcel of property and made an offer to sell it to Mr. Dickinson for £800 and said specifically, "This offer to be left over until Friday, 9:00 am." On the Thursday afternoon prior to that time limit, Dickinson learned that Dodds had been trying to sell or indeed had sold the property to someone else. This prompted Dickinson to make an effort to assure that the acceptance was received before the stated deadline.

He went to Dodds' home and left a written acceptance at that location. The next morning Dickinson went down to the train station to intercept Mr. Dodds as he arrived in town. When Dickinson located him he handed him a written acceptance. Dodds replied that it was too late and that he had already sold the property. This took place before 9:00 am Friday morning, the stated deadline.

The case is important because it illustrates a number of things, one of which is the nature of the offer itself. The offer is a tentative commitment on the part of the person making it and until it is accepted by the other party there is no obligation on the person making the offer. In this case, Mr. Dodds was free to withdraw his offer any time he liked before it was accepted. The real question was whether or not that offer was still open and able to be accepted at the time of the purported acceptance—that is, either when the letter was left at his residence or at the train station the next morning.

In both cases, it is clear that there was no longer an offer open which could be accepted at those times. As stated, Mr. Dodds was free to change his mind if he wanted to and had clearly done so in these circumstances. Note that it is not enough for Mr. Dodds to change his mind. He has to make it clear to the other party that he has done so; otherwise, the offer is outstanding and can be accepted at least until 9:00 Friday morning.

But in this case there was no question but that Dickinson found out Dodds had changed his mind; in fact, Dickinson admitted this in his pleadings when he stated that he went to Dodds' lodgings to accept the contract, "knowing all the while that Dodds had entirely changed his mind."

To sum up, Dodds was not bound simply by promising to hold the offer open until Friday morning. And because Dickinson knew that Dodds had changed his mind before he tried to accept, there was no contract. On the other hand, had Dickinson not been aware, when he made his acceptance, that Dodds was no longer of a mind to sell, there would have been a valid contract.

The essence of a contract is, at least in theory, the meeting of the minds of the contracting parties. The two parties must have a common will in relation to the subject matter of their negotiations and they must have reached an agreement. They must share an understanding of the bargain struck and be willing to commit themselves to the terms of the contract.

Agreement reached—bargain struck

However, if people were bound only to the terms of contracts they fully understood, there would be few enforceable contracts. Few people thoroughly read the

2. (1876) 2 Ch. 463 (Court of Appeal).

major contracts they enter into, such as insurance policies, leases and loans, and of those who do, few fully understand the specific meaning of the documents. So the law does not recognize the excuse that one of the contracting parties did not read the contract or that he or she did not understand it.

Of course, both parties must have had an opportunity to read and understand the contract for it to be valid. That is, the terms of the contract must be unambiguous, so that if they are read with the help of a lawyer a reasonable person can understand their meaning. If the terms are ambiguous, the court will decide that there has been no consensus between the parties and the contract may be declared void. This was the problem with the agreement used to introduce this chapter. Because of the vague nature of the terms, the would-be purchasers were successful in getting back their deposit—there was no contract.

Terms must be clear and unambiguous

Obviously, mistakes happen, and some very complex rules, which we will discuss later, have been developed to handle them. Nevertheless, contract law is based on the assumption that the culmination of the bargaining process is when one party states its position in the form of an offer in the expectation that the other party, through acceptance, will make a similar commitment to be bound by the terms of that offer.

Offer

Offer—tentative promise

The offer contains all of the terms to be embodied in the contract; all that is required of the other party is to give its consent or denial. The offer is a tentative promise on the part of one party to do something if the other party is willing to do whatever the first party requests. When a person offers to sell a car to someone for $500, the offer is a tentative promise by the first party to deliver the car contingent on the second party's willingness to promise to pay $500. The process of making an offer is the communication of a willingness to be bound and the terms and conditions upon which the intention is based.

This aspect of the offer often confuses those involved in commercial activities. People borrowing money, acquiring insurance and so forth frequently have a form placed before them by a salesperson who says, in effect, "This is our contract; sign here." In fact, the document is not a contract at all but only an offer. Once accepted and signed by the customer, the document embodies the terms and conditions of the contract. The offer must contain all significant terms of the proposed contract. The courts do have the power to imply into contracts many of the insignificant terms the parties may not have considered, such as time of delivery, time of payment and so on. Such terms must be incidental to the central agreement, but consistent with the apparent intention of the parties. In fact, it is possible for the courts to infer the entire contract from the conduct of the parties but if important terms are left out, there can be no contract and it will be declared void.

Offer—must include all important terms

The case of *Rossdale v. Denny*[3] involved a long-term lease in the possession of Major Denny for a property known as Marble Arch. After some negotiation, Rossdale made an offer to purchase the lease that contained the term, "This offer is subject to a formal contract to embody such reasonable provisions as my solicitors may approve." Major Denny accepted the offer, but subsequently, the parties had a disagreement and Major Denny refused to go through with the agreement.

The court held that there had been no contract and that Rossdale could not successfully sue Major Denny, since what was purported to be the offer contained terms indicating that the parties were to agree upon important items later. Thus,

---

3. *Rossdale v. Denny* [1921] 1 Ch. 57 (Court of Appeal).

when parties either neglect to include important terms in their agreement or agree to leave something to be negotiated later, they have not entered into a contract. Such uncertainty must be distinguished from offers that are conditional. Often offers are made "subject to" some event taking place. A person may offer to purchase a house "subject to" the sale of their house. These types of provisions are not necessarily uncertain or ambiguous unless the "subject to" clause itself is uncertain as would be the case if the sale was made "subject to my satisfaction." If the terms of the offer are clear and there is nothing else to be negotiated or agreed upon the parties are bound to perform as agreed, once the "subject to" term has been satisfied.

Some types of contractual relationships, often referred to as quasi-contracts, must be viewed as exceptions to the rule that important terms must be clear. Parties seldom agree in advance on the precise cost of the services of doctors, lawyers, mechanics, builders, etc. Although this is a significant term that has not been agreed upon, there is still an obligation to pay. To attempt to evade a mechanic's repair bill on the basis that there was no indication of the ultimate cost is unfair and the courts would not recognize such a defense. Although there is no question but that there is an obligation to pay for the service, the precise amount of the bill can be disputed. The courts would apply the reasonable person test. The customer who has requested the services is only obligated to pay a reasonable amount for them. However, if the customer pays the bill or in some other way indicates acceptance of the amount the total charge is no longer open to question. This exception may be imposed by statute as well. For example, provincial sale of goods legislation[4] requires a reasonable price to be paid for goods where no price was agreed on.

Note exception for service contracts.

Invitation to Treat.

An offer is usually made to an individual or a group of people but it is also possible to make an offer to the world at large, such as a notice offering a reward for the return of a lost item. Generally, however, newspaper, radio and television advertisements are called invitations to treat and are simply invitations to the public to engage in the process of negotiation.

It is sometimes difficult to distinguish between an offer and an invitation to treat. An ad in the newspaper which says, "Automobile tires for sale, two for the price of one," is not an offer at all. The potential customer must go to the shop, look at the tires and determine the value of the deal. The ad is simply an invitation to the reader to visit the place of business and make an offer to purchase some tires. Catalogues and personal ads in the classified section of a newspaper are also invitations to treat.

Invitation not an offer

To identify an invitation to treat as an offer and saddle the person making the invitation with the responsibilities entailed by that offer would short-circuit the whole process. This would put the parties in the position of being liable to be bound by the other parties' acceptance and incur significant legal obligations before they were ready to be serious. If a merchant were to advertise a product having only a limited supply and it was considered an offer, the merchant would be obligated to anyone who accepted even after the goods were sold, creating an impossible situation.

Goods displayed on the shelves of stores, even though the prices of items are clearly marked, are only an invitation to the customer to pick up the desired item, take it to the checkout counter and make an offer to purchase it at the price marked. There is still some controversy over this point, but most jurisdictions (including Alberta) have accepted the principle established in *Pharmaceutical Society of Great*

Display is an invitation, not an offer

---

4. *Sale of Goods Act,* R.S.A. (1980) c. S-2 s. 11.

Britain v. Boots Cash Chemists (Southern), Ltd.[5] In this case, the English Court of Appeal was faced with the problem of deciding whether a statute controlling the sale of certain types of drugs had been violated. The court had to determine whether clearly priced goods displayed on the shelf of a self-service merchandising operation were being offered for sale. The court determined that such a display was an invitation to treat and not an offer.

Another English case, *Fisher v. Bell*,[6] demonstrates the significance of the distinction between an offer and an invitation to treat. A shopkeeper displayed a prohibited type of knife in his window and was charged with "offering for sale" a prohibited weapon. He was acquitted because the display of the knife was not an offer but rather an invitation to treat.

Since the display of an item is merely an invitation to treat, some people might be tempted to make any offer they want. They might take a grease pencil to the store, change the price and make their own offer. However, the principle is that shoppers are being invited to make the offer indicated by the price on the product. If they want to make any other offer, they must bring this fact to the attention of the vendor. Otherwise, such fraudulent price alteration can qualify as a crime.

Offer by Conduct.

Offer may be implied from conduct

A customer in a self-serve store brings the goods to be purchased to a cashier and places the goods and money on the counter. This is an offer implied by conduct. When a person hails a cab, the gesture of raising a hand and calling "Taxi!" constitutes an offer. An auctioneer's comment, "Do I hear $50?" is merely an invitation to the customer to make an offer. When a person in the audience raises a hand or makes some other acceptable gesture, that is the offer, and the auctioneer is free to accept or reject it. A further question, "Do I hear $60?" is an invitation for more offers. The statement "Sold" is an acceptance of the customer's offer.

Auction—an example of the process of offer and acceptance.
AP Photo/Emile Wamsteker/Canapress.

Communication of an Offer.

Before offers can be accepted, they must first be communicated to the offerees; people cannot accept offers they know nothing about. If a lost dog is returned by someone who is unaware that a reward had been offered, he or she has no right to claim the reward since the offer has not been communicated.

Another situation in which the communication of an offer can present a problem occurs when two offers cross in the mail. If one party sends a letter to another offering to sell a car for $500 and the person to whom the offer is sent, unaware of the first letter, sends another letter offering to purchase the car for the same price, there is no contract. Even though the parties are of a similar mind, neither is aware of the other's offer when the letters are sent and so neither could be called an acceptance. If the owner of the vehicle sells it to a third party, the other party would have no complaint. Similarly, if a person fails to bring all the

---

5. *Pharmaceutical Society of Great Britain v. Boots Cash Chemists (Southern), Ltd.* [1952] 2 All E.R. 456 Queen's Bench Div. (Affirmed by Court of Appeal [1953] 1 All E.R. 482).

6. *Fisher v. Bell* [1960] 3 All E.R. 731 (Queen's Bench Div.).

terms of the offer to the attention of the offeree, the uncommunicated terms do not form part of the contract and are not binding on the offeree.

Offer must be communicated

A merchant will often try to include as part of a contract a term exempting or limiting liability for improper performance of the contract. At a parking lot, for example, there is usually a sign disclaiming responsibility for theft or damage to cars or contents left on the lot. A ticket granting admission to a racketball court or to use a ski lift often includes a term disclaiming responsibility for injury, damages or loss of personal property by theft. In both cases the term is only binding where it has been reasonably brought to the attention of the patron at the time the contract is made. The sign in the parking lot must be placed in a well-lit, strategic spot where the driver will see it before or at the time the contract is made.

When a ticket machine is involved the practice is to place the notice of the terms on or near the machine so that the person parking cannot avoid seeing the notice. If a ticket is involved and the terms are listed on the back, there must be a reference on the front of the ticket drawing the patron's attention to it. The ticket must be given at the time the contract is made, not afterwards.

Only the person to whom the offer is made can respond to it. If the offer is made generally, anyone fulfilling the terms can respond. If the offer is made to a group, anyone in the group satisfying the terms can respond to the offer. But if the offer is made to a specific person, no one else can accept it.

Only person(s) to whom offer is made can accept

The End of an Offer.

For the acceptance of an offer to be effective, the offer must be in force at the time of the acceptance. There are several ways for an offer to come to an end before acceptance.

1. *End of a specified time.* If the offer contains a term specifying when the offer will come to an end, the expiration of that time will end the offer. The time limit may be a specific date or a period of time. The offeror can end the offer before the expiration of that date by communicating to the offeree that the offer is revoked. In order to guarantee that an offer be left open until the expiration date, an option can be purchased. Option agreements will be discussed below.

Offer ends when specified

2. *The expiration of a reasonable time.* If no time is specified for the offer to end, it will expire at the end of a reasonable time. The answer to the problem of determining what is a reasonable time is provided by examining the circumstances.

• *at a reasonable time*

OFFER ENDS AFTER REASONABLE TIME

The case involves an insurance claim arising from the plaintiff's house fire. By statute an action associated with any such claim has to be commenced within one year. The fire took place on November 9, and on February 1 the insurance company made a settlement offer of $8900. There was a communication problem and it wasn't until December that the plaintiff's lawyer attempted to accept the settlement offer. The insurance company now refused, and by this time it was too late to start an action on the loss itself, so the plaintiff sued on the strength of the contract that they claimed had been created by the acceptance of the offer to settle. The court found that after nine months the offer had lapsed because it had not been accepted within a reasonable time.

Mitchell v. Bennett, Cole Adjusters Ltd. et al., Mitchell v. Thompson, 33 D.L.R. (4th) 398 (British Columbia Supreme Court)

Thus, one would expect an offer to sell a ship to be held open longer than an offer to sell a load of ripe peaches.

• at death of offeror

3. *Death or insanity of offeror.* If the offeror dies or becomes insane to the extent of being incapable of understanding what he or she is doing, the offer automatically ends and cannot be accepted. This is the case even if the offeree is unaware of the death or insanity.

• when revoked

4. *Revocation of offer.* The offeror may revoke an offer any time before acceptance. For such revocation to be effective, it must be communicated. Thus, revocation is accomplished, very simply, when the offeror tells the offeree that he or she is no longer willing to enter the contract. However, if the offeree accepts the offer before learning of the revocation, there is a valid, binding contract. To make sure, the offeror should specifically revoke the offer and not do anything with the goods involved until it is certain that the revocation has been communicated.

Revocation must be communicated

This was the situation in *Dickinson v. Dodds* used to introduce this section. In that case Dodds sold property he had offered to Dickinson to someone else before that offer had expired. The court held that because Dickinson had found out about the sale and knew "beyond a shadow of a doubt" that Dodds had changed his mind before he accepted, there was an effective revocation implied in the sale of the property to the third party. Although this revocation was done indirectly it was effective nonetheless. It is important to realize that if Dickinson had not learned of the sale before he accepted, Dodds would have been in serious difficulty. But Dodds was "lucky." It would be most foolhardy today to hope for such an indirect revocation and great care should be taken to ensure that the offeree knows that you have changed your mind before you make a contract with someone else. At the very least make the new contract subject to the successful revocation of your prior offer. This case also illustrates the point that even if an offeror promises to keep an offer open for a specified time, he or she is free to revoke it before that time expires if no option has been purchased.

Rejection or counteroffer ends offer

5. *Rejection and counteroffer.* During the bargaining process, several different proposals may be put forward, rejected and then followed by counterproposals. If each proposal and counterproposal remained in effect, the purpose of the bargaining process would be defeated because none of the parties involved would know where they stood. To solve this difficulty, the courts have developed the principle that whenever an offer is put forward and rejected or a counterproposal is put forward, which by implication is a rejection, the first offer is brought to an end. For example, if somebody offers to sell a car to another person for $500 and that person replies, "I'll give you $450," a counteroffer has been made and, by implication, the original offer has been rejected. If the seller rejects the counteroffer, it is too late for the purchaser to reconsider and accept the original offer; it no longer exists. Under such circumstances, an attempt to accept the original $500 offer constitutes a new offer which the seller is free to accept or reject.

Request for information is not a counteroffer

Sometimes it is difficult to tell what constitutes a rejection or a counteroffer. When the offeree is merely requesting information or clarification, that does not constitute a counteroffer or a rejection and the offer remains in force. If the purchaser in the preceding example had asked, "Does the car have whitewall tires?" the courts would interpret the question as a request for information which would have no effect on the original offer. On the other hand, if the purchaser had asked, "Will you take $450?" even though it was worded as a request for information, it was clearly a counteroffer and the original offer would have ended.

The existence of an offer can be affected by other factors as well. For example, the offer will be ended if the activity contemplated by the contracting parties becomes illegal before acceptance or if the goods forming the subject matter of the contract are destroyed without the parties being aware of it.

Offers That Can't Be Revoked.

Often business people find the uncertainty associated with the offeror's right to revoke any time prior to the point of acceptance very inconvenient, especially when they are arranging their business affairs in order to take advantage of the offer.

A typical problem involves land accumulations. When developers wish to build a hotel, mall or other large project, they normally have to acquire the land to be used from several different owners, but they don't want to make any commitments to those owners until they are sure they can get all the parcels of land necessary for the project. They will get offers to sell from each of the land owners, but if those owners are free to revoke there is no certainty for the developers.

In these circumstances a separate, subsidiary contract is entered into called an **option agreement**, wherein consideration is given by the offeree specifically to keep the offer open for a given length of time. The developer now has the certainty necessary to accomplish his goal. Such arrangements are quite common and found in all areas of finance and business. Options can also be put under seal; the use of the seal will be discussed below under "Consideration."

Where option exists, offer can't be revoked

Sometimes the courts are willing to imply such a subsidiary contract. Normally, when a unilateral offer is made in which the performance of the conduct requested is the acceptance of the offer, that acceptance has not taken place until the performance is completed. However, if an employer promises to give her business to an employee if he stays until she retires, the acceptance is made simply by his staying on. If such a unilateral offer can be revoked at any time prior to acceptance, what is to stop the employer from revoking the offer just before she retires and selling the business to someone else? In these circumstances the courts in the United States have found a **subsidiary contract** between the parties that requires the offeror to keep the offer open until performance of the action required for acceptance of the main contract is completed. Thus, once performance has started, the offeror cannot revoke.

In Canada the courts have adopted a similar attitude in tendering situations. It is common business practice to put out a request for bids in order to get the best possible price on a required product or service. This is the normal practice in the construction industry. The traditional legal approach to such a tendering process is that the request for bids is an invitation to treat and the bid by the supplier is the offer. This leaves the party that originally requested the bids free to accept whichever bid is appropriate. The difficulty arises when one of the bidders realizes a mistake has been made, decides upon seeing the other bids that theirs is too low or for whatever reason decides to rethink their bid. Can the person tendering the offer or bid revoke before the final selection and acceptance is made?

Applying the traditional rules of offer and acceptance, an offer can be revoked any time before acceptance. This can cause great damage to the general tendering process where the parties must be certain of the bids when they are considered for acceptance. The Supreme Court of Canada has decided that where the original party requesting tenders has made it clear that they will only consider bids where

Where tenders are requested, bid may not be revoked if so agreed

the tendering party agrees that the bids cannot be withdrawn once submitted, such offers cannot be revoked.[7] The court has found that a subsidiary contract exists, whereby in exchange for including the bid for consideration, the offer cannot be revoked before acceptance. As above, the problem is also avoided where the tendered bid is made under seal.

Standard Form Contract.

The law assumes that the two parties to an agreement are in equal bargaining positions and that both will negotiate the terms of the agreement until a consensus is reached which represents a fair bargain. But any passenger who tried to negotiate with an airline over the terms of a ticket to travel, would not meet with much success. Many large businesses are in a position to impose almost any terms they wish on their customers. They have developed specific non-negotiable terms to be included in their agreements or standard form contracts. These clauses, intended to limit the liability of one of the parties, are called exculpatory or exemption clauses. If customers do not like the terms, they are invited to go elsewhere. If they do accept the terms, they are bound by them because the common law assumes that both parties are in equal bargaining positions.

Bargaining difficult with standard form contract

Statutes and attitude of court mitigate this

To alleviate some of the unfairness of this practice, all jurisdictions in Canada (including Alberta) have passed statutes such as the *Sale of Goods Act.* This statute and various forms of consumer protection legislation will be discussed in Chapter 7. The courts have also tried to relieve some of the harshness of the common law approach by treating exculpatory clauses in standard form contracts very restrictively. Any business which includes in its contracts terms disclaiming responsibility for damage to goods left on the premises would still be held responsible for goods stolen from its premises. Exemption clauses must be very explicit. As can be seen the theory that the offer is part of a negotiating or bargaining process is sometimes misleading.

Acceptance

Entores Ltd. v. Miles Far East Corp.[8]

In this case an American company was dealing with an English company through a Dutch subsidiary and they were negotiating the terms of a contract for electrical components. The method of communication was by telex, which uses telephone lines much like electronic mail or fax machines. There was some difficulty for the courts to determine at what stage the offer was made and when the acceptance had taken place. They finally decided that the offer was made by the Dutch subsidiary by telex and subsequently accepted by return telex by the English company.

The deal went sour, and the English company sued the American company in the English courts for breach of contract. The procedure was somewhat complex, because the English company was asking the court for permission to notify the American company that they were starting an action against them in England. In order to do so the English courts had to determine whether they had jurisdiction—that is, whether the contract had been created in England or Holland.

Normally an acceptance must be communicated back to the offeror before it is effective, and since the acceptance was communicated in England, the contract

7. *Ontario v. Ron Engineering* (1981) 119 D.L.R. (3d) 267.
8. [1955] 2 All E.R. 493.

could be thought of as having been created in England. But there is an exception to this called the "postbox rule," which states that where the mail is used to communicate—and this applies to telegrams as well—the acceptance is effective when and where sent, not when and where received. If this rule applied to acceptances sent by telex, it would make the creation of the contract take place in Holland rather than England.

The court decided that the exception created by the postbox rule was made to address the problems caused by delayed communications between parties, and it was extended to telegrams because the same principles apply. But telex is a form of instant communication like the telephone; there is no reason to extend the exception, and so the general rule applies: the acceptance is effective when and where communicated. The contract, therefore, is created where the acceptance is heard. In this case that is by the offeree in England, and therefore, the English courts had jurisdiction.

This case not only illustrates what happens when the postbox rule comes into play, but also shows that when new, instantaneous methods of communication are involved the postbox rule does not apply.

At the heart of contract law is the concept of consensus and mutual commitment. The manifestation of an intention to commit on the part of the offeror is found in the offer; the offeree's intention to commit is found in the acceptance. The contract is formed and the parties are bound by it at the point of acceptance. The key to understanding acceptance is that the commitment must be total. If a condition or qualification is put on the acceptance, it then becomes a counteroffer, not an acceptance. If a person offers to sell a car for $500 and the response is, "I accept, but you must include new tires," the response is a counteroffer and the seller is now in a position to accept or reject the new offer. Nor is it possible to accept only part of an offer. If a person offers to sell a house and its furnishings at a stipulated price for each, the purchaser cannot say, "I accept your offer, but I only want the furniture." For an acceptance to be valid, it must be an all-or-nothing proposition.

Acceptance must be unconditional

In this connection, serious problems can arise when one party responds to an offer by sending their own order form with different terms typed on it than were included in the original offer. This must be regarded as a counteroffer, and if the goods are sent, that counteroffer with the new terms has been accepted by the seller, who is bound by them. Such a mistake is easily made and care should be taken to watch for such substituted forms.

A further problem arises when an offer contains ambiguous wording which becomes part of the contract on acceptance. Under normal circumstances, the court will do all it can to interpret the ambiguities in such a way as to give effect to the intention of all the parties. In the process, the courts will apply the reasonable person test, but will not go so far as to strike a bargain on behalf of the parties. In the English case of *Scammel v. Ouston*,[9] the parties had referred to a hire-purchase agreement (a device to use the item being purchased as security for payments spread over a period of time), but had failed to include the terms of that agreement in their negotiations for the purchase of a van. Lord Wright of the House of Lords declared that the parties "never got beyond negotiations." Here the parties "never in intention or even in appearance reached an agreement."[10] No matter

9. *Scammel v. Ouston* [1941] A.C. 251 (House of Lords).
10. *Ibid.*, p. 269.

COMMUNICATION OF ACCEPTANCE MAY BE INDIRECT

This dispute involves a tender made by Lanca to the Board of Education for the construction of a school building. The provisions of the tender required that a formal contract be executed within seven days of the notification of the acceptance of the tender. A Board meeting was held at which a resolution to accept Lanca's tender was passed. The president of Lanca was present, to the knowledge of the Board. Some members of the Board, as well as the Board's architect and controller, all spoke at the meeting in terms that implied that the plaintiff was going to be building the school. Two days later the Board rescinded its resolution and awarded the contract to someone else. The question facing the court was whether notice of the acceptance had been given to the plaintiff sufficient to create a binding contract. The answer was yes, and the Board was liable for the breach.

Lanca Contracting Ltd. v. Brant County Board of Education, 26 D.L.R. (4th) 708 (Ontario Court of Appeal)

Acceptance will not cure defective offer

how definite the acceptance, it will not overcome the defect of an incomplete or otherwise defective offer.

Communication of Acceptance.

Offer may be accepted by conduct where specified

Usually, acceptance of an agreement is accomplished by communicating it to the offeror. However, it is possible for an offer to be accepted by conduct. If the offeror has indicated particular conduct to specify acceptance, the offeree must comply with that stipulation for it to be effective. If a person offers to sell a car for $500 and specifies that if the offeree wants to accept, he or she should come and get the keys from the offeror's landlord and drive the car away, paying the offeror upon return from vacation, full compliance with those directions amounts to acceptance. If the offeree acquires the keys from the landlord and drives the vehicle away, the offer has been accepted by conduct and both parties are bound by the contract.

Unilateral contract accepted by completion of performance

A unilateral contract is accepted by performance of the act specified in the offer. A firm in England offered a large sum of money to the first human-powered aircraft to fly across the English Channel. The principals of that firm would not have been impressed by someone planning to perform the feat coming to them to accept the offer. Starting the flight would not constitute acceptance either. For an acceptance to be effective, the cross-Channel flight would have to be completed. This poses a problem because an offer can be revoked at any time before the point of acceptance. Thus, in the period of time between the beginning of performance and its completion, the offeror could legally revoke the offer. For example, a representative of the firm offering the reward for the cross-Channel flight theoretically could have stood on the shore just before completion and shouted, "I revoke." Such an action would be morally repugnant and there is some debate as to whether such conduct would be legally permissible. The American approach is that the offeror is not allowed to revoke once performance has begun.

A selling practice has recently developed in which a merchandiser, without asking, sends a product to the home of a potential customer with a note saying that if the goods are not returned within ten days, the customer will have purchased them. The general rule, however, is that acceptance will not be inferred from silence, even when such silence is specified as the mode of acceptance in the original offer. The common law position is that the offeree is not obligated to respond when unsolicited goods arrive on the doorstep. The recipient is free to ignore the offer or to dispose of the products sent. It is vital to note that if the offeree uses the product in any way, acceptance is complete and the offeree would be bound in contract to the offeror. Many jurisdictions have passed legislation to curb these practices.[11]

Although silence will not normally be taken as acceptance, the courts adopt a different approach when there has been a long history of dealings between the parties. If an offeror says, "If I don't hear from you by Monday, I'll assume we have a deal," the offeree would normally be free to ignore the offer without fear that a binding contract would result. However, if the event in question is just part of an on-going business relationship, the courts are willing to recognize the offeree's failure to respond as requested as an acceptance resulting in a binding contract.

Unsolicited offer not accepted by silence— exception

This principle is often abused, especially when goods or services are being supplied to consumers. Such abuse is involved when a cable supplier notifies a customer that new channels will be supplied at a higher price unless the customer indicates in writing that he or she doesn't want the extra service. Because of the ongoing relationship a failure to respond in these circumstances is considered by courts to be acceptance. Several provinces now prohibit such negative-option schemes.[12] It is important to understand that no such protection is present where ongoing relations between businesses are involved.

Acceptance must be communicated to the offeror to be effective unless it is accomplished by conduct. The result flowing from this general rule is that a contract comes into existence where the offeror learns of the acceptance rather than where it is made by the offeree. If someone in Halifax offers to sell a car to someone in Winnipeg and the offeree accepts over the telephone, the contract comes into existence in Halifax since that is where the offeror heard the acceptance. This has quite an impact; it may determine that Nova Scotia law applies rather than Manitoba law. In addition, the acceptance becomes effective and a contract is formed at the time the acceptance is communicated.

Acceptance must be communicated to be effective

The Postbox Rule.

Difficulties arise when parties deal with each other over long distances using non-instant forms of communication. Because neither party can be absolutely sure of the other's state of mind at a given time, there can be no certainty of the contract's status. The postbox rule, mentioned above, was developed to solve this problem.

When an acceptance is mailed and the use of the postal service is a reasonable means of communication in the circumstances, that acceptance is effective when and where it is deposited in the mailbox. This is a clear exception to the general rule discussed above where an acceptance is not effective until the offeror learns of it. The rule eliminates the difficulties of finding the point of consensus when the parties are communicating at a distance; but it also leads to other problems, the biggest of which is that for a period of time, while the letter of acceptance is still in the mail, the offeror is bound in contract but unaware of that fact.

Mailed acceptance effective when and where dropped in postbox

When the original offer is sent by mail, there is usually little question about a response by mail being appropriate, and thus the postbox rule applies. Difficulty arises when a different means of communication is involved, as is illustrated in *Henthorne v. Fraser*.[13] The plaintiff, Mr. Henthorne, went to the defendant's office

---

11. In Alberta, the only relevant legislation is s. 29 of the *Consumer Credit Transactions Act* S.A. (1985) c. C-22.5, which forbids the issuing of unsolicited credit cards.

12. Such schemes are currently governed only by the common law in Alberta, but they are dealt with in the *Fair Trading Act*, which comes into force effective September 1, 1999.

13. *Henthorne v. Fraser* [1892] 2 Ch. 27 (Court of Appeal).

where he was offered some property, the offer to be left open for 14 days. He took the offer home to think about it and after several days posted a letter of acceptance. In the meantime, the defendant, Mr. Fraser, sold the property to another party and wrote a letter to Henthorne revoking the offer. The two letters crossed in the mail. The court had to decide when, if at all, the acceptance was effective. It decided that a reasonable person would have responded by mail even though the offer had been handed to him, and therefore the acceptance was effective when it was placed in the mailbox.

Only applies where response by mail appropriate

Postbox rule extended to telegrams

As has been mentioned, the postbox rule has been extended to include telegrams; the courts have, however, shown great reluctance to extend it to other forms of communication, such as telex, fax machines and electronic mail, as is illustrated by the *Entores* case above. More significant than when the offer is accepted may be the determination of where it was accepted. If the offeror trying to sell his car in Halifax had been communicating with the offeree in Winnipeg by mail, the postbox rule would apply. The letter of acceptance would have been effective in Winnipeg where it was sent rather than in Halifax where it was received, thus making it more likely that Manitoba law would apply.

Specified Means of Acceptance.

A usual effect of the postbox rule is that for a period of time after the acceptance is mailed, the offeror is bound in contract without knowing it until the acceptance is actually received. If this uncertainty poses a problem, the offeror is free to stipulate another means of acceptance, and the problem can be readily overcome. The offeror is always free to stipulate how the offer is to be accepted and has the right to do this even when the means specified are unreasonable. If the offer states that the acceptance must be by mail, by phone or by telegram, and all other means of communication are prohibited, the offeree must comply if the acceptance is to be effective. If the offeror states that acceptance is to be by mail but does not prohibit other means, the offeree can use a faster means of communication, such as the telephone or a telegram, but if a telegram is used, it will not be effective until received. If the offeror is silent as to the means of acceptance to be employed, a reasonable person test is used to determine if the method used is appropriate. It is usually appropriate to send an acceptance using the same method by which the offer was communicated. Thus, if the offer was mailed, the response should be by mail; if by fax, the acceptance should be given in the same manner.

Communication of a Revocation.

Postbox rule does not apply to revocation

The postbox rule does not apply to a revocation. For a revocation to be effective, it must be communicated to the offeree. If a person offers to sell something to one person, he or she cannot then sell it to someone else with the idea that the sale eliminates any claim the original offeree has to the goods. If a person makes an offer to sell something to someone and then sells it to a third person without revoking the offer to the first, the offer is still open and capable of being accepted by the original offeree.

This is true even when a letter of revocation has been mailed, but not yet received at the time of acceptance. This was Fraser's position in the case of *Henthorne v. Fraser* discussed above. The important point here is that the offer must be revoked by communicating the fact to the offeree. Once the offeree is aware of the revocation, and that the offeror has changed her mind, the offer is no longer open and cannot be accepted. Suppose Chan offers to sell Phillips her car in a letter, the offer to remain open for a week, and the next day she sells it to someone else. She must let Phillips know she has changed her mind. If she mails the letter of revocation, that letter will not be effective until it is received. If Phillips mails the letter of acceptance before receiving the letter of revocation, according to the postbox rule acceptance will be effective when it is dropped in the mailbox and there will be a contract. In such circumstances, Chan will find herself in the position of being bound by two different contracts to sell her car.

CONSIDERATION

Gilbert Steel Ltd. v. University Construction Ltd.[14]

This case illustrates not only the nature of consideration, but also the principle of promissory estoppel, which will be discussed below. Gilbert Steel had supplied construction steel to University Construction on a number of their projects. For one particular project they had a contract for a specified amount of steel to be provided at a set price and of set quality. Unfortunately for Gilbert Steel, their supplier increased the price of steel to them during the project. Gilbert Steel turned to University Construction and sought a new agreement with them to increase the cost of steel. University Construction agreed to pay the higher price.

The steel was delivered and payments were made, but the payments were never enough to cover the extra cost, so that at the end of the project a balance was owing to Gilbert Steel. When Gilbert demanded payment, University refused to pay the extra over the price originally agreed on, taking the position that they didn't receive anything in exchange for their promise to pay a higher amount. Prior to that agreement, Gilbert Steel had been obligated to supply the steel at a set price and subsequent to that agreement the only change was that University Construction was obligated to pay more. Such a one-sided agreement was not a binding contract. In order for a contract to exist, there must be an exchange of promises or commitments between the parties—a one-sided agreement is not enforceable.

The lawyers for Gilbert Steel made several attempts to convince the court that there was benefit on University's side—that is, there was "consideration." They argued first that at the time of the promise to pay the higher price, Gilbert Steel had agreed to give University Construction a good price on a subsequent project. The court found that this was not specific enough and that there was no commitment involved. Gilbert also argued that because University didn't have to pay for 60 days they were getting free credit for whatever they owed during that period of time. They also argued that because the increase in price made the amount owing more, the free credit was worth more than it was before, and this qualified as consideration. The judge's response was "I cannot accept counsel's contention, ingenious as it is, that the increased credit inherent in the increased price constitutes consideration." Finally, Gilbert argued that since the promise to pay the higher price was relied on and steel was delivered, an estoppel was created and, therefore, the higher amount should be paid.

As will be seen from the discussion below, promissory estoppel can arise in situations where an agreement is one-sided and there is no consideration to support

14. (1976) 67 D.L.R. (3d) 606.

it, but such a promise in Canada and England can only be used as a defense when the person making the promise is for some reason suing the other. In this case the person making the promise is University Construction and it is Gilbert Steel, the recipient of the promise, that is suing for breach of contract; promissory estoppel, instead of being used as "shield," is being used as a "sword," and that is not permissible in Canada.

Had University Construction made the higher payments and sued Gilbert Steel to get them back, then promissory estoppel may have been available to Gilbert Steel as a defense.

Consideration—the price one is willing to pay for a promise

Consideration—not necessarily money

Consideration—can be benefit or detriment

Central to contract law is the bargaining process in which people trade promises for promises and all parties derive some benefit from the deal. That benefit, essential to the existence of a contract, is called consideration and is defined as the price one promises to pay for the promise of another. Consideration is not restricted to the exchange of money. A bargain may involve the exchange of anything the parties think is of value. For example, if the parties to a contract agree to exchange a car for $500, there is valid consideration on both sides. The promise to deliver the automobile is a valid consideration as is the promise to pay $500. Thus, before the parties actually exchange the automobile for the cash, they are still bound in contract because the consideration given is the exchange of commitments or promises. If one of the parties fails to honour that commitment, the other can successfully sue for breach of contract.

Because it is sometimes difficult to determine the value a person is getting from a deal, it is often better to look at what the parties are giving or paying. For example, Ali agrees to clean up a public park in exchange for Barbeau's promise to pay $500. Even though this commitment might have been made out of a sense of civic responsibility and results in no personal benefit, Barbeau is still obligated to pay. Both sides have exchanged promises or commitments.

Similarly, the contract is just as binding if the consideration involved is a commitment not to do something as opposed to a promise to do something. For example, if someone promises to pay another $500 to quit smoking, such an arrangement is a valid, binding contract. The consideration on the one side is the promise to pay $500 and the consideration on the other side is the promise to refrain from doing something the party has a legal right to do, that is, smoke.

⌐ CONSIDERATION FOR PROMISSORY NOTE WAS REARRANGING OBLIGATIONS⌐

A woman was indebted to the Bank of Nova Scotia and in the process of the renewal and rearrangement of those debts her husband signed a promissory note to the Bank. Before that time there was no indebtedness on his part. Eventually, the husband and wife separated, and upon the wife's default, the Bank came after the husband for payment on the promissory note. The husband claimed that he had received no consideration in exchange for his promise to be responsible for his wife's preexisting debts. The court found that because pursuant to the husband's signing the promissory note the Bank had given up its rights or claims under the old arrangement, which would not have happened without the husband's promise, consideration did take place.

Bank of Nova Scotia v. Hallgarth et al., 32 D.L.R. (4th) 158 (British Columbia Court of Appeal)

Consideration is a benefit or a detriment flowing between the parties to an agreement as the result of a bargain struck. If the agreement is one-sided and only one of the parties is getting anything from the deal, it is called a **gratuitous promise** and the courts will not enforce it. However, once the gift has been given, the courts will not assist the giver in getting it back. It may well be that such gratuitous promises ought to be honoured from an ethical point of view, but there is no legal obligation to do so and such bare promises will not be enforced by the courts.

Courts will not enforce one-sided contract

When services are performed gratuitously, however, there is still an obligation to do a proper job. If through the negligence of the person performing the gratuitous service, damage or injury results, he or she can be sued in tort. For example, if a skilled carpenter out of the goodness of his heart helps his neighbour repair a roof and because of his negligence the roof leaks and causes damage to furniture and belongings, the neighbour can sue in tort for compensation.

Adequacy of Consideration

It is not necessary that the consideration be fair to both parties. Contract law rests on the foundation that both parties are free to bargain. Once they reach an agreement, the court will assist them in enforcing the resulting contract but will not release either of them from a bad deal. If a person agrees to sell someone a brand new Cadillac for $100, this becomes a valid, binding contract. This does not mean that the courts will never look at the adequacy or fairness of the consideration. If one of the parties claims insanity, drunkenness, unconscionability, fraud or mistake the court may look at the unusually low consideration given in determining the validity of the claim and whether the other contracting party ought to have been aware of the problem.

Consideration
• need not be fair but must be specific

Although the consideration paid does not need to be fair, it must have some legal value. In the case of *White v. Bluett*,[15] a father agreed to give his son money if the boy would stop bothering him. It was held that such a promise had no intrinsic value and therefore was not consideration. Similarly, if a person agrees to give love and affection in return for a promise of money, that is not sufficient consideration. Whatever the parties have bargained for must have some material value for the courts to enforce the bargain.

When two parties strike a bargain, they must agree to a specific consideration or price. Suppose someone agrees to exchange a car for another's promise to "do some work around the house." Such a promise would not be enforceable because the work to be done is not specified. This problem becomes acute whenever a monetary consideration is involved. It is not sufficient to promise to give "some money" as payment for the promise of another. Such a commitment must refer to a specific amount of money. However, there have been cases which establish that there is sufficient consideration if the parties agree to pay the "market value" of an item or where some other objective method or formula for pricing a product at some time in the future is used.[16]

• particularly if money is involved

Existing Duty

The adequacy of consideration becomes important whenever there is an existing duty to do the thing contracted for. For example, Olsen agreed to paint Chang's

15. *White v. Bluett* (1853) 23 L.J. Ex. 36 (Court of Exchequer).
16. *Folley v. Classique Coaches* (1934) 2 K.B. 1 (Court of Appeal).

house for $500 and then said to Chang when the painting was three-quarters finished, "I will not finish unless you promise to pay me another $200." Even if Chang were to agree to this extra payment, it would not be binding because Chang would receive nothing in exchange for the promise to pay the extra $200. Olsen was obligated to finish painting the house before the promise to pay the extra $200 was made. After the promise to pay the extra $200 was made, the obligation remained the same. Olsen's legal position did not change, so therefore there was no consideration.

When a duty to act exists but that duty is owed to a third party, a promise to do the same thing for someone else is enforceable. In the situation above, if Adams, a potential tenant, realized that Olsen's reluctance to finish the job would delay possession of the premises, and thus cause greater expense, and Adams promised to pay Olsen the extra $200, that agreement would be binding. Before Adams' promise to pay the extra $200, Olsen was legally obligated to Chang to finish painting the house. After the promise to Adams, Olsen is now legally obligated to Adams as well as Chang to paint the house. Olsen's legal position has changed because Olsen now runs the risk of having to pay Adams' damages as well as Chang's if the contract is breached. There is a valid consideration here and the contract is binding.

Whenever the existing duty involves a police officer, firefighter or other public servant, there can be no further promise to do what they are already legally obligated to do. A firefighter cannot arrive at a blaze and extract a promise from the victim to pay an extra $500 to put out the fire. Such a contract would be against public policy and unenforceable.

Past Consideration

There are situations when consideration appears to be present but in fact is not. One of these is when the consideration was given in the past. That is, the bargain is struck after the price agreed on has been paid. The classic example of this is when a person rescues someone from drowning and the grateful victim promises to give the rescuer $100. Although it may appear that both parties have given something (the rescuer has performed a service and the other party has promised to pay), such a promise is not enforceable. The key to this problem is in the timing. When the promise to pay the $100 was made, the rescue had already taken place, so where is the bargain? In fact, the rescuer, since the rescue has already been performed, is in exactly the same legal position before the promise as afterwards. Thus, it is often said that "past consideration is no consideration."

Paying Less to Satisfy a Debt

Another situation in which consideration appears to be present, but often is not, is when people who are obligated to pay a certain sum of money negotiate with their creditors to accept lesser amounts in full payment of the debt. Suppose a debtor who owes a creditor $500 payable on or before June 10 approaches the creditor on June 11 and says, "I can't pay you the $500 I owe you. If you will take $300 in full satisfaction of the debt, I will pay you that instead." What is the position of the creditor who takes this money? Can the creditor still sue for the remaining $200? In fact the reduction of the debt is gratuitous. The creditor has received nothing for his promise to take less in full satisfaction of the debt. Under the common law, it was quite clear that where such a one-sided promise was made, it was not binding. Even when partial payment was actually taken, the creditor could then turn around and sue for the remainder.[17] But as a practical business matter, in many situations, such an arrangement to take less is beneficial to the creditor as well as the debtor. The creditor might otherwise have to sue to recover and get nothing. Today most provinces (including Alberta) have passed legislation providing that when a creditor has agreed to take less in full satisfaction of a debt and when the creditor has actually received the partial payment agreed on, the creditor is bound and cannot sue for any deficit.[18] When the creditor has only agreed to take less, however, and the payment has not yet been made, the creditor is still free to change his or her mind and insist on the entire amount being paid. Of course, when the debtor has agreed to pay the lesser amount early or do something in addition to the payment, such as clean up the creditor's property, there is consideration on both sides to support the new arrangement and the creditor is bound by the promise to take less.

Note statutory exceptions

Settlement Out of Court

Using this reasoning, it is possible to assume that when disputes are settled out of court, as they often are, there is no consideration and therefore the parties are not bound by the settlement. It has been argued that if one party receives considerably less than it would have won in a court action, there is really no consideration to support the agreement to take less. In fact, the court will not entertain such an argument. It may be difficult to see what each party has received, but it is clear that both have given up something pursuant to the agreement. In the settlement process, both parties have given up the right to have the matter brought before the court and tried, and that is something of value to each party. Hence, there is consideration on both sides and the settlement is legally binding on them.

Consideration not a factor in out-of-court settlements

Illegal Consideration

There are some policy restrictions on what constitutes good consideration. If a person agrees to pay another to kill a third, such an agreement is not enforceable since the consideration given for the promise of payment is a commitment to perform an unlawful act. In addition, for consideration to be valid, it must be possible to perform the consideration promised. If a person were to promise to bring back someone's relative from the dead in exchange for the payment of $5000, such a promise would be unenforceable due to the impossibility of performance.

Illegal or impossible consideration is no consideration

Request for Services

One situation in which it is difficult to determine consideration at the point of contract is when one party requests the performance of a service before the parties have agreed on a specific payment. When a lawyer or mechanic is hired, often no attempt is made to determine the ultimate price of the job. Even though no consideration has been agreed on in these circumstances, the court will enforce the obligation to pay. If the parties cannot come to an agreement on the amount, the courts will determine what reasonable amount must be paid for the service.

The courts are usually reluctant to enforce any promises when consideration is not present because no bargain has been struck. However, the bargaining nature

Must pay reasonable amount for services

17. *Foakes v. Beer* (1884) 9 App. Cas. 605 (House of Lords).

18. *Judicature Act*, R.S.A. (1980) c. J-1 s. 13.

of the arrangement is present in a request for services; it is just that the parties have not agreed on a specific consideration. Therefore, the courts are willing to enforce an implied promise to pay a reasonable amount.

This is an application of the principle of *quantum meruit*. When goods or services are supplied but the parties have neglected to set out a price, the courts are willing to assess the value of those goods or services and impose an obligation to pay a reasonable price on the person who benefits. *Quantum meruit* means "as much as is deserved," and the courts have shown a willingness to use this principle as a basis of payment in other situations as well. Thus, if a contract involving services is breached by the person benefiting from the services, that person can be required to pay for what has been done. It is likely that recovery on a quantum meruit basis will be denied, however, if the person claiming is the one who breached the contract or if the contract requires the performance of some as yet unmet condition before payment is to be received. The requirement to pay a reasonable price when no specific price has been agreed upon has also been applied to the sale of goods by provincial statute.[19]

Promissory Estoppel

Gratuitous promises usually not enforceable

Another exception to the rule that a promise is only enforceable if consideration is present is based on the principle of **promissory estoppel**, sometimes referred to as **equitable estoppel**. Someone who makes a gratuitous promise to do something for another person is not usually jeopardized if that promise is not performed. Such gratuitous promises are usually not enforceable. But there are situations in which the promisee incurs expenses or other obligations in anticipation of the promise being performed. Unique remedies have been developed to compensate for significant loss.

Promissory estoppel can only be used as a defense

In the United States it is possible to sue for compensation when a person relies on such a one-sided promise and suffers a loss, but in England and Canada such an unfulfilled promise can only be used as a defense to an action initiated by the person who made the promise. In London, England, just before the war, High Trees House Ltd. rented an apartment building from Central London Property Trust Ltd. under a 99-year lease with the intention of renting out the individual flats in that building. The two parties agreed to a set yearly rent of £2500. Because of the outbreak of the World War II, it soon became apparent that High Trees would not be able to rent out all of the flats, and so in 1942 the property owners agreed to lower the yearly rent to £1250. After the war they changed their minds and demanded payment of the entire rent including back rent for the portion that had not been paid since 1942.

The court agreed that for the period after the war, High Trees had to again pay the full rent, but as far as the back rent was concerned, the property owners were bound by their promise to take the lower amount.[20] High Trees was not suing to enforce the promise, rather the property owners were suing for the higher amount in spite of their promise. High Trees used the plaintiff's promise as a defense to its claim. Thus, in Canada and England the principle of promissory estoppel is remedial in nature. In another significant English case, *Combe v. Combe*, Lord Denning made it clear that "It does not create new causes of action where none existed before,"[21] and Lord Asquith, in his concurring judgment, said that promissory estop-

---

19. *Sale of Goods Act*, R.S.A. (1980) c. S-2 s.11.

20. *Central London Property Trust, Ltd. v. High Trees House, Ltd.* [1947] K.B. 130.

21. *Combe v. Combe* [1951] 1 All E.R. 767 (Court of Appeal) 769.

pel could only be used as a "shield but not as a sword."[22] Although there is some dispute about it, promissory estoppel is effectively limited to use as a defense in Canada, which is why in the case of Gilbert Steel used to open this section, the argument of promissory estoppel failed. In the High Trees case, if the company had paid the higher rent by mistake despite Central London's gratuitous promise to take less, High Trees would not have been successful had it tried to sue to retrieve the excess it had paid. This would have been using Central London's promise to take less as a "sword," which it cannot do. In fact, in almost every case where promissory estoppel has been made available as a defense, there was an existing legal relationship, usually contractual, that was modified by the promise. To raise this defense successfully, the victim must also demonstrate reliance on the promise and injury suffered as a result of that reliance.

Sealed Documents

The last major exception to the requirement of consideration is the use of the seal. Seals were originally made by placing some melted wax on a document and impressing a signet ring in it, thus lending authenticity or authority to the document. Different rules came into play when the parties took the trouble to perform this act. The parties to such a sealed agreement were bound by the contract whether or not any consideration was involved. This practice was implemented before modern contract law had developed and before consideration became a requirement. As the modern law of contract came into being, the practice of sealing some documents was retained. A paper wafer has replaced the formal seal and signet impression, although the seal can be almost any form of marking on the document which the parties have identified as a seal. These types of contracts are now considered formal contracts or deeds, and the court will not entertain any suggestion that the promise contained in the document is not supported by consideration. Although it is not necessary to look for consideration when a seal is present, it is important to realize that the existence of the seal does not do away with the other requirements of a valid contract.

Sealed documents do not require consideration

There must be some form of valid consideration in the form of a benefit or detriment flowing between the parties for a legally binding contract to exist. Only when the document embodying the agreement is sealed, or on those rare occasions when the promise of the promisor is being raised as a defense by the promisee will the court not require consideration to be established.

SUMMARY

A contract is an exchange of promises or commitments enforceable in court. All of the essential terms of the contract must be contained in the offer which is a tentative promise by the offeror contingent upon an acceptance by the offeree. Nonessential terms will be implied. The offer will end at a specified time, but it may be revoked earlier simply by notice to the offeree, unless an option agreement has been entered into. In the absence of a specified time limit, the offer will lapse after

---

22. Page 772. British Columbia legislation may have the effect of allowing a person to sue for compensation (use as a "sword") when such promises are relied on as found in that province's *Law and Equity Act*, R.S.B.C. (1996) c. 253 s. 59, ss. 5.

a reasonable time. A counteroffer, rejection, or the death or insanity of the offeror will also cause an offer to lapse.

The acceptance is merely an indication of a willingness to be bound and must be communicated to be effective. The postbox rule is an exception. It provides that, when use of the mail system is appropriate, the acceptance is effective when and where it is dropped in the mailbox. Offer and acceptance lead to consensus, the first element necessary for the existence of a contract.

The second requirement is consideration. Gratuitous promises are not enforceable. Consideration is the price paid by one party to a contract for the promise of the other. Both contracting parties must have experienced some benefit or detriment pursuant to the bargain. The consideration given must be both specific and legal. Past consideration is no consideration. When the agreement is only for the performance of an already existing contractual obligation, there is no consideration. In many provinces (including Alberta), when a person agrees to take less in full satisfaction of a debt, and in fact takes the money, it is legally binding despite the lack of consideration.

A one-sided promise is generally not enforceable. It may, however, be possible to raise the promise as a defense in an action being brought by the promisor under the principle of promissory or equitable estoppel. When there is a request for services with no agreement as to the amount, a reasonable price must be paid under the principle of quantum meruit. When there is a seal, there can be no question about the presence of consideration.

QUESTIONS

1. What is meant by "freedom of contract"? Explain the impact of this principle on the development of contract law.

2. List and explain the elements that must be present for an agreement to qualify as a contract.

3. At what stage in the process of forming a contract are the terms of the contract clearly set out?

4. Explain what is meant by an implied term in a contract.

5. What circumstances might prompt a court to imply terms into a contract?

6. Distinguish between an offer and an invitation to treat.

7. List and explain the various ways an offer can come to an end.

8. What is the effect of the offeror stating in an offer that the offer will remain open for acceptance until a specific date?

9. Give examples of offers that cannot be revoked and explain why.

10. What risks are faced when a person offers to sell certain goods to A and then sells them to B? How can this problem be avoided?

11. What qualities must an acceptance demonstrate to be effective?

12. Explain how a unilateral offer is accepted.

13. Explain the effect of the postbox rule on the principles governing acceptance.

14. How do the courts determine when the postbox rule should be applied?

15. Define consideration and explain what is meant by the term "the exchange of consideration."

16. What difficulty might be faced by a person who has already agreed to do a specific job and then extracts a promise of more pay from the other party?

17. Explain why a contract dispute settled out of court is considered binding even though one party would have obtained more if the action had been taken to court.

18. Explain a person's obligation regarding payment when he or she has requested a service without specifying a particular fee.

19. Describe what is meant by promissory estoppel and the circumstances in which it will arise in contract disputes.

20. How does the presence of a seal affect the requirement that consideration must be present in a contract?

21. Explain under what circumstances a person who fails to properly perform a gratuitous promise can be held legally liable for that failure.

CASES

1. Regina v. Dawood

Mrs. Dawood had been shopping in a department store and came to a display rack containing children's jumpers and blouses. On some of the hangers the jumpers and blouses were combined to make an outfit on sale for a single price, while some of the hangers contained individually priced jumpers and blouses. Mrs. Dawood took a blouse from one of the two-piece outfits and put it on its own hanger with a jumper from one of the individual hangers and took the outfit she had made to the cash register. She had removed any indication of price from the blouse so that the clerk was led to believe that the price from the jumper was the price for the whole outfit. The cashier charged her the lower price which she paid. It is important to note that there was no attempt to hide the blouse in any way but the effect was that she paid for only the jumper. Mrs. Dawood was subsequently charged with theft and the problem for the court was to determine if a crime had taken place.

2. DIS, Data Wiz Information Systems Inc. v. Q. W. Page Associates Inc.

Both the plaintiff and the defendant were in the software development business. The defendant manufactured accounting software and the plaintiff, Data Wiz, developed a data-based information system and sold it through a telemarketing scheme. Data Wiz wanted the exclusive distributorship rights to sell the defendant's accounting software in the United Kingdom and entered into negotiations with the defendant to that effect. These negotiations resulted in a memorandum of understanding and an international distribution agreement being executed by both parties. An important provision of the contract, however, namely the discount that the distributor was to get, was left blank. There was some delay in obtaining the financing and the defendant refused to go forward until the financing was in place, insisting on some significant changes to the memorandum of understanding. What arguments could the defendant bring forth to escape liability under the contract? How could these be countered by the plaintiff?

3. Calgary v. Northern Construction Ltd.

The city of Calgary advertised for tenders for a construction project. One of the terms of the advertisement was that once submitted the bid could not be revoked. Northern Construction submitted the low bid on the job. They then examined their bid and realized they had made an error in their calculations. They showed these documents to Calgary's representatives who agreed that they had made an error. Northern Construction then requested that they be released from their bid. Calgary, however, would not release them from the bid and accepted it as the winning one. Since Northern Construction refused to honour the contract, Calgary was forced to go with the second-lowest bid, and they sued. Explain the legal arguments available to each side and the likely outcome of the action.

4. Michaud v. Grand Falls Golf Course Inc.

Michaud was a contestant in a golf tournament which offered a prize of a new Toyota automobile for a hole-in-one scored on the second hole. Because this was a nine-hole course and the tournament was for eighteen holes, it was necessary for all golfers to go around the course twice. A shotgun start was used for the tournament, which meant that the various golfers started on different tees spread throughout the golf course. To facilitate this setup, each tee had two numbers; at the second hole, the numbers 2 and 11 were posted on a flag beside the tee. Michaud started on Tee #3 and played his eighteen holes by playing from #3 to #9, then around the nine holes a second time, finally playing 1 and 2 again to end the game. It was on the last hole he played, the hole marked #2, that he scored a hole-in-one and as a result claimed his prize.

The Grand Falls Golf Course claimed that for him hole #2 was only #2 the first time around. The time he scored the hole-in-one, it was hole #11 and so he was not entitled to the prize. The general rules of golf state that where a shotgun start is used, the contestant will start at the tee assigned, carry through the eighteen holes, and then go back and make up the original holes missed. Explain the legal arguments on both sides as to whether he is entitled to the car or not. How would your answer be affected if he had scored a hole-in-one on the preceding two holes and, just before he swung on this hole, the appropriate official of the golf course announced that the offer was revoked.

5. Francis v. Canadian Imperial Bank of Commerce

After several interviews with the bank Mr. Francis was offered a position of employment in a letter dated June 9, 1978. He responded on June 15 accepting the offer, by which he was to start work on July 4. When he showed up for work, he was presented with a number of documents that required his signature, including one entitled "Employment Agreement" which he signed along with the others. One of the terms of that employment agreement was that if he should ever be terminated, he was entitled to only three months' notice. After working for the bank for a number of years, his employment was terminated with only three months' notice and he sued for wrongful dismissal. There was no finding in these circumstances that Mr. Francis had done anything wrong, and so the court assessed that under normal circumstances, he would be entitled to 12 months' notice or pay in lieu of notice upon termination given the length of service and surrounding circumstances. Discuss the arguments available to Mr. Francis to support his claim for the higher amount of notice and the arguments available to the bank in response.

6. *Re 6781427 Holdings and Alma Mater Society of U.B.C.*

The holding company in this case leased an area from the Alma Mater Society in the Student Union Building where it operated a cookie shop with a three-year lease containing an option to renew. The renewal provision of the lease required that notice of renewal be given to the landlord in writing before midnight, July 31, 1986. In fact, the holding company approached the general manager of the Alma Mater Society to see if they could expand the area that they were using. The manager could not give a response right away but said he would probably know by September.

When September came the manager said he would not know until December. As a result the holding company missed the July 31 deadline while waiting for a response to their request. In September the Alma Mater Society ordered it to vacate the premises. Explain the arguments available to both parties to explain their positions.

7. *Robichaud v. Caisse Populaire de Pokemouche Ltée*

In this case Mr. Robichaud owed money to a number of different people. In addition, Caisse Populaire had obtained a judgment against him for $3000. As part of the process to consolidate his debts, Avco Financial Services made arrangements with Caisse Populaire and his other creditors. The manager of Caisse Populaire agreed that in exchange for a cheque for $1000 they would discharge Mr. Robichaud's indebtedness. Avco sent a cheque in that amount to Caisse Populaire, but in the meantime the Board of Directors had rejected that deal and the cheque was returned. The question for the court here is whether the Caisse Populaire is bound by its promise to take $1000 in full settlement for the $3787 debt owed. Explain the arguments that are available to both parties. Would it affect your answer to know that this took place in one of the few provinces that had no legislation covering the discharge of debt by payment of a lesser sum?

....

WEBLINKS

Canadian Contract Law Centre
www.wwlia.org/ca-con1.htm

Roger Bachelor's Contract Law Page
qsilver.queensu.ca/~law120

Industry Canada Consumer Information
strategis.c.gc.casc_consu/Consaffairs/engdoc/oca.html

Judicature Act
www.gov.ab.ca/qp/ascii/acts/J01.txt

Formation of Contracts (continued)

OBJECTIVES OF THE CHAPTER

- To describe the various conditions under which people are limited in their capacity to enter into contracts

- To explain what constitutes illegal contracts and those that are against public policy

- To consider the role of intention in determining whether a person is bound in contract

- To illustrate the various forms a contract can take

- To explain when writing is required

When Mr. Guzzo sold his retail fruit market, he signed a written agreement that included the term that he would not become involved in a similar business within five miles of the one he sold for a period of five years. Within a year of the sale, a similar business was opened up by Mr. Guzzo's son within the prohibited five-mile radius. The purchasers suspected that it was really Mr. Guzzo's new business and sued for breach of the non-competition clause in the purchase agreement. The judge decided that the clause was valid, that the arrangement for the new business was no more than a "sham" and that Mr. Guzzo himself was at least indirectly involved in it in violation of the non-competition covenant. The plaintiff was awarded damages of $20 000.[1]

Such non-competition covenants are valid only if they are reasonable and in the public interest; otherwise they are void. That the terms of the contract be legal is only one requirement of a legally binding contract which will be discussed in this chapter.

The previous chapter examined consensus and consideration as requirements of a legally binding contract. This chapter will discuss the other elements that must be

1. *The Lawyers Weekly*, April 7, 1987, pp. 1 and 8.

present in order to have an enforceable contract. They are capacity, legality, intention and the requirement that some contracts be evidenced in writing.

CAPACITY

Our lawmakers have always recognized that some people are more vulnerable than others and thus require special protection. Over the years, several categories of people have been protected by having their freedom to enter into contracts severely restricted or, in some cases, eliminated completely.

Infants

The age of majority or the age at which a person is considered to be an adult is 21 in common law. The age at which a person becomes an adult in Canada today is controlled by statute and varies from province to province (18 in Alberta[2]). In common law, people who are under the age of majority have always had their freedom to enter into contracts severely limited for their own protection. In some jurisdictions, such as B.C., this protection is governed by special statute. Alberta does not have such a statute, and so the common law rules apply.

Age of majority varies with provinces

The general principle in all jurisdictions is that infants (persons under the age of majority) who enter into contracts are not bound by the agreements although the adults with whom they contract are bound. The application of this principle has proven to be quite complicated because there are two opposing factors to be weighed by the courts. The first objective is to protect infants from their own inexperience in business matters and the second is to avoid placing undue hardship on the other parties to the contracts. The law of infancy tries to balance the protection of infants against harm resulting to merchants when infants abuse this protection.

It is important to distinguish between the artificial incapacity imposed on the youth who is a functioning member of society and the actual incapacity of the child who is incapable of understanding what is happening. Most problems arise when dealing with young people who are approaching the age of majority. The test for infancy is objective. When an adult deals with a customer who is under the age of majority, it makes no difference if the adult was under the impression that the other party was an adult. The court is only concerned with the fact that the person was under the statutory age of majority. As a general rule, whenever an infant enters into a contract with an adult, the adult is bound by the contract but the infant can escape. The contract, therefore, is voidable. For example, an adult named Myers offers to sell a car for $500 to a minor called Prokop who accepts the offer. Myers would be bound by the contract but Prokop would be free to either honour the agreement and purchase the car or refuse to go through with the deal.

Infants not bound by contract, but adults are

Infants are bound by contracts for the acquisition of necessaries. **Necessaries** are things required to function in society, such as food, clothing, transportation or lodging. For an adult to enforce a contract with an infant, it must be demonstrated to the court that the goods sold to the infant could be classified as necessaries and that the infant needed them. This point is often quite difficult to prove since if it can be shown that the infant already had an adequate supply of the goods they are not necessaries. Although transportation can be a necessary, the courts are extremely reluctant to find that the purchase of a car qualifies as a necessary. The courts have held that medical, dental and legal services, toiletries, uniforms and even a house can be

2. *Age of Majority Act,* R.S.A. (1980) c. A-4.

necessaries in different situations. What is or is not a necessary has varied with the social status of an infant. For example, fine jewelry was held to be a necessary for a wealthy man's son in the nineteenth century.[3] This distinction is of less significance now. If the merchant succeeds in establishing that the contract was for a necessary, the contract will be binding on the infant. However, the infant is only required to pay a reasonable price for the necessary. If it can be demonstrated that the merchant has charged an exorbitant amount, the infant will not be required to pay the contracted amount but only that which is deemed fair and reasonable under the circumstances.

Infants must repay money borrowed and used for necessaries

The question arises as to whether an infant can refuse delivery when necessaries have been ordered. It is clear that when educational, medical or legal services are involved, the contract is binding on the infant even if the services have not yet been delivered. However, it is not yet clear in Canadian common law whether the same principle applies to goods. The *Sale of Goods Act* does require infants to pay a reasonable price for necessaries in the form of goods that have been sold and delivered.[4]

Another problem arises when money is loaned for the purchase of necessaries. Is a contract to repay the money binding on the infant? When the borrowed money has actually been used by the infant for the purchase of a necessary, the creditor can insist on repayment. However, if the infant declares that the money will be used for necessaries but in fact uses it for a different purpose, the creditor cannot enforce repayment. Thus, money loaned to an infant to pay for school tuition cannot be recovered by the creditor if it is used for gambling. Government student loans are exceptions because they are supported by legislation requiring repayment regardless of what the money is used for.

Beneficial Contracts of Service.

Infants bound by contracts of service which substantially benefit them

A contract in which an infant agrees to do something for someone else is binding if it can be demonstrated that taken as a whole the contract is for the benefit of the infant. The classic example of this is an apprenticeship agreement. In the case of *Roberts v. Gray,*[5] an infant entered into a contract with a well-known billiards player to be his assistant and, in the process, be taught to play the game. This contract was held to be binding on the infant since it was beneficial to him. However, in the case of *DeFrancesco v. Barnam,*[6] in which a young girl had agreed to be an apprentice to a dancing master, the contract was determined to be not binding. The court ruled that the girl had been taken advantage of by having to provide significant labour for the dancing master with little or no commitment on his side to teach anything. The contract was held to be not in her best interests and was therefore not binding. These common law provisions are of less significance today because provincial and federal governments have passed legislation covering apprenticeship arrangements which override common law provisions.

It is often difficult to assess when contracts of service are binding on infants. It is clear that contracts involving infants' services as part of a business or trade, or contracts made by infants to facilitate a business or trade, are not binding on the infants. For example, if an infant were to purchase a truck to facilitate a delivery business, that contract would not be binding on the infant. But most simple employment contracts are considered beneficial contracts of service and thus the infant is bound by them.

3. *Peters v. Fleming* (1840) 6 M & W 42.

4. *Sale of Goods Act,* R.S.A. (1980) c. S-2 s. 4.

5. *Roberts v. Gray* [1913] 1 K.B. 520 (Court of Appeal).

6. *DeFrancesco v. Barnam* (1890) 45 Ch.D. 430 (Court of Appeal).

RATIFICATION OF INFANTS' CONTRACTS

In this case the minor borrowed money and secured the loan by way of a chattel mortgage on both a car and a motorcycle. This loan was defaulted. When he came of age, he actually assisted the creditor in seizing and selling the motorcycle, and because of this the creditor held he had ratified the contract and thus he had to make payment on the full amount. The court disagreed, saying that the ratification required something more than simply helping out as the goods used to secure the loan were seized. It was not appropriate that the plaintiff be in a worse position by cooperating than he would have been by not cooperating.

Bayview Credit Union Ltd. v. Daigle, 3 D.L.R. (4th) 95 (New Brunswick Court of Queen's Bench)

Infants' Voidable Contracts.

The voidable nature of an infant's contract means that the infant can get out of the contract. But when the infant reaches the age of majority, he or she can ratify the contract, either in writing or by implication. The process of ratification breathes new life into old agreements, making them binding. For example, if an infant agrees to pay $500 for an automobile, this contract is voidable. If, however, on coming of age, the infant makes a written statement or indicates by actions that he or she intends to be bound by the contract, it is binding.

Infant can ratify contract at age of majority

Some types of contracts are voidable at the option of the infant. These contracts require positive steps on the part of the infant to overcome their effects. The infant must take action shortly after reaching majority to indicate that he or she will no longer be bound by the agreement if the subject of the contract is a continuing benefit. Continuing agreements include acquired interest in land through lease arrangements, partnership agreements or holding shares in a company. Infants who have agreed to marriage settlement arrangements become bound by them unless they are repudiated at the age of majority. There are some types of contracts, however, that are not binding on the infant under any circumstances. If a contract contains a clause amounting to a penalty against the infant or if the contract, taken as a whole, can be said by the court to be prejudicial to the interests of the infant, the contract is simply void.

Although these principles may seem reasonably straightforward, their application has created a good deal of confusion. To appreciate the reasons for this, it is necessary to think of the contractual relationship progressing through prescribed stages. At the first stage, when the parties have entered into the agreement but the infant has not yet obtained any benefit from it and has not yet paid, the infant can get out of the agreement. This is an **executory contract**. If the infant has received the goods but has not yet paid for them, he or she is not necessarily bound by the agreement. This is a **partially executed contract**. When the goods are in the infant's possession, the infant will be required to return them or pay for them and upon return is entitled to return of any money already paid. If the infant has passed those goods on to a third party or the goods have been destroyed, the merchant will not be entitled to repayment, nor can the merchant insist that the party to whom the goods have been given return them.

Conflict may arise when the contract has been **executed**. Can infants change their minds once they have obtained the benefit under the contract and insist on the return of their money? In Canadian law, the conclusion seems to be that infants

Where contract bestows no benefit infant can escape even executed contract

are bound by the agreement unless it can be demonstrated that what was received was of no value at all.[7] An infant can insist that payment be returned if there is total failure of consideration or if the infant gained nothing from the deal.

Parents' Liability.

Parents not responsible for infant's contracts except where authorized

There is a popular misconception that liability will rest with the parents if a child fails to pay a debt. Parents are not responsible for the torts of their children, nor are they responsible for their contractual obligations in the absence of specific legislation creating such a responsibility. If an infant enters into a contract, it is that infant's responsibility alone. The adult contracting with the infant cannot turn to the parents if the infant does not live up to the contract. The parents are in no way obligated to honour the infant's defaulted promises whether or not those promises are binding on the infant except in rare circumstances where liability is imposed by statute. Only when the merchant is under the impression that he or she is dealing with an infant who is the agent of the parents may the parents be liable for the agreement. This is a simple question of agency and the infant's authority to bind parents as agent will be dealt with in a subsequent chapter. Merchants can overcome this difficulty by having the parent guarantee the infant's obligation at the time the contract is entered into. A guarantee is a written commitment whereby the guarantor agrees to pay the debt if the debtor does not. Since the very purpose of the guarantee is to encourage the merchant to go through with the contract, these guarantees have been held to be binding on the parents in Canadian law.

Legislation.

Infants Relief Act causes confusion

To bring a sense of order to the complicated aspects of infancy law, the British Parliament passed the *Infants Relief Act* in 1874 which purported to make infants' contracts other than for necessaries and beneficial contracts of service "absolutely void." But the courts didn't apply the plain meaning of these words which ended up only adding to the confusion.

Only the province of British Columbia followed the English example by passing a similar statute. But British Columbia has recently significantly changed their *Infants Act* making all contracts with infants **unenforceable** against the infant but enforceable against the adult. The practical effect is to make B.C.'s approach similar to that of the rest of the provinces, but there is still one very significant difference. In B.C., all infants' contracts, including those for necessaries, are unenforceable. Thus the distinction between necessities and other forms of infants' contracts has been eliminated in that province. The B.C. act also provides for the ratification or repudiation of infants contracts upon reaching the age of majority. Other provinces have also made some changes to the common law, such as requiring ratification of infants' contracts to be in writing; but none have made such sweeping changes as British Columbia. In particular, Alberta has not followed B.C.'s lead in making all contracts with infants unenforceable against the infant. Alberta has also not passed legislation requiring ratification of infants' contracts to be in writing.

Infant's Liability for Torts.

The law of infancy is advantageous to infants but it often puts merchants in very vulnerable positions. In response to this, merchants have been tempted to try to avoid the protection given to infants in contract law by suing them in tort. Tort liability is

7. *Coull v. Kolbuc* (1969) 68 W.W.R. 76 (Alta. Dis. Ct.).

a completely different type of action based on different principles and responsibilities. It is a basic tenet of tort law that an infant is as liable as an adult for torts committed although the standard of behaviour expected may differ. Once it has been established that an infant has failed to live up to the level of responsibility society deems appropriate, the infant will be held responsible for those inappropriate actions.

It is true that an infant cannot be sued for breach of contract when non-necessaries are involved. However, many of the situations classified as breaches of contract would be, except for the existence of the contract, considered torts. If an infant cannot be sued for breach of contract, why not sue for negligence instead?

The courts will not allow adults to change to a tort action just to get around the incapacity problem in contract law. If it is appropriate to sue for breach of contract then the plaintiff must do so and if the infant is protected by the defense of incapacity, then that is the end of the matter.

Adult cannot avoid protection given to infant by suing in tort

On the other hand, if the infant used the subject matter of the contract in some way completely beyond the contemplation of the contract and carelessly caused injury or damage to those goods, the adult would be able to sue for negligence since the act complained of was not anticipated in the contractual relationship. For example, if an infant rents an automobile and then damages it while trying to plow a field, the merchant would be able to sue the infant for negligence since the use to which the automobile was put was completely outside what was anticipated in the contract. However, if the infant had an accident while driving the rented automobile on the highway, the adult could not sue for tort even if the infant were clearly negligent because that activity could have been anticipated by the contract. In short, the adult cannot circumvent the protection afforded to the infant in contract law by suing for tort instead. It should be further noted that an infant is responsible for other tortious conduct as well. If a tort such as fraudulent misrepresentation is involved, the adult may have another avenue to pursue in seeking redress from an infant with whom he or she has contracted.

Except where tort arises independent of contract

Insanity and Drunkenness

Hardman v. Falk [8]

Nora Falk and her sister Ethel Swenson lived with their 87-year-old mother on her farm located on Annacis Island in the Fraser River. They were approached by a real estate agent to purchase the farm, and after negotiating an extremely attractive price for the women, they finally explained that they didn't own the property, their mother did.

This offer to sell the property was embodied in an option agreement for which the purchasers paid one dollar. The four of them went upstairs to the mother's bedroom to obtain her consent. The deal was explained to her and she nodded at the appropriate times indicating her understanding, but when it came time to sign the document, the daughters explained that she was too old and feeble to sign her name and therefore she was assisted to make a mark consisting of an X on the paper beside her name.

In fact the real estate agency, through their solicitor and agent, were assembling land for the Annacis Island Industrial Estates and when they had acquired similar options on various farms in the vicinity, they exercised those options accepting the offers and then were prepared to go through with the deals. Nora Falk and

8. [1955] 1 D.L.R. 432 (B.C. Supreme Court). Affirmed [1955] 3 D.L.R. 129.

Ethel Swenson, however, refused to honour the agreement they had entered into with their mother's consent. They claimed that their mother's mind was gone and the agreement wasn't worth the paper it was printed on.

It was clearly established through evidence that the aged mother did not have the mental capacity to form a contract and was incapable of understanding what was going on. But the court held that there was nothing in the circumstances that should have alerted the plaintiffs to that fact, and although the daughters claimed to have told the plaintiffs about their mother's mental condition, that was denied by them and the court rejected that testimony by the daughters. The court decided that because the plaintiffs were not in a position where they knew or ought to have known of the insanity of the person that they were contracting with, the contract was valid and binding. Age, by itself does not prompt a person to inquire as to that person's mental capacity. The court also looked at the $1 that was paid for the option and concluded that because the dollar was being paid for the privilege of paying more for the property than what it was worth there was no problem with the consideration paid for the option.

Remember that there are two contracts here. The first is the option to hold the offer open, and the second the actual agreement to purchase the land. Normally the courts, once they determine that some consideration was paid, do not enter into a debate as to whether it was adequate or not; however, when a person who is insane is involved, the court will ask whether that person has been taken advantage of. In this case, because a higher price was paid than should be expected, there was no question of the mother being taken advantage of. The court was not sympathetic to the position of the daughters, since a decision in their favour would amount to legal blackmail; it was clear the daughters were attempting to use the courts to get an even higher price for their property.

This case illustrates the two things that must be established when trying to get out of a contract when one of the parties was insane: first, that the person is so mentally incapacitated that they don't know or understand what they are doing; and second, that the contractor knew or ought to have known of the insanity.

Insanity applies if person did not understand—and if other party knew or ought to have known of incapacity

The law extends its protection to those incapacitated because of insanity in a way similar to the protection given to infants. To qualify for this protection, it must be shown that the person could not understand the nature of the act being performed. For example, if a man is under the impression that he is Napoleon and thinks he is selling his horse when in fact he is selling his car, he would be declared insane because he does not understand that he is selling his car. To escape contractual liability on the basis of insanity, the insane person or a representative must prove not only insanity but that the person he or she was dealing with knew or ought to have known of the incapacity. This is the point illustrated in the case of *Hardman v. Falk* discussed above.

Drunkenness treated like insanity

People who lose their ability to reason through intoxication are treated in the same way as the insane. Such intoxication is usually caused by alcohol but the same principles apply for other intoxicants, such as drugs. For a defense of intoxication to be considered, it must be demonstrated that the person was so incapacitated that he or she could not understand the nature of the transaction and that the other person knew or ought to have known of the incapacity. The person trying to escape a contract on the basis of drunkenness must be able to show that, on reaching sobriety, the contract was repudiated. An intoxicated person who purchases shares is not permitted, on becoming sober, to wait and see whether the stocks go

Must repudiate upon becoming sober

up or down before repudiating the contract. Hesitation to repudiate makes the contract binding. This requirement of repudiation also applies to insane people who regain their sanity. Usually an insane person will be held responsible for contracts for necessaries, but, as was the case with infants, he or she will only be obligated to pay a reasonable price for them.

A person who is of weakened intellect or otherwise vulnerable but not insane is still to some extent protected. Unconscionable transactions, the legal principle providing this protection, will be discussed below.

Bound by purchase of necessaries

Native Indians

The capacity of Native Indians living on reserves (status Indians) is still limited to some extent by the *Indian Act*.[9] Although they may seem discriminatory these provisions remain because they are viewed as protections exempted from the operation of the *Charter of Rights and Freedoms* by Section 35 which recognizes and affirms existing aboriginal and treaty rights.

Status Indians still protected under Indian Act

Corporations

There are several situations in which the law recognizes the existence of an artificial person or legal entity separate and apart from the individuals who make it up. The most common example of such an artificial person is a modern business corporation or limited company. In fact, the corporation as a person does not really exist. It is a legal fiction, albeit a convenient one, for the world of commerce. Whenever we deal with a corporation, and most consumer activities do involve sales transactions with corporations, we are dealing with a fictional person who is considered to be a separate legal entity. When we purchase something from a department store such as The Bay, our contract is with The Bay itself and not with The Bay's shareholders. Corporate law will be dealt with in a subsequent chapter. At this point the problem to be considered is the method by which corporations enter into contracts.

Corporation—separate legal person

The method of incorporation varies from province to province and in some provinces the power or capacity of corporations to enter into contracts has been limited. This was a significant feature of corporate law in many provinces in the not very distant past. This lack of capacity is much less important in Canadian corporate law today, because several provinces have recently changed the method of incorporation used or have otherwise reformed their corporate law legislation with the effect that such corporations have the capacity of a natural person.[10] Incorporation under federal and provincial legislation will be examined in depth in Chapter 13.

Corporate capacity—usually no longer a problem

It must be emphasized, however, that there are many special corporations and other government bodies in Canada, including Crown corporations, created by specific provincial or federal legislation which are intended to carry out government policy. The Canadian National Railway, Canada Post, Petro-Canada, Air Canada and Canada Mortgage and Housing Corporation are some examples. The normal rules of contract law apply to these bodies but their powers are often limited by specific legislation, and outsiders dealing with them must be alert to the possibility of their limited capacity. In the absence of such statutory provisions, the merchant is free to assume that the government body or corporation in question has the

Capacity of government bodies and Crown corporations limited by legislation

9. *Indian Act,* R.S.C. (1985) c. I-5.

10. *Business Corporations Act,* S.A. (1981) c. B-15 s. 15.

power to do whatever it has agreed to do. Legislation will override any common law contractual principle, so anyone dealing with a Crown corporation or government body in any unusual way is well advised to check the legislation which created it.

Aliens

Capacity of enemy aliens limited in times of war

Any contract with a citizen of a country against which war has been declared is void under common law if it can be shown to have a detrimental effect on Canada. A citizen of an enemy country, whether a resident of Canada or of a hostile territory, is classed as an enemy alien. Even people who just reside in that country or who have businesses there may be included. Most frequently the people concerned would be foreigners doing business in Canada when war breaks out. If the effect of the contract is not detrimental to the country in any way, the contract is merely suspended for the duration of the hostilities; otherwise, it is void. The Canadian government usually passes legislation to cover this area of law which overrides the common law provisions whenever hostilities break out.

Contracts with foreign governments or their representatives were traditionally thought to be unenforceable even in times of peace because of a foreign government's immunity from prosecution in Canadian courts. This immunity is based on the fact that the sovereignty of the foreign government would be lost if subjected to the jurisdiction of our courts. This provision was particularly important when dealing with matters of state that were of diplomatic importance. However, since foreign governments are now more frequently involved in simple commercial enterprises that have nothing to do with matters of state, the courts have been willing to treat them as any other party to commercial transactions. These principles are now embodied in legislation.[11] Representatives of foreign governments, such as ambassadors and their families, have traditionally been immune from prosecution in our criminal courts and continue to be. A court will not issue a writ against such a person in a civil matter and their property is immune from seizure. Of course, these representatives can waive this immunity if they wish, but anyone dealing with people with diplomatic immunity ought to be aware of the protection they have been given.

Married Women

Capacity of married women no longer limited

In the past, married women were incapacitated in much the same way as infants and the insane under the common law. However, legislation has abolished these common law restrictions. Married women now have the same legal capacity to enter into contracts as any other adult person.

Unions

Trade unions have capacity to contract for union activities

Historically, unions were denied the capacity to enter into contracts because of their illegal status, but modern legislation in all provinces has given trade unions the capacity to enter into contracts relevant to their union responsibilities. Trade unions in many jurisdictions are, with some qualifications, considered legal entities much like corporations and can sue or be sued in their own capacity.[12]

---

11. *State Immunity Act*, R.S.C. (1985) c. S-18.

12. Section 23 of the *Labour Relations Code*, S.A. (1988) c. L-1.2, states that, for the purposes of the *Code*, a trade union is capable of prosecuting and being prosecuted, and suing and being sued.

Bankrupts

People who have filed for or been placed in bankruptcy also have their contractual capacity significantly limited before they are discharged. Bankruptcy will be discussed in a subsequent chapter.

LEGALITY

The objectives of an agreement must be legal and not contrary to the public interest for the agreement to qualify as a binding contract. It is easy to understand that a contract to commit a crime would be void, but there are many other types of activities that, while not illegal, are considered immoral or contrary to the public interest. The courts have taken several different approaches when faced with the problem of immoral or illegal contracts.

Under normal circumstances, the courts will help the parties to a contract which is found to be void return to their original positions. This may include the refund of deposits or the return of property. However, with illegal or immoral contracts that the courts find offensive (for example, contracts involving blatantly unacceptable conduct such as an agreement to purchase a prohibited drug), not only will the courts declare the contract void, but they will refuse to deal with the parties. If money or property has changed hands, the courts will not assist the parties to get it back. But, for example, if one or both of the parties has acted innocently, the courts may not view the contract as offensive, and may therefore be willing to assist the parties in getting back any money or property that was exchanged.

Contracts lacking legality— courts may assist parties

If contract is also offensive, courts will not assist parties

Illegal Contracts

Contracts can be jeopardized because they are inconsistent with either federal or provincial statutes. Workers' compensation legislation is designed to provide for safer working conditions and to compensate workers injured on the job. Any agreement between the worker and employer that circumvents the provisions of this legislation would be void. Much consumer protection legislation is designed to prevent unacceptable sales tactics and other inappropriate behaviour and prohibit contracts that try to override and defeat these protective mechanisms. Such contracts or the offensive portions, if they can be separated from the main agreement, are simply void.

Statutes which restrict the right of parties to contract often contain provisions setting out the rights of the parties in the event of a violation of the statute. Unfortunately, many statutes do not state the consequences of such violations. In such instances, the courts are left to apply the common law provisions related to illegal contracts. The courts have developed a flexible attitude when violations occur because of the variation in the degree of acceptability of the violations. Depending on the severity of the infraction, the courts may declare the contract void and assist the parties to return to their original positions. In some circumstances, the courts may enforce the contract. For example, most cities have legislation requiring that tradespeople such as roofers and painters acquire licenses to practise. When work has been performed by a tradesperson who does not have a license and the courts determine that the object of the bylaw is merely to generate revenue, they may enforce the contract and simply require that the tradesperson acquire the license after the fact. If the purpose of the bylaw is to protect the public from the unqualified

Statute may set out consequences

Businesses must be licensed to operate in a
municipality.　　Photo by Al Harvey/The Slide Farm

or the unethical, however, the unlicensed tradesperson will not be able to enforce the contract. If the legislation itself sets out the consequences of an infraction, this will override any discretion available to the court.

Contracts Against Public Policy

There is little difficulty in applying these principles when a crime is involved or a statute exists that prohibits certain conduct or types of contracts. However, some types of agreements have been treated as tainted because they are not considered to be in the public's best interests. These agreements may not violate any law. They may vary in seriousness from those not in the public interest but not particularly immoral to those most members of the public would find offensive. Contracts or the offending portions, that are not particularly disagreeable but which the courts feel should be set aside in the best interests of

Contracts determined not to be in public's best interests may not be binding

the public are simply declared void. If a deposit has been paid, money has been advanced or property has changed hands, the parties will be able to recover their expenditure. The parties to such contracts have not committed a crime for which they could be arrested or sued, but the courts simply refuse to promote activities they have determined should not be encouraged by enforcing such agreements. The courts will not only declare very offensive agreements void, but they will not help the parties return to their original positions.

The following is a list of some of the types of contracts that have been determined to be either illegal or against public policy.

Examples of contracts against public policy

1. *Contracts to commit a crime or a tort.* For example, if Mullins offered Nowak $100 to claim that Abercromby did a poor job of repairing his house, that would be defamation.

2. *Contracts involving immoral acts.* For example, although prostitution is not illegal in Canada, a prostitute could not expect the courts to enforce a bargain made with a client because the act is considered immoral.

3. *Contracts that obstruct justice.* If the effect of the contract is to interfere with the judicial process, it is against public policy. For example, suppose Sawchuk is sent to jail for producing illegal alcohol. Fischer had promised to pay him a salary of $1000 per month if he was sentenced to jail. That contract would be deemed to be against public policy and therefore void. Sawchuk could not force payment from Fischer for the time he spent in prison. Enforcing such a contract would defeat the whole purpose of the jail term.

4. *Contracts that injure the state.* An example of this would be a contract to sell steel to Germany during World War II.

5. *Contracts that unduly restrain trade.* Business people often enter into contracts with provisions that prohibit certain types of business activities. If such a provision is reasonable and necessary to protect the interests of the parties, it is enforceable, but if the provision is unreasonably restrictive or against the public interest, that provision of the contract is void. For example, Beaudoin purchases a barbershop from Ahmed for $50 000. A considerable portion of the

purchase price may be for the customer relations established by Ahmed. If Ahmed then opens another barbershop next door, it would destroy the goodwill aspect of the contract. It would be reasonable for the buyer to include a provision in the contract prohibiting the seller from carrying on a similar business for a specified time (for example, three years) and within a specified geographical area (for example, five kilometres). If the time and distance restrictions agreed to were not excessive, this would be classed as a reasonable restraint of trade and the contract would be valid. In the example used to introduce this chapter, the agreement prohibiting Mr. Guzzo from opening a similar business within five years was held by the court to be a reasonable restraint of trade. His violation of this clause cost him $20 000.

Essentially, some interest must need to be protected, the restrictions must be no greater than necessary to protect that interest, and the restrictions must not be against the interests of the public. The agreement is against the public interest when it interferes with free trade, driving up prices, decreasing service or having any other effect whereby the public may be harmed. If it is possible to separate the restrictive covenant from the rest of the agreement, then only that part of the contract will be void, when it unduly restrains trade. The purchase price and all other terms of the agreement would be the same but the seller would have no restrictions at all and would be free to open a similar business anywhere. In the example above, if the provision in the contract for the purchase of the barbershop prohibited Ahmed from opening another shop anywhere in Canada or imposed an unreasonably long period of time such as ten years, this provision of the agreement would be void. Ahmed would then be free to open a new barbershop wherever or whenever he wanted.

Restrictive covenants can also be imposed if the success of a business depends to some extent on the loyalty of its employees. If the employees could do the business considerable harm either by taking away customers when leaving employment or by revealing trade secrets to new employers, the employer will often impose a restraining term in the contract of employment. Again, such a restriction must be reasonable in nature and not against the public interest. It also must not have the effect of completely preventing the former employee from earning a living. Generally the courts are more reluctant to enforce restrictive covenants when they are found in employment contracts.

Restrictive covenants must be reasonable

6. *Contracts that restrict competition.* The federal *Competition Act*[13] specifically prohibits agreements which have as their primary purpose or objective the "undue" restriction of competition. Thus, if two merchants agreed not to sell a particular commodity below a certain price, or not to open up branches that would compete with each other in specified communities, and they were the only ones selling the products in that community, such agreements would be void and such a conspiracy may be punishable as a criminal act. This is another example of a contract in restraint of trade. The federal *Competition Act* prohibits a number of other unacceptable business practices, some of which will be discussed in a subsequent chapter.

7. *Contracts that are bets and wagers.* This area is covered by statute and varies from province to province. Horse track betting, provincial lotteries, bingo games, video lottery terminals, etc., are permitted if the appropriate permission or license is obtained. But activities such as off-track betting, poker games in which

13. *Competition Act,* S.C. (1984-85-86) c. 91.

the house takes a cut and other types of gambling activities are usually prohibited. Historically, gambling was considered a great sin needing strict control, but today with changing public attitudes and the general acceptance of lotteries and other games of chance, it is better to view these provisions as controlling the practice rather than preventing immoral and socially unacceptable practices. Unfortunately, our laws are still in a state of transition.

It should be noted that provisions prohibiting gambling have application beyond games of chance. For example, insurance policies are essentially a special type of wager. The difference between a wager and insurance is that in order to win, the insured must also lose in the sense that the subject matter of the insurance contract is destroyed or damaged. The intent of insurance is not to give a person a windfall but to compensate for the loss by spreading the risk. Therefore, it is necessary to show that the party insuring the property has an **insurable interest** in the subject of the policy. An insurable interest means that the insured has something to lose if the anticipated event takes place. An insurance policy taken out on one's own house is valid and, if the house burns down, the owner is compensated for the loss. But if an individual takes an insurance policy out on someone else's house and has nothing to lose if it burns down, that person would not be permitted to collect on the policy since it is only a wager. The terms of the policy are void because there is no insurable interest. Contracts for the sale of shares suffer the same problem. If the contract merely requires the parties to pay each other the difference if the share price goes up or down, it is void as a wager. To avoid this problem, the contract must provide that the share will actually change hands.

8. *Contracts that promote litigation.* The courts have always been careful to ensure that they are used only to fulfill their declared public purpose: to settle disputes between the parties who come before them. Entering into agreements to use the courts for an ulterior motive is illegal. One party paying another to proceed in a court action against a third party would be an illegal and unenforceable agreement. If Chase carelessly drove over Park's foot and Roscoe were to offer to pay Park to sue Chase because of a dislike for Chase, such an agreement would be unlawful, being against public policy. If a person approached the victim of an accident and offered to pay all of the legal fees in exchange for a promise of half of the eventual court award, such an agreement would be unlawful.

Contingency fee arrangements permissible because they make courts accessible

Lawyers, however, in most provinces quite often enter into contingency fee arrangements with their clients whereby the lawyer agrees to bear the burden of the cost of the action and the risk of loss if the client will agree to pay a certain percentage of the award. This agreement appears to be permissible because it does not promote litigation but serves to make the courts more accessible to those who normally could not afford to proceed. At the time of writing Ontario remains the last jurisdiction in North American not to permit contingency fees and that is expected to soon change.

9. *Contracts injuring public service.* An example of this type of contract is if someone tried to pay a politician to vote a certain way in the legislature.

10. *Contracts in restraint of marriage.* Any contract that has as its object the prevention of marriage is against public policy. An agreement to pay someone $100 000 in return for a promise never to marry would not be binding.

These are some of the categories held to be either illegal or against public policy. This list is neither complete nor exhaustive. It may well be, for example, that new types of activities made possible by changing technology could also be declared either illegal or against public policy.

INTENTION

Osorio et al. v. Cardona[14]

Osorio and Cardona were friends who had recently come to Canada from Colombia and often went to the horse races together. On July 10 a wagering scheme known as the Sweep Six was offered at the racetrack. This wager involved betting on six races and predicting the winners. Both Osorio and Cardona had tickets on the Sweep Six, and after the third race they discovered that both their tickets were still in the running. This meant that they had a significant chance of winning.

They entered into an agreement to the effect that if either of them won, the winner would pay the other 30 percent (this was later modified because of the odds involved so that if Cardona won, Osorio would only receive 20 percent but if Osorio won, Cardona would receive 30 percent). In fact Osorio's horse was knocked out in the next race but Cardona's went on to win $735 403.

After several days of trying to avoid Osorio, Cardona finally told him that he would have to take $60 000 or nothing (the 20 percent share would have been $147 000). There was also some threat involved that Cardona would leave the country and go back to Colombia and Osorio would get nothing. Osorio agreed to take the $60 000. This was given to him, but then he sued for the remainder.

There is no question about the fact that the parties had agreed to split the money in the way outlined. The problem is whether such an agreement is binding on the parties.

The first point to note is that the contract between the parties is not a bet or a wager; rather, it is an agreement to pool the winnings, so there is no problem with legality. The problem is whether the parties intended to be legally bound and intended legal consequences to flow. This has to be determined from the conduct of the parties. The courts try to give effect to the reasonable expectations of the parties in such an agreement and so the test of whether this is intentional or not is objective and it doesn't matter what the actual state of mind of the parties was.

Cardona had always acted towards Osorio in a way that led Osorio to believe that he was serious and that he intended the agreement to be in force. The renegotiation of the split from 30 percent to 20 percent indicates that they were in serious negotiations and so the court decided that there was an intention to be legally bound and therefore a contract existed between the parties.

The final question that arises is whether the agreement to accept $60 000 with that sum actually paid over to Osorio ended the obligations between the parties, and while this might be so under normal circumstances, it was the threat of Cardona leaving and giving Osorio nothing that had forced him to take the lower payment. Such an agreement, extracted by threat to pay nothing, was

---

14. 15 D.L.R. (4th) 619 (B.C. Sup. Ct.).

unconscionable and therefore the agreement was unenforceable. Osorio was able to collect the other $87 000.

This case illustrates not only what is meant by the requirement that the parties intend to be legally bound by their agreement but also that the test to determine the presence of intention is an objective rather than a subjective test whereby the court seeks to enforce the reasonable expectations of the parties.

Parties must have intended legal consequences from agreement

Another element necessary to establish the existence of a binding contract is the requirement that the parties must have intended that legal obligations and rights would flow from their agreement. If a person invited a friend over for dinner who failed to show up for some reason, the delinquent guest would probably be quite surprised if the would-be host were to sue for breach of contract. In such a social relationship, neither party intended to create a legal obligation.

The statement that the parties must have intended to be bound is a little misleading, however, in that the court is less concerned with whether the promisor intended to be bound than with whether the promisee's reasonable expectations have been protected. The test is objective. It is no defense for promisors to state that they were just kidding or even to produce evidence to the court to support the contention that they did not think the contract would be binding. The courts will direct their attention to the person who is being promised something and ask whether that person should have known that the other party was not serious. Only if the court concludes that the promisee should have realized there was no serious intent to be legally bound will the agreement not be enforceable. In the example above, the guest invited to dinner would not normally expect a binding contract to be in place to force an appearance. The following situations illustrate instances in which this problem arises and indicate the courts' probable responses.

Courts will enforce reasonable expectations

Courts will accept stated intention

1. *Stated intention of the parties.* If the parties clearly state that they do not wish to be legally bound by their agreement, the court will grant this wish. Such a statement must be embodied in the terms of the contract and be very clear as to the intention. An example of a case in which the courts have honoured such a desire is *Rose and Frank Co. v. J. R. Crompton and Bros. Ltd.*[15]

Courts will presume intention in commercial transactions

2. *Commercial relations.* If the relationship between the contracting parties is primarily commercial in nature, the courts will presume that the parties intended to be legally bound by their agreement. The contract will be binding on them in the absence of any evidence to the contrary.

Courts will presume no intention in domestic and social relations

3. *Domestic and social relations.* When an agreement is between members of a family, or friends involved in domestic (non-business) activities there is a presumption that the parties do not intend legal consequences to flow from the agreement. This is probably the result of a policy of non-interference in family disputes, but the effect is to make such agreements not binding in the absence of clear indication that the parties intended otherwise. If members of a family informally agree to make payments to each other, such as a child agreeing to pay room and board, the courts would assume that there is no intention to be legally bound and would not enforce the agreement. However, if the parties had gone to the trouble of having a lawyer draw up a formal contract, then the court would be satisfied that the parties did intend that legal consequences would flow from their agreement and would enforce the contract.

---

15. *Rose and Frank v. Crompton* [1923] 2 K.B. 261 (Court of Appeal).

The courts will presume there is no intention to be legally bound in purely social relationships.

4. *Social and business relations.* Problems arise when the relationship involved is a mixture of social and commercial, such as when people jointly enter a contest and dispute over the distribution of the prize. This problem could become more prevalent in Canada with the proliferation of lotteries with large prizes. In such cases, the court must treat each situation on its individual merits. In fact, the courts turn to the reasonable person test to determine whether it is reasonable for the parties trying to enforce the agreement to think that a legally binding contract had been created. This was the problem in the Osario case used to introduce this section, and the court had to use the reasonable person test to determine whether they were serious in their agreement to share the winnings. In an Alberta case, the court decided that an agreement between co-workers regarding the sharing of Calgary Flames hockey tickets was unenforceable because there was no intention that the arrangement would have any legal consequence.[16]

> Reasonable person test applies where social and business mix

5. *Exaggerated claims.* Another area in which the problem of intention arises is when exaggerated claims are used to sell goods. Often the advisor or salesperson will say something like "This is the best product in Canada" or "This is the best deal in the city." Most people expect dealers to exaggerate the qualities of their products and the defense is often raised that these claims are mere advertising "puffs" and that there was never any intention that they should be taken seriously. Many of these situations are now controlled or prohibited by statute.

> —and when dealing with exaggerated claims

When an exaggerated claim forms part of the contract, the court must determine the intention of the parties. Again, the courts turn to the reasonable person test and simply ask if a reasonable purchaser would have recognized the claim to be an exaggeration. In the case of *Carlill v. Carbolic Smoke Ball Company,*[17] the defendant manufacturers made a product which they claimed would protect users from influenza. They offered £100 to anyone who used their product as prescribed and still contracted influenza, and stated in an advertisement that £1000 had been deposited in the Alliance Bank, Regent's Street, which showed their sincerity in the matter.

Mrs. Carlill used the product, got influenza, and claimed the money; but the company reneged, stating that the advertisement was an advertising puff that merely indicated some enthusiasm for the product and was not meant to be taken seriously by the public. The court held that depositing money to back up the claim had taken it out of the category of an advertising puff. It was determined that a reasonable person would have thought the advertisement was serious, so the offer was valid. There was intention, and Mrs. Carlill's use of the product and contracting the illness were appropriate forms of acceptance; thus there was a valid contract.

Form of the Contract

We have established that the essential ingredients of contracts are consensus, consideration, capacity, legality and intention. Nevertheless, the courts must sometimes consider an additional factor before they will enforce a contract. Historically,

16. *Eng v. Evans* (1991) 83 Alta. L.R. (2d) 107 (Q.B.).

17. *Carlill v. Carbolic Smoke Ball Co.* [1892] 2 Q.B. 484; [1893] 1 Q.B. 256 (Court of Appeal).

the form of the contract was very important. Promises were enforceable because they were contained in sealed documents or deeds. The seal is significant now because it eliminates the need to show consideration. As a general rule, in the common law system today there are no **formal** requirements that must be met for a contract to be enforceable, although many jurisdictions still require that in specific situations the documents used must be sealed. Deeds to transfer interests in land are an example. In Alberta, for example, transfers of land (and other instruments) signed on behalf of a corporation must be sealed with the corporate seal.[18]

People are often surprised to find that verbal agreements are every bit as binding on them as those in writing. While there is some truth in the old saying that a promise is worthless if it is not in writing, it cannot be overemphasized that most verbal agreements have the same legal status as a written one as long as it meets the requirements described in this and the previous chapter. The courts are even willing to find an implied contract exists by looking at the conduct of the parties.

Verbal contracts binding but writing advised

The importance of the written document is practical, not theoretical. It is always a good idea to put the terms of an agreement in writing so that if a dispute arises something permanent establishes the terms to which the parties agreed. In the absence of such a document, it is surprising how differently people remember what they have agreed to. If the dispute between the parties does end in litigation, the parties will be in a better position to prove their case if they can produce written evidence to support their claim. In some circumstances, however, a contract *must* be evidenced in writing for it to be enforceable.

Writing required to enforce some contracts

Statute of Frauds

Statute of Frauds requires writing for enforcement in courts

During the reign of Charles II in the seventeenth century, many unscrupulous land dealers cheated others out of their property by perjuring themselves in court. To prevent this abuse, parliament enacted the *Statute of Frauds* which required that certain types of transactions be evidenced in writing before the courts would enforce them. The *Statute* has remained in force in Britain over the years and has become part of the law of most of the common law provinces in Canada, including Alberta. Because of the illiteracy prevalent at the time the *Statute* was enacted, it led to much abuse and caused as many problems as it solved. Significant modification to the *Statute* has been made in the United Kingdom, British Columbia and Manitoba, but in the rest of Canada the act has remained essentially as passed. British Columbia recently repealed its *Statute of Frauds* altogether and included those provisions that were retained in the *Law and Equity Act*.[19] Manitoba has similarly repealed its *Statute*

WRITING STILL NEEDED IN MANITOBA

Two parties were negotiating by telephone and at the conclusion of the conversation a deal was struck. But before any documents were drawn up the vendor changed his mind, and the purchaser sued. The court held that despite the fact that the *Statute of Frauds* had been repealed, there was the usual expectation of the parties that the contract dealing with the sale of land would not be effective until put into writing and, therefore, that expectation was honoured.

Megill-Stephenson Co. v. Woo, 59 D.L.R. (4th) 146 (Manitoba Court of Appeal)

---

18. *Land Titles Act,* R.S.A. (1980) c. L-5 s. 152.3.

19. R.S.B.C. (1996) c. 253, s. 59.

of Frauds; there is no general writing requirement in that province.[20] It must be emphasized that failure to comply with the *Statute* does not invalidate the contract; it merely prevents the parties from using the courts to enforce it.

The following is a discussion of the types of contracts generally included under the *Statute of Frauds* in Canada. The actual wording varies between provinces.

1. *Contracts not to be performed within one year.* When the terms of the agreement make it impossible to perform the service stipulated in the contract within one full year from the time the contract is entered into, there must be evidence in writing for it to be enforceable. For example, if Sasaki agrees to paint Monette's house one year from the following Monday, that contract must be evidenced by writing to be enforceable. Failure to have evidence in writing will make it no less a contract but the courts will refuse to enforce it. British Columbia and Ontario have eliminated the requirement of writing in this area.

   When contract cannot be performed in one year

2. *Land dealings.* Any contract that affects a party's interest in land must be evidenced in writing to be enforceable. It is often difficult to determine just what types of contracts affect interest or ownership in land and what types do not. Any sale of land or part of it, such as the creation of a joint tenancy in land, must be evidenced in writing. Any creation of an easement or right of way or estate, such as a life estate, is also covered by the *Statute.* But contracts for services to the land which do not affect the interest to the land itself are not covered. For example, if a carpenter agrees to build a house, such an agreement may affect the value of the land but not the interest in the land itself and so need not be evidenced in writing to be enforceable. Similarly, when permission is given to someone to come on the land (licensee) or when someone is lodging in another's home, these types of agreements need not be evidenced in writing. This provision of the *Statute of Frauds* has also been modified in some jurisdictions. In Alberta, it appears that "the requirement of writing does not apply to leases of less than three years, if the rent to be paid is at least two-thirds of the annual value of the premises."[21] In addition, the *Land Titles Act* provides that where land is leased for more than three years, a lease in the prescribed form must be executed.[22] The practical result is that leases for more than three years must be in writing (in the prescribed form) and be registered at the Land Titles Office.

   When the title to land is involved

3. *Guarantees and indemnities.* When moneylenders are not satisfied with the creditworthiness of a debtor, they may insist that someone else sign as well. This means that the creditor wants another person to add his or her credit to the transaction and assume responsibility for the repayment of the debt. The arrangement can be in the form of a guarantee or an indemnity. If the third party incurs a secondary liability for the debt, it is called a guarantee. The guarantor promises that if the debtor fails to pay the debt, he or she will assume the responsibility and pay. Note that in this type of transaction the obligation is secondary or contingent; there is no obligation on the guarantor until the debtor actually fails to pay the debt.

   When guarantee is involved

   An indemnity describes a relationship in which the third party assumes a primary obligation for the repayment of the debt or other obligation along with the debtor. As a result, both owe the debt and the creditor can look to either

20. *An Act to Repeal the Statute of Frauds*, L.M. (1982-83-84) c. 29.

21. Ziff, Bruce. *Principles of Property Law.* Toronto: Carswell, 1993, at p. 213.

22. *Land Titles Act,* R.S.A. (1980) c. L-5 s. 98.

for repayment. When a third party says, "I'll see that you get paid," there is an assumption of a primary obligation and the promise is an indemnity. The distinction between the two is important because, in most provinces, the *Statute of Frauds* requires that a guarantee be in writing but not an indemnity. If the court classifies the nature of the third-party agreement as an indemnity, there is no requirement of writing. The distinction can be vital when a person has made only a verbal commitment to pay the outstanding loan of the debtor. In Alberta, very specific requirements must be satisfied before a guarantee will be given effect by the courts.[23]

When promise is given in consideration of marriage

4. *Promises in consideration of marriage.* It is not necessary that a promise to marry be evidenced in writing to be enforceable. This provision covers those situations in which a promise is contingent on another's commitment to marry. Thus, a parent's promise to give a child a new car upon marriage would have to be evidenced in writing to be enforceable. This provision has been abolished in Ontario and British Columbia. In those provinces where the provision is still in place, its operation must be viewed as very restricted because of overriding family law legislation.[24]

When an executor promises to meet the debts of an estate out of own pocket

5. *The promise of an executor.* The *Statute* states that when the person appointed to look after the distribution of the assets of a person after death, known as the executor of the estate, promises to pay for a debt of the deceased out of his or her own pocket, there must be evidence in writing for the agreement to be enforceable. The executor is often a member of the family of the deceased and may feel a moral obligation to pay some of the debts even though no legal obligation exists. There are often considerable delays in paying out the debts of the deceased and such a promise may be given to avoid unpleasant pressure from creditors. This provision has also been abolished in British Columbia.

When goods sold over specific value

6. *Others.* The original *Statute of Frauds* required that whenever the purchase price of goods sold exceeded a specified minimum, there had to be evidence in writing for the sale to be enforceable. This provision has been included in the *Sale of Goods Act* in many jurisdictions in Canada, including Alberta. It is usually sufficient evidence in writing if a receipt or sales slip has been given or if delivery of the goods has been accepted. The definition of goods and the sale of goods generally will be discussed in Chapter 7. Parliament and the provincial legislatures have passed many statutes which require the transaction itself to be in writing to be valid. Some examples are the *Bills of Exchange Act*, insurance legislation, consumer protection legislation, some of the legislation dealing with employment relations and the carriage of goods and passengers.

What Constitutes Evidence in Writing.

Writing must contain all essential terms

It is not necessary that the entire contract be in writing to satisfy the *Statute of Frauds*; the courts have held that only the main or essential terms must be evidenced in writing. This usually means a description of the parties to the agreement, a description of the property involved and a statement of the price paid. It must be remembered that if the parties have included any other unusual or essential terms in their agreement, those terms must also be evidenced by writing. Care has been taken throughout this presentation to avoid saying that the contract itself

---

23. *Guarantees Acknowledgement Act*, R.S.A. (1980) c. G-12.

24. In Alberta, see the *Matrimonial Property Act*, R.S.A. (1980) c. M-9.

has to be in writing. It does not. The only thing that the act requires is that there be some evidence in writing.

This evidence can come into existence after the contract. If someone is trying to avoid responsibility under an agreement because it is not "in writing," it would be unwise to write a letter to the other party to that effect. Such a letter may qualify as the required evidence in writing and thus defeat the objective of getting out of the deal. The *Statute* also requires that the evidence in writing be signed but only by the person who is trying to deny the existence of the obligation. The written evidence need not be in a single document but can be contained in a compilation of documents, the whole of which indicates the existence of the contract.

- and may arise after agreement

- and be signed by party to be charged but need not be in the same document

IN PRACTICE

Agreements Enforceable Without Formal Contracts

Businesses may be bound by agreements even if the parties don't sign formal contracts.

In *Silvio Construction Co. vs. 678192 Ontario Ltd.*, Madame Justice Jean MacFarland decided that, even though the defendant had agreed that a formal contract should be prepared and that contract was never signed, the agreement was still binding.

Owned by Louis Meier, 678192 bought a large tract of land in Aurora, Ont. The idea was to build a subdivision called Hunters Hill Estates.

In the summer of 1987, Silvio Construction Co., owned by Domenic Lombardi, was asked to tender on the construction of roads, sewers and watermains for the project. After some preliminary negotiations, he submitted a bid of $1 093 889.

Early in January 1988, Lombardi was told he had the job and he agreed to a small reduction in the price.

When he heard nothing further, Lombardi wrote to Meier in March to demand that the contract be signed immediately.

In the first week of April, the construction company wrote again, saying that since the work was seasonal it had to begin right away.

Meier agreed to meet at his offices. At the meeting it was agreed Silvio would do the job.

Most of the agreement had been set out in the April letter, so a notation was made at the bottom of the letter.

This read: "I, the undersigned president and director of 678192 Ontario Ltd., do hereby agree to the above condition in principle, subject to a contract agreement prepared by Ray Floyd."

There was still a question of the final price, as the Town of Aurora had changed some of its requirements.

According to Mark Klaiman, the Toronto litigation lawyer who represented Silvio at trial, the formal contract was prepared by Floyd, who headed the consulting engineering firm on the project.

Lombardi signed it but Meier refused.

At trial, Meier claimed he had "made an agreement to make an agreement," so there was nothing legally binding.

He said many details were not settled, such as start and completion dates, final cost and terms of payment.

The judge did not accept his evidence.

"One would think on Mr. Meier's version of the meeting that he must have attended a different meeting," she said.

"All the essentials were set out in Lombardi's letter, save the starting date. ... There were no additional terms to be left to the formal contract; the essentials were agreed upon.

"The formal contract was nothing more than a standard form into which the essential particulars agreed to at the April meeting would be inserted."

Lombardi was awarded $65 000 in damages, based on the justice's estimate of his lost profit.

The principle in the case according to Klaiman is that "if all the essential terms are agreed to, that is sufficient for a binding contract. The parties do not need a more formal contract document."

But although Meier lost the case, all was not lost for him.

During negotiations, a buyer offered to buy the property, netting Meier more than $2 million profit.

Source: James Carlisle, "Agreements Enforceable Without Formal Contracts," The Financial Post, October 26, 1993, p. 17. James A. Carlisle is a partner in the litigation firm of Beard, Carlisle.

For example, if a person agreed to sell a house to another for $100 000 and the seller then refused to go through with the deal, it would be necessary for the purchaser to produce a document signed by the seller which identified the property, the purchaser, the amount of money involved and any other unique or essential terms. It is only when all of these requirements are satisfied that there is sufficient evidence in writing to satisfy the *Statute* and thus make the contract enforceable in the courts. (See In Practice box, "Agreements Enforceable Without Formal Contracts.")

Effect of the Statute.

Contract still valid even where no writing, just unenforceable

It is vital to remember that under the *Statute of Frauds*, if a contract is not in writing that does not make the contract void, it is merely unenforceable. This means that the contract is still binding on the parties, but the courts will not assist the parties to enforce it. If the parties have already performed, or if there is some other remedy available that does not require the court's involvement, the contract will still be binding, even in the absence of evidence in writing. The courts will not assist a person who has performed to get out of a contract. Nor will the court order the return of money even when there is no evidence in writing of the contract. In effect, the party only did what was required under the contract. Similarly, when there is a lien (a right to seize property) or when there is a right to set off a debt against the obligations established within the contract, the parties themselves may be in a position to enforce it without the help of the courts and in that sense the contract is binding even though there is no evidence in writing.

Part Performance.

When part performance consistent with contract involving land, writing not required

The court will waive the requirement of writing if the parties can produce evidence to show that a contract dealing with an interest in land has been partially performed. There are some important limitations to this principle. The part performance must be evidence of the existence of the contract and consistent only with the existence of the contract. The payment of money owed under the contract will not usually be acceptable as proof of part performance because the payment of money is consistent with any number of different obligations.[25] A good example of acceptable part performance when land has been sold is the starting of construction. The permission to enter onto the land and start building is consistent with the sale of the land and so the part performance will be accepted by the courts as sufficient evidence to support the contract.

PART PERFORMANCE SATISFIES STATUTE

In this case, the Supreme Court of Canada overturned the decision of the Supreme Court of Alberta, Appellate Division, and restored the judgment of the trial judge, by ruling that the building of a house on the lands in question was "unequivocally referable" to the verbal agreement which existed. The verbal agreement, between the plaintiff and the deceased landowner, required the latter to leave his lands, in his will, to the plaintiff, in return for services rendered over a period of 26 years. The deceased died intestate (i.e., without a will), but the Supreme Court of Canada found that there was part performance and that the verbal agreement was therefore enforceable.

Brownscombe v. Public Trustee (1969) S.C.R 658.

25. In B.C., the requirements to satisfy part performance are not as stringent, and part payment is acceptable and not restricted to contracts dealing with interests in land.

SUMMARY

Contracts with infants in most provinces are voidable except for contracts for necessaries and beneficial contracts of service. Insanity or drunkenness will only cause a contract to be invalid when the person was so insane as to not know what was happening and when the other contracting party knew or ought to have known of that incapacity. Corporations, enemy aliens in time of war, trade unions, government agencies, bankrupts and even Native Indians under some circumstances may have their capacity to enter contracts limited to some extent.

Contracts that are illegal or against public policy may also be invalid or unenforceable. Agreements to commit crimes or immoral acts, to obstruct justice, to injure the state, to promote litigation, to injure public service, and to restrain marriage, and in some circumstances bets or wagers—any of these may be held to be illegal or against public policy. Contracts that restrain trade, such as price fixing, are generally prohibited, but contracts in which one party agrees not to carry on business in competition with another are valid if they can be shown to be reasonable in terms of the interests of the parties and the public.

Both parties must intend to be legally bound by their agreement. In family and other social relationships there is a presumption of no intention but this can be challenged by evidence that shows an intent to be bound. In commercial relationships, intention is presumed. In unusual situations, the reasonable person test is used to determine intention.

Contracts dealing with land that will not be performed within one year (except leases for three years or less), and contracts involving guarantees, in consideration of marriage, and by the executor of an estate to personally pay a debt are examples of contracts that, under the *Statute of Frauds*, must be evidenced in writing to be enforceable. When part performance is established, such agreements are enforceable.

....

QUESTIONS

1. Explain the circumstances in which an infant may escape liability for a contract and the circumstances in which an infant is bound by a contract.

2. What is the significance of an infant's contract being designated as a beneficial contract of service?

3. What is the responsibility of parents for the actions of their infant children in both tort and contract law?

4. What are the rights and obligations of the parties involved when an infant makes a contract with an adult for non-necessaries?

5. Explain the circumstances in which an infant can be sued for tort even though a contract between the parties is involved.

6. What must an insane or drunk person establish to escape liability under a contract?

7. Describe how the provisions of the *Indian Act* limit the capacity of status Indians to enter into contracts.

8. Explain what care business people must exercise when entering into contracts with Crown corporations or government bodies.

9. Describe how the courts treat a contract to commit a crime.

10. Give five examples of contracts deemed by the courts to be against public policy and describe the effect of such a designation.

11. Are all contracts which restrain trade unlawful? Explain.

12. Explain how the courts' treatment of domestic agreements differs from their response to commercial transactions when the question of intention arises.

13. Describe tests the courts will use in determining whether the parties were serious in their statements.

14. What is the significance of a written document in contractual relations?

15. Explain why some people have suggested that the *Statute of Frauds* has led to more frauds than it has prevented.

16. Give examples of the types of contracts currently included under the *Statute of Frauds*.

17. What must be evidenced in writing to satisfy the requirements of the *Statute of Frauds*?

18. Under what circumstances will a contract falling under the jurisdiction of the *Statute of Frauds* be enforceable even though it is not evidenced by writing?

CASES

1. Re Collins

Mrs. Collins was divorced from a famous rock star and living in Vancouver with his two children. As part of the divorce she received a substantial payment along with a support payment for each child. She persuaded Mr. Collins to purchase a large house in the city, which he did, but he arranged that the house be held in trust for the two minor children. Mrs. Collins became concerned about her financial position and persuaded the two children to transfer the title of the house to her. At the time of the trial the oldest child who had reached the age of majority confirmed the sale, but the youngest child was still under age. Evidence was presented that this contract was for the benefit of the child, giving the children the security they needed until they reached the age of 25. Evidence indicated that the child had received independent legal advice and a psychiatrist testified that this was truly the desire of the child to make sure the mother had financial security. Explain the arguments that support the transfer of the house and the arguments against it.

2. Lenson v. Lenson

The father owned a farm in Saskatchewan and his son, the plaintiff, lived on that farm along with his wife. For a number of years, they had a crop sharing arrangement which was essentially a lease on the property paid for by the son sharing the crop with his father. This arrangement had been going on for some time when the son alleged they had entered into an oral agreement whereby he would buy the farm for $100 000 and be given the land immediately around the farmhouse as a gift. According to the son's testimony, he and his wife gave up several opportunities to buy surrounding property and made considerable improvements on the land in question, but eventually there was a falling-out between the parties and the father denied that any agreement existed. Explain what difficulties the son will face in trying to establish his claim to the land and how those difficulties can be overcome.

3. Ouston et al. v. Zurowski et al.

A number of plaintiffs including Ouston were persuaded to invest in a scheme run by the defendant, "Kulnan Investment Corp.," which was a pyramid investment scheme. Such a scheme is similar to a chain letter, where one person higher on the chain makes money based on others whom they persuade to join the chain for a fee. The idea is that the person joining the chain will get higher in that chain as others join and make a considerable amount of money on those they recruit. The problem with such schemes is that the last people to join lose all their money.

The plaintiffs testified that they were told when they were brought into the scheme by Zurowski that if the board should stop, Zurowski would make sure they got their money back—that is, that if the pyramid scheme failed, he would reimburse the defendants. The scheme did fail because of local publicity that discouraged any further meetings and the attraction of any further investors. Pyramid schemes are illegal under the *Criminal Code*.

In this action Ouston and the other plaintiffs seek to have their money returned. Explain what arguments they can put forward to support this request and the likely attitude of the court in granting remedies.

4. Canadian American Finance Corp. v. King

The Canadian American Finance Corporation markets a registered scholarship savings plan for profit. King was employed to market the plan as director of agencies. King set up a separate company to market the plan. The agreement between the Canadian American Finance Corporation and King included a non-competition clause which said that once the relationship was terminated King could not enter into competition with the corporation for a period of two years in Canada or Bermuda. King eventually quit and went to work for a rival company in Alberta and British Columbia. Comment on the arguments available to both parties as to the validity of this non-competition clause.

5. Fairgrief v. Ellis

The plaintiff agreed to be a housekeeper for the defendant on the understanding that his house would go to her when the defendant died. This agreement was never put down in writing but it is clear that this was the understanding of both parties during the course of their association. The defendant's wife arrived and the plaintiff was required to leave, but the defendant promised to pay her $1000 to replace the previous agreement. The plaintiff agreed to this and when the money was not paid, she sued for $1000. Explain the likely outcome. Would her suit have succeeded if she had sued on the original agreement?

6. Fobasco Ltd. v. Cougan

The plaintiffs and the defendants were business associates and the defendants bought Toronto SkyDome baseball tickets for several years and gave them to the plaintiffs, who reimbursed them. After 1986 that social and business contact ceased and the defendant stopped supplying the tickets. The plaintiffs sued, claiming the defendant had agreed to continue to supply the tickets, while the defendant stated that no such agreement had been made. Give the arguments that can be raised by the defendant in this case to avoid any obligations to the plaintiffs.

7. Performance Systems Inc. v. Pezim

The defendant was involved in promoting a restaurant chain in Canada which required buying a franchise from a similar American company. The American company loaned the Canadian company $50 000 on the strength of a promissory note guaranteed by the defendant. There was some dispute about whether the agents who consented to the guarantee on behalf of the defendant were authorized to do so, but it was held that the defendant could not deny that he had guaranteed the promissory note despite the fact that the guarantee had not been signed until several months after the $50 000 was advanced. When the Canadian company ran into difficulties and was unable to repay the loan, the American company demanded that the defendant honour the guarantee. What arguments would the defendant raise in defense of this action? Explain the likely outcome.

LEGISLATION

Alberta

Age of Majority Act, R.S.A. (1980) c. A-4
Apprenticeship and Industry Training Act, S.A. (1991) c. A-42.3
Dependent Adults Act, R.S.A. (1980) c. D-32

Federal

Indian Act, R.S.C. (1985) c. I-5
State Immunity Act, R.S.C. (1985) c. S-18

Note: Age of majority varies with provinces.

WEBLINKS

Alberta Dependent Adults Act
www.gov.ab.ca/qp/ascii/acts/D32.txt

Alberta Dependent Adults Act Amendment 1996
www.gov.ab.ca/qp/ascii/acts/96/CH13.txt

Alberta Age of Majority Act
www.gov.ab.ca/qp/ascii/acts/A04.txt

Apprenticeship and Industry Training Act
www.gov.ab.ca/qp/ascii/acts/A42p3.txt

Factors Affecting the Contractual Relationship

OBJECTIVES OF THE CHAPTER

- To describe the nature and effect of a mistake in a contract
- To explain misrepresentation and its consequences on a contract
- To consider the implications of duress and undue influence
- To outline the rules governing privity and assignment

Mr. Hoy purchased a 50-year-old house from Mr. and Mrs. Lozanovski after having a builder friend inspect it and indicate that it was sound. Soon after he moved in, he discovered that the house was infested with termites; it had to be completely renovated at a cost of $25 000 before he could live in it. Mr. Hoy sued the Lozanovskis, claiming damages in this amount for fraudulent misrepresentation. The judge held that there was no fraud since the Lozanovskis did not know of the termites when they sold the house. Even if they had, the judge said, they would not be liable since they were silent (they had made no statements that the house was free from such infestation) and the purchaser had not relied on any representations from them but had had his own builder inspect the house. To obtain damages, Mr. Hoy not only had to demonstrate that the misrepresentation was fraudulent rather than innocent but also that he had relied on the representation in question. In this case, not only was there no reliance on the representation, there was no representation at all.[1] Misrepresentation is just one of the factors to be considered in this chapter that can affect the rights of the parties to a contract.

1. *Hoy v. Lozanovski* as reported in *The Lawyers Weekly*, April 3, 1987.

The two previous chapters examined the process of forming contracts. This chapter will discuss the extent of the responsibilities and obligations of the original parties to an agreement, what happens when the parties disagree as to the nature and effect of the contract, and how those obligations are affected when an innocent third party or a stranger to the contract becomes involved.

MISTAKE

The purpose of contract law is to give effect to the reasonable expectations of the parties to an agreement. The courts, therefore, are reluctant to relieve the parties to a contract of their obligations merely because they have made a mistake. The courts will, however, in the event of mistake interfere when it is clear that to do otherwise would lead to an unjust result. This is especially true when it is clear that because of the mistake the parties have failed to reach a consensus and there is no complete agreement between them. Mistake in this sense is restricted to situations where the contract in general or its terms are different from what the parties originally intended. The mistake must go to the identity of the parties, the subject matter itself, or the terms, not the effect of the agreement or the law surrounding it. If a person buys a property in the belief that a new highway will soon be built nearby and it turns out that the purchaser was mistaken in this belief, that mistake would not be grounds for claiming that the contract should be set aside. The purchaser made an incorrect assumption, but there is no problem with the agreement or its terms. However, if a purchaser thought that he or she was buying certain property, Blackacre, when in fact it was different property all together, Greenacre, this would be a mistake as to the subject matter of the agreement itself and could be raised as a defense when being sued for breach of contract.

A mistake in law is normally not a defense. If either party misunderstands the legal effect of the agreement, he or she will not be able to escape the contract on the basis of mistake. Generally, the courts will not interfere with a contract unless it can be demonstrated that the mistake claimed is a very serious one. It must be a factual mistake as to the subject matter or the identity of the parties, or a misunderstanding of the agreement that is so fundamental it destroys the element of consent. Thus, a mistake involving the parties must concern the existence or identity of those parties and a mistake involving the subject matter must concern the identity or existence of the subject matter.

The area of mistake in law is very confusing and over the years the courts have reversed or modified their position many times. The discussion below is an attempt to summarize the important aspects of the law in this area. The approach taken concentrates on three different ways that a mistake can be made. It should be remembered that if a contract is found to be void, it is no contract at all, but if it is voidable, the contract does exist but one of the parties has the option of getting out of it. When an innocent third party has acquired goods that are the subject of a voidable contract, that party gets to keep the goods, but if the contract was void—that is, there never was a contract—the person who sold the goods to the third party never had title to them and those goods must be returned to the original owner.

Misunderstanding that destroys consensus results in void contract

Mistake must be part of agreement, not just as to effect of agreement

Mistake must relate to nature of agreement, not the law

Mistake must be serious

Shared Mistake

A **shared mistake** takes place when the two parties are in complete agreement but they have both made the same mistake regarding a fundamental aspect of the subject matter of the contract. There are two circumstances in which the courts will declare such contracts to be void. The first is when the subject matter of the agreement does not exist at the time the parties enter into the contract.[2] Thus, if the parties enter into an agreement for the sale and purchase of the cargo of a ship without knowing that the cargo had been destroyed the night before, the contract is void because of the shared mistake. The second situation is when the vendor is in no position to convey title to goods because the prospective purchaser already has title. In the case of *Cooper v. Phibbs*,[3] a contract was held void because, although both the vendor and the purchaser thought the vendor had title to a fishery, it turned out that the purchaser already owned it. The contract was void because of this shared false belief about the subject matter of the agreement.

Fundamental shared mistake about subject matter—void

The court will not allow the careless party to escape responsibility when a shared mistaken belief about a fundamental aspect of the contract is the result of negligence on the part of one of the parties. This principle was clearly established in *McRae v. Commonwealth Disposals Commission*,[4] and legislation has also been passed incorporating provisions to this effect in the *Sale of Goods Acts* in all the common law provinces in Canada.[5]

Careless party responsible when mistake is result of negligence

When the parties make a mistake about only the value of what they are dealing with, it normally will not affect the enforceability of the contract. For example, if both vendor and purchaser think that they are dealing with some ordinary furniture and, in fact, a rare and valuable Hepplewhite table is included, the contract would be binding nevertheless.

Rectification.

If the written document does not reflect the common intention of the parties to the contract, the courts are willing to correct or rectify the document. For example, if two parties had agreed to the sale of land for $50 000 and a clerical error made the document read $5000, the court would add the missing zero and require the parties to perform the corrected agreement. The parties had entered into the contract, and the written document was merely evidence of the contract. Therefore, the court is free to rectify the written document.

Courts may correct a mistake in recording agreement

However, there must be the clearest evidence that both of the parties agreed to something different from what was embodied in the written document to obtain rectification by the courts. If the parties to an agreement intended to buy and sell some oats but because of some confusion wrote "hops" the courts would not rectify such an agreement. Both intended to write "hops" even though what they should

---

2. *Couturier v. Hastie*, (1852) 8 Ex. 40 (Court of Exchequer).

3. *Cooper v. Phibbs*, [1867] L.R. 2 H.L. 149 (House of Lords). In the case of *Hyrsy v. Smith*, the Ontario High Court of Justice has taken this principle even further. In that case, both the vendor and the purchaser of land thought the vendor had title to all of the land that was the subject matter of the contract. But the vendor had title to only part of the land and thus only that part was conveyed to the purchaser. In the subsequent action, the court held that a common mistake going to the "root of the contract" had taken place, the contract was void, and rescission was granted. *Hyrsy v. Smith* [1969] 2 O.R. 360.

4. *McRae v. Commonwealth Disposals Commission*, (1951) 84 C.L.R. 377 (High Court of Australia).

5. Section 9 of the *Sale of Goods Act*, R.S.A. (1980) c. S-2, states that if specific goods have perished when a contract for their sale is made, without the knowledge of the seller, then the contract is void.

have been agreeing on was oats and so "hops" it is. The court will refuse a request to rectify the written document because it is in fact a correct record of their agreement. If both parties had oats in mind and a secretary simply used the wrong word, that would be a situation for the use of rectification; but in this case, both parties had hops in mind and the wording of the contract stands. It is important to remember that the courts are not rewriting the agreement during rectification. They are simply correcting a written document so that it corresponds to the demonstrated intention of the two parties. Rectification of the contract may be available as a remedy in other situations as well such as where a unilateral mistake is caused by the fraud of the other party.

Misunderstanding

A different type of mistake occurs when the parties have a misunderstanding about the terms of the agreement itself and neither party is aware of the other's different understanding of the agreement. When one party to an agreement thinks that the agreement is to do something else, the courts will usually apply the reasonable person test to determine which interpretation of the contract is more reasonable. The court will then adopt the more reasonable position as the correct interpretation of the contract. This point is discussed below in more detail under the heading "Rules of Interpretation." Only if the error is a serious one and the court cannot choose between the two positions because both are equally reasonable will the contract be declared void. For example, if there is an agreement to buy a 1984 Chrysler and the purchaser thinks this term means a 1984 Chrysler sailboat when the item for sale is a 1984 Chrysler automobile, a misunderstanding about a fundamental term of the agreement has taken place. The court will examine the relationship between the parties, including the comments made at the time of the agreement, to determine if one interpretation is more reasonable than the other. If the parties discussed the condition of the motor and the transmission, and what gas mileage was obtained, the position of the seller would seem more reasonable since such comments would normally be associated with a car rather than with a sailboat. But if, after examining all the factors, it is still not possible to choose one position as the more reasonable, the court would probably find that there is no contract. If the error is serious, involving an important term of the agreement, and the interpretations are equally reasonable, consensus is not present and there will probably be no contract between the parties.

Misunderstanding may void contract if serious enough

MEANING OF "SALE" CLARIFIED

In a listing agreement, a vendor agreed to pay a real estate agent a commission on the sale of property if that sale or exchange, however effected, was procured by the agent. The agent procured an offer, including a deposit, and requested payment according to the agreement. Unfortunately, the deal fell through, and the vendor had to sue the purchaser for the deposit and for specific performance. The Supreme Court of Canada had to decide whether the agent was still entitled to the commission. The Court, after looking at the practice in the industry and the various contracts involved, concluded that the completion of a contract of sale was not enough; the sale itself had to go through, despite the fact that the vendor obtained compensation in the form of a deposit from the reluctant purchaser.

H. W. Liebig & Co. Ltd. v. Leading Investments Ltd., 25 D.L.R. (4th) 161 (Supreme Court of Canada)

One-Sided Mistake

Moss v. Chin[6]

In this case Mrs. Moss was a pedestrian in a crosswalk when struck by a car driven by Mr. Chin. She was severely injured and unconscious. A government official, called a public trustee, was appointed to act on her behalf and start a legal action against the person causing her injuries.

Since the defendant was insured by the Insurance Corporation of B.C., they defended the action. Her claim was for $300 000 in damages, most of which was for pain, suffering and future care. In the process of negotiations between the parties, Mrs. Moss suffered a seizure and it became apparent that she would not live long. When the lawyer for the public trustee learned this, he got permission to settle the matter right away with ICBC, for if she died her right to sue would die with her. An offer to settle was made by ICBC the day after the plaintiff died. The public trustee and the solicitor, while failing to inform ICBC of her death, accepted the offer on her behalf. ICBC paid out the money, but eventually learned what had happened and brought an application to the court to have the settlement set aside.

The court found that the agreement had been entered into on the basis of a unilateral mistake. Normally, a unilateral mistake is simply the problem of the person making it and will not affect the rights of the other parties. In effect, the person making the mistake has misled himself and there is no remedy. If there is fraud involved, however, or as in this case, where one party deliberately sets out to make sure the other does not discover a mistake, the court has the power to interfere. The court ordered that the contract be rescinded.

This case is interesting because it illustrates the difference between a unilateral mistake and other forms of mistakes and shows that even when such unilateral mistakes are made, under some limited circumstances there may be a rescission of the contract.

A one-sided or unilateral mistake takes place where one of the parties makes a mistake in relationship to the contract and the other party is aware that this mistake is being made. This was the situation in *Moss v. Chin* above. As a general rule there is no recourse for a person who makes such a one-sided mistake. Thus, if a purchaser is under the impression that the car being purchased is equipped with a V8 engine when in fact it has only a four-cylinder engine and the seller is aware of the purchaser's misconception, the seller is under no legal obligation to disabuse the purchaser of any incorrect assumptions. This is an example of the principle of *caveat emptor* ("Let the buyer beware"). But if the seller has misled the purchaser into believing that the car is equipped with a V8 engine, the situation is quite different and the principles of misrepresentation or breach of contract apply. It should be noted, however, that when the offeror makes an obvious error in relation to his or her offer, the purchaser will not be allowed to take advantage of this obvious error and snap up the offer. Thus, if a vendor to the knowledge of the purchaser intended to offer her property for $22 500 and wrote $12 500 instead, the court would hold that the resulting agreement was not enforceable. The purchaser should have realized that the vendor was making a mistake and the courts will not allow the purchaser to take advantage of it.

Caveat emptor applies when purchaser misleads himself or herself

Caveat emptor lot buyer be war

---

6. 120 D.L.R. (4th) 406 (British Columbia Supreme Court).

When a one-sided mistake takes place, the person making the mistake usually only has a remedy when he or she has been misled and then the normal course of action is to claim for misrepresentation with its associated remedies. Even when there has been misrepresentation it may be important for the victim to establish that the misrepresentation led to a mistake with respect to the contract. If goods are involved and they have been resold to an innocent third party the remedy of rescission for misrepresentation will not be available. However, if a mistake sufficient to affect consensus has taken place, the contract may be void allowing recovery of the goods involved even from an innocent purchaser.

Contract may be void when one party makes mistake sufficient to affect consensus

Such a one-sided mistake can occur when there is incorrect identification of one of the parties to a contract. If the person claiming that a mistake has taken place actually thought the deal was with someone else and can demonstrate that identity was an important aspect of the agreement, the court will declare the contract to be void. However, if the party using mistaken identity as a defense was just in error about some attribute of the other party, this will not affect the existence of the contract. For example, if a vendor thought that jewelry was being sold on credit to Ms. Paré, a wealthy movie star, and in fact the merchant was dealing with Ms. Paré who was a waitress and not associated with the movie industry at all, the contract would be binding and title would go to the purchaser. If the jewelry is resold, the ultimate purchaser would acquire good title. Of course, the seller would still have recourse against Ms. Paré if she did not pay for the jewelry. But if the seller thought that the purchaser was Ms. Paré, a wealthy and well-known movie star, and in fact the purchaser was Ms. Capozzi, a waitress, a mistake has been made about the identity of the person with whom the seller is dealing, and there would be no contract. In the first instance, the seller knew whom he was dealing with but was mistaken about some of the person's qualities or attributes; in the second situation, the seller was fooled into thinking the purchaser was somebody else entirely. Therefore, there is no contract.[7] If a mistake is made in the actual performance of a contract with, for example, more paid than is owed, the court can order the excess returned because the creditor has been unjustly enriched.

If mistake about attributes— valid contract

If mistake about identity— void contract

Non Est Factum.

If misled about nature of document signed—void

Whenever it is clear that one of the parties, even though he or she was careful, was unaware of the nature of the contract, the courts have the right to declare the agreement void on the basis of *non est factum* ("It is not my act"). In these cases, the defendants hold that the signed documents do not represent what they thought they were signing, thus, there is no consensus. For this defense to succeed and the contract to be void, it must be shown that the mistake about the document went to the very nature of that document rather than merely to its terms. It is unlikely today that such a defense will be successful unless it can be shown that the error was caused by misrepresentation.

For example, if Ms. Paré was fooled into thinking she was signing an autograph when in fact it was a mortgage on her property, that mistake would be significant enough to give rise to the defense of *non est factum* and the agreement would be void. Even when an innocent third party acquired the rights under the mortgage, she would not be bound by it. However, if she thought she was signing a mortgage document requiring 8 percent interest when in fact she had signed one requiring 20 percent interest, she would not be able to rely on the defense of *non est factum*. A personal remedy against the person who misled her, such as rescission or

7. *Cundy v. Lindsay* (1878) A.C. 459 (House of Lords).

misrepresentation, may be available, but such remedies would be of no value against an innocent third party who acquired these mortgage rights.

When it can be demonstrated that a person was in any way careless in signing a document, he or she would not be permitted to rely on the defense of *non est factum*. Negligence on the part of the person claiming *non est factum* when the other party is clear of any wrongdoing may be a bar to this defense. Failure to read the document will likely be enough to constitute such negligence but this must be determined case by case.[8] The finding of a court that a one-sided mistake has resulted in a void contract is usually limited to those circumstances where the victim has been intentionally misled into making that mistake.

—but not where negligence present

Rules of Interpretation

The test to determine whether a mistake has taken place or not is objective. The courts are not concerned with what the parties thought they were agreeing to but rather with what the parties should have been aware of when they made the agreement. In such instances, the courts use the reasonable person test. Instead of declaring the contract void because one of the parties has made a mistake about the meaning of a term, the courts will look at the wording to determine what a reasonable person would have understood the term to mean. In those rare circumstances in which there is no reasonable interpretation of the agreement or the positions taken by the two parties are equally reasonable, the courts can declare the contract to be void.

Reasonable person test applies when misunderstanding is not fundamental

In the case of *Raffels v. Wichelhaus*,[9] the contract concerned a crop being transported on a particular ship called *The Peerless*. It happened that there were two ships by this name both leaving the same port but at different times. The seller intended one of these two ships and the purchaser had in mind the other. There was no way of applying the reasonable person test to this case and, since the disagreement was fundamental, the contract was declared void. In the vast majority of cases, however, the courts will simply impose a reasonable interpretation on the agreement.

Whenever there is a dispute involving the meaning of a specific term, the courts have a choice of applying the literal meaning of the term or adopting a more liberal approach by trying to determine the parties' intent. The courts will apply the literal meaning of the wording chosen by the parties if there is no ambiguity. If the term is ambiguous, the court will look at what was behind the agreement and apply the most reasonable meaning of the term to the contract.

Courts apply literal meaning to specific wording

Determining the literal meaning of the words is not as simple as it might first appear. Even dictionaries often have several different meanings for particular words. Determining the intention of the parties may also be difficult because of the conflicting positions taken by the parties to the dispute. The court will often look at how the terms are normally used in the particular industry involved. The court will also look at past dealings between the parties as well as their dealings at the time the contract was formed to determine what they intended by the words they used. The key to the court's approach to such ambiguous terms in an agreement is to choose the most reasonable interpretation. But whenever the courts are faced with a choice of two equally reasonable interpretations, one of which will result in a declaration

Ambiguous wording interpreted liberally

8. *Marvco Color Research Ltd. v. Harris et al.* (1983) 141 D.L.R. (3d) 577 (S.C.C.).

9. *Raffels v. Wichelhaus* (1864) 2 H. & C. 906 (Exchequer Division).

that there is no contract and the other giving life to the contract, the courts have a preference for the term that will keep the contract alive.

Courts will not permit outside evidence to contradict clear wording

Another rule courts use in these situations is the **parol evidence rule**. This rule states that when the written term of a contract is clear and unambiguous, the parties will not be permitted to introduce outside evidence to contradict the clear meaning of the contract. For example, if a seller agreed to sell a "1984 Chrysler automobile" and that specific clause was used in the contract, the purchaser would not be permitted to introduce outside evidence later to show that the agreement concerned a 1984 Chrysler sailboat. Had the parties agreed to use the term "1984 Chrysler" instead, the statement would be ambiguous and the court would be free to consider outside evidence brought in by the purchaser, as discussed above. An ambiguous term is just one of the exceptions to the parol evidence rule.

Another situation in which the courts will allow outside evidence despite the clear terms of the contract is when the evidence to be introduced is of a fraud or some other problem associated with the formation of the contract. Other exceptions to the parol evidence rule include evidence of a condition precedent (a condition that has to be met before the obligations set out in the contract are in force); evidence of a collateral contract (a separate contractual obligation that can stand alone, independent of the written one); evidence of a subsequent agreement entered into by the parties after the written one; or the absence of an intention that all of the contract would be embodied in the written document. When the evidence contradicting the terms of the agreement falls into one of these categories, the court can be persuaded to hear it, despite the parol evidence rule.

It does not occur to most contracting parties to provide terms in their offer for every possible eventuality. In such circumstances, the courts will imply terms to the contract which the parties may have overlooked or neglected to include. For example, if a seller offers to sell an automobile for $500 and a purchaser accepts the offer without coming to terms about the date of delivery or when payment is due, the two parties would probably assume it was implicit in the agreement that the car would be delivered in a reasonable time and that payment would take place upon delivery. The courts will not make an agreement for the parties; they will simply imply insignificant terms the parties would have included if they had thought of them.

Courts will imply terms where appropriate

The courts are even more willing to imply such terms when there is a considerable amount of tradition associated with a particular industry. When parties within the industry enter into agreements with each other, the courts are willing to

---

TERM IMPLIED INTO CONTRACT

Two parties entered into a joint venture agreement for the development of computer software. Unfortunately, nowhere in the agreement did they make any provision for the termination of the relationship. One of the parties terminated without notice, causing significant damage to the other, who sued. The court held that although there was no termination provision, termination by either party on reasonable notice should be implied into the contract, for clearly the parties should not have expected their agreement to be perpetual. But then again, the notice was not given at all, so the terminating party was responsible for at least some of the damages.

Rapatax (1987) Inc. v. Cantax Corp., 145 D.L.R. (4th) 419 (Alberta Court of Appeal)

imply terms to the contracts that are consistent with the practices of their trade. Some terms may be implied automatically by statute. The *Sale of Goods Act* has set down in rule form the terms that are implied in a contract for the sale of goods when the parties have not addressed them.[10] As well, some consumer protection legislation imposes terms in contracts whether or not the parties have agreed to them.[11]

Equity.

The law of equity permits a court to actually use the principles of fairness and equity to justify the imposition of new terms on the parties even though the contract is declared void. Such imposition happened in the case of *Cooper v. Phibbs*[12] discussed under "Shared Mistake." In that case, a vendor sold a fishery to a purchaser without realizing that the purchaser already owned it. In fact, the vendor had done a considerable amount of work to prepare the property for sale but since the agreement was void he received nothing for his work. The court, however, applied the principles of equity, granted the would-be vendor a lien against the property and ordered the owner to pay him for the work he had done. The courts have maintained the right to set the contract aside when justified by either of the parties' conduct even if the mistake involved does not affect the foundation of the agreement and the contract is otherwise valid.

MISREPRESENTATION

Metropolitan Stores of Canada Ltd. v. Nova Construction Co.[13]

Metropolitan Stores had occupied space in the Antigonish Mall for seven years when the owners of the mall sold it to Nova Construction. Metropolitan and Antigonish had entered into a verbal agreement but a lease had never been signed, and Nova, upon taking over, tried to evict Metropolitan, resulting in litigation between the two parties.

In the process of attempting to reach a settlement, a new lease was negotiated for a 20-year term. One of its provisions was that no stores in competition with Metropolitan would be allowed to locate in the mall; but the clause would not apply if there was any expansion to the existing shopping centre.

When questioned about this, the representative of the mall explained that the only expansion that would take place would be within the present boundaries of the mall, and that another clause in the agreement protected Metropolitan from competition within those boundaries. The representative knew that this was false, and seven years later the mall purchased surrounding property, expanded into that area and leased property to another department store similar to Metropolitan, in direct contravention of the intent of the lease. They claimed that the exemption clause permitted this.

10. See, for example, ss. 15–18 of the *Sale of Goods Act, R.S.A.* (1980) c. S-2.

11. One example is found in s. 6 of the *Direct Sales Cancellation Act,* R.S.A. (1980) c. D-35, which states that a buyer may cancel a sales contract, without any reason, at any time, within 10 days of receiving a copy of the written sales contract.

12. *Cooper v. Phibbs* [1867] L.R. 2 H.L. 149 (House of Lords).

13. 50 D.L.R. (4th) 508 (Nova Scotia Supreme Court, Appeal Division).

In the original lease agreement between Metropolitan and Nova, the area of the present mall was specifically covered by the non-competition clause. So when Metropolitan was told that any expansion was going to take place within the present boundaries of the mall, they didn't worry about a competing department store moving in because they were protected by the provision setting out the mall boundaries. In effect, Metropolitan was tricked into signing a lease that did not protect them the way they thought it would. Metropolitan claimed that the lease had been breached and stopped paying rent; again Nova tried to evict them.

Metropolitan first tried to claim that the lease ought to be interpreted so that this expansion and leasing to the other department store would be considered a violation of it. The judge looked at that and found that the wording of the lease was clear. There was no ambiguity and so he was not free to do that. However, he did find that a fraudulent misrepresentation had taken place which induced Metropolitan to enter into the contract. Although the parol evidence rule restricts any outside extrinsic evidence from being considered which conflicts with plain meaning and unambiguous wording of the contract, there are several exceptions, one of which is evidence of fraud inducing the parties to enter into the contract. Such fraud was found in these circumstances.

This case is unusual because the normal remedies for misrepresentation are either rescission or, when fraud is present, rescission and/or damages. In this case, however, Metropolitan asked for rectification of the contract, that is, for the contract to be rewritten to include the terms as they understood it, making the expansion with the inclusion of the rival department store a breach of their lease. The trial judge thought this was going too far, but the Court of Appeal was willing to rectify the agreement, added the appropriate words to the lease and declared Nova in breach of that lease. Rectification—the rewriting of a contract on behalf of one of the parties at the expense of the other—is a drastic remedy, but because of the fraud, it was appropriate.

Misrepresentation is a misleading statement that induces a contract

Misrepresentation is a false statement of fact that persuades someone to enter into a contract. The false statement can be made fraudulently, when the person making the statement knew it was false; negligently, when the person should have known the statement was false; or completely innocently, when the misrepresentation is made without fault.

The concepts of misrepresentation and mistake frequently overlap. The rules of misrepresentation come into effect when one party can show that the mistake was a direct result of being misled by the other party. Remedies are available to victims of misrepresentation which are unavailable to those suffering from mistake. It is necessary to show that the mistake destroyed the very foundation of the contract to escape a contract on the basis of mistake. But the person claiming misrepresentation needs only to show that he or she had been misled about some material or important aspect of the contract to receive a remedy. Some other qualifications to this principle must also be considered.

Allegation of Fact

Misrepresentation must be fact not opinion—nor promise

The statement that forms the basis of the misrepresentation must be an allegation of fact. Only statements made about the current state of things which prove to be incorrect can be considered misrepresentation. A promise to do something in the future or a statement of opinion will not normally qualify as misrepresentation.

For example, the promise to paint a neighbour's house and then not doing so, or the statement that the neighbour's house is the nicest in the area are not actionable under misrepresentation. Even though they may be misleading, they involve statements of promise or opinion rather than statements of fact. However, if someone promises to do something in the future and it can be shown that he or she had no intention of fulfilling that promise at the time of making it, a misrepresentation has taken place. The person will be held liable for the promise. When an expert in the area covered by the contract gives an opinion on the matter being dealt with and the other party relies on this special knowledge, the opinion will be taken as an allegation of fact and will lead to a misrepresentation action. If a real estate appraiser states incorrectly that a home is worth more than any in the neighbourhood, such expert opinion can be misrepresentation. Also, if one of the parties expresses an incorrect view of some rule or interpretation of law, it will generally not be a misrepresentation unless that person is an expert, or made the statement knowing it was wrong.

Opinion by expert may be misrepresentation

Misrepresentation must be of fact, not law

Silence or Non-disclosure

Silence or non-disclosure is not usually actionable, but in some special situations, a duty to disclose information does exist. For example, insurance contracts require the parties acquiring insurance to disclose a great deal of personal information that affects the policy. People who apply for life insurance are required to disclose if they have had heart attacks or other medical problems, whether or not the question is specifically asked. The sale of new shares involves a similar obligation of disclosure to an investor in a prospectus. If the terms require that the parties disclose all information to each other as a condition of the agreement, the contract can be rescinded if they fail to do so. Professionals also have an obligation to disclose certain information at their disposal that might affect the actions of their clients.

Silence not misrepresentation unless there is a duty to disclose

Actions for misrepresentation may be available when one of the parties to a contract does something to hide the facts. A person anxious to sell a car might be tempted to hide a noisy transmission by using a heavier grade of oil, but such an act might well invite a claim of misrepresentation. It is not necessary that the statement be written or verbal; misrepresentation can occur even if the method of communicating it is a gesture such as a nod of the head. Misrepresentation is normally only available as a cause of action when an actual representation has been made. When individuals mislead themselves, *caveat emptor* applies and there is no cause for complaint. It is for this reason that the action against the vendors of the property infested by termites failed in the example used to introduce the chapter. Mr. Hoy, the purchaser, went to considerable trouble to inspect the property and so, in effect, misled himself about its condition. The vendors had made no representation in relation to it.

False Statement

It is not only necessary to demonstrate that the misleading comment qualifies as an allegation of fact but it must also be shown that the statement is incorrect and untrue. Even when a person technically tells the truth but withholds information that would have created an entirely different impression, this can amount to misrepresentation. For example, if a used car salesperson tells a potential purchaser that

Partial disclosure may be misrepresentation

the transmission of a particular car has just been replaced but fails to say it was replaced with a used transmission, this partial truth can be misrepresentation.

Statement Must Be Inducement

A victim of misrepresentation must show that he or she was induced into entering a contract by a false statement. If the victim knew that the statement was false and entered into the agreement anyway, either because he or she did not believe the statement or it did not make any difference, the misrepresentation is not actionable. Similarly, if the person thought the statement was true but would have entered into the contract even if he or she had known it was false, there is no misrepresentation. The false statement must affect the outcome of the agreement and the victim must have been misled into doing something that he or she otherwise would not have done for there to be an actionable misrepresentation.

As a Term of the Contract

If the misleading statement complained of has become a term of the agreement, the normal rules of breach of contract apply. If Osterman agreed to sell Nasser a 1957 Ford Thunderbird for $10 000 but the car turned out to be a 1957 Ford Fairlane, Nasser is free to sue Osterman for breach of contract. But if a person bought a particular property because the vendor said that the municipal council had voted to build a new highway nearby, it would be a rare contract that would include such a provision as a term of the agreement. Because the statement is an inducement to buy, not a term of the contract, the victim must rely on the rules of misrepresentation to obtain a remedy. The remedies available will depend on whether the statement was made inadvertently, fraudulently or negligently.

Even so, the courts today are more open to the suggestion that such representations have become terms of the contract. As a result contracts often have terms stating that there are no other representations other than those in the written agreement. Many provinces in their consumer protection legislation not only have provisions controlling misleading and deceptive trade practices but also state that the representations of salespeople are specifically made part of the contract.[14] The topic of consumer protection legislation will be discussed in a subsequent chapter.

Innocent Misrepresentation

An innocent misrepresentation is a false statement which the person who made it honestly believes to be true. Because the person making the misrepresentation is in no way at fault, remedies are limited. The only recourse available to the victim is to ask for rescission. As soon as the victim realizes what has happened, he or she can either choose to ignore the misrepresentation and affirm the contract or rescind the contract.

Rescission.

Rescission returns both parties to their original positions; the subject matter of the contract must be returned to the original owner and any monies paid under the contract must also be returned. The courts will also require the party who is returning the subject matter of the contract to return any benefit derived from the property

14. For example, s. 4 of the *Direct Sales Cancellation Act*, R.S.A. (1980) c. D-35, states that any representations made by salespeople are deemed to have been made by them as agents of the seller.

while it was in his or her possession. Similarly, a person can be compensated for any expenses incurred. Damages are not available as remedies because both parties are innocent. Although rescission is an important remedy, because it is equitable, it is quite restricted in its application. Rescission is not available in the following situations:

1. *Affirmation.* Victims of misrepresentation who have affirmed the contract are bound by the affirmation and cannot later insist on rescission.

2. *Impossible to restore.* The remedy of rescission is not available if the parties cannot be returned to their original positions because the subject matter of the contract has been destroyed or damaged. Since neither party is at fault with innocent misrepresentation, the court will not impose a burden on either one of them but will simply deny a remedy.

3. *Third-party involvement.* Rescission will not be granted if it will adversely affect the position of a third party. When the subject matter of the contract has been resold by the purchaser to a third party who has no knowledge of the misrepresentation and otherwise comes to the transaction with clean hands, the courts will not interfere with that person's possession and title to the goods.

> Rescission not available if contract affirmed
>
> —restoration impossible
>
> —or it will affect third party

Fraudulent Misrepresentation

If a misrepresentation of fact is intentional and induces another person to enter into a contract, the victim of the fraud can sue for damages under the tort of deceit in addition to seeking the remedy of rescission. The problem with fraudulent misrepresentation is to determine just how intentional the false statement has to be. In the case of *Derry v. Peek*,[15] it was established that fraud has taken place when the false statement was made "1) knowingly, or 2) without belief in its truth or 3) recklessly careless whether it be true or false."[16] There have been some difficulties over the years in interpreting just what these words mean, but essentially it is fraud if it can be demonstrated that the person who made the false statement does not honestly believe it to be true. The persons making the statement cannot avoid responsibility by claiming they did not know that what they said was false or because they did not bother to find out the truth. Even if the victim of the misrepresentation could have found out the truth easily but relied instead on the statement of the defendant, there is still fraud. There is no onus on the victim of the misrepresentation to check the truthfulness of the other party.

When a person innocently makes a false statement and later discovers the mistake, he or she must without delay inform the other person of the misrepresentation. Failure to do so will turn an innocent misrepresentation into a fraud. A person who, during the process of negotiating the terms of a contract, makes a statement which was true but, because of changing circumstances, later becomes false must correct the statement upon finding out the truth.

Once it has been established that the false statement was intentional and thus fraudulent, the courts can award rescission or damages:

1. *Rescission or avoidance.* The victim of fraudulent misrepresentation retains the right to have the parties to the contract returned to their original positions and to be reimbursed for any out-of-pocket expenses.

> Rescission and/or damages for torts are remedies for intentional misrepresentation

> Remedies for fraudulent misrepresentation– rescission

15. *Derry v. Peek* (1889) 14 App. Cas. 374 (House of Lords).
16. *Ibid.*, p. 374.

• damages

2. *Damages for deceit.* The victim of fraudulent misrepresentation can seek rescission as well as monetary compensation for any loss incurred as a result of the fraud. When damages are awarded the courts try to put the victim in the position he or she would have been in had the contract not been entered into. Note that no property is being returned and that the courts are not attempting to return both parties to their original positions, as with rescission. Rather, the courts try to compensate the victim financially for the loss suffered; this payment is made at the expense of the person who is at fault. A victim of fraud can seek damages even after the contract has been affirmed. The victim does not lose the right to demand monetary compensation simply by giving up the right to claim rescission. On rare occasions the victim of a fraudulent misrepresentation can seek punitive damages, that is, damages intended to punish the wrongdoer rather than compensate the victim.

Contract void when
consensus destroyed

Whether the misrepresentation is innocent or fraudulent, the contract itself can be considered void if the misrepresentation is serious enough to cause the victim to make a mistake that goes to the very foundation of the agreement and destroys consensus. For example, if the false statement causes the victim to make a mistake about the identity of the other party or the nature of the agreement, the contract can be declared void. A void contract means that there never was a contract. If the contract involved the sale of property which was resold to a third party, it will be returned to the original owner because the person from whom it was obtained did not have title to convey. Note that in the Metropolitan Stores case discussed above they went even further and awarded rectification (rewriting) of the contract as a remedy.

Negligent Misrepresentation

Until relatively recently, it was thought that negligent misrepresentation when fraud was not involved must be treated the same as innocent misrepresentation. Thus the remedies were limited to rescission.

Damages may be available
in cases of negligent
misrepresentation

However, since the decisions of the House of Lords in *Hedley Byrne & Co. Ltd. v. Heller & Partners,* Ltd.,[17] the Supreme Court of Canada in the case of *Haig v. Bamford,*[18] and subsequent related cases, it appears that if it can be shown that the parties should have known what they said was false even though they honestly believed it was true, then the rules and remedies discussed in Chapter 2 under the tort of negligence apply and damages will be available. Even when the negligent statement becomes a term of the contract or arises out of a contractual relationship, the plaintiff may have a choice about whether to sue in contract or sue in tort for negligence. The Supreme Court of Canada made it clear that such "concurrent liability" may exist, although with some important limitations such as not permitting the plaintiff to circumvent the protection provided in an exemption clause by suing in tort instead.[19] Of course, when the misrepresentation has become a term of the contract and a breach results, damages as well as other contractual remedies are available.[20] It should also be noted that if a breach of contract can be established, damages are one of the remedies available. Thus, it appears that only when the misrepresentation is truly innocent and without fault is the victim restricted to the remedy of rescission.

17. *Hedley Byrne v. Heller* [1963] 2 All E.R. 575 (House of Lords).

18. *Haig v. Bamford* (1976) 72 D.L.R. (3d) 68 (Supreme Court of Canada).

19. *Central Trust Co. v. Rafuse et al.* (1986) 31 D.L.R. (4th) 481 (S.C.C.). and *B. G. Checo v. B.C. Hydro* (1993) 99 D.L.R. (4th) 577.

20. *Beaufort Realties v. Chomedey Aluminum Co.* (1981) 116 D.L.R. (3d) 193 (N.B.C.A.).

DURESS RESULTS IN VOIDABLE CONTRACT

Through a complicated series of transactions, a family made arrangements to develop several hectares of land owned by the parents. Serious difficulties arose between the parties, and a son threatened physical harm to one of his siblings. Fearing that threat, which was not taken seriously by the sibling, the parents conveyed certain properties and created other advantages for the son. When an action was brought to enforce the agreement made by the parents and the defense of duress was raised, the trial court found the contract void on that basis. However, the Court of Appeal reversed this, finding the contract voidable. The distinction is important: a void contract is no contract, and nothing done by the parties can give it life afterwards; if a contract is voidable, however, the conduct of the victims can revive it if they continue to perform its terms after the duress has passed. But the Court, though it found the contract voidable rather than void, did not find affirmation of the contract in the conduct of the parents, for they had not known they had the right to rescind the contract until the two years had passed. This case also points out the fact that when duress is involved, the force or threat does not have to be directed at the other party in the contract; it can be directed at some other person.

Byle v. Byle, 65 D.L.R. (4th) 641 (British Columbia Court of Appeal)

DURESS AND UNDUE INFLUENCE

Duress

When people are forced or pressured to enter into contracts against their will by threats of violence or imprisonment, duress is present and the contracts are voidable. The person who used duress is bound by the contract but the injured party may have the contract set aside.

Duress involves threats of violence or imprisonment—contract voidable

Originally, the definition of duress was limited to situations in which there were actual threats of violence or imprisonment, but the courts of chancery expanded this definition to include threats of criminal prosecution and threats to disclose embarrassing or scandalous information.

In Canada, duress has been expanded further to include threats to a person's goods or property. A person who is unlawfully in possession of property belonging to another and uses that possession as a lever to force the rightful owner of the property to enter a disadvantageous agreement would find that the resulting contract is voidable due to duress. If O'Rourke threatened to run a lawnmower borrowed from Tong over rocky ground unless Tong sold him a particular plant he had grown, this would qualify as duress in Canada. To succeed, it is necessary to show that the threat was the main inducement for entering into the agreement.

Even though the threat of loss of employment and other financial losses can amount to economic duress and be actionable, it is important not to mistake the normal predicaments in which we all find ourselves for improper pressure or duress. If a person has no choice except to use a particular taxi because it is the only one on the street or has to deal with the only airline or telephone company that services a particular area, these accepted conditions of the marketplace do not amount to duress. Even the threat of suing when the person doing so has a legitimate right to sue is not duress. Rather, it is the legitimate exercise of the rights of that person.

Economic advantage not enough

A third party's position cannot be jeopardized if the victim of duress seeks a remedy. Thus, if a purchaser improperly pressures someone into selling a gold watch and then resells that watch to an innocent third party, the watch cannot be

Voidable contract cannot affect third parties

retrieved. Because a voidable contract is still a contract, the title is passed on to the third party. Had the watch been stolen from the original owner and then sold to an innocent third party, the original owner would not have given up title to the watch and could, therefore, retrieve it.

Undue Influence

The types of pressure brought to bear on people are often more subtle than those described by duress. When pressure from a dominant, trusted person makes it impossible to bargain freely, it is regarded as undue influence and the resulting contract or gift is voidable. Because it is sometimes difficult to prove that a person was improperly pressured to enter into a contract, the courts have developed rules to establish the existence of undue influence. Certain categories of relationships result in a presumption of undue influence and if the presumption is not rebutted the contract will be set aside. These categories are:

1. Adult contracting with infant child or adult contracting with parent with mental disability

2. Solicitor contracting with client

3. Doctor contracting with patient

4. Religious advisor contracting with parishioner

5. Trustee contracting with beneficiary

6. Guardian contracting with ward

Of these relationships, the religious relationship seems to be one of the most suspect in the opinion of the courts. In the case of *Allcard v. Skinner*,[21] a woman entered a religious order and gave it all her property. The court determined that there had been undue influence when the contract was entered into and would have set the contract aside except that she had affirmed the contract after leaving the relationship. It is interesting to note that in this case there was clear evidence that there had been no overt attempt on the part of the religious order to influence this

UNDUE INFLUENCE PRESUMED

Barney was a friend and client of John Farlow, a solicitor, and in the past had lent him money. In this transaction, Farlow persuaded Barney to guarantee a loan of $50 000 he was getting from the Rochdale Credit Union. Barney did so reluctantly. Farlow died and the credit union demanded payment from Barney. The Ontario Court of Appeal found undue influence on the part of Farlow in persuading his client to guarantee the loan and because Farlow rep-resented both parties, the credit union was also responsible for that undue influence and Barney did not have to pay the debt. The case illustrates how in transactions between solicitor and client undue influence is presumed but it is also interesting because the third party, Rochdale Credit Union, is affected by that presumption.

Rochdale Credit Union Ltd. v. Barney, 14 D.L.R. (4th) 116 (Ontario Court of Appeal)

---

21. *Allcard v. Skinner* (1887) 36 Ch.D. 145 (Court of Appeal).

woman, but the court decided that the situation itself had robbed her of her ability to act voluntarily.

In the above relationships, the presumption of undue influence is automatic, and it is up to the other contracting party to overcome that presumption if the contract is to be binding. Note that as a general rule, parents contracting with adult children or husbands and wives contracting with each other are excluded from these categories.

If the relationship involved does not fall into one of the protected classes listed above, there can still be a finding of undue influence on the basis of unique circumstances. The court attempts to determine whether the surrounding circumstances cast doubt on the voluntariness of the agreement, in which case the court may still presume undue influence.

In other relationships, more evidence is needed for undue influence

A husband or a wife signing a guarantee for the indebtedness of their spouse might be such a situation. If the court makes that presumption, it falls on the party trying to enforce the contract to show that there was no domination or unfair advantage taken of the other party. When the relationship does not fall into the special categories and it is not possible to presume undue influence from the unique circumstances, parties trying to escape contracts may still present evidence to satisfy the court that undue influence was in fact exerted and that they were coerced. This can be difficult to prove since the victim must show that a relationship of trust developed because of the relationship between the contracting parties, and that that trust was abused. When it can be shown that the person trying to enforce the contract took advantage of the fact that he or she was being relied on for advice, the courts may find that there was undue influence. Even when undue influence has been established, the contract will be binding if the person trying to enforce the contract can show that the undue influence was overcome and that the victim either affirmed the contract or did nothing to rescind it after escaping the relationship. The courts may refuse a remedy if the person trying to escape the contract is not altogether innocent of wrongdoing.

It is advisable for contracting parties who are concerned with this problem to get legal advice before entering into an agreement. When it can be demonstrated that the potential victim followed independent legal advice, it is very likely that the courts will enforce the agreement. It must be stressed that the terms of the agreement must be reasonable in such circumstances. The courts will resist enforcing a contract that conveys great advantage to one of the parties, whether or not legal advice has been taken.

Independent legal advice desirable, but contract must be fair

Unconscionable Transactions

Woods v. Hubley

This is also a case dealing with an insurance company and a person injured in an automobile accident. Mrs. Woods was a passenger in a car driven by her mother when it was struck from behind and extensively damaged by a car owned by Brenda Hubley and driven by Michael Hubley. There was no question but that the Hubleys were responsible. Mrs. Woods suffered pain in her back and neck area for which she eventually had to have surgery to repair the spinal injury.

About a week before the surgery the insurance adjuster contacted her by telephone offering her a $3500 settlement—"Take it or leave it"—and she agreed, signed a release and was paid the $3500. Unfortunately, even after the operation, her condition got worse and she brought an application to the court to have the release set aside. This was done and she was awarded damages of over $500 000.

Several problems had faced the court. First, there was a question of whether the release could be set aside, whether damages could be awarded when the limitation period had expired, and finally, the amount of damages that ought to be awarded. On appeal those three issues had to be dealt with again, and the appeal court decided that the release that she signed along with the agreement should be set aside on the basis of "unconscionability." She had been taken advantage of. In fact, the trial judge found that the adjuster had deceived and misled Mrs. Woods and prevented her from having a fair opportunity to consult a lawyer. "He effectively dissuaded her from seeking the services of a lawyer, thereby taking advantage of her ignorance and her need." The trial judge quoted Hallet J. from the case of *Stevenson v. Hilty (Canada Ltd.)* where he found that a transaction can be set aside as unconscionable where the evidence shows (1) that there is an inequality in the bargaining positions of the parties arising out of ignorance, need or distress of the weaker party, (2) where the stronger party has consciously used the position of power to achieve an advantage and (3) the agreement reached is substantially unfair to the weaker party. These elements were established in this case, and therefore the settlement agreement was set aside.

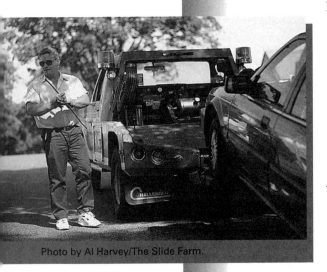

Photo by Al Harvey/The Slide Farm.

As far as the limitation defense is concerned, it is interesting to note that the act governing limitations in Nova Scotia (*Limitations of Actions Act*)[22] generally gives the judge considerable discretion to decide to waive it where not to do so would considerably prejudice the plaintiff. For this reason the limitation was waived. The appeal court did not interfere with the amount of damages awarded.

This case illustrates the direction that the principle of unconscionability is going and that many transactions found to be unfair and prejudicial to one of the parties are set aside on the basis of "unconscionability" as discussed below.

Contract may be unconscionable and voidable if parties in unequal bargaining positions

The concept of **unconscionable transactions** has received a greater acceptance by courts in recent years. This is an equitable doctrine that permits the court to set aside a contract in which one party has been taken advantage of because of factors such as desperation caused by poverty or intellectual impairment that falls short of incapacity. To escape from such a contract, it must be shown that the bargaining positions of the parties were unequal, that one party dominated and took advantage of the other, and that the consideration involved was grossly unfair.

In fact the courts are showing a willingness to expand this concept and apply it in situations where they feel an injustice has been done or where the results of the agreement are simply unfair as was in *Woods v. Hubley* discussed above. It must be remembered that simple economic advantage will not qualify. If a person having limited assets can't get a loan from anyone else and must pay 20 percent interest, that in itself will not make the contract unconscionable. There must be evidence that the debtor was taken advantage of because of some problem such as lack of sophistication, age, or desperation and then it must be shown that the resulting deal was not

22. R.S.N.S. (1989) c. 258.

reasonable. If the 20 percent interest charged was reasonable given the risk, the contract is not unconscionable.

There is some overlap in the principles of unconscionable transactions and undue influence. Although legislation has been passed in most common law provinces prohibiting unconscionable transactions, in most instances the statutory provisions are limited to loan transactions.[23] The recent acceptance of this equitable doctrine developed by the courts makes the defense of unconscionability available even when the contracts in question do not involve the loan of money.

PRIVITY OF CONTRACT AND ASSIGNMENT

Privity

When two parties enter into a contract, they create a world of law unto themselves. Contracting is a bargaining process and only those participating in the bargain can be affected by it. It is a fundamental principle of contract law that the parties to a contract do not have the power to impose benefits or obligations on third parties or outsiders who are not parties to the contract. The contracting parties have created a private agreement and outsiders to it can neither enforce it nor be bound to perform its terms. This principle is called privity of contract.

Contract only affects parties to it

The case of *Donoghue v. Stevenson*[24] referred to in Chapter 2 illustrates the application of the privity principle. In that case, a woman bought a bottle of ginger beer with a decomposed snail in it for her friend. Because the person who bought the ginger beer was not the person who consumed it, the victim could not sue the owner of the café for breach of contract since there was no contract between them. Under normal circumstances, merchants can be sued for breach of contract for selling faulty products even though they are unaware of the problem. If there is no contract, the victim must sue the manufacturer in tort for negligence, not for breach of contract.

Exceptions—Apparent and Real

Privity has caused some severe difficulties in normal commercial relationships and, therefore, there are several exceptions to the rule of privity of contract, both real and apparent. Note that our law clearly establishes that the original two parties to the contract can enforce the terms when they bestow a benefit on a third party even though the third party cannot enforce the contract. Thus, if Aguilar agrees with Balzer to mow Carriere's lawn, Carriere cannot enforce the agreement but Balzer certainly can. The court may provide either damages or money compensation calculated on the basis of what it would cost to have somebody else mow the lawn.

Original party to contract can enforce it where benefit to be bestowed on outsider

The original contracting parties are also free to enter into a new agreement which changes the terms of their original contract. A **novation** is an example of such a change and takes place when a new party is substituted for one of the original parties to the contract. This does not violate the rule of privity since the original parties must both agree to such a change, although such agreement is sometimes inferred from the conduct of the parties. These examples are only apparent exceptions to the privity rule.

Novation involves new agreement

23. See, for example, the *Unconscionable Transactions Act*, R.S.A. (1980) c. U-2.
24. *Donoghue v. Stevenson* [1932] A.C. 562 (House of Lords).

Land.

Where interest in land involved, rights run with land

The principles of real property law have developed independently of contract law, resulting in major differences. One such difference is that the rights created usually run with the land instead of with the parties and the concept of privity does not apply. Restrictions and obligations tied to the property, even those which have been entered into by contract with some other outside party, are binding on the new purchaser when property is transferred or sold. An easement, the right someone has to cross or be on the property, is binding on any subsequent owner of that property. Similarly, even if the purchaser of a building is unaware of a tenant occupying a leased apartment, the purchaser is bound by that lease and cannot evict the tenant.

Obligation to register interest

Much of this area of land law is now covered by provincial statutes which impose obligations to register these interests.[25]

Agency.

Agents create contracts between principal and third party

Agency involves the creation of contractual relations between a principal and a third party through the services of a go-between called an agent. Although all of the arrangements may have been made by the agent, the contract is created between the principal and the third party, so this is not a true exception to the privity rule. For example, when a person goes to a department store to buy a jacket, the purchase will be arranged by a sales clerk. The clerk will write down the terms of the agreement and receive payment for the merchandise, but the contract is between the store and the individual buying the jacket. The sales clerk merely acts as an intermediary

—but limited by authority

or an agent. However, if the clerk tried to sell the store, the contract would not be binding because such an action would be beyond the authority given to the clerk. If dissatisfied, the third party or customer would sue the principal, the department store. The only circumstance in which the third party can sue the agent is when the agent has gone beyond his or her authority. The topic of agency will be discussed in a subsequent chapter.

Trusts.

A difficult problem to resolve under common law was a situation in which someone wanted to transfer the benefits flowing from owning property to a third party while conveying the property itself to someone else. The courts of chancery created the

Trusts allow a third party to benefit from the property of another

concept of **trust** to deal with such situations. A trust involves three people: the person conveying the property, called the settlor; the person looking after the property, called the trustee; and the person benefiting from the trust, often called the beneficiary. Trusts allow people to bestow benefits on third parties through contracts which have been created with other parties.

Beneficiary can enforce trust agreement against trustee

The effect of a trust is that the beneficiaries will be able to enforce their rights under that trust. Beneficiaries can force their trustees to make appropriate payments. Trusts are often created by people who want to ensure that their family is adequately taken care of after their death. If the rules of privity applied, trustees would be in a position to keep the property which they had been given only to take care of once the creator of the trust died. The third party, or outsider to the agreement, would not be able to enforce that agreement. This would be an entirely unfair result. An exception to the privity rule was created and beneficiaries are able to enforce trusts.

25. See, for example, the *Land Titles Act,* R.S.A. (1980) c. L-5, which sets out the registration requirements, if any, for different interests in land, and the effect of registration.

A similar situation exists with life insurance policies. By statute, the beneficiary of such a policy can force the insurance company to pay even though the person they had originally contracted with, the insured, is dead.[26]

Beneficiary can enforce insurance contract

The Supreme Court of Canada has created another potentially important exception to the privity of contract rule. It is clear that, even when the relationship involved is based on contract, an injured party can sue for breach of contract as well as in tort for negligence when the circumstances are appropriate. It is normal for the parties to a contract to include terms in their agreement called exculpatory clauses that have the effect of limiting their liability. This limitation would apply if one party was suing the other party to the contract for breach of contract or for negligence by the other party.

Employees protected by exculpatory clauses

This was the case in *London Drugs Ltd. v. Kuehne & Nagel International Ltd.*[27] In this case, a clause in the contract limited liability to only $40 maximum. Kuehne & Nagel had contracted with London Drugs to store a large transformer and, because of mishandling by their employees, that transformer suffered significant damage. It was clear that the plaintiff could not recover from Kuehne & Nagel because of the $40 exculpatory clause and so sued their employees instead in tort for negligence, since they were the ones who had actually caused the damage. Applying the privity principle, the $40 exculpatory clause could be used to limit the liability of the other party to the contract, Kuehne & Nagel, but not their employees who were not party to the contract. The Supreme Court had to decide whether it would make an exception to the privity rule and extend the protection created by this exculpatory clause to the employees of Kuehne & Nagel.

The decision of the Supreme Court of Canada to override the privity rule and give the employees the protection of an exculpatory clause in a contract to which they were not a party is a significant departure. It may become even more important if this is in an indication of a willingness on the part of the Supreme Court to depart from privity in other circumstances as well.

Another area where the rule of privity of contract may be breaking down is in the field of product liability. In *Donoghue v. Stevenson*[28] the consumer of the ginger beer could not sue the merchant because she was not the one who purchased it and there was no contract between them. Some provinces have passed legislation allowing the consumer of such products to sue the seller in contract law where the defective product causes injury even when the injured person is not the purchaser and not party to the contract. The courts have also extended the right to sue in contract law in product liability cases by finding collateral contracts created by advertising brochures giving the purchaser a right to seek redress in contract law back past the retailer to the manufacturer. These topics will be discussed in Chapter 7 under "Consumer Protection Legislation."

Assignment

Just as a person buying goods under a contract is then free to resell them, so can a person receiving a benefit under a contract transfer that benefit to a third party. This is called the **assignment of contractual rights** and the benefit transferred is known as a **chose in action**. While the practice of transferring such rights was originally not permitted because of privity, it is now an essential part of our commercial world.

Contracting party can assign rights

26. See, for example, s. 264 of the *Insurance Act,* R.S.A. (1980) c. I-5.

27. *London Drugs Ltd. v. Kuehne & Nagel International Ltd.* [1993] 1 W.W.R. 1 (S.C.C.).

28. *Supra.*

With assignment the contract itself does not bestow a benefit on a third party as discussed above; rather, assignment involves the transfer of a right or benefit after the right to the benefit has been obtained in the contract from the other party. The contract itself makes no reference to this subsequent transaction. In such a transaction, of the original parties to the contract the one transferring the rights and claims derived under it is called the **assignor** and the outsider to whom those rights are being conveyed is the **assignee**.

For example, Joe bought a car from Sam's Used Cars, agreeing to make a series of payments at a set rate of interest, and then Sam, for a price, transferred or assigned that benefit (the right to receive series of payments and interest) to Daisy Finance. In these circumstances Joe might be surprised at the change but must now make his payments to Daisy, not Sam.

It must be emphasized that only the benefits or claims under a contract can be assigned, not the obligations. In this example, if the car broke down Joe would still have recourse against Sam the seller no matter what kind of deal Sam made with Daisy. The assignor cannot escape contract responsibilities by transferring them to an assignee in this way.

Historically, the third party—Daisy in this example—could not enforce her claim directly against the debtor. If not paid she had to get the original party (the assignor) to enforce the contract. What actually happened was that the assignee would sue the original party, but would have to "join" the assignor as a party to that action, so in effect they both were suing. While this is effective, it is a very cumbersome process and legislation has been passed allowing such an assignee of contractual right to enforce those rights directly. This is referred to as a **statutory assignment**. The statute simply states that when certain qualifications are met, the assignee of the contractual rights has the right to enforce that claim directly against the debtor rather than having to join the assignor in the action as a party to it. The qualifications that must be met are:

Qualifications for statutory assignment

1. The assignment must be absolute and unconditional. This means that if the assignor is owed $500 by the debtor, the entire $500 claim must be assigned to the assignee, not part of it. The assignment must also be complete; it cannot be used merely as a security.

2. The assignment must be in writing with adequate identification of the parties, the amounts involved and the signature of the assignor.

3. Proper notice of the assignment in writing must be given to the original debtor and that notice must contain all the pertinent information, including the names of the parties.

When these qualifications are met, the assignee can sue the debtor directly. The common law provinces of Canada have all adopted a version of this legislation.[29]

If any of these qualifications are not met, it is still possible to enforce the agreement indirectly by joining the assignor in the action as described above. This is called an **equitable assignment**. For example, Chadha owes Ace Rental Co. $500 for the use of equipment. Ace Rental Co. is not really in the business of lending money and so assigns that $500 debt to Wolanski Finance Co. This process is called factoring of accounts receivable. If the assignment is complete, meaning the entire $500 debt has been assigned; the assignment is in writing and is signed by the appropriate

---

29. In Alberta, the relevant legislation is the *Judicature Act*, R.S.A. (1980) c. J-1, s. 21.

officer of Ace Rental Co.; and written notice has been given to Chadha, then Wolanski Finance Co. can enforce the debt directly. Thus, Wolanski Finance Co. can sue Chadha in its own right if he fails to make his payments.

But if these requirements are not met, Wolanski Finance Co. is not able to sue Chadha directly in the event of default. Rather, it is forced to join with Ace Rental Co. as a party to the action and, in effect, ride on the coattails of Ace Rental's suit to force Chadha to pay. Great care should be taken in business transactions of this nature to make sure all the qualifications are met, because it is much easier to proceed with a statutory assignment. One of the reasons statutory assignment is possible, in the face of the privity of contract doctrine, is because the contract itself is not being assigned; rather, only the rights derived under the contract are being transferred to a stranger or outsider.

Some things, by their very nature, cannot be assigned. Any claim for maintenance or alimony which might cause the assignor to become destitute and certain claims against government bodies cannot be assigned.[30] In other circumstances, the contract itself may prohibit assignment. In these cases, the assignee has obtained no rights under the contract and the debtor would be well advised to pay the money to the court and let the court decide who should receive the funds.

Another important area of prohibited assignments developed out of the concept of **champerty**, or selling the right to sue. In an attempt to discourage wholesale litigation and abuse of court procedures, laws were established to discourage people from buying and selling the right to sue. The assignment of the right to litigate is invalid. For example, a person whose foot has been run over by another cannot sell the right to sue to a third person but would have to proceed with the action personally. However, the award of damages set out in the court order does create an obligation which can be assigned.

In some situations, the consent of the other contracting party must be obtained before an assignment can be made, especially when personal skill and knowledge are involved in the performance of the contract. It is important to note that only the advantages or rights obtained under a contract can be assigned, not the obligations. If one party has obtained a contract to paint a house, the payment to be derived under the contract may be assigned but the obligation to paint the house remains the responsibility of the contracting party. That is not to say, however, that it must be performed personally. In many situations, it does not matter whether the person who contracted performs the contracted duties personally or not. For example, a builder may subcontract many construction jobs such as framing, bricklaying, plumbing or electrical work. This is called **vicarious performance** and is permissible as long as the contract is of such a nature that personal performance is not required. However, if an impresario contracted with a famous performer to appear at the National Arts Centre and that performer sent an understudy instead, the impresario would be able to sue, even if it could be demonstrated that the understudy was just as good. In such circumstances, personal performance by the contracting party is required.

It is vitally important to realize that the assignee is in no better position than was the original party to the contract, whether the assignment is statutory or equitable. The expression used to describe this circumstance is that the assignee is subject to the equities between the original parties. If the right or claim that the original party to the contract had was tainted in some way, then the assignee obtains tainted

Some things cannot be assigned

• the right to sue

• or in the case of skillful performance, consent required

Assignee subject to equities at time of notice of assignment

30. See, for example, s. 135 of the *Workers' Compensation Act,* S.A. (1981) c. W-16, which states that workers' compensation benefits may not be assigned without the approval of the Workers' Compensation Board.

rights. If a fraud involved in the original agreement would have given the original debtor a good defense if sued by the assignor, the debtor has the same defense when sued by the assignee. If the assignor has committed fraud or failed to perform the contract properly, or if the original debtor can establish another independent claim against the assignor's claim, these issues can all be raised as defenses against the assignee's claim as well. Being subject to the equities between the original parties is a significant limitation on the power of the assignee to enforce any claims on the contract.

Subsequent claims do not affect assigneec

To eliminate the possibility that any subsequent claims might arise between the original parties and unfairly undercut the position of the assignee, a qualification has been developed to provide more equitable results. The general rule is that with a statutory assignment the rights or equities the assignee is subject to are determined when the debtor receives notice of the assignment. Any subsequent rights or claims arising between those parties, except those dealing with the performance of the contract itself, will not affect the rights or claims of the assignee.

A return to the example of the Ace Rental Co.'s assignment of Chadha's $500 debt to Wolanski Finance Co. will illustrate this point. Suppose Chadha defaulted on the debt and is sued by Wolanski Finance Co. and his defense is that he did not pay because the equipment rented did not live up to Ace Rental Co.'s guarantee. Wolanski Finance Co. would not be able to enforce the debt against Chadha. Chadha's defense against Ace Rental Co. is good because the company failed to fulfill its contractual obligation. The claim Ace Rental has against Chadha is tainted. Wolanski Finance has obtained tainted rights and is in no better position to enforce the debt than Ace Rental would have been.

If, after the notice of the assignment of the debt to Wolanski Finance, Chadha did some work for Ace Rental for which he was not paid, Chadha could not raise this as a defense when sued by Wolanski Finance for the original $500. Chadha's claim for wages arose after he received notice of the assignment and, therefore, will not affect the position of Wolanski Finance. On the other hand, if a debtor chooses to ignore a notice of assignment, he or she assumes the risk of having to make all future payments to the assignee. If the debtor continues to pay the original assignor, he or she will still be required to pay the entire amount owing to the assignee. Notice of assignment should never be treated lightly.[31]

Debtor must pay first who gives notice of assignment

The notice given by the assignee to the debtor serves another important purpose. A company in financial difficulty might be tempted to fraudulently assign the same claim against a debtor to several different assignees. In such circumstances, priority is determined by the order in which the debtor receives the notices. A qualification on this rule is the principle that one assignee cannot gain priority over another by giving notice while knowing of the existence of a prior claim. Only assignees who are ignorant of any other attempts to assign can obtain priority by giving notice to the debtor of the assignment.

Involuntary assignment in cases of death and bankruptcy

The principles discussed so far relate to voluntary assignments. There are some circumstances in which the assignment of rights can take place involuntarily. For example, rights and obligations are automatically transferred to the administrator or executor of the estate when a person dies. This representative steps into the deceased's shoes and is not restricted by the privity of contract rule unless the terms of the contract require personal performance by the deceased. The second situation of involuntary assignment is when a party to a contract goes bankrupt. Under bankruptcy legislation, all of the bankrupt's assets are transferred to a

31. Rights of an assignee and the consequences of notice are also dealt with in the *Personal Property Security Act*, S.A. (1988) c. P-4.05, s.41.

trustee called the receiver who will then distribute them to pay the creditors as much as possible.

Negotiable Instruments

Another exception to the privity of contract rule recognizes the commercial realities of modern business. As commerce developed, it became necessary to devise a method to freely exchange and pass on claims for debt which had been incurred in the process of business. When these claims met certain qualifications, they were defined as **negotiable instruments** and through them unique rights were bestowed on the parties.

These rights will be discussed in detail in Chapter 9. Briefly, the negotiable instrument could be freely passed from one person to another, conveying with it all the rights associated with the original agreement between the parties, and no notice of the transaction would be required. This flexibility is completely inconsistent with the doctrine of privity of contract and the law of assignment discussed above. The most significant innovation of negotiable instruments was that better rights or claims than those held by the initial parties could be passed on. As discussed under assignment, it was clear that even when it was possible to assign contractual rights, the assignee was subject to whatever equities existed between the original two parties. Thus, if a defense such as fraud was available against the original party to the contract (the assignor) it was available against the assignee as well. This is not the case with negotiable instruments. Even when a defense of fraud is available against the initial party to a transaction, a third party to a negotiable instrument who satisfies the qualifications to be a "holder in due course" can enforce the contract despite the existence of the fraud.

> Negotiable instruments true exception to privity

> Negotiable instruments give rights to holder

SUMMARY

For a mistake to affect the validity of a contract, it must go to the nature of the agreement or the existence of the subject matter, not just to the effect of the agreement when performed. When both parties are making a common error as to the existence of the subject matter at the time the contract is made, there is no contract. If an error is made in recording the terms of the contract, it can be corrected by rectification. When the mistake is not shared but there is a misunderstanding between the parties, the court will adopt the most reasonable interpretation of the contract. When the mistake is one-sided, *caveat emptor* applies unless the mistake is so fundamental as to destroy consensus between the parties.

When a person is induced to enter into a contract by a false statement, such a misrepresentation is actionable. When the misrepresentation is innocent, the remedy is rescission. When the misrepresentation is fraudulent, the victim may sue for damages for the tort of deceit. Damages may also be available when negligence can be demonstrated. When duress or undue influence is involved, the contract is voidable.

Under privity of contract, only the original parties to the contract are bound. Any benefit going to a third party must be enforced by the original party to the agreement. A novation is when a new party is substituted for one of the original parties and is enforceable only when there has been agreement by all. Contracts dealing with interests in land create rights that flow with the land. Agency arrangements involve contracts between the principal and a third party, the agent acting merely as a go-between. The trust is a true exception to the privity rule because the beneficiary can enforce it even though he or she is not a party to the original agreement. Under assignment, only the benefits, not the obligations, in a contract can be sold (assigned) to a third party and those benefits must be enforced through the original contracting party, the assignor. Only when it qualifies as a statutory assignment can the assignee enforce the assigned rights directly.

QUESTIONS

1. Distinguish between a mistake about the effect of a contract and a mistake about its nature. Explain the significance of this distinction.

2. Distinguish mistake, shared mistake, misunderstanding, and one-sided mistake.

3. What approach will the courts usually take when the mistake involves disagreement about the meaning of the contract?

4. What bias will the court display in choosing between two equally reasonable interpretations of vague wording in a contract?

5. Explain the parol evidence rule.

6. What must a party to a contract show to obtain rectification of a document?

7. Under what circumstances will a unilateral mistake cause a contract to be a nullity?

8. Under what circumstances would a person raise a claim of *non est factum*? What restrictions are there on its availability?

9. Explain what is meant by *caveat emptor*. What is this principle's significance in relation to unilateral mistake?

10. What happens when a misrepresentation becomes a term of the contract?

11. What is the distinction between fraudulent, negligent and innocent misrepresentation? Why is the distinction important?

12. Under what circumstances can silence or a statement of opinion become misrepresentation?

13. What factors may affect the availability of the remedy of rescission?

14. Describe the relationship between misrepresentation and mistake.

15. What is the significance of determining whether a contract is voidable rather than void?

16. Distinguish between duress and undue influence and give examples of each.

17. What is meant by privity of contract?

18. Explain what is meant by the term "novation."

19. Explain the relationship of the privity principle to land transactions, agency, trusts, assignment and the position of employees.

20. What qualifications must be realized before there can be a statutory assignment?

21. What limitations are placed on the rights and obligations of the assignee when a contract is assigned?

22. What is meant by "the assignee takes subject to the equities"? When is it appropriate to determine these equities?

23. What is the significance of a negotiable instrument in terms of the rights conveyed to third parties?

CASES

1. Chrispen v. Topham

The facts in this case are quite simple. A man and woman had agreed to live together in his house with the woman agreeing, in writing, to pay a monthly rent. About a year after this arrangement began, she left owing a considerable amount of unpaid rent. In this action, the man sued to recover the unpaid rent and other expenses in the amount of $3282.90. The woman, on the other hand, made a counterclaim saying that the parties had also agreed to share the domestic or household duties and that over the year the man had completely failed to perform any of these duties. She claimed that she was entitled to compensation in the amount of $3595.50. Explain what kinds of arguments the man in these circumstances can raise in defense and any responses to those arguments that the woman can raise.

2. Corporate Properties Ltd. v. Manufacturers Life Insurance Co.

In this case, Bloor West leased property from Manulife and in turn sublet that property to Corporate Properties Ltd. The arrangement was that Bloor West would pay Manulife a certain set percentage of its gross revenues that was earned from the property. Corporate Properties, which initially owned Bloor West but eventually through refinancing sold their interest, had agreed to a different calculation for paying rent to Bloor West. But Corporate Properties, instead of paying their rent to Bloor West, paid it directly to Manulife. Instead of basing the rental payment on what Bloor West earned from the property, they based it on what they earned from the property, which was considerably more—thus, from their perspective, creating an overpayment for a considerable period of time. When they discovered this in 1983, they demanded repayment of the overages paid. While the matter was in dispute, they, under protest, made further payments for the period between 1984 to 1986.

The ambiguity is whether the term "gross annual income" refers to that received by Bloor West or the income from the properties obtained by Corporate Properties. Certainly Corporate Properties treated it for years as if it referred to their gross income from the properties. Explain the arguments available to all of the parties and whether Manulife will have to repay these overpayments.

3. Hayward v. Mellick

Mellick had 59 hectares of land that he wanted to sell. In the process of negotiations with Hayward, he represented to Hayward that the farm had approximately 65 acres of workable farmland. Relying on this representation, Hayward purchased the farm and later learned that the farm had only 21 workable hectares. In fact, Mellick had never measured the farm and it was only his own personal belief that it had 26 workable hectares. But he never told Hayward that he was not sure. Hayward sued for compensation. Discuss the legal position of the parties. How would your answer be affected by the knowledge that the written contract included an exemption clause that stated, "It is agreed that there is no representation, warranty, collateral agreement or condition affecting this agreement or the real property or supported hereby other than as expressed herein, in writing"?

4. Junkin & Junkin v. Bedard & Bedard

Mr. and Mrs. Junkin hired an agent to sell their motel and told the agent that their gross revenue for the previous year was $16 000 and the net profit was $9700. The judge found that Mrs. Junkin knew this information was false and that she had given it to the agent to persuade prospective purchasers. This information was given to the Bedards, who relied on it when they decided to purchase. When they discovered that it was incorrect, they sued the Junkins asking for damages. Explain the likely outcome.

5. Pettit & Johnston v. Foster Wheeler Ltd.

Roderick Ashley Ltd. was supplying materials for Foster Wheeler Ltd. at a project at the University of Alberta in Edmonton. Mr. Pettit had supplied $14 000 worth of financing to Roderick Ashley Ltd. Pursuant to that agreement, Pettit took an assignment of all accounts of Roderick Ashley. Notice of this assignment was given to Foster Wheeler Ltd. who was told to make all payments to Mr. Johnston, Pettit's lawyer, who would hold the money in trust for him. Some payments were made, but on December 27 the Bank of Nova Scotia sent a letter to Foster Wheeler Ltd. stating that it had received a general assignment of book debts of Roderick Ashley as collateral security for a debt and that any payments to be made to Roderick Ashley should now be paid to the Bank of Nova Scotia. Accordingly, Foster Wheeler immediately paid the $7345 outstanding to the Bank of Nova Scotia instead of paying to Pettit and Johnston. Pettit and Johnston then sued Foster Wheeler for this amount, claiming that it should have been paid to them. Explain the likely outcome.

6. Re Royal Bank of Canada and Gill et al.

The younger Mr. Gill was fluent in English and a sophisticated businessman who had worked in a credit union for a number of years as well as managing his father's berry farm. To take advantage of a business opportunity, he arranged with the Royal Bank to borrow $87 000. During the negotiations, it became clear that he could get a more favourable rate of interest if his father guaranteed the loan. In fact, the son had done a considerable amount of banking on behalf of his father, who was also a customer of the same bank. The elder Mr. Gill could not read, write or speak English and relied on his son in all his business dealings. The documents were prepared and the son brought his father to the bank to sign. At no time did he explain to his father that he was signing a personal guarantee, and the evidence is clear that the father had no idea what he was signing other than that it was a document associated with a loan transaction. Mr. Gill, Sr., had implicit faith in his son's handling of his business affairs. Mr. Gill, Jr., on the other hand was so excited about the deal that he apparently never explained the nature of the documents to his father. It is clear in this situation that at no time was there any misrepresentation to the father or the son on the part of the bank. When the loan was defaulted, the bank turned to the father for payment. Explain the arguments of the father and the bank as to whether Mr. Gill, Sr., should be held responsible for this debt and the likely outcome.

7. Stott v. Merrit Investment Corp.

Stott was a sales representative working in the securities business for the defendant. He was approached by a customer who wanted to start an account to speculate in gold futures, a very risky business. The account was started and some successes were achieved but then the market reversed itself and the customer lost heavily. The customer ended up indebted to the company for $66 000. Stott was called into his supervisor's office and asked to sign an agreement stating that Stott would be fully responsible for that amount if the customer could not pay. He suggested that he should have legal advice and was told, "You are probably right but if you don't sign, it won't go well with you at this firm and it would be very difficult for you to find employment in the industry." Stott signed the document and continued to work for Merrit. Deductions were taken off his income for this debt over the employment period. Several months later, he said that he had received legal advice and offered to settle the debt for 25 percent of the outstanding amount. Even when he resigned two years after the event, it was clear that he felt some obligation under the agreement. Some time after he left and obtained other employment, he refused any further responsibility and sued Merrit for the amount that had been deducted from his income to pay this debt. Merrit countersued for the amount still outstanding. What are the legal arguments to support each position? Would your answer be different if you were to learn that it was the practice in the industry to hold sales representatives responsible to some extent for such bad accounts?

WEBLINKS

High Court of Australia: McRae v. Commonwealth Disposals Commission (1951) 84 CLR 377
www.austlii.edu.au/do2/disp.pl/au/cases/cth/high_ct/84clr377.html

Supreme Court of Canada: Rulings: BG Checo International Ltd. v. British Columbia Hydro and Power Authority
www.droit.umontreal.ca/doc/csc-scc/en/pub/1993/ vol1/html/1993scr1_0012.html

Supreme Court of Canada: Rulings: London Drugs Ltd. v. Kuehne & Nagel International Ltd.
www.droit.umontreal.ca/doc/csc-scc/en/pub/1992/vol3/html/ 1992scr3_0299.html

The End of the Contractual Relationship

6

OBJECTIVES OF THE CHAPTER

- To describe the various degrees of performance and their effect on contractual obligations
- To summarize the various conditions that constitute a breach of contract
- To outline the process of discharging by agreement
- To define frustration in contractual terms
- To list the remedies available to the victim of a breach of contract

Standard had an agreement to supply 133 precast concrete panels for Dywidag which were later to be erected at a building site by a general contractor within a limited time period. Unfortunately the first nine of these concrete slabs failed to meet the specifications set out in the contract. Dywidag cancelled the contract on 24 hours' notice against Standard's protests. The Supreme Court of B.C. had to decide whether the breach committed by Standard in failing to produce the first nine panels properly was a breach sufficient enough to justify the termination of the whole agreement. This is a problem that often arises when performance of the contract is being done by installments and there is a failure of all or some of those installments. At what stage is the other contracting party entitled to treat the contract as ended and make other arrangements?

In this case the court decided that this was an example of repudiation of the contract through conduct. Although Standard protested that they were willing and wanted to perform, they proved themselves unable to do the job. This failure was significant enough for Dywidag to lose confidence in them treat the contract as over and turn to another source.[1] Breach of contract is just one of the ways in which a contract can be discharged that will be discussed in this chapter.

---

1. *Standard Precast Ltd. v. Dywidag Fab Con Products Ltd.*, 56 D.L.R. (4th) 385 (British Columbia Court of Appeal).

Contractual obligations can come to an end or be discharged in four ways. These are by performance, breach, agreement between the parties to end or modify, and frustration. This chapter will examine each of these.

PERFORMANCE

Contractual obligations are discharged and a contract is ended when each party satisfactorily performs or completes its part of the bargain. Historically, the failure of one party to perform the terms of a contract relieved the other party of any obligation to perform its part of the bargain since the obligations of the parties were interdependent. If a lump sum payment was to be made for services rendered, no payment would be due unless that service was performed exactly as specified in the contract. Thus, a person who agreed to paint a building in exchange for payment upon completion would not be entitled to anything if only a portion, even if it was a major portion, of the building were painted. The obligation to pay was dependent on the completion of the painting. This was a harsh rule and over the years several exceptions to it have developed.

Substantial Performance

When a party has performed most of the obligation under the agreement but has left out some element of performance that is trivial in its effect on the contract, the courts will treat the contract as performed. For example, if Jones contracts to deliver 1000 boxes of tomatoes to Sharif but delivers only 999 boxes, the contract is substantially performed and Jones is discharged from the obligation to deliver tomatoes to Sharif. However, Sharif has the right to deduct the value of that one undelivered box or to get it from somebody else and seek compensation from Jones for the expense of doing so.

Contract discharged when contract substantially performed

There are some types of contracts in which only complete and exact performance will suffice. For example, if Aarons has a contract to drill a water-producing well for Parada and drills 29 dry holes, this will not qualify as substantial performance because those dry holes are worthless to Parada. Only the delivery of a producing well will qualify as performance. Payment is said to be conditional on the exact performance as required in the contract.

But some contracts must be performed exactly

Tender of Performance

The general rule in common law is that when a person has tendered performance of a contract, it counts as if the contract had been performed. This means that if a person is ready, willing and able to perform a contractual obligation and attempts to do so, but the other party refuses to accept it or prevents it, the first party is taken to have completed the contractual obligation and is discharged from it. The person who has attempted performance is then in a position to sue the other party for damages. Tendered performance means that the person performing must actually attempt to deliver the specified goods or attempt to perform the specified service.

When performance is refused or made impossible—that constitutes breach

It should be noted that in many service arrangements, the service does not have to be provided personally; vicarious performance will suffice. If Watson contracts to clean Nyberg's windows and his employees are refused entrance by Nyberg when they show up to do the job, performance has been tendered and the contract is discharged. There are some types of contracts for which personal services are required and sending a substitute would not be an appropriate tender of performance. The compensation granted for refusal to accept delivery or service will cover only the damages suffered, not the cost of goods or services since these costs have not been incurred. If Chan agreed to paint Smith's house, showed up to do it on the specified day and was refused entrance, he has discharged his obligation. But when he sues he will only be entitled to the lost profit from the job, not the total price since he has not incurred the expenses associated with the job such as paint, brushes, solvent and the like. In some situations, however, where goods have been sold and the title to those goods has actually transferred to the purchaser, the whole purchase price must be paid. Even though the goods may not have been delivered, they now belong to the purchaser. When title changes hands in the sale of goods will be discussed in the following chapter.

Where debt owed and money refused—money still owed but creditor bears expense

The effect of tendering proper payment of debt is different. It does not extinguish the debt but simply relieves the debtor of the obligation to seek out the creditor to make payment. It thus becomes the creditor's responsibility to ask the debtor for payment and to bear the cost of doing so. Even if it becomes necessary for the creditor to sue, the costs of the court action are the creditor's responsibility if it can be shown that the debtor properly attempted to pay the debt.

Payment must be in legal tender

Proper performance of a contractual obligation in which the payment of money is involved requires the tendering of cash. Cheques, even certified cheques, are acceptable only when the parties have agreed to allow cheques to be used to pay debts. This may be an actual agreement between the parties or it may be an accepted business practice. If there is any question about the acceptable form of payment, it is advisable to present cash. If the contract requires a specified amount to be given, exactly that amount must be tendered. The person paying does not have the right to demand that the other party produce change. A creditor need only accept a limited number of coins in payment of debt. The *Currency and Exchange Act* [2] states that creditors need only accept up to 25 pennies, five dollars' worth of nickels and ten dollars' worth of any larger coins. There is no limit on what qualifies as legal tender when gold coin or paper money is offered as long as official Canadian bank notes are used.

Delivery must be at a reasonable time and place

The delivery of money, goods or services must be tendered at a reasonable time and place. Usually this means during normal business hours at a person's place of business, unless it has been otherwise specified in the contract. Thus, if Jones has a contract to deliver five tonnes of ripe tomatoes to Sharif by July 10, Jones would be expected to make that delivery to Sharif's packing house rather than to Sharif's home or office. The delivery should also take place during the usual working day. Sharif would not be obligated to accept delivery at 6:00 p.m. on Saturday unless such time was permitted in the contract.

The general rule is that if a condition of the contract specifies a time for performance, the time specified is absolute. Failure to perform within that specified time will be fatal to the contract. If a person had an option to purchase property that must be exercised by July 30 and attempts to exercise that option on August 2, it would be too late. Rights under the option agreement would have expired. If a bid or tender for a job must be submitted by 11:00 a.m., it must be submitted by that

2. R.S.C. (1985) c. C-52.

time, not a few seconds later as happened in *Smith Brothers and Wilson v. B.C. Hydro Authority*.[3] Even a bid tendered that close in time could not be considered.

In circumstances in which the parties have not specified a time for performance, they are obligated to perform within a **reasonable time**. The definition of reasonable time will vary with the nature of the agreement, the parties and the type of goods or services involved. A reasonable time would be shorter for an agreement to buy shares in a company trading on the stock exchange than for the purchase of a farm. If the time has not been specified and one of the parties feels that the other has been delaying too long, the appropriate action is to serve notice on the delaying party that performance must take place within a specified but reasonable length of time and that failure to perform in that time will discharge the agreement.

The courts of equity have developed a more lenient approach towards specific time requirements in the contract. The courts are much less likely to find that the contract has been discharged because of a failure to perform on time when the parties are seeking an equitable remedy, such as specific performance or injunction. These and other remedies for breach of contract will be discussed below.

Independent Obligations

In most contractual relationships, the obligation of one party is dependent on the performance of the other party to the contract. If one person agrees to sell another a car for $500, the obligation of the purchaser to pay the $500 will not arise until the car is delivered. If there is no delivery, there is no obligation to pay the $500. Similarly, if the purchaser is not willing to hand over the $500, there is no obligation on the part of the seller to hand over the car. In some relationships, however, the contractual obligations borne by the parties are independent or severable from each other. This means that if one of the parties fails to perform an obligation under the agreement, the other party will not be relieved from the obligation to perform. The tenant of leased property has an obligation to pay rent and the landlord has an obligation to make repairs when they become necessary. If the tenant notifies the landlord that certain repairs have to be made and the landlord fails to make those repairs, the tenant is not relieved of the obligation to pay rent. This obligation is independent of the landlord's obligation to make repairs. This condition can be overcome by specifying in the contract that the obligations are interdependent. Note as well that when residential tenancies are involved this may be determined by statute.[4]

May be obligation to perform despite breach

A similar result occurs when the contract requires delivery in several installments. For example, if a supplier has an obligation to deliver a tonne of coal per month for a year, that contract can be treated as a series of individual contracts, one for each installment. If the supplier fails to make one delivery, the other contracting party is not relieved of the obligation to pay for the deliveries received. Again, the parties can specify in the contract that the obligation to pay is concurrent or dependent on the other party's complete performance of all the other provisions of the contractual relationship. In some situations, however, a supplier's failure to deliver an installment such as the first installment is so important that failure to deliver it would undermine the whole contractual relationship. This failure would amount to a repudiation of the contract and there would be no obligation to accept

Performance by installments

3. B.C.S.C. February 24, 1997, reported in *The Lawyers Weekly*, Vol. 16, No. 42.

4. In Alberta, the *Residential Tenancies Act,* R.S.A. (1980) c. R-15.3 does not state that the obligations are interdependent. This means that tenants cannot withhold rent when they believe that the landlord is not fulfilling its obligations.

any further deliveries. This was the situation in *Standard Precast Ltd. v. Dywidag Fab Con Products Ltd.* used to introduce this chapter. But even in these circumstances, the purchaser is obligated to pay for the installments that have already been received.

BREACH

Breach of contract involves the failure of the breaching party to perform properly its contractual obligations. Such a breach can take place in two ways: (1) by improper or incomplete performance of the obligations set out in the agreement and (2) by refusal to perform. Refusal, also called repudiation, will be discussed below. In the example used to introduce this chapter, the failure to deliver the appropriate concrete panels was serious enough so that it was treated as a breach of the whole contract. Such a breach may be either a major or a minor infraction.

Conditions and Warranties

Breach of condition—party relieved

Breach of warranty—performance required

Breach accepted—performance required

Warranties can become conditions and vice versa

Terms essential to the substantial performance of a contract are called **conditions**. Terms which are insignificant or peripheral to the central obligation of the contract are called **warranties**. The failure to perform a condition of the contract generally permits the other party to treat his or her obligation as ended and sue for breach of contract. But the improper performance of a warranty does not relieve the other party of the obligation to fulfill his or her side of the agreement. The victim of such a breach of warranty has the right to sue the other party for whatever it costs to overcome the deficiency in performance but still must perform his or her part of the agreement.

Although the breach of a condition will normally allow the victim of the breach to treat the contract as discharged, there is an obligation to perform if the partial performance is accepted. Acceptance means that the party has accepted some benefit under the agreement, knowing that the agreement has been breached. For example, if Beaman has a clear obligation to deliver to Singh a portrait of Singh's mother and delivers a landscape painting instead, this would normally be a breach of a condition. However, by accepting the painting, Singh then has to live up to the obligation to pay but retains the right to sue for any damages suffered. A breach of condition in a contract that has been accepted by the other party is treated as a breach of warranty.

Terms that might normally be considered insubstantial or unimportant can be upgraded to the status of conditions by the parties so declaring in their agreement. For example, suppose someone orders a new automobile and stipulates that it come in a certain shade of red. Such a term would normally be a warranty and the purchaser must accept delivery of the automobile and make payment even if the car is delivered painted in a different shade. But the purchaser can write into the purchase contract that the colour of the automobile be a condition of the contract. If a certain colour vehicle is used for a trademark (as is done by Mary Kay Cosmetics), having a car that colour may be the most important aspect of the transaction for the purchaser. If the colour is made a condition of the contract, failure to deliver a car in the appropriate colour would be a breach of a condition and the purchaser would be able to refuse delivery.

Similarly, a term that would normally be a condition can be relegated to the position of a warranty by the parties so specifying in the agreement. The *Sale of*

Goods Act states that in transactions governed by the *Act*, the court has the option of treating a term specified as a warranty as a condition.[5]

Exemption Clauses

A warranty clause is often included in a purchase document which summarizes the seller's obligations under the contract. The term "warranty" as used here is usually thought of as an assurance of quality and a willingness to stand behind the product. In fact the seller is trying to limit his or her obligations under the contract by making what would normally be a major term into a minor one. Because they are declared to be warranties instead of conditions when these limited obligations are not honoured, victims cannot return the goods or withhold payment for them if there has been a breach.

The term "warranty" used in this way means actually an **exemption clause,** often referred to as an **exclusion** or **exculpatory clause**. It is an attempt by the sellers of goods or services to significantly limit or eliminate their liability under an agreement. The courts will generally enforce exemption clauses because the object of contract law is to carry out whatever the parties have freely bargained to do. But they do so reluctantly. If there is any ambiguity in the terms of the exemption clause, the narrow or restrictive meaning will be used.

For example, if a restaurant has a sign above the cloakroom stating, "Not responsible for lost or stolen clothing," bringing this term to the customer's attention would make it part of the **contract of bailment** in which goods are being cared for by someone else. If clothes left there are damaged by fire or water instead of being stolen or lost, the proprietor would not be able to rely on the sign to avoid liability because of the narrow interpretation the courts would apply. Similarly, if a briefcase left with the proprietor was stolen, the proprietor would not be able to rely on the exemption clause because it was not clothing that was stolen.

Exemption clauses attempt to limit liability

Exemption clauses strictly interpreted

EXEMPTION CLAUSE STRICTLY INTERPRETED

A Purolator employee delivered an expensive medical machine going to Meditek to the wrong address. As a safeguard Purolator employees fill out delivery sheets indicating where the goods have been delivered to and the signature of a recipient so that missing goods can be traced in the event of misdelivery; in this case, however, the delivery sheets had been falsified and it was impossible for Purolator to trace the goods. It was only after a prolonged delay, during which Meditek acquired a different machine, that the goods were found, but Meditek refused delivery and sued Purolator for damages including the cost of the extra machine. Purolator claimed their liability was limited by an exemption clause in the Meditek contract that limited Purolator's liability, "whether or not from negligence or gross negligence." The court found that Purolator was not protected by the clause, since the actual damage was caused by a willful act of the employee to falsify the delivery sheets. Such exemption clauses are strictly interpreted against the breaching party, and although this one covered even gross negligence, it did not cover willful or fraudulent conduct.

Meditek Laboratory Services Ltd. v. Purolator Courier Ltd., 125 D.L.R. (4th) 738 (Manitoba Court of Appeal)

---

5. *Sale of Goods Act,* R.S.A. (1980) c. S-2, s. 14.

Exemption clauses are intricate and involved because the people who draft them try to cover all possible eventualities knowing that the courts will take a restrictive approach in their interpretation. Consumer protection legislation that significantly limits the scope of exemption clauses is becoming much more common.[6]

Must be brought to the attention of party at time of contract

Exemption clauses usually form a part of the written document, but they could be included in a sign or notice. In any case, the terms must be brought to the attention of the customer at the time the contract is made. If the clause is on the back of the ticket or receipt, there must be a reference on the front directing the holder to read the back. Even when the exemption clause is part of a written contract, if it is in any way unique or unusual it must be brought to the attention of the other contracting party.

The key point to remember when dealing with exemption clauses is that one party cannot unilaterally impose a restriction of liability on the other. Both parties must agree to it as part of the contract. An exemption of liability sign at a car park, train station or dry cleaners must be in clear view so that a reasonable person would notice it when entering the premises or undertaking a contractual obligation. It is only then that the term will form part of the agreement, and even then the words will be interpreted narrowly. When goods are sold, especially manufactured goods, the seller will often include such an exemption clause in the form of a "limited warranty." It is important to note that under the *Sale of Goods Act* and other consumer protection legislation, the sellers' right to restrict their obligations in such sales may be extremely limited.

Fundamental Breach

Exemption clauses will not completely eliminate liability

Suppliers of goods or services try to limit their liability as much as possible. But the courts have shown a considerable reluctance to allow suppliers to eliminate their liability entirely. It is in these circumstances that the concept of **fundamental breach** has developed. Fundamental breach means that some types of failure to perform are so basic to the contract that they destroy any semblance of performance of the contract, leaving one party bereft of any benefit from it at all. In the face of such a breach, an exemption clause will in most cases not protect the breacher from liability for damages. Thus, if a new car is plagued with problems to the point that it is not capable of being driven, the purchaser will be entitled to return it and get a refund in spite of any exemption clause or "warranty." The breach has been fundamental; what was received was something essentially different from what was bargained for. "A car is not a car if it has to be towed."[7]

Exemption clauses ineffective in cases of fundamental breach

The courts have refused to give effect to exemption clauses in cases of fundamental breach. When goods are involved they have allowed the victim of the breach to rescind the contract and return the goods. For example, a customer took his suit in a bag to a dry cleaner which had a sign stating that they were not responsible for any failure to perform their contractual obligations. If he were to come back the following week and after paying the dry cleaning bill discover that his suit had never been taken out of the bag, it is doubtful that a court would allow the dry cleaner to keep

6. Alberta's current consumer protection legislation does not significantly limit the scope of exemption clauses. The *Fair Trading Act,* which takes effect September 1, 1999, similarly does not restrict the effectiveness of exemption clauses. Section 6(3)(c) does, however, state that it is an unfair practice for a supplier to include harsh, oppressive or excessively one-sided terms or conditions in a consumer transaction. Would a court use this provision to strike down an exemption clause in a consumer transaction?

7. *Burkitt, L.J., Yeoman Credit, Ltd. v. Apps* [1961] 2 All E.R. 288 (Court of Appeal).

the payment. The basic or fundamental objective of the contract had been to clean the clothes and the exemption clause will not relieve them of this obligation even if brought to the customer's attention. The customer would never have expected such a limitation to extend to the very heart of the contract, the act of cleaning the suit.

The justification for this policy is based on two different lines of reasoning and there was, until recently, considerable debate over this apparent interference with the freedom of contracting parties to agree to whatever they want. When the doctrine was developed, it was thought to be a rule of contract law that the parties could not contract out of all liability. If the breach was so basic that it changed the nature of the agreement, the exemption clause would simply be overruled. This approach has been rejected and the accepted view today is that the judge will examine the entire contract as well as the exemption clause and imply from the terms whether the parties intended the exemption clause to cover this fundamental breach. As a result, it is now feasible to draft an exemption clause that excludes all liability, but the normal practice of the lower courts has still been to interpret it, if they can, in such a way as to not give it effect when a fundamental or basic obligation of the contract is breached. This is referred to as the construction approach. The Supreme Court of Canada, in *Hunter Engineering*,[8] has made it clear that a properly worded exemption clause could overcome even a fundamental breach, and Dickson C.J.C. went so far as to regret the development of the concept of fundamental breach stating that the problem could better be addressed by finding such exemption clauses unconscionable when it was appropriate to do so.

Exemption clauses— disregarded if enforcement would be unconscionable

In commercial dealings, people often look at a contract technically and think that they are only bound by the restrictive wording of the contract. They sometimes try to find ways to get around the wording of the agreement in order to avoid performing when it becomes less attractive to do so. Courts have always resisted such an approach and will vary from a narrow interpretation to a more expansive one depending on the merits of the case. Recently the courts have become even more flexible when enforcing contractual obligations by requiring the parties to adhere to a standard of conduct based on good faith.

A group of Ontario doctors owned a building and agreed to let a medical lab (the MDS Group) lease a part of that building. The lease included a restrictive covenant that the landlord, King Street Medical Arts Centre Limited, would not permit any other tenant to provide medical lab services at the site, although the doctors would not be restricted from doing their own medical lab work. During the term of the lease the landlord requested MDS to pay a much higher rent and the lab refused.

A number of the doctors who were shareholders in the landlord company then took one of the rooms in the facility and used it as a collection point for sending samples to another lab and effectively destroyed the business of MDS, the first lab. In addition they encouraged their patients to have lab work done at a different facility. This collection point didn't violate the terms of the lease, as the lab work wasn't actually done on the premises nor were any samples taken from patients there.

The Ontario court held that the doctors had a duty to act in good faith in performing their contractual obligations and an injunction was granted stopping the practice. While they might not be technically in violation of strict wording of their agreement, they certainly had breached their obligation to act in good faith in relation to the MDS group.[9]

8. *Hunter Engineering Co. v. Syncrude Canada Ltd.*, 57 D.L.R. (4th) 321; *Beaufort Realties v. Chomedey Aluminum Co.* (1981) 116 D.L.R. (3d) 193 (S.C.C.).

9. *MDS Health Group Limited v. King Street Medical Arts Centre Limited*, reported in *Lawyers Weekly*, Vol. 14, No. 47.

Repudiation

Fletton Ltd. v. Peat Marwick Ltd.[10]

Peat Marwick Ltd. came into possession of 2797 washer/dryer units from an import company that had become insolvent and entered into an agreement to sell these units to Fletton Ltd. One of the conditions of the agreement was that Fletton, the purchaser, would obtain product liability insurance on the units or an unqualified legal opinion that there could be no liability to the receiver, Peat Marwick. Peat Marwick wanted the insurance because they had knowledge that there were electrical and mechanical problems with the units that made them susceptible to catching fire. Canadian Standards Association approval had been removed from them and so this was a serious problem.

Fletton then tried to find a carrier for this insurance but was unable to arrange a policy satisfactory to both parties. In August Peat Marwick repudiated the contract and had, in fact, found another purchaser at a considerably higher price. Fletton sued for breach of contract. The remedy they sought was specific performance, an order for the breaching party to perform the contract and deliver the units.

At trial the judge found that although Peat Marwick had repudiated, Fletton had not accepted the repudiation but had continued to demand performance of the contract and had kept trying to obtain the appropriate insurance. Faced with such repudiation, Fletton either had to accept the repudiation and sue for breach, or ignore the repudiation and continue to demand performance, which they did. They were bound by their choice. When they finally sued for breach of contract, it was determined that they were in no position to do so, since they had failed to arrange for the insurance as required in the contract. They could not rely on Peat Marwick's repudiation as a breach since they had ignored it and demanded performance.

This case illustrates the danger of anticipatory breach. You have a right to demand performance or to sue for breach but if you do demand performance, you had better be prepared to perform your side of the agreement or you may be the one that is in breach.

Repudiation occurs when one of the parties to a contract indicates to the other "an intimation or an intention to abandon and altogether to refuse performance of the contract."[11] Repudiation that takes place after performance is due is just one more way that a contract can be breached, but if this refusal occurs before performance is due, it is called **anticipatory breach** and is treated somewhat differently.

Victim is discharged and can sue if repudiation occurs before due date —or demand performance and wait

In such circumstances, it makes little sense to insist that innocent parties continue to perform their part of the agreement. The courts, therefore, allow the victim to treat the contract as breached, sue and refuse to go through with any further performance. Alternatively, the victim of the repudiation can insist that the contract be fulfilled by performing his or her side of the agreement and waiting until the performance date to see if the other party carries through with the threat of non-performance. If the repudiating party fails to perform, the innocent party can then sue for breach of contract and the party repudiating will be held responsible for damages incurred after the repudiation.

---

10. 50 D.L.R. (4th) 729 (British Columbia Court of Appeal).

11. Comment of Lord Coleridge, C.J. in *Freeth v. Burr* (1874) L.R. 9 C.P. 213 (Court of Common Pleas).

Once the choice is made either to ignore the repudiation and insist on per-formance or to accept it and treat the contractual obligations as ended, that choice is binding. This can have serious consequences for the victim's legal position. If the innocent party insists on performance of the repudiated contract and is then unable to perform for any reason, it will be the victim that will be subject to a breach of contract action as in the *Fletton* case discussed above.

Victim is bound by choice

When a repudiation in the form of an anticipatory breach does takes place the innocent party also runs the risk of being affected by changing circumstances. In the case of *Avery v. Bowden*,[12] the defendant chartered the plaintiff's ship and agreed to supply it with a cargo at the Russian port of Odessa. However, when the ship arrived, the defendant refused to supply a cargo and insisted that the boat leave. The cap-tain stayed in port hoping that the supplier would change his mind. The Crimean War then broke out, before the expiration of the specified time in which the cargo had to be supplied, which made it impossible to go through with the original con-tract even if the defendant had changed his mind or had not repudiated. The owner of the ship sued for breach of contract.

Changing circumstances may affect repudiation

Although the court agreed that the plaintiff would have had the right to treat the contract as discharged by breach once the defendant had clearly indicated that he was not going to go through with the agreement, the defendant had cho-sen not to acknowledge the repudiation. Therefore, the contract had not been breached since the time specified for performance had not yet expired when the war broke out. The contract was discharged by frustration, not by breach. Frustration will be discussed later in the chapter.

Repudiation can be **express** or **implied** from the conduct of the parties. Repudiation is implied if the subject matter of an agreement is sold to a third party or if an effort has been made to sell the goods. It is clear that the owner does not intend to honour the original agreement. Repudiation may also be implied by an actual breach of the terms of the agreement. Failure to perform one part of an ongoing contract, such as an important installment, may be taken as repudiation of the rest of the contract. The failure to perform must be of a condition and serious enough for the victim to assume that the rest of the agreement will not be per-formed as was the case in *Dywidag* at the beginning of this chapter.

Repudiation may be implied by conduct

DISCHARGE BY AGREEMENT

Gregorio v. Intrans-Corp.[13]

Gregorio, a truck driver, ordered a truck from the dealership Intrans for $100 000. It was purchased from the supplier Paccar, who obtained it from the U.S. manu-facturer. This agreement was entered into on May 12, 1984. Financing was arranged on July 3 removing the only condition on the sale, and so there was a binding contract as of that date. On August 2 when the truck was delivered, Gregorio was required to sign certain documents, including a warranty which purported to give a one-year limited warranty, but excluded all other implied warranties and other liability for consequential damages for failure to perform.

---

12. *Avery v. Bowden* (1855) 5 E. & B. 714; affirmed (1856) 6 E. & B. 953 (Court of Exchequer).

13. 115 D.L.R. (4th) 200 (Ontario Court of Appeal).

The *Sale of Goods Act* will be discussed in the next chapter, but it should be noted that this statute implies certain warranties and conditions into such contracts which protect the purchaser unless the parties specify otherwise in their agreement. This is what the August 2 warranty signed by Gregorio purports to do.

The truck turned out to be a lemon. After several attempts to fix it, Gregorio sued to get his money back in 1987. He succeeded in doing so, because the contract for the purchase was entered into on May 12, 1984, and the August 2 warranty was an attempt to modify that agreement. Since Gregorio received no consideration for the changes, he was not bound by the agreement. The contract for purchase was the May 12, 1984, agreement and because it was silent as to warranties the *Act* implied warranties and conditions in it. Gregorio was entitled to rescission because of the implied condition that the goods be fit for their purpose. A contract can be modified by agreement, but it is vitally important that all of the elements be present. In this case consideration was missing and Gregorio was not affected by the changes.

Contracts can be modified or ended by agreement

There is no difficulty in entering into an agreement to end or modify a previous contract. This is referred to as discharge by agreement. As in creating any contractual relationship, all of the ingredients necessary to form a contract must be present. It may be important to determine whether the old agreement has been ended and a new one substituted or whether the old agreement has been merely modified. Generally, if it is only a minor term that is altered, the old agreement continues, but the change of a major term will result in a new contract, depending, of course, on what the court determines is the intention of the parties. Terms in the original agreement that are not referred to in the new one will still be in place if the agreement has been modified, but they will no longer apply if a new agreement has been created. If the *Statute of Frauds* required the original agreement to be in writing, then any modifications to it must also be in writing. A verbal agreement to discharge such a written contract would be valid, but the new contract must be in writing.

Must have consensus

The requirements of consensus and consideration are most frequently called into question by the courts when a contract to discharge or modify an agreement is challenged. One party to a contract cannot unilaterally impose modification or termination on the other. A merchant might be tempted to charge an excessive amount of interest to a customer who does not pay a bill on time. There is no problem if this had been agreed to in the original contract, but if the merchant imposes such a term after the fact, such as on the bill requesting payment, it will not be binding on the customer. This does not excuse the customer from the debt, but the courts will protect customers from excessive interest rates imposed unilaterally after the fact.

Must have consideration

Consideration is necessary to support a new agreement to discharge or modify the first contract. If both parties have something left to do under the original contract which the agreement to modify relieves them of, there is valid consideration on both sides to support the change. This is called **bilateral discharge** or mutual release. The problem arises where the discharge or modification is one-sided. When one of the parties agrees to a modification of the agreement that is wholly for the benefit of the other or agrees to allow the other party not to perform all or part of their obligations under the contract while still performing their side, such a one-sided change or **unilateral discharge** is not binding on the parties. There is no consideration to support it and so no contract to change or discharge the original contract.

This was the reason the limited warranty provision agreed to later did not bind Gregorio in *Gregorio v. Intrans-Corp.* discussed above. Of course, if extra work is agreed to or the new agreement is put under seal, consideration is not a problem. Even when the discharge is entirely one-sided, the person relying on such a gratuitous promise to relieve them of their obligation may still be able to raise that promise as a defense if the other party changes their mind and insists on performance of the original agreement. This would be a situation where the defense of promissory estoppel may be raised which was discussed in Chapter 3.

When the parties discharge the contract on the payment of some substituted consideration, they have reached an **accord and satisfaction**. "Satisfaction" refers to the additional consideration given to support the discharge. To illustrate this point, consider the situation in which Aiello agrees to paint Newcombe's house for $500 to be paid in advance. After payment Aiello tells Newcombe that she is no longer able to paint the house. If Newcombe were to tell Aiello that there was no need to worry about it, would he be bound by those words? The release would not be binding because there is no consideration.

Unilateral discharge requires accord and satisfaction

But if Aiello were to agree to paint Newcombe's fence instead, there would be an accord and Newcombe would obtain satisfaction. The agreement is supported by new consideration and this arrangement would be binding on both parties. Airlines often find themselves in this position when they have overbooked a flight. They will usually ask for volunteers to give up their seats and go on a later flight. Inducements are offered such as free flights and deluxe accommodation. Those that volunteer have reached an accord and satisfaction with the airline.

The classic example of a one-sided attempt to change a contractual obligation is when a debtor approaches a creditor and offers to pay less than the full amount of debt owed. Creditors are often tempted to take partial payment of the debt owed, rather than getting nothing or having to sue. If this payment is made before the date due the consideration is in the early payment, but when it is made after the due date, where is the consideration for the creditor taking partial payment as discharge for the debt? Can the creditor still sue for the shortfall?

According to the case *Foakes v. Beer*[14] the answer is yes—when part payment is accepted, the full debt is not abolished unless there is additional consideration. The creditor would still be able to sue for the unpaid amount. This result is not very desirable from a business point of view, since arriving at such accommodation makes for more efficient business relationships. Creditors would often prefer to be able to take such a partial payment rather than get nothing and debtors must be certain of the discharge before they are willing to make the payment. As a result, most provinces have adopted legislation which largely overrules the precedent set in *Foakes v. Beer*. If partial payment is offered and taken as full payment of a debt, the creditor cannot sue for any deficit. Nothing forces the creditor to accept the lesser amount, but if it is taken the creditor must be satisfied with it.[15]

Partial payment of debt acceptable if taken

Contractual Terms

Contracts that involve ongoing relationships between parties may not provide for the termination of those relationships. In these cases, the courts will imply a provision requiring each party to give the other reasonable notice of the termination of the agreement. Reasonable notice will vary depending on the nature and subject matter

14. *Foakes v. Beer* (1884) 9 App. Cas. 605 (House of Lords).

15. See the discussion in Chapter 3, starting at p. 142.

of the contract, such as the payment period in the lease or the length of the term of employment. The contract can also provide that either party has the right to end their obligations, usually by simply giving the other notice. When the contract does specify the circumstances under which it will end, the provision will be binding.

Contract may provide for its own discharge

Conditions precedent

The contract itself can specify conditions under which the obligations of the parties may begin or end. These are generally called **conditions precedent** and **conditions subsequent**. Conditions precedent exist when the parties specify in their agreement some event or requirement that must be satisfied before either party to the contract is obligated to do anything. The agreement will not be binding on either party if that event fails to take place. For example, if Nishi were to agree to buy Fafard's house, subject to the sale of her own house, the contract is conditional on that event. Thus, if Nishi fails to sell her house, she is not obligated to go through with any agreement for the purchase of Fafard's house. When a condition precedent is not satisfied, there is no contractual obligation on either party. For this reason "subject to" clauses in contracts can be extremely important.

Conditions subsequent

Conditions subsequent exist when terms are included in a contract that bring the obligations of the parties to an end upon some event or condition taking place. Whereas conditions precedent prevent the obligations set out in the agreement from resting on the parties, conditions subsequent bring those obligations already resting on the parties to an end.

For example, if Agar agreed to pay Nguyen $400 per month for janitorial services "until Nguyen ceases to be a full-time student," this term is a condition subsequent. Agar will be obligated to pay until Nguyen finishes school. In this way, a contract can provide for its own end. The contract can also set out other ways for such contractual obligations to come to an end, such as simply allowing for one party to serve a specific period of notice on the other to that effect. But the parties can also agree to end, modify or substitute obligations with a new agreement. Contracts can also end by operation of law, as would be the case when of one of the parties dies or goes bankrupt. Bankruptcy will be discussed in Chapter 8.

FRUSTRATION

British Columbia (Minister of Crown Lands) v. Cressey Development Corp.[16]

Cressey bought land from the B.C. government which was conveyed to him upon payment of $2 million in September 1988. This was all done on the expectation that the property would be rezoned by the municipality so that it could be developed. In fact, the rezoning did not take place, and the court held that it frustrated the contract. The contract was ended and the title re-transferred to the B.C. government, which was ordered to return the money.

Note that there are several cases similar to this where rezoning has not taken place or permits not granted and the reason for the failure is that the developer failed to submit proper forms or plans, or failed to take the necessary steps to obtain the approval. When this happens it is an example of self-induced frustration which is simply a breach of contract.

16. 97 D.L.R. (4th) 380 (British Columbia Supreme Court).

Here, however, there was no suggestion of any failure on either party's part. An unexpected event beyond the control of either party led to frustration of the contract. In cases like this the contractual obligations cease to exist. A further question arises, however, as to what then ought to happen between the parties. In the present instance the B.C. government had the use of the money for a considerable time, so the court held that they should be required to pay interest to Cressey for the use of that money. Cressey also argued that they had done a considerable amount of work in preparation for the development of the property, for which they wanted compensation.

Under the *Frustrated Contracts Act* in place in most jurisdictions, where one party does work and it confers a benefit on another, even though the contract is frustrated compensation must be paid by the benefiting party. In this case, however, the court held that although the work had been done and the effort expended, no benefit had been received by the government, and therefore Cressey was not entitled to compensation.

The case illustrates not only how a contract can be ended by a frustrating event, but also the rights of the parties once such frustration has taken place.

A founding tenet of contract law was strict liability for contractual obligations. Historically, only performance would satisfy the terms of a contract and any failure to perform, even if it was through no fault of the parties, would result in the victim of that failure having the right to sue for breach. This is a harsh doctrine and the principle of frustration has been developed over the last century to alleviate some of the hardships. When, after the creation of the contract, some unforeseen outside event interferes with the performance of the contract, making the basic object of the agreement unobtainable, the contract is said to be discharged through frustration.

> Frustrating event may end a contract

This interference can make the performance of the agreement impossible or it might result in the performance being something essentially different from what the parties had anticipated when they entered into the agreement. It is easy to understand frustration when performance of the contract is made impossible, such as when a person agrees to paint a house which is subsequently destroyed in a fire. The difficulty arises when performance is still possible but the difference in the effect of performance is significant enough to amount to frustration.

In the case of *Krell v. Henry,*[17] the parties agreed to the rental of an apartment to view the coronation parade of Edward VII. A small deposit was paid at the time the contract was entered into, but the coronation parade was cancelled before the balance was paid because of the King's sudden illness. It was still possible for the parties to go through with the performance of the contract and for the tenant to occupy the flat, but to do so with no coronation parade to watch would be something essentially different from what the parties had in mind when they entered into the contract. Although performance of the contract was possible in a literal sense, it was no longer possible to obtain the purpose or object of the contract itself. Thus, the contract was said to be frustrated.

It must be noted, however, that frustration requires the essential nature of the contract to have changed; it is not enough that performance is just more difficult.

Care should be taken not to confuse frustration with shared mistake. There is no contract if the parties make a mistake about the existence of the subject matter

> Shared mistake not the same as frustration

---

17. *Krell v. Henry* [1903] 2 K.B. 740 (Court of Appeal).

at the time they enter into the agreement. There is no contract at all if a ship is destroyed, unbeknownst to the parties, before they enter into an agreement involving that ship or its cargo. With frustration, however, the interference takes place after the parties have entered into the agreement.

Frustration commonly arises in the following circumstances:

1. *Performance of a contract becomes impossible because the subject matter of the agreement is destroyed or is otherwise unusable.* Contracts may be frustrated when a person who has agreed to supply personal services becomes ill or dies, or when the specific article that formed the object of the contract is destroyed before the agreement can be performed.

   In the case of *Taylor v. Caldwell,*[18] there was an agreement between the parties to rent out a music hall. The hall burned down six days before the performance was to take place. The court held that the contract was discharged through frustration.

2. *An event that forms the basis of a contract fails to take place.* An example of this is *Krell v. Henry* cited earlier.

3. *Acts of the government interfere with performance.* Government policy can interfere with the performance of a contract in several different ways. A perfectly appropriate commercial contract with someone in another country may become unlawful through a declaration of war between the two countries; contracts involving the manufacture and production of particular drugs or foodstuffs may become illegal by statute; a contract may anticipate the acquisition of a licence or permit which the government does not grant as happened in the *B.C. v. Cressey* case discussed above; and all levels of government have the power in certain circumstances to expropriate the property that may form the basis of a contract.

Circumstances Not Constituting Frustration

Self-induced frustration is breach

Self-induced frustration is caused by one of the parties to the contract and, although it may appear to be frustration, it is treated as a breach. For example, if Moser has a contract to build an apartment building for Wu but the city refuses to grant Moser a building permit, we would expect the contract to be frustrated. However, if the building permit is refused because Moser failed to submit the appropriate plans as required by city bylaw, the frustration is self-induced. Moser is responsible for the misfortune; the refusal of the city to grant a permit will not provide an excuse for Moser's failure to perform the contract.

Similarly, if the parties have anticipated the frustrating event or have provided for one of the parties to bear the risk of such an eventuality, these contractual terms will prevail and the parties will not be able to claim that their agreement has been frustrated. It is only when the event is an unforeseen interference not caused by either party that the courts are willing to find frustration.

Increase in costs is not frustration

Finally, the contract is not frustrated if the unforeseen outside event only makes the performance of the contract more costly or more difficult. In the case of the *Tsakiroglou and Co. Ltd. v. Noblee and Thorl G.m.b.H.,*[19] the defendant agreed to sell and deliver a cargo of Sudanese groundnuts from a port in the Sudan to Hamburg. Then the Suez War broke out which prevented the defendant from using the Suez

18. *Taylor v. Caldwell* (1863) 3 B. & S. 826 (Court of Queen's Bench).
19. *Tsakiroglou and Co. Ltd. v. Noblee and Thorl G.m.b.H.* [1962] A.C. 93 (House of Lords).

Canal to deliver the cargo. It was not shipped; the purchaser sued for breach of contract and the seller claimed frustration.

The court held that, although it was more difficult and costly to ship the cargo around Africa, the essential nature of the contract remained intact and frustration did not apply. The seller was held liable for breach of contract. The contract would probably have been frustrated if the parties had specifically referred to the Suez Canal in the contract.

Similarly, if a farmer agrees to sell 50 boxes of Golden Delicious apples to a buyer and then her crop is destroyed by hail, this is not frustration unless the terms of the contract specifically stated that the apples were to come from her trees. The source of the apples was not a term of the contract and the farmer can simply obtain them from another farmer or on the open market and thus fulfill her contractual obligation.

Effect of Frustration

When a contract was frustrated under common law, the general principle was, "Let the loss lie where it falls." In other words, the party who had done work or provided services before the frustrating event would bear the loss and could not seek compensation from the other party. Similarly, money already paid as a deposit was lost.

Let loss lie where it falls under common law

This approach was considered unsatisfactory and the House of Lords modified this position in the *Fibrosa* case.[20] An English company had agreed to supply a Polish company with machinery to be delivered four months later. A prepayment of £1000 was made by the Polish company but, before the contract could be performed, World War II broke out and the contract was frustrated. The Polish company sued for the return of the prepayment.

The court declared that when there has been a complete failure of consideration resulting in one of the parties receiving nothing, any prepayment or deposit must be returned. This modification is the present common law position, but it is only a partial solution. It is still an all-or-nothing situation, with no option to apportion the loss between the parties whenever that might be the more appropriate course of action. Most common law jurisdictions have passed legislation to overcome these inadequacies.

The use of coins as legal tender is limited.
Photo from Prentice Hall Archives.

Legislation

The English *Law Reform Act*[21] states that a prepayment made before the frustrating event discharging the contract took place must be returned. The court, however, is given the right to allow the other party to retain a portion of that prepayment to compensate for expenses incurred. This provision of the *Act* eliminates the all-or-nothing consequences of the *Fibrosa* decision. However, the performing party is out of luck if it incurred expenses and there was no prepayment unless performance or part performance resulted in a substantial benefit to the other party.

Legislation allows deposits to be split

20. *Fibrosa Spolka Akeyjna v. Fairbairn, Lawson, Combe, Barbouk Ltd.* [1943] A.C. 32 (House of Lords).

21. *Law Reform Act* [1943] 6 and 7 Geo. 6, c. 40.

REIMBURSEMENT FOR EXPENSES WHERE CONTRACT FRUSTRATED

The plaintiff's truck was sent to the defendant for some $28 000 worth of repairs. The repairs were partially completed when a fire destroyed the both the shop and the truck, thus frustrating the repair contract. The court, however, ordered that the company be reimbursed for the expenses they incurred in repairing the vehicle before the fire, as established under Ontario's *Frustrated Contracts Act.*

Can-Truck Transportation Ltd. v. Fenton's Auto Paint Shop Ltd., 101 D.L.R. (4th) 562 (Ontario Court of Appeal)

The provisions of this legislation were adopted by Alberta, Manitoba, New Brunswick, Newfoundland, Ontario, Prince Edward Island and the Northwest Territories in their frustrated contracts statutes. British Columbia and the Yukon have also adopted a *Frustrated Contracts Act,* but their legislation allows the courts to go further. The British Columbia and Yukon courts can split the costs incurred between the parties whether or not a prepayment or deposit has been paid and even when no significant benefit has been bestowed. The various frustrated contracts acts in place also provide that, when one party has received a benefit from the other before the frustrating event takes place, the court has the power to order the benefiting party to pay the party creating that benefit an amount equal to its value.[22]

In the *B.C. v. Cressey* case discussed above, it was argued that the work done by Cressey bestowed a benefit on the B.C. government before the frustrating event, but this argument failed. Therefore no compensation was paid to Cressey under the act. Other statutes also modify the common law application of the frustration principle. At common law frustration does not apply to leases, but most jurisdictions have clearly stated that in residential leases frustration will apply.[23] British Columbia extends the application of frustration to commercial leases as well. When goods are being sold, the *Sale of Goods Act* provides that if the goods, through no fault of the parties, perish before the risk passes to the purchaser, the contract is avoided.[24] This means that the contract is not binding on the purchaser and any moneys paid have to be returned.

REMEDIES FOR BREACH OF CONTRACT

Rescission and Rectification

A breach of a condition in a contract does not automatically end all obligations of both parties to that contract. The victim of the breach has the right to ignore the breach and continue to treat the contract as if it were in force. If Mouzakis agreed to sell Smith a car and delivered a boat, Smith can choose to take the boat. It takes

22. The relevant Alberta legislation is the *Frustrated Contracts Act,* R.S.A. (1980) c. F-19. Section 3 states that sums paid before the contract was discharged are recoverable, and that sums payable before the contract was discharged cease to be payable. Section 4 states that if the party to whom the sums were paid or payable incurred expenses before the parties were discharged, then the court may allow the party to retain, or to recover, an amount not exceeding the amount of the expenses. Section 5 states that if either of the parties has obtained a benefit under the contract, then the court may allow the party conferring that benefit to recover the value of the benefit. There is no provision in the Alberta act which goes as far as the British Columbia and Yukon legislation.

23. See, for example, s. 32 of the *Residential Tenancies Act,* R.S.A. (1980) c. R-153.

24. See s. 10 of the *Sale of Goods Act,* R.S.A. (1980) c. S-2.

both parties to discharge a contract by breach of condition. Even if the victim of the breach elects to treat the contract as discharged, this does not end the obligations of the breaching party. The nature of those obligations is changed; the breaching party becomes liable for the remedies that are discussed below.

The remedies of rescission and rectification available to victims in contractual relationships were discussed in Chapter 5. These remedies usually come into play when problems with the formation of a contract affect its validity. A contract lacking consideration, legality or capacity can be rescinded and the parties can ask the courts to return them to the position they would have been in had they never entered into the contract. Similarly, if duress, undue influence, misrepresentation or mistake has led to a lack of consensus, rescission may be available. Rescission is also available when there has been a repudiation in the form of an anticipatory breach or when goods have been returned because they are defective. Rescission is only possible if the breach of the agreement is significant and the parties can be returned to their original positions.

Unlike other remedies available in contract law, rescission involves returning the parties as near as possible to the position they would have been in had the contract not been made, as opposed to putting the victim in the position he or she would have been in had the contract been properly performed. Rescission looks backward.

Rectification is another remedy available to correct defects in the formation of contracts but it is not available as a remedy for defective performance. As was discussed in Chapter 5, rectification is the process by which the court corrects the wording of a written document that has incorrectly recorded the terms of the agreement. This incorrect wording may have been caused by mistake or fraud. Rescission and rectification are equitable remedies developed in the Courts of Chancery.

> Remedies available where formation of contract was defective

Remedies Provided in Contract

Liquidated Damages.

It is possible for a contract to provide a consequence if one of the parties fails to honour its terms. These consequences may be quite varied. For example, the contract may include a term stating that arbitration will determine compensation to be paid in the event of disputes. The contract might also delineate the maximum amount of compensation to be paid by the breaching party, such as when establishments post signs indicating they are not responsible for losses over a specified amount. Failure to make an installment payment will often trigger a term of the contract called an **acceleration clause**. Upon default of payment, this clause makes all the entire outstanding debt due and payable immediately.

The most common alternative remedy specified in a contract is a **liquidated damages** clause, which states that the responsible party will pay a certain amount of money if a breach occurs. The amount is called a **deposit** when the money is advanced at the outset of the agreement. Suppliers of goods or services will often insist that purchasers make prepayments with the understanding that the supplier will be able to retain the deposit if the purchaser fails to perform the contract. It must be clear that the deposit is intended to be liquidated damages and that it is to be forfeited upon failure to perform. For example, the vendor of an automobile will usually require the buyer to pay a substantial deposit when ordering to secure the purchase. If the purchaser fails to go through with the deal when the car arrives, one of the remedies available to the vendor is to retain the deposit.

> Deposits to be forfeited upon breach

The temptation to take a large deposit entails significant risk. To qualify as liquidated damages, a deposit must be an honest attempt by the parties to estimate the damages that would be suffered if the contract were breached. If the amount involved crosses the line from being an honest attempt to estimate the possible injury or damages that would be suffered to an attempt to punish or impose a penalty for failure to perform, the provision may be void. A $1000 deposit on a new car might be fair in view of the cost of advertising, the time lost, the extra interest payments and so on. But a $10 000 deposit on a $15 000 car is no longer an attempt to compensate for possible loss or injury but becomes an attempt to punish the breaching party for failure to go through with the contract. Such a penalty clause, being excessive, is unconscionable and void. The $10 000 would not be a deposit at all and the prepayment would be returned subject to an action for damages for the injury actually suffered. Even when no prepayment is involved, a liquidated damages clause may be brought into question if the object is to punish rather than to compensate and the amount involved is exorbitant.

Deposit must not be penalty

Down Payments.

Another difficulty the courts must face is to distinguish between a **deposit** and a **down payment**. When a prepayment is meant to be forfeited in the event of a breach of contract, this sum is usually called a deposit. But when there is no intention that the amount be forfeited, the prepayment becomes an installment or a down payment. A down payment must be returned to the purchaser even if it is the purchaser who breaches the contract. The vendor then retains the right to sue for compensation for the injuries suffered. Of course, possession of the down payment will often give the vendor a lever to force the other party into settling the dispute.

Deposit is forfeited—down payment is not

The term applied to a particular prepayment does not always determine its nature. Even when the parties have consistently referred to a particular payment as a deposit, the courts will not treat it as such unless they can find a clear intention by both parties that the amount was to be forfeited in the event of a breach. And if the courts do determine that this was in fact the intention, the amount of the deposit must reflect an honest attempt by the parties to estimate their damages rather than to impose a penalty.

Damages

The remedy of damages or monetary compensation was developed by the common law courts, but it is not always appropriate when a contract is breached. Although the Courts of Chancery developed other remedies, the significance of damages as a remedy for breach of contract must be emphasized since it is still the most important remedy available to the courts, largely because it does not require the supervision of the court as the other remedies do. Courts assess what loss the victim of the breach has suffered and order the breaching party to pay an amount that will compensate for that loss to try to put the victim of the breach in the position he or she would have been in *if the contract had been properly performed.*

Damages in contract law designed to compensate

Victim of breach compensated as if contract had been properly performed

For example, if a person bought defective paint from a supplier which blistered when put on the house, necessitating repainting, the court would not only award the cost of the paint as damage but also take into consideration the amount it would cost for a painter to scrape the blistered paint off and repaint the house. The courts will then order the vendor to pay a sum sufficient to put the purchaser in the position he or she would have been in if the paint had not been defective.

Limitations on Recoverable Damages

Although damages are designed to compensate a person for losses suffered, not all injuries suffered are recoverable. Remoteness and mitigation are two limitations on the recoverability of damages.

Remoteness.

In the important case of *Hadley v. Baxendale*,[25] the plaintiff asked the defendant, a shipper, to send the crankshaft of a steam engine to the manufacturer to be used as a sample for a new one. The shipper was asked to send it quickly but failed to do so. Unbeknownst to the shipper, the plaintiff's entire plant was shut down while waiting for the crankshaft. This caused great expense to the plaintiff, who sued the shipper.

The defendant claimed that he could not be responsible for the unusual damage because he had no knowledge of it. The court used the reasonable person test to determine the extent of the shipper's responsibility for damages and held that the shipper was only responsible for the usual damages that could be expected if the contract was breached.

The principle that has developed from this and other cases is essentially that a breaching party is only responsible for those damages which, at the time the contract was entered into, seem a likely outcome if the contract were breached. Thus, the breaching party is also responsible for any unusual damages for special circumstances when communicated to him or her at the time the contract is entered into. In short, the breaching party is responsible in contract law for any damages that can be reasonably foreseen at the time the contract is entered into.

One area in which the problem of remoteness often arises is in a claim for damages to compensate for lost profits. The breaching party must be aware of the details of the other person's business at the time the contract is entered into for a claim of lost profits to be considered. Goods purchased for some unusual or specialized purpose may have a greater-than-normal potential to cause injury, but it is only when that unusual or specialized purpose is communicated to the vendor that the vendor can be held responsible for all of the damages suffered.

If Seto bought sealant from Mishra to waterproof the foundation of his house, Mishra would not be liable if it failed to do the job unless he knew what the sealant was to be used for at the time it was purchased.

When a contract is breached, damages are awarded in order to compensate for monetary losses. It is only recently that courts have shown a willingness to award monetary compensation for mental distress. Punitive damages are generally not available for breach of contract.

Must pay reasonably anticipated losses

Unique circumstances must be communicated

Mitigation.

Victims of breach have an obligation to mitigate their losses, that is, to keep them as low as is reasonably possible. If a vendor has an obligation to deliver and install goods at a person's house but leaves them on the front lawn instead, the purchaser must mitigate the loss by bringing the goods in and having them installed. The purchaser will not be able to claim for all of the injury suffered if he leaves the goods out on the lawn to be destroyed by the weather. The purchaser can sue the vendor for the cost of installing the goods but he is limited to the amount of loss that would have been suffered if he had acted reasonably in the circumstances.

Victims must mitigate their losses

---

25. *Hadley v. Baxendale* (1854) 156 E.R. 145 (Court of Exchequer).

Another situation in which losses must be mitigated is in the case of wrongful dismissal. A person who is dismissed from employment without just cause and without proper notice has a right to sue for wrongful dismissal. The amount of damages that may be recovered will be equal to the amount of notice that should have been given or the pay that should have been received in lieu of notice.

The dismissed employee does have an obligation to go out and try to find another job, and, if one is found, the damages that can be claimed from the employer will be reduced by the amount earned during the time of required notice. If the fired employee does not attempt to find another job and the court determines that one could have been found, it will reduce the amount of compensation for wrongful dismissal by the amount that would have been earned if the person had found other employment. However, the onus is on the breaching party to show that the fired employee failed to mitigate, which may not be easy to do. It is also important to note that the person who is required to mitigate is not obligated to take personal risks. The obligation to mitigate means simply that the victim of the breach must take all reasonable steps to minimize losses suffered.

Equitable Remedies

The following are examples of remedies that have been developed by the Courts of Chancery to deal with special situations in which the ordinary remedy of damages would not be adequate for the injuries suffered in a breach of contract situation.

Specific Performance.

Court can order performance of contract

Specific performance occurs when the court orders the defaulting party to live up to the terms of the contract. A person who buys a house and then finds that the vendor refuses to go through with the deal could sue the vendor for the expenses incurred and the cost of finding another house. If the purchaser has to pay more for a comparable house, the purchaser will be able to claim the difference as part of the damages. If the purchaser particularly liked the original house because of its unique design or location, monetary compensation may not be an adequate remedy. In such circumstances, the courts may grant specific performance and order the vendor to convey the house to the purchaser for the agreed-upon price.

—but only where damages would be inappropriate

SPECIFIC PERFORMANCE NOT AVAILABLE WHERE THIRD PARTY HURT

Mr. Galway offered a property for sale through a real estate agent. An offer was made to Island Properties, one that had to be accepted by a specific date. On the specified date, not knowing that an acceptance had been telegraphed by Island Properties, Galway entered into another contract to sell the property to Pegasus. Island Property asked for a court order of specific performance to have the property reconveyed to them. But although the court found that the contract between Galway and Island Properties was valid and binding, it also found that the prop-erty had been conveyed to Pegasus. The problem was whether an order of specific performance was available now that the property was in the hands of an innocent third party. The Newfoundland Court of Appeal held that so long as there was no notice of the prior transaction and no bad faith on the part of that third party, specific performance would not be available to wrest the property from them.

Island Properties Ltd. v. Entertainment Enterprises Ltd. et al., 26 D.L.R. (4th) 347 (Newfoundland Court of Appeal)

If a vendor reneges on an agreement to sell a new Ford automobile to a purchaser, it is usually possible for the customer to acquire an identical vehicle from a different dealer; the difference in price can be charged to the breaching vendor. Specific performance will not be available to the victim of the breach because the automobile is not unique and because monetary compensation is sufficient. But if the item being sold is an antique or one of a kind, money would not compensate the purchaser and specific performance would be available.

The courts will not order the defaulting party to perform the requirements of a contract that requires personal service. If a famous painter has a contractual obligation to paint a portrait and then refuses to do so, the courts will not order specific performance. Similarly, the courts will not award specific performance as a remedy in any situation that would require close supervision to ensure that the contract is properly performed. Nor will specific performance be available where it would hurt a third party.

Courts will not force performance of contracts for personal services

In the past it was thought that because every parcel of land is unique, specific performance would always be available as a remedy for breach of a contract to purchase land if sought by the victim. This has been changed by the Supreme Court of Canada, however, and now the purchase of land will be treated the same as other forms of property as regards the remedies available.

Injunction.

If a person agrees specifically not to do something and then goes ahead and does it anyway, the appropriate remedy may be an **injunction**. An injunction involves the court ordering the defaulting party to stop the offending action. The injunction is not limited to breach of contract; it may be available in any situation in which wrongful conduct is involved.

Courts may order breaching conduct to stop

In rare circumstances, the courts may issue a **mandatory injunction** when a person does something to violate a contractual term and thereby creates an ongoing problem. For example, if neighbours have a contract between them promising not to build over 15 metres high and one of them builds a structure 20 metres high, the courts may issue an injunction requiring removal of the structure. Such mandatory injunctions are not common.

As with specific performance, there are many instances in which the courts will refuse to issue an injunction. The courts will not order an injunction that would make it impossible for the person defaulting on the contractual agreement to earn a living any other way. A football team might be able to require one of its players to agree not to play for any other football team, but it would not be able to enforce by injunction a requirement that the football player not be employed by any other person at all. Similarly, the courts will not issue an injunction when damages provide a sufficient remedy. An injunction is not designed to punish someone for breaching a contract but to prevent further injury. An injunction will also not be awarded where it will cause harm to a third party.

But not where damages more appropriate

Accounting.

It is often difficult for the victim of the breach to determine just what kind of injuries he or she has suffered, especially when the offending party has taken advantage of some opportunities or rights belonging to the victim. This can happen when there is a fiduciary relationship between the contracting parties, that is, a relationship in which the person dishonouring the contract has a duty under the terms of the agreement to act in the best interests of the other party. In these circumstances, the

Court may order accounting

court can order that the defaulting party disclose all financial dealings and records so that the injured party can determine what he or she is entitled to claim. The court will then order the offending party to pay over any profits made from the wrongful conduct to the injured party. So the court, instead of awarding damages on the basis of what has been lost by the victim, awards damages on the basis of what has been wrongfully obtained by the breaching party.

Quantum Meruit.

Court may order payment for part performance

In some situations, the contract is breached before the amount agreed to in the contract is due and payable to the injured party. The courts have the power to award compensation for the value of work performed on the basis of *quantum meruit* if the injured party has done a considerable amount of work towards earning that payment. Care must be exercised, because the same does not apply if the breaching party has done some work but payment for this work is not due at the time the breach takes place. The courts are extremely reluctant to grant any compensation for the breaching party's partial performance of the agreement unless the contractual obligations have been substantially performed.

It is important to note that whether or not any partial payment was due and owing before the default takes place depends on how the contract is worded. The courts will often find that, under the terms of the agreement, the victim of the breach was entitled to some payment for what was performed before the breach. The courts are also willing to find that the victim of the breach can rescind the contract if its terms do not contain an implied promise to pay for partial performance. Once rescinded, the contract no longer exists and the courts are then free to imply a promise to pay the victim of the breach for the partial work done.

Suppose Scholz agrees to build a house for Banerjee according to Banerjee's specifications and the contract makes clear that no money is due until the job is complete. If Scholz refuses to complete the second half of the job, Banerjee would simply get someone else to finish it. If Scholz sues for compensation for the amount of work done, Banerjee can defend by saying no amount of money was due or payable until the job was completed and, since it was not completed, no money is owed. In these circumstances, the court is unlikely to find a provision in the contract allowing for partial payment and Scholz will be out of luck. But if Banerjee had refused to allow Scholz to finish the house, the court would have no hesitation in awarding compensation to Scholz for the work done.

Undue delay

Some general requirements must be met before the courts will grant an equitable remedy. If there has been **laches**, an undue delay on the part of the person seeking the equitable remedy, the courts can refuse to grant the remedy. The plaintiff will still be able to pursue any common law remedy such as damages without penalty for delay, provided the action is brought within the limitation period in place, as discussed in Chapter 1. The courts can refuse to award an equitable remedy in any situation in which it would cause hardship to the parties or to some other person, or would be inappropriate for any other reason. A person seeking equity must come to the court with clean hands. The remedy will be denied when the person seeking the equitable remedy is guilty of some wrongdoing. These requirements apply to all equitable remedies.

Hardship

Clean hands

Another factor that may affect the right of the victim of a breach of contract to bring an action in court is the *Limitations of Actions Act* discussed in Chapter 1. The limitation periods outlined in such statutes also apply to the field of contracts, thus limiting the availability of the remedies discussed after the passage of specified time periods.

Finally, it should be noted that when a judgment or an equitable remedy has been awarded and a defendant refuses to comply, the defendant may be held in contempt of court and can be jailed. The remedies to enforce a judgment outlined in Chapter 1 are available to the victim of a breach of contract as well.

Contempt

SUMMARY

Performance, including substantial performance, will bring a contract to an end. When one party properly tenders performance and is refused, the contract is normally discharged. When money is involved, however, it is still owed, but the creditor must bear the cost of its collection. When a condition is breached, the victim may treat the contract as discharged and sue. A breach of warranty, however, means the contract is still binding but the victim can sue for damages. When a party repudiates an agreement before performance is due, it is an anticipatory breach and the victim has the option of either treating the contract as discharged immediately or waiting to see if the contract is performed.

A contract is ended by agreement when all of the requirements of a contract including consideration and consensus are present. If one of the parties has already performed and promises not to insist on performance by the other, that promise is not enforceable. It may, however, be raised as a defense under the principle of promissory or equitable estoppel. The contract may provide for its own end with conditions precedent or conditions subsequent. An unexpected intervening event that makes the contract impossible to perform or something essentially different from what the parties expected may discharge the contract by frustration. In most jurisdictions (including Alberta), when there is frustration, the normal result of "Let the loss lie where it falls" has been modified by statute to allow the courts to apportion any monies advanced to compensate for expenses or losses incurred. Self-induced frustration is merely breach of contract.

The victim of a breach of contract is entitled only to the damages that were reasonably within the contemplation of the parties when they entered into the agreement and then only after all has been done to mitigate the loss. When the contract itself sets out the damages to be paid, it must be an honest attempt to forecast the loss to be enforceable. Similarly, a prepayment in the form of a deposit cannot be a penalty. The equitable remedy of specific performance requires the breaching party to carry out the terms of the agreement. An injunction is a court order that the breaching party stop doing something inconsistent with the terms of the contract.

QUESTIONS

1. Describe the various ways in which a contractual relationship can come to an end.

2. Under what circumstances would a breaching party who had partially performed the terms of the contract be entitled to receive part payment?

3. Describe the differences between a condition and warranty. What is the significance of the distinction?

4. How may the victim of the breach of a condition lose the right to rescind the contract?

5. What constitutes adequate tender of performance?

6. What recourse is available to one party to a contract when performance is made impossible by the other party's conduct?

7. What options are available to the victim of an anticipatory breach? Explain the advantages, disadvantages and risks associated with these options.

8. How do the courts approach an exclusionary or exculpatory clause in a contract?

9. What is meant by fundamental breach and what are the two different philosophies developed by the courts in applying this principle?

10. What two factors are most likely to be absent when a claim that a contract was discharged or modified by agreement is challenged in court?

11. Explain what rule the case of *Foakes v. Beer* established. How has it been modified by statute since then?

12. Distinguish between contractual terms that are conditions precedent and those that are conditions subsequent.

13. Define frustration. List three ways frustration can take place.

14. What is the significance of a court's determination that a contract was frustrated through the fault of one of the parties?

15. Explain how the House of Lords' decision in the *Fibrosa* case modified the previously accepted common law rule on the obligations of the parties in the face of a frustrating event. Explain how this decision was further modified by statute.

16. Distinguish between a deposit and a down payment. What is the significance of this distinction?

17. What must be the demonstrated intention of the parties for money paid under a term of a contract to be categorized as a deposit?

18. Explain what limitations on the recovery of damages were developed from the case of *Hadley v. Baxendale*.

19. Describe what is meant by mitigation. Explain how the obligation to mitigate damages limits the ability of the victim of a breach to obtain damages.

20. Distinguish between specific performance and injunction. Explain the restrictions on their availability.

CASES

1. Sumpter v. Hedges

The plaintiff agreed to erect certain buildings for the defendant for a lump sum payment to be paid upon completion. The plaintiff failed to finish the work and asked for reimbursement for the amount he had done. The defendant refused. The plaintiff then sued for payment for the work he had done. What factors would the court need to determine before they decided the case? Explain the likely outcome.

2. Betker v. Williams

Mrs. Williams owned property in Cranbrook, and listed the property for sale with Mr. Klinkhammer, a real estate agent. It was advertised as a residential lot in the local newspaper, with a clear indication that a house could be built on it. The property was bought by Mr. Betker, who in the process specifically asked Mr. Klinkhammer if it would be appropriate for a solar home and he received a positive reply. Four years after the sale they discovered that a house could not be built on the property because it was too small for a septic tank and had no access to the city sewer line.

It turned out that neither the Williams nor the realtors were aware of this problem. The Betkers learned that they could not build a house on the property and they brought an action against the realtors and Mrs. Williams. There was a term in the agreement stating that there were no representations other than those contained on the written agreement itself but this provision had not been specifically brought to the attention of the purchasers. Explain the arguments available to both parties and the appropriate remedies that might be sought.

3. Bell v. St. Thomas University

Bell was enrolled at the defendant university in a four-year program leading to a bachelor of social work. The program required the successful completion of a field practice course called Social Work 410. He took this course but failed it in 1987. The university calendar contained a provision about the repeating of courses that stated, "Students may without special permission register for a course already taken in order to meet a prerequisite or other degree requirement or in order to improve their grade." But in this case before allowing Bell to repeat Social Work 410, the department required him to fulfill certain conditions. He made several attempts to comply but these attempts were rejected and he was not permitted to retake the course.

Explain what options were available to Mr. Bell in these circumstances. Would your answer be any different if you understood that the course required Mr. Bell to interact with the community, including people at risk, and that his failing grade, and the terms and conditions imposed, related to making sure that no damage was done to the people he was dealing with?

4. Capital Quality Homes, Ltd. v. Colwym Construction Ltd.

The defendant paid a $13 980 deposit to the plaintiff for some undeveloped land in Windsor, Ontario. The agreement involved the conveyance of 26 separate building lots and the plaintiff was required to deliver 26 individual deeds of conveyance, one for each building lot. After the contract was entered into by the parties but before it was executed, legislation was passed bringing planning consent for the land in question under the control of a designated committee. The parties disagreed about who bore the obligation to get the required consents.

At the closing date, the defendant was unable to deliver the individual deeds required even though the plaintiff was ready to pay the required funds. It should be noted that this change of law took place only 33 days before the closing date for the transfer of the property and it is questionable whether it was possible to obtain the required consent in time.

The plaintiff sued for the return of the $13 980 deposit paid. Explain the likely outcome. Would your answer be affected if the reason consent was not obtained was that the defendant had made no effort to obtain the required consents?

5. Strata Corp. NW 1714 v. Winkler

Winkler was a contractor who agreed to erect a building on behalf of Strata Corporation according to certain specifications. When it was built, it failed to meet those specifications. There was insufficient depth of fill under the concrete floor; the floor itself was not of sufficient thickness; and Winkler had also failed to properly waterproof the walls. Strata Corporation claimed damages in the amount of $170 000—what it would take to rebuild the building to the stated specifications. The judge made a finding of fact that if the court awarded the $170 000 it would far exceed any reduction in value caused by the work that had been done improperly. Explain the arguments available on both sides and the likely outcome.

6. Meunier v. Cloutier

In 1977 Cloutier sold the St. Charles Hotel in Timmins to Meunier and in the process signed a non-competition clause whereby he promised not to compete in the hotel business for five years in the Timmins area. The clause had a provision that damages of $50 000 would be paid in the event of a breach and specifically stated that this was by way of liquidated damages and not as a penalty.

Within the prohibited period Cloutier and his wife returned to Timmins and opened a hotel in his wife's name to which Mr. Cloutier had made a substantial financial contribution. Explain the arguments available to the parties and what the court is likely to do in these circumstances. How would it affect your answer to know that Mr. Cloutier made it clear in his evidence that little attention was paid to the amount to be paid in the event of a breach and it had been agreed upon with little thought?

7. Computer Workshops v. Banner Capital Market Brokers

Banner, the defendant in this action, was in the brokerage industry and was developing a computer software network to handle his business. The plaintiff, Computer Workshops Ltd., entered into an agreement with Banner to provide him with the necessary hardware and software equipment to do the job. After 25 of the 100 computers agreed to were delivered, Banner discovered that Computer Workshops was negotiating with Banner's competition to provide them with a similar system with similar capabilities. Banner learned that in those discussions certain confidential information that he had given to Computer Workshops had been disclosed to their competitor. Banner refused to take the rest of the computers.

Computer Workshops sued for breach. Explain the arguments on both sides and any defense that might be available to Banner in these circumstances.

LEGISLATION

Alberta
Frustrated Contracts Act, R.S.A. (1980) c. F-20

Federal
Currency Act, R.S.C. (1985) c. C-52

WEBLINKS

Canada: Department of Justice: Dispute Resolution Project
canada.justice.gc.ca/Orientations/Methodes/index_en.html

Canadian Dispute Resolution Corporation (Quebec)
profil-cdi.qc.ca/scrd/scrde.htm

Alberta Arbitration and Mediation Society
www.agric.gov.ab.ca/sperg/arbitrat.html

Arbitration and Mediation Institute of Ontario Inc.
www.interlog.com/~amio/

B.C. International Commercial Arbitration Centre
www.ei.gov.bc.ca/Directory/Trade&Inv/centres/bcicac.htm

Institute for Dispute Resolution, University of Victoria
dispute.resolution.uvic.ca/

Society of Professionals in Dispute Resolution
www.igc.apc.org/spidr/

Alberta Frustrated Contracts Act
www.gov.ab.ca/qp/ascii/acts/F20.txt

REFERENCES FOR PART 2

Cheshire, G. C., C.H.S. Fifoot, and M. P. Furmston. *The Law of Contracts.* 9th ed. Ed. M. P. Furmston. London: Butterworth, 1976.

Fridman, Gerald Henry Louis. *The Law of Contract in Canada.* 2nd ed. Toronto: Carswell, 1986.

Fridman, G.H.L. *Sale of Goods in Canada.* 3rd ed. Toronto: Carswell 1986.

Linden, Allen M. *Canadian Tort Law.* 4th ed. Toronto: Butterworths 1988.

Owen, David G. *Philosophical Foundations of Tort Law.* Oxford, Clarendon Press, 1995.

Smyth, J. E., D. A. Soberman, and A. J. Easson. *The Law and Business Administration in Canada.* 8th ed. Toronto: Prentice Hall Canada, 1998.

Wright, Cecil A., Allen M. Linden, and Lewis N. Klar (ed. Priscilla Darrel). *Canadian Tort Law.* 8th ed. Toronto: Butterworths 1985.

Loewen Group's Contract Disputes

R ay Loewen had built a powerful empire in the funeral services business over the past decade. His style had been aggressive and competitive as his company, The Loewen Group, acquired 800 small funeral operations in Canada and the United States. All was going remarkably well until a family-owned funeral business in Jackson, Mississippi, that Loewen had been negotiating with launched a lawsuit over an $8 million contract dispute. The trial in Mississippi turned into an attack against big business, the rich and powerful, and the defense claimed to a largely non-white jury that Loewen, a Canadian, had stolen millions from "poor black Americans."

The jury found against Loewen, and it assessed a penalty of $500 million, more than the company was worth. The impact of the decision was devastating on his company, with an immediate 35 percent drop in stock values and a corresponding loss in their credit bond rating. The company then had to struggle to raise the $125 million deposit required by the court before it could launch an appeal. The case was finally settled for a payment of $175 million, but Ray Loewen is still reeling from the injustice.

Although the video does not go into the details of the dispute between the two companies, there is some suggestion of an abuse of judicial power in this case. It is unusual for a court to award punitive damages in a breach of contract dispute unless there has been fraudulent misrepresentation. The case also points up the dangers of doing business in another legal jurisdiction. It would also be unusual in Canada for a breach of contract case to be heard before a jury and then for a jury to award such exorbitant punitive damages.

Source: "Funeral Biz," *Venture,* Show Number 569; telecast date December 10, 1995. Running time: 7:05.

DISCUSSION QUESTIONS

1. The video refers to both fines and penalties. Is there a distinction between the two terms?
2. When is a penalty usually used as a remedy?
3. Should there be limits on the amount of a penalty that can be placed on a company by the courts?
4. Should governments attempt to regulate this kind of takeover operation?
5. The impact of such a verdict can be devastating to a company. How should a company protect themselves from such a risk?

Commercial Transactions

The world of commerce involves myriad individual transactions which taken together create markets that establish the economic structure of our society. Whether these transactions are associated with complex commercial activities or simple purchases, they are all controlled by an involved set of rules embodied in both the common law and legislation. This section examines that complex body of rules. Chapter 7 examines transactions involving the sale of goods, the *Sale of Goods Act* and the various statutes that are now in place intended to protect the consumer. Chapter 8 looks at secured transactions and the legislation controlling activities involving the transfer of title to property and the other means used by creditors to ensure that they get paid first by a debtor. Chapter 9 is devoted to negotiable instruments, cheques, bills of exchange, and promissory notes which are used to facilitate those transactions.

Photo by M. A. Kulla/First Light.

Sales and Consumer Protection

OBJECTIVES OF THE CHAPTER

- To review the main features of sale of goods acts
- To outline the legislation designed to protect consumers

Mrs. Knuude was an 80-year-old homeowner who was approached by a door-to-door sales representative for a home improvements company. The representative told Mrs. Knuude she had a problem with her windows that needed fixing. After four hours of extremely-high-pressure selling which included a refusal to leave unless the contract was signed, the sales representative left with a contract signed by her for repair and installation of an aluminum soffit, eavestroughs, flashing, repairing a damp wall and weatherstripping all the doors and windows in the house. Mrs. Knuude signed a $300 cheque as a deposit but stopped payment on it immediately after the salesman left.

The next day, workers from the firm came to do the work and she insisted they leave. This brought the sales representative back, who, by devious means, persuaded her to reinstate the contract. The work was done. She again refused to pay and the company sued for the money owed under the contract.

The judge determined that this was a clear case of fraud; that the contract was not binding on her as it was unconscionable; and that it did not conform to the requirements set out in the provincial consumer protection act.[1] This is an example of the unscrupulous business practices engaged in by some people that have led to the increase in legislation designed to protect consumers, the subject matter of this chapter.

---

1. *Dominion Home Improvements Ltd. v. Knuude* 20 C.L.R. 192 (Ont. District Ct.).

The preceding four chapters have been devoted to a general examination of the law of contracts. It should be apparent that this body of law has been developed by the courts rather than enacted through legislation. Although some incidental statutes modify particular aspects of contract law, it is still accurate to say that the law of contracts is based primarily on case law. There are, however, two particular areas where legislation has been enacted that profoundly affects the contractual relationship. The first part of this chapter is devoted to legislative statutes relating to the sale of goods. The second part of the chapter deals with consumer protection legislation.

THE SALE OF GOODS

The *Sale of Goods Act*

A large body of case law has developed in the area of contractual disputes involving the purchase and sale of goods. This body of case law was codified and enacted by Parliament in 1893 as the *Sale of Goods Act*, part of the general legal reforms in nineteenth-century Britain. This statute was adopted with only minor variations by every common law province in Canada.

People seldom think about the technicalities of contract law when they buy and sell items in the marketplace. They quite often neglect to set out all the terms necessary to cover the various eventualities that may arise in their transactions. Major terms of the agreement may be specified but small details are often taken for granted by the parties. The courts may imply missing terms when disputes arise that involve unstated details.

Act implies terms into contract

For example, the parties may not specify a date for payment when one person sells a car to another because each would assume that payment would be made on delivery of the car. These omissions put quite a burden on the courts and a great body of precedent law has been developed to fill in the gaps left by parties to contractual relationships. A major purpose of the *Sale of Goods Act*[2] is to provide a standardized approach for the courts to use as they imply omitted terms in disputed contracts.

It must be emphasized that the *Act* is only intended to fill the vacuum left by parties who neglect to specify all the terms of their agreement. It is not the courts' responsibility to impose new terms or conditions on the parties. It must be emphasized as well that the *Sale of Goods Act* is not limited to retail or consumer transactions, but applies to all situations where goods are bought and sold. Even significant commercial transactions involving goods such as a railway locomotive or other large piece of machinery are covered by the *Act*.

A major feature of the *Sale of Goods Act* is that terms specified in the contract will generally prevail over the provisions set out in the legislation. Generally, the parties can contract out of the operation of the *Sale of Goods Act* and thus override its provisions,[3] except in consumer sales, which will be discussed below.

Parties can contract out of provisions of *Act*

2. *Sale of Goods Act,* R.S.A. (1980) c. S-2. References to the *Sale of Goods Act* or the *Act* throughout this chapter refer to this Alberta legislation.

3. See, for example, *ibid.*, s. 13(1), which states that stipulations as to time of payment shall not be deemed to be of the essence of a contract of sale, unless a different intention appears from the terms of the contract. Furthermore, s. 55 of the Act says that any right, duty or liability that would arise by law under a contract may be negatived or varied by express agreement.

A second point to note about the *Act* is that it is merely a summation of the common law and complements the normal rules of contract law described in the four previous chapters. These apply to sale of goods contracts as well. To be bound by the contract for the sale of goods, the parties must show that a consensus was reached through offer and acceptance, that consideration was exchanged, that neither party was incapacitated, that the terms of the contract were legal and not against public policy, and that the parties intended legal consequences to flow from their transaction. The presence of mistake, misrepresentation, undue influence or duress can affect the obligations of the parties. The rules of breach and privity also apply.

Consensus and reasonable price often assumed by court

The requirement of consensus is somewhat modified by the *Sale of Goods Act*. Under normal circumstances, the parties must agree on a price; failure to state a price would result in a non-binding agreement. The *Sale of Goods Act* permits the parties to omit reference to a price or a method of calculating it and requires that a reasonable price will be paid for the goods in question.[4] The *Act* clearly states, however, that in circumstances where, unbeknownst to the seller, specific goods have perished at the time the contract is entered into, that contract is void.[5] This is consistent with the approach set out under "Shared Mistake" in Chapter 5.

Goods and Services.

Because the types of transactions affected by the *Sale of Goods Act* are quite restricted, it must be determined to which contractual relationships the *Act* applies. It must first be established that goods are the subject of the contract. **Goods** are tangible items such as watches, televisions, books and so on. The term "goods" does not include real estate but does include crops still growing on land. Buildings and building materials are subject to the *Sale of Goods Act* unless they are attached to the land and then they are treated as part of the real property and not subject to the *Act*. The *Act* does not apply to such non-tangible items as the sale of a **chose in action** (the right to sue another) or to the exchange of pieces of paper representing negotiable instruments, stocks, bonds and so forth.

Act applies only to sale of goods—not services

Contracts for services or the exchange of negotiable instruments, stocks, bonds and other documents representing rights or claims are excluded from the

---

SALE OF GOODS ACT DOES NOT APPLY TO SERVICE

Borek commissioned a large painting from Hooper, an artist. Unfortunately, about three years after it was purchased the painting showed serious problems of discoloration and surface deterioration. Borek sued for breach of warranty as to quality under the *Sale of Goods Act*. This case was first heard in Small Claims Court, which had awarded damages under the *Act*. When it went to the Divisional Court, that decision was reversed. The superior court held that the *Act* did not cover this transaction, as it did not involve a sale of goods, but of labour and skill; and the court recognized a similar provision implied into the contract in that there was a warranty with respect to quality and fitness for purpose and the case was sent back for retrial at the small claims level.

Borek v. Hooper, 114 D.L.R. (4th) 570 (Ontario Court [General Division], Divisional Court)

---

4. *Ibid.*, s. 11; Section 11(3) does state that what is a reasonable price is a question of fact dependent on the circumstances of each case.

5. *Ibid.*, s. 9.

jurisdiction of the *Act.* Therefore, transactions involving both goods and services can pose a problem. Although a will is a physical item that becomes the client's property, a major portion of the lawyer's fee is for the service rendered in drawing it up. When an artist is commissioned to paint a portrait, the primary component of the transaction is the service provided by the artist even though the consumer receives a tangible item. In such circumstances, the *Sale of Goods Act* will not apply.[6] If the customer were to resell the portrait to a third party, that transaction would be covered by the *Sale of Goods Act* since the entire amount paid is for the physical item transferred. There is no service component in this resale. When the service rendered involves the installation of goods, however, as in the repair of an automobile, the *Sale of Goods Act* applies to the goods portion of that contract.

Transfer of Goods.

The *Sale of Goods Act* applies when it can be demonstrated that the parties intended that the actual possession and property of the goods would transfer to the purchaser. The *Act* does not apply when the goods are used merely as security for a loan.[7] If the person borrowing the money retains possession of such goods and will regain title to those goods upon payment of the money borrowed, the *Act* does not apply because it is not a sales transaction. This point may seem obvious, but the tool used to accomplish the granting of security for a loan is often a bill of sale which purports to sell the goods in question to the creditor loaning the money. These transactions are covered by Alberta's *Personal Property Security Act*[8] and will be discussed in the following chapter.

Goods must be transferred

The *Sale of Goods Act* does apply when the seller of the goods is also providing credit. This type of sale is referred to as a **conditional sale** in which the eventual transfer of the property is anticipated in the agreement. The buyer obtains possession of the goods but the title or property of those goods remains with the seller until the final payment is made. At that time, the title is transferred to the buyer as well. Since this type of contract envisions a sale of the goods involved, albeit delayed, the *Sale of Goods Act* does apply. The financing aspect of the transaction, however, is covered by the personal property security legislation.[9]

Monetary Consideration.

It is also necessary that monetary consideration be given for the goods for the *Sale of Goods Act* to apply.[10] Money must change hands. The *Act* does not cover barter transactions. Often goods are traded in when new ones are purchased, but as long as some money is exchanged in addition to the trade-in, the *Sale of Goods Act* applies.

Act does not apply to barter

Requirement of Writing.

Some formal requirements must be met for the sale of goods to be binding on the parties. Originally, the *Statute of Frauds* contained provisions which affected the

---

6. In cases where both goods and services are provided, the court must determine if the essence of the contract was the materials or the work provided. See *Keillian West Ltd. v. Sportspage Enterprises Ltd.* and *Vogel,* 23 Alta. L.R. (2d) 99 (Q.B.), where the court decided that a contract for the printing of 20 000, 44-page programs was a contract for goods, not services, and was therefore subject to the *Act.*

7. *Ibid.,* s. 59(3).

8. *Personal Property Security Act,* S.A. (1988) c. P-4.05.

9. *Ibid.*

10. *Sale of Goods Act,* R.S.A. (1980) c. S-2 s. 3(1).

Requirement of writing

sale of goods. These provisions are now covered in sale of goods acts in the various provinces. In Alberta, a sale of goods above $50 must be evidenced in writing for the transaction to be legally enforceable.[11] When the total value of goods purchased at any one time exceeds the prescribed limit, this section of the *Sale of Goods Act* will apply. As is the case with the *Statute of Frauds*, failure to comply with this portion of the *Act* does not make the contract invalid but the courts will not enforce it. This distinction can be significant when the parties have the right to self-help or set-off. If the value of the purchase exceeds the specified amount and there is no evidence in writing, the contract will be enforceable if something has been given in earnest. This means that the buyer has given something of value to bind the contract.[12] Similarly, the contract will be enforceable in court when there has been part payment or part performance, which means that some of the goods have been accepted by the buyer.[13]

Title and Risk

Distinction between sale and agreement to sell

There is a distinction between a **sale** and an **agreement to sell**, although both are covered by the *Sale of Goods Act*. Sale refers to a situation in which the title and goods are transferred immediately. When the goods or title will be transferred at some future time, either because the goods have not yet been manufactured or because something remains to be done to them, the transaction is referred to as an agreement to sell.[14]

Normally risk follows title

The sale of goods involves the transfer of both possession and property rights of the goods from the seller to the buyer. Disputes between parties are often concerned with determining at what stage the property (or title) transferred from the seller to the buyer. Determining the precise time of exchange is important because the *Sale of Goods Act* provides that risk follows title.[15] **Risk** refers to any potential loss due to the destruction or damage of the goods. As with other sections of the *Act*, the parties can change who bears the risk by agreement.

Specified Risk.

There are three common methods of specifying contractually who will bear the risk if it is to be anyone other than the title holder.

Exceptions to assumption of risk

1. *C.I.F. contracts (cost, insurance and freight).* In this type of contract, the buyer may obtain title at an early stage in the transaction but the seller has assumed responsibility to pay for the costs involved in the shipping of those goods as well as arranging insurance to a specific point in the process, such as to the transport service or the destination.

2. *F.O.B. contracts (free on board).* With F.O.B. contracts, the parties have specified that the seller will bear the risk until the goods are placed on board the carrier chosen to transport them to the buyer. At that point the buyer assumes the risk.

3. *C.O.D. contracts (cash on delivery).* This type of contract entitles the seller to maintain both the proprietary rights (or title) as well as control over the

---

11. *Ibid.,* s. 7.
12. *Ibid.,* s. 7(1)(a).
13. *Ibid.,* s. 7(1)(a).
14. *Ibid.,* s. 3(4).
15. *Ibid.,* s. 23(1).

possession of those goods until they are delivered to the buyer's premises and paid for. The risk stays with the seller until delivery is complete.

Another method by which the seller may maintain control of the goods and risk during shipment is through a bill of lading. A **bill of lading** is a document given by the transporter or carrier of the goods to the shipper as a form of receipt. The person designated as the consignee on a bill of lading has the right to take delivery of the goods at their destination. A straight bill of lading usually names the buyer as the consignee on the document; the shipper/seller no longer has control and the risk shifts to the buyer during shipping. When **order bills of lading** are used, shippers name themselves as consignees and retain the right to receive the goods at their destination or to designate that right to someone else. Sellers who have maintained control in this way bear responsibility for the goods until they have reached their destination subject to any other provisions that may be in the contract of sale itself. It should be noted that the use of order bills of lading provides sellers with maximum flexibility and facilitates arrangements such as financing in which the goods are used as security.

Bills of lading may determine title

Transfer of Title.

The timing of the transfer of the property or title of the goods can control more than risk. Whoever has the proprietary interest will also determine whether the seller can sue for the entire price of the goods or merely for damages upon default by the buyer. The time of the transfer of title and the risk will be implied according to the following rules when no contrary intention is indicated by the parties.[16]

Remedy may depend on who has title

RULE 1

Rules for determining title

> When there is an unconditional contract for the sale of specific goods in a deliverable state, the property in the goods passes to the buyer when the contract is made and it is immaterial whether the time of payment or the time of delivery or both be postponed.

This rule states that when the contract involves the sale of a specifically identified and finished item, the proprietary interest transfers to the buyer at the time the contract is made. For example, if Lynch walked into Amann's T.V. Store on Thursday night, pointed to a television set and said, "I want to buy that one," the property in that television would transfer to Lynch as soon as the offer was accepted by Amann. If Lynch decided to pick up the set the following night, Lynch would still have the proprietary interest and the risk in the set during the interim. Lynch would bear the loss if the set were destroyed by fire early Friday morning and it was not Amann's fault. Note that who actually pays will usually be determined by the nature of the insurance coverage.

Title transfers immediately

RULE 2

> When there is a contract for the sale of specific goods and the seller is bound to do something to the goods for the purpose of putting them into a deliverable state, the property does not pass until the thing is done and the buyer has notice thereof.

---

16. These provisions are taken from Section 21 of the Alberta *Sale of Goods Act.*, R.S.A. (1980) c. S-2.

Contracts will often require that the seller make some modification, such as repair or service, before the buyer takes possession of the goods. The title to these goods is transferred only after the work has been performed and the buyer has been given notice of the completion of the work. This notice usually comes in the form of delivery of the goods, but it would probably be sufficient notice for the seller to telephone the buyer and say, "Your goods are ready." In the example used earlier, if Lynch required that Amann repair a scratch on the television set before taking delivery, the title and risk would still be with Amann at the time of the fire on Friday morning and Amann would bear the loss. This would be true even if Amann had finished repairing the components or the scratch the night before if Lynch had not yet received notice.

RULE 3

When there is a contract for the sale of specific goods in a deliverable state but the seller is bound to weigh, measure, test or do some other act or thing with reference to the goods for the purpose of ascertaining the price, the property does not pass until the act or thing is done and the buyer has notice thereof.

The provisions of this rule are similar to those set out in Rule 2. However in this instance some evaluative process must be completed and notice given before property in the goods and thus risk can pass. For example, if Schmidt agreed to purchase a particular truckload of potatoes from Naslund, it would probably be necessary to weigh the load to determine the exact price. Title to the potatoes would only transfer to Schmidt after the weighing was completed and notice given.

RULE 4

When goods are delivered to the buyer on approval or "on sale or return" or other similar terms, the property in them passes to the buyer:

(i) when he signifies his approval or acceptance to the seller or does any other act adopting the transaction, or

(ii) if he does not signify his approval or acceptance to the seller but retains the goods without giving notice of rejection then if a time has been fixed for the return of the goods, on the expiration of that time, and, if no time has been fixed, on the expiration of a reasonable time, and what is a reasonable time is a question of fact.

This rule covers situations in which goods are taken by the buyer to test for a trial period before deciding to keep them. It becomes difficult to determine when the proprietary interest transfers in these circumstances. It is straightforward when the buyer contacts the seller to say the goods are acceptable, but, if the buyer fails to do so, the proprietary interest can still transfer to the buyer. If the buyer tries to resell, modify or install the goods, these acts are inconsistent with the seller maintaining title to the goods. In other words, if the buyer acts as if he or she owns the goods, the buyer does own them, and title transfers. Otherwise, the title transfers when the trial period agreed on is over. If no period was agreed on, a reasonable time must pass before title transfers.

In our earlier example, if Amann had allowed Lynch to take the television home and try it for four days, title would not transfer to Lynch until the expiration of those four days, unless Lynch notified Amann before that time that he was happy with the goods. However, if Lynch built the television set into the wall of his den, that action would be inconsistent with Amann still having title to the goods. Title would pass to Lynch. If the title had not passed during those four days and the goods were damaged or destroyed, the risk would remain with the seller unless the parties had agreed otherwise.

RULE 5

> (i) When there is a contract for the sale of unascertained or future goods by description and goods of that description and in a deliverable state are unconditionally appropriated to the contract either by the seller with the assent of the buyer, or by the buyer with the assent of the seller, the property in the goods thereupon passes to the buyer.

> (ii) The assent may be expressed or implied and may be given either before or after the appropriation is made, and if pursuant to the contract the seller delivers the goods to the buyer or to a carrier or other bailee, whether named by the buyer or not, for the purpose of transmission to the buyer and does not reserve the right to disposal, he shall be deemed to have unconditionally appropriated the goods to the contract.

The goods covered by Rule 5 are those that have not been manufactured at the time the contract was entered into or that exist but have not yet been separated out and identified as the particular goods to be used in a given transaction. Suppose that, in the example used earlier, Lynch had walked into Amann's television store, pointed toward a particular television and said, "I want a set like that one," and Amann had agreed to supply Lynch with a television from a stock of new sets in the back of the store. This situation would be covered by Rule 5 because no particular television set had yet been appropriated to the contract. Rule 5 also applies when a person orders a new car from the factory to be manufactured to particular specifications because the goods are not in existence at the time the contract is entered into.

When goods are not yet manufactured or not identifiable as the goods in question, unconditional appropriation and assent needed

Only when the goods have been manufactured or separated out and unconditionally committed to the buyer with the buyer's assent does title pass. While notice to the buyer that the goods are ready may be the most common method of satisfying the assent or approval provision, assent is often implied from the circumstances. Thus, if a person were to leave her car with a dealer for the installation of a new stereo cassette player, she will be taken to have assented to the selection of the stereo when it is installed since she left her car there for that purpose.

The parties can specify an intent contrary to that set out in the *Act* in relationship to who bears the risk. In addition to the traditional methods (C.I.F., F.O.B. and C.O.D. contracts discussed above), care must also be taken to examine other contractual terms to determine whether the parties have contracted out of the provisions of the *Sale of Goods Act* dealing with risk. For example, if the parties clearly state in their contract that the goods are to remain at the risk of the seller until they are delivered to the buyer's place of business, that stated intention will prevail over the implied provisions of the *Act*.

Rights and Obligations of the Parties

Hunter Engineering Co. v. Syncrude Canada Ltd.[17]

As part of its tar sands extraction project in Northern Alberta, Syncrude used a large conveyor belt to carry sand over long distances. Syncrude contracted with Hunter Engineering in the United States to supply a number of the gear boxes needed to convert the power generated by large motors to the gears that move the conveyor belt. Syncrude specified their needs and the items were designed by Hunter and manufactured by a subcontractor in the United States.

Syncrude also contracted directly with Allis-Chalmers for the purchase of 14 conveyor systems, including a number of gear boxes manufactured to the same specifications by the same subcontractor that Hunter had used in the United States. About a year after the gear boxes acquired from Hunter, and two years after the ones acquired from Allis-Chalmers, went into service, they failed, and upon inspection cracks were found indicating that there would be future failures in the other gear boxes. Syncrude had all the gear boxes redesigned and rebuilt, and repaired the damage.

In this action Syncrude sought compensation from Hunter U.S. and Allis-Chalmers. The two firms admitted that the gear boxes were too weak for the service required, but they denied liability because both of their contracts contained a clause specifically limiting their liability to a limited period of time. The court had to deal with whether the *Sale of Goods Act* applied to the contract.

The firms argued that even though dealing with large pieces of equipment created significant damages, the *Act* did apply to this contract, unless its provisions were specifically barred by wording to the contrary. The provision of the *Act* that was important was the implied condition that the goods were fit for the purpose for which they were used when the skill and ability of the supplier of those goods was relied on, as was the case here. The problem is whether the parties had excluded the operation of this provision of the *Sale of Goods Act* because of their specific contract language.

The court held that as far as Hunter U.S. was concerned, they did not specifically exempt the operation of the statutory conditions or warranties, and that therefore Section 15 of the *Act* did apply and Syncrude's action against Hunter was successful. Syncrude had relied on their expertise; the gear boxes were not reasonably fit for their purpose and Hunter had not specifically contracted out of their responsibility.

In the contract with Allis-Chalmers, however, there was a provision excluding any other statutory warranties or conditions other than those specifically included in the contract, and since the warranty set out in the contract had expired there would be no warranty unless the breach was so fundamental as to override the provisions of this exclusionary clause. The court held that even though the breach was fundamental, it could be caught by the exclusionary clause, therefore Allis-Chalmers was not liable to Syncrude.

This case has several interesting aspects. It illustrates that the *Sale of Goods Act* applies to business transactions on a massive scale, as well as normal consumer transactions; that there are provisions in the *Act* implied into contracts of sale giving protection to purchasers; and that it is possible for parties to contract out of those provisions if they wish.

17. 57 D.L.R. (4th) 321 (Supreme Court of Canada).

It also illustrates the operation of the concept of fundamental breach and exclusionary clauses. Exclusionary clauses are designed to limit the operation of the fitness and quality provisions of the *Sale of Goods Act*. The doctrine of fundamental breach has been designed to overcome that, but the courts have made it clear that the principle of fundamental breach is a rule of construction, meaning that it really depends on what the parties intended as to whether exemption clauses can be applied even to fundamental breaches. This is one of the few cases in which the Supreme Court of Canada has made it clear that an exemption clause worded correctly can exempt liability for even a fundamental breach. Note, however, that it will be extremely rare for a court to make such a finding.

The *Sale of Goods Act* has provisions intended to supply terms that affect the very substance of the contractual relationship between the parties. These terms are referred to in the *Act* as conditions or warranties. As was discussed previously, conditions are important terms of the contract, the breach of any of which entitles the victims to consider themselves no longer bound. Breaches of warranties do not release victims from their obligations under the contract. Parties are free to agree that a term that would normally be considered a warranty become a condition. The opposite is possible as well. But under the *Sale of Goods Act* the courts retain the power to treat a term designated as a condition as a warranty and one designated as a warranty as a condition.[18]

Conditions and warranties under Sale of Goods Act

The victim of a breach of a condition has the option to ignore it or to treat it as a breach of warranty. The victim of a breach may lose the right to have a contract discharged by a breach of condition by accepting the goods. In our example of the television set purchased from Amann's television store, Lynch would be entitled to return the set and demand a refund if he had specified as a condition of the contract that the television have a remote control device and he did not discover until he got it home that his set did not have one. Although Lynch had taken delivery of the goods and taken them home, he was unaware of the breach of condition and therefore cannot be said to have accepted the goods. But once Lynch became aware that the set had no remote control, plugging it in and using it over the weekend is inconsistent with Amann still owning the set. Lynch would then have accepted the goods with full knowledge of the breach of condition. It is likely that he would only be able to sue for damages and would be required to perform his part of the contractual obligation.

Acceptance causes victims of breach to lose right of discharge

Title

The *Sale of Goods Act* implies several terms into sales agreements which cover a seller's right to sell goods to a buyer. Section 15(a) of the *Sale of Goods Act*[19] states that it shall be a condition of a contract for sale that the seller has the right to sell the goods or, when dealing with an agreement to sell, that the seller will have that right at the time the property is to pass. Thus, Amann breaches a condition of the contract if he does not own the television set he tries to sell to Lynch and has no right to acquire it. Lynch would be free from any further obligation under the contract.

Seller must convey good title

18. *Sale of Goods Act*, R.S.A. (1980) c. S-2 s. 14(2). The common law discussed in this and the next paragraph is set out in s. 14 of the *Act*.
19. *Ibid.*

• and quiet possession

Section 15(b) requires that the seller provide **quiet possession of the goods** as a warranty of the contract. This means that the goods must be delivered in such a condition that they can be used and enjoyed by the buyer in the way they were intended, free from any interference. If the seller does not have the right to sell the goods because they belong to somebody else and the rightful owner seizes the goods from the buyer, this would contravene both part (a) and part (b) of Section 15.

Some overlap exists between the two provisions. However, Section 15(b) is somewhat broader than Section 15(a), because quiet possession may be interfered with for reasons other than mere title. For example, it is quite possible that the buyer could be restrained from using a product which violates a copyright, patent or trademark. This is not a problem of title, because the seller did own the goods and did have the right to convey good title, but the patent infringement interfered with the buyer's quiet possession of the goods and therefore violated an implied warranty in the contract.

• and goods free from charge or encumbrance

Section 15(c) of the *Act* specifies that it shall be an implied warranty of the contract that the goods shall be free from any charge or encumbrance in favour of any third party not declared or known to the buyer. When personal goods are used as security in loan transactions, the creditor obtains the right to seize the goods and sell them if the debt is not honoured. This is a charge or encumbrance, often called a **lien**. The lien or charge gives the creditor the right of seizure even when the goods are passed on to innocent third parties. Transactions in which personal property is taken as security should be registered. Creditors obtain rights of priority when these formal requirements are met. For this reason, it is always prudent to search the title of a motor vehicle before purchasing it. Even a buyer who fails to do such a search and later discovers a charge or encumbrance against goods purchased has the right to sue the seller for breach of this implied warranty. If it is not possible to obtain a remedy against the seller because the seller is insolvent or unavailable, the priority of the creditor will prevail and the buyer will be required either to pay off the lien against the goods or to surrender the goods to the creditor.

Description

Goods must match description

Goods are often sold by catalogue, mail order or other forms of distance shopping. In such circumstances, the goods have to be sold by description. The written text is often accompanied by a picture or illustration. Section 16 of the *Sale of Goods Act* provides that, when the sale is accomplished by description, there shall be an implied condition in contracts that the goods delivered must correspond with the description or illustration provided. If Afsari based her order for a new camera from a catalogue on an illustration showing a Nikon camera and the camera that Afsari eventually received was a Pentax, there has been a breach of the implied condition that the goods correspond with the description.

Most sales of manufactured goods are by description

Although there is some dispute over just what sale by description means, there is little doubt that the term is broad enough to cover the sale of virtually all manufactured goods, even when the customer makes the selection as would be the case in a self-service store. The manufacturer has produced many identical, essentially indistinguishable items, so the buyer relies on the general description given by the manufacturer as to what those goods can do. The fact that she chooses one over another does not lessen that reliance. Even when the buyer inspects a sample of the goods in addition to relying on the description contained on the box, in the brochure or in the catalogue, the buyer would be entitled to claim that a

PRODUCT LIABILITY WHERE SELLER RELIED ON

Eli Lilly Canada sold a herbicide to the Caners, who applied it to their crop. In the first year this was done, the crop grew with large areas of weed infestation, the herbicide having failed to do the job. The next year, after consulting with Eli Lilly, they treated the field with the herbicide again and the result was essentially that the crop didn't grow at all. Eli Lilly claimed that in the first year the Caners didn't follow the instructions properly and failed to apply the herbicide evenly, and that in the second year Mr. Caner sowed his crop too deeply. The court found that the instructions provided were imprecise, and therefore under the *Sale of Goods Act* the warranty as to fitness and quality was breached. It is interesting that at the trial level the court found contributory negligence and reduced the award accordingly, but at the appeal level the judge specifically said that contributory negligence as found in the *Tortfeasors and Contributory Negligence Act* of Manitoba did not apply to sale of goods actions.

Caners v. Eli Lilly Canada Inc., 134 D.L.R. (4th) 730 (Manitoba Court of Appeal)

condition had been breached if the goods matched the sample but failed to correspond with the description.[20]

Fitness and Quality

Another condition the *Sale of Goods Act* implies into a sale by description is that the goods provided must be of a **merchantable quality**.[21] This means that the goods must be free of any defect that would have persuaded the buyer not to buy them at the agreed-upon price if the buyer had known of the defect at the outset. If a sample has been examined, there is no implied condition for defects the examination ought to have revealed. Note that with the broader approach taken by the courts as to what qualifies as sale by description, this provision will apply to virtually all sales of manufactured goods.

> Goods must be of merchantable quality

A similar provision requires that, if the buyer has relied on the skill or judgment of the seller to advise on the suitability of a particular product for an intended purpose, there is an implied condition that the product will be reasonably fit for that purpose.[22] This was the section applicable to the *Hunter* case discussed above. For example, if Florio bought a particular kind of paint from McGregor's Paint Company after asking if it was suitable for concrete and later found that the paint peeled, Florio would be able to sue McGregor for compensation because of the breach of the implied condition that the goods would be reasonably suitable for their intended purpose.

> Goods must be suitable for purpose of purchase when salesperson relied upon

There are two situations in which this provision of the *Act* does not apply. If it is not in the course of the seller's business to supply this type of product[23] or if the buyer requests the product by trade name,[24] the seller is not responsible. The courts, however, have adopted a broad interpretation of this latter provision. In the case of *Baldry v. Marshall,*[25] they suggested that, to avoid liability, the request for

20. *Ibid.,* s. 16.
21. *Ibid.,* s. 17(4).
22. *Ibid.,* s. 17(2).
23. *Ibid.*
24. *Ibid.,* s. 17(3).
25. *Baldry v. Marshall* [1925] 1 K.B. 260 (Court of Appeal).

an article by its trade name must be made in such a way that it is clear that the skill of the seller is not being relied on. Similarly, the courts have moved in the direction of finding that there is sufficient reliance on the skill and ability of the seller whenever the customer goes to a specific store to purchase the goods.

It should also be noted that this section is broad enough to cover not only goods sold for special purposes but also goods to be used under normal conditions. The courts' liberal approach means that the provisions related to fitness and quality apply in most sale of goods situations. The principle of *caveat emptor* discussed in Chapter 5 applies to transactions that come under the *Sale of Goods Act*. It must be remembered, however, that *caveat emptor* only means that the buyer is required to be careful in these transactions; he or she still has the right to expect a certain level of quality and protection when such care has been shown. Alberta courts have found sellers liable for breach of the implied condition that the goods will be reasonably fit for their purpose in cases involving the sale of a sandwich that contained a piece of wood,[26] a truck that was plagued by constant breakdowns[27] and a laptop computer that frequently broke down.[28]

Sample

Goods must match sample and be free of significant hidden defects

The *Act* uses a similar approach for the purchase of goods after examination of a sample.[29] When a buyer places an order after being given an opportunity to inspect a sample of the goods, the bulk of the goods must correspond in quality to the sample inspected, and the buyer must be given an opportunity to compare the original sample to the goods delivered. The goods must also be "free from any defect rendering them unmerchantable." That is, the goods must be free from any hidden defects which would have persuaded the buyer not to buy them at that price if he or she had been aware of the defects when inspecting the sample.

For example, if the load of bricks Tsang bought from Cashin after first inspecting a sample brick looked fine but, in fact, had not been baked properly and disintegrated after being used in Tsang's building, the bricks would be of unmerchantable quality. In these circumstances, Tsang would be able to sue Cashin for the breach of the implied condition that the goods be free from any hidden defect that would render them unmerchantable.

Parties free to contract out

It must be reemphasized that, under the terms of the *Sale of Goods Act*, the parties are generally free to include clauses which override the provisions set out in the *Act*. This can be very important especially when it is realized that the actual loss experienced may far exceed the cost of the goods involved, as would likely be the case when contaminated food has been purchased and consumed. Most sales contracts dealing with manufactured goods contain warranty provisions which include exculpatory clauses that limit or eliminate any responsibility on the part of the seller for defects in the product. When parties to a contract include such exculpatory or exemption clauses, they too will override the provisions of the *Act* unless prohibited by provincial legislation. In the *Hunter* case discussed above, the exemption clause was effective with respect to Allis-Chalmers, but not with respect to Hunter, which had not excluded the implied conditions of the statute. Several provinces, including Ontario and B.C., have enacted legislation prohibiting the

---

26. *Coote v. Hudson's Bay Company and Swift Canadian Co. Ltd.* (1977) 6 A.R. 59 (Alta. District Ct.).

27. *Rosseway v. Canadian Kenworth Ltd.* 6 Alta. L.R. (2d) 177 (Alta. District Ct.).

28. *Gadd v. London Drugs Ltd. et al.* (1991) 123 A.R. 335 (Alta. Prov. Ct.).

29. *Sale of Goods Act*, R.S.A. (1980) c. S-2 s. 18.

seller from excluding or limiting these provisions of the *Sale of Goods Act* relating to fitness and quality in consumer sales transactions. (Consumer protection legislation will be discussed below.) It should also be noted that sellers sometimes go beyond the minimum requirements of law, providing generous return policies for goods when the purchaser is not satisfied. These are store policies going beyond the legal requirements set out here. Alberta has no such legislation and, as discussed above, s. 55 of the *Sale of Goods Act* allows the parties to a sales contract to exclude any implied term.

Other Implied Terms

The *Sale of Goods Act* implies a term in the contract that the buyer shall pay a reasonable price for the goods delivered if the parties fail to stipulate a price.[30] When the parties have not agreed otherwise, there is also an implied term in the contract that delivery and payment are regarded as concurrent conditions.[31] Stipulations as to time of payment shall not be deemed to be of the essence of a contract of sale, unless a different intention appears from the terms of the contract.[32] Whether any other stipulation as to time is of the essence of the contract depends on the terms of the contract.[33] When the contract contains no provision for when the seller is to send the goods to the buyer, the seller is bound to send them within a reasonable time.[34] Tender of delivery will be ineffective unless made at a reasonable hour, which is a question of fact.[35] In most cases, this would be during business hours. The place of delivery is the seller's place of business, unless the contract indicates otherwise.[36]

Where price omitted— reasonable price

If the seller delivers a quantity of goods less than he contracted to sell, the buyer may reject them, or accept them and pay for them at the contract rate.[37] If the seller delivers a quantity of goods larger than he contracted to sell, the buyer may accept the goods contracted for and reject the rest, reject all of the goods delivered, or accept all of the goods, in which case he must pay for them at the contract rate.[38] The provisions affecting delivery, place, time and quantity of the goods are often made conditions by the parties.

When quantity delivered is wrong, buyer has choice

Remedies on Default

The seller has several options when the buyer has defaulted or breached. The seller holds an **unpaid seller's lien** against the goods if they have not been paid for and are still in the seller's possession.[39] This means that, even though the proprietary interest in the goods has transferred to the buyer who is, therefore, entitled to possession by the terms of the agreement, the seller has the right to retain the goods until payment is received. If credit arrangements for payment have been made, the seller

Unpaid seller's lien and stoppage in transitu

30. *Ibid.,* s. 11(2).
31. *Ibid.,* s. 29.
32. *Ibid.,* s. 13(1).
33. *Ibid.,* s. 13(2).
34. *Ibid.,* s. 30(4).
35. *Ibid.,* s. 30(7).
36. *Ibid.,* s. 30(2).
37. *Ibid.,* s. 31(1).
38. *Ibid.,* s. 31(2).
39. *Ibid.,* s. 41(1).

is only entitled to a lien against the goods when the purchaser has defaulted on the credit terms. An unpaid seller is also entitled to retain possession of the goods when the buyer becomes insolvent. A person is deemed to be insolvent when he has ceased to pay his debts in the ordinary course of business or cannot pay his debts as they become due.[40]

Seller protected in case of bankruptcy

Similarly, if the seller has delivered the goods to a transporter or shipper and they are en route to the buyer, the seller retains the right of **stoppage *in transitu*.**[41] This means that when the buyer becomes insolvent, the seller can stop the delivery of the goods and retake possession of them as long as they have not yet reached the buyer.

Unless the contract has a provision authorizing the resale of the goods in such circumstances, the seller must notify the buyer of an intention to resell the goods. If payment is not made within a reasonable period of time, the seller can then resell. There is no requirement that notice of resale be given when the goods are perishable.[42]

This right of lien and the right to stop the goods in transit can be very important to the seller because, once the goods get into the possession of the buyer, they become part of the buyer's estate and may be claimed by other creditors. Under the *Bankruptcy and Insolvency Act*, however, a supplier of such goods has the right to retake those goods if, within 30 days of delivery, the debtor has become bankrupt or a receiver has been appointed and, of course, providing the debtor or trustee still has them.[43]

Seller can sue for price in cases of default or refusal of delivery once title has passed

Sellers can sue for breach of contract whenever the buyer defaults on the contract of sale, whether or not the buyer is insolvent. Sellers have at their disposal all of the contractual remedies described in Chapter 6. The seller has the right to sue for the price of the goods when the proprietary interest has passed to the buyer.[44] It must be remembered that the proprietary interest or title in the goods may transfer in advance of the actual possession. When the title has passed but the buyer refuses to accept delivery of the goods, the buyer is rejecting his or her own goods and may still be required to pay the entire purchase price. If the time specified in the contract for full payment passes, the seller can sue for the full purchase price of the goods sold even when the title has not yet passed. Buyers would be wise to refuse delivery only when the seller has breached some condition of the contract. Otherwise, by refusing delivery, the buyer takes the risk of not getting the goods but still being required to pay full price for them.

Seller still entitled to sue for damages for breach

The seller may be able to claim for damages for breach of contract to compensate for loss even in situations in which it is not possible to claim the purchase price of the goods.[45] But it is often difficult for the seller to claim lost profits on the sale as damages. To do so, the seller may be required to show that the product could not have been sold to anyone else. If this cannot be proven, the damages will be limited to the costs incurred in the process of resale. In many cases, it may not be worthwhile to sue for damages if suing for the purchase price of the goods is not permitted. The seller also has an obligation to mitigate losses or keep damages as low as possible. This usually means that the seller must take steps to resell the goods immediately. Delay might lead to a claim that there was a failure to mit-

40. *Ibid.*, s. 2(2).

41. *Ibid.*, s. 44.

42. *Ibid.*, s. 48.

43. *Bankruptcy and Insolvency Act*, R.S.C. (1985) c. B-3 s. 81.1.

44. *Sale of Goods Act*, R.S.A. (1980) c. S-2 s. 49.

45. *Ibid.*, s. 50.

igate. The obligation to mitigate damages generally does not require that the seller spend any further money to sell the goods.

The remedies available to the buyer if the seller defaults are those of general contract law. The buyer can have the contract rescinded in cases of misrepresentation. Damages may also be available if the misrepresentation is fraudulent or negligent. When the misrepresentation becomes a term of the agreement, it is treated as any other condition or warranty under the *Act.* If the seller has breached a condition of the sales contract, the buyer can repudiate. When the purchase price has not yet been paid, the buyer can refuse to pay it. When the purchase price has been paid, the buyer can demand its return. When the term breached is a warranty, the buyer must fulfill his or her side of the contract but can withhold sufficient payment to compensate for losses incurred. The buyer can commence an action for damages if he or she has already paid. When the seller fails to deliver the goods to the buyer, the damages will usually be based on the difference between what the buyer had agreed to pay for the goods and the cost of obtaining those goods from another source.[46] But when there are additional injuries suffered because of the delay in obtaining the goods, the buyer will be able to claim them as well.

(margin note) Purchaser's remedies those of contract law

Goods supplied by the seller that fail to meet the standard of quality required in the contract or as set out in the *Act* can cause substantially different sorts of injuries. These injuries can be claimed as damages for breach of contract as long as they were reasonably within the contemplation of the parties at the time the contract was entered into.[47] Thus, someone who suffers food poisoning because of poor-quality food at a restaurant can seek compensation for their injuries under the *Sale of Goods Act* provisions. When the goods being sold are unique in their nature, the buyer may also be able to claim a remedy of specific performance and force the seller to go through with the sale rather than pay damages in compensation.[48]

(margin note) Extent of damages depends on circumstances

Finally, it should be mentioned that most provinces have recently enacted an *International Sale of Goods Act.*[49] The federal government is a signatory to a United Nations convention along with many other nations, and the provincial legislation is intended to implement that international treaty. A great deal of trading today is done in the international arena and these statutes bring the same kind of structure and certainty to import and export dealings as the *Sale of Goods Act* provides domestically.

CONSUMER PROTECTION LEGISLATION

Rushak v. Henneken[50]

Mrs. Rushak went with a friend to purchase a used car. She had a look at a very attractive 1982 Mercedes sports model. (The trial judge later said that the car was "of such peerless beauty that ... she appears to cast a hypnotic spell upon all who had dealings with her.") The salesperson was Mr. Henneken, who was also the owner of the car lot.

---

46. *Ibid.,* s. 51(3).
47. *Hadley v. Baxendale* (1854) 156 E.R. 145 (Court of Exchequer).
48. *Ibid.,* s. 52.
49. In Alberta, the legislation is the *International Conventions Implementation Act,* S.A. (1990) c. I-6.8.
50. 84 D.L.R. (4th) 87 (British Columbia Court of Appeal).

The car had been imported from Germany, and Mr. Henneken knew that cars from Germany often had a problem with rust. Although another salesperson Mrs. Rushak had talked to pointed out some minor rust and advised her to take it to a Mercedes dealer for inspection, when she talked to Mr. Henneken he said that he knew the owner, that the car was one of the best of its kind in Vancouver and that it was generally a very nice car, a "good vehicle." In fact the car had been taken to a mechanic who had inspected it for a fee and given it a fairly favourable response, reporting only that there was some surface rust and very minor under-body rust. But he, too, had recommended that it be inspected by a Mercedes dealer.

Instead it was merely put up on a hoist, where Mrs. Rushak's friend examined it, and Mr. Henneken and one of his employees also took a look. Everyone thought it looked pretty good. She bought the car.

Unfortunately, she couldn't get used to the standard transmission, put it into storage and about a year later tried to sell it. At that time she discovered that it was in sad mechanical shape and so badly rusted it would cost about $10 000 just to patch up. She sued Mr. Henneken.

The court found that, because everyone maintained throughout the entire process that she ought to have the car inspected by Mercedes and that no pressure was put on her to purchase the car, there was no common law liability or any liability under the *Sale of Goods Act*. The judge did find, however, that Mr. Henneken's statement that the car was one of the best in Vancouver and that it was a good vehicle, was deceptive under the *Trade Practices Act*. This was supported at the appeal level and he was required to pay damages to Mrs. Rushak.

Note that there was no suggestion of wrongdoing here on the part of Mr. Henneken. He honestly held the belief that what he stated was true and clearly encouraged Mrs. Rushak to have the car inspected before taking it. This illustrates how important and extensive consumer protection legislation is. The judge in this case said, "While it used to be said that what is described in general terms as 'puffery' on the part of the salesman does not give rise to legal consequences, I am not satisfied that the same can be said today in light of the provisions of the *Trade Practices Act*. 'Puffery' cannot in my view excuse the giving of an unqualified opinion as to quality when the supplier has factual knowledge indicating that the opinion may in an important respect very well be wrong."

Consumer transaction made by ultimate consumer

The second major area in which legislation has interfered with contractual relationships and modified the case law developed by the courts is when **consumer transactions** are involved. Consumer transactions involve goods or services that are not being obtained for resale or other business activity. The products or services are being acquired by the ultimate consumer for personal use. Corporations are not considered consumers for the purposes of this legislation.

Although consumer protection statutes vary greatly, they do have common objectives: they impose standards and responsibilities on manufacturers and suppliers of goods, they control the use and disclosure of information and they control unethical or otherwise unacceptable business practices. The rest of this chapter will examine these areas and consider the regulatory bodies created to enforce these statutes. Although provincial statutes predominate, there is also considerable federal legislation in the field.

Consumer protection legislation imposes contracts

The main purpose of the *Sale of Goods Act* is to imply terms into a contract which the parties have omitted; consumer protection legislation, on the other hand, is designed to impose restrictions on the conduct of the parties by enforcing, controlling, modifying, limiting or otherwise altering the effects of contractual relationships entered into between merchants and consumers. A form of consumer protection legislation has been present in our legal system for centuries but, in the past several decades, statutes have been passed which have expanded this area to its modern dimensions. These statutes and recent court decisions have significantly modified the law relating to consumer transactions.

Until recently, the common contractual themes of *caveat emptor* and freedom of contract dominated consumer transactions. But consumers are vulnerable to unscrupulous or careless merchandising and manufacturing practices. This growing abuse and an increase in the inequalities of the bargaining positions of individual consumers in relation to large corporate manufacturers and merchandisers led legislators to place limits on these previously accepted principles. For example, consumer protection legislation (unlike the *Sale of Goods Act*) generally does not allow a party to release or waive her rights, benefits or protection under the legislation.

Although some still retain separate acts, most provinces have concentrated their consumer protection legislation into a single *Consumer Protection Act*. Some provinces have added a second act, referred to as the *Trade Practices* or *Business Practices Act*. Current Alberta consumer protection legislation includes the *Collection Practices Act, Consumer Credit Transactions Act, Direct Sales Cancellation Act,* and the *Unfair Trade Practices Act*.[51] The *Fair Trading Act* S.A. (1998) c. F-1.05, introduced in and passed by the Alberta legislature in the spring of 1998, will replace and repeal all of these *Acts*. The *Fair Trading Act* is to come into force on September 1, 1999. Once effective, Alberta's consumer protection legislation will largely be included in a single statute. Other legislation, such as the *Sale of Goods Act*, R.S.A. (1980) c. S-2, and the *Unconscionable Transactions Act*, R.S.A. (1980) c. U-2, will, however, still remain in effect.

Responsibility for Goods Sold

Consumer protection provisions have been incorporated into the sale of goods acts of the provinces. The requirements that the seller have good title, and that goods correspond to their description and are fit and of merchantable quality are of great value to the consumer. In several provinces, such as Ontario and British Columbia, the right to contract out of these provisions in consumer transactions by exculpatory clauses has been eliminated.[52] This is not the case, however, in Alberta, where the *Sale of Goods Act* specifically states that the parties, by agreement, can "negative or vary" rights, duties or liabilities that would arise under a contract of sale by implication of law.[53]

The result of these provisions is that, in Alberta, merchants can rely on exemption clauses to relieve themselves of the obligation to deliver quality goods to the buyer. But if there is no relevant exemption clause, then buyers can sue for breach of contract and receive compensation for the damage done when products are unfit. Damages are usually simply a refund of the purchase price. Other expenses incurred while using the defective product may be recoverable as well, if they were reasonably foreseeable when the contract was made.

Effect of exemption clauses limited by statute

51. *Collection Practices Act,* R.S.A. (1980) c. C-17; *Consumer Credit Transactions Act,* S.A. (1985) c. C-22.5; *Direct Sales Cancellation Act,* R.S.A. (1980) c. D-35; and the *Unfair Trade Practices Act,* R.S.A. (1980) c. U-3.

52. *Sale of Goods Act,* R.S.B.C. (1996) c. 410 s. 20 ss. 2 and *Consumer Protection Act,* R.S.O. (1990) c. C31 s. 34 ss. 2.

53. *Sale of Goods Act,* R.S.A. (1980) c. S-2 s. 55.

Victims of unsafe products are entitled to sue the manufacturer in tort for negligence. But if the victim was also the buyer of the product that led to the injury, a breach of contract has taken place and, under contract law, the seller too is liable. When a patron at a restaurant in Vancouver developed botulism and suffered serious and disabling illness, he successfully sued, not for tort, but under the provisions of the *Sale of Goods Act*.[54] Similarly, in Edmonton, when a customer bought a meat sandwich that contained a piece of wood, the court found that the seller breached the implied term that the food would be reasonably fit for human consumption, and awarded the buyer damages for the injuries suffered.[55]

There is a considerable advantage in establishing the right to sue in contract rather than tort. A tort action requires that the person bringing the action establish **Tort liability requires fault** that the defendant was at fault in some way, which is often difficult to do. A breach of contract, on the other hand, requires only that the plaintiff establish that a term of the contract was breached. It is no defense for the merchant to show there was **Contractual liability does not** no negligence. He or she is required to perform the terms of the contract and fail- **require fault** ure to do so causes liability for damages. Where personal injury has resulted, the damages payable under such a breach of contract action can be substantial.

A difficulty arises when the injured user of the product did not buy it but received it from someone else. Because of the principle of privity of contract, only those **Contractual liability limited** who are party to the contract are permitted to claim breach of contract and sue **to immediate parties** for damages. The case of *Donoghue v. Stevenson* discussed in Chapter 2 has had a great impact on the development of the law of negligence in general and of product liability specifically.

Recall that Mrs. Donoghue consumed a contaminated bottle of ginger beer given to her by a friend but could not sue the seller because she was not privy to the contract of purchase. Even though it was clearly established that the seller had no idea that the ginger beer was defective and that there was no way he could have known it, he would have been liable for breach of contract if Mrs. Donoghue had purchased the product from him. Since this was not the case, the victim turned to the manufacturer of the ginger beer and successfully sued in tort for negligence.

This case is important because it establishes users' ultimate right to sue manufacturers in tort for damages caused by the products they produce even though there is no contractual relationship between them. It is important to note that in Canada, the user must still usually prove that the manufacturer or manufacturer's servant was actually negligent in the manufacture of the product. Fault must be demonstrated. In product liability cases involving a blatant defect, plaintiffs have invoked the doctrine of *res ipsa loquitor,* shifting the burden of proof to the manufacturer, and forcing it to prove that it was not negligent. (*Res ipsa loquitor* was discussed in Chapter 2.) However, the Supreme Court of Canada has recently cast doubt on the availability of *res ipsa loquitor* so future cases may be more difficult to establish.

The ultimate consumer is not always the person who purchased the product and because of privity, such a person cannot sue the seller for breach of contract. In view of this, New Brunswick and Saskatchewan have extended their consumer protection legislation beyond the immediate parties to the contract.[56] In these provinces, the requirements of fitness and quality extend to anyone the seller could reason-

54. *Gee v. White Spot* (1986) 32 D.L.R. (4th) 238.

55. *Coote v. Hudson's Bay Company and Swift Canadian Co. Ltd.* (1977) 6 A.R. 59 (Alta. District Ct.).

56. *Consumer Product Warranty and Liability Act,* S.N.B. (1978) c. C-18 s. 23; *Consumer Product and Warranties Act,* R.S.S. (1978) c. C-30 s. 14(1).

ably foresee might use the product. The impediment of privity of contract in product liability cases is overcome. The seller is liable for injuries even if it can be demonstrated that the he or she had no way of knowing about the defects in the product. The Alberta *Sale of Goods Act* does not contain such provisions, and only a buyer of goods is protected by the implied contractual terms set out in the legislation.

Another significant development in Canadian law in this area is exemplified by the Ontario case of *Murray v. Sperry Rand Corp.*[57] In this case, the purchaser of a harvester was able to sue the manufacturer as well as the vendor for breach of contract even though the machine was purchased from a retailer. The court found that, because of false claims made in the advertising brochures supplied by the manufacturer, there was a breach of a **collateral contract** existing between the purchaser and the manufacturer; that is, one that exists between the ultimate purchaser and manufacturer in addition to the primary contract between the retailer and the purchaser. Normally, the principle of privity of contract prevents consumers from suing anyone for breach of contract but the person who sold the goods to them. The contract is between the purchaser and the retailer, not between the purchaser and the wholesaler or manufacturer. The significance of *Murray* is that privity of contract was circumvented through the application of collateral contracts. Since the manufacturer had advertised directly and the consumer had been influenced to buy by the advertisement, a direct relationship had been created between the manufacturer and the purchaser. This relationship took the form of a separate or collateral contract imposing obligations on the manufacturer to deliver a product that lived up to the claims stated in the advertisement. This willingness to find collateral contracts based on the advertising and promotional claims of the manufacturer may help to overcome the obstacle of privity of contract in product liability cases if it is followed in other jurisdictions. The Supreme Court of Canada has recently shown a willingness to abandon the privity principle in other situations.[58]

> Collateral contracts can protect ultimate purchasers

Some useful products, by their very nature, are hazardous. The obligation of the manufacturer and seller of such products is to make them as safe as possible, warn the potential user of the dangers and provide information on their proper use. An injured consumer can sue the manufacturer for negligence when these steps are not followed. A warning incorporated into the product label must alert the consumer to the hazards associated with the product. If the warning is inadequate, the manufacturer and seller are liable for the injuries that result.[59]

> Duty to warn when product hazardous

For products whose hazard is obvious, such as a sharp carving knife, there is likely no duty to warn. Federal legislation dealing with the merchandising of dangerous products will be covered later in this chapter.

Normally, the responsibilities set out here relate to the sale of goods only but leases are being used increasingly as an alternative method of financing consumer purchases. Several jurisdictions have modified their consumer protection legislation to extend this kind of protection to long-term lease arrangements as well.[60] In Alberta, the *Sale of Goods Act* does not apply to leases, but other statutes, such as the *Unfair Trade Practices Act*, do cover such agreements.[61]

---

57. *Murray v. Sperry Rand Corp.* (1979) 23 O.R. (2d) 456 (Ontario High Court of Justice).

58. *London Drugs Ltd. v. Kuehne & Nagel International Ltd.* [1993] 1 W.W.R. 1 (S.C.C.).

59. *Lambert v. Lastoplex Chemicals Ltd.* (1972) 25 D.L.R. (3d) 121 (Supreme Court of Canada).

60. *Sale of Goods Act,* R.S.B.C. (1996) c. 410, s. 18.

61. *Unfair Trade Practices Act,* R.S.A. (1980) c. U-3. The definition of "consumer transaction" in s. 1(c) includes leases of goods.

Unacceptable Business Practices

Another major thrust of consumer protection legislation is to prohibit or control certain unacceptable business practices, such as making misleading or false statements to persuade people to buy a product. Unless the misleading statement actually becomes a term of the contract, the consumer's only course of action in common law is to rely on the remedies available for misrepresentation, and when the misrepresentation is innocent, rescission is the only remedy—and that remedy may be lost due to the circumstances of the sale. To obtain damages as a remedy, one must prove the misrepresentation to be either fraudulent or negligent.

In Alberta, this issue has been addressed by the *Unfair Trade Practices Act*.[62] Section 4(1)(d) of the *Act* sets out several unfair acts or practices, including any representations or conduct that have the effect of deceiving or misleading a consumer, such as representations that

1. the goods or services have performance characteristics, ingredients, quantities, uses or benefits that they do not have;
2. the goods are of a particular standard, quality, grade, style or model if they are not;
3. the goods have been used to an extent that is different from the fact;
4. the goods are new if they are not;
5. the goods have a particular prior history or usage if they have not;
6. a specific price, benefit or advantage exists if it does not;
7. a part, replacement, repair or adjustment is needed if it is not; and
8. the consumer transaction involves or does not involve rights, remedies or obligations if the representation is deceptive or misleading.

A consumer who has suffered damage or loss due to an unfair act or practice may commence an action against any supplier who engaged in or acquiesced in the unfair act or practice.[63] In such an action, the court has the power to make several different types of orders, including an award for damages (even punitive damages) or an order for specific performance, restitution or rescission.

It must be remembered that the provisions of the *Act* apply even if there is an agreement to the contrary. Furthermore, any waiver or release of the rights, benefits or protections provided under the *Act* is against public policy and void.[64]

The provisions of the *Act* apply even when the parties involved have been relatively innocent, as in the Rushak case discussed above. No one in that case faulted Mr. Henneken's honesty, but the statements he made still qualified as a deceptive practice and he was required to pay damages to Mrs. Rushak. This would likely also be the result under the Alberta legislation.

Government bodies have been given significant powers

The Director of Trade Practices is given considerable power under the *Act* to investigate complaints of unfair acts or practices, and to deal with suppliers who have committed unfair acts or practices.[65] The Director may enter into an undertaking with a supplier that requires the supplier to cease committing an unfair act or practice and to compensate consumers who suffered damages from the unfair act or practice.[66] The Director may even commence a court action against a supplier ei-

---

62. *Ibid.*
63. *Ibid.*, s. 11.
64. *Ibid.*, s. 21(1).
65. *Ibid.*, ss. 5-9.
66. *Ibid.*, s. 10.

ther on his own behalf or on behalf of a consumer.[67] The court may require a supplier to advertise any order of the court under the *Act*.[68] The common law provisions concerning false and misleading claims in consumer transactions have been considerably strengthened by the provisions of legislation such as the *Unfair Trade Practices Act*.

In some provinces government can initiate action

Unconscionable Transactions.

One of the facts of modern society is that the merchants selling goods and services are increasingly large corporate bodies. This change further emphasizes the considerable inequality in the bargaining positions of the two parties in consumer transactions. When this inequality becomes so great that the consumer is taken advantage of because of desperation, poverty or mental weakness, the courts are now able to interfere with the resulting contract by setting it aside, modifying its terms or ordering the refund of money.

Unconscionable transactions or unfair bargains controlled

The legislation permitting the courts to do this exists in every province; in Alberta, the relevant statute is the *Unconscionable Transactions Act*.[69] It is important to note that this legislation applies only to the lending of money. To be able to rely on the provisions of this *Act*, it is necessary to demonstrate that the cost to the debtor was excessive and that the transaction was harsh and unconscionable in the circumstances.[70]

One of the factors the courts must take into consideration is the risk borne by the creditor. Even when it can be demonstrated that the borrower was of weak intellect or in desperate straits and that an unreasonably high rate of interest was charged, the court must also be satisfied that the rate of interest was excessive considering the risk faced by the creditor. If somebody is desperate because no one else will lend him money, the transaction will probably not be considered unconscionable because even a high rate of interest would not be considered excessive in such a risky situation.

Creditor's risk considered

Transactions that may be considered unconscionable are also dealt with in s.4 of the *Unfair Trade Practices Act*.[71] If the supplier subjects a consumer to "undue pressure" in trying to get him to enter into a consumer transaction, that will be deemed an unfair act or practice. Another example of an unfair act or practice occurs when a consumer transaction is entered into by a supplier when the consumer was not reasonably able to understand the character or nature of the transaction, and the supplier took unfair advantage of the consumer's inability to understand.

The *Fair Trading Act*, which was introduced in the Alberta legislature in the spring of 1998, will expand the scope of actions that may be considered unfair practices to include, among others, the following:[72]

1. A supplier charging a price for goods and services that grossly exceeds the price of similar goods or services, without advising the consumer of the difference in price and the reason therefor.
2. A supplier charging a price for goods and services that is materially higher than any estimate given, unless the consumer has consented to the higher price.

67. *Ibid.*, s. 13 and s. 14. See *Alberta (Director of Trade Practices) v. Edanver Consulting Ltd.* (1993) 6 W.W.R. 719 (Alta. Q.B.).

68. *Ibid.*, s. 17.

69. *Unconscionable Transactions Act*, R.S.A. (1980) c. U-2.

70. *Ibid.*, s. 2. See *Krocker et al. v. Midtown Mortgage & Loans Ltd. et al.,* 52 D.L.R. (3d) 286 (Alta. S.C.T.D.), where the court held that money lent at a rate of interest more than double the rate that the borrower could have obtained from other lenders was harsh and unconscionable.

71. *Unfair Trade Practices Act*, R.S.A. (1980) c. U-3.

72. *Fair Trading Act*, S.A. (1998) c. F-1.05.

3. A supplier including terms or conditions that are harsh, oppressive or excessively one-sided, in a consumer transaction.

In addition to these legislative provisions, the common law doctrine of unconscionability in contract law has recently become much more accepted and, thus, as discussed in Chapter 5, important in these situations. In the case introducing this chapter, Mrs. Knuude was able to escape her contractual obligations because she was taken advantage of and unreasonably pressured by the sales representative. This made the contract unconscionable under the common law. The sales representative also committed unfair acts or practices under the *Unfair Trade Practices Act.*

Door-to-Door Sales.

Door-to-door sales controlled

Another type of activity which all provinces vigorously control is door-to-door sales. In Alberta, the relevant legislation is the *Direct Sales Cancellation Act.*[73] Pursuant to the *Fair Trading Act,*[74] the *Direct Sales Cancellation Act* will be repealed, as provisions regarding direct sales contracts are included in the new legislation.

Because door-to-door selling often involves a great deal of pressure, one of the main provisions of this legislation is for a cooling-off period. The period allows the buyer to rethink the transaction in the absence of pressure and then to cancel the sales contract without any disadvantage, even without any reason. The Alberta legislation allows the buyer to cancel the sales contract up to 10 days after she receives a copy of the written sales contract.[75] (A sales contract is not concluded until it is signed by the buyer.)[76] Cancellation of a sales contract has the same effect as rescission. Within 15 days of cancellation, the seller must make a full refund to the buyer.[77]

A misleading statement by a salesperson becomes part of the contract.

Photo by Paul Barton/First Light.

The buyer may also cancel the sales contract up to a year from the day she signed the contract[78] if the seller was required to be registered or licensed but wasn't, if the sales contract does not contain all of the required information, or if the goods (or services) are not all provided (not started) within 30 days of the delivery date specified in the sales contract.

Sellers may be required to be registered or licensed under the *Licensing of Trades and Businesses Act.*[79] By retaining the power to refuse to issue a licence or to cancel or suspend a licence, the government can exercise considerable control over sellers. A practical result of the licensing requirement is that buyers should ask for identification from door-to-door sellers. Identification confirming current registration or licensing increases the probability of successfully resolving any difficulties that the buyer may encounter in dealing with the seller (e.g., licensed sellers may be bonded).

73. *Direct Sales Cancellation Act,* R.S.A. (1980) c. D-35.

74. *Fair Trading Act,* S.A. (1998) c. F-1.05.

75. *Direct Sales Cancellation Act,* R.S.A. (1980) c. D-35 s. 6.

76. *Ibid.,* s. 1(2).

77. *Ibid.,* s. 8(1).

78. *Ibid.,* s. 6.1.

79. *Licensing of Trades and Businesses Act,* R.S.A. (1980) c. L-13.

Referral Selling.

Another activity often prohibited or controlled by legislation is referral selling. With this practice, the seller has the purchaser make a list of friends and acquaintances that the salesperson then uses, often accompanied by introductory letters, to put pressure on those prospects. The purchaser is usually persuaded to provide this list of referrals by a promise of a discount for each referral that bears fruit. Several provinces, including Ontario and British Columbia, have controlled or completely prohibited this type of activity because it is susceptible to so much abuse. Referral selling (other than in the insurance industry) is not directly controlled or prohibited in Alberta, although such selling may, depending on the circumstances, be subject to the provisions of some of the consumer protection legislation in place, such as the *Direct Sales Cancellation Act*.

Referral selling controlled

Control of Specific Businesses

There are many other examples of consumer protection legislation designed to guard against abuses in particular industries. *The Consumer Protection Act* of British Columbia has provisions controlling mortgage transactions, food plan transactions, the practice of discounting income tax returns, solicited and unsolicited credit card transactions and door-to-door transactions dealing with the sale of goods and services. Nova Scotia has similar legislation for income tax refund discounting and credit cards. Saskatchewan has legislation controlling the sale of training courses and other provisions dealing with unsolicited goods and credit cards. Manitoba's legislation controls prearranged funeral services, credit cards and unsolicited goods. Ontario's *Consumer Protection Act* requires the cost of consumer borrowing to be clearly set out, not only in the actual contract but in all advertising as well. It also removes any obligations on the consumer who uses unsolicited goods or credit cards sent to him or her and has provisions which prohibit misleading advertising. In Ontario the maximum fines for offenses are $25 000 for an individual and $100 000 for a corporation. All of these jurisdictions have legislation designed to curtail and control abusive practices used in areas such as debt collection.

In Alberta, there are many similar examples of consumer protection legislation designed to guard against abuses in particular industries. One example involves credit cards, which are dealt with in Part 4 of the *Consumer Credit Transactions Act*.[80] This legislation forbids the issuance of unsolicited credit cards, limits the liability of customers who lose their credit cards, and sets out the information the credit grantor must provide before issuing a credit card.

The Consumer Credit Transactions Act, in Part 5, also deals with leases of personal property. Written copies of such leases must be provided, by the credit grantor, to the lessee. The legislation sets out what information must be included in the written lease.

Two interesting issues are dealt with in the *Fair Trading Act*, which has been discussed earlier in this chapter.[81] The supply of goods or services pursuant to a "negative option practice" is forbidden in Part 2, Division 3, of this legislation. Effective September 1, 1998, a consumer will not be liable to pay for any goods or services received under a negative option practice, unless she agrees to do so in writing.

Part 4 of the future legislation deals with marketing through electronic media. The statute does nothing but authorize the making of regulations to control such

---

80. *Consumer Credit Transactions Act*, S.A. (1985) c. C-22-5.

81. *Fair Trading Act*, S.A. (1998) c. F-1.05.

marketing. No such regulations have been made as of the date of publication of this book.

Methods of Control.

Several methods used to control abusive activity

Controlling these unacceptable activities through legislation is accomplished by several methods. As in the *Direct Sales Cancellation Act*, businesses may be required to register with a government body that has the power to withdraw registration for misbehaviour. The government department that has the job of overseeing legislation may also have the power to enforce it by applying to the court for an appropriate order. Pursuant to the *Unfair Trade Practices Act*, for example, the Director of Trade Practices may apply to the court, either on the Director's own behalf, or on behalf of a consumer. To facilitate control and enforcement, the government body may also have the power to investigate and seize records. Under the *Unfair Trade Practices Act*, the Director may, for example, apply to the court, without notice to the supplier, for an order allowing the Director to enter any building and to search for, examine and remove relevant books or papers of the supplier.[82] Another method of enforcement is to create new rights and obligations between the parties and to give consumers the right to enforce those obligations by suing the other party. Such is the case in the *Direct Sales Cancellation Act*, as discussed above. Finally, the legislation may levy penalties against anyone convicted of an offence as in the *Unfair Trade Practices Act*.[83] The *Fair Trading Act* will dramatically increase the penalties for breaches of this legislation; the maximum penalty is a fine of up to the greater of $100 000, or three times the amount obtained by the party as a result of the offence, and imprisonment for up to two years.[84]

Loan Transactions

We reviewed above the provisions of the *Unconscionable Transactions Act*,[85] which prohibits loans where the cost of borrowing is excessive and the transaction is harsh and unconscionable. *The Criminal Code*[86] also prohibits the charging of excessive rates of interest. Alberta has also enacted the *Consumer Credit Transactions Act*.[87]

PROPER DISCLOSURE OF INTEREST RATES REQUIRED

The defendant law firm drew up certain promissory notes on behalf of Elcano Acceptance that they used in their business. The notes stated interest calculated at the rate of 2 percent per month. Section 4 of the *Interest Act* provides that any contract where interest is payable must be stated at an annual rate; otherwise, it is not permissible to collect more than 5 percent interest. Because of this, the plaintiff finance company was not able to collect the interest due and payable from the customers as per the promissory notes and successfully sued the law firm for negligence.

Elcano Acceptance Ltd. v. Richmond, Richmond, Stambler & Mills, 79 D.L.R. (4th) 154 (Ontario Court of Appeal)

---

82. *Unfair Trade Practices Act*, R.S.A. (1980) c. U-3 s. 7.
83. *Ibid.*, s. 18.
84. *Fair Trading Act*, S.A. (1998) c. F-1.05.
85. *Unfair Trade Practices Act*, R.S.A. (1980) c. U-3.
86. *Criminal Code*, R.S.C. 1985, c. C-46, s. 347.
87. *Consumer Credit Transactions Act*, S.A. (1985) c. C-22.5.

EXCESSIVE INTEREST CHARGES PROHIBITED

Mrs. Banks needed a short-term loan and arranged through her accountant for a loan from Mrs. Milani. The terms were that she would borrow $32 000 but repay $35 000 one month later and pay interest on the $35 000 at 18 percent. It was clear that neither party intended to break the law, but this amounted to an annual rate of interest of 250 percent because of the $3000 bonus involved. The court held that this rate of interest violated Section 347 of the *Criminal Code*. The court also found that the 18 percent in-terest charged was, by itself, unconscionable. As a re-sult, Mrs. Banks was required only to repay the $32 000 she actually received and the interest payable on that was established at the rate normally charged litigants on money due called the "pre-judgment in-terest rate." Had the parties been aware they were breaking the law, they would have been subject to criminal penalties.

Milani v. Banks, 98 D.L.R. (4th) 104 Ontario Court (General Division)

This legislation requires that the true cost of borrowing be disclosed to the consumer in various types of transactions. (The federal *Interest Act* has similar requirements.[88]) The *Consumer Credit Transaction Act* regulates such matters as the calculation of credit charges, the contents of advertisements published by credit grantors and the disclosure required in various types of written agreements. Neither this *Act* nor the *Fair Trading Act* requires moneylenders to be registered.

True cost of borrowing must be disclosed

A related issue is businesses that supply information on the creditworthiness of customers. They provide a very useful function from the merchant's point of view, but the harm that could be done to the customer through carelessness or abuse is great. Most provinces have introduced legislation controlling credit-reporting bodies. This legislation varies from province to province, but typically the reporting agency must be registered, giving the government agency some direct power over them. The acts usually set out what types of information reports can include and make it an offense to include any information known to be incorrect. The consumer is usually given the right to inspect the file and the right to remove or correct any incorrect information. In some jurisdictions, the credit-reporting body can only give a report to a merchant when the consumer has requested it in writing. This gives the consumer complete control over the dissemination of information regarding creditworthiness.

Credit-reporting practices controlled

There is currently no legislation in Alberta regulating credit reporting agencies. The *Fair Trading Act*,[89] does deal with this issue, in Part 5. The legislation regulates the contents of credit reports, the furnishing of such reports to creditors, the disclosure of personal information to the individual, the correction of errors in an individual's file and the remedy available to an individual who has suffered a loss because of breach of the legislation by a credit reporting agency.

Debt Collection Processes

Creditors will often turn to methods other than court action to pressure debtors to pay their obligations. Often, they turn to debt collection agencies. Collection prac-tices range from the simple sending of a bill marked "Overdue" to harassment.

88. *Interest Act*, R.S.C. 1985 c. I-15.

89. Bill 20, *Fair Trading Act*, S.A. (1998) c. F-105.

Abusive debt collection practices controlled

Since there are many situations in which collection practices can become abusive, methods of controlling them have been developed. Most common law remedies available to the victims of excessive debt collection practices are based on tort actions for such offenses as defamation, assault and battery, trespass and even false imprisonment. As a general rule, common law remedies for abusive debt collection processes are ineffectual. Accordingly, the provinces have passed legislation to regulate debt collection processes. (It should also be noted that the threat of criminal prosecution to pressure a debtor to pay is a violation of the *Criminal Code* and can result in prosecution of the person making the threat.)

The relevant legislation in Alberta is the *Collection Practices Act*.[90] It requires collection agencies, and collectors employed by collection agencies, to be registered and licensed. A licence may not be issued unless security is provided by the collection agency or collector. Licences may be suspended or cancelled if the holder does not comply with the legislation. Fines may also be levied for violations of the statute or its regulations.

Collection agencies must keep proper accounting records, and deposit all money collected into a trust account. Money collected must be remitted to the creditor by the 20th day of the month following the month in which the money was collected. The legislation, in s. 13, sets out prohibited practices for collection agencies and collectors. For example, telephone calls for the purpose of demanding payment can only be made between 7 a.m. and 10 p.m. The Alberta legislation, however, is not as extensive as some of the other provinces' legislation, as there is no restriction on the number of telephone calls that can be made, no prohibition of collect telephone calls, no prohibition on communicating with employers, friends or relatives, and no required (prescribed) form of demand letter that must be used by collection agencies (although collection agencies may be ordered to stop using letters that are misleading).

Consumer Service Bodies

Role of government agencies

Most of the consumer protection statutes referred to in this chapter empower a government body or agency to implement the legislation. The authority given to such departments usually includes the right to hear and investigate complaints, seize records, search premises, suspend licenses, impose fines or some other corrective action and initiate civil actions on behalf of the consumer. In Alberta, the relevant government agency is the Consumer Affairs Division of Alberta Municipal Affairs Department.

In some jurisdictions, these bodies have become clearing-houses of consumer information, with a mandate to collect and disseminate that information to the public. Consumer bureaus can collect information on dangerous products, consumer business scams or unacceptable practices. They may get involved in advertising to educate the consumer.

Also private agencies

Private organizations, such as the Better Business Bureau, are also designed to be clearing-houses for such information. It must be remembered, however, that the Bureau is supported and sustained by the business community and thus has a vested interest in serving that community. The theory is that it is in the best interests of the business community to maintain high standards by weeding out disreputable businesses. The Better Business Bureau and similar organizations serve that function for members of the business community who join them.

---

90. *Collection Practices Act*, R.S.A. (1980) c. C-17.

Federal Legislation

Sumner Sports Inc. v. Pavillon Chasse & Peche (440) Inc.[91]

Although this case takes place in Québec, where the specific rules of contract law are somewhat different from those in the rest of Canada, it is included here for its reference to the application of the *Combines Investigation Act* (now the *Competition Act*), a federal statute that applies throughout Canada.

The nature of the agreement entered into between the plaintiff and the defendant was that Sumner would not retail their hunting and fishing gear within the city of Laval or a 10-mile (16.1-kilometre) radius thereof for a period of ten years. The agreement also provided that Sumner would sell their goods exclusively to Pavilion in that area for that ten-year period. Pavillon, for their part, agreed not to sell their products in the Lower St. Lawrence area for ten years or in the City of Ottawa for five and also only to sell products purchased from Sumner. In effect, the two companies agreed not to carry on business in competition with each other.

This action was brought by Sumner because Pavillon failed to sell the agreed-upon quantities of goods that they had promised to purchase from Sumner. In their defense Pavilion argued that the contract was illegal anyway, because it violated the provisions of the *Combines Investigation Act* and so the court had to determine whether the provisions of the *Act* had been violated because of the agreement.

The court found that although they had agreed to restrict competition between them, there was no evidence that it in any way impeded the operation of the marketplace generally. It is necessary for it to be an offense under the *Combines Investigation Act* to find that competition has been "unduly restricted." For that there must be some evidence to show that both parties control a large segment of the market, such that access to suppliers is cut off or other competitors are driven from the market and unable to function. No such evidence was presented and so there was no undue interference with competition. In fact the court found that Pavillon had breached the contract.

Note that although this case dealt with the application of the *Combines Investigation Act,* the principles apply today because of similar provisions in its successor, the federal *Competition Act.* This case is presented as an example of how the *Act* works and to show that not all situations where parties enter into agreements restricting competition will be illegal or in violation of the *Act.*

Although the most dramatic developments in consumer protection legislation have taken place provincially in recent years, there are some significant and effective statutes federally as well. The Department of Consumer and Corporate Affairs was established by the *Department of Consumer and Corporate Affairs Act*[92] with a mandate to enforce legislation and provide service to consumers. The *Act* establishes that the department is to be concerned with consumer affairs, restraint of trade and bankruptcy as well as providing systems to educate and protect consumers. The Department has established extensive research facilities to identify unsafe products. It has also become active in consumer matters at the provincial level, hearing and investigating complaints and communicating with consumers and merchants.

---

91. 72 D.L.R. (4th) 317 (Quebec Court of Appeal).

92. *Department of Consumer and Corporate Affairs Act,* R.S.C. (1985) c. C-37.

Competition Act.

Competition Act controls
abuses

One of the most important federal acts related to the protection of consumers is the *Competition Act* [93] (formerly the *Combines Investigation Act*). The *Act* is primarily intended to prevent business activities that interfere with the operation of the free market system and thus the public is indirectly protected from unfair pricing.

To enforce the provisions of the *Competition Act*, the *Competition Tribunal Act* sets up a competition tribunal which functions like and has the power of a court. Violations are prosecuted with the potential imposition of significant penalties. These penalties include fines or imprisonment for periods of up to five years. Significant powers of investigation and enforcement are given to the director appointed under the *Act*, and for certain kinds of offenses the director can bring matters before the tribunal to be dealt with at that level.

Mergers controlled

One of the main purposes of the *Act* is to control mergers. Mergers are no longer treated as inherently bad; the tribunal just reviews them to determine whether they will have the effect of substantially limiting or lessening competition.

Mergers can take three forms. Horizontal mergers take place when firms that would normally compete directly with each other join together into one operation, for example when one department chain buys out another. In this case, the competition tribunal would look not only at the anti-competitive effect of such a merger but also at any efficiency that might be gained and balance these factors in terms of public benefit. Vertical mergers take place when a supplier and retailer are merged, for example when a supplier of foodstuffs purchases a chain of retail grocers. There is a temptation on the part of such a merged operation to "squeeze" competitors that buy foodstuffs from the same supplier by charging higher prices, giving poorer service or otherwise favouring its own retail operation. The tribunal has the power to review such effects. Conglomerate mergers are mergers of companies that are not in direct competition; the main concern here is whether such a merger eliminates or limits potential competition.

Abusive trade practices
prohibited

The *Competition Act* has specific provisions prohibiting certain anti-competitive, abusive trade practices. This *Act* seeks to prevent one company that is dominant in a particular market from using its position to impose anti-competitive forces in that market. For example, suppose a dominant company in a market has a sale or uses loss leaders in such a way as to drive its competitors out of business. This is known as predatory pricing and is prohibited.

Other, more indirect activities that have a similar effect are also prohibited. For example, the vertical price squeeze involves a vertically integrated supplier raising prices so that other retailers purchasing from them have to sell the goods at a higher price, thus reducing their profit margin. This price increase affects the supplier's own retail operation as well; however, its profit is made at the wholesale level at the expense of the retail level. A similar prohibited practice involves a newly vertically integrated company that refuses to supply other retailers as it has in the past in order to enhance the competitive position of its own retail operation. A third variation involves manipulating freight prices to give an advantage to its own retail operation at the expense of the competition.

The *Act* also contains provisions restricting agreements between merchants that unduly restrict competition. Thus, if two merchants agree not to sell specific goods in the other's area and they are the only source of those goods, this would likely violate this portion of the *Act*. In the Sumner case discussed above, their non-competition agreement was not in violation of the *Act*, because there was no evidence that they had any impact on the overall market situation.

---

93. *Competition Act*, S.C. (1984-85-86) c. 91.

Other examples of prohibited activities are bid rigging (a group of bidders gets together and agrees ahead of time who will be the low bidder); blacklisting someone in professional sports; agreements between banks controlling interest rates; and suppliers discriminating between customers with rebates and special discounts for only some.

The *Act* also prohibits such direct offensive practices as misleading advertising in any form; double-ticketing, which means that more than one price ticket is displayed on an item (goods must be sold at the lowest price); and bait-and-switch advertising by which customers are enticed into a store by unreasonably low advertised prices and when the goods are not available, the customers are switched to higher-priced items. The *Act* also controls referral selling schemes, pyramid selling schemes and selling for higher prices than advertised, and requires that, when promotional contests are involved, the chances of winning be clearly stated.

Previously, one of the most common complaints about both federal and provincial consumer legislation was that it was toothless. Ineffectual enforcement provisions often made it more profitable to break the law than to follow it. Many provincial consumer protection statutes have been significantly strengthened through increased maximum fines and the introduction of other methods of enforcement, such as allowing consumers to sue in their own right for violation of the legislation.[94] Jail sentences for violation (up to five years) go a long way towards making the *Competition Act* effective. The *Competition Act* also contains provisions allowing consumers the right to sue offending parties for damages suffered due to misleading or deceptive sales practices described in the *Act*, and provides for significant fines (up to $10 million) for the commission of offenses.

Effective penalties available

Other Federal Legislation.

Several other federal statutes have the effect of protecting the consumer. *The Food and Drug Act*[95] is intended primarily to control the sale of food, drugs and cosmetics unfit for consumption or use. The legislation also prohibits misleading or deceptive claims associated with the sale, labelling, and advertising of these products. The *Act* also creates several categories of drugs which are controlled in various ways. For example, unsafe drugs, such as thalidomide, cannot be sold in this country. The sale of other dangerous but useful drugs that may be abused or misused is also restricted and controlled. The *Controlled Drugs and Substances Act* makes it an offense to traffic in controlled drugs such as amphetamines. As with the *Competition Act*, the presence of strict enforcement provisions makes legislation very effective.

Food and Drug Act carries strict penalties

The *Hazardous Products Act*[96] similarly controls the manufacture, importation and sale of products inherently dangerous. The *Act* creates two categories of substances: those which are restricted and those which are merely controlled.

Effective control over hazardous products

The products restricted by Part 1 of the *Act* cannot be imported, advertised or sold in Canada. Children's toys, clothing and furniture that are excessively flammable, toxic or otherwise dangerous are prohibited under this section. Examples

94. The *Fair Trading Act*, enacted by the Alberta legislature in the spring of 1998, allows for fines of up to $100 000, or of three times the amount obtained by the defendant as a result of the offence, whichever is greater, and for imprisonment for up to two years, for any person convicted of an offence under the *Act* [cl. 165(1)]. This legislation, effective September 1, 1999, will enable consumers to commence legal action for relief if they suffer damage or loss as a result of a supplier committing an unfair practice (s. 13).

95. *Food and Drug Act*, R.S.C. (1985) c. F-27. See also the *Controlled Drugs and Substances Act*, S.C. (1996) c.19.

96. *Hazardous Products Act*, R.S.C. (1985) c. H-3 (and amendments R.S.C. (1985) 3 Supp. c. 24).

of other items controlled by Part 1 are products containing carbon tetrachloride meant for consumer use and glass soft drink containers over 1.5 litres that do not meet required specifications.

Part 2 of the *Act* lists goods that can be imported, marketed and sold in Canada as long as the regulations set down are followed. Products such as cradles, cribs, carpets, kettles, toys and pacifiers are controlled under this section, as well as many other products. This *Act* also provides for analyses of products and authorizes inspection processes to uncover violations. Enforcement provisions allow for search and seizure and prosecution for violations. Some hazardous products are covered by their own legislation such as the *Explosives Act*,[97] the *Pest Control Products Act*[98] and the *Motor Vehicle Safety Act*.[99]

The *Weights and Measures Act*,[100] the *Consumer Packaging and Labelling Act*[101] and the *Textile Labelling Act*[102] are intended to force proper disclosure of information and thus help consumers make comparisons between products. There are also examples of federal and provincial legislation designed primarily for a purpose other than consumer protection which do have consumer protection aspects to them. For example, the *Bills of Exchange Act*[103] was designed to regulate the use of negotiable instruments such as cheques and promissory notes. But, in response to a certain abuse of negotiable instruments in consumer transactions, the *Act* has been amended to create a consumer note. This amendment significantly lessens the advantage to the creditor or merchant when negotiable instruments are used in consumer transactions. This *Act* will be discussed in considerable detail in Chapter 9.

SUMMARY

When the contract involves the sale of goods, a number of terms are implied into that contract by the *Sale of Goods Act*, unless the parties have agreed otherwise. The *Act* only applies when goods are being sold. The *Act* provides that risk follows title and supplies five rules to determine when title is transferred. Other provisions specify that the seller must convey good title and quiet possession, and that the goods must be free of any lien or charge and be of merchantable quality. When a sample has been shown or where goods are sold by description, the goods must match the sample or description. In certain situations, the seller has an unpaid seller's lien and has the right of stoppage *in transitu*.

When consumer transactions are involved, a number of statutes are in place to protect consumers. Consumer protection acts, trade practices acts, unconscionable transactions acts and direct sellers acts are examples of such legislation. These statutes control unacceptable business practices such as misrepresentation and other forms of misleading advertising, and prohibit unconscionable transactions, that is, when a merchant takes advantage of a customer in a weak bargaining position. Specific activities are also controlled. Door-to-door selling is controlled by imposing a cooling-off period, moneylenders are required to disclose the true cost of

97. *Explosives Act*, R.S.C. (1985) c. E-17.

98. *Pest Control Products Act*, R.S.C. (1985) c. P-9.

99. *Motor Vehicle Safety Act*, R.S.C. (1985) c. B-10.

100. *Weights and Measures Act*, R.S.C. (1985) c. W-6.

101. *Consumer Packaging and Labelling Act*, R.S.C. (1985) c. C-38.

102. *Textile Labelling Act*, R.S.C. (1985) c. T-10.

103. *Bills of Exchange Act*, R.S.C. (1985) c. B-4.

borrowing to their customers and abusive debt collection practices are restricted. Effective September 1, 1999, Alberta's laws in this area will be changed due to the new *Fair Trading Act*.[104] The federal government has passed legislation controlling inappropriate practices with the *Competition Act* and controlling and restricting dangerous products in acts such as the *Hazardous Products Marketing Act*.

QUESTIONS

1. Explain the purpose of the *Sale of Goods Act* in relation to the obligations of the parties to a sale of goods transaction.

2. What three qualifications must be met before the *Sale of Goods Act* applies to a transaction?

3. What is the distinction between a sale and an agreement to sell? What is the significance of that distinction?

4. When does the risk transfer to the buyer in a sale of goods transaction? Explain the exceptions to this general rule.

5. What is a bill of lading? How can it affect who bears the risk in a sale of goods transaction?

6. Indicate when title transfers in the following situations:

   a. When the contract for sale is unconditional and the goods involved are in a deliverable state at the time the purchase is made

   b. When the subject of the contract involves specific goods to which the seller is obligated to do something, such as repair, clean or modify, to get them into a deliverable state

   c. When the contract for sale involves specific, identified goods which must be weighed or measured before being given to the buyer

   d. When the goods are delivered to the buyer on approval

   e. When goods purchased by description have not been selected, separated out or manufactured at the time the sales contract is entered into

7. The *Sale of Goods Act* imposes terms relating to goods matching samples or descriptions, and meeting standards of fitness, quality and title. Explain the nature of these implied terms and their effect on the parties. Indicate which terms are conditions and which are warranties. Explain the significance of the distinction.

8. Explain what merchantable quality means.

9. Explain the effect of an exculpatory clause included in a contract which is inconsistent with the terms set out in the *Sale of Goods Act*.

10. Explain the rights of the seller when the buyer of goods

    a. becomes insolvent;

---

104. *Fair Trading Act*, S.A. (1998) c. F-1.05.

b. defaults on the contract of sale while the goods are still in the hands of the seller;

c. becomes insolvent after the goods have been given to a third party to deliver but before they are received by the buyer.

11. Explain why it might be more difficult for a seller of goods to sue for damages than for price.

12. Under what circumstances may a buyer refuse delivery of goods?

13. The *Sale of Goods Act* in each province implies certain terms into contracts of sale relating to the fitness and quality of the product. What are the approaches used in various Canadian jurisdictions to make these provisions mandatory in consumer transactions?

14. How does the concept of privity of contract limit the effectiveness of many consumer protection provisions? How have some jurisdictions overcome this problem?

15. What common law provisions are available to protect consumers from unscrupulous business practices? Describe the limitations inherent in these provisions and the steps that have been taken to overcome these limitations.

16. Explain the object of the *Unconscionable Transactions Act* and the limitations to its application.

17. What statutory provisions have been introduced in Alberta to control door-to-door selling, referral selling and the practice of purchasing tax refunds?

18. Describe the methods outlined in federal and provincial consumer protection statutes to control businesses prone to abuse. Discuss the effectiveness of these tactics.

19. What services are provided to consumers through organizations set up by the federal and provincial governments? Discuss whether these services are adequate.

20. Describe the practices controlled by the *Competition Act* and explain how that control is accomplished.

CASES

1. Kelly v. Mack Canada Inc. et al.

David Kelly bought a used truck from Mack Sales, a dealership. The truck proved incapable of the job for which it was required. Kelly had been told that the truck had a rebuilt engine; this was not the case. After significant repairs, Mack Sales agreed to take it back as a trade-in on a new Mack truck with a new vehicle warranty from the manufacturer, Mack Canada Inc. Again the truck was not up to the task. It was in need of constant repair with a considerable amount of downtime. Mack Canada had warranted the truck to be free from defects with the obligation that they would repair or replace any defective parts.

Kelly sued both the dealer, Mack Sales, under the *Sale of Goods Act* and the manufacturer, Mack Canada, under the manufacturer's warranty. He claimed return of the purchase price and costs incurred. Explain the arguments that both the dealer and the manufacturer will use in these circumstances and Kelly's likelihood of success.

2. Re Royal Bank of Canada and Saskatchewan Telecommunications

Tritec built prefabricated buildings and was in the process of building several for Saskatchewan Telecommunications. When finished, the buildings were to be transported to northern Saskatchewan and bolted to timbers in the ground. But during the construction Tritec were put into receivership by the Royal Bank of Canada. Tritec had defaulted on payments due Royal Bank, and the Bank, as the secured creditor, took over the operations and seized the unfinished buildings.

Saskatchewan Telecommunications, who had been making monthly progress payments from the date of the signing of the contract, then paid Royal Bank $20 000 to get the buildings, but did so under protest, and with the understanding that if the court determined that title to the buildings had already passed to Saskatchewan Telecommunications they would get back the $20 000.

Explain the arguments available to both sides to decide whether title had passed to Saskatchewan Telecommunications.

3. Lasby v. Royal City Chrysler Plymouth

Mrs. Lasby, after considerable dealing with the defendants, through their salesperson, Mr. MacDonald, decided to purchase on MacDonald's recommendation a Dodge 600. They had been given the impression that the car had a big engine and that it was executive-driven. After getting it home, they found out the engine had four cylinders, not six as they thought, but didn't do anything about it when they were assured by Mr. MacDonald that it was the largest four-cylinder engine made.

A few months later when she was having it serviced, Mrs. Lasby mentioned to her mechanic that it had the big engine. He told her that it had in fact the smaller engine and there was a much bigger engine than hers. She asked Royal City for her money back but the dealership refused to either return her money or take the car back .

Under these circumstances explain Mrs. Lasby's options. What would be the appropriate remedy? How would your answer be affected by learning that by the time of the trial, the car was 22 months older and had been driven a further 40 000 kilometres?

4. Harry v. Kreutziger

Harry was a Native Indian with a Grade 5 education, a hearing defect and a retiring manner. He owned a fishing boat worth very little except for the fishing license that went with it. With the license, the boat was worth about $16 000. Kreutziger persuaded Harry to sell the boat and license to him for $4500, saying that, as a Native Indian, Harry would have little trouble getting another license.

Harry sued to have the contract set aside. What would be the nature of Harry's complaint against Kreutziger? What defenses would be available to Kreutziger in response to Harry's action? Predict the outcome.

5. W.W. Distributors & Co. v. Thorsteinson

A salesman and his manager approached a young engaged girl and her mother at their home one evening and, after using some very-high-pressure sales tactics, sold them some cooking utensils. The mother was persuaded to sign the contract after being told that it was not really important. By so doing, the mother became a party to the agreement, even though it had been made clear to the salesman that her only involvement was to lend her daughter $50 towards the purchase.

The daughter was led to believe that she was getting very good value for her money but experts clearly established that the price was over 75 percent more than the maximum value of the goods involved. The next day, unable to contact the plaintiff, the mother stopped payment on the cheque. When this was discovered, the salesman went by the home and was informed that the mother and daughter were repudiating the agreement. The company immediately commenced an action to recover the purchase price and the various penalties and service charges built into the agreement.

Explain the arguments which could be raised on both sides and the likely outcome. What effect would it have on your answer to learn that the engaged girl was under the age of majority? What legislation provisions have been put into place in most jurisdictions to curb this type of abuse?

6. Gee v. White Spot Ltd.

Mr. Gee went to the White Spot restaurant and ordered a meal. Unfortunately, the food was contaminated and Mr. Gee suffered botulism poisoning. He sued White Spot, claiming compensation for the serious damages he suffered. What arguments might Mr. Gee raise to establish liability on the part of White Spot under the *Sale of Goods Act*? What arguments might White Spot raise to refute such liability?

7. Regina v. Birchcliff Lincoln Mercury Sales Ltd.

Birchcliff operated a car dealership with a service centre where a sign was posted stating "Customer labour charges are based on $38.00 per flat rate hour." The sign was there because Ford, the manufacturer, insisted that such notices be posted in clear sight at their dealerships.

In fact a flat rate of $38 per hour was not charged for the services given; rather, for each job reference was made to a standard industry guide that set out the number of hours the job ought to take and the charges were based on that guide. Even if the time spent on a particular job was less than that set out in the standard guide, the amount stated in the guide was charged.

Explain the nature of the complaint in these circumstances and the likely consequences that Birchcliff would face.

LEGISLATION

Alberta

Collection Practices Act, R.S.A. (1980) c. C-17
Consumer Credit Transactions Act, S.A. (1985) c. C-22.5
Direct Sales Cancellation Act, R.S.A. (1980) c. D-35
Fair Trading Act, S.A. (1998) c. F-1.05.
Financial Consumers Act, S.A. (1990) c. F-9.5
International Conventions Implementations Act, S.A. (1990) c. I-6.8
Sale of Goods Act, R.S.A. (1980) c. S-2
Unconscionable Transactions Act, R.S.A. (1980) c. U-2
Unfair Trade Practices Act, R.S.A. (1980) c. U-3

Federal

Bills of Lading Act, R.S.C. (1985) c. B-5
Competition Act, R.S.C. (1985) c. C-34 (and amendment 2d Supp. 610)
Competition Tribunal Act, R.S.C. (1985) c. 19 (2d Supp.) Part 1
Consumer Packaging and Labelling Act, R.S.C. (1985) c. C-38
Controlled Drugs and Substances Act, S.C. (1996) c.19
Food and Drugs Act, R.S.C. (1985) c. F-27
Hazardous Products Act, R.S.C. (1985) c. H-3 (and amendments 3d Supp. c. 24)
International Sale of Goods Contracts Convention Act, R.S.C. (1991) c. 13
Weights and Measures Act, R.S.C. (1985) c. W-6

WEBLINKS

United Nations Office of Legal Affairs, International Trade Law Branch
www.un.or.at/uncitral/

World Trade Organization
www.wto.org

The Better Business Bureau Central Web Server for U.S. and Canada
www.bbb.org/

Consumer Connection—Office of Consumer Affairs, Industry Canada
strategis.ic.gc.ca/sc_consu/consaffairs/engdoc/oca.html

Market Place on CBC TV
www.tv.cbc.ca/market/

Alberta Municipal Affairs Consumer Tipsheets
www.gov.ab.ca/~ma/hca/html/constips.htm

Alberta Sale of Goods Act
www.gov.ab.ca/qp/ascii/acts/S02.txt

Alberta Consumer Credit Transactions Act
www.gov.ab.ca/qp/ascii/acts/C22P5.txt

Alberta Direct Sales Cancellation Act
www.gov.ab.ca/qp/ascii/acts/D35.txt

Alberta Unconscionable Transactions Act
www.gov.ab.ca/qp/ascii/acts/U02.txt

Alberta Unfair Trade Practices Act
www.gov.ab.ca/qp/ascii/acts/U03.txt

Priority of Creditors

OBJECTIVES OF THE CHAPTER

- To describe the methods and process of securing debt
- To outline the rights and obligations of the parties to a security transaction
- To consider the effect of builders' liens and bankruptcy

Calderbank was the driving force in Skyhook Operations Ltd., a company incorporated to carry out helicopter logging. Calderbank held 50 percent of the shares and two investors, Rodenbush and Rooke, held the other 50 percent. The bank had granted Skyhook Operations a $25 000 line of credit as well as a fixed loan of $112 000; the investors had signed a personal guarantee for this debt.

At the end of a year's operation, the line of credit was at its limit and Skyhook had defaulted on its fixed loan payments. Calderbank met with the bank manager to request an increase in the line of credit. He assured the bank manager that the investors would be putting another $20 000 into the business. Calderbank also confided to the bank manager that he was planning to start up another company to compete with Skyhook. When asked why, he stated that he wanted to run the business his way and get 100 percent of the profits.

The bank manager sought and obtained a promise from Calderbank that any funds from the extended line of credit and the additional funds injected by Rooke and Rodenbush would be used only for the operation of Skyhook and not for the new company. When he received this assurance, he extended the line of credit to $40 000. When the bank manager received the investors/guarantors' approval for the change in the line of credit, he did not tell them about the new company that Mr. Calderbank intended to start, believing that the information was given to him in confidence. Rooke and Rodenbush invested a further $20 000 into Skyhook.

Shortly afterwards, Calderbank exhausted the line of credit, and took these funds and the extra funds invested by Rooke and Rodenbush and diverted them to his new company. When the investors learned of this action, they informed the bank that they would not be responsible for any further debts of Skyhook. Skyhook failed, and shortly thereafter Rooke and Rodenbush learned that the bank manager had known all along of Calderbank's intention to form the competing company and had not told them. They refused any responsibility for the guarantee and the bank brought an action to enforce it.[1]

Personal guarantees are common and a vital aspect of doing business in Canada today. Since corporations are separate legal entities and responsible for their own debts, creditors usually insist on having personal guarantees from real individuals with substantial assets before they will loan money to such entities. The creditors want to ensure that people will be responsible for the debt in the likely event that the new company does not succeed. It is vitally important that people understand that when they sign such a personal guarantee there is a real possibility that they will be called on to pay back the debt.

In the above case, however, the court found that the investors were not bound by the guarantee they had signed. Because a guarantor's position is so vulnerable, the law has imposed an obligation on the creditor not to make new arrangements with the debtor that will put the guarantor at greater risk without first obtaining the guarantor's permission for the change. Part of the creditor's obligation is to disclose any unusual factors that the creditor is aware of which might persuade the guarantor not to agree to the change. The bank manager's failure to disclose that Calderbank was about to start another company in competition with Skyhook amounted to misrepresentation and therefore Rooke and Rodenbush were not required to pay the guarantee. The personal guarantee is one of the important topics discussed in this chapter.

A considerable industry has developed around the practices of lending money and granting credit. This chapter will examine the various methods that have been developed to ensure that money owed is properly repaid and the legislation that has been created to control such transactions. Although there is some overlap, this area is primarily under the jurisdiction of the provinces. Provincial legislation varies considerably from province to province, but there are many common principles which, along with significant variations, will be examined in this chapter. The main focus, of course, will be on Alberta legislation.

METHODS OF SECURING DEBT

Certain steps should be taken to protect a moneylender's interests because a simple contractual arrangement cannot guarantee that the lender will be repaid.

Security helps assure creditor of repayment

1. *Toronto Dominion Bank v. Rooke et al.* (1984) 3 D.L.R. (4th) 716 (B.C.C.A.).

Because a debtor who becomes insolvent and unable to honour a debt is unlikely to hold enough assets to cover all the outstanding creditor claims, a lender stands to lose part or all of the loan. To persuade a creditor to lend money, a debtor must often ensure that the creditor will be paid before other debts are cleared, even in the event of insolvency. Several methods have been developed to satisfy this requirement. When the parties are successful in creating a priority system of one creditor over the others, the party with priority is said to be a secured creditor.

Personal Property

Real property includes land and buildings

Personal property can be used as security

Both real and personal property have been used to create security. **Real property** includes land and any buildings or items attached to the land, called fixtures. Non-real property is called personalty or **personal property**; similar methods have been developed to allow personal property to secure the payment of money owed. Personal property can be divided into **chattels,** which are tangible, movable things, and intangible rights called **choses in action**. The creditor of a dishonoured debt has the right to initiate an action to recover the money. This right or claim is a **chose in action**. A cheque or a promissory note is actually a chose in action because the paper merely represents an obligation to pay and a right to sue for failure to do so. Both a chattel and a chose in action can be used to secure a debt. The most common method in consumer transactions is to take tangible real property or chattels as security.

The oldest system for using personal property as security is a pledge or a pawn in which a creditor (pawnbroker) takes possession of a particular item as security and holds it until repayment. The creditor has possession of the goods but the debtor still has title and remains the owner. Only when there is no repayment does the pawnbroker acquire the right to sell the goods to recover the amount lost.

Personal property security involves right to take possession upon default

In most circumstances, it is inconvenient and contrary to the intention of the parties for the creditor to take possession of the goods to be used as security. If a person were to purchase a new car on credit, it would be silly for the car to remain in the possession of the creditor until the debt was paid off. It is now customary for personal property to be used as security in the same way as real property is used. The creditor in such circumstances has the right to seize the goods upon default while the debtor continues to enjoy the possession and use of those goods. Only when the debtor fails to repay the loan can the creditor take possession of the personal property. It must be emphasized that, even in those contracts which state that the title to the goods transfers to the creditor, the primary nature of the transaction is the loan of money, not the conveyance of any interest in the goods used as collateral.

Recent Developments.

Over the years, business people have developed several different methods of using personal property as security by using the tenets of common law. Some of the most significant of these methods are conditional sales, chattel mortgages and the assignment of book accounts. Because these methods developed gradually and independently of each other, the principles which apply are usually unique to the form of security taken. Similarly, legislation passed to control each form of security has contained significant variations. In the recent past, most jurisdictions had separate conditional sales acts, bills of sale acts for chattel mortgages and assignment of book accounts acts. The result was considerable confusion and sometimes injustice. Many of these statutes had different conditions under which registration must take place, different time limits, different places for registration, different remedies and no unified system of enforcement.

In reaction to this situation, most provinces (including Alberta) now have, or are preparing to put in place, legislation adopted from the United States called personal property security acts. The significance of these acts is that one set of regulations controls all types of personal property used as security. There can still be contractual differences between conditional sales, chattel mortgages and the other types of secured transactions covered by this legislation, but the formal requirements and procedures for all of these types of securities are the same. As well, a personal property security act allows other, less common forms of personal property such as licenses, shares and bonds to be used as security and treated in a uniform way.

Personal property security acts rationalize the area

Before looking at the personal property security acts, we will examine conditional sales, chattel mortgages and the assignment of book accounts. In the provinces and territories that use the personal property security act, conditional sales, chattel mortgages and assignment of book accounts are still important because they usually form the contractual basis of the security arrangement; the various personal property security acts in place only create a unified approach to enforcing the rights and obligations set out in those contracts. In those provinces where there is no personal property security act, there is a separate statute for each of these types of security.

Conditional Sales.

Some contracts involving the sale of goods include special provisions whereby the seller retains title as a form of security until the last payment is made. A conditional sale takes place in two stages. The first stage involves the purchaser entering into the contract and taking possession of the goods. The sale is conditional in the sense that when the last payment is made, the condition is satisfied and title then follows. When title eventually passes to the purchaser the second stage of the contract of sale is complete.

Conditional seller retains title until payment is completed

If the purchaser defaults, the seller has available all of the normal remedies for breach of contract, including judgment and damages. The conditional sale arrangement, however, gives the seller the additional remedy of retaking the goods and reselling them to recoup the loss. If Lee buys a new car under a conditional sale agreement from Palmers Fine Cars Ltd., Lee gets to take the car home and then makes regular payments to Palmers. When the last payment is made Lee gets title to the car as well. If Lee can't make the payments, Palmers has the right to retake the car because they hold the title. In effect they are simply retaking their own car. Generally there is no requirement that they get a court order to do this. The right to retake is set out in the conditional sale agreement and is inherent in the fact that the seller has retained title.

Upon default, conditional seller can retake goods

A common practice among creditors who are involved in conditional sale agreements is to assign them to third parties. Although purchasers are often surprised when they find they are required to pay someone other than the seller, this is a common and entirely acceptable business practice. The assignment of contractual rights was discussed in Chapter 5. Note that such an assignment only changes to whom the purchaser pays the money, not the other obligations in the contract of sale. For example, Palmers Fine Cars Ltd. may assign their conditional sale agreement with Lee to Ace Finance Company. Upon Ace giving notice of the assignment, Lee would make further payments to Ace. But if something went wrong with the car, Lee would still look to Palmers Fine Cars Ltd. to fix it.

Assignee of conditional sales agreement only acquires benefits

The conditional seller remains obligated to the purchaser for the performance of the contract. The purchaser can even withhold payment from the assignee if the default is serious, since the assignee is in no better position than was the assignor. To avoid this problem for the assignee, the contract will often include a promissory note signed by the purchaser. The inclusion of negotiable instruments can have a significant impact on the rights and obligations of the parties. Negotiable instruments are discussed in Chapter 9.

Mortgages on Personal Property.

Real property mortgage—in Alberta, just an encumbrance

A common method of providing security for the lender when land and buildings are involved is for borrowers to grant mortgages on their real property. In Alberta, real property mortgages are simply registered against title as encumbrances or charges. Title remains with the borrower. Elsewhere, the mortgage transaction means the borrower temporarily transfers title to the land to the lender while retaining possession of the property as security for the money owed. Title is returned when the debtor repays the loan. Mortgages of real property will be discussed more extensively in Chapter 15.

Chattel mortgage

—title to goods transferred to secure loan

A **chattel mortgage** is a similar arrangement where the subject matter taken as security is in the form of tangible, moveable personal property called a chattel such as a car or a boat. Both the chattel mortgage and conditional sale provide security to the creditor while the debtor maintains possession of the goods. The chattel mortgage is much more flexible than a conditional sales agreement which is restricted to those situations where the credit is being extended by the seller of the object being used as security. A chattel mortgage can be used to create security by anyone extending credit such as a bank or finance company and the goods used as security need not be newly purchased.

Repossession available upon default

To create a chattel mortgage a **bill of sale** is given by the debtor to the creditor, in effect giving that creditor title to the goods until the loan is repaid. In the event of default the bill of sale is proof of title and gives the creditor the right to repossess the goods. Note that a bill of sale is also used in a true sale or transfer of goods and it is not always apparent from the documents just which kind of transaction is taking place.

In the event of default the creditor has the same kinds of rights as with a conditional sale.

Assignment of Book Accounts.

Accounts receivable can be used as security for a loan

Intangible property or a chose in action can also be used as security. A typical method of creating security for businesses is through a general assignment of accounts receivable or book accounts. Merchants often have outstanding accounts with customers who owe them for past transactions. The right to collect such accounts is of considerable value to the merchant and so can be used as security when that merchant wants to borrow money. The right to collect outstanding accounts is conditionally assigned to the creditor. As long as the merchant debtor makes payment to the creditor, the merchant will be able to collect on the accounts receivable in the normal way. The creditor's security rests with the right to step in and collect them directly in the event of a default.

Legislation

A serious problem arose with chattel mortgages and conditional sales when innocent third parties became involved. With these security arrangements the goods are in the possession of the debtor and it looks as if that debtor has the rights of the owner, that is, the right to resell the goods or even to use them to secure another loan. There was no way for an innocent third party to know of the danger. If the innocent third party buys the goods from the apparent owner who then fails to make proper payment to the creditor, there are two competing claims on the goods, each of which appears to have fairness and justice on its side.

For example, if Sam buys a violin from Joe on credit, arranging to make payments using the violin as security, and then sells that violin to Jane, both Jane and the unpaid seller Joe have legitimate claims against the violin. A similar problem arose with the assignment of book accounts since there was nothing to stop the merchant from assigning those book accounts to one creditor as security and then to turn around and use them again to secure another loan with a different creditor.

In response to this problem, legislation was passed in all English-speaking provinces requiring such security arrangements to be registered. Historically, each type of transaction had its own statute with different registration requirements and procedures; there were conditional sales acts, bills of sale acts and assignment of book accounts acts (in Alberta, the *Conditional Sales Act, Bills of Sale Act* and the *Assignment of Book Debts Act* respectively). Now, in most jurisdictions (including Alberta), these have all been replaced by one statute, the *Personal Property Security Act* or PPSA, creating one unified system.

Registration establishes priority

The objective of a secured transaction is to give first claim on the assets to the secured creditor in the event of default. There are some difficulties with this process because the principle involves giving one creditor priority over other parties. A creditor who has followed the appropriate procedures is able to prevent other, perfectly innocent parties from receiving what they would normally be entitled to. Security is an understandable objective from the point of view of the secured creditor, but it may seem very unjust to unsecured creditors. It would defeat the whole purpose of security if an innocent outsider could purchase goods used as security, from the debtor and obtain good title. And it would be equally unjust if a secured creditor were able to take the goods back from an innocent third party who had purchased them from a fraudulent debtor.

The unique solution that was developed to protect the security interest of creditors requires them to register the security at a designated government registry. If this is done properly it provides a place for others to check to make sure the goods they are buying or taking as security are free of any charges or liens. The legislation puts an obligation on creditors, in order to protect their privileged position, to properly and accurately register that security (usually by name and by serial number of the goods taken as security). The onus is then on third parties dealing with the goods to check with the registry. If they do, they are warned of the security and the creditor's priority. If they don't bother to check, they take the goods subject to that security. In the example used above in which Lee bought a car from Palmers Fine Cars, if Lee were to resell that car to Davis and then default on the payments, Palmers would have the right to retake possession of the car from Davis, but only if they had properly registered the security arrangement at the appropriate government registry. Davis should have checked before purchasing the car.

Onus on third party to search registry

Although creditors have their normal contractual remedies available upon default by the debtor, the whole point of secured transactions is to also give them the right to realize on that security. When tangible goods have been taken, this usually involves the right to retake possession and to resell the goods. These rights are very carefully controlled by the legislation in place. The following examination concentrates on the provisions of the *Personal Property Security Act*.[2]

---

2. *Personal Property Security Act*, S.A. (1988) c. P-4.05

The Personal Property Security Act.

Re Foster[3]

Mr. Foster obtained his license to drive a taxi in the City of Mississauga. One of the conditions attached to the license was that it was not transferable until three years from the date it was issued. But Mr. Foster needed money and made arrangements for four loans with four different creditors using the taxi license as security in various forms.

Mr. Foster didn't recover from his financial problems and made an assignment in bankruptcy just 11 days before the restriction on the license which prohibited him from transferring it expired. All four creditors and Mr. Foster's wife claimed a right to the license and in this action these claims were put forward.

The court first had to deal with the question of whether a license could be a form of property under the *Personal Property Security Act*. The court held that although there were some limitations on the license, including the possibility that it might be suspended or revoked, it still represented a valuable asset, and therefore qualified as property under the *Act*.

The next problem for the court was to decide which party had priority in their claim. (Note that Mr. Foster's trustee in bankruptcy made no such claim because he didn't want to get involved.) The wife's claim was disposed of on the basis that it was generally against her husband and didn't attach to any specific asset in priority over a secured creditor. That left the four creditors who had taken the license for security on loans.

In the first one the license was simply treated as a security for the loan. In the second the agreement between the parties purported to lease the license to the creditor with an option to purchase. The third purported to be a sale to the creditor of an interest in the license with the creditor to get the whole thing in the event of default. The fourth was the sale of the license to the creditor for its stated value which was then leased back to Foster.

The court held that the first three transactions, where money was loaned, and the license was used as security, fell under the *Personal Property Security Act* and the provisions of that *Act* had to be complied with in order to establish priority. Only the first creditor properly registered his security interest. The second and third creditors made a minor but fatal mistake when registering their interest by leaving Mr. Foster's middle initial off the registration document. The whole purpose of a personal property security act is to provide for a method to alert people to secured interests in property and in order to do that, the interest must be properly registered. Ontario's *Act* specifically required that the middle initial be included in the registration. Since it wasn't, those two secured interests were not valid. The final transaction where the license was sold with a lease back was a simple sale and didn't require registration so this creditor was entitled to the license, subject to the interest of the first creditor. It is interesting that before trial, the first and fourth creditors got together and made a settlement between them in which the first creditor got the license and so the court didn't have to decide between them.

This case illustrates several important points concerning secured transactions. First, that something as intangible as a license can be used to secure a loan and is covered by the *Personal Property Security Act*. The *Act*, therefore, is much more flexible than the old method. Second, various different kinds of transactions in rela-

3. 89 D.L.R. (4th) 555 (Ontario Court, General Division).

tionship to property are caught as security transactions under the *Act*, providing greater flexibility. It also illustrates the importance of properly following the procedures for registration of secured interests and how claims can be lost for minor mistakes.

As indicated above, Alberta has replaced the *Conditional Sales Act, Bills of Sale Act* and *Assignment of Book Debts Act* with one statute called the *Personal Property Security Act.* The agreement between the parties may be a chattel mortgage, conditional sales agreement or a general assignment of book accounts, but, regardless of the form the personal security takes, the parties need only follow the provision of this one *Act.* The *Act* is designed to cover any situation in which a creditor is given a secured interest against the personal property assets of a debtor to ensure repayment of a loan or obligation.

It should be noted that this combined legislation results in a much broader application than is found in more specific legislation such as the *Conditional Sales Act* or *Bills of Sale Act.* Here, title in the property (called the collateral) need not actually change hands to create a security. The security is any situation in which the creditor (called the secured party) receives priority or an assurance of payment before other creditors of the debtor. These rights and obligations are not affected in any way by who has title to the goods. The *Act* permits a security interest to be created for every transaction (except for some specified situations) that in substance creates a security interest, without regard to its form or to the person who has title to the collateral.[4] In addition to the traditional chattel mortgages and conditional sales, the *Act* covers, for example, floating charges, pledges, trusts, assignments, consignments, leases, and transfers of chattel paper where they secure payment or performance of an obligation.[5] This flexibility is illustrated in the *Foster* case used to introduce this section.

The *Act* does not apply to liens, charges or other interests given by an *Act* or rule of law in force in Alberta.[6] Examples include possessory liens such as unpaid seller's liens,[7] garagemen's liens[8] and bailee's liens.[9] As well, the legislation does not cover, for example, insurance policies, assignments of wages, transfers of interest in land, or transfers of an interest in a right to damages in tort.[10]

The *Personal Property Security Act*, then, is intended to replace a number of confusing and complex statutes governing secured transactions by one all-encompassing and standardized *Act.*

> *Act* creates one cohesive process

One of the primary objectives of the *Act* is to give effect to the contractual obligations entered into by the parties. Throughout this examination of the *Personal Property Security Act*, it is important to keep in mind that the rights and obligations set out in the original contractual agreement between the parties remain important.

> Contract prevails

The method of creating a secured relationship under this statute is unique. There are three stages. First, the parties enter into the contractual agreement; second, the secured interest must attach to the collateral which has been identified to provide the security; and third, the secured interest must be perfected.

> Security must attach to collateral

4. *Personal Property Security Act,* S.A. (1988) c. P-4.05 s. 3(1)(a).

5. *Ibid.,* s. 3 (1)(b).

6. *Ibid.,* s. 4(a).

7. *Sale of Goods Act,* R.S.A. (1980) c. S-2 s. 41.

8. *Garagemen's Lien Act,* R.S.A. (1980) c. G-1.

9. *Possessory Liens Act,* R.S.A. (1980) c. P-13 s. 4.

10. *Personal Property Security Act,* S.A. (1988) c. P-4.05 s. 4.

For attachment to take place, value must have been given, the debtor must have rights in the collateral and, except for the purposes of enforcing rights between the parties to the agreement, the security interest becomes enforceable.[11] Usually, this means that a security interest will not attach until a security agreement has been signed (or the secured party has possession of the collateral), the debtor has rights in the collateral, and the secured party has advanced funds. So, for example, if a person requiring a business loan makes an agreement with a bank to that effect and uses a car as collateral for the loan, that security does not attach until the debtor has actually received the money from the bank. The contractual agreement must be a "security agreement,"[12] that is, an agreement that creates or provides for a security interest that secures payments or performance of an obligation. The security agreement must contain a description of the collateral by item or kind, a statement that a security is taken in all of the debtor's present and after-acquired personal property, or a statement that a security interest is taken in all of the debtor's present and after-acquired property except specified items or kinds of personal property.[13] These security agreements usually take the form of the more traditional conditional sales, chattel mortgages or assignment of book accounts discussed above, but they need not be restricted in this way. The attachment process will give the secured party (the creditor, in this instance, the bank) certain rights and remedies in relationship to the car, such as the right to retake the goods upon default. But those rights and obligations apply only in the relationship between those two parties (creditors and debtor). The car could not be retaken from an innocent third party such as a subsequent purchaser.

For the creditor to obtain priority over third parties, the secured transaction must also be perfected. This perfection can be accomplished in one of two ways. The first is by registering the creation of the security obligation as discussed above.[14] This process has been simplified so that a single form is used. The form and required content of the financing statement varies to some extent from province to province, but in general the form requires the complete name and address of the parties, and the type and description (including the serial number) of the security used. A copy of a financing statement has been included at the end of this chapter as Appendix 8-1.

The second way the transaction can be perfected is by the creditor obtaining physical possession of the collateral used, as would be the case with a pledge or pawn. The whole purpose of requiring registration is to provide a method whereby a third party will not be misled by the debtor when he or she is in possession of the collateral property. This, of course, is not a problem if the property used as collateral is in the possession of the creditor. Therefore registration is not required for perfection or to protect the rights of innocent third parties. In these circumstances, if more than one secured interest is perfected by registering different financing agreements against the same collateral, the priority between those secured parties is generally determined by the date registration takes place.

Perfection required to prevail against outsiders

Rights and Remedies upon Default.

Royal Bank of Canada v. J. Segreto Construction Ltd.[15]

Two corporations borrowed money from the Royal Bank and executed promissory notes to ensure repayment. As part of the agreement each corporation put up

11. *Ibid.,* s. 12(1).
12. *Ibid.,* s. 1(1)(pp).
13. *Ibid.,* s. 10(1).
14. *Ibid.,* s. 25.
15. 47 D.L.R. (4th) 761 (Ontario Court of Appeal).

certain construction equipment as security for the loan and financial statements were properly registered under the *Personal Property Security Act* to that effect. The debtors defaulted on the loan, and the Royal Bank seized the construction equipment which had been put forward as security. This equipment was then sold at public auction, but didn't bring in enough to cover the amount owing. The Bank then sued the two corporations for the shortfall.

Unfortunately for the Bank, when they seized and sold the construction equipment, they failed to notify the debtor when and where it was to be resold as required under the *Personal Property Security Act.* The court held that this failure completely prohibited the Bank from claiming any deficit and they had to be content with the proceeds of the sale.

This case is reasonably straightforward, but it illustrates a very important point. When a default does take place and goods were used as security, the normal course of action is to seize or repossess those goods and sell them for whatever is owing. But the legislation protects the position of the debtor from abuse and requires that the debtor be notified of when the sale will take place and be given a certain period of time in order to make arrangements to reclaim the goods. Since this did not happen in this case, there was no right to sue for a shortfall. Again we see the importance of carefully following the procedures set out in the *Act* in order to protect both the rights of the debtor and the rights of the secured creditor.

It must always be remembered that, when a default takes place, the normal common law remedies set out in the original contract are available. Only when the secured party enforces his or her rights in relationship to the collateral property do the provisions of the legislation come into play. Under the personal property security legislation, the creditor, in the event of default, has the right to take possession of those goods and have them disposed of (sold) for the amount owing. But, of course, these rights have to be set out in the original contract between the parties.

> All normal contract remedies available upon default

> Upon default, creditor can take possession and dispose of collateral

> Repossession also available

As a general rule, once there has been a default, the secured party or creditor can take possession of those goods in any way that does not violate the law. When the original contract sets out the right as in a conditional sales agreement the creditor or an agent acting on his or her behalf, usually a bailiff, can come onto the property of the debtor and seize possession of the chattels used as security, providing that no force is used.

As discussed in Chapter 1, the *Civil Enforcement Act*[16] resulted in the privatization of the execution process of seizure in Alberta, such that a bailiff employed by a civil enforcement agency seizes the property of the enforcement debtor. The *Act* also governs the obtaining of possession of the security by a secured creditor (after the required demand for payment and notice[17] have been given to the debtor). Seizure in such cases must also be made by a civil enforcement agency (unless a receiver has been appointed, either privately by agreement or by way of court order).[18]

A seizure pursuant to the terms of a security agreement continues until possession of the property is surrendered to the secured creditor, or the seizure has been released.[19] While the property is in the possession of the secured creditor, "reasonable care" must be used in its custody and preservation.[20] If the goods require

> Creditor must take care of collateral in his or her possession

16. *Civil Enforcement Act,* S.A. (1994) c. C-10.5.

17. *Bankruptcy and Insolvency Act,* R.S.C. (1985) c. B-3 s. 244.

18. *Civil Enforcement Act,* S.A. (1994) c. C-10.5 s. 9(3)(b).

19. *Personal Property Security Act,* S.A. (1988) c. P-4.05 s. 58(6).

20. *Ibid.,* s. 17(1).

any repair, processing or preparation, such reasonable expenses will be added to the amount the debtor owes.[21]

Once the secured creditor has obtained possession of the property, she may dispose of it.[22] The proceeds from the disposal are applied first against the reasonable expenses of enforcing the security agreement, then against the obligation secured by the security interest of the secured creditor. The balance is dealt with according to the legislation; any surplus must be paid to the debtor.[23] If there remains a deficiency outstanding to the secured creditor after disposition of the proceeds, the debtor will, in the absence of a contrary agreement or legislation, be liable for the deficiency.[24]

As a result, most security agreements state that the debtor will be liable for any deficiency that exists after the goods are sold. Secured creditors, however, are not always allowed to enforce security agreements that make the debtor liable for the deficiency. Part 6 of the *Law of Property Act*[25] forces the secured creditor to make an election to either seize the goods or sue for the amount owing under the security agreement. She cannot both seize and sue.

Part 6 applies to "consumer goods," which are defined as goods used or acquired for use primarily for personal, family or household purposes.[26] Only transactions resulting in the creation of a purchase money security interest for consumer goods are affected by Part 6. A purchase money security interest is a security interest taken in consumer goods by a seller to secure payment of all or part of its purchase price (including credit charges).[27] Part 6 is therefore applicable only where the actual seller of the goods retains a security interest in them, and not where the purchase money is advanced by a lender who then takes a security interest in the goods.[28]

If the secured creditor elects to enforce a purchase money security interest against consumer goods by way of seizure, and the goods are seized, the secured creditor may not maintain an action for the purchase price of the goods.[29] That is, when the consumer goods are seized, the holder of a purchase money security interest is then restricted to her right of repossession and sale. The secured creditor, with respect to a purchase money security interest, is therefore forced to make an election as to which remedy to pursue. The case law states that this election takes place at the time of seizure, and that once the secured creditor has effected a seizure, she cannot later release it and pursue another remedy.[30]

Collateral that has been seized may be disposed of by private or public sale—as a whole or in commercial units or parts.[31] In any event, the sale must be undertaken in good faith and in a commercially reasonable manner.[32] The secured

---

21. *Ibid.*, s. 17(2).

22. *Ibid.*, s. 60(1).

23. *Ibid.*, s. 61(1).

24. *Ibid.*, s. 61(4).

25. *Law of Property Act*, R.S.A. (1980) c. L-8.

26. *Ibid.*, s. 47(a); *Personal Property Security Act*, S.A. (1988) c. P-4.05 s. 1(h).

27. *Law of Property Act*, R.S.A. (1980) C. L-8 s. 47(f).

28. Rutman, R.C., Summers, B.W., et al. (1996). *Creditors' Remedies in Alberta*. Toronto: Thomson Canada Ltd., Paragraph 15.75.

29. *Law of Property Act*, R.S.A. (1980) c. L-8 s. 49(2).

30. Rutman, R.C., Summers, B.W., et al. (1996). *Creditors' Remedies in Alberta*. Toronto: Thomson Canada Ltd., Paragraph 15.81.

31. *Personal Property Security Act*, S.A. (1988) c. P-4.05 s. 60(2).

32. *Ibid.*, s. 66.

creditor must, however, follow certain requirements, including giving 20 days' notice of the sale to the debtor and other interested parties.[33] The notice must describe the collateral, state the amount owing (including any interest and reasonable expenses) and include a statement that the debtor can redeem the collateral or reinstate the security agreement upon payment of the appropriate amounts; but if these amounts are not paid, the collateral will be disposed of and the debtor may be liable for any deficiency.[34] It was the failure to follow requirements such as these that caused the creditors in the *Segreto* case discussed above to lose their right to sue the debtor for a deficiency. Furthermore, if a secured creditor does not satisfy the stipulated requirements, and a debtor therefore suffers losses, then the debtor may be successful in suing the creditor to recover them.

A secured creditor also has a right to retain the collateral in satisfaction of the obligations secured, if the appropriate steps are taken. To do so, the secured party must give notice of the intention to take the collateral, to parties entitled to receive a notice of disposition of collateral.[35] These parties may give the secured party written notice of objection to the retention within 15 days and, if such notice is given, the secured party must dispose of the collateral as discussed above.[36] The secured party may, however, make an application to the court for an order that the notice of objection is ineffective.[37]

Secured creditor may opt to retain collateral

If no notice of objection is made, the secured party is deemed to have irrevocably elected to take the collateral in satisfaction of the obligation secured by it. She is then entitled to dispose of the collateral free from all rights and interests of the debtor and of any person who received the notice of the intention to retain.[38]

Procedures such as those described above may appear very cumbersome, and the legislation itself is very complex, but in actual practice it works quite well and relatively simply. For example, where a personal property security act is in place (as in Alberta) and a person goes to a bank or credit union using a car as security, the security becomes attached to the car once the contract has been entered into and the monies advanced. The credit union then perfects the security by registering the financing statement with a registry agent. Thereafter, if the debtor tries to sell that car, the buyer may search the registry and should find the registered security against the vehicle. If the third party buys the car anyway, and there is a default, the creditor will be able to recover the vehicle even from an innocent third party. This is the essence of the creditor's security.

Once there is a default, the credit union has the option of either pursuing its normal breach of contract remedies or taking possession of the vehicle. If it chooses the latter, it can't use force to do so, and once the vehicle is repossessed it must keep it in good repair; but thereafter it can choose to dispose of the car (sell it) to recover the amount of money owing.

First notice of such disposition must be given to the debtor and any other interested parties, that is, creditors, so they have a chance to redeem it by paying off any money owing. Any surplus from the sale after paying off the principal, interest, legal fees, repair expenses, etc., will go to the debtor and in most cases any deficiency (shortfall) can be recovered from the debtor. Alternatively, the credit union can

33. *Ibid.*, s. 60(4).
34. *Ibid.*, s. 60(5).
35. *Ibid.*, s. 62(1).
36. *Ibid.*, s. 62(2).
37. *Ibid.*, s. 62(6).
38. *Ibid.*, s. 62(3).

choose to retain the car by serving notice of its intention of so doing. If the credit union chooses this route, it can do whatever it wants with the car but the debtor's obligation ends. If there is a deficiency, the creditor will not be able to claim it against the debtor.

In those provinces where a personal property security act is not yet in force, at a practical level very similar rights exist. A creditor can use an item of personal property such as a car or boat, even accounts receivable as security for a loan. The creditor must register the transaction and in the event of default has the right to repossess the goods even from an innocent third party and resell them. The problem is that these provisions are found in separate bills of sale, conditional sales and assignment of book accounts acts. The purpose of the *Personal Property Security Act* is to overcome this duplication and confusion and bring all such uses of personal property as security under one system and one statute and to allow more flexibility as to what can be used as security.

Personal property security acts unify and simplify process

The Bank Act.

Before the passage of personal property security acts, a major disadvantage of chattel mortgages and conditional sales was that they had to be attached to specific goods or, in the case of the assignment of book accounts, to specific claims. These goods or claims usually could not be resold without violating the terms of the contract and defeating its objectives. Often much of the value of a business is tied up in its inventory or in the goods being manufactured. Being able to sell those goods is the essence of the business. Another difficulty was that only certain types of personal property could be used as security and then only in very structured ways.

These problems are now largely overcome in provinces with personal property security acts, but originally provisions were incorporated into what is now the federal *Bank Act*[39] to solve these problems and to give the banks more flexibility in their financing operations. The *Act* allows banks to use items such as crops that are still being grown and goods that are still being manufactured as security. This kind of financing arrangement requires that the goods be sold to repay the loan. Normally, not all of the products from the farming or manufacturing process are sold at the same time, but Sections 426 and 427 allow goods to be sold and new goods to be produced as part of an ongoing process without altering the nature of the security. This was much more difficult, if not impossible, to arrange under prior provincial legislation. This is now possible because of the much greater flexibility under the personal property security acts. There is now also more overlap with the *Bank Act* and, as a result, more potential conflicts. People also must worry about two different sets of rules. One important feature of the *Act* is that the loan is registered with the local branch of the Bank of Canada.

Anticipated crops can be used as security

This banking legislation also permits banks to continue to use the normal types of secured transactions available to everyone such as chattel mortgages, guarantees, real estate mortgages, assignment of debts and so on.

Floating Charges

Although a corporation is an artificial creation, it has the same rights and obligations as a person. A corporation can be either a creditor or a debtor in a secured transaction. As with an individual, the corporation as a debtor can grant security to a creditor in all of the standard ways, such as a real estate mortgage, guarantee,

39. *Bank Act*, S.C. (1991) c. 46.

lease, consignment, chattel mortgage, conditional sale, assignment of book accounts and so on.

A debenture is one form of security unique to corporations. A **debenture** is a document acknowledging debt that corporations often use to assume a debt obligation involving more than one creditor. Since the debenture is merely an acknowledgement of debt, it can take several forms and can be either secured or unsecured.

A common practice is for corporations to secure a debenture through a **floating charge**. Typically, there will be a mortgage against the specific property and a floating charge as well. A floating charge is not fixed against any specific item or goods; rather the property of the corporation generally, such as inventory, is taken as security in such a way that the corporation can continue to deal with it. The company is free to purchase new goods and sell its inventory in the normal course of business as long as it is not in default of its agreement. The customers of such a firm take the goods they purchase free and clear of any encumbrance. It is only upon default or some other crystallizing event that the floating charge descends and attaches to the specific goods described in the debenture. The debenture document sets out the nature of the security and under what condition the floating charge becomes fixed. The requirement of registration is present with floating charges as well.

Crystallizing events may include the making of an unauthorized payment, such as a dividend to the shareholders, or the sale of a valuable asset used as security, such as a factory, offices or other building owned by the debtor. If any other creditor manages to obtain a security fixed to the specific goods before the floating charge becomes fixed, the fixed charge will have priority.

For the creditor the advantage of a floating charge is to give it priority over general creditors; the advantage of the floating charge to corporations involved in manufacturing is that it allows them to use their work in process, inventory and other assets as security but does not interfere with their business.

Since the personal property security acts in place in most jurisdictions allow inventory and other changing assets to be used as security, in those jurisdictions the floating charge is of diminishing importance, having been superseded by the *Personal Property Security Act.*[40]

> A debenture acknowledges debt

> Floating charge not fixed on goods until default

Bulk Sales

Certain similarities exist between the protection given to secured creditors and the protection given to general or unsecured creditors in bulk sales transactions. A **bulk sale** involves a merchant selling all or almost all of a business's inventory, equipment or other assets in other than the ordinary course of business.

For example, it is a bulk sale if Alberti owns a hardware store and sells not only all of its merchandise to Nystrom but some of the display tables as well. Such an action by a debtor is obviously inconsistent with continuing in business and means that assets that would have been available to satisfy the claims of creditors may have been taken beyond their reach. If Alberti has an unsecured creditor named Jamal, Jamal would expect to have a claim against the store's merchandise and fittings to satisfy the debt. But if they are sold to Nystrom there is nothing left for Jamal when

> Creditors protected when merchant sells the bulk of business

---

40. *Personal Property Security Act*, S.A. (1988) c. P-4.05. In Alberta, s. 10(4) of the *Act* indicates that a description of collateral as inventory is adequate as long as the debtor is holding the goods as inventory. Section 10(1) confirms that after-acquired personal property can be the subject of a security interest. Section 3(1)(B) specifically states that the *Act* applies to floating charges.

Alberti defaults. Under common law, in these situations unsecured creditors might be left in the position of getting nothing.

Bulk sales acts regulate bulk sales activities

The western provinces have repealed their bulk sales acts[41] but all of the other common law provinces and the territories have bulk sales acts in force to protect general creditors. Although these statutes vary somewhat from province to province, they have a common objective. A *Bulk Sales Act* puts an obligation on the purchaser in a bulk sales transaction to ensure that the general creditors have first claim on the proceeds of the sale.

The legislation also gives the creditors a say in the price paid for the goods to prevent the bulk seller from selling them at an unreasonably low price. The method used is to require the purchaser to acquire a list of creditors from the seller, to notify them of the sale and if they wish, to have the proceeds of the sale put into the hands of a trustee for distribution to those creditors. Failure to comply will make the sale void as against the creditors, effectively requiring the purchaser to account to those creditors for the value of the goods.

Other Legislation

Fraudulent conveyance void

Other legislation has been enacted to protect creditors against frauds committed by debtors. Debtors are often tempted to hide property or otherwise protect it from the claims of creditors. Giving or selling property to a friend or relative to avoid the debt becomes a void transaction. The creditor can seek out the fraudulently transferred property and get it back from the purchaser. If the transfer is a proper sale from the point of view of the purchaser, that is, an arm's-length transaction in which the purchaser is unaware of any debts owing to the creditors and a fair price was paid, it is exempted from the legislation. In these circumstances, the third party is called a *bona fide* purchaser for value.

Fraudulent preference void

Another way in which a debtor might attempt to cheat a creditor is by paying one creditor in preference over another. The unpaid creditor can challenge this type of fraudulent preference. Legislation embodying these provisions varies from province to province; the statutes are called variously *Fraudulent Conveyances Act*, *Fraudulent Preferences Act*, *Assignment and Preferences Act* and *Fraudulent Creditors Act*. They are designed primarily to prevent debtors from unfairly making payments or transferring property in such a way as to keep it from the just claims of creditors. The Alberta *Act* reads as follows.

> 2. ...every gift, conveyance, assignment, transfer, delivery over or payment of goods, chattels or effects or of bills, bonds, notes or securities or of shares, dividends, premiums or bonus in any bank, company or corporation, or of any other property, real or personal, made
>
> (a) by a person at a time when he is in insolvent circumstances or is unable to pay his debts in full or knows that he is on the eve of insolvency, and
> (b) to or for a creditor with intent to give that creditor preference over the other creditors of the debtor or over any one or more of them,
>
> is void as against the creditor or creditors injured, delayed, prejudiced or postponed.[42]

The federal *Bankruptcy and Insolvency Act* discussed below also has provisions prohibiting settlements (fraudulent transfers) and preferences, provisions that apply uniformly throughout Canada. The wordings used in the federal and provin-

---

41. In Alberta, the *Bulk Sales Act* was repealed in 1992.

42. *Fraudulent Preferences Act*, R.S.A. (1980) c. F-18 s.2.

cial acts vary considerably, which may make it more effective in any given situation to proceed under one statute than under another.

GUARANTEES

Another method creditors use to ensure the repayment of a debt is the **guarantee**. When corporations are involved, the use of guarantees is very common as a means of circumventing the limited liability characteristic of incorporation, making the principals of a corporation directly responsible for loans and other obligations. In consumer transactions they are a frequently used method of putting a more substantial debtor under obligation to ensure the repayment of a loan or other debt, as when parents are asked to guarantee the loans of their children.

The essential nature of a guarantee is that the creditor can turn to some third party who has assumed an obligation to ensure the debt is repaid. The borrower produces a relative, friend or business associate who is willing to take responsibility for the debt.

A guarantee involves a secondary obligation that arises only in the event of a default. It is not a guarantee when a third party agrees to be directly responsible for paying a debt or to indemnify the creditor for any loss; such an obligation is not secondary but primary, the debtors sharing the responsibility, and is referred to as an **indemnity**.

The distinction, although subtle, can be important. As we discussed in Chapter 4, the *Statute of Frauds* requires that certain types of contracts be evidenced in writing to be enforceable in the courts. In most provinces, only the guarantee must be evidenced in writing, but in British Columbia both indemnities and guarantees must be evidenced in writing. And in Alberta[43] most personal guarantees must be entered into in the presence of a notary public and a certificate to that effect must be produced which states the notary public is satisfied the guarantor understands the nature of the obligation entered into—and when this is not correct, the guarantee is unenforceable.[44]

Since a guarantee is a separate contract, all of the elements of a contract must be present including offer and acceptance and consideration. Usually part performance of the contract, such as advancement of funds, is sufficient indication that the creditor has accepted the guarantee.

Finding the required consideration, however, is often a more difficult problem. The consideration requirement is satisfied when it can be shown that the creditor has either done or refrained from doing something, such as advancing goods or money, or forbearing to take the remedies available to enforce an existing debt, in exchange for the guarantor's promise. There is little difficulty in identifying consideration if a merchant refrains from advancing the goods involved until the guarantee has been received. It is when the creditor extracts the guarantee after the subject matter of the contract has been delivered or the creditor's obligations under the contract have been performed that the question of consideration arises.

If Kotsalis borrows money from the Business Bank and the manager of the bank asks for a guarantee after giving the money to Kotsalis, the requirement of consideration will probably not be satisfied. When a guarantor adds a seal to the document, this prevents any future claim by the guarantor that he or she is not

Margin notes:

Guarantor must pay when debtor defaults

Evidence in writing of guarantee required

Contractual requirements must be met for guarantor to be bound

---

43. *Guarantees Acknowledgement Act,* R.S.A. (1980) c. G-12.

44. *Bank of British Columbia v. Shank Investments et al.* (1985) 34 Alta. L.R. 379 (Q.B.).

bound because there was no consideration. As we discussed in Chapter 3, when a seal is present, consideration is conclusively presumed. Similarly, if the debtor is in default and a guarantee is obtained which persuades the creditor not to sue, there has been an appropriate exchange of consideration, even if it appears to flow to the debtor, not the guarantor. That is, the creditor has refrained from suing.

Rights and Obligations of the Parties

The creditor has significant duties to protect the interests of the guarantor. At the outset, it is important for the creditor to ensure that the guarantor understands the full nature of the guarantee he or she is signing. Guarantors often escape their obligation by claiming misrepresentation, *non est factum*, or undue influence. When in doubt, the creditor should insist that the guarantor obtain independent legal advice.

Creditor must not weaken the position of the guarantor

Significant changes may release guarantor

Creditor can reserve rights against guarantor

After the guarantee has been created, the creditor is obligated to do nothing to weaken the position of the guarantor; therefore, the agreement must be strictly adhered to. Subsequent dealings between the creditor and debtor are the most common grounds for ending a guarantor's obligation. The principle is that any substantial change in the nature of the contract between the creditor and debtor without the guarantor's consent will relieve the guarantor of any obligation. If the creditor simply delays bringing an action to give a defaulting debtor a chance to pay, this will not be considered a substantial change in the relationship. But if, rather than simply being a gratuitous forbearance by the creditor, the change was entered into by agreement, the change in the agreement would be significant enough to relieve the obligations of the guarantor. The creditor can avoid this problem by making a specific statement reserving rights against the guarantor at the time of extending the repayment period. The effect will be that the guarantor will continue to be bound by the original agreement. When there has been no default but the creditor agrees to a different method of payment, imposes a higher rate of interest or changes the size of installments, such changes can release the guarantor from obligation.

The guarantor is also released from obligation when other forms of security, such as chattel mortgages, are released. For example, if Kotsalis were to go to the Business Bank requesting a loan and the bank required that Bruno guarantee the loan in addition to taking a chattel mortgage against Kotsalis's car as security, such an arrangement would cease to be binding on Bruno if the bank subsequently allowed Kotsalis

GUARANTOR RELEASED BECAUSE OF CHANGE

Farries Enterprises owned certain property and gave Royal Trust a mortgage on it to secure a loan. Reid also guaranteed the loan. Afterwards Farries sold the property to a third party, who agreed to assume the mortgage and the responsibilities under it. Unfortunately, they ran into financial troubles and got Royal Trust to extend the loan for a year at higher interest. But they still defaulted on the loan, so Royal Trust seized the property and had it sold. In this action Royal Trust sued Reid for the difference between what was owing and what the property was sold for, claiming Reid was still responsible as guarantor. The court held that Reid was no longer responsible, since the nature of the agreement changed when the time was extended and the higher rate of interest agreed to, and Reid had not consented to this.

Reid et al. v. Royal Trust Corporation of Canada, 20 D.L.R. (4th) 223 (Prince Edward Island Supreme Court, Appeal Division)

to sell the car. Similarly, Bruno would be released if the bank advanced Kotsalis more money or agreed to a change in the nature of the repayment terms without Bruno's consent. However, the guarantor is still bound if the agreement between the guarantor and the creditor permits such modification.

Thus, a contract that allows the debtor to borrow more money continues to be binding on the guarantor even though the nature of the debt continually changes. This is called a **continuing guarantee** and will not release the guarantor unless the pre-arranged limit of funds is exceeded. Even when the guarantor does consent to such a change, he or she may not be bound. If the creditor is aware of special circumstances which, if known to the guarantor, would cause him or her to withhold consent to the change and the creditor fails to disclose this information to the guarantor, it can constitute misrepresentation and void the guarantee. This is what happened in the Skyhook case discussed at the beginning of the chapter. To be considered misrepresentation, the withheld information must be of some substantial and unusual nature and not simply the normal kind of information that would pass between business associates. In the Skyhook case, the information that the driving force behind the company, Calderbank, intended to start another company in competition was of such a significant and unusual nature as to void the guarantee.

When a default occurs, the creditor can turn to the guarantor for payment but the creditor usually first informs all the parties involved, giving them the opportunity to satisfy the obligations. When the debtor has put up some other form of security, such as a chattel mortgage on a car, the creditor is not normally obligated to seize the chattel before looking to the guarantor for payment, unless it has been otherwise agreed to in the contract. A guarantor who pays the debt is subrogated to the rights of the creditor, which means, in effect, that the guarantor steps into the creditor's shoes. Any remedy or right available to the creditor is thus available to the guarantor, including the right to seize a chattel used as security for the debt and to sue the debtor and take advantage of the proceedings available to assist in collecting the debt.

Guarantor assumes rights of creditor upon payment

Since the obligation of the guarantor is contingent upon default by the debtor, any defense available to the debtor is also available to the guarantor. If breach of contract, fraud or misrepresentation on the part of the creditor has barred an action by the creditor against the debtor, the creditor cannot then look to the guarantor for payment, because the guarantor is entitled to the same defenses as those available to the debtor. Note, however, that if the reason the guarantee was required was because of the infancy of the debtor, the guarantor will normally not be allowed to use that infancy as a defense against the creditor.

Defences of debtor are available to guarantor

The basic rights and obligations associated with guarantees are founded in common law, but because the relationship is one of contract, those obligations can be modified by agreement. It is characteristic of guarantee arrangements that provisions are included that attempt to exempt the creditor from the basic obligations discussed here, but like all exemption clauses they are interpreted very carefully by the courts. Great care should be taken when entering into a guarantee to determine the extent of such exemption clauses and how they modify the obligations of the parties.

BUILDERS' LIENS

A person who supplies goods or services that will be incorporated into another person's property faces two potentially significant problems in common law. First, if the contract is with the owner of the property who defaults on the agreement, the only course of action available to the supplier under common law is to sue. Even though the supplier's goods or services are incorporated into the property of the person with whom the contract was established, the supplier has no prior claim to recover the amount owed over the claim of any other general creditor. A second problem often facing the supplier of the goods or services is that there may not be a contract with the owner of the property at all. In the construction industry, for example, the owner of a property will often hire the services of a general contractor who will then enter into independent contracts with tradespeople and suppliers to complete the project. As discussed in Chapter 5, the principle of privity of contract establishes that, without such a direct contractual relationship, these suppliers have no claim against the owner of the property who benefits from their work. The subcontractors and wage earners must look to the general contractor for satisfaction.

To alleviate these difficulties the *Mechanics' Lien Acts*, the *Builders' Lien Acts* and, in Ontario, the *Construction Liens Act* were passed. The resulting liens are variously called mechanics' liens, builders' liens or construction liens. This text will use "builders' liens."[45]

Lien against property available to supplier of goods and services

The principle and object of such legislation is to create a lien in favour of the supplier of goods and services and against the property to which those goods and services have been supplied. This lien or charge is entirely a creation of the legislation and provides direct access to the property even when there is an intervening general contractor. It gives suppliers of goods and services priority in the event of insolvency or default on the part of the owner or contractor. It should be further noted that the people who can file liens and thus obtain security and priority against the property of the landowner are typically contractors, subcontractors, wage earners, suppliers of materials and, in some provinces (including Alberta),[46] a lessor of equipment used on the property.

Registration.

Lien must be registered within time specified

In Alberta, the legislation provides that a contractor, subcontractor, wage earner or supplier who does work or furnishes material has a lien against the property involved.[47] But before anyone can take advantage of that lien, it must first be preserved and then perfected. The lien is preserved by registering it at a land titles office. Registration of a lien must take place within 45 days from the day the last of the materials is furnished or that the performance of the services is completed.[48] Failure to register the lien within the 45-day period is fatal to that lien, although the supplier of the goods or services could still seek any available contractual remedy.

Only when the lien has been registered does the lien claimant have a claim against the holdback discussed below. But after the lien has been preserved by registration, the claimant must take steps to have the lien perfected. In this regard, the lien claimant must commence an action under the *Act* to enforce the lien within 180 days from the date the lien is registered.[49]

Holdbacks.

It would cause significant hardship on property owners if suppliers of goods and services could use builders' liens to force them to pay whenever the suppliers did not receive proper payment from the general contractor. To eliminate the possibility of

45. In Alberta, the relevant legislation is the *Builders' Lien Act*, R.S.A. (1980) c. B-12.

46. *Ibid.*, s. 4(4).

47. *Ibid.*, s. 4(4).

48. *Ibid.*, s. 30.

49. *Ibid.*, s. 32(1).

property owners having to pay twice, the legislation requires that the owner of the land retain a certain percentage of the contract price in reserve to satisfy any builders' liens that may eventually be registered. This retained amount is called a **holdback.**

<aside>Owner must hold back part of contract price</aside>

The percentage that must be retained varies from a low of 10 percent to a high of 20 percent, depending on the province. This amount must be retained for a specified period of time, from 30 to 60 days in the various jurisdictions. The amount that must be retained in Alberta is 10 percent for 45 days.[50] The time the holdback must be retained equals the period in which the builders' lien must be filed, which eliminates the possibility of a valid builders' lien being filed after the expiration of the holdback period. The owner is thus able to pay out the holdback amount at the end of the holdback period without incurring any risk. Although the total amount of claims in the form of builders' liens may exceed the total amount retained in a holdback, the owner cannot be required to pay more than has been held back as long as all of the provisions set out in the legislation have been complied with and he or she has had no notice of disputes before making payments. The holdback provision in the legislation gives some protection to the builders' lien claimant and ensures that the owner of the property does not have to pay twice for the work done.

<aside>Owner's liability limited to holdback</aside>

Many provinces have amended their legislation to require that a certificate of substantial completion be made when the job is finished. In Alberta, a contract or a subcontract is substantially performed when the work under the contract or subcontract, or a substantial part of it, is ready for use or is being used for the purpose intended, and when the work to be done under the contract or subcontract is capable of completion or correction at a cost of not more than 3 percent of the first $500 000 of the price, 2 percent of the next $500 000 of the price and 1 percent of the balance of the price.[51] The *Act* then allows a contractor (or a subcontractor, with respect to his own contract), to issue a certificate of substantial performance.[52] The owner must retain a holdback equal to 10 percent of the value of the work actually done, and materials actually furnished, for a period of 45 days from the date of issue of a certificate of substantial performance, or the date of completion of the contract if a certificate of substantial performance is not issued.[53] Before the owner can pay out the holdback to the contractor, the lien must come to an end. This happens automatically if the lien has not been preserved or perfected within the specified periods.[54] It can also come to an end when the claimant's action is dismissed, by payment into court of the monies claimed or when the claimant is paid what is owed.[55]

Rights of the Parties.

A person who has filed a properly registered builders' lien has the right to enforce it against the owner of the property in the event of default. The property owner's obligations are satisfied by the retention of the holdback amount for the time required by the legislation. If a builders' lien is registered before the property owner has paid an amount payable under the contract, then the owner is required not to pay out further funds to the general contractor until the matter is settled, even if this amount exceeds the holdback percentage.[56] In the event of a dispute, the owner of

<aside>Liability may exceed holdback with notice of lien</aside>

50. *Ibid.*, s.15(1).
51. *Ibid.*, s. 2.
52. *Ibid.*, s. 15.1.
53. *Ibid.*, s. 15(1).
54. *Ibid.*, ss. 31 and 32.
55. *Ibid.*, ss. 33–35.
56. *Ibid.*, s. 15(1) and (2).

the property who has paid all of the funds owing to the general contractor except the holdback percentage, or who has withheld an amount greater than the holdback percentage because a builders' lien has been registered, should then pay that money into court so that the court can resolve the dispute.[57] The owner of a property who ignores this obligation and pays directly to the general contractor assumes a considerable risk because he or she may also be required to pay the builders' lien claimants.

If no builders' liens are registered within the statutory time specified, the owner of the property is free to pay the retained amount to the general contractor.[58] If the owner of the property fails to make proper payments to the builders' lien claimants, the registration of the lien gives the claimant priority against the property. A person who holds a mortgage at the time of the creation of the builders' lien will retain a prior claim. But, if the registered mortgage is for funds, not all of which have been dispersed, the priority will only be for those funds already given to the owner before the registration of the builders' lien.[59] Subsequent mortgagees or purchasers of the property will be subject to the builders' lien. As with other forms of registered security, the builders' lien gives the holder the right to have the property sold to satisfy the debt,[60] although this would be extremely rare because of the relatively small size of the holdback.

Lien creates priority over subsequent creditors

Because a builders' lien holder has priority over subsequent parties obtaining interest in the property,[61] the filing of such a lien puts tremendous pressure on the owner of the property to have the lien removed by satisfying the lien claimant. Subsequent purchasers or mortgagees will be reluctant to deal with the property as long as the builders' lien is registered against it. However, the owner may not be

PRIORITY OF SECURED CREDITORS

Royal Life was a mortgagee, having loaned money for a township development. This mortgage was properly registered and was to be paid out as a series of advances over the life of the project. Several advances were made and then the contractor defaulted on the payment to the subcontractor, who properly filed a builders' lien against the property. Further advances were then made. The court had to determine who had priority: Royal Life, who had security by way of the registered mortgage, or the subcontractor, who had security by way of the lien. The court held that the lien in effect provided notice to Royal Life and that they, therefore, lost priority of claim with respect to any funds that were advanced after the properly registered lien. What is interesting in this case is that

the builders' lien was eventually removed and further funds were advanced. Because of the unique features of the Ontario legislation, the court held that even these further advances were subject to other liens eventually registered against the property. It is at least clear in all provinces that priority between mortgages and builders' liens is not established by comparing the time of registration of the mortgage to that of the lien; what matters is when the money is advanced. If money is advanced after the registration of a builders' lien, priority for that portion is lost.

Boehmers v. 794561 Ontario Inc., 105 D.L.R. (4th) 473 (Ontario Court, General Division)

57. *Ibid.*, s. 18.
58. *Ibid.*, s. 18(1).
59. *Ibid.*, s. 9(2) and (3).
60. *Ibid.*, s. 45(2).
61. *Ibid.*, s. 9(1).

able to pay disputed claims without incurring liability to the other claimants. Under these circumstances, the owner can pay the amount of the claim or holdback into court and ask the court to remove the lien. The court will do this because the lien has accomplished its purpose; the payment of valid claims is now assured because the funds are in the possession of the court. Using the court also prevents the frivolous or abusive use of builders' liens to tie up property and bring pressure to pay when it is not justified because the owner needs to pay only the disputed amount into court and ask that the property be freed from the lien. The owner is still free to dispute the claim of the builders' lien when the holder applies to the court for the money.

When claim is disputed, owner may make payment to court

The existence of the lien itself does not determine liability. The lien is merely a tool designed to help suppliers of goods and services enforce their rights when there has been a default. The lien holder must demonstrate through a civil action that the claim is justified. This prevents builders' liens from being used as a means of harassment or bluff. The onus is on the builders' lien claimant to follow through with the claim and sue for payment. Some provinces allow the owner of the property to send a notice to the builders' lien holder demanding that action be commenced within a very limited period of time (30 days in Alberta).[62] Failure to do so means the claimant loses the protection of the lien. The owner is permitted to say to the lien holder, in effect, "Put up or shut up."

Judgment must be obtained to execute lien

Generally speaking, all lien holders or claimants are treated the same. When the amount available is less than the total amount of the claims, they share the loss equally, each being paid the same percentage of the amount of claim.[63] In all common law provinces, wage earners have been given a priority over other builders' lien claimants, but this priority is limited to the wages earned in a specific time period. In Alberta, this period is six weeks.[64]

Some claims may have priority

A supplier of goods and services who has not complied with the legislation loses the right to a builders' lien and reverts to the position of any other creditor. The supplier must sue the defaulting party for breach of contract. Several provinces, including Alberta, have declared that any funds paid to the general contractor by the owner constitute a trust fund with the suppliers of goods and services as beneficiaries of that trust.[65] This decision is significant because it provides both civil and criminal remedies when the general contractor breaches that trust. It also protects these funds from any claims levied against the general contractor by other creditors who had nothing to do with the project for which funds were paid. Such outside creditors have no claim against the funds in the hands of the general contractor; because of this trust provision, they must be kept for the lien claimant. Only after the payment of all wage earners, subcontractors and suppliers will outside creditors receive payment from these funds.

Ontario has taken this idea further and declared that "not yet paid" funds in the hands of the owner are a trust for the benefit of the lien claimants as well. The effect of the legislation is to prevent the owner of the property from unjustly benefiting from the goods and services which enhance the value of the property without paying for them. Alberta does not have legislation to this effect.

Legislation prevents unjust enrichment

It should also be noted that similar legislation creates liens to the benefit of other suppliers of goods and services such as garage mechanics, appliance repairers, and warehouse owners.

---

62. *Ibid.*, s. 32.2(1).
63. *Ibid.*, s. 47(5).
64. *Ibid.*, s. 47(3)(b) and (4)(c).
65. *Ibid.*, s. 16.1.

BANKRUPTCY

While the bulk of this chapter is devoted to the position of a secured creditor, consideration must also be given to the position of an unsecured creditor. When the value of the security is not great enough to cover the debt, a secured creditor is an unsecured creditor for that outstanding amount. In these circumstances, the creditor is usually just one of many and must rely on the normal debt collection methods discussed in Chapter 1. The creditor has the right, before judgment is obtained, to apply to the court for an attachment order.[66] An attachment order may[67]

A growing number of businesses face bankruptcy.
Photo by Al Harvey/The Slide Farm.

1. prohibit any dealing with exigible property of the defendant;
2. impose conditions or restrictions on any dealing with exigible property of the defendant;
3. require the defendant or a person who has possession or control of exigible property to deliver it to a specified person;
4. authorize the issuance of a garnishee summons by the clerk; or
5. appoint a receiver.

If property subject to an attachment order will depreciate substantially in value or will be unduly expensive to keep under attachment, or if it is otherwise necessary or prudent to sell or dispose of the property, the court may authorize the sale or other disposition of the property.[68]

In general, however, the creditor must proceed to judgment to recover the money owed by the debtor. After judgment, the creditor has many remedies available to enforce the judgment, including garnisheeing wages and having property of the debtor seized to satisfy the judgment, as discussed in Chapter 1. It must be emphasized, however, that there is considerable truth in the adage that you can't get blood from a stone. If the debtor has no money, such procedures may only consume more of the creditor's resources without any substantial return. If the debtor owes more money than there are assets to recover, a real alternative is the process of bankruptcy.

Bankruptcy—to pay creditors and rehabilitate debtor

Legislation has been created to provide a way in which debtors who are unable to pay off their debts can be forgiven of their obligations. The legislation saves a productive member of society from facing a lifelong burden of insurmountable debt. It also protects the interests of creditors and provides for the punishment of fraudulent debtors.

The *Bankruptcy and Insolvency Act*[69] is a federal statute uniformly applicable throughout Canada. In 1992, it was the subject of significant amendment and introduced a further objective which was to help viable businesses to survive restructuring. It should be noted that some people and bodies are exempt from this legislation; banks, trust companies and railways, for example, are not covered by the *Bankruptcy and Insolvency Act*.

---

66. See Part 3, Prejudgment Relief, of the *Civil Enforcement Act*, R.S.A. (1994) c. C-105.
67. *Ibid.*, s. 17(3).
68. *Ibid.*, s. 21.
69. *Bankruptcy and Insolvency Act*, S.C. (1992) c. 27.

Bankruptcy must be distinguished from **insolvency**, which simply means that a person is unable to pay his or her debts. **Bankruptcy** is the process by which debtors convey their assets to a trustee in bankruptcy who then deals with them for the benefit of the creditors. One of the changes introduced by the 1992 *Act* was to expand the legislation to cover the pre-bankruptcy stage of insolvency. When a debtor voluntarily assigns property to a trustee in bankruptcy, it is referred to as an **assignment**.

Assignment—voluntary transfer of assets to trustee

Bankruptcy can also take place against the debtor's wishes. A creditor who is owed more than $1000 can petition the court to force the debtor into bankruptcy. The court grants a **receiving order** which results in the forceful transfer of the assets of the debtor to the trustee. This is a statutory assignment of the debtor's assets and includes any real property. This transfer ensures that the creditors will get paid at least some of what they are owed. It also ensures that any assets that do exist are preserved and distributed fairly among the creditors. The relevant section is Section 71(2):

Receiving order—forcible transfer of assets to trustee

> 71(2) On a receiving order being made or an assignment being filed with an official receiver, a bankrupt ceases to have any capacity to dispose of or otherwise deal with his property, which shall, subject to this Act and to the rights of the secured creditors, forthwith pass to and vest in the trustee named in the receiving order or assignment. ...

To obtain a receiving order, the creditor must show that the debtor has committed an **act of bankruptcy**. Significant acts of bankruptcy include the voluntary assignment of assets to a trustee in bankruptcy, fraudulent transfers of money or assets to keep them out of the hands of the trustee, a fraudulent preference given to one of the creditors, trying to leave the jurisdiction without paying debts and general insolvency.

The new *Bankruptcy and Insolvency Act* provides an alternative to bankruptcy. It allows the debtor to propose to the creditors another method for satisfying their claims. Two separate procedures are involved, depending on whether the insolvent debtor is a commercial or a consumer debtor. Commercial debtors, including under the new legislation corporations, are permitted to make a reorganization proposal to their creditors.

Commercial and consumer proposals—alternative to bankruptcy

This process has three stages. First the debtor files a notice of intention to file a reorganization proposal. Within 10 days, the debtor must file a statement of projected cash flow and then, within 30 days, the reorganization proposal itself. This filing is followed by a meeting of the creditors who accept or reject the proposal. Two-thirds of the creditors by value and a majority by number must approve the proposal. If they do, all are bound by it, including secured creditors who have approved the proposal. If the creditors reject the proposal, the insolvent debtor is deemed to have made an assignment in bankruptcy from the day the notice of intention was filed and the normal bankruptcy procedures follow. The effect of filing the notice is to stop any creditors, including secured creditors who have not yet acted upon the security, from taking any action against the debtor at least until the date of the vote, about two months later. The time may be extended with the permission of the court for a period up to five months. In effect, during this period, the insolvent debtor is protected from the creditors and if the proposal is accepted by an appropriate number of them, that protection continues.

Consumer debtors are similarly protected when they make a consumer proposal. The insolvent debtor goes to a professional administrator who examines the debtor's finances, prepares the proposal and any reports required, and provides counselling for the debtor. With the administrator's help, the insolvent debtor files a consumer proposal which provides protection against unsecured creditors. With consumer proposals, an actual meeting of the creditors is not necessary. Creditors are given notice of the proposal and, if they do not demand a meeting, the proposal is deemed to be accepted by them. It is then up to the consumer to live up to the terms set out in the proposal. These terms must include a payment to the administrator at least once every three months; the administrator in turn must make payments to the creditors. As long as the debtor lives up to the terms of the proposal, action cannot be taken against him or her by unsecured creditors, public utilities, landlords, etc. Even those supplying ongoing services such as power, gas, telephone must continue supplying them. But if the debtor defaults, the proposal is annulled and the debtor will then face the normal bankruptcy procedures.

Trustee distributes assets or proceeds of sales to creditors

Once the trustee has been given the assets of a bankrupt debtor, it is the trustee's responsibility to divide them so that all the creditors get a fair share. This task may not be easy because some of the creditors may be secured and others may be general creditors. Even in the case of bankruptcy, a secured creditor remains in a better position than the other creditors. Normally the trustee will sell the asset used as security and pay off the secured creditor. When there is a shortfall, the secured creditor becomes a general creditor for any outstanding amount. When the goods are sold for more than is owing, the excess will be paid out to the other creditors. When the trustee and the creditor agree on a value, the creditor may be permitted to take the item used as security for that value and become a general creditor for any shortfall.

A significant change under the new *Act* is the position of a supplier of goods to a bankrupt. Previously, once such goods became part of the estate of the bankrupt, the seller simply became a general creditor for the purchase price and could not seek the return of the goods unless there was some added security arrangement. Under the new *Act*, such a supplier has the right to demand the return of the goods upon learning of the bankruptcy or receivership, provided this is within 30 days of delivery of those goods and the debtor or trustee still has them.

Supplier of goods can reclaim

The position of farmers, fishers and aquaculturists is somewhat different because of the nature of the goods they supply. Crops and fish become commingled with those supplied by others and are no longer identifiable. In this case, the supplier becomes a secured creditor for the unpaid amount and has priority over all claims of other creditors, except the supplier of specific goods as discussed above, provided the products were delivered within 15 days and the claim filed within 30 days of the bankruptcy.

The trustee must also evaluate the worth of each claim of the various creditors. If the trustee feels that a claim has no substance, the creditor will not share in the proceeds unless the creditor successfully challenges that decision in court. After the secured creditors have received what they are entitled to, the trustee distributes the remaining assets, or the proceeds from the sales of those assets, to the other creditors. There is a system of priority amongst these creditors, some claims being preferred over others. The following claims are paid in the order listed to the preferred creditors: funeral expenses, costs associated with the bankruptcy process, claims for arrears in wages for a limited amount and time period, municipal taxes, arrears in rent for a limited period, some direct costs incurred by creditors in the execution process, amounts owed to Workers' Compensation (note that workers' compensation claims may actually rank as a secured creditor under the new *Act*), unemployment insurance and income tax which should have been deducted from salaries, and other claims of the Crown. General creditors are paid only after these obligations have been met.

Priority Among Creditors

Re Speedy Roofing Ltd.[70]

In this case Mr. Pompeo and Mr. Gaggi were the sole shareholders of Speedy Roofing Ltd. and through years of operation, Speedy Roofing became indebted to one of their suppliers, Roofmart. Eventually Roofmart became concerned and insisted on security for the indebtedness and mortgages were provided on the homes of the wives of Mr. Pompeo and Mr. Gaggi.

In 1983 the financial problems of Speedy became insurmountable, and the Bank forced the company into bankruptcy. Shortly before this, however, Speedy Roofing had paid Roofmart over $80 000 to have the two mortgages discharged. In this action the Royal Bank is claiming that the payment from Speeding to Roofmart amounted to a fraudulent preference.

The *Bankruptcy Act* specifically prohibits payments that favour one creditor over another and the court has the right under the *Act* to order the funds repaid if they are made within three months of the bankruptcy. The court in this case did make such an order, and Roofmart was required to repay the $80 000 paid for the discharge of the mortgages over to the trustee in bankruptcy, who then made it available to all of the creditors.

The case illustrates that the purpose of the bankruptcy legislation is to obtain as much as possible for all of the creditors. It may be in the best interests for the bankrupt to make sure one of the creditors gets paid in preference to another, but such payment is an offense under the *Act* that can be reversed.

People going through bankruptcy often try to keep some of their property out of the hands of creditors by transferring it to friends or family as a gift or for a nominal amount. The trustee in bankruptcy can reverse these **fraudulent transfers** (or **settlements** as they are called in the *Act*).

The relevant sections for the *Bankruptcy and Insolvency Act* are as follows:

> 91(1) Any settlement of property, if the settlor becomes bankrupt within one year after the date of the settlement, is void against the trustee.

> 95(1) Every conveyance or transfer of property or charge thereon made, every payment made, every obligation incurred and every judicial proceeding taken or suffered by any insolvent person in favour of any creditor or of any person in trust for any creditor with a view to giving that creditor a preference over the other creditors shall, if the person making, incurring, taking, paying or suffering it becomes bankrupt within three months after the date of making, incurring, taking, paying or suffering it, be deemed fraudulent and void as against the trustee in the bankruptcy.

Fraudulent transfers and preferences prohibited

For example, if Kincaid transfers his house or his car to his wife's name to avoid creditors, this action will not likely prevent the trustee in bankruptcy from including the house or car in the assets available to the creditors. This transfer is classed as a settlement and is therefore void. People who become insolvent may choose to pay only one or two of their creditors because they expect to deal with them

---

70. 45 D.L.R. (4th) 142 (Supreme Court of Ontario in Bankruptcy).

SETTLEMENT AND FRAUDULENT CONVEYANCE BY BANKRUPT PROHIBITED

On March 6, 1980, a successful business person transferred his interest in his matrimonial residence to his wife and continued to live there with her. One of his companies, Textile Industries Ltd., ran into financial difficulty. He had signed a guarantee for the indebtedness of this corporation and so was personally responsible for its debts. In 1977 an action was commenced against the company that eventually led to the man claiming bankruptcy. It was clear at the time of transfer to the wife that the matter was going to go to trial and that the man was facing substantial loss. In May 1980 judgment was given against Textile Industries and the respondent as guarantor. The question that the court had to decide here was whether the transfer of the interest in the matrimonial home amounted to a prohibited settlement under the provisions of the *Bankruptcy Act*. A settlement occurs when a person transfers property to another in order to preserve some benefit for him- or herself. The court held that this was exactly what had happened and voided the transaction. The court was also asked to determine whether, under the provincial *Fraudulent Conveyances Act*, this was a fraudulent conveyance—that is, a case of a debtor conveying property to another in order to defeat or defraud creditors. This also was found to have taken place and was additional grounds on which the transaction was set aside.

Re Fancy, 8 D.L.R. (4th) 418 (Ontario Supreme Court, Bankruptcy)

---

later or because they think that failure to pay those creditors will do them more harm. Showing preference to one creditor over another is unfair to the unpaid creditors and is classed as a **fraudulent preference** which is also prohibited under the *Act* (see Section 95 above). Such a transaction would be void and the preferred creditor can be forced to return the goods or funds so that they are equally available to all the creditors, as in the Speedy Roofing case discussed above. As part of the bankruptcy process, the debtor must file an affidavit setting out all debt, creditors and assets.

Limitations on undischarged bankrupts

The debtor is classified as an **undischarged bankrupt** once the assignment in bankruptcy has been made or a receiving order obtained. This status prohibits the bankrupt from borrowing over $500, and that amount only for necessaries, without disclosing that he or she is an undischarged bankrupt. A bankrupt is also not permitted to sit on the board of directors of any corporation. Failure to comply with these provisions can lead to imprisonment. Once the bankrupt has gone through the entire process and the creditors have received all they can from the assets, the bankrupt is in a position to be discharged from the bankruptcy. The court may issue an order discharging the bankrupt if it is satisfied that the request is appropriate. When an individual is involved, the bankruptcy procedure contains an automatic application for discharge. When it is the first bankruptcy, that discharge is generally automatic.

Eventually a bankrupt may be discharged

Upon discharge, the debtor is freed from most previous claims by creditors and is in a position to start over. Any assets subsequently obtained by the discharged bankrupts are theirs to do with as they wish and unpaid creditors cannot claim against them. Some obligations survive the discharge. For example, debtors who have been ordered to pay maintenance for dependents will continue to bear that obligation even after being discharged from bankruptcy. Similarly, any fines resulting from the conviction of an offense are still owing.

Discharge not granted if bankruptcy offense committed

Debtors who commit bankruptcy offenses are liable to be imprisoned. The court will not discharge a bankrupt who has committed such an offense. In addition to settlements such as fraudulent preferences and fraudulent transfers, the *Bankruptcy and Insolvency Act* sets out several other bankruptcy offenses: lying while under examination by the trustee in bankruptcy, hiding or concealing property, misleading or falsifying records, or otherwise trying to cheat the creditor. The court will also be reluctant to discharge bankrupts who have paid creditors less than 50 cents on the dollar. Under such circumstances, the court can put conditions or restrictions on the bankrupt, granting only a conditional discharge. In the Supreme Court of Canada, Estey J. commented on the purpose of the bankruptcy process and said,

> The purpose and object of the *Bankruptcy Act* is to equitably distribute the assets of the debtor and to permit his rehabilitation as a citizen, unfettered by past debts. The discharge, however, is not a matter of right and the provisions of ss. 142 and 143 plainly indicate that in certain cases the debtor should suffer a period of probation.[71]

Note that this reference relates to a prior act but similar provisions are in the current statute.

Bankruptcy proceedings also apply to corporations but, unless the corporation can pay back the full amount owed or has completed the "proposal" process outlined above, it cannot receive a discharge for the bankruptcy. Instead, it faces dissolution. It should be noted that other statutes, both federal and provincial, such as the *Winding-up and Restructuring Act,*[72] *Companies' Creditors Arrangements Act,*[73] *Builders' Lien Act*[74] and *Business Corporations Act,*[75] are available to disgruntled shareholders and creditors of corporations.

Bankrupt corporations are dissolved

Corporations that go into **receivership** are often not involved in bankruptcy at all. When a corporation borrows significant funds from a lender, the creditor will usually set out certain terms in the agreement which will trigger a provision that allows the creditor to appoint a receiver to take over the business without going through the bankruptcy procedure if the provisions of the agreement are not met. Such an assignment of assets to a receiver is not actually a bankruptcy, but the effect can be every bit as devastating to the business. The rights of creditors to appoint such receivers have been limited to some extent by the recent revisions to the *Bankruptcy and Insolvency Act* discussed above.

Receivership may be based on contract

DISCHARGE OF BANKRUPT NOT ALWAYS UNCONDITIONAL

A bankrupt professional who maintained a very high lifestyle looked forward to a reasonable income after his discharge as well. The court, on determining that in fact no payments had been made to the trustee in bankruptcy, ordered that under these circumstances he shouldn't be entitled to an unconditional discharge and required him to consent to a judgment for $80 000—in effect, make a commitment to pay back a significant amount to his creditors. The court has the discretion to place such conditions on the discharge of a bankrupt.

Re McAfee, 49 D.L.R. (4th) 401 (British Columbia Court of Appeal)

71. *Industrial Acceptance Corp. v. Lalonde* [1952] 3 D.L.R. 348 (S.C.C.).

72. *Winding-up and Restructuring Act*, R.S.C. (1985) c. W-11.

73. *Companies' Creditors Arrangements Act*, R.S.C. (1985) c. C-36.

74. *Builders' Lien Act*, R.S.A. (1980) c. B-12 (as amended S.A. (1985) c. 14).

75. *Business Corporations Act*, S.A. (1981) c. B-15.

Legislation also exists to assist in the orderly payment of debt. If the account owed is less than $1000 or if the debtor obtains the consent of the creditors, the debtor can make arrangements to consolidate all of the debts and pay all of the creditors back at one rate with one payment. Government agencies available to assist in this process can be helpful for both the debtor and the creditor.[76] It must be remembered that the creditor is in the business of making money, not destroying the debtor. If the debtor cannot pay, the creditor gains nothing by harassment. The two main purposes of the *Bankruptcy and Insolvency Act* and the other legislation discussed in this chapter are to ensure that the creditor realizes as much of the amount owed as possible and to rehabilitate the debtor. The legislation also provides punishment for fraudulent activities by the debtor and provides a uniform system of laws throughout Canada. The idea is to restore the debtor as a productive working member of the community as soon as possible.

SUMMARY

Security involves giving the creditor some assurance that he or she will be paid even when other creditors are not. With a conditional sales agreement, the creditor retains title while giving the debtor possession of the goods. With a chattel mortgage, the debtor gives up title to the creditor while keeping possession. In both cases, in the event of default, the creditor may retake the goods. Assignment of book accounts can also be used as security. In many provinces (including Alberta), the statutes controlling these traditional approaches have been replaced by the *Personal Property Security Act* which allows both chattels and intangible forms of personal property to be used as security. The security must first attach but the priority is usually established by perfection (involving registration or taking possession of the property). In the event of default, the creditor can retake the goods and resell them and/or sue for the debt. In some situations, the creditor must choose one or the other but cannot do both. A floating charge allows a debtor to bring new goods into the security group and dispose of others out of it. It is only with default that the charge attaches and prevents further dealing with the goods.

A guarantee is a contingent liability in which someone agrees to be responsible when a debtor fails to pay. An indemnity involves a co-responsibility for the debt. If a guarantor pays the creditor, he or she steps into the shoes of the creditor and can seek redress from the debtor.

A builders' lien gives the supplier of services or materials (when not paid) the right to register a lien against the building in which the materials or services were used. The owner of the property, when paying the general contractor, must hold back a certain amount to make sure all debts are paid.

Bankruptcy can take place voluntarily through assignment or involuntarily through a receiving order. It involves the transfer of the debtor's assets to a trustee in bankruptcy who sells the assets and distributes the proceeds to the creditors. The debtor, after meeting certain qualifications, can apply to be discharged. Discharge relieves responsibility for these prior debts.

76. In Alberta, Credit Counselling Services of Alberta Ltd. (CCS) assumed responsibility for the Orderly Payment of Debts Program and consumer debt counselling from Alberta Municipal Affairs on May 1, 1997. CCS is a non-profit organization whose funding by the provincial government will decrease progressivily over five years, after which it will operate without any government financial assistance.

QUESTIONS

1. Distinguish between the following:

   a. A chattel mortgage and a mortgage on real estate

   b. A chattel mortgage and a conditional sale

   c. Real property and personal property

   d. Chose in action and a chattel

2. What significant problem associated with the practice of taking goods as security is alleviated by the registration requirements introduced by legislation? Describe the resulting obligations on all parties.

3. What obligations are imposed on the secured creditor who retakes goods used as security when a debtor defaults?

4. Explain the rights and obligations of all parties when a secured transaction agreement is assigned to a third party.

5. Why is the security allowed banks under the *Bank Act* significantly different from other forms of secured transactions? How are the registration requirements different?

6. In what ways was the passage of the *Personal Property Security Act* a significant departure from the traditional treatment of secured transactions?

7. Distinguish between the security contract, the attachment and the perfection, and explain the significance of each step.

8. Under the *Personal Property Security Act* how is a security perfected and what is the significance of such a perfection?

9. In the event of a default, explain what the rights of a secured party are and what limitations there are on those rights.

10. Explain the difference between retention and disposal on the part of the secured party in the event of default and explain the procedure and limitations associated with each alternative.

11. What kinds of property can be used as collateral under personal property security legislation?

12. Explain the rights of debtors after they have defaulted and the secured party has taken possession of the collateral.

13. What happens upon default when a floating charge has been used to secure a debt? How does this form of security affect the priorities between types of creditors?

14. Explain the position of the secured creditor in relation to the debtor and other creditors in the following situations in which assets have been used as security. Indicate provincial variations in your response.

    a. The amount still owing to the secured creditor is less than the value of the asset used as security.

b. The amount still owing to the secured creditor is greater than the value used as security.

15. What obligations does the guarantor of another person's debt incur? What protection is available to guarantors in subsequent dealings between the creditor and debtor?

16. When a debtor defaults on a loan and the guarantor is required to pay, what rights does the guarantor have in relation to the debtor?

17. What significant difficulty facing the supplier of goods and services in the construction industry is overcome by the creation of the construction, mechanics' or builders' lien? Include an explanation of the significance of the declaration that any money paid by the owner to the contractor is held in trust.

18. What remedies are available to a supplier of goods and services who has filed a builders' lien?

19. How is the claimant's position affected when the lien has not been properly registered?

20. Define the objectives of bankruptcy legislation and explain how these objectives are accomplished. Explain what role the process of discharge and the function of the trustee in bankruptcy have in the realization of these goals.

CASES

1. Re Purschke et al. and Avco Financial Services Canada Ltd.

Sandra Harris entered into a chattel mortgage with a bank in 1985. The bank registered this chattel mortgage, but the serial number was recorded incorrectly. Ms. Harris then granted another chattel mortgage to Avco in 1986 which was properly registered. Before Avco registered the mortgage they contacted the bank for a credit check on Ms. Harris and were told that the bank had a chattel mortgage already on the vehicle. After Avco registered their chattel mortgage, they contacted the bank telling them that they had done a search, found the incorrect number and had registered their mortgage ahead of the bank. Avco seized the motor vehicle and after correcting the serial number the bank challenged Avco's right to the car. Explain the arguments available on both sides.

2. Boehmers v. 794561 Ontario Inc.

The numbered company 794561 was a general contractor building a series of townhouses for the property owner. This contractor defaulted in its payments to subcontractors, and several liens were registered against the property. Royal Life was a creditor with a secured mortgage for $3 895 000. Of this money, $1 606 586 had been advanced before the first liens were registered. Subsequent to the registration and perfection of those liens, Royal Life made a further series of advances, bringing the amount up to the $3 895 000 total. In these circumstances, explain the priority of creditors (the secured mortgagee or the lien claimants) in relationship to the property and any funds available.

3. First City Capital Ltd. v. Hall et al.

Karsha Holdings Ltd. was a company whose sole shareholders and officers were Hall and deHaan. When the company needed word processing equipment, it went to First City Capital where it borrowed a considerable amount of money. First City Capital required a personal guarantee for the funds to secure this equipment. The equipment was purchased through seven lease arrangements. A few years later, Hall sold her interest in Karsha Holdings to deHaan. Shortly after that, Karsha Holdings defaulted on its payments to First City Capital for the seven leases as well as on a separate indebtedness to the Royal Bank of Canada. This indebtedness was also secured against the assets of the corporation. First City Capital had failed to perfect the security arrangements with Karsha Holdings (the seven leases), which it should have done by registration, and the Royal Bank had perfected its interest. The Royal Bank, therefore, seized the word processing equipment and First City Capital turned to Hall on the personal guarantee for payment.

Explain the legal position of Hall in these circumstances and what arguments she could raise in her defense. How would your answer be affected by the knowledge that a term in the personal guarantee with First City stated that Hall would be required to pay "notwithstanding that the lease or any other arrangements shall be void or voidable against the lessee ... including ... by reason ... of ... failure by any person to file any document or take any other action to make the lease ... enforceable"?

4. Red Deer College v. W.W. Construction, Lethbridge, Ltd.

Red Deer College owned property and hired *W.W. Construction* as the general contractor to complete certain buildings on that property. W.W. then hired several subtrades to continue with the work. A number of liens were registered against the project and Red Deer College not only held back the 15 percent required by law but also refused to pay out any further money to the defendant. The defendant then failed to complete the project and abandoned it. Red Deer College had to get other people to finish the job. In this action, W.W. Construction claimed for money owed less the 15 percent holdback. Explain the legal obligations of Red Deer College.

5. Jaron Construction Ltd. v. McNeil et al.

The owner of a construction project properly held back the appropriate amount from a general contractor who subsequently abandoned the project. The owner then completed the project himself but at considerably increased cost which he deducted from the amount of holdback he had retained. When the subcontractors hired by the general contractor who had abandoned the project registered their mechanics' liens, only this reduced amount of the holdback was made available to them. They sued the owner, claiming the entire amount of holdback. Explain the rights of the parties involved. If the owner had neglected to hold back any funds, how would this have affected your answer?

6. Finning Tractor and Equipment Company Limited v. Mee

In April 1976, Morrill and Sturgeon Lumber Company signed a conditional sales agreement with Finning Tractor to purchase a new caterpillar wheel loader. The agreement was guaranteed by Mee. The purchaser defaulted after some payments were made. Finning chose to seek payment from the guarantor instead of seizing the tractor under the conditional sales agreement. Explain the liability of the guarantor in these circumstances. Would your answer be any different if you learned that Finning had neglected to register the conditional sales agreement and therefore had lost its priority against other secured creditors?

7. Re Bank of Montreal and International Polyeurothane Company Ltd.

International Polyeurothane entered into a 30-month lease with a landlord. Subsequently, they acquired goods to be used at the premises and granted the Bank of Montreal a chattel mortgage covering the items. The company became insolvent and the landlord had the sheriff seize these goods for unpaid rent. The municipality issued a similar order for unpaid taxes, as did the Workers' Compensation Board for an overdue assessment. Explain how these claims would affect the right of the Bank of Montreal to repossess the goods under their chattel mortgage security. Set out the priorities between the parties.

8. Mitsui & Co. (Canada) Ltd. v. Royal Bank of Canada

Pegasus operated a business supplying helicopter services in and around Nova Scotia, and pursuant to that objective they leased two helicopters from Mitsui. As part of their agreement, Pegasus had an option to purchase the helicopters on paying a reasonable market price as determined by Pegasus. Pegasus became bankrupt and the trustee in bankruptcy and a receiver claimed a prior right to the helicopters.

Explain the arguments available for both sides. How would your answer be affected by the knowledge that in Nova Scotia under the *Conditional Sales Act,* "Any contract for the hiring of goods by which it is agreed that the hirer shall become or have the option of becoming the owner of the goods upon full compliance with the terms of the contract" is a conditional sale and Mitsui had not registered interest under the *Act*?

....

LEGISLATION

Alberta

Builders' Lien Act, R.S.A. (1980) c. B-12 (as amended S.A. (1985) c. 14)
Civil Enforcement Act, S.A. (1994) c. C-10.5
Civil Service Garnishee Act, R.S.A. (1980) c. C-11
Collection Practices Act, R.S.A. (1980) c. C-17
Debtors' Assistance Act, R.S.A. (1980) c. D-5
Fair Trading Act, S.A. (1998) c. F-1.05.
Fraudulent Preferences Act, R.S.A. (1980) c. F-18
Garagemen's Lien Act, R.S.A. (1980) c. G-1
Guarantees Acknowledgement Act, R.S.A. (1980) c. G-12
Personal Property Security Act, R.S.A. (1988) c. P-4.05
Possessory Liens Act, R.S.A. (1980) c. P-13
Wage Assignments Act, R.S.A. (1980) c. W-1
Warehousemen's Lien Act, R.S.A. (1980) c. W-3
Woodmen's Lien Act, R.S.A. (1980) c. W-14

Federal

Bankruptcy and Insolvency Act, R.S.C. (1985) c. B-3 (see Amendment S.C. (1992) c. 27)
Companies' Creditors Arrangements Act, R.S.C. (1985) c. C-36

Garnishment, Attachment and Pension Diversion Act, R.S.C. (1985) c. G-2
Wages Liability Act, R.S.C. (1985) c. W-1

....

WEBLINKS

Royal Bank—Services for Small Business & Entrepreneurs
www.royalbank.com/english/sme/index.html

Scotiabank Business Banking
www.scotiabank.ca/BusinessBanking.html

mbanx—Business Banking Plan
www.mbanx.com/canadam/svbb.html

TD Business Banking Centre
www.tdbank.ca/tdbank/bizexch/index.html

Canadian Imperial Bank of Commerce: Small Business Information Exchange
www.cibc.com/SmallBusiness/

Alberta: Personal Property Security Act
www.gov.ab.ca/qp/ascii/acts/P04P05.txt

Canada: Bank Act (Part 1)
canada.justice.gc.ca/FTP/EN/Laws/Chap/B/B-1.01

Canada: Bank Act (Part 2)
canada.justice.gc.ca/FTP/EN/Laws/Chap/B/B-2

Business Development Bank of Canada
www.bdc.ca/

Office of the Superintendent of Bankruptcy
strategis.ic.gc.ca/sc_mrksv/bankrupt/engdoc/superint.html

Canada: Bankruptcy and Insolvency Act
canada.justice.gc.ca/FTP/EN/Laws/Chap/B/B-3

Alberta Municipal Affairs—Consumer Tipsheets
www.gov.ab.ca/~ma/hca/html/constips.htm

APPENDIX 8-1 Financing Statement

REGISTRIES
Personal Property

FINANCING STATEMENT

See Information Guide for help in completing this form.
Please type in CAPITAL LETTERS. Use 'X' to select options.

Office use only
Affix registration # label

TYPE OF REGISTRATION (Choose one only)

SA PPSA Security Agreement (Answer Questions 1 - 3 below)
1. How many years do you want this registration to last?   Type no. of years (1 - 25), or 'X' for infinity
2. Will this registration cover a trust indenture?   If yes, type 'X'
3. Will this registration cover a security agreement registered before Oct. 1, 1990? If yes, where was it registered?   Central   Vehicle   Corporate
Complete the Court Order, Other Changes and Additional Information form as described in the Information Guide.

SG Sale of Goods Act s.27 (1.1) or Factors Act s. 8 (2) (Answer Questions 1 - 2 below)
1. How many years do you want this registration to last?   Type no. of years (1 - 25), or 'X' for infinity
2. Will this registration cover a Bill of Sale registered before Oct. 1, 1990?   If yes, where was it registered?   Central   Vehicle
Complete the Court Order, Other Changes and Additional Information form as described in the Information Guide.   DD   MM   YY

WE Writ of Execution - Alberta   In which judicial district was writ issued?   Date of Judgment?

FW Writ of Execution - Federal   In which judicial district was writ issued?   Date of Issue?

MP Matrimonial Property Order

Other Specify type

DEBTOR #1   Business   Individual   Birthdate (if known)

Business Name **or** Last Name   First Name   Middle Name   DD   MM   YY

Street Address   City   Prov.   Postal Code

DEBTOR #2   Business   Individual   Birthdate (if known)

Business Name **or** Last Name   First Name   Middle Name   DD   MM   YY

Street Address   City   Prov.   Postal Code

SECURED PARTY   Business   Individual

Secured Party Code   Business Name **or** Last Name   First Name   Middle Name

Street Address   City   Prov.   Postal Code

COLLATERAL: SERIAL NUMBER GOODS (If PPSA, applicable only to consumer goods or equipment)

Serial #   Year   Make and Model   Category

COLLATERAL: GENERAL

REGISTERING PARTY   (Complete only if other than SECURED PARTY above) Business   Individual

Registrant Code   Business Name **or** Last Name   First Name   Middle Name

Street Address   City   Prov.   Postal Code

AUTHORIZED SIGNATURE   Area Code & Phone #   Call Box

Type Name of Person Signing

Signature   Your Reference #   Page   Of
                                                                                      1

CONTROL #   **RO** 2560558

+ AG 1767 (Rev Jan 94)

Negotiable Instruments

OBJECTIVES OF THE CHAPTER

- To examine the special nature of negotiable instruments

- To distinguish the various types and their purposes

- To describe how negotiable instruments are endorsed and transferred

- To discuss the rights and responsibilities of the parties

Mrs. Jordan was a bank clerk who had convinced her husband and Mr. Courage, the manager of the local branch of the Toronto-Dominion Bank, that she was a wealthy and successful business executive. In fact, she was using bank accounts of several relatives to move money from account to account to support her speculation in the stock market. Such a practice is known as "kiting" and involves drawing cheques on a succession of accounts to cover funds drawn from those accounts. Because there is a time delay in clearing the cheques and the final cheque covers the deficit caused by the first cheque, it is difficult to detect that there is an amount outstanding.

Mrs. Jordan gave several gifts and benefits to Mr. Courage and involved him in some of her profitable speculations to encourage him to protect information regarding her transactions. Managers of two other banks had become suspicious of the activity in Mrs. Jordan's account and warned Mr. Courage that she might be kiting cheques. He ignored their warnings but pressed her to cover an overdraft in the amount of $350 000. Mrs. Jordan persuaded her husband to give her a blank cheque signed by him and drawn on the Teacher's Credit Union which she filled in for $359 000 and gave to Mr. Courage at the Toronto-Dominion Bank to cover the overdraft. This cheque was subsequently dishonoured and signalled the end of this series of transactions.

The Toronto-Dominion Bank branch of which Mr. Courage was the manager then sued Mr. Jordan for the face value of the cheque drawn on his account. If negotiable instruments had not been involved, the bank would not have been able to enforce payment of the cheque any more than Mrs. Jordan could. Because of her fraud, she could not have collected. But because a cheque is a negotiable instrument, the situation was quite different. If an innocent third party acquires a cheque in good faith, it can be enforced against the drawer, Mr. Jordan, even if the intervening party has been fraudulent.

This raised the question of whether Mr. Courage had acted in good faith. The court looked at his involvement with Mrs. Jordan and decided that, while he may not have been directly dishonest, he certainly had not acquired the cheque in good faith and, therefore, the bank could not enforce it against Mr. Jordan.[1]

This complicated set of transactions illustrates the most significant characteristic of negotiable instruments—that is, their enforceability in the hands of innocent third parties and the corresponding extreme vulnerability of those who make such negotiable instruments and allow them to be circulated. In this chapter, we will examine negotiable instruments and the rights and obligations of the parties to them.

Negotiable instruments are freely transferable and a substitute for cash

Cheques, bills of exchange (often called drafts) and promissory notes are all **negotiable instruments**. They are in common use today because of several characteristics that greatly facilitate the commercial process. Negotiable instruments represent the right to claim funds from a particular debtor or financial institution. They are used as a substitute for money and allow for its exchange without the necessity of handling large amounts of cash. They can be transferred between parties not associated with the original transaction without the requirement of any notice and without diminishing the right of the eventual holder to collect on the negotiable instrument from the original parties. Another important characteristic of negotiable instruments is their capacity to create creditor/debtor relationships. Since a negotiable instrument gives the holder a claim for the stated amount against the maker of the instrument, and sometimes the financial institution it is drawn on as well, the negotiable instrument represents a creditor/debtor relationship until the claim is satisfied. Whenever a significant period of time is involved between the creation of the instrument and its discharge through payment, the negotiable instrument becomes an effective method of advancing credit, with the added advantage of being freely transferable between creditors. Negotiable instruments can provide for payment by installment and require the payment of interest. They have become a standard part of business transactions and it is important to understand the legal principles involved and to know the rights and obligations of the parties. The use of negotiable instruments today is in decline to a considerable extent because of the use of credit cards and electronic transfers of funds. While these inroads are significant, the study of negotiable instruments is still important because of their unique character.

They facilitate the advancement of credit

1. *Toronto Dominion Bank v. Jordan* [1985] 61 B.C.L.R. 105.

NEGOTIABILITY

Essential Characteristics

Our discussion of contract law demonstrated that it is possible to assign contractual rights but it is necessary to notify the debtor of the transfer before the assignee can enforce payment directly. The element that makes negotiable instruments an effective substitute for money in many situations is their free transferability from one party to another without having to notify or acquire the consent of the original parties to the transfer.

Negotiable instruments are freely transferable

To facilitate their transferability, negotiable instruments have acquired a second characteristic that makes them unique in the field of special contractual relationships. As you will recall, a problem with the assignment of contractual rights from the point of view of the outsider or assignee is that the assignee is in no better position than the assignor. When the debtor has a good defense against the assignor, it will hold against the assignee as well, thus allowing the debtor to avoid payment. This possibility obligates the assignee to investigate and accept the risks associated with the dealings between the original parties since the assignee is subject to them. A negotiable instrument is unique because, when it is transferred through negotiation to a third party who meets certain qualifications, that third party may take the instrument free of any problems which may exist between the original parties to it. The holder of the negotiable instrument may have better claims than the person from whom it was received. Even if the debtor under the instrument has a good defense against the original creditor, it cannot be used against an innocent third party, who is called a **holder in due course**, and the debtor will have to pay. This is the essential prerequisite to making negotiable instruments freely transferable because it removes much of the risk and uncertainty that might otherwise interfere with their use.

Third party acquires better rights than original parties

A negotiable instrument can only be an effective substitute for money if the person using it does not have to worry about disagreements between the initial parties. For example, if you were to go to a movie and give the teller a $10 bill for your ticket, you would be very surprised if the teller demanded to know whether that bill had ever been involved in a breach of contract or a fraudulent transaction, the assumption being that, if it had, the teller could refuse it because it had lost its value.

Of course, money cannot work that way but must stand on its own as payment, independent of any previous dealings. It must be clearly understood that money is legal tender created by special statute and must not be confused with negotiable instruments, and to say that negotiable instruments are a substitute for money is not to say that they are equivalent. As explained in Chapter 6, when a contract requires the payment of money, a cheque—even a certified cheque—will not be satisfactory performance unless this is agreed to by the other party.

Money and negotiable instruments, however, come from common roots, and money nicely illustrates the essential quality of negotiation. A negotiable instrument can only be an effective substitute for money when the party receiving it is not obligated to go behind the instrument and examine the dealings of the parties to it but need only be concerned about the instrument itself.

The primary factors to keep in mind when studying negotiable instruments are the following:

1. They are a claim for funds against the person designated on the instrument.

2. They are freely transferable.

3. They may be used as an instrument of credit.

4. They may bestow greater rights or claims on the bearer of the instrument than on the party from whom the instrument was received.

Historical Context

Although variations of negotiable instruments have been used for thousands of years, the antecedent of modern forms developed in the Middle Ages. As trade grew in Europe, it became impractical and dangerous for merchants to carry large amounts of gold and silver as they travelled from one trading centre to another. They began to deposit their money at financial institutions designed for that purpose. When it became necessary for one merchant to give another money in the process of trade, the merchant would instead present a document which ordered the financial institution storing the merchant's money to pay out a certain sum to the person indicated on the document. Since their primary objective was to transfer money, these documents became known as bills of exchange. Their use effectively reduced the risks associated with trading since promises were being exchanged rather than actual funds. The rules associated with negotiable instruments were originally developed by the merchant guilds and included in their body of law called the "Law Merchant." These laws were adopted by the English courts and became an integral part of the common law system.

Negotiation an outgrowth of trading guilds

The Bills of Exchange Act.

Bills of Exchange Act summarizes common law

As part of the general legal reforms that took place in Britain in the last half of the nineteenth century, the numerous cases dealing with negotiable instruments were codified into one cohesive statute and enacted as the *Bills of Exchange Act* by the British Parliament in 1882. This *Act* was adopted by most common law jurisdictions and the Canadian *Bills of Exchange Act*, which the federal government passed in 1890, contained only minor changes.

The statute remains very similar today.[2] The *Act* simply codified already-existing principles dealing with negotiable instruments and did not change much of the common law. However, because of some minor changes, the *Act* makes it clear that common law principles apply except when specifically contrary to the provisions of the *Act.* The fact that the common law still applies despite the legislation can be important in those situations not anticipated in the *Act.* Since 1890, the only significant amendment to the *Bills of Exchange Act* has been a 1970 addition concerned with "consumer notes."[3] Under the *Constitution Act (1867)*, only the federal government has the power to pass legislation regarding bills of exchange and promissory notes. The provinces may have legislative provisions which indirectly affect them but the provisions governing negotiable instruments are uniform throughout Canada.[4]

Negotiable instruments under federal jurisdiction

---

2. *Bills of Exchange Act*, R.S.C. (1985) c. B-4.

3. *Bills of Exchange Amendment Act*, R.S.C. (1970) 1st Supp. c. 4.

4. *Constitution Act (1867)*, s. 91 ss. 18.

TYPES OF NEGOTIABLE INSTRUMENTS

Although the *Bills of Exchange Act* deals only with bills of exchange (drafts), cheques and promissory notes, it must be remembered that the *Act* is merely a codification of the common law. In fact, under the common law other types of instruments can qualify as negotiable instruments or take on many of the characteristics of negotiable instruments. For example, bonds made payable to a designated person or to his or her order have been held to be negotiable instruments. Similarly, security certificates where no restrictions are noted have been specifically designated as negotiable instruments in Alberta.[5] The discussion in this chapter will be limited to bills of exchange, cheques and promissory notes, although it should be remembered that the principles discussed will also apply to all other types of negotiable instruments.

There are other types of negotiable instruments

Negotiable instruments are orders or promises. The fundamental nature of a cheque or a bill of exchange is that it is an **order** or direction given by one person to another, usually a bank, to pay funds to a third. The nature of a promissory note, on the other hand, is primarily that of a **promise** that funds will be paid by the maker at some future date. Thus cheques and bills of exchange fall into the category of orders and promissory notes are promises.

Orders and promises

Bills of Exchange

Although not in common use today except in some particular businesses, the bill of exchange is important to understand since its features relate to the other forms of negotiable instruments discussed below. A bill of exchange is an order made by one person to another to pay an amount of money to a third; it is often called a draft. The person drawing up the instrument is called the **drawer**. It is the drawer who orders the **drawee**, usually a financial institution, to make payment to a third party, known as the **payee**. Normally, the drawer has already established some sort of business arrangement, such as an account, with the person or institution being ordered to pay. Otherwise, the order would simply be ignored. However, in some circumstances, a bill of exchange is used as a means of collecting a debt and then the drawer orders the debtor to make payment to a third party. The idea is that, if the debtor fails to do so, his or her credit rating will be harmed. Although the instrument is addressed to the drawee, it is physically transferred to the payee and the payee then presents the instrument to the drawee for payment.

Bill of exchange is order instrument

If the bill is made payable on demand, the normal course of action is for the payee to present the instrument to the drawee as soon as possible for payment. However, when the instrument is made payable at some future time, the payee or subsequent holder of the instrument must wait until the bill reaches the date designated for payment before the funds can be obtained. If the bill has not yet matured or where payable on demand the payee or subsequent holder wishes to delay immediate payment for some other reason, another option is available. It is still important for the holder of the instrument to determine whether the bill will be honoured when the date of maturity is reached. The holder of the bill has the right to take the instrument to the drawee, even before maturity, to determine whether the drawee will assent to the order given by the drawer. Thus, the drawee accepts the obligation to pay out on the instrument the amount specified at the date of maturity, indicating this by a signature, the date and the word "Accepted"

Bill paid upon maturity

Once accepted—drawee primarily liable

5. *Business Corporations Act*, S.A. (1981) c. B-15 s. 44(3).

written on the bill of exchange. When the drawee has done this, he or she has accepted the bill and is referred to subsequently as the acceptor rather than the drawee. If the drawee refuses to accept the instrument, it is said to be dishonoured and the holder must then seek redress from the drawer. Redress can be sought immediately without waiting until the maturity date. But if the instrument is accepted, the drawee becomes primarily liable on the instrument and the drawer no longer has any control over the payment of the bill.

It is interesting to note that, before acceptance takes place, the drawee owes no obligation to the payee to honour the instrument since there is no direct relationship between the drawee and the payee or subsequent holder. It is only because of the relationship that exists between the drawer and drawee that the drawee is willing to accept the order and pay out to the holder of the instrument. The drawer retains control of the situation and can countermand the order, provided the bill has not been honoured through payment or accepted by the drawee. The drawee will respect the countermand and refuse to honour the instrument.

For example, if Garcia buys a boat from Saito and gives Saito a bill of exchange, payable three months later, drawn on Ace Trust Company where Garcia has an account or line of credit, it is quite likely that Saito would go to Ace Trust Company as soon as possible to find out whether Ace would honour the bill three months hence. Ace Trust Company would indicate their willingness to honour the instrument at maturity by their representative writing "Accepted" across the instrument, accompanied by the date and the signature of the appropriate signing officer. If they refuse to do this, the bill would be dishonoured and Saito would then turn to Garcia, the original drawer of the instrument, for satisfaction. But if Ace Trust Company does accept the bill, Garcia can no longer issue any instructions to Ace Trust Company in relation to it. In effect, the primary debtor is now Ace Trust Company. Since they have assumed the debt and the obligation to pay, Garcia has lost control of the situation.

In fact, the *Bills of Exchange Act* states that the position of the acceptor is the same as that of the maker of the promissory note.[6] If Garcia were to discover that there had been some fraudulent misrepresentation on the part of Saito, Garcia could countermand the order to Ace Trust Company any time before acceptance. But once Ace Trust Company has accepted the bill and become the primary debtor, it owes an obligation to Saito to honour the instrument independently of Garcia and so is uninterested in any difficulties that exist between Garcia and Saito. If there has been fraud, Garcia has the right to sue Saito for compensation, but he cannot prevent Ace Trust Company from paying out on the accepted bill of exchange. It is possible for the "acceptor" of the bill to make a qualified acceptance. When the acceptance is qualified, as in "acceptable when car repair complete," the bearer of the instrument can submit to the qualification or treat the bill of exchange as dishonoured and look to the drawer for satisfaction.

Bills of exchange can be used to accomplish two purposes. First, they are an extremely effective method of transferring funds between parties without the necessity of carrying cash, and, second, they can be used to create a creditor/debtor relationship. Demand **drafts** and sight **drafts** are usually used to transfer funds, the demand draft being payable when it is presented and the sight draft payable three days after being presented. The advantage of the sight draft is that it gives the drawee time to assemble the funds after it has been presented. A bill of exchange payable at some future time is called a **time draft**.

Drawee has no obligation to payee before acceptance

Order to pay can be countermanded before acceptance

6. *Bills of Exchange Act*, R.S.C. (1985) c. B-4 s. 186(2).

Although the bill of exchange was traditionally the most significant type of negotiable instrument, its use in modern times has dwindled because of business people's increased reliance on another negotiable instrument, the cheque, and more recently the move to electronic methods of banking. However, the bill of exchange is still a valuable tool of commerce and there are many circumstances in which, because of tradition or the need for the unique qualities of this instrument, the bill of exchange is still important today.

Cheques

A **cheque** is a bill of exchange drawn on a bank and payable on demand. It is drawn up by the drawer and made payable to the payee. Thus, a cheque may be viewed as a type of bill of exchange; it has the same general characteristics but is limited to situations in which the drawee is a bank and payment can be demanded immediately. It should be noted that the definition of "bank" for the purposes of the *Act* has been broadened to include other institutions such as credit unions and some trust companies.[7] Since a cheque is payable on demand, its primary purpose is to exchange funds conveniently rather than to function as an instrument of credit. However, cheques that are postdated can be used to create a creditor/debtor relationship over substantial periods of time. Because a creditor/debtor relationship is inconsistent with a cheque being payable on demand, a postdated cheque does not acquire all of the characteristics of a negotiable instrument until the date specified on the instrument.

Cheque is bill of exchange, drawn on bank, payable on demand

Cheques primarily used for exchange of funds

As a result, a unique feature of postdated cheques is that the drawer retains the right to countermand it up to the stated date, even against an innocent third party, and anyone acquiring the instrument before that date takes it subject to that right. Thus, if on June 3, Robinson were to make a cheque drawn on his account at the Royal Bank payable to Devji postdated to June 10, and if Devji were to take that cheque to her own bank (the Bank of Commerce) on June 7 and receive cash for it, the Bank of Commerce would receive a negotiable instrument but would take it subject to Robinson's right to countermand. If Robinson were to countermand the cheque on June 8 because of some fraud, the Bank of Commerce would not be able to demand payment as a holder in due course from Robinson. Its only option would be to turn to its depositor, Devji, for repayment. Once the date has arrived, the instrument can be further negotiated and the person acquiring possession will be in the position of any other holder of a negotiable instrument.

However, it is important to note that, because the Bank of Commerce took the instrument with an irregularity on its face, it would be subject to the countermand even when it attempted collection after June 10, when the irregularity was no longer apparent. When a bank has sufficient funds in a customer's chequing account to cover a cheque drawn on it or has agreed to a line of credit, that bank has an obligation to honour the cheque. Whenever it fails to do so, the bank can be required to pay substantial damages to the customer because of that failure. If there are not enough funds to cover a cheque, the bank will not honour the cheque and the liability is in the hands of the drawer. It is a criminal offense to issue a cheque where there are not sufficient funds (N.S.F.) or where you know there will not be sufficient funds to cover it when it will be presented for payment.

One important feature of a cheque set out in Section 167 of the *Bills of Exchange Act* is that the authority of the bank to pay a cheque drawn on it is effectively ter-

Banks can stop payment on cheque in event of death or countermand

---

7. *Bills of Exchange Act*, R.S.C. (1985) c. B-4 s. 164.

minated when either of two events take place. When the customer who has drawn the cheque dies, the authority of the bank to honour that cheque is terminated as soon as it has notice of the death. The bank's authority to pay out on a cheque also ends when the customer orders a stop payment or countermands payment on the cheque.[8] Many banks require their customers to agree to reimburse the bank if the cheque is inadvertently paid after such a countermand.

It is common practice today to require that payment be stopped (countermanded) in person, as opposed to over the phone, and in writing with all of the information including the amount accurately stated. Accuracy is required because computers are used to identify the cheque. Even a small discrepancy in the information provided may cause the computer to miss the cheque and let it go through. Although the cheque remains valid until the end of the six-year limitation period the bank as a mater of policy will not pay out after six months. Any older cheque is said to be staledated and a holder must go back to the original drawer for payment.

Certification.

When cheque certified by payee, it cannot be countermanded

While founded on English legal principles, the banking system in Canada has borrowed many of its procedures from American banks. This dual heritage has not only caused confusion but has also created a significant legal dilemma because the Canadian banking system has adopted the American practice of certifying cheques. The *Bills of Exchange Act* is silent on certification so its legal consequences are still to some extent the subject of debate. Certification requires the certifier to take a cheque to the bank on which it is drawn and have the bank indicate on the cheque that they will pay the amount shown on the cheque to any holder. This procedure is similar to the acceptance of a bill of exchange.

A cheque can be certified in either of two circumstances. A cheque may be presented to the bank for certification by the payee or some subsequent holder of the instrument and the result is similar to a bill of exchange being accepted by the drawee. That is, the drawer of the cheque will lose control over the instrument and the bank will assume primary liability to pay the payee or holder. The drawer could not stop payment on such a certified cheque even given fraud on the part of the payee. But a more common practice is for the drawer to have the cheque certified by the bank before transferring it to the payee. Common sense would seem to argue that this situation should lead to a different result since at the time of the certification the instrument has net yet been delivered to the payee. In fact, in practice, the banks treat a cheque certified by the drawer as they treat one certified at the request of the payee or subsequent holder, that is, as an accepted bill of exchange. Several recent court decisions have adopted this practice as correct in Canadian law and, therefore, it is likely that a certified cheque, whether certified at the request of the original drawer or by the payee or subsequent holder, will be treated as equivalent to an accepted bill of exchange with the bank being the primary debtor and the drawer losing all control. To avoid any possible problem, some banks have adopted the practice of giving their customers a bank draft rather than certifying a cheque at the request of the drawer. Of course where the cheque has been certified by the drawer and not yet delivered to the payee, there is no problem of cancelling or countermanding that certified cheque since it is returned to the bank in the process and there is no danger of a subsequent holder showing up demanding payment.

8. *Ibid.*, s. 167.

A CERTIFIED CHEQUE IS LIKE CASH

Office Plus Interiors entered into an agreement to purchase office furniture from Centrac for $48 000. Centrac demanded payment by certified cheque. Mr. Stanway, a principal of Office Plus, deposited a cheque for $76 000 from another source in their account at the Canadian Imperial Bank of Commerce. He then asked the bank to certify an Office Plus cheque for $48 000 to Centrac, which they did without checking to see if the deposited cheque would be honoured. Centrac took the cheque and delivered the furniture to Office Plus. When it was learned that the $76 000 cheque deposited earlier would not be honoured, the representatives of the CIBC phoned Centrac and told them not to bother trying to negotiate the $48 000 cheque, as they had stopped payment on it. But Centrac did present it for payment and when it was dishonoured Centrac sued CIBC for payment. The court held that when the bank had certified the cheque, it was giving Mr. Stanway something equivalent to cash, and therefore CIBC was required to honour it. "Once certification was made any attempt made by the bank to avoid payment was too late." The bank in this case may have made an error in not checking out the first $76 000 cheque, but they couldn't hide behind that error.

Centrac Inc. v. Canadian Imperial Bank of Commerce, 120 D.L.R. (4th) 765 (Ontario Court of Appeal)

Promissory Notes

Bills of exchange and cheques are orders to third parties but promissory notes fall into another category of negotiable instruments. They are promises to pay the amount set out on the instrument. The person signing the promissory note, the debtor, is referred to as the maker and the person designated on the instrument as entitled to the funds is referred to as the payee. Because only two parties are involved, the main function of promissory notes is only to advance credit. They are an important form of negotiable instrument used by financial institutions and are common in consumer transactions.

Promissory notes are promises to pay

Because promissory notes are used for the granting of credit, it is acceptable and quite common for them not only to bear interest but to be paid by installment. When this is done it is important for the maker to have each installment indicated on the promissory note as an endorsement so no subsequent holder can have any doubt that the installments have been paid. Alternatively, separate promissory notes or postdated cheques can be made out for each installment. The abuses associated with promissory notes in consumer creditor transactions led to the 1970 amendments to the *Bills of Exchange Act* which created consumer notes and which are discussed below.[9]

The maker of a promissory note corresponds to the acceptor of a bill of exchange having the direct obligation to honour the instrument when it comes due.[10] The other provisions of the *Bills of Exchange Act* also apply to promissory notes, which can be negotiated to third parties who, if they meet the qualifications of a holder in due course, will acquire better rights under the instrument than the original payee possessed. It is this characteristic that makes promissory notes so attractive to institutions in the business of lending money. Traditionally, a customer would purchase a commodity from a merchandiser and make arrangements to pay for the goods by installment. This sale usually took the form of a conditional sale

Promissory notes often used for consumer credit

9. *Ibid.,* Part V.
10. *Ibid.,* s. 186(2).

as described in Chapter 8, but, in addition to the conditional sale agreement, the customer would be required to sign a promissory note. The merchandiser would then sell or assign the conditional sale agreement to the third-party credit institution and, along with that assignment, negotiate the promissory note to that same institution. That institution would then become an innocent third party or a holder in due course and could rely on the promissory note, independently of any problems between the merchandiser and the customer. If the merchandise proved defective, so that the customer would normally not be required to pay the merchant, this would not affect the position of the credit institution which could still demand payment on the note. This particular advantage to the credit institution has been significantly reduced by the passage of the 1970 amendment to the *Bills of Exchange Act* dealing with customer notes which will be discussed below.[11]

A simple IOU is not a negotiable instrument. A person who signs a document, "I owe you $500, (signed) J. B. Samra," has acknowledged a debt but has made no promise to pay. Use of the words "payable on demand," or if it is designated payable at some specified date, make the instrument a promissory note.[12]

NEGOTIATION

Negotiation involves transferring negotiable instruments to people who were not original parties to the transaction. The process can take place in two ways depending on the method used to create the instrument in the first place. If the negotiable instrument was created as a bearer instrument, the negotiation of that

Bearer instrument negotiated through transfer

Order instrument must be endorsed to be transferred

instrument can be accomplished simply by transferring it from one person to another. A **bearer instrument** is created by the drawer stating on its face that the amount specified is payable "to bearer," the bearer being the person in physical possession of the instrument at any one time. An **order instrument** is made payable to a specific person or to his or her order. In this case, the person designated as the payee on the instrument (the person who is to receive payment) must endorse it on the back before it is delivered to a third party. Negotiation of an order instrument is a two-stage process requiring both endorsation and delivery of the endorsed instrument to the third party. Negotiation of a bearer instrument, on the other hand, is a single-step process accomplished simply by delivering it to another person. A negotiable instrument is endorsed by the designated payee signing the back of the instrument. The normal practice is for a cheque to be made payable to a specific person. For example, if Paquette draws a cheque made payable to Quon, Quon could negotiate that cheque to Naidu by signing the back of it and delivering it to Naidu. If this endorsation is only a signature, the cheque becomes a bearer instrument and Naidu could transfer it without further endorsement. If Quon not only signed his name but as part of the endorsement stated that the cheque is payable to Naidu or to the order of Naidu, then the instrument remains an order instrument and Naidu must go through the two-stage process of endorsing it and delivering it to some third party to negotiate it further.

In fact, there are many different types of endorsements which can be attached to a negotiable instrument, each of which is designed to accomplish a different purpose. An instrument that becomes a bearer instrument can be made an order instrument again by the bearer so stating in a "special endorsement" on the in-

11. *Ibid.,* B-4 Part V.
12. *Ibid.,* 176.

strument. It should be noted that an instrument originally created as a bearer instrument cannot be made an order instrument through endorsement. The various types of endorsements and the liability of the endorsers are discussed below.

Requirements for Negotiability

Bank of British Columbia v. Coopers & Lybrand Ltd. et al.[13]

In the early 1980s it was common practice for investors to obtain tax advantages through MURBs (multi-unit residential buildings). To facilitate this scheme, Community Builders Ltd. sold 29 units to a series of investors, taking a document purporting to be a promissory note back. (In fact the actual construction of the deal was more complex in order to facilitate the tax shelter requirements of the MURBs.) Each of the investors paid $10 000 in cash and signed two of these promissory notes payable to Community for $22 400 and about $15 000 varying somewhat unit to unit. All of the notes taken together had a face value of well over a million dollars. These notes were then assigned by Community Builders to the Bank of British Columbia as security. They were not actually transferred to the bank; rather, copies of them were given to the Bank and the Bank had the right to demand production of the actual documents at any time. The Bank advanced almost $800 000 to Community secured by the assigned promissory notes. Eventually the Bank requested that Community endorse the notes and deliver them to the Bank, but before this took place Community went into receivership. An action was commenced by the Bank against the investors for the value of the promissory notes.

In fact the Bank lost their action, and the reasons are quite instructive. First of all, although they had the right to become holders of the negotiable instruments, they did not do so. There was no endorsement and no delivery of the promissory notes to them. Therefore, they had them by right of assignment only. That means they were in no better position than Community and did not obtain the rights of a holder in due course. This nicely illustrates the distinction between assignment and negotiation of negotiable instruments. The Bank would have been in a much better position as a holder in due course of the notes rather than an assignee.

The second reason is even more telling, since the promissory notes themselves provided for interest to be paid on them *from the moment construction was completed.* A promissory note must be for a sum certain in money. That sum certain becomes uncertain when interest is payable from the construction completion date. It is not possible to know what amount is due without the introduction of extrinsic evidence—that is, when the construction was complete. Therefore, these notes do not qualify as negotiable instruments at all and the Bank could not be a holder in due course. It may be possible to charge interest on a promissory note, but that interest must be clearly calculable from the information on the face of it.

The following is a summary of the general characteristics these instruments must exhibit to be negotiable as a negotiable instrument:

13. 15 D.L.R. (4th) 714 (British Columbia Supreme Court).

Promise to pay must be unconditional

1. *Unconditional commitment.* Any instrument that requires an event to take place or qualification to be met before the promise to pay is binding on the maker of that instrument will not qualify as negotiable. These instruments must meet the obligation of being freely transferable so that subsequent holders do not have to look to the dealings of the original parties. If it were possible to make such instruments conditional, the holders would never know for certain if the condition had been met, thus defeating the purpose of negotiation. If Quon were to draw a cheque made payable to Paquette "if the barn has been painted" and Paquette then transferred this instrument to Naidu, Naidu could not tell if the condition had been met from the instrument itself. Naidu would have to inquire of one of the original parties and, because this is inconsistent with the purpose of negotiability, the cheque would not qualify as a negotiable instrument.

Instrument must be in writing and signed

2. *Signed and in writing.* The instrument must be able to stand on its own. It must be in writing and the name of the maker or drawer must appear on the face of the document. Because the legislation does not require that the person signing the document be the one promising to pay, it is quite permissible to have it created and signed by an agent and still qualify as a negotiable instrument. The purported principal will not be bound, however, if the agent has exceeded both actual and apparent authority. Such an unauthorized agent would be personally liable on the instrument. When a person is signing a negotiable instrument on behalf of a company or employer it is vital that they make it crystal-clear that they are acting on behalf of another. Even stating their position in the organization such as "President" or "Secretary" is not enough. The person signing on another's behalf must write "per" in front of their signature after stating the name of the principal or state below their signature that they are signing on behalf of a stated principal. Failure to do this will make the signer liable on the instrument in their personal capacity as if they were the drawer or maker.[14]

A NEGOTIABLE INSTRUMENT MUST BE UNCONDITIONAL

The plaintiff and the defendant had agreed to buy a hotel together, but when it came time to pay the deposit, the defendant didn't have the money. It was agreed, therefore, that the plaintiff would lend the defendant $25 000 for this purpose, but that there would be a promissory note made by the defendant in favour of the plaintiff for that amount, payable on demand. A letter was attached to this promissory note explaining that if the sale went through, the loan would be credited towards the plaintiff's share of the purchase. If it didn't go through, the defendant would have to pay the deposit. In fact, the transaction was not completed, and the plaintiff lost his deposit and refused to honour the promissory note, claiming the note was conditional. The court agreed. The note and the letter had to be taken as one agreement, and it was clear from the letter that the note would only have to be paid if the deal collapsed; this made it conditional, and the *Bills of Exchange Act* defines a promissory note as an unconditional promise pay a sum certain of money. This was not a promissory note. The plaintiff then was allowed to change his pleading so he was suing for breach of contract rather than for payment on a promissory note.

Pennefather v. Zanet, British Columbia County Court, October 7, 1988, as reported in *The Lawyers Weekly*, Vol. 8.

14. *Bills of Exchange Act*, R.S.C. (1985) c. B-4, s. 52.

3. *Payable at a fixed time or on demand.* An instrument can be made payable on demand by so stating on the instrument or by making no indication at all of a time for payment. A cheque is an example of a negotiable instrument payable on demand. The holder of the instrument is free to present the instrument for payment at any time during normal business hours. An instrument not payable on demand must be payable on some certain date or at some determinable time as specified on the instrument. Thus, if Quon were to make a note payable 90 days after his death, this would satisfy the requirement since his death is a certainty and so the date is determinable. However, care must be exercised because payment dates determined on some event carry considerable risk. For example, a note which is made payable 90 days after marriage is based on an event that is not a certainty. The note would be conditional and therefore not negotiable. In Canada, an instrument payable "at sight" is quite different from a note payable on demand or presentation. When it is made payable at sight, the payment is really due three days after it is presented, allowing the debtor three days of grace to gather the funds.

> Instrument must have a specified time for payment or be payable on demand

4. *For a fixed amount of money.* A negotiable instrument must be for a certain amount of money specified on the face of the instrument. The payment of that money can be made in installments, and interest can be added, but the amount owing must be certain. Thus, a promise by Quon to pay his inheritance to Paquette is not a negotiable instrument because the amount owed is not specified. In the case used to introduce this section the interest payable on the promissory note was to start after the completion of construction and there was no way to know when that was completed on the face of the note. The note therefore did not qualify as a negotiable instrument because it was not for a "sum certain" that could be calculated on the face of the instrument. In an Alberta case, the words "plus accrued interest thereon," without more, were held to render the sum secured uncertain, thereby preventing the instrument from being a promissory note. This prevented the plaintiffs from being entitled to recover as holders in due course of a promissory note.[15]

> Instrument must be for a fixed sum

The amount to be paid must also be payable in Canadian funds if the instrument is to be presented for payment in Canada. The amount could be calculated in other currency, but it must be possible to pay that amount in the equivalent Canadian funds. Thus, an instrument promising to pay $500 in U.S. currency will not qualify as a negotiable instrument in Canada but one promising to pay $500 U.S. will. Here the equivalent in Canadian funds can be delivered since there is no requirement that it be paid out in U.S. currency.

5. *Delivery of the instrument.* Even if the instrument has been drawn up, it does not qualify as a negotiable instrument until it has been physically transferred to the payee. This first transfer to the payee is called the **issue** of the instrument and all subsequent transfers are called **deliveries**. If delivery has been induced by fraud or if the instrument was stolen before it was issued, the debtor is not obligated to honour it. However, if the instrument gets into the hands of an innocent third party who qualifies as a holder in due course, such delivery will be conclusively presumed.

> Instrument must be delivered to payee

6. *The whole instrument must pass.* The entire claim specified on the face of the instrument must be passed to a subsequent holder for the instrument to remain negotiable. If the claim on a cheque is for $500 and the payee delivers that

> Partial claims not permitted

15. *Royal Bank of Canada v. Bauman* (1986) 46 Alta. L.R. (2d) 68 (Q.B.).

cheque to a third party but states in the endorsement that only $300 of the $500 claim is to pass, the instrument will not be a negotiable instrument in the hands of that third party. It should be noted that the third party will still have a claim against the debtor based on the assignment of contractual rights. This condition does not affect the right of the payee to discount the instrument. For example, if Quon were to transfer to Paquette all of the claim on a negotiable instrument made out for $500 for only $300, the instrument would remain negotiable since the entire instrument is passing. Quon has simply sold it for less than its face value. But if Quon transferred only part of the $500 claim to Paquette, retaining the right to collect some of the amount specified, this action would destroy the instrument's negotiability. If a promissory note is involved and installments have been made, those payments must be recorded on the instrument and then the amount still owing must be transferred.

Only when all of these requirements have been met will the document in question qualify as a negotiable instrument. It is important to remember that even when the instrument does not qualify as a negotiable instrument, the claimants may still have significant legal rights under the principle of assignment discussed in Chapter 5.

When negotiable instruments are used for consumer purchase, they must be so marked.
Photo by Dave Starrett/Prentice Hall Archives.

RIGHTS AND OBLIGATIONS OF THE PARTIES

The right to enforce a negotiable instrument varies not only with the status of the holder of the instrument but also with the type of defense being raised. To understand the rights and obligations of the parties to a negotiable instrument, it is best to examine them from the point of view of the person seeking to enforce the instrument. The following is an examination of the position of a holder in due course, a remote holder and a payee.

Holder in Due Course

Holder in due course acquires better rights

Throughout this chapter, the unique position of a holder in due course has been emphasized. We stated that a person who is not a party to the negotiable instrument but who acquires possession of it and otherwise qualifies as a holder in due course can actually acquire better rights or claims under that instrument than previous possessors held. Thus, if ever a problem such as misrepresentation or breach of contract existed between the maker of the instrument and the original payee, the holder in due course takes the instrument independently of any of these problems and will be able to enforce it despite their presence. The essential and unique nature of negotiable instruments is embodied in the person of the holder in due course. It is because of this special and privileged position that negotiable instruments are so attractive and useful as a medium of exchange and a method of advancing credit.

Not all third parties to negotiable instruments are holders in due course. The qualifications which must be met to obtain the status of a holder in due course are set out in Section 56 of the *Bills of Exchange Act.* These qualifications can be summarized as follows:

1. A holder in due course must have received the negotiable instrument through negotiation and cannot be one of the immediate parties. In *Bank of British Columbia v. Coopers & Lybrand Ltd.*, discussed above, although the Bank had a right to obtain delivery of the notes they never bothered to exercise that right. The notes were never actually delivered to the Bank and so they never did become a holder in due course and as a result had no better claim to those notes than the other creditors.

Qualifications of a holder in due course:
• received through negotiation

2. A holder in due course must have taken the instrument complete and regular on its face. If important portions of the instrument, such as the amount payable, had been left blank when the holder acquired possession of it, or if the instrument had been obviously altered—for example, if the amount payable has been increased—the holder will not qualify as a holder in due course. If Dedrick persuades Yoshida to issue a cheque with the amount left blank and Dedrick fills in $5000 and negotiates that cheque to Ramji, Ramji will be able to enforce the instrument if he otherwise qualifies as a holder in due course. If Dedrick fails to fill in the blank, Ramji will have acquired an incomplete instrument and if Ramji fills in the amount, he will also not qualify as a holder in due course and, therefore, will not be able to enforce it against Yoshida. However, assume Yoshida had given Dedrick a cheque for $500 and Dedrick added a zero, making it $5000. If the added zero was not apparent to Ramji when he received it through negotiation, he would qualify as a holder in due course and be able to enforce the cheque against Yoshida but only in its original form for $500. If the alteration was obvious, Ramji would not qualify as a holder in due course because the instrument was not regular on its face. Similarly, if the instrument is marked paid or cancelled, the person who takes it in such a condition will not qualify as a holder in due course.

• complete and regular

3. The holder must have acquired possession of the instrument before it becomes due and payable. An instrument is overdue if the date specified on the face of the instrument has passed, whether that date is fixed or determinable. (A grace period of three days should be included in this calculation whenever applicable.)

It is a little more difficult to determine whether an instrument is overdue or not if it is payable on demand. A bill of exchange which is payable on demand is said to be overdue when it appears on the face of it to have been in circulation for an "unreasonable length of time."[16] What qualifies as an unreasonable length of time is a question of fact. When a promissory note payable on demand is involved, the *Bills of Exchange Act* specifically states that the mere fact that the note has not been presented for payment within a reasonable period of time will not make it overdue when negotiated. The holder still qualifies as a holder in due course. The difference in the way that demand bills and notes are treated illustrates an essential difference in their natures. When a cheque or bill payable on demand is drawn, a third party is expected to take payment quickly. But when a promissory note is involved, even if it is payable on demand, the original parties to it would not expect payment to be demanded immediately. A promissory note, bill of exchange or cheque becomes overdue as soon as it is presented for payment and refused. The status of a holder in due course is affected only if the instrument is negotiated in such a way that the holder should know that the payment has been refused. For example, suppose Dedrick holds Yoshida's promissory note which is payable on demand for $500 and is refused when Dedrick presents it for payment. If he

• acquired before due and payable

---

16. *Bills of Exchange Act*, R.S.C. (1985) c. B-4, s. 69 ss. 2.

then negotiates that note to Ramji at a significant discount and arouses Ramji's suspicions that there is a likelihood that Dedrick had previously tried to get payment on the note, then Ramji would not qualify as a holder in due course because he took delivery of it after it was overdue. Of course the right to seek payment from the original drawer or maker of the instrument continues until action is prohibited by reaching the end of the limitation period, six years in the case of negotiable instruments.

• without knowledge of dishonour

4. The holder must have acquired the instrument without knowing that it had been dishonoured previously. If the drawer of a cheque stops payment on it because of the payee's fraud, the payee cannot get around this by making a deal with an associate who hopes to enforce it against the original drawer as a holder in due course. Because the third party is aware of the countermand which constitutes dishonour of the cheque, he or she does not qualify as a holder in due course. On the other hand, if the third party who otherwise qualifies as a holder in due course is not aware that the cheque had been countermanded and is not in a position to have known, his or her status as a holder in due course will not be affected. The same principles apply when a bill of exchange or a promissory note is involved.

• without knowledge of defect of title

5. The holder must have no knowledge of any defect of title. A "defect of title" is some problem, usually between the payee and the original drawer of the instrument but also possibly between the payee or other holder, which affects the right to possess the instrument. A holder of the instrument who is aware that the person who negotiated it had a defect of title is not a holder in due course. Defect of title problems may result from fraud, duress, undue influence and some kinds of incapacity. For example, if Yoshida were drunk at the time of drawing up a promissory note payable to Dedrick and Dedrick was aware of Yoshida's condition, Dedrick's title to that negotiable instrument would be defective. If Dedrick then negotiated this promissory note to Ramji and Ramji was aware that Yoshida was drunk when the instrument was drawn up, Ramji would have notice of the defect of title and would not qualify as a holder in due course. Defect of title defenses are discussed in more detail below.

• good faith

6. The holder must have acquired the instrument in good faith. There is considerable overlap between this qualification and qualification 5, but essentially this one is broader because it requires honesty on the part of the holder in due course. The holder of an instrument who has no specific knowledge of a defect of title or other problem associated with the instrument but suspects that someone is being cheated would not be acting honestly by demanding payment. It is important to point out that Section 3 of the *Bills of Exchange Act* states that the person is deemed to be acting in good faith when the act is honest but negligent. A person will not lose the status of a holder in due course merely because he or she has acted carelessly in taking possession of a negotiable instrument.

It is for this reason that the bank in the example used to introduce the chapter could not claim to be a holder in due course and enforce the cheque against Mr. Jordan. The manager of the bank had been so involved with Mrs. Jordan that he could not be said to be acting in good faith. As a consequence, Mr. Jordan did not have to pay.

• for value

7. Value must have been given for the negotiable instrument. Value in this sense is defined in the *Act* as valuable consideration and has essentially the same

meaning as it does in contract law. However, this definition also includes "an antecedent debt or liability" as consideration.[17] This exception is to avoid the problem of "past consideration is no consideration" when negotiable instruments are given for already-existing debt or liabilities. It is not necessary that the holder in due course be the one to provide such valuable consideration. Section 54 of the *Bills of Exchange Act* clearly states that a holder is deemed to be a holder for value whenever value has been given for the instrument. Thus, if Yoshida issued Dedrick a promissory note for $500 in exchange for a motor vehicle and Dedrick gave this negotiable instrument as a gift to Ramji, Ramji's status as a holder in due course would not be affected by the fact that it was obtained as a gift because Dedrick had given valuable consideration for the instrument.

Real Defense.

Only when these requirements are met can the holder claim to be a holder in due course, but even meeting these requirements does not ensure payment. The maker of the instrument has various defenses available which can be raised against the different categories of holders seeking to enforce a negotiable instrument. A **real defense** is one which is good against any holder, even a holder in due course, because it involves a problem with the instrument itself.

Real defenses can defeat holder in due course

When the signature of the drawer has been forged or signed by an agent who has no actual or apparent authority to do so, the drawer or maker will not be liable on the instrument. A drawee is not liable for a forged acceptance nor is an endorser liable for an unauthorized or forged signature. It should be noted that, when the instrument has been endorsed, the person endorsing it cannot rely on the forgery of one of the immediate party's signatures as a defense against a subsequent holder. An endorsement encourages subsequent holders to believe the negotiable instrument is what it purports to be. Even when the signature is valid, if other material parts of the negotiable instrument, such as the amount, have been forged, this will constitute a real defense, although the original drawer will be liable to a holder in due course for the contents of the original unaltered instrument. When a signature is valid but has been given for another purpose (the drawer thought a letter was being signed), and someone subsequently forges a negotiable instrument around that signature, such forgery will constitute a real defense. Negligence on the part of the drawer in these circumstances will preclude raising the defense against an innocent holder in due course.

Drawer not liable in cases of forgery

It is interesting to note that, when the forgery is the signature on a bill of exchange or cheque and the drawee or bank pays out under the impression that the instrument is valid, it cannot then turn to the purported drawer for compensation. The drawee or bank in such circumstances is normally the one who bears the loss. Recent cases have established, however, that where a bank has an agreement with a customer requiring him or her to check accounts, to examine the cheques cashed, and to notify the bank of any discrepancy, his or her failure to do so within the required period (for example within 30 days of the cheque being cashed) can make the customer responsible for the loss.

A second type of real defense occurs when the instrument has been **discharged**. The discharge can take place in several ways:

Discharge of instrument is a real defense

1. Through payment in due course at the appropriate time which is apparent to the holder.

17. *Ibid.*, s. 52(b).

2. When the holder renounces in writing any claim to that bill (this only constitutes a real defense if the holder in due course has notification of this renun-
ciation).

3. When the instrument itself has been cancelled in such a way that it is apparent
on the face of it.

4. When the instrument has been materially altered without the consent of the parties in such a way that it is apparent on the instrument.

Lack of delivery of incomplete instrument is a real defense

Another real defense is lack of delivery of an incomplete instrument. The initial delivery is referred to as issuing the negotiable instrument to the payee. But
when this has not taken place (if the instrument has been stolen from the drawer
or if it has been delivered into the hands of the payee by someone purporting to act
as an agent but without either actual or apparent authority to do so), the drawer
would have a good defense against anybody except a holder in due course. Only
when the instrument is incomplete as well as not being issued to the payee can the
drawer claim a real defense and thus defeat even a holder in due course's attempt
to enforce the instrument. If Rasmussen were to go to Cohen's office and notice a
cheque on the secretary's desk made payable to him but with the amount left blank,
and if Rasmussen took the cheque and later filled in what he considered to be the
appropriate amount and then negotiated that instrument to Jaswal as an innocent
holder in due course, Jaswal could not enforce payment. If the instrument had
been complete with the appropriate amount filled in before Rasmussen took it,
Jaswal would be able to enforce the instrument against Cohen because, if a complete
instrument gets into the hands of a holder in due course, delivery is "conclusively
presumed."

Incapacity is a real defense

Some forms of **incapacity** provide another type of real defense against a holder
in due course. The *Bills of Exchange Act* makes it clear that what constitutes capacity in a given jurisdiction corresponds to the principles of contract law.[18] Essentially,
if a contract is void because of the incapacity of one of the parties, a negotiable instrument will also be unenforceable against that incapacitated party. A negotiable
instrument that has been drawn up by a minor is unenforceable because of his or
her incapacity under contract law.

Remember, however, that in some circumstances, infants are obligated to honour
contractual rights. Thus, the holder of the instrument may be able to sue the infant,
not on the basis of the negotiable instrument, but on the basis that the contract was
for necessaries. Of course the infant's obligation in such circumstances is to pay a
reasonable price for the necessaries which may or may not correspond to the
amount set out on the negotiable instrument.

When insanity or drunkenness is involved, such incapacity will not necessarily
amount to a real defense and may not be available against an innocent holder in due
course, unless the person has been declared insane under statutory power. Such a
person would not be liable to even a holder in due course because the incapacity
is absolute. The *Bills of Exchange Act* clearly establishes that a corporation with limited capacity in provinces using a registration system of incorporation or created by
special statute will not be liable on a negotiable instrument drawn on it pursuant to
a contract that is beyond its capacity to enter into.[19] Most provincial corporations
now have full capacity but, as will be discussed in Chapter 13, some corporations created by special statute may have their capacity limited in this way.

18. *Ibid.*, s. 46.
19. *Ibid.*, s. 46 s. 2.

It is important to point out that, when incapacity is claimed as a defense, it is only available to the person incapacitated and will not invalidate the negotiable instrument. Thus, a drawee who pays out or accepts the instrument and a payee or subsequent endorser will be liable despite the incapacity of the original drawer or maker of the instrument. If an infant has a bank account, draws a cheque on it and delivers it to a payee, that payee can present it to the bank and the bank is fully entitled to honour the cheque if there are sufficient funds on deposit. If the infant countermands the cheque, there would be no recourse against either the bank or the infant on the basis of the negotiable instrument. The liability of the infant would have to be established on the basis of a contract for necessaries. If the instrument is in the hands of a holder in due course, that holder in due course can enforce it against any endorser or against the acceptor, since once those parties have accepted or endorsed, they cannot claim the incapacity of the original drawer or maker as a defense.

Under some circumstances, **mistake** can be a real defense. But this mistake must go to the nature of the instrument itself. That is, the purported drawer or maker of the instrument must have been under the impression that he or she was signing something other than a negotiable instrument when the signature was affixed to the document. This is an example of the defense of *non est factum*. This defense will not be available when the mistake was caused by the negligence of the drawer or maker. Since the principle puts an obligation on the drawer or maker to make an effort to determine the nature of the document being signed, it may well be that the only situation in which *non est factum* will be available as a defense on a negotiable instrument is when the drawer or maker has been actively misled about the nature of the instrument signed.

Mistake can be a real defense

Finally, any **material alteration** on the instrument will amount to a real defense, if it is apparent to the holder. Thus, a negotiable instrument with scratches on it or which otherwise indicates an erasure or alteration cannot be enforced at all against the original drawer or maker. Only when the alteration is not obvious can the instrument be enforced against the original drawer, and then only on the terms of the original instrument before any alterations. When such a real defense is available, the instrument cannot be enforced against the maker, even by someone who meets all of the other requirements set out for a holder in due course. Such obvious material alteration causes the instrument to be discharged as indicated above.

Apparent alteration prevents enforcement

Other Holders

The holder of an instrument who is not an immediate party to it and fails to meet the qualifications listed above is known as a **remote holder**. But even a remote holder may be in a better position to enforce the instrument than was the original payee. Basically, a remote holder must not only refute any claimed real defenses as listed above but also establish that good title was held on the instrument. A defect of title defense (which is a problem with the way the instrument was acquired) can be effectively used against a remote holder. Many of the rules governing contracts are brought into play with this defense. Some examples of **defect of title defenses** are as follows:

Real defenses and defective title defenses available against remote holder

1. When fraud, undue influence or duress is used to obtain the instrument.

2. When the consideration given for the instrument is illegal.

3. When there is incapacity in the form of insanity or drunkenness on the part of the maker or drawer and the person to whom it is issued knows or ought to know of the condition of that person, this constitutes a defect of title defense rather than a real defense.

4. When a complete instrument is not properly delivered. When an instrument is properly delivered but is issued in blank and completed by a subsequent holder, there is no difficulty since the authority to so complete is presumed. However, when the given authority to complete is violated, such as when the wrong amounts or dates are put in the blanks, this also constitutes a defect of title defense.

5. When the instrument has been discharged in such a way that it is not apparent to the holder. Thus, if a promissory note is being paid by installment and the last payment is made but there is no indication of the receipt of these payments on the instrument and it gets into the hands of a third party, the fact that it has been paid is only a defect of title defense. Similarly, if the holder has renounced claim on the instrument, even when it is acknowledged in writing, it is a defect of title defense if it is not indicated on the instrument itself.

There is one circumstance under which a remote holder can obtain the same kind of rights as a holder in due course. If it can be demonstrated that someone has held the instrument previously who qualified as a holder in due course, then the remote holder who now possesses it will have all the rights and claims of a holder in due course, acquiring those rights from the previous holder in due course through assignment. In these circumstances, the holder is called a holder through a holder in due course and has all the rights of a holder in due course. The remote holder will only lose those rights if the holder actually participated in the fraud or illegality that is being raised in the defense.[20] Also under the *Act* when the payee deposits a cheque in her bank, that bank becomes a holder in due course.

A BANK CAN BE A HOLDER IN DUE COURSE

Milligan issued a cheque in the amount of $1253 in favor of Meier, drawn on a branch of Canada Trust. The cheque was intended to be a loan. Meier endorsed the cheque and presented it at a branch of Capital City Savings and Credit Union Limited. The teller telephoned Canada Trust and verified that there were sufficient funds in the account and that there were no stops or holds on the funds that were on deposit. Capital City Savings then credited Meier's account.

Milligan subsequently instructed Canada Trust to stop payment on the cheque. Capital City Savings sued Meier and Milligan. The Small Claims Division of the Provincial Court allowed the claim against Meier, but dismissed the claim against Milligan.

On appeal, the Court of Queen's Bench held that Capital City Savings was a holder in due course of the cheque. The court concluded that the effect of the *Bill of Exchange Act* is to enable a bank to enforce payment of a cheque against the drawer notwithstanding a stop payment, in the absence of any real defences such as fraud, illegality or discharge. The rationale for the law is "…to permit the effective use of the fundamental facilities and services banking institutions provide."

Capital City Savings and Credit Union Ltd. v. Milligan (1989) 94 A.R. 47 (Q.B.).

20. *Ibid.*, s. 56.

Payees

Immediate parties seeking to enforce a negotiable instrument have no better rights than are available in ordinary contract law. The contract itself governs the relationship. It is possible to use not only real and defect of title defenses, discussed below, against an immediate party but any other defense that would normally be available in contract law. These additional defenses are called "mere personal defenses," an example of which is the **right of setoff**. A right of setoff involves the person being sued having some other separate claim against the person suing that may not be related to the bargain involving the negotiable instrument at all.

Mere personal defenses available against payee

For example, if Nimmo were an employee of Deheer's Used Cars and bought a used automobile from Deheer for $1000 by issuing a promissory note to Deheer, Nimmo would be entitled to set off against that claim any amount Deheer may owe him as salary or commission. So if Nimmo were owed $800 in commissions from Deheer, the two amounts when set off against each other would result in Nimmo being required to pay only the remaining $200 to Deheer on the negotiable instrument. Thus, when a person is being sued by an immediate party to a negotiable instrument, setoff may be used as a defense.

Another typical example of a mere personal defense is when there has been a **partial failure of consideration**. Contracts require the exchange of consideration between the parties. When a negotiable instrument is involved, some consideration must be exchanged for it pursuant to the terms of the contract. If the parties fail to perform the terms of the contract properly, the drawer or maker of the instrument can use that failure as a defense against the person with whom the contract was made. This is simple **breach of contract**. It should also be noted that rights based on contract apply to any parties involved that are immediate to each other. Thus even where one holder delivers the negotiable instrument to another, the rights between those holders is based on contract law and subject to personal defenses.

Endorsers

The unique features of negotiable instruments come into play when those instruments get into the hands of third parties. The process of transferring the instrument is through delivery to third parties. When the instrument is in bearer form, negotiation can take place through delivery only, but when it is made out to a specific person or order, negotiation takes place through delivery and endorsement. Endorsement is a notation, usually on the back of the instrument, which includes the endorser's signature. The general rule is that when a party affixes an endorsement to a negotiable instrument, he or she is obligated to see that it is paid. If an instrument, after endorsement by the third party, gets into the hands of a holder in due course who presents it for payment but is refused by the drawer or drawee, that holder in due course can then turn to anyone who has endorsed the instrument and demand payment. An endorser who has had to pay in this way can then enforce the instrument against the defaulting drawer or any previous endorser. When it is a bearer instrument being negotiated through delivery, the person taking such an unendorsed instrument still has the right to seek compensation from the person who negotiated the instrument to him or her. The difference is that the holder in due course can seek redress only from the immediately preceding party, not from a person who held the instrument and negotiated it without endorsement before the person who negotiated it to the holder in due course. Thus, if Burkholder made a promissory note payable to bearer and it was then passed to Sakich, Rahal, Diaz and

Negotiation of order instrument involves delivery and endorsement

Endorser is liable if instrument is refused by drawer

Black, all without endorsement, and if Black could not collect from Burkholder, he must then turn to Diaz. Even if Black qualifies as a holder in due course, he cannot demand payment from Sakich or Rahal, who have not endorsed the note.

The liability of an endorser on a dishonoured instrument is only established when certain qualifications are met by the person seeking redress. As a general rule, the holder of the instrument is required to give **notice of dishonour** to any endorser from whom payment is sought and that notice must be given by the close of the following business day after the instrument has been dishonoured. Failure to give such notice in the prescribed period of time will eliminate that holder's right to sue the endorser of the instrument. In very limited circumstances (in Québec or if a negotiable instrument requires payment in a country different from where it was drawn), a more formal type of notice must be given called "protest" which is done before a notary public.

Holder must give notice of dishonour

Forms of Endorsement.

Other objectives are accomplished through the type of endorsement affixed to a negotiable instrument. As a result many different forms of endorsement have been developed. The following is a summary of the different forms of endorsement:

Different kinds of endorsement

1. *Endorsement in blank.* This is a simple signature and will change an order instrument into a bearer instrument.

2. *Special endorsement.* This endorsement, in addition to the endorser's signature, also specifies the name of the party to whom the instrument is being negotiated; the instrument remains an order instrument.

3. *Restrictive endorsement.* This endorsement contains the endorser's signature as well as some restriction on the further negotiation of the instrument, for example, "Pay to B. R. Gatz only" or "For deposit only." This type of endorsement renders an instrument no longer negotiable.

4. *Qualified endorsement.* An endorsement which contains the words "without recourse" or their equivalent eliminates the normal liability associated with the process of endorsement. By including such words, the endorser is no longer liable in any way to a subsequent holder of the instrument if that instrument is dishonoured. At the same time, an endorser can remove the requirement that normally falls on a holder of a dishonoured instrument to provide notice of such a dishonour simply by including the words "notice of dishonour waived" or "protest waived." In such cases, the holder of a dishonoured instrument need not meet the technical requirements of giving notice in order to protect his or her right to seek redress from the endorser.

5. *Conditional endorsement.* Although the original negotiable instrument cannot be conditional in any way, it is possible for the endorser to make a conditional endorsement. Thus, if Jackson endorses an instrument, "Pay to J. Galati only if car properly repaired," this is a valid endorsement. If J. Galati negotiates the instrument to Jang, Jang is entitled to assume the condition has been fulfilled and can demand payment from either Galati or Jackson. If Jang does demand payment from Galati and the condition has not been met, Galati could not look to Jackson for reimbursement.

6. *Accommodation endorsement.* Although the process of endorsement normally takes place in conjunction with the negotiation of an instrument, there are

some circumstances in which it may be appropriate to have another endorser who has been neither a holder of the instrument nor a party to it add his or her credit. Such an accommodation endorser incurs all of the liabilities of an endorser to a holder in due course.[21]

There are two other situations in which it may appear that an endorsement has taken place. Often the drawee on a bill of exchange will be requested to pay out on the instrument without being certain of the identity of the person presenting it for payment. In such circumstances, a third party who is known to the drawee may be asked to verify that the person presenting the instrument for payment is who he or she claims to be. This third party then identifies the person presenting the instrument for payment by so stating on the back of the instrument. Although this may seem to be an endorsement, an "identifying endorser" is liable only if the identification proves incorrect. This identification by endorsement process can also have a role to play as the instrument is negotiated from one holder to another when the person taking delivery of the instrument is unsure of the identity of the person negotiating it to him or her.

A second situation that appears to be an endorsement is when the drawee bank requires the person presenting the cheque for payment at the bank upon which it is drawn to sign the back of the instrument in order to receive the money. This appears as a simple blank endorsement and has been mistaken as such by bank employees in the past. In fact, the holder of the instrument is presenting it to the bank for payment. Since this is not part of the negotiation process, the signature is not an endorsement. The signature is no more than an acknowledgment of receipt of the money. The bank when presented with such an instrument simply has the right to honour or reject it. If the bank, through its representatives, chooses to honour it, that is the end of the matter as far as the holder presenting it for payment is concerned. If it turns out later that the bank has a problem, they must look to their depositor, the drawer of the cheque, for compensation and not the holder of the instrument who presented it for payment, even though the signature now appears on the back of the cheque.

Acknowledging receipt of funds not endorsement

It must be noted that the more common situation is for the payee to deposit the cheque at his own bank for collection. This is an entirely different situation and the payee depositing is an endorser and liable as such to the bank.

The Drawee

The person on whom a bill of exchange is drawn (the drawee) or, in the case of a cheque, the bank, has no liability on the instrument. Since it is made by the drawer or maker and issued to the payee directly, there is no relationship between the drawee and the payee or subsequent holder of the instrument. The only reason a drawee or bank will honour such an instrument is because of prior arrangements made with their depositor, the drawer. When such arrangements have been made and the drawee fails to honour them by paying out on the instrument, he or she can be sued, but only by the drawer. This is the reason a drawer can stop payment on a cheque and the bank does not hesitate to do so. However, if the drawee or bank pays out because of its own error, it cannot look to the innocent holder who presented the instrument for payment for reimbursement but must turn to their depositor.

Drawee has no liability on instrument

---

21. *Bills of Exchange Act*, R.S.C. (1985) c. B-4 ss. 54, 130.

When drawee accepts, becomes primarily liable

The position of the drawee dramatically changes when a bill of exchange is presented for acceptance. Once the drawee has accepted the obligation on the bill, a direct relationship has been established between the drawee and the person presenting it. Once this happens, the acceptor is personally liable and must honour the instrument, even if there have been problems or difficulties in the relationship between drawer and payee. The acceptor cannot claim the signature of the drawer is invalid, claim there is not enough money on deposit to cover the debt, or challenge the drawer's capacity to sign. Similarly, the drawee (now acceptor) cannot claim that the payee's rights in relationship to the instrument are in any way limited after acceptance. However, the act of acceptance on the part of the drawee in the case of a bill of exchange does not eliminate the responsibility of the drawer. Although the acceptor has assumed primary liability to the holder and must pay, the drawer has guaranteed payment by the drawee, and the holder can turn to the drawer for payment if the acceptor fails to pay. The bank is in the same position as an acceptor when they have certified a cheque.

Drawer remains liable after acceptance

CONSUMER BILLS AND NOTES

The fact that negotiable instruments bestow better rights on innocent third parties than on the original party has led to considerable abuse, especially in the area of consumer transactions. The problem developed out of the practice of merchandise being sold to consumers through a conditional sales agreement which included, as part of the transaction, a promissory note signed by the consumer. The merchant would then discount this right or claim against the customer to a financial institution who then would collect the payments. This arrangement poses no problems as long as there is no defect in the product, but if the customer is dissatisfied in some way he or she could not refuse to pay since the financial institution could demand payment on the promissory note as a holder in due course, despite any contractual dispute between the customer and the merchant.

The practice even developed of retailers and finance companies working together to set up this kind of protection. Where the courts were satisfied that they were working in collusion the finance companies were said not to be operating at arm's length and therefore did not qualify as holders in due course, but this still left the potential for much abuse. The *Bills of Exchange Act* was amended by the addition of a section dealing with *Consumer Bills and Notes* [22] to prevent this type of abuse.

A consumer note is a promissory note signed by a person purchasing goods or services for a non-commercial purpose (not for resale or use in any business). A consumer bill is any bill of exchange or cheque given for the advancement of credit. In such a consumer transaction, a cheque postdated for more than 30 days is included as a consumer bill. In this way, a bill of exchange or cheque used just to transfer funds is not covered but one used to establish a creditor/debtor relationship is. This legislation is designed to protect consumers by requiring that all consumer bills or notes be stamped on the face as such. This removes the advantages of negotiable instruments in the hands of holders in due course. Even when the consumer bill or note gets into the hands of a holder in due course, the original drawer or maker of that instrument can raise most of the defenses available in a normal breach of contract action.

Where consumer note— more defenses available

While this amendment effectively curbs the abuse associated with the use of promissory notes and other forms of negotiable instruments in consumer purchases,

22. *Ibid.,* Part V.

it also interferes with the basic purpose of negotiable instruments, that is, free transferability without the need to look beyond the face of the instrument. Since the consumer bill or note must be clearly stamped on its face "Consumer Purchase," this problem is generally overcome. Any third party who might come into possession of a negotiable instrument used in this way has clear notice that it is a consumer bill or note with its attendant higher risk and can avoid problems associated with it simply by refusing delivery.

The *Act* makes it clear that negotiable instruments used for this purpose must be clearly marked "Consumer Purchase," but also recognizes that there may be circumstances in which this does not take place. It is possible for an innocent third party not to know that the instrument was used in a consumer purchase if the merchant fails to stamp the instrument as required. When a holder in due course has received no notice that the instrument has been involved in a consumer purchase, that innocent third party acquires all the rights of a holder in due course dealing with a normal negotiable instrument and can enforce it against the drawer, independently of any contractual dispute between the customer and the merchant. However, the merchant who has failed to stamp the instrument is subject to prosecution and the payment of a significant fine, and is liable to compensate the drawer for damages.

Instrument must be marked

The following example illustrates the operation of consumer notes. If Degraaf purchased a used car from Galer's Fine Cars Ltd. by entering into a conditional sales contract and signing a promissory note for $5000, Galer would have the right to negotiate that promissory note and assign the conditional sale agreement to Quinn's Finance Company. If it turned out later that Degraaf was the victim of fraudulent misrepresentation (in relationship to the purchase of the car from Galer's Fine Cars Ltd.), before 1970, Degraaf would still be forced to pay the $5000 to Quinn's Finance Company because Quinn was the holder in due course of the promissory note and took it independently of any problems between the immediate parties to the instrument. However, subsequently to the 1970 amendment, Galer would have been required to stamp "Consumer Purchase" on the face of the promissory note; this fact would be obvious and effective notification to Quinn that the promissory note did not convey with it the rights normally associated with a negotiable instrument. In such circumstances, Degraaf could not only sue Galer for fraud but also refuse to honour the promissory note. If Quinn sued, Degraaf could raise the fraudulent misrepresentation as an effective defense. On the other hand, if Galer had failed to stamp the note "Consumer Purchase" and Quinn was not aware that it had been obtained in this way, Quinn would be the holder in due course of a normal negotiable instrument and would still be able to enforce payment against Degraaf. However, Galer would be subject to prosecution and would be required to pay a fine as well as being subject to an action to recover any money that had to be paid to Quinn to honour the promissory note.

LETTERS OF CREDIT

69971 Manitoba Ltd. v. National Bank of Canada[23]

Mr. Barrin imported various items of produce from foreign countries through Barrin Produce (the numbered company above). In this case they were importing oranges from a Spanish company and required an international letter of credit from

23. 122 D.L.R. (4th) 609 (Manitoba Court of Appeal).

their bank, the National Bank of Canada, in order to facilitate the transaction. The arrangement was that the Spanish company would transport the oranges directly to Barrin Produce but the bill of lading for the oranges would be transferred through a Spanish bank to the National Bank of Canada and subsequently to Barrin Produce. The standard practice would be that when the National Bank received the appropriate documentation including the bill of lading and released it to Barrin, title to the oranges would transfer and then the National Bank would become obligated on the letter of credit to pay the Spanish exporter. Payment would be made by the National Bank, when satisfied the documentation they had received was correct.

When the documents were delivered to the National Bank by the Spanish bank, they included the completed bill of lading and a bank draft requesting payment as required under the letter of credit. Unfortunately, the documentation received was not correct. There were several errors, including an important one on the bill of lading that listed the goods delivered as oranges and lemons instead of just oranges as required. The Bank was aware of this discrepancy but failed to bring it to Barrin's attention when they transferred the bill of lading to Barrin.

When Barrin discovered the problem and the defective nature of the produce he asked his bank not to honour the letter of credit and not pay out on the bank draft. His bank refused and paid out the amount owing to the Spanish supplier. The National Bank took the position that as soon as they released the proper documentation including the bill of lading to Barrin, that transferred ownership in the goods to Barrin and committed the bank to honour their international letter of credit. The money was paid to the Spanish supplier and Barrin account at the Bank was debited accordingly. An action was brought by Barrin against the National Bank for wrongfully honouring the international letter of credit.

The principle is quite clear that such letters of credit have to be honoured if the documentation required pursuant to it is properly submitted and correct on the face of it. In this case it was not correct on the face of it, the money should not have been paid out, and therefore the Bank was liable to Barrin for their error. It is interesting to note, however, that the actual damages that were paid by the Bank to Barrin was not the amount debited against the account, but the actual losses he suffered in the transaction.

This case nicely illustrates the nature of letters of credit and how they are used. It also shows how they are used in conjunction with bank drafts and bills of lading and how they have become extremely important in international trade.

In international trade the bill of exchange or draft and other forms of negotiable instruments are still extensively used, but today it is becoming more common to use a letter of credit. The letter of credit is a guarantee from the importers bank that the price stated will be paid upon presentation of appropriate documentation confirming delivery thus giving assurance to the seller that they will be paid by their customer. This letter of credit is normally delivered to the exporter by the importer who upon delivery of the goods submits the appropriate documentation to the importer's bank and receives payment. Sometimes, especially when the importer's bank is in a foreign country, the exporter will require that a bank that he or she has confidence in, usually in his or her own country, become involved as a confirming bank. The exporter's chosen confirming bank then receives the letter of credit directly from the importer's bank and commits to the exporter that they will honour it upon receiving the appropriate documentation. The confirming bank plays a role very much like that of endorsing a negotiable instrument in that they add their guarantee to the letter of credit. The exporter then simply submits the appropriate documents indicating performance to his or her bank and receives payment.

If Chan was exporting pianos from Hong Kong to Weiss in Canada, to satisfy Chan, Weiss might ask the Royal Bank to generate a letter of credit to support this transaction. The letter of credit would guarantee payment to Chan of a specific amount (for example, $200 000) upon the production of certain documentation. This required documentation might include a proof of insurance, bill of lading, customs declaration, and invoice. It might even require a certificate of inspection from some third party to indicate that the goods are as expected. This letter of credit would be given to Weiss by the Royal Bank and Weiss would deliver it to Chan, who would upon shipping the goods present the appropriate documents including the letter of credit and collect the money from the Bank.

More likely than not, however, Chan would want his own bank involved in the transaction. If he only involves his bank in an advising capacity where it assumes no liability, it is referred to as an advising bank, but where Chan wants his bank to guarantee payment it is called a confirming bank. If he were to choose the Hong Kong bank as the confirming bank, he would inform Weiss of this requirement at the outset and when making arrangements for the letter of credit with the Royal Bank Weiss would also provide the Royal with the particulars of the Honk Kong Bank as confirming bank. The Royal Bank contacts the Hong Kong Bank directly making arrangements for the confirmed letter of credit. The Hong Kong Bank then sends a confirmed letter of credit to Chan who then ships the pianos. Chan then submits the appropriate documents confirming delivery to his bank, the Hong Kong Bank, which after careful inspection, and if satisfied, makes the appropriate payment. These documents are then sent to the Royal Bank which pays the Hong Kong Bank and appropriately debits the account of Weiss.

This may seem like a very complex process but it is really quite simple in that the two traders each choose banks that they trust to hold and transfer the funds. The effect is quite similar to that of a bank draft but this process is often more convenient and more flexible. The case used to open this discussion illustrates the process and what should happen when incorrect documentation is submitted to the bank on which the letter of credit is drawn. In that case, as held by the court, the National Bank of Canada should have withheld payment because of the bill of lading stating that oranges and lemons were delivered rather than just oranges.

Often drafts are used in conjunction with this process, the letter of credit authorizing the creditor to obtain payment by drawing a draft on the issuing or confirming bank. In the above example Chan, upon presenting the appropriate documentation showing that the pianos were shipped, would then draw a bill of exchange (a draft) naming the Royal Bank as the drawee and him or his bank as the payee which he could then give to his bank for collection.

Letters of credit are primarily used in international trade, but they are very flexible and because of this quality it is not uncommon to find them being used in domestic business transactions as well. Letters of credit are also used in other ways, for example to in effect guarantee that one party to a contract will properly perform. If there is a breach the victim has recourse to the bank that has issued the letter of credit. This is referred to as a standby letter of credit.

SUMMARY

Negotiable instruments are freely transferable instruments, and are used effectively as a substitute for money and as a method of advancing credit. When the negotiable instrument gets into the hands of an innocent holder in due course, that person can acquire better rights than the immediate parties to the instrument had. The federal *Bills of Exchange Act* regulates negotiable instruments. These instruments are promissory notes in which a maker promises to repay a payee; bills of exchange or drafts in which a drawer orders a drawee to pay a payee; and cheques which are bills of exchange drawn on a bank, payable on demand. A certified cheque is similar to an accepted bill of exchange in that the drawee or bank accepts a direct responsibility to the holder of the instrument to pay.

A negotiable instrument is negotiated by endorsement and delivery if it is an order instrument but by delivery alone if it is a bearer instrument. Several obligations must be met for the instrument to qualify as negotiable. It must be a signed instrument containing an unconditional commitment to pay a fixed amount of money at a fixed time or on demand. It is also necessary that the instrument be delivered and that the whole instrument pass. To qualify as a holder in due course, a person must have received the instrument for value, an instrument complete and regular on its face, through negotiation, before it was due and payable, in good faith and without knowledge of any defect of title or notice of dishonour. Only real defenses can be used against a holder in due course whereas real defenses and defect of title defenses can be used against other holders. Endorsers of the instrument are liable on default by the original drawer only if properly notified of the default. Because of abuse it was necessary to amend the *Act* so that negotiable instruments used to extend credit in consumer transactions did not convey the same rights as regular negotiable instruments. Such consumer notes must be clearly stamped as such by the merchant. Letters of credit are a similar method of transferring funds where one bank issues a letter of credit on behalf of their client to a confirming bank that guarantees payment to a creditor of the first bank's client.

QUESTIONS

1. What two important characteristics of negotiable instruments have led to their prevalent use in business activities today?

2. What is the difficulty associated with the assignment of contractual rights that is overcome when a negotiable instrument is used? Explain how the position of a holder in due course differs from that of an assignee of contractual rights.

3. Describe how negotiable instruments differ from money. Describe how negotiable instruments are similar to money.

4. Describe the *Bills of Exchange Act* and how it came about as a Canadian statute. Which level of government passed it and has jurisdiction in this area?

5. What is meant by a bearer instrument? Contrast this to an order instrument. Indicate how an order instrument can become a bearer instrument.

6. Explain what is meant by negotiation of a negotiable instrument and how this is accomplished. What qualifications must an instrument meet to be negotiable?

7. What is the difference between a bill of exchange, a promissory note and a cheque? Give an example of when each would be used and give examples of two other kinds of instruments that sometimes qualify as negotiable instruments.

8. What is the process of acceptance of a bill of exchange and the significance of acceptance? What types of bills of exchange would you probably see presented for acceptance? Explain the nature of the relationship before acceptance between the payee and the drawee. How does this change once acceptance has taken place?

9. What is meant by the dishonour of a negotiable instrument? What obligation falls on the holder of that instrument when such dishonour takes place?

10. When a payee presents a bill of exchange for acceptance to the drawee and it is accepted, how does this acceptance affect the position of the drawer of the instrument?

11. Under what circumstances will the authority of a bank to pay out on a cheque be terminated?

12. Will a bank honour a stop payment order made against a certified cheque?

13. What is the primary purpose of promissory notes?

14. Distinguish between real defenses, defect of title defenses and mere personal defenses. Indicate the circumstances in which these distinctions can be significant when dealing with negotiable instruments.

15. Define what is meant by a holder in due course, the characteristics this person must have to qualify and the significance of being so designated. Explain how the knowledge of a holder of a negotiable instrument can affect his or her right to claim to be a holder in due course.

16. When a person does not qualify as a holder in due course but acquires the instrument through a holder in due course, what defenses are available to the original maker or drawer of the instrument?

17. Explain the significance of the 1970 amendments to the *Bills of Exchange Act* creating consumer notes.

18. Explain how a letter of credit differs from a negotiable instrument.

19. Distinguish between a standby letter of credit and a normal letter of credit.

20. Explain the role of a confirming bank when letters of credit are involved.

CASES

1. National Bank of Canada v. Tardivel Associates

Mr. Tardivel and Mr. Didonato decided to participate together through their corporations in a quick real estate deal to flip some property. Mr. Didonato invested $23 000 and Mr. Tardivel assured him that he would get $35 000 within four weeks. Didonato drew a cheque on his corporate account, but Tardivel was unable to provide the appropriate documentation to support the investment. Didonato got cold feet, refused to go through with it and refused to hand the cheque which was signed and complete over to Tardivel. However, when Didonato was out of his office for a few minutes, Tardivel took the cheque without permission. He cashed it and immediately took $20 000 out of that account and wired it to someone else. The next day Didonato stopped payment on the cheque and when Tardivel's bank presented the cheque for payment by Didonato's bank it was refused, the stop payment being honoured. Tardivel's bank was left holding the bag.

Tardivel's bank sued both Didonato on the cheque and Tardivel for the money that had been drawn on the account, a shortfall of almost $20 000. The problem here is whether or not Didonato's company is responsible on the cheque. Give the arguments for both sides.

2. Royal Bank of Canada Ltd. v. Pentagon Construction Maritime Ltd.

Maramichi Glassworks Ltd. was a customer of the Royal Bank. It was in financial difficulty when it assigned any benefits flowing under a contract it had with Pentagon Construction Maritime Ltd. to the Royal Bank. Maritime was informed of this arrangement and made two cheques totalling approximately $20 000 payable to Maramichi Glassworks. Maritime made it clear to Maramichi that unless Maramichi performed the appropriate services contracted for, the cheque would not be honoured. Maritime also made this clear to the Royal Bank as well. Maramichi Glassworks did not live up to its contractual requirements and Maritime put a stop payment on these two cheques. The Royal Bank tried to collect but the cheques were dishonoured. In this action, the Royal Bank sued Maritime for payment of the cheques. Explain the arguments of both parties and the probable outcome.

3. Eastern Elevator Services Ltd. v. Wolfe

Wolfe was dissatisfied with his employment and discussed the possibility of working with an another employer, Pace. An agreement was worked out whereby a separate company, Eastern Elevator Services Ltd., would be incorporated and employ Wolfe. But Wolfe had to give Eastern a $5000 cheque to show how sincere he was, the understanding being that the cheque would not be cashed unless Wolfe failed to honour the agreement and did not take up his new position of employment. The deal fell through, Wolfe did not become an employee and he stopped payment on the cheque. Eastern sought a court order that Wolfe be required to pay out on the cheque.

Explain the arguments available to Wolfe as to why he should not be required to honour the cheque and more, why he should not be required to pay the $5000. Would your answer be any different if the cheque had got into the hands of an innocent third party who was a qualified holder in due course?

4. A. E. LePage Real Estate Services Ltd. v. Rattray Publications

In 1985 Rattray agreed to lease certain premises from A. E. LePage on Yonge Street. Pursuant to that agreement Rattray delivered a cheque to LePage for $20 825.89 as a deposit. It was drawn on a branch of the CIBC. A. E. LePage was acting for London Life, the owner of the property. The offer was taken by LePage to London Life for their signature. Rattray changed his mind and stopped payment on the cheque, but because of a mistake at the CIBC branch, the stop payment order was ignored when the cheque was brought in for certification by a representative of LePage. The cheque was subsequently deposited in LePage's trust account at the Toronto Dominion Bank, but when it was sent to the CIBC branch, they refused to honour it.

Indicate the arguments on both sides of this case as to whether or not A. E. LePage should be able to require the bank to honour this cheque. Explain Rattray's position. Would your answer be any different if the cheque had been certified by Rattray in the first place and then presented to LePage?

5. Stienback Credit Union Ltd. v. Seitz

Mr. Seitz was a businessman in Winnipeg who agreed to provide bridge financing for the Winnipeg Lions Club to cover the expenses for a fundraising concert it was planning. He wrote a $100 000 cheque and gave it to the Lions Club which presented it to the Royal Bank for deposit. Before crediting the Lions Club account with the money, the bank phoned Seitz's credit union to confirm that it would honour the cheque even though there were not quite enough funds in the account. The credit union assured the bank that the cheque would be guaranteed and that it was unnecessary to certify it. It turned out later that the concerts were a disaster and Mr. Seitz tried to stop payment on the cheque. Explain the arguments available to both parties.

6. Canadian Imperial Bank of Commerce v. Burman and MacLean

On May 4, 1979, the defendant, Burman, bought a car from the defendant, MacLean, for $3700. Burman made two cheques payable to MacLean to cover the price but both were dated May 6, 1979. About 6:30 p.m. on May 4, MacLean took these two cheques to the Bank of Commerce at Sydney River, where he had an account. The cheques were drawn on the Bank of Montreal. The CIBC took the cheques and gave MacLean $3700 for them. It turned out that MacLean had fraudulently represented the nature of the vehicle. Instead of having 53 100 kilometres on the odometer it had 136 800 kilometres. Burman went to the Bank of Montreal and issued a stop payment order before the bank opened on May 7, 1979.

The CIBC in this action is seeking to force Burman to honour the $3700 cheques. Explain the arguments available to Burman, and explain the likely outcome.

7. Enoch Band of the Stony Plain Indian Reserve No. 135 v. Morin

Morin worked as an employee of the Enoch Band and one of her responsibilities was to requisition cheques for the payment of students who were members of the band in various schools. Eventually these students would cease to be eligible for the band supplements but Morin kept on making out the cheques, forging the students' endorsements on the cheques when necessary and depositing them in her own account. All of the cheques were properly drawn on the band, signed by the band's authorized signing officers and made payable to the existing individuals, but they were intercepted, cashed and deposited by Morin. When the cheques came back to the band they were honoured.

The scheme was eventually discovered, Morin was fired and this action was commenced against the Bank of Montreal by the band seeking repayment of the monies debited from their account, representing the cheques with the forged endorsements.

Explain the arguments available on both sides. Which one of these two innocent parties should be the one to bear the loss? Would your answer be different if you knew that when the Enoch Band learned of the problem, they neglected to give written notice to the Bank of Montreal of the forgeries as required under the *Bills of Exchange Act* until the action commenced, a delay of over a year?

LEGISLATION

Federal
Bank of Canada Act, S.C. (1991) c. 46
Bills of Exchange Act, R.S.C. (1985) c. B-4

WEBLINKS

Canada: Bills of Exchange Act
canada.justice.gc.ca/FTP/EN/Laws/Chap/B/B-4

Canada: Bank of Canada Act
canada.justice.gc.ca/FTP/EN/Laws/Chap/B/B-2

Citizenship and Immigration Canada
cicnet.ingenia.com

REFERENCES FOR PART 3

Bennett, Frank. *Bennett on Bankrupty*. 5th ed. North York, Ont.: CCH Canadian Ltd., 1998.

Falconbridge, J. D., B. Crawford. 8th ed. *Banking and Bills of Exchange*. Toronto: Canada Law Book, 1986.

Sarna, Lazar. *The Law of Bankrupty and Insolvency of Canada*. Montreal: Jewel Publications, 1997.

Bankruptcy

When a company goes into bankruptcy, the creditors of that company also feel the impact, whether they are moneylenders or suppliers. The *Bankruptcy and Insolvency Act* has protected such groups to some degree. Government officials use the *Act* to monitor bankruptcies and regulate the process. Several companies in the past decade have sought further court protection to allow time for restructuring on the off chance that by doing so they can recover and keep the company's assets intact.

A Montreal lawyer discovered an obscure statute enacted in the 1930s allowing companies in trouble to protect their assets from creditors when they became insolvent. The *Companies' Creditors Arrangement Act* was initially enacted to protect business people, particularly farmers, who were hard hit by the Great Depression. It is a loosely constructed piece of legislation that does not provide for monitoring or careful regulation except by the overworked courts. In the dozen years since it has been revived the CCAA has acquired a dismal track record, because companies that have few assets left to salvage often rely on it. Essentially, it encourages "companies in trouble (to use) the court to stay afloat."

Consumers Distributing is a case in point. By invoking the CCAA in the name of restructuring, the company was able to delay the bankruptcy procedure. In the meantime they continued to sell off stock and acquire merchandise from their suppliers when it was clear that they would never have the means to pay for the goods. Olympia and York dragged the bankruptcy process out five years by invoking the CCAA, and managed to accumulate $30 million in legal and accounting fees in the first six months of the process.

When such stalling tactics are over there is little likelihood of there being anything left for creditors.

Source: "Bankruptcy," *Venture,* Show Number 625; telecast date: January 12, 1997. Running time: 8:03.

DISCUSSION QUESTIONS

1. What controls are set out in the *Bankruptcy and Insolvency Act* that are missing in the CCAA?

2. Should there be some kind of limitation period placed on government statutes so that they must be reviewed for their currency and suitability?

3. Should legislation be prioritized so that the courts are required to apply all the terms of one *Act* before the terms of another come into play?

4. Does the *Bankruptcy and Insolvency Act* do enough to protect creditors?

5. Do these statutes too easily allow people and institutions to escape their ethical obligations?

Employment and Agency

Business activity, in addition to the production of products or services, normally involves interaction with customers, suppliers, creditors and others. These activities are carried out by employees or other representatives and the legal rules and principles associated with these relationships are the subject of this section. Chapter 10 deals with the master/servant relationship or employment. It looks at the responsibilities that employees and employers have to each other, statutes which set standards and establish the rights of such workers and the special labour legislation controlling the collective bargaining process. Chapter 11 examines the agency function where one person represents another in transactions with a third. The law of agency is much more significant than is sometimes appreciated, since in the corporate environment all transactions must be entered into by such representatives.

Photo from Manitoba Archives.

Employment

16

OBJECTIVES OF THE CHAPTER

- To distinguish between employees and contractors
- To review the laws concerning employment relationships
- To describe the requirements for collective bargaining and trade union action

Jack Gibson was 67 when he was hired by a food distribution company on a two-year contract which included $3000 a month, car expenses and a membership at an exclusive golf and country club. As the sales manager, he was required to supervise other sales staff, and telephone and visit various supermarkets in the area to see that they were properly stocked with the company's products. Gibson's employer went away for two months and, when he returned, he discovered that certain stores were not properly stocked and that the company had lost the account of a major customer. When asked about this, Gibson told his employer that stores were being regularly called, visited and serviced.

The employer doubted this and hired a private detective to follow Gibson. From the reports of the detective, the employer learned that Gibson regularly visited the golf club. He called Gibson into his office and asked specifically how many calls had been made during the time corresponding to his surveillance. When Gibson answered "Fifty," the employer presented him with the detective's report and challenged him on the information. Gibson then admitted that he had not made the calls because of health problems. Gibson went on vacation for a while and on his return was fired. He sued for wrongful dismissal. The court said that, while Gibson's failure to perform his duties may have supported his dismissal, it was his dishonesty that caused a fundamental breach of the employment contract.[1]

---

1. *The Lawyers Weekly*, November 6, 1987, p. 6.

A contract for employment is one of the most important in which a person will become involved. This chapter is devoted to exploring the different legal ramifications of the employment relationship.

Employment law deals with business relationships in which one person works for another. But not all work done by one person for another is classed as employment. When someone acquires the services of a plumber to fix a faucet, a doctor to diagnose and treat an illness or a lawyer to draw up a will, the plumber, doctor and lawyer are performing services on behalf of the person paying them but they are not normally employees. The relationship is based on contract, but not on an employment contract, and the person doing the job or providing the service is called an independent contractor. Usually it is when someone works for another regularly that an employment arrangement results. Even then, if the person is paid by the job or by commission, it is sometimes difficult to determine where the independent contractor relationship ends and employment begins.

The third category in business relationships is called agency and will be discussed in detail in the next chapter. Each of these relationships imposes different legal rights and obligations on the parties; understanding which body of rights governs a particular relationship can be of vital importance.

Not all work is employment

WHAT IS EMPLOYMENT?

Jaremko v. A. E. LePage Real Estate Services Ltd.[2]

Mr. Jaremko was a real estate salesman paid by commission working for A. E. LePage who was discharged without notice on June 9, 1983. He was fired for not disclosing an interest he would acquire in property that he was selling if the deal went through. Mr. Jaremko had agreed to participate with the purchasers in financing the purchase of the building by investing the commission that he would make in the project. His employer took the position that he should have disclosed that interest to both the seller Bucyrus and LePage.

In fact this was a very minor part of the financing and Mr. Jaremko did write a letter on A. E. LePage stationery and sent it to the seller disclosing that he had an interest or a potential interest in the property, but hadn't disclosed his interest to A. E. LePage. The reason the deal went through is that A. E. LePage had decided to work out a deal with the purchasers whereby they would lease a large portion of that building for their offices. It was pretty clear from the circumstances that Mr. Jaremko had intended to disclose the information to LePage but just hadn't got around to it when he was discharged.

When he sued A. E. LePage for wrongful dismissal, their arguments were essentially that he was not an employee and that he was discharged for cause. As far as the first argument is concerned, the court took pains to point out that although Mr. Jaremko was paid by commission and was in control of his own time, he was an integral part of the organization, subject to company discipline, had to adhere to company policy, had offices supplied by LePage, worked exclusively for them and otherwise was generally under their control. The judge found that a master/servant relationship did exist. As far as the cause was concerned, the court found that his minor interest in the transaction was properly disclosed and found

2. 39 D.L.R. (4th) 252; affirmed 60 D.L.R. (4th) 762 (Ontario High Court of Justice).

it somewhat ironic that A. E. LePage would complain under these circumstances when they in fact had failed to disclose to the seller their interest in the property which was that they intended to lease it from the purchaser. In fact the purchaser made no complaint.

LePage also argued that another incident, either on its own or combined with this incident, amounted to cause. Mr. Jaremko had received a secret commission on another deal. In fact that deal involved a seller offering him a bonus without him seeking it out. In any case this matter had been dealt with between the A. E. LePage management and Mr. Jaremko, who had apologized and assured them that it wouldn't happen again. That matter had been dealt with.

For our purposes, this case illustrates the distinction between an independent contractor and an employee or servant and how each case must be considered independently. You cannot simply say that if a person is paid by commission, the person is an independent contractor. You must look beyond that. It also illustrates cause and how the conduct of both parties has to be examined in determining whether there is justification for dismissing an employee.

The Control Test.

Employee controlled by employer

The traditional method of determining whether an employment relationship exists is to assess the degree of control exercised by the person paying for the service. A person who is told not only what to do but how to do it is classed as an employee. But if the person doing the work is free to decide how the job should be done, the position is that of an independent contractor. For example, if Fong hires Kirk to paint a house, Kirk could be either an independent contractor or an employee. If Fong tells Kirk what tools to use, when to work and how to perform the job, then Kirk is an employee. If Kirk supplies the tools, and determines what time to start work and the best way to perform the job, then Kirk is probably an independent contractor. Whether the person is paid a wage or salary or is paid by the job is also taken into consideration in determining employment. Courts will also look at who owns the tools used, and who profits or runs the risk of loss from the work performed.

Independent contractor works independently

The employment relationship involves a contract in which the person being hired agrees generally to serve the employer. That is, the person acquiring that service has the right to supervise and direct. On the other hand, an independent contractor is entering into a contract to do a particular job and does not contract to serve the other person. In other words, employees work for their employer whereas independent contractors work for themselves. In the Jaremko case used at the start of this discussion it was clear to the court that Mr. Jaremko was working for A. E. LePage and not himself.

The Organization Test.

Organization test substituted for control test

In recent years, the courts have supplemented the control test with the organization test. This involves deciding whether the person to be designated an employee can be said to be part of the employer's organization. If the person is part of the employer's organization and subject to group control, then that person is considered an employee.[3]

---

3. John G. Fleming, *The Law of Torts*, 8th ed. (Sydney: The Law Book Co. Ltd., Australia, 1992), p. 372.

Mr. Justice Spence, when voicing a majority decision for the Supreme Court of Canada in *Cooperators Insurance Association v. Kearney*,[4] adopted the organizational test as put forward by Fleming. He indicated that there are many situations in which a person might be an independent contractor for most purposes but could still be a servant in some specific instances.[5] This ruling has prompted the courts to find employment relationships in areas which were traditionally considered purely independent. A person can now be determined to be a servant when engaging in one activity although the general relationship remains that of an independent contractor. Such an approach would likely be restricted to situations where the court was determining questions of vicarious liability but it may play a role in questions of termination and notice as in the Jaremko case used to start this discussion.

Definition of employment broadened

Many statutes contain a definition of employment but it is important to note that the definition is valid only for the purposes of that particular act. There is no general legislated definition of an employee. The courts, when faced with issues involving wrongful dismissal, liability or duties between the parties, must first determine the nature of the relationship. If there is no applicable statutory definition it is left to the courts to apply these principles to determine if the relationship is one of employment or not.

Agency, employment and independent contractors are three distinct types of relationships. There is a great temptation to think of these three categories as mutually exclusive. It may be generally true that a person cannot be an employee and an independent contractor at the same time for the same employer, but that is not so with an agent. An **agent** is someone who enters into legal relationships with others on behalf of a principal and such agents can be employees as well. It is important to realize that employees often find that their job responsibilities include acting as an agent representing the employer in dealings with suppliers, customers and other third parties. Although the customer may deal with a clerk, the sales contract that results is between the clerk's employer and the customer; the clerk merely functions as an agent for the principal. It is also common for an agent to be an independent contractor of the principal rather than an employee. Insurance agents, real estate agents, stockbrokers, lawyers and many other professionals offering advice and service are independent agents, not employees. It also does not follow that all employees are agents, just those who enter into contractual relationships on behalf of their principals. A manager who orders the produce for a grocery store is both an employee and an agent, but the person packing the groceries is generally only an employee.

An employee can be an agent

An agent can be independent

These distinctions are important, because the liability of the parties may be determined by which of these relationships exists. If an individual qualifies as an employee, not only will the employer's liability for the employee's wrongful conduct be greater than for an independent contractor or agent but the legislation providing protection, rights and benefits to employees will also apply. If an agency relationship exists, the agent's actions in creating new legal relationships done with authority will be binding on the principal.

The legal principles governing the independent contractor are embodied in the general rules of contract law already covered in Chapters 3 to 6. This chapter will examine the law of master and servant, the federal and provincial legislation, the trade union movement and collective bargaining. The law of agency will be discussed in the following chapter.

4. *Cooperators Insurance Association v. Kearney* (1965) 48 D.L.R. (2d) I.
5. *Ibid.*, p. 21.

THE LAW OF MASTER AND SERVANT

Over the years the common law developed special rules governing employment, which was then referred to as a master/servant relationship. Today employment is governed primarily by the general provisions of contract law, but many of the special rules developed by the common law courts to deal with the unique problems associated with the employment relationship have been retained. Also, a number of specialized statutes have been passed further defining the responsibilities and obligations the parties have towards one another.

Employer must provide safe working conditions

The main responsibility of the employer in addition to wages is to provide a safe workplace and good working conditions for the employee. The employee is entitled to leave the job when conditions are dangerous. It is not enough that the employee dislike the conditions; the danger must be real in the eyes of a reasonable person. Some types of jobs, such as construction, involve a certain amount of inherent danger and the employer's obligation in these circumstances is to take reasonable steps to minimize that danger. This duty requires not only the erection of protective fences and the supplying of appropriate safety equipment but also extends to hiring competent people. If the employer knowingly hires a careless or improperly trained person who causes an accident which injures another employee or some other person, that employer could be held responsible for the injury suffered. The workers' compensation rules discussed below now significantly modify these responsibilities towards other employees.

Other obligations of employer

The employer is also obligated to compensate the employee for any reasonable expenses incurred in the course of employment, such as gasoline for a car, parts for repair work and so on. The employer must also provide work, direction and the agreed-upon wages for the employee. The employee must be informed of any special terms in the contractual relationship such as bonus arrangements and employee benefit packages.

Obligations of employee

The employee also has obligations to fulfill. The employee must possess the skills claimed and exercise them in a reasonably competent and careful manner. The employee has an obligation to follow any reasonable order pertaining to the employment and must treat the property of the employer carefully. The employee must be honest, loyal and courteous; an employee who does the work required but acts in an insubordinate or disloyal way can be fired. Similarly, an employee must be punctual and work for the time specified in the contract. There may also be an obligation to act in the best interests of the employer; an employee who becomes aware of financial opportunities in the course of performing his job, must offer them first to the employer. In the same way, if the employee uses company time or facilities without permission to do something which earns a profit, the employee is obligated to pay that profit to the employer.

General contract law applies to employment

Employment contracts are often not formal or written documents. As with any form of contract, it is always good advice to have the contract in writing clearly stating the provisions that are important for the parties. These provisions may include not only the rate of pay, hours of work, a description of what services are required and for what period, but also more unique terms such as a restrictive covenant, or how much notice is to be given upon termination.

As with other contracts these terms cannot be imposed on the employee after the employment has begun. All of the ingredients necessary for a contract to exist must be present. Problems may arise if after working on the job for some time the employee is persuaded to accept a new employment contract which includes a restrictive covenant or a limited period of notice to be given upon termination. These provisions are often not binding on the employee because of a failure of consideration.

In some provinces, if the term of a contract of employment is for a definite period of time and will not be completed in one year, the contract must be in writing to satisfy the requirements of the *Statute of Frauds*.[6] Also, when a restrictive covenant is included that commits the employee not to work in a particular geographic area or in a particular industry after leaving the position, it has to be for a reasonable time and area, be the most appropriate way of protecting the employer's interests and not be against the public interest. For example, if an employer invents a special production method, the secrecy of which could only be maintained by requiring that the employees commit themselves not to work in a similar industry for a period of time, a restrictive covenant in the contract of employment to that effect would likely be valid. But in general the courts are much more reluctant to enforce restrictive covenants in employment contracts because of the danger of denying the employee the ability to earn a livelihood and because of the normally weaker bargaining position of the employee.

Restrictive covenants must be reasonable

Termination

An employment contract may provide for its own discharge or parties can mutually agree to bring it to an end. However, most contracts of employment are for an indefinite period of time with no reference to notice requirements, and rules have been established by which contracts can be terminated at the instigation of either party. An employee can be terminated with reasonable notice when there is no special employment contract or collective agreement, to the contrary. Alternatively, the employee can be given pay comparable to what would have been earned if proper notice had been given. Such monies are called **pay in lieu of notice**.

Reasonable notice of termination required of both employer and employee

Most people have little difficulty appreciating an employee's right to leave a job, but they may forget that an employer has the right to dismiss an employee for any reason, providing appropriate notice is given. An employee can leave a job for any reason, just as an employer can terminate the relationship for any reason as long as sufficient notice is given. Provincial and federal human rights legislation including the *Charter of Rights and Freedoms* restricts this right of an employer to terminate.[7] When the dismissal amounts to a violation of the provisions of provincial or federal human rights statutes, such as discrimination on the basis of sex, religion, colour or age, employers are liable to the enforcement provisions of that legislation and may find themselves involved in a wrongful dismissal action.[8]

One important difficulty in employment relations is determining what constitutes proper notice. The employment contract itself may have a provision setting out what is proper notice for termination of that agreement. In the event that no such term is included, common law has provided that **reasonable notice** must be given. The amount of time constituting reasonable notice varies with the circumstances. In the past if a person were hired on a weekly basis, one week's notice was appropriate. And a person who was hired on a monthly basis would require only one month's notice. However, this is no longer the case; the courts will take other factors into consideration, such as length of service, the type of job, the employee's

What constitutes reasonable notice varies with circumstances

6. The general requirement that contracts to be performed beyond one year be in writing does not apply in British Columbia, Ontario or Manitoba.

7. *Constitution Act (1982)* Part 1; *Canadian Charter of Rights and Freedoms*, Sections 15, 16 and 28.

8. For example, *Human Rights Code*, R.S.O. (1990) c. H.19 s. 5: *Human Rights, Citizenship and Multiculturalism Act*, R.S.A. (1980) c. H-11.7 s. 7.

qualifications and age and the nature of the job market, to determine what constitutes reasonable notice.[9] As a result, in some cases involving long-term, senior managers, the required notice period may be as long as two years. Note that long-term notice periods have recently been applied to much-lower-level employees as well.

Newly hired employees during a probationary period are usually not entitled to very much notice. However, there are two important exceptions. A probationary employee who has not been informed of the basis on which his performance will be evaluated, or an employee who has been persuaded to leave another job but is terminated after a short time may be entitled to a significantly greater period of notice. In addition to these common law provisions, most provinces have included provisions for minimum notice of dismissal in their employment standards regulations. For example, Alberta's *Employment Standards Code* stipulates that employers must give their employees written notice of termination of at least one week, if employed more than three months but less than two years. If employed two years but less than four years, the minimum notice increases to two weeks, and this minimum notice continues to increase with length of service until it peaks at 8 weeks if the individual has been employed more than ten years.[10] Trade unions usually insist that provisions relating to the circumstances under which employees can be dismissed and to the nature of notice or pay in lieu of that notice be included in the collective agreements they negotiate with the employer.

Notice not required when there is just cause

An employer who can demonstrate that an employee is being fired for **just cause** is not required to give notice. An employee can be dismissed without notice for such things as serious absenteeism, consistent tardiness, open disobedience, habitual negligence, incompetence, harassing other employees, drinking on the job or immoral conduct on or off the job that reflects badly on the employer. Even swearing at the

employer has been determined to be serious misconduct sufficient to justify dismissal. In the example used to introduce this chapter, it was the employee's dishonesty in lying to his employer about how many calls he had made that justified the dismissal. Such dishonesty need not be tolerated by the employer no matter how sympathetic the plight of the employee. Great care must be taken when dismissing employees for dishonesty such as fraud or theft to ensure that the accusations are accurate and the evidence firm. The courts have awarded significant damages for wrongful dismissal including punitive damages when the charges have proved false. Also, care should be taken to ensure that when a person is dismissed because of immoral or

---

REASONABLE NOTICE CAN BE SIGNIFICANT EVEN FOR NEW EMPLOYEES

Mr. Isaacs had a good education and a successful career with another company when he was persuaded to move to MHG International to be its purchasing agent. He was hired in anticipation of a large project involving the construction of a petrochemical plant. That project was abandoned, and seven months after he was hired Mr. Isaacs was terminated. He sued for wrongful dismissal. The question facing the court was how much notice should have been given.

Although Isaacs had only been working for the company for seven months, the court held that he was entitled to nine months' notice or pay in lieu of notice. This was upheld at the appeal level on the basis that he was persuaded to leave secure employment for this new job.

Isaacs v. MHG International Ltd., 7 D.L.R. (4th) 570 (Ontario Court of Appeal)

---

9. *Bardal v. The Globe and Mail Ltd.* 24 D.L.R. (2d) 140 (H.C.).

10. *Employment Standards Code*, S.A. (1996) c. E-10.3 s. 56.

inappropriate activities, it is not a case of discrimination. The human rights tribunals of the various jurisdictions are very active in prosecuting such violations.

In the past employees who became seriously ill could be discharged without notice if they could no longer perform their job. Although it was not the employee's fault, the employer was not required to pay for work that was not performed. In effect the employment contract was frustrated. Today, however, there is a legislated duty to accommodate disabled workers that are still able to work and human rights commissions are very willing to rule against employers who fire workers because of illness or disability too quickly. The *Human Rights, Citizenship and Multiculturalism Act* of Alberta states the following:

7(1) No employer shall
(a)   refuse to employ or refuse to continue to employ any person, or
(b)   discriminate against any person with regard to employment or any
      term or condition of employment,
because of race, religious beliefs, colour, gender, physical disability, mental disability, marital status, age, ancestry, place of origin, family status or source of income of that person or of any other person.

In enforcing the above provision, the courts have ruled that employers have a legal duty to take reasonable steps to accommodate an employee's individual needs. However, this legal duty does not apply if the only way to resolve the problem will cause the employer "undue hardship"; that is, hardship that is substantial in nature.

The employer must take great care to comply with the human rights legislation and the *Workers' Compensation Act* provisions designed to protect disabled or injured workers. Today, most businesses have some form of illness and long-term disability insurance or policy in place to deal with this problem. But this is a double-edged sword. By having benefits such as these, they have anticipated the possibility of the worker becoming ill or disabled and can no longer claim that the employment contract is frustrated. Employers today must ensure that disabled workers who can work are accommodated and that those that can't have access to such benefits.

Although an employee is entitled to refuse to work because of dangerous working conditions, failure to perform a reasonable order is also grounds for dismissal without notice. Employers are well advised to let employees know when the level of performance is unacceptable as soon as it becomes apparent. It may appear to be easier to let the matter go, but the employer may then be faced with the argument that the employer's conduct and acceptance of the employee's performance led that employee to believe that the level of performance was appropriate. This argument will be especially difficult to overcome if bonuses or wage increases were given to the employee in the past despite the poor performance.

Dismissal without notice must be based on the wrongdoing of the employee or his or her failure to perform the job. Running out of work for the employee to do does not justify discharge without notice, even temporarily, unless specified in the employment contract. Provisions in collective agreements often cover layoffs and recalls, and several provinces have included provisions covering temporary layoffs in their employment standards legislation.[11] Alberta's *Employment Standards Code* stipulates that on the 60th consecutive day of a temporary layoff, employment terminates and the employer must pay the employee termination pay on that day. However, if wages or other payments are made to or for the benefit of the employee during the layoff, employment may terminate when the payments cease.[12] But in the absence of one of these factors an employee who has been temporarily laid off is

---

11. For example, *Employment Standards Code*, S.A. (1996) c. E-10.3 ss. 62-63.
12. *Ibid.*, s. 63.

IN PRACTICE

Top Court Orders Compensation for Wrongful Hiring

First there was wrongful dismissal, now there is wrongful hiring.

The Supreme Court of Canada ruled yesterday that workers can sue their employers if they are hired based on misleading and inaccurate information during a job interview.

In a 6-0 ruling, the top court ordered Ottawa computer software giant Cognos Inc. to pay $67 224 plus interest to accountant Douglas Queen for making false representations when they hired him in 1983 from a secure, well-paying job in Calgary.

Queen was hired to help develop an accounting software package, but two weeks later, the company decided to shift research funds into a more successful product.

Justice Frank Iacobucci ruled the company should have told Queen, who was let go about 18 months later after a number of fill-in jobs, that the project was not yet a reality because senior management had not approved financing or conducted a feasibility study.

"[Queen] had a relatively secure and well-paying job in Calgary and he would not have chosen to move across the country if there was a substantial risk that the employment opportunity described to him would no longer exist after his arrival in Ottawa," wrote Iacobucci.

The court said employers must tell job applicants all "highly relevant information" about the nature and existence of the job and must ensure their statements are accurate.

Queen's lawyer Peter Bishop said employees now have a legal right to accurate information when they consider taking a new job.

"An employer can't just paint a bright rosy picture and give you the sun and the moon and then you take the job on and find that it's a totally different situation."

Source: Stephen Bindman, "Top Court Orders Compensation for Wrongful Hiring," *Southam News*, 1993.

Wrongful dismissal can be grounds for court action

entitled to treat that as termination with its accompanying right to notice and compensation.

An employee who has been discharged without just cause or reasonable notice can sue for **wrongful dismissal** (or even "wrongful hiring"—see In Practice box). It should be noted that, if an employer fires a person without just cause, the person could not successfully claim wrongful dismissal if it later came to light that there had been just cause even though the employer was not aware of it.

JUST CAUSE CAN BE LEARNED AND ADVANCED AFTER THE FACT

King's employment was terminated because the transport company was being reorganized and he was offered a year's pay in lieu of notice. He sued for wrongful dismissal. Shortly after he had been given notice of his termination, he had informed his employer that another employee who was his subordinate had theft and alcohol problems and that he had not reported this as required. The court in this case had to decide whether this failure on the part of King amounted to cause and whether the company was allowed to raise it after giving him notice of termination and the offer of a year's severance pay. The court held that King's failure to report did constitute cause and could be used as grounds for his dismissal. Therefore, his action for wrongful dismissal failed, and he got nothing.

King v. Mayne Nickless Transport Inc., 114 D.L.R. (4th) 124 (British Columbia Court of Appeal)

EVEN EMPLOYEES CAN BE REQUIRED TO GIVE LENGTHY NOTICE

Savoy and Deringer were employees of Tree Savers, a relatively small company working in the oil industry. After giving Tree Savers' management two weeks' notice, they left and incorporated a company in competition with Tree Savers. Savoy and Deringer had been key employees at Tree Savers—Savoy was described as the whole sales arm of the company—and when they left they took some documents with them, including lists of contacts. Ducharme, who gave them financial aid and advice, and the company they created, Trojan, were also defendants. The court had to decide whether Savoy and the others were in violation of their fiduciary duty to their former employer. The answer was yes, and an injunction was issued ordering them to stop their offending conduct. Ducharme was also found liable for inducing them to breach their contract. The court decided that because the two men were senior, key employees, they should have given their employer 18 months' notice, and the damages awarded were calculated on this basis.

Tree Savers International Ltd. et al. v. Savoy et al., 87 D.L.R. (4th) 202 (Alberta Court of Appeal)

It is just as wrong for an employee to leave without proper notice as it is for the employer to terminate without proper notice. Although an employer has the right to sue an employee who leaves without giving reasonable notice, it is generally not worth the effort unless the employee is key in the organization such as a senior executive or salesperson. But where the employee holds a key position or possesses unique skills, and the employer experiences difficulty finding a replacement, losses may well be incurred, motivating the employer to sue for damages. In some situations, however, employees are entitled to leave without notice. An employee has the right to quit immediately if the employer gives an unreasonable or dangerous order, if the working conditions are dangerous and the employer refuses to correct them, or if the employer involves the employee in illegal or immoral activities.

When employees can leave without notice

Most cases in which former employees are sued involve accusations that a fiduciary duty has been breached or confidential information has been disclosed that has harmed the employer. For ordinary employees there is no general fiduciary duty and so nothing restricts departing employees from working for a competing business or even starting a competing business of their own. Only the existence of a restrictive covenant in their contract of employment will impose such an obligation and then only if it is considered reasonable and not against public policy. That competition, however, must start after they leave. An employee cannot start a business in competition with his or her employer before that employment is over. If information is gathered, customer lists copied, or customers solicited before termination, the departing employee can be sued. Similarly, if the departing employee takes confidential information and misuses it, that conduct is also actionable. Managers and other executives do have a fiduciary duty to their employer and may find themselves somewhat restricted in what they can do even after they leave their employment. It is much preferable for the employer to set out such restrictions clearly in the original employment contract.

Although there are conflicting cases in this area, it appears that an employer can breach a contract of employment without realizing it. When an employer unilaterally changes the nature of a job and requires an employee to do something entirely different or demotes that employee, the contract of employment may have been breached as much as if the person had been fired. Such breach of the employ-

Constructive dismissal— employer breaches contract when nature of job is changed without consent

ment contract on the part of the employer is known as **constructive dismissal**. In these circumstances, the employee may be entitled to treat the contract of employment as ended and sue for wrongful dismissal. On the other hand, if the employee accepts the change and the employment relationship continues, the parties have by mutual agreement simply changed the terms of the contract. This is not actionable.

A troublesome issue surrounds just how large or small the changes, made unilaterally by the employer, must be to constitute a constructive dismissal. If the employer maintains the salary rate but reduces the benefits package, is that a constructive dismissal? The Alberta Court of Appeal has decided that a reduction in benefits reducing annual compensation by 8%, where salaries are maintained, does not constitute a fundamental breach of an employment contract amounting to a repudiation of the contract.[13] The breach may constitute a minor breach compensable by damages, but does not necessarily constitute a constructive dismissal. In light of this decision, employees would be well advised to seek legal advice to determine whether a pay reduction is a constructive dismissal.

Of course, if the employer intentionally changes the employee's conditions of employment or job in order to humiliate or otherwise make that employee uncomfortable so that he will leave voluntarily, this is also constructive dismissal. Even when it was the conduct of the other employees that made continued employment impossible, such as the sexual harassment of female workers, if the employer does nothing to correct the situation that may be constructive dismissal. In a situation that amounts to constructive dismissal, the employee has an obligation to mitigate the damage. This obligation may extend to accepting the new position offered by the employer. Of course, there is no such obligation if accepting that new job would cause humiliation or otherwise create an impossible working situation, especially if bad relations have been created because of the way the termination took place.

Compensation based on notice that should have been given

The compensation awarded by the court for wrongful dismissal is usually calculated on the basis of the difference between the notice the person was given and the notice that should have been given. If a person who would normally have been entitled to three months' notice is fired without cause, he or she would be entitled to an amount equal to what would have been earned in those three months if the appropriate notice had been given. The court will reduce the amount of the award if the person obtains other employment within that period of time. There is an obligation to try to do this since the employee must try to mitigate his or her losses. In determining the damages to be paid, the court will in rare situations take into consideration damage done to the person's reputation or mental distress resulting from the way the dismissal took place and false claims made by the employer. The court will even award punitive damages against the employer where appropriate. (See *Deildal v. Tod Mountain Development Ltd.*, 28 C.C.E.L. (2d) 1 (B.C.C.A.), where damages equalling 33 months' pay was awarded. A notice period of 15 months would have been appropriate, but the employer's unfounded allegations of gross incompetence and misappropriation of funds made it difficult for the employee to find alternative work. An additional 12 months' notice was thus justified. A sum equalling six months pay was also awarded as aggravated damages.)

Obligation to mitigate losses

A person who is dismissed from a corporation will normally sue the corporation itself for damages. But, if the individual implementing the decision to discharge the

---

13. *Hamilton & Olsen Surveys Ltd. v. Otto*, 12 Alta. L.R. (3d) 431 (Alta. C.A.). Leave to appeal to S.C.C. dismissed.

employee has committed a tort, such as defamation, that conduct is also actionable against both the corporation and the manager who made the defamatory statement.

Claims for damages in wrongful dismissal actions will often include lost fringe benefits and pension rights if they were part of the employment contract. Damages are the appropriate remedy for wrongful dismissal and it is rare for the court to order that an employee be given back the job. Reinstatement is more common when collective agreements are involved since disputes are usually settled by an arbitrator and are not under the jurisdiction of the courts. Some jurisdictions have provided for reinstatement in non-union situations by statute. The *Canada Labour Code* is one example but such reinstatement is still rare.

Although employers have the right to dismiss employees for incompetence or misconduct, they must be extremely careful in so doing. An employer must have the clearest evidence of the misconduct or incompetence and with the latter must demonstrate that the employee has been given a reasonable opportunity to improve. Failure to substantiate just cause will likely result in a successful action by the employee for wrongful dismissal and may include an award of punitive damages and compensation for mental distress.

Liability of Employer

An employer can be held liable for the tort committed by an employee during the course of employment. This is the principle of vicarious liability discussed in Chapter 2. Even though the employer has done nothing wrong, the employer is responsible for the wrongful conduct of the employee under the theory that, since the employer has benefited from the work of the employee, the employer should be responsible when that work causes injury.

But the employer's liability does not forgive the employee for the conduct that forms the basis of the tort. In fact, the employee, the employer or both can be required to compensate the victim. The employer may have done nothing wrong under these circumstances but the employer does bear responsibility to compensate anyone injured by an employee in the process of work.

It must be emphasized, however, that vicarious liability imposed on an employer is limited to torts committed during the course of employment. An employer is not liable for conduct not connected to the employment (when the employee was "on a frolic of his own"). The problem of whether the tort was committed during the course of employment is not determined only on the basis of whether the incident occurred during working hours. The real question is whether the act complained of was part of the employment activity. If Pawluk is asked by his employer to deliver a letter to Caron on his way home from work and, rushing to do so, he carelessly knocks over and injures a fellow pedestrian, the pedestrian could sue not only Pawluk but his employer as well. The negligent act occurred during the course of employment even though it did not happen during working hours. But if the same employee decides to go across the street to do his personal banking during working hours and carelessly injures someone in the process, the injured person could sue only Pawluk and not his employer. In this case, Pawluk is "on a frolic of his own." He is not involved in employment activities, even though the accident occurs during working hours, so there is no vicarious liability.

An even more fundamental question than whether the tort was committed during the course of employment is whether there was an employment relationship at all.

Employer liable for torts committed by employee while on the job

In general, if there is no employment relationship, there is no vicarious liability. This is why the tests discussed above for determining if an employment relationship exists are so important. (Some exceptions to the requirement that employment is needed for vicarious liability will be discussed in the next chapter.) Some jurisdictions have legislated vicarious liability in special situations. For example, in Alberta and some other provinces, the owner of a motor vehicle is vicariously liable for any torts committed by someone to whom the vehicle has been loaned. The driver "shall be deemed to be the agent or servant of the owner of the motor vehicle and to be employed as such, and shall be deemed to be driving the motor vehicle in the course of his employment."[14]

When an employer is held vicariously liable for the torts committed by an employee, that employer will generally have the right to turn to the employee to compensate for the losses suffered. This remedy is often hollow, however, since the employee is usually in no financial position to pay such compensation.

Legislation

As a consequence of the relatively weak position of individual employees in the employment relationship, employees have tended to band together to exert greater pressure on the employer. Such collective action is now governed by legislation and will be discussed under "Collective Bargaining" later in this chapter. A considerable amount of legislation has also been passed which is designed to protect employees, whether unionized or not, by setting minimum standards of safety, remuneration, hours of work and other benefits. Conditions of employment normally fall under the provincial jurisdiction, but there are a number of activities such as banking, the military, activities on Indian reserves, the post office, telephone and broadcast companies, airlines, railroads and steamships that fall under federal jurisdiction. Employees working in these federally regulated sectors of the economy are protected by the provisions of the *Canada Labour Code* and the *Canadian Human Rights Act.* Most provinces have concentrated their employee welfare legislation into one statute, generally called the *Employment Standards Act* or *Labour Standards Act.* Alberta's *Employment Standards Code* will be used here as an illustration.[15]

Employment Standards.

Machtinger v. HOJ Industries Ltd.[16]

This case involves two employees, Mr. Machtinger and Mr. Lefebvre. They had provisions in their employment contracts whereby they were to be given minimal notice upon termination. Mr. Lefebvre was to be given two weeks' notice and Mr. Machtinger was entitled to no notice at all. Both had been working for the employer for a number of years and if it were not for these clauses in their contracts, by the judge's estimate, they would be entitled to seven months' notice in the case of Mr. Machtinger and seven-and-a-half months in the case of Mr. Lefebvre. In addition to these factors, under the *Employment Standards Act* of Ontario they would be entitled to four weeks' notice. Another section of that act provides that this requirement is a minimum, not a maximum.

14. *Highway Traffic Act,* R.S.A. (1980) c. H-7 s. 181.

15. *Employment Standards Code,* S.A. (1996) c. E-10.3.

16. 91 D.L.R. (4th) 491 (Supreme Court of Canada).

In fact the employer gave both of these employees four weeks' notice, despite what their contract said, thus satisfying the minimum requirement of the *Act*. Both employees brought a wrongful dismissal action against the employer demanding compensation.

The Supreme Court of Canada held that any contractual term that did not comply with the minimum standards set out in the *Act* was a nullity, and therefore the employment provisions found in the contract were void. The court then observed that the *Employment Standards Act* merely set the minimum standard, and since the reasonable amount of notice that these people would have been entitled to under the common law was seven and seven-and-a-half months, that longer notice requirement prevailed.

This is a very interesting case illustrating how employment contracts can have provisions in them that override the common law, but those provisions must not override the minimum standards set out in the statute. It also illustrates that when such a contractual provision doesn't meet the minimum standards set out in the statute, it is void and the courts are not bound to consider even the spirit of that provision; the court could award the much more generous "reasonable amount" found in the common law. Great care must be taken by employers who attempt to reduce this common law notice period to make sure that what results is not in violation of the statue. They must provide for a longer notice period than the minimum there set out. And in general it should always be remembered that in all provinces the *Employment Standards Act* or its equivalent sets standards that are a minimum, not a maximum.

It must be emphasized at the outset that statutory provisions set a minimum standard only. The *Code* further stipulates that any agreement that the protections or remedies available under the legislation do not apply is against public policy and void.[17] Where the parties have agreed to a higher standard or where a higher standard is imposed by the common law, that higher standard will normally prevail.[18] But even the minimum statutory provisions do not treat all employees equally. The government may, by regulation, exempt certain employments or modify certain provisions in respect of an employment.[19] In other words, employers may be excused from paying minimum wage to real estate brokers or articling students, and overtime may be calculated differently for ambulance attendants and taxicab drivers.[20]

Payment of Earnings.[21]

Earnings is defined as including wages (salary, commission or other remuneration), overtime pay, vacation pay, general holiday pay and termination pay. Wages and overtime are to be paid at least monthly; payment being made within 10 days of the end of each pay period. Employers are not entitled to make deductions for faulty work; nor are deductions for cash shortages allowed if individuals other than the employee have access to the cash. Employers are required to notify employees of any change in pay rate before the start of a pay period, allowing employees the opportunity to refuse to work for any lower rate and to demand and collect the

17. *Employment Standards Code*, S.A. (1996) c. E-10.3 s. 4.

18. *Ibid.*, s. 3.

19. *Ibid.*, s. 6.

20. *Employment Standards Regulation*, AR 14/97.

21. *Employment Standards Code*, S.A. (1996) c. E-10.3 Part 2, Division 1.

EMPLOYMENT STANDARDS ACT SETS MINIMUM STANDARDS

In February, 1992 Smith resigned his position, giving seven months' notice. It was clear that he was trying to be helpful to the company and give them time to train a replacement and he also volunteered to come in on an on-call basis after the employment ended. The company, on the other hand, rejected that notice period, fired him immediately and gave him eight weeks' pay as provided under Alberta's *Employment Standards Act*. Smith applied for permission to sue for wrongful dismissal, relying on the considerably longer notice period found in common law. The court looked at the *Employment Standards Act* and found that there was a provision that entitled the employer upon receiving such notice to give pay in lieu of notice based on the time periods as set out in the *Act*. The problem was whether this barred Smith's common law action. The court found that the company's action in effect rejected Smith's resignation and notice and instead terminated his employment pursuant to the provisions of the *Act*. The *Act* sets only a minimum notice period and does not affect an employee's right to seek a greater remedy that might be available under the common law. Smith therefore had the right to sue for wrongful dismissal and seek greater damages, that is, a longer notice period than that set out in the *Act*.

Smith v. Hostess Frito-Lay Co., 116 D.L.R. (4th) 378 (Alberta Court of Appeal)

old pay rate if not so notified. The *Code* also requires employers to provide employees with a statement each pay period, detailing hours of work (regular and overtime), earnings paid, and deductions made. Employment records must be retained for at least three years.

Hours of Work and Overtime.[22]

Unless there is an accident or emergency, or urgent work is necessary, employees are to work no more than 12 hours in a day. A rest period of 30 minutes is required for every shift exceeding five hours in length. One day of rest per week is to be given, but these days off can be accumulated and taken consecutively, so long as at least four days off are taken after 24 consecutive workdays. Overtime pay is at least 1.5 times the regular wage rate for all overtime hours worked, unless time off in lieu of overtime is taken in accordance with an overtime agreement between the employer and employee. Overtime is to be paid if an employee works more than eight hours in a day, or more than 44 hours in a week. Note that the *Employment Standards Regulation* has modified this entitlement for employees working in various sectors, including the trucking industry, nursery industry, oil well servicing industry, ambulance industry, etc. Other employees do not receive overtime entitlement at all, such as employees engaged in supervisory or managerial capacities.[23]

Vacation and Holiday Entitlements.[24]

An employee becomes entitled to an annual vacation of at least two weeks after each of the first four years of employment (with vacation pay equal to 4 percent of gross regular earnings or two weeks' salary). The entitlement increases to a minimum three weeks' vacation (with 6 percent of gross regular earnings or three weeks' salary) after five years of service. General holidays in Alberta are New Year's Day,

22. *Ibid.*, Part 2, Division 3 and 4.
23. *Employment Standards Regulation*, AR 14/97.
24. *Employment Standards Code*, S.A. (1996) c. E-10.3 Part 2, Division 5 and 6.

Alberta Family Day, Good Friday, Victoria Day, Canada Day, Labour Day, Thanksgiving Day, Remembrance Day, Christmas Day and any other day designated by the employer. Only employees who have worked for an employer 30 days in the 12 months preceding the holiday are entitled to general holidays and general holiday pay. The employee then receives a regular day's pay if the holiday falls on a regular workday and the employee is not required to work. If required to work, the employee is entitled to regular pay plus time-and-one-half. Part-time employees are also entitled to holiday pay if the holiday falls on one of their regularly scheduled workdays and they do work.

Maternity and Adoption Benefits.[25]

To be eligible for these benefits, the employee must have been employed by the employer for at least 12 consecutive months. Eighteen weeks' maternity leave (without pay) is allowed to the mother. Paternity leave is not available under the Alberta legislation. Adoption leave, however, is available to either parent, but it is only eight weeks in length and only applies where the child being adopted is under three years of age. The *Code* requires the employee to give two weeks' notice of the employee's intent to commence leave and to return to work. The employer is required to reinstate the employee or provide alternative comparable work at the same level of pay when the employee resumes employment at the conclusion of the leave.

Termination.[26]

As under the common law, the *Code* recognizes that an employer can terminate the employment of an employee by providing notice or pay in lieu of notice or a combination of the two. Where the *Code* and the common law differ is in the calculation of the amount of notice. The *Code* does not consider the nature of the employment, but only its length, when determining adequate notice. It requires an employer to give one week's notice to an employee who has worked more than three months but less than two years for the employer. As service length increases, so does notice/pay: over two years' service—two weeks' notice/pay; over four years' service—four weeks' notice/pay; over six years' service—five weeks' notice/pay; over eight years' service— six weeks' notice/pay; over 10 years' service—eight weeks' notice/pay. An employee likewise is required to provide the employer notice of his intention to terminate employment of at least one week if employed from three months to two years; two weeks if employed for two years or more. The *Code* sets out several situations where notice is not required, such as where the employee is being fired for just cause, or where the employment was seasonal and the season has been completed. The employee is not required to give notice where the employee leaves in response to a reduction in wage rate, or in response to dangerous working conditions. In such situations, the employee is reacting to a breach of the contract by the employer.

Employment of Minors and of Persons with Disabilities.[27]

Regulations made pursuant to the *Code* currently allow children under 15 years of age to work in Alberta within certain restrictions. Parental consent is generally required and the hours of work are limited to two hours on school days and eight hours on non-school days, and no work is allowed between 9:00 p.m. and 6:00 a.m.

---

25. *Ibid.*, Part 2, Division 7.

26. *Ibid.*, Part 2, Division 8.

27. *Ibid.*, Part 2, Division 9 and 10.

Similarly, young persons aged 15–17 years can work after midnight only with parental consent and with adult supervision. The Director of Employment Standards may issue a permit that enables employees who have disabilities to work for an employer for less than minimum wage, but only if this is a satisfactory arrangement between the employer and employee.

Complaints.[28]

Employees may file their written complaints with Employment Standards at any time while employed or within six months after their employment is terminated. The employment standards officer may dismiss the complaint if it is frivolous, vexatious or unsubstantiated, but this determination may be appealed. The officer is to attempt to mediate a settlement but if no agreement is reached and the officer determines that earnings are due to the employee, the officer may order payment to be made. On the other hand, if the officer determines that the employee was improperly terminated or laid off (because of garnishment of wages or because the employee requested anything to which he was entitled under the *Code*, etc.), the matter is to be referred to the Director. The Director is authorized to order reinstatement, compensation or both.

Recovery Provisions.[29]

The orders made by employment standards officers and by the Director are generally subject to appeal. Nonetheless, these orders may be filed with the Clerk of the Court of Queen's Bench and enforced as an order of the Court. If the employer is a corporation, the directors are personally liable for any unpaid wages earned during a period not exceeding six months. Collection is enhanced by Third Party Demands that enable the Director of Employment Standards to direct third parties who owe money to the employer to remit those sums to the Director instead. These monies can then be paid out to employees to compensate them for unpaid earnings. Collection is also enhanced by the creation of a deemed trust that gives the employees collectively a prior claim to $7500 of the employer's assets.

Most jurisdictions have passed similar legislation, but the provisions vary substantially from province to province. For example, Ontario's *Act* provides that when a person has been temporarily laid off for a period longer than 35 weeks of the year, he can treat this layoff as a termination. Alberta's *Code*, on the other hand, declares that a temporary layoff exceeding 60 days constitutes a termination. Accordingly, it is necessary to review the provisions of the relevant statute to determine the entitlements of a particular employee. Note that these statutes set minimum standards that do not override the common law requirements of reasonable notice. If parties agree to less than the statutory minimums, that agreement is against public policy and void, a problem that was illustrated in the *Machtinger* case used to introduce this section. Employers must be careful to comply with the legislation. As well, collective agreements can provide employees with greater earnings or benefits, but the statutory minimums must be satisfied.

Employees who face termination have a real concern. Recent case law makes it imperative that employees seek legal advice before claiming termination pay under the *Employment Standards Code*. The application for these minimal benefits may foreclose one's ability to later sue for damages for wrongful dismissal. If an employment standards officer determines that the complainant was terminated for cause, not

28. *Ibid.*, Part 3, Division 3.
29. *Ibid.*, Part 4.

only will the complainant's claim for termination pay under the *Code* fail, but if the employee later tries to sue for damages for wrongful dismissal, the Court may decide that the issue was already settled.[30] This is because the employment standards officer has already decided that the termination was not wrongful. Issue estoppel may cause the Court to dismiss the wrongful dismissal suit altogether without even hearing the details. Such were the results in the *Fayant*[31] and *Wong*[32] cases where the pleadings were struck out after issue estoppel was successfully raised.

Human Rights.

An area of employment law that is becoming much more significant is the area of protection of employee rights. With the passage of the *Charter of Rights and Freedoms* as well as federal and provincial human rights legislation, employers are required not only to ensure that they do not discriminate in their hiring and employment practices, but also to take active steps to ensure that these basic rights are protected. Although the *Charter* does not apply directly to most employment situations, it does have an important indirect effect, since the *Canadian Human Rights Act* and the various provincial human rights acts (including Alberta's *Human Rights, Citizenship and Multiculturalism Act*) must be consistent with the provisions of the *Charter*. Indeed, as mentioned in Chapter 1, the courts have gone so far as to read into these statutes provisions that they deem should have been included because of the *Charter*. Thus, homosexuals have been accorded protection under the *Canadian Human Rights Act* even though no such provision was included at the time.[33] Although these statutes apply to most social activities, their greatest contribution is in the field of employment. The statutes vary from jurisdiction to jurisdiction but they all contain provisions prohibiting discrimination on the basis of such factors as race, national or ethnic origin, colour, religion, sex, and in some cases age, marital status, physical or mental disability including stature and pardoned criminal convictions. (A review of Alberta's legislation follows, to illustrate how human rights legislation operates.)

Alberta's *Human Rights, Citizenship and Multiculturalism Act* prohibits discrimination on the following grounds: race, religious beliefs (including aboriginal spirituality), colour, gender, age, place of origin, ancestry, physical or mental disability, source of income, family status and marital status. The last three grounds were added to the list in 1996. Divorcees and single parents, as well as lower income Albertans receiving benefits such as social assistance or pensions, are all now afforded protection against discrimination by the *Act*.

If a violation occurs, the complainant can either complete a form or send a letter to the Human Rights and Citizenship Commission. A 12-month time limit, running from the date of the incident, applies. An appointed conciliator attempts to find a mutually agreeable solution. If that fails, an investigator is assigned. If the investigator determines that the complaint has merit, the matter may be referred to a Human Rights Panel. The Panel's decision has the same force as a court decision but the Panel's powers are limited. It can order the contravention to cease and the respondent to refrain from committing a similar contravention, and it can make available to the complainant the rights and opportunities denied. The Panel can take action to place the complainant in the position he should have been in but

Federal and provincial legislation prohibit most forms of discrimination

---

30. *Rasanen v. Rosemount Investments Ltd.,* 17 O.R. (3rd) 267 (Ont. C.A.).

31. *Fayant v. Campbell's Maple Village Ltd.,* 3 W.W.R. 171 (Alta. Q.B.).

32. *Wong v. Shell Canada Ltd.,* 35 Alta. L.R. (3d) 1 (Alta. C.A.).

33. *Haig v. Canada* [1993] 2 S.C.R. 995.

for the contravention. It can order compensation be paid the complainant equaling the wages or income lost or expenses incurred as a consequence of the contravention. Reinstatement of an employee wrongfully terminated is within its power, but awarding damages is not.

The *Act* prohibits discrimination with regard to any term or condition of employment based on the employee's race, religion, etc. It also prohibits the refusal to hire or fire any person based on one of the prohibited grounds for discrimination.

Another area the legislation addresses is discrimination during pre-employment inquiries. Job applications and advertisements must be reviewed by employers to ensure that they do not directly or indirectly express a limitation or preference based on race, colour, gender, etc. The forms used cannot require an applicant to furnish information concerning their gender, age, marital status, etc. Accordingly, unless a bona fide occupational requirement exists that would justify such a request, employers should refrain from requesting photographs or requesting the applicant's gender, previous name, marital status, date of birth, and religion to be supplied in the application form.

Harassment is a form of discrimination that occurs when one subjects another person to unwelcome verbal or physical conduct because of their colour, gender, age or other characteristic. Unwanted physical contact, jokes or insults are harassment when they negatively affect the working environment. Sexual harassment is just one example.

A particular problem arises when an employee is terminated because of harassment of other employees before the employer has developed a company policy for dealing with such harassment. Failure to take action to protect the employee would make the employer subject to a complaint to the tribunal. But to terminate the harassing employee without such a policy might leave the employer open to a wrongful dismissal action by the fired employee in the courts.

It is vital for employers to be proactive and take positive steps to develop a harassment and discrimination policy that makes it clear such conduct will not be tolerated and spells out what disciplinary steps might be taken.

Many employers have gone beyond dealing with just sexual harassment and have included in their harassment policy any situation where one party in the organization inappropriately misuses the power of his or her position over another.

This positive obligation on the employer to protect the employee from wrongful conduct of others in the workplace has been taken further. Employers now have an obligation to take steps to accommodate employees with special needs. Employers are expected to make reasonable efforts to accommodate employees' individual needs, but this duty does not apply if resolving the problem would cause the employer undue hardship. Employers with only a few employees are not faced with obligations as great as those imposed on large employers that must bear the expense of changing the physical environment of the office or plant to accommodate disabled employees such as the visually impaired or wheelchair-bound. Work schedules may have to be modified to accommodate a worker who, because of chronic illness such as AIDS or partial disability, can only do limited work, or even work only part-time. When religious beliefs require time off work for holidays, the employer will be required to change the work schedule to accommodate the employee. Where religious regalia such as a turban must be worn, rules should be changed to allow this. But where there is a bona fide occupational requirement that a person be of a particular stature, wear a hard hat, etc., that occupational requirement will prevail, especially if it is safety-related. But it is vital that that requirement be a necessary part of the job.[34]

Employers are not to discriminate on the basis of gender. The *Act* specifically ensures that men and women working in the same establishment and performing "similar or substantially similar work" be paid at the same rate.[35] Any pay differentials must be based on factors other than gender. It is also illegal for employers to reduce a rate of pay to equalize pay rates. Employees who were paid less than their counterparts are given the choice of suing to obtain the pay differential for the preceding 12 months or filing a complaint under the *Act*.

Note that discrimination in the workplace has prompted the passage of various Employment Equity Acts as well. Statutes have been enacted requiring that public sector employers and in some cases, private sector employers, take active steps to correct imbalances that historically have existed in various types of professions and employment. When there is a predominance of males or females in a particular occupation such as nursing or engineering or when racial groups or disabled workers are underrepresented, employers are required to have a plan to redress the imbalance. This usually means giving preferential treatment to those job applicants or candidates for advancement who belong to underrepresented minority groups. Such affirmative action programs are extremely controversial, as they generally involve reverse discrimination, which is just as distasteful when directed at individuals who belong to the overrepresented group. In fact, Ontario has recently repealed its *Employment Equity Act*. It is difficult, however, to imagine any other solution than affirmative action programs to the historical problem of imbalance in the workplace, and so such programs are specifically authorized under Section 15, Subsection 2 of the *Charter of Rights and Freedoms*.

A very difficult problem arises with mandatory retirement policies in place in many jurisdictions in both private and public sector employment. The *Charter* and many provincial human rights codes prohibit discrimination on the basis of age. It is generally thought a good thing to require people to retire in order to open up new jobs for the youth. While this may be attractive from a social policy point of view, from the point of view of the person being required to retire at 65, it can be a disaster, especially when they may not be in a financial position to do so and are still in good health and able to do their jobs.

Some jurisdictions are moving to do away with mandatory retirement, but the Supreme Court of Canada in several important decisions has held that where such a mandatory retirement policy is allowed under provincial human rights legislation, it does not violate the provisions of the *Charter of Rights and Freedoms* and is permissible. In areas of public service, although such forced retirement clearly is discrimination on the basis of age and prohibited under Section 15, because it is for the social good, it is "reasonable" under Section 1 and permissible. In the private sector, the *Charter* does not govern employment relations, and the provincial human rights statutes that permit this kind of discrimination are not in contravention of the *Charter* for the same reason.[36]

The obligations of employers in the field of employee rights are changing at a significant rate. Furthermore, more employees are now demanding implementation of policies such as those that will prevent the various forms of harassment that can take place in the workplace, accommodate disabled workers or give same-sex

34. *Human Rights, Citizenship and Multiculturalism Act*, R.S.A. (1980) c. H-11.7 s. 7(3).

35. *Ibid.*, s. 6.

36. *Harrison v. University of British Columbia*, 77 D.L.R. (4th) 55 (S.C.C.). and *Dickason v. University of Alberta* (1992) 2 S.C.R. 1103.

couples the same benefits as others. Employers should therefore take care when determining which policies to implement.

In addition to the human rights legislation discussed above, every province and the federal government has legislation ensuring that a woman can get time off without pay for maternity purposes and be guaranteed that she will have a job to come back to without losing seniority. An example of this legislation is the Alberta *Employment Standards Code* discussed above.[37] It is illegal to discriminate against a woman because of pregnancy for this would constitute gender discrimination. Accordingly, employers should refrain from asking women at job interviews whether they are pregnant or plan to have children. Employers also cannot fire or demote an employee because of pregnancy.[38]

Child Labour Regulations.

Use of children in workforce tightly regulated

Some of the most significant labour legislation deals with child labour. Every jurisdiction in Canada has legislation designed to control the use of children in the workforce although not every jurisdiction sets a minimum age for work. These provisions vary not only between provinces but also within a province and with the nature of the work involved. For instance, in Alberta, adolescents (aged 12 to 15 years) are restricted to working as delivery persons, clerks in offices or retail stores, or workers in an occupation approved by the Director. In hotels, restaurants and shops, the minimum age is 15 years and the young employee must be in the continuous presence of at least one adult.[39] The *School Act* requires children to stay in school until reaching 16 years of age, and employment of children during normal school hours is generally prohibited. Two exceptions that excuse children from school attendance are vocational training through employment and approved work experience programs.[40] The federal government does not set a minimum age of employment, but does set guidelines designed to control abuses, such as restricting the hours in which a child can work and requiring that a certain wage level be maintained.[41]

Workers' Compensation.

Workers' compensation— compulsory insurance coverage

The common law was often unable to provide an appropriate remedy for an employee injured on the job. This was especially true when the accident resulted from the employee's own carelessness. All provinces and the federal government have now passed workers' compensation legislation which provides a compulsory insurance program covering accidents that take place on the job. The legislation sets rates of compensation to be paid for different types of injuries and establishes a board that hears and adjudicates the claims of injured employees. The system is essentially a no-fault insurance scheme in which benefits are paid to injured workers or to their families in the event of death, and careless conduct on the part of the worker will not disqualify an injured employee from receiving compensation. The program is

37. *Employment Standards Code*, S.A. (1996) c. E-10.3 Part 2 Division 7. The maternity leave period varies with the jurisdiction, but in Alberta it is 18 weeks in length with a prenatal period varying from six to 12 weeks and a postnatal period of six weeks.

38. *Human Rights, Citizenship and Multiculturalism Act*, R.S.A (1980) c. H-11.7 s. 7(1), s. 38(2).

39. *Employment Standards Regulation*, AR 14/97 Part 5.

40. *Employment Standards Code*, S.A. (1996) c. E-10.3 s. 66.

41. For example, under the *Canada Shipping Act*, R.S.C. (1985) c. S-9 s. 273, the minimum age in that industry is 15, with exceptions.

financed by assessments levied by the various workers' compensation boards in each province against the employers. The amount levied can vary with the risks associated with the industry involved. Some types of industries are exempted from workers' compensation coverage, such as farming operations, secretarial services and travel agencies. If one is self-employed, coverage is not automatic; however, one may purchase personal coverage and thus receive the same compensation benefits injured workers receive. British Columbia has extended workers' compensation coverage to almost all workers in the province.

A significant aspect of workers' compensation legislation in most jurisdictions is that the worker gives up the right to any other compensation which would normally be available under common law. Thus, even if it can be established that another worker or the employer was negligent, the employee covered cannot sue. The employee is limited to the benefits bestowed by the workers' compensation legislation, which might be considerably less than what the employee would have received through normal litigation.

Worker gives up right to any other compensation and cannot sue

A significant limitation on the availability of workers' compensation is that the injury complained of must have arisen in the course of the employment. While this restriction is not normally a problem, in cases of disease it is often difficult to determine that the disease, such as emphysema for example, was caused by the work of the employee.

Health and Safety.

In conjunction with workers' compensation legislation, the federal government and the provinces have passed legislation controlling health and safety conditions in the workplace. The objective of this legislation is not only to help the worker by providing a safer working environment but also to keep the premiums paid by employers into the workers' compensation fund at a manageable level by reducing the number of claims. In some jurisdictions, health and safety requirements are embodied in general labour statutes, as in the *Canada Labour Code*. In other jurisdictions, separate statutes are in place dealing with employment, and health and safety as in Alberta's *Occupational Health and Safety Act.*[42] The main thrust of these statutes is

1. *To provide safer working conditions.* This is done by requiring fencing of hazardous areas, safety netting, proper shielding of equipment, environmental control and so on.

2. *To ensure safe employment practices,* such as requiring the supply and use of hard hats, goggles and protective clothing.

3. *To establish programs to educate both the employer and the employee* on how to create a safer working environment for all concerned.

These objectives are facilitated through the establishment of a board with the power to hear complaints and enforce correction. These statutes also provide for inspectors who have the power to inspect and investigate working conditions in any place of employment without a warrant. When these inspectors encounter dangerous conditions, such as lack of fencing or shielding, poor safety practices such as failure to use hard hats or safety lines or environmental contamination caused by hazardous chemicals, fumes or dust, they have the right to order the problem cor-

Safety boards ensure regulations are adhered to

42. *Occupational Health and Safety Act,* R.S.A. (1980) c. O-2.

rected or, if it is serious enough, to require that the activity stop altogether and the job be shut down. When serious injury or death results from violation of these provisions, provinces are more willing to initiate prosecution. Important changes to Ontario's legislation have increased the maximum fines levied and resulted in directors of corporations being held personally responsible for harmful and dangerous practices.

Employment Insurance.

Employment insurance is federal jurisdiction

The provision of insurance coverage for unemployed workers would normally fall under the jurisdiction of the provinces under the *Constitution Act 1867.* But an amendment to that *Act*, made with the consent of all the provinces, gives the federal government that responsibility. The *Employment Insurance Act* sets up a scheme whereby both employers and employees pay into a government-supplemented fund.[43] Upon being laid off, an employee applies to and is paid out of this fund for a specific period of time, called the entitlement period. The payments made are insurance premiums. This means that a claimant is only entitled to receive payments when the required qualifications are met and then only such benefits as are permitted under the legislation. The benefits received may bear little or no relation to the amount paid in, although the total benefits the employee is entitled to will be based on the number of weeks worked before the claim and the amount of wages he or she had been receiving. It is now very difficult for a person who voluntarily leaves employment to receive unemployment insurance benefits, or employment insurance benefits as they are now called. No benefits will be paid to those who are on strike or locked out, but those who can't work because others are on strike will receive benefits provided they otherwise qualify. A severance package from the employer will also limit eligibility and no benefits will be paid until the severance period is over. Benefits are also paid under the act to those who are unable to work because of illness or disability and for pregnancy and adoption. As with other federal programs, the worker may appeal any decisions made such as entitlement to benefits to an administrative body set up under the legislation. The rights of individuals before such administrative tribunals will be discussed in Chapter 16.

Employee must meet qualifications to receive benefits

Other Legislation

Many other statutes affect the employment relationship. Most jurisdictions have legislation controlling the apprenticeship process and trade schools. (NAIT and SAIT are, for example, governed by the *Technical Institutes Act*, S.A. (1981) c. T-3.1.) Some jurisdictions have legislation controlling the licensing of private employment agencies and restricting the types of payments they can receive from their clients. And, as has been discussed in other chapters, legislation such as the *Bankruptcy and Insolvency Act* and the *Mechanics'* or *Builders' Lien Acts* provide security to the worker in the payment of wages. All jurisdictions have legislation dealing with special categories of employees, such as teachers and public servants.

COLLECTIVE BARGAINING

The most significant impact on labour legislation in Canada has come from the process of collective action brought about by unionized workers. Although a

43. *Employment Insurance Act*, S.C. (1996) c. 23.

significant part of the Canadian workforce is unionized in both the public and the private sector, this percentage has been declining in recent years. The trade union movement today finds itself in the position of fighting to hold onto what it has gained and to resist the trend of changes in various statutes that are detrimental to its interests.

The modern trade union movement can trace its roots back to the Industrial Revolution in Britain and the resulting shift in population from rural to urban areas. The conditions under which people lived and worked were appalling; both adults and children were required to work long hours in unsafe conditions for small returns. These circumstances gave rise to a significant movement to organize workers to pressure employers to provide safer conditions and better wages. The government's initial reaction was repression. The courts treated attempts to organize workers as criminal conspiracies and participants were severely punished. The subsequent history of organized labour is a chronicle of the gradual acceptance of the trade union movement as a legitimate economic force that had to be given a respectable place in the economic and social structure. These changes were accompanied by significant legislative advances in both Britain and Canada. The establishment of organized labour in the United States followed a roughly parallel course but, although the resistance of employers was as great, the governing legislation was not as repressive.

The resistance of employers to trade unions and the corresponding demands of employees for their "rights," which were often based more on emotion than economic reality, resulted in confrontation. This spirit of conflict and confrontation is most evident when an employer first faces the prospect of dealing with a trade union. This is the recognition process and a considerable amount of violence is often associated with such union organization of the work force.

Because of growing public intolerance of this violence, the U.S. Congress passed the 1935 *National Labor Relations Act* also known as the *Wagner Act*.[44] The main thrust of the *Act* was to eliminate conflict between management and labour at the main point of contention, the process of recognition. The *Wagner Act* required that the employer not interfere in any way with the organization process. A trade union successful in persuading over 50 percent of the employees to join was recognized as the official bargaining agent for all of the employees in that workforce by the government agency created by the legislation. The employer was then required to negotiate with the trade union in good faith. The primary objectives of the *Wagner Act* were to promote labour peace and to give some stability and structure to the field of labour relations in the United States.

> Legislation designed to reduce conflict

A major problem in Canada was that each province and the federal government had the power to pass labour relations legislation for its own jurisdiction. Different rules and regulations proliferated before World War II. In 1944, after a considerable amount of labour strife, the federal government passed the *Wartime Labour Relations Regulations* by an order-in-council.[45] This order incorporated most of the provisions set out in the *Wagner Act*, and most Canadian provinces added the provisions of this federal legislation to their provincial statutes after the war.

> Canada followed example of U.S. legislation

It should be noted that the Canadian legislation, in addition to following the lead of the *Wagner Act* in controlling **recognition disputes** (disputes arising between unions and employers during the organization process), included provisions that reduced conflict in interest disputes and rights disputes as well. An **interest dis-**

> Types of disputes— recognition, interest, rights, jurisdiction

---

44. The *National Labor Relations Act* is also known as the *Wagner Act* (1935) 49 Stat. 449.

45. *Wartime Labour Relations Regulations of 1944*, P.C. 1003. Because of the war emergency the federal government had the power to pass general legislation for Canada.

pute is a disagreement between the union and employer about what should be the terms of their collective agreement. A **rights dispute** is a disagreement over the meaning or interpretation of a provision included in a collective agreement. Another type of dispute that can arise is a **jurisdictional dispute** which is a dispute between two unions over which one should represent a particular group of employees or over which union members ought to do a particular job. For example, should carpenters or steel workers put up metal-stud walls in an office building? The employer is usually caught in the middle in jurisdictional disputes and has little power to affect the situation.

The federal collective bargaining legislation is embodied in the *Canada Labour Code*.[46] This legislation covers those areas over which the federal government has jurisdiction, such as railroads, shipping and dock work. Each provincial government has passed collective bargaining legislation covering areas in which it has jurisdiction. These acts are variously called *Labour Codes, Trade Union Acts, Labour Relations Acts, Industrial Relations Acts* and *Labour Acts*. The statutes cover most labour relations situations arising within the jurisdictions of the provinces as set out in Section 92 of the *Constitution Act (1867)*. Some types of activities such as public services, schools and hospitals have unique federal or provincial legislation specifically designed to cover labour relations within that industry, such as the *Public Service Employee Relations Act*, which establishes the dispute resolution mechanisms for Alberta's public sector.[47]

In all jurisdictions special labour relations boards have been established to deal with disputes associated with the collective bargaining process. These bodies take the place of courts. It is important to remember that although they quite often look and act like courts, they are not. Rather they are part of the executive branch of government, and as such they can be used as an instrument of government policy. Labour relations boards have the advantage of expertise in labour matters. Also, resolution of disputes is usually much quicker than would be the case in the courts. Administrative tribunals such as these will be discussed in more detail in Chapter 16.

Important questions arise with respect to union membership, collective bargaining and the *Charter of Rights and Freedoms*. The Supreme Court has decided that there is no constitutional right to belong to a union, to strike or even to bargain collectively. These rights have been created by statute and the limitations imposed by government do not violate Section 2(d) of the *Charter* guaranteeing freedom of association. However, picketing is protected to some extent by Section 2(b) of the *Charter* guaranteeing freedom of expression. In short, these rights have been gained politically and not through the courts, and political action must be relied on to retain them.

Because Canadian labour statutes vary considerably from jurisdiction to jurisdiction it is impossible to examine them all in detail. However, an examination of the Alberta *Act* will follow.

Both federal and provincial legislation cover collective bargaining

Organization of Employees

Certification.

Certification of bargaining unit set out in *Wagner Act*

While in some Canadian jurisdictions, it is possible for employers to voluntarily recognize a trade union as the bargaining agent for their employees, the most

---

46. *The Canada Labour Code*, R.S.C. (1985) c. L-2.
47. *Public Service Employee Relations Act*, R.S.A. (1980) c. P-33.

common method of union recognition in Canada results from the certification process adopted from the *Wagner Act* of 1935. For a union to obtain certification as the **bargaining agent** for a group of employees referred to as the **bargaining unit**, it must apply to the labour relations board for certification and satisfy the board that a certain percentage of the workforce are members of the union.

In Alberta if the applicant can show that 40 percent of the workforce has either joined the union or has signed a petition to show their support, it can apply for certification. A representation vote is then held and a majority vote supporting the union is necessary for it to obtain certification. Alternatively, the union may approach the employer directly and ask the employer to voluntarily recognize the union by agreeing to bargain with the union. The employer and union can then negotiate a collective agreement that will define the group of employees covered.

Majority of workers must support union

Bargaining Agent.

An essential feature of the legislation in all jurisdictions is the requirement that there be only one bargaining agent for a given unit of employees. The trade union that obtains certification has exclusive bargaining authority for the employees it represents and a unionized employee has no opportunity to negotiate personally with an employer as would be the case under the common law. Any contract negotiated by the union with the employer is binding on all of the employees in the designated unit. As a result, a trade union must meet several other qualifications to obtain certification. It must be established that the workforce the trade union intends to represent is an appropriate bargaining unit. Labour relations boards discourage bargaining units that are either too small or too large, or that contain groups of employees with conflicting interests. Management employees are thus excluded. Also the trade union cannot be guilty of any discriminatory practices. A union that has applied for certification to be the bargaining agent for a group of workers and has failed must wait 90 days from the time of the previous application or get the Labour Relations Board's consent before trying again.

Certification gives exclusive authority to bargain

Unfair Labour Practices.

Canadian Broadcasting Corp. v. Canada (Labour Relations Board)[48]

ACTRA is a union representing writers, journalists and performers, and in 1988 its president was Dale Goldhawk, a journalist employed by CBC and the host of Cross Country Checkup on CBC Radio. The union publishes a regular paper called ACTRA Scope which is distributed across Canada.

As president, Goldhawk wrote an article stating the union's position on free trade, an important issue in the ongoing election debate taking place at that time. Reference was made to this article in several other general publications across Canada. The CBC's position was that they couldn't have one of their journalists taking such a partisan stand in an election. Journalists were required to be balanced and impartial. Goldhawk was made to resign from the CBC.

ACTRA took the position that this was an unfair labour practice interfering with the formation or administration of a trade union and prohibited under the *Canada Labour Code*. They put that position to the Canadian Labour Relations

48. 121 D.L.R. (4th) 385 (Supreme Court of Canada).

Board, which agreed, finding against the CBC. The CBC took this to the Supreme Court of Canada, which also agreed that an unfair labour practice had taken place.

It is interesting to note that as the dispute progressed, Goldhawk and ACTRA presented a compromise proposal which would have had Goldhawk acting as president but not as spokesperson for the union. This was rejected by CBC and it was the rejection of that compromise position that the Canadian Labour Relations Board found constituted the unfair labour practice.

This case nicely illustrates how important it is for the delicate balance between trade unions and employers to be maintained. A distance must be kept between the employer and the union to ensure that the employer in no way interferes with the formation or operation of the trade union. Firing somebody because he became president of a trade union could not be tolerated. The case also illustrates the role played by administrative tribunals in the field of labour relations. This case went first to such a tribunal and the question the Supreme Court of Canada dealt with was whether the Labour Relations Board had acted within their powers in reaching the decision that they did. The Supreme Court found that they had.

Rules of conduct reduce conflict

The primary objective of labour legislation is to create an orderly process for the organization and recognition of trade unions. Specific rules of conduct are laid down for both labour and management in an effort to reduce or eliminate the conflict which often takes place in such circumstances. Prohibited conduct, called unfair labour practices, can include threats or coercion of employees by either the union or management, the threat of dismissal for joining a trade union and the requirement that an employee refrain from joining a trade union as a condition of employment. There are certain sensitive times during the certification and bargaining cycle when the *Code* prohibits unilateral changes in rates of pay and terms and conditions of employment. These include the period immediately following the filing of an application for certification and the period following service of a notice to bargain upon the employer. If the employer does resort to retaliatory action or unfair labour practices, the Board has the power to order the practice be stopped and the employees be compensated and reinstated, and, in extreme cases, the Board may grant certification without a vote.

Threats, coercion, dismissal—unfair labour practices

Unfair labour practices can result in certification without a vote

However, the Labour Relations Board will not usually take this step unless the union can demonstrate that it has the support of a majority of the employees. For example, if an employer named Schneider learned that Takeda was trying to get a union certified and fired Takeda as a lesson to all the other employees, this would be an unfair labour practice. It is likely that a certification vote would not reflect the true feelings of the employees because of this intimidation, so the board may grant certification without a vote.

Requiring that an employer not coerce or intimidate employees does not eliminate the employer's right to state his or her views during the electioneering process that precedes a certification vote. Freedom of expression as set out in the *Charter of Rights and Freedoms* requires that, as long as such statements are merely statements of opinion or fact and do not amount to threat or coercion, they are permitted. But it is an unfair labour practice for an employer to participate in, or interfere with, the formation or administration of a trade union. The employer must not contribute financial or other support to a trade union, for this undermines the union's independence.

Although the legislation provides for a process whereby an employer can eventually be forced to recognize and bargain with a certified trade union, the provisions do not give the union representatives the right to trespass on the employer's property to carry out union activities, nor do they have the right to carry out those activities while on the job. However, employers will often permit their premises to be used for such purposes because then at least they know what is going on. Once the trade union has successfully completed the certification process, it becomes the certified bargaining agent for all the employees in the bargaining unit. As such, the employer is forced to recognize the trade union and bargain with it. The trade union has the right to serve notice on the employer requiring that the employer begin collective bargaining.

Employers often wish to join together to bargain collectively with a trade union. In Alberta, such **employers' organizations** can form in one of two ways. Employers may voluntarily authorize a consultant or employers' organization to bargain as their agent. An employer can withdraw from the informal process at any time to bargain on its own behalf. Section 60 of Alberta's *Labour Relations Code* S.A. (1988) c. L-1.2 outlines a more formal procedure. An employers' organization may be authorized in writing to bargain on behalf of the signatories. This organization continues to represent those employers until the dispute is settled or a strike or lockout occurs. Employer organizations are most frequently found in areas such as construction which have a number of small employers. Local trade union organizations are often affiliated with much larger, parent unions which generally bring considerable benefits to the local bargaining units, such as providing funds in a prolonged strike and making available a pool of expertise to assist in negotiations.

Employer organizations help employers bargain with unions

Bargaining

Collective Agreements.

Once a union is certified as a bargaining agent for a group of employees, the next step is for the union and the employer to get together and bargain towards a collective agreement. If they have never had a collective agreement before, either party can give notice to commence bargaining within 30 days after the notice is given. This notice can be given any time after certification is granted. If the union has been certified for some time and a collective agreement is already in force, the parties are still free to give the other notice to commence bargaining, but this notice can only be given within a relatively short period of time before the end of the previous agreement, specifically between 60 and 120 days before the existing collective agreement expires, unless the collective agreement specifies a longer period.

Either party can give notice to commence collective bargaining

Once this notice has been given, the parties must begin to bargain or negotiate with each other "in good faith." There is some question as to what this term means, but if the parties meet with a willingness to explore compromises and try to find an area of agreement, they are bargaining in good faith. It does not mean that either party has to agree to the other's terms. The *Code* requries the parties to make "every reasonable effort" to reach an agreement, and if either party feels the other is failing to bargain in good faith, a complaint can be filed with the Board.

Parties must bargain in good faith

Ratification.

A bargain is the result of a successful negotiation process. The agreement is put into writing, approved by the employer and presented to the union membership for

Agreement must be ratified by both employer and employees

EMPLOYER MUST BARGAIN IN GOOD FAITH

The employer operated a mine in the Northwest Territories and put forward an offer to contract with its unionized employees. The offer was rejected and a bitter 18-month strike followed in which a number of workers died. Some employees were dismissed, and the company, when pressured as part of the eventual settlement package to at least provide for due process in the dismissals, steadfastly refused. After attempts at mediation, an industrial inquiry commission, and intervention by the Minister, there was still no settlement to the strike. The union went to the Canadian Labour Relations Board, complaining that the employer failed to bargain in good faith. The Board agreed, and ordered the employer to renew the original offer made before the strike. The employer refused and appealed the Board's decision. The Supreme Court of Canada upheld the Labour Relations Board's right to find that the employer had not bargained in good faith and upheld their right to impose the settlement. The Supreme Court Justices observed that it was not necessary that the Labour Relations Board's finding of lack of good faith to be correct, only that it was not patently unreasonable because it was within the Board's jurisdiction to make such a finding.

Royal Oak Mines Inc. v. Canada (Labour Relations Board), 133 D.L.R. (4th) 129 (Supreme Court of Canada)

ratification. If a majority of the union membership ratifies the agreement, it becomes a collective agreement binding on both parties. The agreement is a contract, but because of the modifying legislation it must be viewed as a special form of contract with unique features, such as the method of its enforcement. When bargaining has begun, the *Code* automatically extends the terms of a contract that would otherwise expire. Due to this bridging, the employer is not permitted to change the terms and conditions of the employment, such as wages, benefits or hours of work. When it is clear that the parties cannot reach an agreement, it is possible in some jurisdictions for the labour relations board to impose a first contract, but Alberta's *Code* does not go so far.

Mediation.

Mediation assists
negotiation process

A very important aspect of the Canadian labour relations system is third-party intervention in the negotiation process. This is called conciliation or, in Alberta, **mediation**. Either party has the right to make application to the appropriate government agency for the appointment of a mediator at any time during collective bargaining. This person then meets with the two parties and assists them in their negotiations. The hope is that communications between the two parties will be greatly facilitated by this third-person go-between.

An initial 14 days of formal mediation is provided for in the *Code* and no strike or lockout is permitted until a further 14-day cooling-off period has passed following any vote on the mediator's report. During mediation, settlement is encouraged. The mediator has the choice of issuing a report containing recommendations or not issuing a report. If the parties accept the recommendations, the recommendations become binding.

If only one party accepts the recommendations, it can apply to have the Board conduct a vote of the side that rejected the offer. Individual employees, or in the case of an employers' organization, individual employers, vote by secret ballot. A recommendation accepted by this vote forms the new collective agreement. But if the vote fails, the parties must decide whether to continue negotiations, consider a strike or lockout, or submit to some other method to resolve their dispute.

The *Code* establishes three means of resolving disputes: proposal votes, voluntary arbitration and setting up a disputes inquiry board.

Proposal votes enable each side to ask the Board to take a proposal to the opposite party for a secret vote. This can be done just once, by each side, during the course of the dispute. If, for example, the employer asks the Board to poll the employees individually and they vote to accept the offer, the offer becomes the basis of a new collective agreement.

Voluntary arbitration can resolve a dispute but is only available where both parties agree to submit to arbitration. Arbitration differs from mediation in that the arbitrator does have the power to make a decision binding on the parties. The arbitration board (consisting of one or three persons) will hold a hearing, listen to submissions and then decide on the terms and conditions for the collective agreement.

A **disputes inquiry board** may be appointed by the Minister of Labour. Such boards are convened to settle disputes either before or after a strike or lockout begins.

Contract Terms

When the negotiations between the parties have been successful, certain requirements must be contained in the collective agreement. The agreement must be for a fixed term; if the parties have placed no time limit on the agreement, it will be deemed to be for one year. Collective agreements may have an automatic renewal clause so that if no notice to bargain is given at the appropriate time, the contract will automatically be renewed, usually for another year.

Contract must be for a fixed term

The parties will often find themselves bargaining well after the new contract should have come into force. When they reach an agreement it may operate retroactively, but only if the new agreement so provides. For example, if Sami is involved in collective bargaining with her employees whose agreement expires on December 31, it is possible that the parties would still be bargaining in the following April. If Sami and her employees finally reach an agreement in June, to run for one year, the agreement could be retroactive to the prior January 1 and expire on the following December 31. The agreement would only be in effect for a further six months after the date the agreement was reached. Alberta's legislation does not require new collective agreements to be retroactive; retroactivity is a matter to be negotiated by the parties.

Arbitration.

All collective agreements must contain provisions which set out a method for the settlement of disputes arising under the agreement. This is usually accomplished through a grievance procedure ultimately leading to **arbitration.** The contract will set out a process involving a series of structured meetings in which the parties negotiate a settlement. When no settlement can be reached, the matter is submitted to an arbitrator (or panel of arbitrators) who will hold a hearing and make a decision that is binding on both parties. This grievance process is used to resolve disputes not only over the interpretation of the contract provisions but also as a response to individual employee complaints of violations of their rights by the employer. If an agreement does not contain a grievance and arbitration procedure, the parties are required to follow the model procedure set out in Section 134 of the *Labour Relations Code.*

Interpretation of contract disputes to be arbitrated

While both arbitration and mediation involve the intervention of an outside third party, the distinction is that the parties are not required to follow the recommendations of a mediator but the decision of the arbitrator is binding on both parties. Arbitration, therefore, is a substitute for court action. Each party in an

Decision of arbitrator binding on both parties

DISPUTES ARISING FROM COLLECTIVE AGREEMENT MUST BE ARBITRATED

Otis Elevator terminated Mr. Bourne, who was in a trade union and subject to a collective agreement between Otis and the union. Bourne sued for wrongful dismissal. This action was brought to determine whether the court had jurisdiction to hear such a case. The judge in this case decided that since Bourne was a trade union member and there was a collective agreement, the court had no jurisdiction. These types of disputes are determined by the provisions of the agreement, and since it is required under legislation that all collective agreements have arbitration provisions, any dispute arising under that agreement must be settled by arbitration. It is clear that had this matter gone to arbitration, it would have been appropriately resolved there.

Bourne v. Otis Elevator Co. Ltd., 6 D.L.R. (4th) 560 (Ontario High Court of Justice)

arbitration hearing is given an opportunity to put forth its side of the argument and present evidence before the arbitrator makes a decision. Arbitrators are not required to follow the stringent rules of procedure that normally surround judicial proceedings. In Alberta, their decisions are final and binding; there is no appeal to the Labour Relations Board or the courts. The collective agreement replaces any individual contract that may have existed previously between the employer and employee, so all disputes between the parties must be handled by the grievance procedure and arbitration. This method of dispute resolution is compulsory. It is

No strike when contract in force

not permissible for the parties to indulge in strikes or lockouts to resolve a dispute over the terms of the contract once it is in force.

Other Terms.

In addition to the terms specifically relating to conditions of work, rates of pay, vacations, termination and the like that are the main object of the collective bargaining process, there are various other terms which often appear in collective agreements.

Statutes cover other terms

The federal government and some provinces have passed legislation which requires the contract to cover how technological changes in the industry will be handled. British Columbia now requires that union/management committees be set up to handle such conflicts. Throughout Canada the parties can agree to terms that provide for union security, such as the **union shop clause**. This clause simply requires that new employees join the union within a specified period of time. In some jurisdictions, particularly in industries such as construction or longshoring, the agreement may require that the employee be a member of the union before getting the job. This requirement is called a **closed shop clause**. In some areas employees retain the right not to join a union but are still required to pay union dues. This arrangement is referred to as the **Rand Formula** or **the agency shop**. Many statutes permit the collective agreement to contain a **checkoff provision** which means that the parties have agreed that the employer will deduct union dues from the payroll. A fifth option, **maintenance of membership**, requires those who are already union members to pay dues and maintain their membership, but new employees need not join the union.

Strikes and Lockouts

Job action may involve lockout, strike, work to rule

Some sort of job action will probably result if the parties cannot agree on what terms to include in the agreement. A **lockout** is action taken by the employer to prevent employees from working and earning wages. A **strike** is the withdrawal of services by employees. Although a strike usually consists of refusing to come to work or intentional slowdowns, other forms of interference with production may also be classified as strikes. For example, post office employees announced just before Christmas 1983 that they would process Christmas cards with ten-cent stamps on them despite the fact that the appropriate rate was thirty-two cents per letter. This action was taken to draw attention to the fact that certain commercial users of the postal system got a preferential bulk rate not available to the public. The courts declared that the action was a strike and since a strike would have been illegal under the circumstances the union reversed its position. Employees can pressure an employer by strictly adhering to the terms of their agreement or by doing no more than is minimally required. This behaviour is called **working to rule** and will often prompt a lockout. Strikes and lockouts are both work stoppages, but they are initiated by different parties.

Because the object of the *Wagner Act* and subsequent legislation was to eliminate conflict and stabilize the labour relations climate as much as possible, the right to strike and the right to lockout have been severely limited by current legislation. It is unlawful for a strike or lockout to occur while an agreement is in force. Strikes and lockouts can only take place after the last agreement has expired and before the next one comes into effect. Any strike or lockout associated with the recognition process is illegal. Similarly, any strike that results from a conflict between two unions about which one should be the bargaining agent for a particular employee (jurisdictional dispute) is also illegal. Both of these kinds of disputes are dealt with through the certification process described above. Only when the dispute is part of the negotiation or bargaining process and concerns the terms to be included in the collective agreement (interest dispute) is a strike or lockout legal.

Strike or lockout can only occur between contracts

Strike and lockout only legal in an interest dispute

If a dispute concerning the interpretation of a term of an agreement between the parties (rights dispute) arises after the contract is in force, and negotiation cannot resolve it, the dispute must be settled by grievance and arbitration. Any strike associated with such a dispute is illegal. Even when the dispute between the parties is an interest dispute, there are still some limitations on strike action. No strike can take place until after the mediation process and cooling-off period. A vote authorizing strike action must be taken and a specified period of notice must be given—for example, 72 hours in Alberta and British Columbia. The employer must give the same notice to the employees when a lockout is about to take place. The notice must also be served on the mediator. Its purpose is to give the other side advance notice and provides an opportunity for a last-minute settlement. If the strike or lockout does not begin on the date set out in the notice, a new 72-hour notice is required. Futhermore, the strike or lockout must occur within 120 days of the vote or a new vote is required. In some jurisdictions, such as Québec and British Columbia, the employer is prohibited from hiring replacement workers during a strike. This restriction puts considerably greater pressure on the employer to settle the dispute and goes some way in reducing the violence associated with such labour-management confrontation. Ontario has recently repealed a similar provision while the federal government has introduced amendments to the *Canada Labour Code* that partially prohibit the use of such replacement workers. Replacement workers can, however, be hired in Alberta, but as soon as the strike or lockout is over, union employees are to be reinstated in preference to any employee hired as a replacement during the dispute.

No strike until after mediation and cooling-off period

Picketing

Once a strike or lockout has taken place, one of the most effective techniques available to trade unions is picketing. But as with striking, the use of picketing is severely limited and controlled. Picketing involves strikers standing near or

Right to picket limited by legislation

Strikes and lockouts are the ultimate weapons in a labour dispute.

Photo by Jeff McIntosh/Canapress.

marching around a place of business trying to dissuade people from doing business there. Picketing is permissible only when a lawful strike or lockout is in progress. Employees who picket before proper notice has been given or somewhere not permitted under the labour legislation of the province are in violation of the law. A picketer responsible for communicating false information to those who might cross the picket line can be sued for defamation.

When the information communicated does not try to discourage people from crossing the picket line, the action may not qualify as picketing. For example, postal employees handing out pamphlets to customers in front of post offices stating the preferred rates charged to bulk users may not be classed as picketing even though it is embarrassing to the employer.

Picketing must be peaceful and merely communicate information. Violence will not be tolerated. A tort action for trespass may follow the violation of private property and, if violence erupts, the assaulting party may face criminal and civil court action. But if the striking worker keeps his or her conduct strictly within the confines set out in the legislation, in most jurisdictions no tort action can be taken against that worker or against the union itself. When picketing goes beyond the narrow bounds permitted in common law and legislation, the employer can resort to the courts or labour relations boards to get an injunction to limit or prohibit the picketing. Under some circumstances, the number of picketers used may be excessive. When mass picketing goes beyond simple information communication and becomes intimidation, at the request of the employer the courts or labour relations boards will restrict the number of picketers. Employees face considerable risk of personal liability for damages caused when they involve themselves in illegal picketing.

No tort action for legal picketing

Strong tradition of union solidarity makes picketing effective

Picketing may seem to be an ineffectual weapon, limited as it is to those types of activities specifically prescribed under the statutes or permitted by the common law. It must be appreciated, however, that there is an extremely strong tradition among union members and many others never to cross a picket line. Others simply wish to avoid the unpleasantness of a confrontation. This observance is perhaps the most effective tool available to a union. Employers must deal with other businesses who employ union members such as suppliers, truck drivers, electricians, plumbers and telephone service people. Because most collective agreements have terms which protect union members from punishment for refusing to cross a valid picket line, it is unusual for a member of one union to cross the picket line of another. It eventually becomes very difficult for an employer to continue in business surrounded by a picket line.

Some provinces permit secondary picketing

One of the more difficult problems associated with picketing is determining which locations can be legally picketed. Employees in every jurisdiction can picket the plant or factory where they work. In some jurisdictions, such as New Brunswick, secondary picketing can be extended to any place at which the employer carries out business.[49]

These provisions are significant because the striking employees are able to picket not just their own workplace, but also other locations where the employer

49. *Industrial Relations Act*, R.S.N.B. (1973) c. I-4 s. 104.

carries on business. In any case, unrelated businesses cannot be legally picketed even if they are located on the same premises as the one struck. Of course, whether the picketing is directed towards such an unrelated business in a given dispute is a question for the court or board to decide in each case. But the more extensive the picketing, the more effective the economic pressure placed on the employer. Secondary picketing is not allowed in Alberta.

Anyone has the legal right to cross a picket line. Customers are free to continue doing business with an employer involved in a strike or lockout; suppliers are free to continue supplying goods and services to the employer if they can persuade their employees to cross the picket line; and the employer has the right to continue normal business activities. Unfortunately, picketers can lose sight of these basic rights when they think their picket line is not being effective. As a result, a considerable amount of intimidation, coercion, violence and injury still takes place despite all the precautions introduced into the labour relations system in Canada.

No legal obligation to honour picket line

Public Sector and Essential Services

The provisions discussed under the heading of collective bargaining relate to people employed in private industry. However, many people are employed either as part of the public sector or in service industries which are considered essential to society, such as power companies, hospitals, police and fire departments. Employees falling into these categories are treated differently from those employed in private industry, and special legislation governs their activities. Public servants are subject to the *Public Service Employee Relations Act,*[50] whereas the *Police Officers' Collective Bargaining Act* applies to police in Alberta.[51] Although labour issues and disputes in these occupations are virtually the same as those in the private sector, the government and the public regard the position of public service employees as quite different. Normal collective bargaining with its attendant pressures in the form of strikes, lockouts and picketing can be viewed as interference with the government's right to govern because the government itself is either directly or indirectly the employer. Strikes by police, firefighters, hospital workers, schoolteachers and other public servants are usually considered inappropriate by members of the public.

Public sector employees have limited rights to job action

Every province has special legislation to deal with these groups. Most provinces permit collective bargaining to some extent but only a few allow public sector employees to participate in strikes and picketing, the others substituting some form of compulsory arbitration of disputes. The *Labour Relations Code*, for example, has special rules applicable to certain essential services. Parties employed in these essential services must submit their unresolved bargaining disputes to compulsory arbitration boards. Such no-strike-or-lockout rules apply to hospital employees and firefighters. These rules can also be applied whenever Cabinet declares a dispute to be a public emergency. Of course, in all labour disputes the government retains the right, either by existing statute or by the passage of a specific bill, to impose a settlement or an alternative method of resolving the dispute such as compulsory arbitration.

In recent times there has been great pressure to reduce costs. Governments have sometimes responded by unilaterally reducing the salaries, benefits and work of

50. *Public Service Employee Relations Act,* R.S.A. (1980) c. P-33.
51. *Police Officers' Collective Bargaining Act,* S.A. (1983) c. P-12.05.

their employees whether or not they have a collective agreement. The governments of Ontario and Alberta have both recently exercised their legislative power to impose such changes.

Union Organization

Trade unions must be democratic organizations in which policy is established by vote and executives and officers are elected. Members can be expelled or disciplined for misbehaviour such as crossing picket lines after being instructed not to by the union executive. Expulsion can be devastating for a worker since many collective agreements provide for a **union shop** in which all employees must be members of the union. Some jurisdictions have passed legislation stipulating that a person who loses his or her union membership for reasons other than failure to pay dues will be able to retain employment.[52] There are some employees whose religious beliefs prevent them from joining or contributing to organizations such as trade unions, which presents a real dilemma in a union shop situation. Alberta exempts such individuals from paying dues to the union; instead the same amount must be paid to a registered charitable organization.[53]

Unions can expel for misbehaviour

Trade unions are subject to the human rights legislation in place in their jurisdiction. In some jurisdictions, the labour legislation provides that they can lose their status as a trade union if they discriminate. Unions have an obligation to represent all their members fairly. Employees who feel unfairly treated by the union or who feel that the union is not properly representing them in disputes with employers can lodge complaints before the provincial labour relations board and the union may find itself required to compensate the wronged employees.

Trade unions controlled by labour relations boards

From this discussion, it seems that labour relations boards have considerable power. In fact, this power varies from province to province and in some jurisdictions the courts still have a significant role to play. In others, such as Alberta, the power to resolve disputes in labour relations matters has been given entirely to the provincial labour relations board.

Trade unions were once considered illegal organizations with no status separate from their membership and therefore no corporate identity. Most provinces have passed legislation giving a recognized trade union the right to sue or be sued on its own behalf, at least for the purposes outlined in the labour legislation.

SUMMARY

The employee provides service to the employer generally whereas the independent contractor contracts to do a specific job. The employer is vicariously liable for the acts of the employee done during the course of employment. The employer must also provide a safe working place, direction and wages. The employee must follow these directions, and honestly, carefully, and loyally carry them out. In the event of termination, both parties are obligated to give the other reasonable notice. After a long period of employment this notice period can be quite lengthy. No notice is required where there is just cause for dismissal such as dishonesty or incompetence. In the event of wrongful dismissal, the employee is required to mitigate losses by trying to find other employment.

52. *Canada Labour Code*, R.S.C. (1985) c. L-2 s. 95(e).
53. *Labour Relations Code*, S.A. (1988) c. L-1.2 s. 27.

There are a number of federal and provincial statutes controlling such things as minimum wage, hours of work, termination, child labour, discrimination, employment standards, health and safety standards, employment insurance and workers' compensation. Provincial and federal human rights statutes are primarily effective in the area of employment and not only prohibit discrimination in its various forms but also require positive action on the part of employers to accommodate the religious beliefs or special needs of their disabled or ill workers.

A major area of legislated intervention in the field of employment is collective bargaining. The organization of the employees by unions into bargaining units is controlled by the certification process. After a majority vote of the employees, the government certifies the union as the official bargaining agent for those employees and the employer is required to bargain fairly with them. Only when that bargaining process breaks down, and after an attempt at mediation, is a strike or lockout permitted and then only after a majority vote and proper notice. During the strike, persuasive picketing is allowed but no physical confrontation. Once the contract is in place, any disputes arising under it must be dealt with through an arbitration process provided for in the agreement.

QUESTIONS

1. Distinguish between an employee, an independent contractor and an agent.

2. Explain how a court will determine whether a person is an employee rather than an independent contractor.

3. Summarize the employer's obligations to the employee and the employee's obligations to the employer under common law in a master/servant relationship.

4. Explain what is meant by a restrictive covenant and what factors determine whether it is enforceable or not.

5. What is the proper way to terminate an employment contract that is for an indefinite period of time?

6. How is the appropriate notice period to terminate a master/servant relationship determined?

7. Under what circumstances can an employee be dismissed without being given notice? When can an employee leave employment without giving notice?

8. What risk does an employer face who ignores an employee's incompetence over a period of time?

9. What factors will a court take into consideration when determining compensation in a wrongful dismissal action? Indicate any other types of remedies which may be available to the victim.

10. Explain what is meant by vicarious liability. Describe the limitations on its application and how vicarious liability will affect the liability of the employee.

11. Describe how the *Employment Standards Code* protects basic workers' rights.

12. Explain how human rights legislation applies to areas of employment.

13. Explain what is meant by a duty to accommodate in the field of human rights and how that can effect employers.

14. Explain the object and purpose of workers' compensation legislation. How does the legislation attempt to accomplish these objectives? Explain what the position of the parties would be if only the original common law applied.

15. What is the significance of the American *National Labor Relations Act* (*Wagner Act*) in Canada?

16. Distinguish between recognition disputes, jurisdiction disputes, interest disputes and rights disputes.

17. Explain the difference between mediation and arbitration. Describe how these tools are used in Canadian labour disputes.

18. Once a collective agreement is in place, what effect will it have on the individual rights of employees? How will it affect employers?

19. Strikes and lockouts are limited to what kind of disputes? How are the other types of disputes between union and employer dealt with?

20. Distinguish between a strike and a lockout. Describe the type of job action that can constitute a strike.

21. Explain what steps must take place before a strike or lockout is legal.

22. Explain what is meant by picketing. Under what circumstances is this type of job action available? What limitations have been placed on picketing in Alberta?

23. What is the legal position of a person who wishes to cross a picket line?

....

CASES

1. Greaves v. Ontario Municipal Employees Retirement Board

Mr. Greaves had been working for the defendant for about 12 years as a money manager, eventually becoming a vice-president in charge of various financial and investment areas. In 1993 the employer was reorganized. The court found that the reorganization was appropriate for business purposes, but as a result Mr. Greaves' overall responsibilities were reduced. Finally, two vice-presidents junior to Mr. Greaves were promoted to positions higher than Mr. Greaves. He resigned even though he was asked to stay on at the same salary. He sued for wrongful dismissal. Explain the arguments available to both parties.

How would your answer be affected if you understood that hard feelings between Greaves and his supervisor, unrelated to the job, had made the work environment very unpleasant and the changes in his job were the result of that vindictive action by that supervisor? (See *Vanderleest v. City of Regina*, 91 D.L.R. (4th) 538, Saskatchewan Court of Queen's Bench.)

2. Clare v. Canada (Attorney-General)

Clare was an employee of the federal government who was fired from his job for incompetence after 23 years of service. After a number of years of satisfactory service in various capacities with the federal public service, the plaintiff received an unsatisfactory evaluation in his performance appraisals for three consecutive reviews. On the basis of this performance, the plaintiff was fired from his position.

During that time, his wife had suffered from a series of major illnesses and nearly died. He was also having serious problems with his son including physical confrontation. As a result, Clare was experiencing an extreme amount of stress in his life. In addition to his personal troubles, he had a personality conflict with his immediate supervisor which introduced work-related stress. During this period, Clare was receiving counselling and had asked to participate in a federally sponsored program designed to help employees experiencing these kind of difficulties. The plaintiff sought reassignment which was refused and so after 23 years of service he was fired from his position.

Explain the legal position of the parties and whether the dismissal was justified in the circumstances. Would your answer be different if it were established that he had experienced family problems over his entire work history with the department, and that several of his transfers from one department to another had been to accommodate a "problem or troubled employee and that his performance had never been fully satisfactory."

3. DiCarlo v. DiSimone et al.

The plaintiff was in a car owned by his employer and driven by a fellow employee when they were in an accident while in the process of work. They collided with a car driven by Lilian Watson and owned by her husband Alfred. Both drivers were found to be negligent and partially at fault in the accident. The plaintiff sued for damages from both drivers, his employer and Mr. Watson, the owner of the other vehicle. Describe the arguments that can be used by the employee and employer and any limitations on the amount that can be collected from the Watsons.

4. Parks v. Atlantic Provinces Special Education Authority

Parks had been employed as a residence counsellor since 1976 at a school catering to physically and mentally handicapped children and students up to the age of 21. This job was very physically demanding in that he often had to lift the residents, help them to do exercises, help with their personal care, provide assistance on outings, and cope with medical problems and emergencies. The school was originally just for the blind but the job became more and more onerous as the function of the school broadened. Mr. Parks' job got progressively more difficult.

After nine years Mr. Parks suffered a herniated disc in his neck caused by lifting patients. In 1987 he developed problems with his left knee. After some time off work on a disability pension, he wanted to return to work in May 1989, but it was clear that he wouldn't be able to do the same heavy lifting that he had done before. His employment was terminated and he sued for wrongful dismissal.

Explain the arguments on both sides and how much notice Mr. Parks would be entitled to in these circumstances.

5. Québec Human Rights Commission v. City of Québec

The City of Québec operated a municipal jail which employed female guards or matrons to work with prisoners as well as male guards who were also policemen. These male guards were paid a higher rate of pay than the female matrons. The police officers were assigned this duty as part of their general police functions. They were usually assigned this lighter duty because of such factors as age, seniority and health. The women, however, were hired specifically to do that job. Explain the arguments available on both sides to support the difference in pay.

6. United Association of Journeymen Apprentices, Local 264 v. Metal Fabricating and Construction Ltd.

The union and the employer entered into an agreement which was to remain in force until April 1984. In March 1984 the employer served notice on the employee that the agreement was to be considered terminated at the end of April. The parties then began to bargain for a new collective agreement. This bargaining went on for three years; during that time, the terms of the old agreement were adhered to. At the end of the three years (in 1987), the employer made certain changes to working conditions without the consent of the union. Does the employer have the right to do so? Explain the arguments available to both parties as to whether the terms of the old collective agreement were in place and binding on the parties in Spring 1987.

7. United Steel Workers of American L. 7917 v. Gibraltar Mines Ltd.

In this case, a number of truck drivers were suspended because they refused to drive their trucks. One of the truck drivers was a union official. The truck drivers claimed that the conditions were unsafe. They had to drive up a ramp beside an open pit. The weather conditions made the ramp slippery. A protective device, called a berm, which was designed to keep the trucks from falling into the pit, was missing for a stretch of about 130 metres. The company claimed that it was an illegal strike and suspended the truck drivers. The drivers brought an application to be reinstated.

Explain the arguments on both sides and the probable outcome. Would your answer differ with the added information that, upon learning that the mining operation was still functioning, a union official set up a picket line and encouraged the entire crew to stay off the job?

8. Amalgamated Clothing and Textile Workers Union (Toronto Joint Board) v. Straton Knitting Mills Ltd. et al.

When the union in question tried to organize the workers at the respondent's premises, the co-owner held three meetings with the employees in an attempt to dissuade them from joining the union. He told them it was not necessary for them to have a union, that it would be divisive, that they would have to pay union dues, that there was the possibility of a strike and that it might result in the loss of contracts for the company which would mean less work for the employees. The company also changed the pay scale which resulted in higher wages. A petition was circulated to oppose the union, but there was some suggestion that management was behind it. Part of the message that got through to the employees was that the employer did not want a union, that if it came there would be layoffs, short weeks and perhaps closure of the business. What course of action would you recommend to the union in these circumstances?

9. 683481 Ontario Ltd. v. Beattie

In this case the numbered company operated a warehousing business, storing steel for a number of different companies. In 1989 the parent company entered into an agreement with Stelco to exclusively store their steel. They did so and then the United Steel Workers of America Local 1005 went on strike against Stelco. This was a lawful strike and they included the warehouse in their picketing. The warehouse company brought an application for an injunction to stop the picketing. Explain the arguments on both sides.

LEGISLATION

Alberta

Blind Workers' Compensation Act, R.S.A. (1980) c. B-7
Employment Standards Code, S.A. (1996) c. E-10.3
Human Rights, Citizenship and Multiculturalism Act, R.S.A. (1980) c. H-11.7.
Labour Relations Code, S.A. (1988) c. L-1.2
Master and Servants Act, R.S.A. (1980) c. M-8
Occupational Health and Safety Act, R.S.A. (1980) c. O.2
Public Service Act, R.S.A. (1980) c. P-13
Public Service Employee Relations Act, R.S.A. (1980) c. P-33
Workers' Compensation Act, S.A. (1981) c. W-16

Federal

Canada Labour Code, R.S.C. (1985) c. L-2
Employment Insurance Act, S.C. (1996) c. 23
Fair Wages and Hours of Labour Act, R.S.C. (1985) c. L-4
Old Age Security Act, R.S.C. (1985) c. O-9
Public Sector Compensation Act, S.C. (1991) c. 30
Public Service Employment Act, R.S.C. (1985) c. P-33
Public Service Staff Relations Act, R.S.C. (1985) c. P-35
Wages Liability Act, R.S.C. (1985) c. W-1

WEBLINKS

Charter of Rights and Freedoms
www.solon.org/Constitutions/Canada/English/ca_1982.html

An Annotated Bibliography for Canadian *Charter of Rights and Freedoms* Research
www.law.utoronto.ca/conlit/bibliog2.htm

Canadian Human Rights Commission
www.chrc.ca/

Human Resources Development Canada: Employment Insurance
www.hrdc-drhc.gc.ca/ei/common/home.shtml

WWW Virtual Library: Labour and Business History
www.iisg.nl/~w3vl/

Public Service Alliance of Canada
www.psac.com/

Supreme Court of Canada Ruling: *Queen v. Cognos* Inc.
**www.droit.umontreal.ca/doc/csc-scc/en/pub/1993/vol1/html/
1993scr1_0087.html**

Alberta Labour Relations Board
www.gov.ab.ca/~a/rb/

Alberta Department of Labour
www.gov.ab.ca/~/ab/

The Sims Group: Administrative, Tribunal and Labour Management Consultants
www.simsgroup.com

Alberta Workers' Compensation Board
www.wcb.ab.ca/index.html

Alberta Employment Standards Code
www.gov.ab.ca/qp/ascii/acts/E10P3.txt

Alberta's Labour Relations Code
www.gov.ab.ca/qp/ascii/acts/L01P2.txt

Alberta's Human Rights and Citizenship Commission
www.gov.ab.ca/~mcd/citizen/hr/hr.htm

Agency

OBJECTIVES OF THE CHAPTER

- To identify the agency relationship
- To discuss the rights and responsibilities of an agent and a principal
- To explain the implications of a fiduciary relationship

Mr. Snarey was a "well-respected agent" working for the Mutual Life Assurance Company of Canada when he was approached by a customer who wanted to take advantage of one of the investment opportunities offered by the company. Mr. Snarey persuaded the customer to part with $16 000 by way of a cheque made out to Mr. Snarey. The customer was told that his money was going into an "investment vehicle offered to the public by Mutual Life." Actually, the company did not offer this kind of investment plan and never had. This was simply a scheme used by Mr. Snarey to cheat a trusting customer out of a considerable amount of money. When the customer discovered the fraud, he turned to the Mutual Life Assurance Company for compensation. In the resulting action, it was determined that Mr. Snarey had devised and conducted a fraudulent scheme. Because he was an agent of Mutual Life with the actual authority to enter into this general type of transaction with the company's customer, the company was vicariously liable for his conduct and had to pay compensation to the client.[1]

---

1. *The Lawyers Weekly*, May 1, 1987, p. 21.

Fraudulent misrepresentation is one of the few circumstances in which a principal will be held vicariously liable for the acts of an agent even in the absence of an employment contract between them, providing that agent is acting within the authority he has been given by the principal. This case illustrates that such an agency relationship can have a tremendous impact on the principal. A discussion of how agency relationships are created and the obligations which arise between the parties is the topic of this chapter.

The subject of agency is a vital component in any discussion of business law. The legal consequences that stem from an agency relationship are of utmost concern to business people because at least one of the parties in most commercial transactions is functioning as an agent. Agency law is the basis of the law of partnership and an understanding of it is essential for coming to terms with corporate law. These subjects will be dealt with in the next two chapters.

Agent represents and acts for principal

An agent's function is to represent and act on behalf of a principal in dealings with third parties. Although by far the most common type of legal relationship in which agents represent principals is in the creation of contracts, agents also find themselves involved in other types of legal relationships. Real estate agents do not usually have the authority to enter into contracts on behalf of vendors but they function as agents nonetheless because they participate in the negotiations and act as go-betweens. Other professionals, such as lawyers and accountants, also create special legal relationships on behalf of their clients or principals which are not necessarily contractual in nature. The term *agency* refers to the service an agent performs on behalf of the principal. This service may be performed as an employee, as an independent agent, or gratuitously. When an agent is acting independently, the business performing the service is often called an agency, such as a travel agency, employment agency or real estate agency.

Agency refers to service performed by an agent

The discussion in this chapter will focus on the law of agency and in most cases no distinction will be made between people functioning as agents as part of an employment contract and those acting independently. In any case it is important not to think of the agency function found within an employment relationship as just another aspect of that employment. The duties and obligations imposed on agents go far beyond the employment relationship and must be understood as a separate function or set of obligations.

THE AGENCY RELATIONSHIP

The agency relationship can be created by an express or implied contract, by estoppel, by ratification or gratuitously, the key element being the granting of authority.

Formation by Contract

Agency relationship usually created through contract

Usually an agency relationship is created through a contract, called an agency agreement, between the agent and the principal. It is important not to confuse this contract with the contract created by the agent between the **principal** and the **third party**, which is the object of the agency relationship. Because the agency agreement is a special application of contract law, the principles outlined in Chapters 3 through 6 apply. The authority of the agent to act on behalf of the principal may be set out in an agency agreement. Similarly, the payment the agent is to receive for services rendered may be set out in the contract. There are no formal require-

Basic rules of contract apply to agency contracts

ments for the creation of such a contract, which can be either verbal or in writing. An agency contract that is to last over one year must be evidenced in writing to satisfy the requirements of the *Statute of Frauds* except in jurisdictions such as British Columbia, Manitoba and Ontario where this requirement has been abolished. (See the discussion of the *Statute* in Chapter 4.) The *Bills of Exchange Act* requires that the agent's authority be set down in writing when the agent will be signing checks and other negotiable instruments. Even though it is not generally required, it is always best to put an agency agreement in writing to assist in resolving potential disputes between the parties later. There is no requirement that agency agreements be under seal unless the agent will be sealing documents with third parties on behalf of the principal or when required by statute, such as in some provinces when an agent actually sells land for a principal. An agency agreement in writing and under seal is called a **power of attorney**.

All the elements of a contract, such as consensus, consideration, legality, intention to be bound and capacity on the part of both parties, must be present for an agency agreement to be binding. The lack of any one of these elements may have serious ramifications for the agreement between the agent and the principal. But problems with the agency agreement may not have any effect on the binding nature of any agreement the agent enters into on behalf of the principal. Thus, if Clarke is underage and acts as Jiwan's agent in the sale of Jiwan's car to Skoda, the agency contract between Clarke and Jiwan may be voidable because of the incapacity of Clarke. But the contract between Jiwan and Skoda for the purchase of the car is still binding. Only when agents are so young, drunk, insane or otherwise incapacitated that they do not understand what they are doing does the contract between the principal and third party become doubtful on the basis of incapacity or lack of consensus.

An agency agreement may take the form of an employment contract or an independent contractual relationship between the principal and agent. In either case, defects in the agency agreement will not usually have a negative effect on the binding nature of the contract between the principal and the third party.

Formation Without a Contract

Unlike many other areas of the law, the essential requirement for the formation of an agency relationship is merely the consent of both parties. It is quite possible for a principal to be bound by an agent's actions even when no contract exists between them. This point explains why the contract for the purchase of the car is binding between Jiwan and Skoda despite the infancy of the agent, Clarke. The resulting contract between a principal and a third party is binding even when a person serves as an agent gratuitously. It must be emphasized that most agency relationships are created by binding contracts which have been expressly entered into by the parties or implied from their conduct. Often these are simply employment contracts.

Consent the only essential requirement for agency

AUTHORITY OF AGENTS

The most significant part of any agreement between a principal and agent, and the source of most disputes, is the extent of the authority given to the agent by the principal to create a binding relationship with a third party. An agent's authority can be derived from the principal in several ways.

Actual Authority

The agency relationship is established when a principal grants authority to an agent to act on his or her behalf. This power is limited and is called the agent's **actual authority**. When the agency agreement is in writing, the written document will set out the limitations on the agent's authority. When the principal sets out the specific nature of the agent's authority, it is called **express authority**. But the actual authority of the agent is not limited to that expressed by the principal; it will also include an **implied authority** conveyed by the principal. As in other forms of contracts, certain provisions in the agency agreement are implied from the circumstances and form part of the contract. A person who is appointed as an agent to perform a specific function for a principal also has the authority to enter into contracts necessarily incidental to the main activity he or she has been engaged to perform. A person who is hired as a purchasing agent has the authority to carry out the customary and traditional responsibilities of purchasing agents. This actual authority is granted through implication. Of course, normally no such authority is implied if the principal has specifically stated that the agent does not have it. Still, there may be apparent authority as discussed below.

In the example used to introduce this chapter, the contract entered into by Mr. Snarey was just the kind of contract he was authorized to conclude with his clients. Because of this actual authority, the principal was liable for his fraud.

The agreement between principal and agent should set out specifically the express authority the agent has to bind the principal and should avoid the need to imply authority where possible. An agent who exceeds this actual authority may be liable for any injury his or her conduct causes the principal. It would be incorrect, however, for principals to assume that they cannot be bound by actions of their agent which exceed the actual authority the agent has been given.

Apparent Authority

A principal who behaves in a way that makes it appear to a third party that an agent has the authority to act on the principal's behalf is bound by any legal relationship entered into based on that **apparent authority**. The agent's actions may exceed the authority given, or may even have been specifically prohibited, but when the principal has told a third party or led him or her to believe by conduct that the agent has authority to so act, this apparent authority will bind the principal.

The existence of apparent authority based on the conduct or statements of the principal is an application of the principle of estoppel. When a person claims that a certain condition exists, such as, "George is my agent and has my authority," estoppel comes into effect. Such a statement may be wrong, but when it has been relied upon, the person making the statement cannot later claim that what was said was incorrect to escape responsibility. Estoppel applies when a principal has done something to lead the third party to believe that an agent has authority to act on his or her behalf. When a principal leads a third party to believe the agent has authority in this way, that principal is said to have "held out" that the agent has authority to act on his or her behalf. If a third party has relied on this representation, the principal cannot then claim that the agent had no authority.

The most important example of the application of estoppel is in the field of agency. It is important not to confuse this principle of estoppel with equitable or promissory estoppel as described in Chapter 3. Equitable estoppel involves a promise or commitment to do something in the future. Here we are dealing not with a promise but with a claim or a statement of fact made by the principal.

When an agent acts with apparent authority, the principal must look to the agent, not the third party, for compensation for any injuries. Only when the agent has acted beyond both actual and apparent authority is the principal not bound by the agent's actions. If Pedersen operates a used-car dealership and employs Mohammed as sales manager, customers could presume that Mohammed has the authority to sell cars and to take trade-ins because these are the responsibilities that sales managers of car lots normally assume. If Pedersen instructs Mohammed not to accept any trade-in over $2000 without first getting Pedersen's express approval, Mohammed's actual authority has been limited. Suppose Kim wants to trade in a 1985 Mercedes on a 1983 Cadillac and Mohammed, in a burst of enthusiasm, gives a $5000 trade-in on the deal. Could Pedersen later claim that the contract was not binding because he did not give permission for the trade-in? No. Pedersen behaves as if Mohammed is his sales manager, leading Kim to believe that Mohammed has the ordinary authority and power of a sales manager. The agent acted within his apparent authority and the contract was binding on the principal. If, however, the agent had sold Kim the entire car lot, this would be beyond both his actual and apparent authority and would not be binding on Pedersen.

A principal can also be bound by the actions of an agent that would normally be beyond the agent's authority if the principal has sanctioned similar actions in the past. Kim's chauffeur, Green, would not normally be expected to have the authority to purchase automobiles on behalf of his principal. For several years, however, Green has purchased cars from Pedersen's Used Cars on behalf of Kim. The deals have always gone through without any problems, leading Pedersen to believe that Green had authority to make this kind of purchase. Even if Kim specifically told Green not to buy any more cars, if Green returned to Pedersen's car lot and purchased another car, the contract would be binding on Kim because of the apparent authority possessed by the chauffeur. The existence of this apparent authority is based on the statements and conduct of the principal, not the agent. When the misleading indication of authority comes from the agent rather than the principal and the action is otherwise unauthorized, the third party will have no claim against the principal. Only when the agent has no actual and no apparent authority is the principal not bound and then the third party must turn to the agent for compensation.

The reasonable person test has a significant role to play in determining the existence of apparent authority. The usual authority associated with the position in which an agent has been placed is based on this test. The reasonable person test is also used to determine whether the third party should have been misled into believing that the agent had authority by the statements and conduct of the principal.

To determine whether a principal is bound in contract with a third party by the actions of an agent, a person must first ask, "Was the agent acting within the actual authority given by the principal?" If the answer is yes, then there is a contract, providing all the other elements are present. If the answer is no, then the question to ask is, "Did the principal do anything to lead the third party to believe that the agent had the authority to act?" In other words, was the agent acting with apparent authority? If the answer is yes and the third party relied on that apparent authority, there is a contract between the principal and the third party. It is only when the answer to both of these questions is no that there is no contract and the third party must look to the agent for redress.

Most find it difficult to understand the difference between implied and apparent authority, and in most cases the distinctions is not important. When a principal has specifically stated that the agent does not have authority, however, there can be no authority implied. In spite of such a declaration there may still be apparent

Agent acting on apparent authority will bind principal

Previous acceptance of agent's actions

Reasonable person test used to determine existence of authority

authority present on the basis of the principle of estoppel because of the principal's comments or conduct in relation to the third party. The principal has led the third party to believe that the agent has authority and now cannot deny that fact.

Ratification

If principal ratifies unauthorized agreement it is binding

A principal can still **ratify** a contract even if the agent has acted beyond both actual and apparent authority. If a mechanic working at Pedersen's Used Cars were to sell one of the cars on behalf of Pedersen, it is quite likely that the contract would not be binding since a reasonable third party would not expect a mechanic to have the authority to sell cars. However, if Pedersen liked the deal and wanted the sale to proceed, he could force the third party to honour the contract through **ratification** even though the agent had exceeded both actual and apparent authority. The effect of such ratification is to give authority to the mechanic to act on behalf of the principal retroactive to the time he entered into the sale. The result can seem unfair because the principal is not bound when an agent goes beyond the authority given and the third party can do nothing to change that. The third party, however, is bound if the principal ratifies the deal. In fact, the rights of the parties have been qualified to a great extent. The third party has the right to set a reasonable time limit within which the ratification must take place. In the case of a mechanic selling a car without authority, if the customer, after learning of this lack of authority, approached Pedersen to try to get out of the deal, Pedersen could ratify the agreement at once which would force adherence to the contract. But in the absence of such immediate ratification, the customer is not required to have this possibility dragging on for any length of time. The customer is free to say, "You have until noon tomorrow to decide." In the United States, once the third party repudiates, it is too late for the principal to ratify. This may indicate the future direction in Canada, but we are not there yet.

Third party can set time limit for ratification

Agent must have been acting for a specific principal

Another requirement for ratification is that the agent must have been acting for the specific principal who is now trying to ratify. A person cannot enter into a contract with a third party while purporting to be an agent and then search for a principal to ratify. The customer would be free to repudiate the purchase since the would-be agent did not have a particular principal in mind when entering into the contract. There is, therefore, no one to ratify the agreement.

Principal must be capable of entering contract
• when it is entered into

The principal has to be fully capable of entering into the contract at the time the agent was claiming to act on his or her behalf. A principal who did not have the capacity to enter into the original deal because of drunkenness or insanity does not have the power to ratify upon becoming sober or sane. The natural extension of this qualification can cause a serious problem for the people who initiate the process of incorporating a corporation. Often, promoters who are planning an incorporation will enter into contracts, such as the purchase of property on behalf of the proposed corporation, assuming that once the company is formed it will ratify the agreements. But there was no corporation at the time the contract was entered into. For a corporation to ratify a contract, it must have been in existence and capable of contracting at the time the would-be agents entered into the contract on its behalf. The promoter, because she by implication warrants that she had the authority to act for her principal, would be held responsible for any injuries suffered by a third party. Legislation in some jurisdictions has modified this principle to allow a corporation to ratify a contract entered into on its behalf before its incorporation.[2]

2. For example, the *Alberta Business Corporation Act*, S.A. (1981) c. B-15 s. 14.

A further restriction on the ability to ratify is that the parties must be able to still perform the object of the contract at the time of the ratification. For example, if an agent enters into a contract on behalf of a principal to insure a building against fire, the principal cannot ratify the agreement after a fire. There is no building to insure when ratification is attempted, so there can be no contract. The contract the agent enters into must not make any reference to the need for ratification. If the contract includes terms such as "subject to principal's approval" or "subject to ratification," it becomes merely an agreement to enter into an agreement. The contractual requirement of consensus is not satisfied and there is no contract.

when it is ratified

Consensus necessary for contract

Inadvertent Ratification.

The ratification process can work against the principal in other ways. It is possible for the principal to ratify the contract inadvertently by accepting some sort of benefit under the agreement knowing where it came from. If Kim's chauffeur bought a new Rolls Royce on Kim's behalf without the actual or apparent authority to do so, Kim would normally not be bound by such a contract. However, if Kim were to use that car in some way, such as driving it to work or going for a ride in the country before returning it to the dealer, Kim would have accepted some benefit under the contract. The principal could then argue that the contract of purchase had been ratified and Kim would be bound to go through with the purchase of the automobile provided that, at the time she received the benefit, Kim knew that the purchase was made on her behalf.

Ratification can take place inadvertently

Agency by Necessity

At the heart of agency law is the requirement that the principal and the agent must both consent to the agent's acts on behalf of the principal. It is the application of this requirement that renders an agent's act performed without actual or apparent authority not binding on the principal without ratification. As a result, the courts are extremely reluctant to impose agency relationships on principals against their will. However, there are a few situations in which the courts are willing to impose an agency relationship on the principal despite the clear lack of consent. This is called **agency by necessity**.

The doctrine had more application in the past than it does today when communication systems are so much more effective. The classic illustration of agency by necessity is the captain of a ship putting into port and selling damaged cargo for the best possible price in order to preserve some value for the owners. The owners cannot later attack the sale as being unauthorized and claim the return of the cargo or compensation from the third party. Nor can they claim compensation from the ship's captain on the basis of unauthorized action. In this circumstance, the ship's captain was authorized to act by the principle of agency by necessity. Today, modern communication systems allow the captain to get instructions from the owners about what should be done with the cargo, thus avoiding the need to act unilaterally and rely on agency by necessity. Merely finding another person's property in danger does not, in and of itself, create an agency by necessity relationship. There must be some duty or responsibility placed on the agent to care for those goods before an agency by necessity relationship can arise. Even then the courts will be reluctant to impose such an obligation on the principal.

Agency by necessity rarely used today

It is common for a spouse to have the actual or even apparent authority to act on behalf of their spouse when dealing with merchants especially for the purchase of necessities and other household goods. When the marriage breaks down, those

except in some family matters

merchants who, because of past dealings, have been led to believe a person has authority to act for a spouse, may rely on that apparent authority. In the absence of notice to the contrary, the authority continues even when the spouse has been specifically prohibited from making such purchases.

In some circumstances, authority can be implied by operation of law against the will of the other party. A wife who is deserted by her husband is presumed to have the authority to bind him to contracts with third parties for the purchase of necessities. What is or is not a necessity will vary with the lifestyle and status of the family. Today, this principle must be viewed in the light of modern family law legislation which usually provides a more satisfactory remedy. In some jurisdictions, this principle has been abolished altogether.

THE RIGHTS AND RESPONSIBILITIES OF THE PARTIES

The Agent's Duties

The Contract.

When an agency agreement has been created by contract, the agent has an obligation to act within the authority given in that agreement. An agent violating the contract can be sued for breach and will have to compensate the principal for any losses suffered. An agent who goes beyond the authority given in the agency agreement and uses apparent authority to create a binding contract between the principal and a third party can be held responsible for compensating any losses suffered. The agent is also obligated to perform any other functions set out in the agency agreement. Failure to do so may be a breach of contract. However, if the performance of the agency function requires the commission of some illegal act or one against public policy, the agent is not required to perform.

An agent owes a duty of care to the principal. If the agent's conduct falls short of claimed skills or below the level of performance expected from a reasonable person, the agent will be liable to the principal for any damages suffered. For example, if Khan hires Gamboa to purchase property on which to build an apartment building, Gamboa must not only stay within the authority given but must exercise the degree of care and skill one would expect from a person claiming to be qualified to do that type of job. If Gamboa buys a property for Khan that is later discovered to be zoned for single-family dwellings, then Gamboa would be liable to compensate Khan because the failure to ascertain that vital information would fall below the standard of care expected from somebody in this type of business.

Agents usually have considerable discretion in carrying out agency responsibilities as long as they act to the benefit of the principal. However, an agent cannot go against the specific instructions received, even if it might be in the principal's best interests to do so. If a stockbroker is instructed to sell shares when they reach a specific price, the broker must do so even though waiting would bring the principal a better price.

Delegation.

Generally, the agent has an obligation to perform the agency agreement personally. An agent is not permitted to delegate responsibility to another party unless there

Agent must perform as required by principal

Agent owes duty of reasonable care

Agent cannot delegate responsibility

is consent to such delegation, either express or implied by the customs and traditions of the industry, in which case the agent can appoint someone else to perform that function. The agent still has the responsibility to see that the terms of the agency agreement are fulfilled. The authority of an agent is commonly delegated to sub-agents when that agent is a corporation or large business organization such as a law firm, bank, real estate agency or trust company.

Accounting.

Because the agent is acting on behalf of the principal, any monies earned pursuant to the agency function must be paid over to the principal. If the agent acquires property, goods or money on behalf of the principal, there is no entitlement to retain any of it other than the authorized commission. Even when the agent has some claim against such funds, the agent must first convey them to the principal. If the agent, Brose, collects $500 from Witze while acting for Campbell, that money must be paid over to Campbell. Even if Witze owes Brose money from some other deal, Brose must pay over any money collected to the principal. To facilitate this process, the agent also has an obligation to keep accurate records of all agency transactions.

> **Agent must turn money over to principal**

> **Agent must account for funds**

Fiduciary Duty.

Ocean City Realty Ltd. v. A & M Holdings Ltd. et al.[3]

Mrs. Forbes was a licensed real estate salesperson working for Ocean City Realty Ltd. She was approached by Mr. Halbower to find a commercial building in downtown Victoria. After some investigation, Mrs. Forbes approached the owners of a building to determine whether it might be for sale. A & M Holdings Ltd. entered into an arrangement with her whereby they agreed to pay a commission if she acted as their agent in selling the building.

Negotiations followed and a sale was concluded between A & M and Mr. Halbower. This agreement included the payment of a commission of 1 3/4 percent of the sale price which was $5.2 million. Unknown to the seller, A & M, Mr. Halbower insisted that Mrs. Forbes pay back to him $46 000, which was half of her commission. Mrs. Forbes went to her principal, Ocean City Realty, to discuss the appropriateness of the deal, and her supervisor told her that she should go ahead with it and gave her a letter for Mr. Halbower in which he authorized Mr. Halbower to withhold $46 000 from the commissions being paid, on the understanding that the money was owed to him by Mrs. Forbes. There was some delay in completing the transaction and when A & M discovered the secret deal between Mrs. Forbes and Mr. Halbower, they refused to pay any commission.

The problem in this case was that Mrs. Forbes had a fiduciary obligation to act in the best interests of her principal, A & M. She argued that A & M ended up paying exactly what they expected to. She was the one who gave up part of her commission so the deal could go through. That didn't hurt A & M but helped them. The court held, however, that one of the key elements in the duty of the fiduciary is to disclose all pertinent information with respect to the transaction that would be considered important by the principal. In this case, the knowledge that she was paying part of her commission back to Halbower was important to A & M and it may have determined whether they would go through with the deal or not.

---

3. 36 D.L.R. (4th) 94 (British Columbia Court of Appeal).

In effect, they thought that Halbower was paying one price when in fact he was paying less for the property. They were entitled to this information and it may have influenced their decision. Therefore, the fiduciary obligation of the agent had been breached and the agent was entitled to no commission at all.

One is very sympathetic with the position of Mrs. Forbes. She was reluctant to pay over part of her commission to Mr. Halbower; she only did so to preserve the deal, and she argued that because of that she wasn't making more but less out of it. If she didn't complete this deal, it is quite likely the property would have been sold by another real estate agent to somebody else and she would have gotten nothing. And so it is clear that she was acting in her own self-interest above the interest of the principal. This case strongly illustrates the nature of fiduciary duty where a person owing that duty must submerge personal interests in favour of the interests of the principal they represent.

Agent must act in best interests of principal

The relationship between the principal and agent is based on **fiduciary** duty, or trust. Therefore, the agent has an obligation to act only in the best interests of the principal. The relationship is often referred to as an **utmost good faith** relationship. Often the principal is particularly vulnerable because of the trust put in the agent. The agent has an obligation to keep in strict confidence any communications that come through the agency function. The agent cannot take advantage of any personal opportunity that may come to his or her knowledge through the agency relationship. Even if the agent is in a position where some personal benefit will be lost, he or she must act in the principal's best interests. If the agent does stand to benefit personally from the deal, this must be disclosed to the principal. If there is a failure to disclose, the principal can seek an accounting and have any funds gained by the agent in such a way paid over to the principal.

Agent cannot act for both principal and third party without consent of both

If any information comes to the agent in the course of duty that could benefit either the principal or the agent, that information must be disclosed to the principal. It was this failure to fully disclose all information to her principal that was the undoing of Mrs. Forbes in the Ocean City case used to introduce this section. Even though she actually lost money because of the special deal made without the principal's knowledge, that was information the principal was entitled to have and she lost her commission as a result. An agent cannot act for both a principal and a third party at the same time. It would be very difficult for an agent to extract the best possible price from a third party on behalf of a principal when the third party was also paying the agent. The common practice of agents accepting gifts such as holidays, tickets to sporting events and liquor is an example of the same problem. If the principal discovers the agent accepting payment from the third party, the principal is entitled to an accounting and the receipt of all such funds. This policy holds true unless the agent has fully disclosed the fact that he or she is acting for both parties at the outset and receives consent from both of them. In the same way, the agent can only overcome this fiduciary duty and be allowed to keep any personal gain in any of these situations by fully disclosing the nature of the transaction and his or her involvement as well as gain, and receiving the consent of the principal to proceed. This can

Agents have a duty to act in the best interests of their principals.
Photo by Angelika Baur/Prentice Hall Archives.

AGENT'S FIDUCIARY DUTY REQUIRES FULL DISCLOSURE

The plaintiffs listed their home for sale and Mr. Murray submitted an offer for $29 000 below the list price. His friend, Charman, a real estate agent (not the listing agent) wrote a letter accompanying this offer trying to persuade the Baillies to accept this lower offer. They did so, but before the home was transferred, Murray decided he preferred another home listed by Charman and bought that. Charman decided he wanted to take over the deal and had a company that he was principal of take delivery of the property from the Baillies. At the time he substituted the name of the company for his friend Murray in the transaction. He did not tell the Baillies that he had any interest in that company. When they eventually found out what had happened, they brought this action claiming that Charman had violated his fiduciary duty to the plaintiffs. The court agreed.

Charman, as the selling agent, would not normally have such a duty to the vendors, but he took on a fiduciary obligation to the Baillies when he wrote that letter persuading them to take the offer by Murray. After that he had an obligation to disclose, especially his conflict of interest, when he had his company purchase the house. Because he failed to do so and made personal profit, he had to give up not only the commission he made on the original sale of the Baillies' house to the company but also the commission he made on the resale of the property by the company to the eventual purchaser. Also, he had to hand over the profit the company had made. The standards imposed on a fiduciary in these circumstances are significant.

Baillie v. Charman, 94 D.L.R. (4th) 403 (British Columbia Court of Appeal)

cause considerable difficulty in the field of real estate when the agent involved usually represents the seller. Often, however, the purchaser doesn't realize this and they rely on that agent to protect their interests as well often to their detriment. In some western provinces this difficulty is largely overcome by requiring the purchasers to have their own agent acting for them and splitting the commission.

Another example of a violation of a fiduciary duty is what can happen when an agent is hired to purchase property or goods. In such circumstances, the agent cannot sell his or her own personal property to the principal as if it came from a third party even if that property fully satisfies the principal's requirements. This kind of deal would be enforceable only if the agent fully disclosed the ownership of the property and charged a fair price. A similar problem can arise in real estate

Agent must not profit at principal's expense

AGENT OWES FIDUCIARY DUTY TO PRINCIPAL NOT THIRD PARTY

Adams-Eden was a furniture manufacturer that obtained insurance through the services of an insurance broker who arranged this insurance with Kansa. There was a fire and Adams-Eden made a claim to Kansa on its insurance. At first Kansa refused to pay on the basis that they had not been properly informed about prior claims and other material information. They eventually settled their claim and paid Adams-Eden, thinking they would be able to maintain an action for negligence against the insurance broker. This case is to decide whether the insurance broker owed Kansa a duty to disclose the information. The court held that there was no such duty between the broker and the insurer. The broker was the agent of the furniture company, not the agent of the insurance company. In these circumstances Kansa's only remedy would have been not to pay out on the claim.

Adams-Eden Furniture Ltd. v. Kansa General Insurance Co., 141 D.L.R. (4th) 288 (Manitoba Court of Appeal)

transactions. Suppose the agent hired to sell a house recognizes it as a good deal and purchases it in such a way that it looks as if it has been bought by a third party, for example, by a corporation or a partner. The agent then has the advantage of a good price and the commission as well. The problem is that the agent is not acting in the best interests of the principal by getting the best possible price for the property. In such a situation, the agent would be required to pay back both profits and commission to the vendor of the property. (See In Practice box.)

Agent must not compete with principal

In the same way, the agent must not compete with the principal, especially if a service is being offered or if the agent also represents another principal selling the same product. The agent must give the principal all of the benefit resulting from

---

IN PRACTICE

Agent Must Hand Over House

TORONTO—A real estate agent has been given until Oct. 1 to move out of a house in Markham, Ont. that she bought while acting for a would-be purchaser.

In ordering Linda Chow to yield possession of the house she and her husband purchased for $920 000 through a company they owned, an Ontario Supreme Court judge found that Mrs. Chow had breached a fiduciary obligation to her clients.

"While still an agent and fiduciary, she had a conflict of interest with her principal which she failed to disclose," Madame Justice Janet Boland ruled, adding: "She deliberately deceived her principal and used information gleaned through the course of acting as his agent in usurping the opportunity to purchase the property for herself."

The court was told that in the fall of 1987, plaintiff Yin Hang Lee, a retired businessman, sought Mrs. Chow's assistance in finding a new home in the Bayview Avenue area for about $1-million.

Mrs. Chow showed Mr. Lee and his wife the house on Old English Lane in Markham, northeast of Metropolitan Toronto, that became the subject of the court case, and then represented the couple in two weeks of negotiations. At the end of those talks, the parties were only $10 000 apart, with the vendors asking $905 000 and the Lees offering $895 000.

Judge Boland found that the Chows bid $915 000 for the property on Dec. 14, 1987, less than a week after Mrs. Chow presented a $905 000 oral offer on behalf of the Lees. The final $920 000 price was agreed to four days later.

The judge said the first indication the Lees had that Mrs. Chow was no longer acting for them was on the day of the sale, when they found an envelope containing their deposit in their mailbox.

In finding the real estate agent in breach of her fiduciary relationship, the judge said an agent has a duty "to avoid placing herself in potential conflict of interest with her principal unless the principal has full and complete disclosure.

"The value of the agency relationship would be completely destroyed if agents were allowed to occupy a position of trust and then act in direct competition with their principal."

Judge Boland added that the concept of conflict of interest "not only requires disclosure but it also implies that the fiduciary is prohibited from using his position to reap personal gain." In the case at bar, the agent had used confidential information—the price the vendors were willing to accept—that had been obtained in acting for her clients.

In finding the defendants—Mr. and Mrs. Chow and their company—"constructive trustees" for the plaintiff, the judge ordered the house turned over to Mr. Lee "on or before Oct. 1, 1990, upon payment of the sum of $920 000."

A spokesman for the Toronto Real Estate Board said yesterday the median price of Toronto-area homes rose about 40 percent from December, 1987, to April, 1989, and despite a recent market decline is still about 25 percent above late 1987 levels.

Source: Thomas Claridge, *The Globe and Mail*, August 8, 1990.

the performance of the agency agreement. The agent must not collect any profits or commissions that are hidden from the principal. Such wrongful conduct on the part of the agent who is an employee amounts to just cause for dismissal.

Duties of Principal

The Contract.

The principal's primary obligation to the agent is to honour the terms of the contract by which the agent was hired. The principal must adhere to the terms of remuneration that have been agreed to in the contract. If the contract is silent as to payment, an obligation to pay a reasonable amount can be implied. The amount of effort put forth by the agent as well as the customs and traditions of the industry will be taken into consideration to determine what constitutes reasonable payment. If the agreement provides for payment only on completion of the particular job for which the agent has been hired, no payment will be forthcoming unless that act is performed. Thus, if an agent is to receive a commission upon the sale of a house, even if the agent puts considerable effort into promoting a sale, there is generally no entitlement to commission if no sale occurs.

> Principal must honour terms of contract and pay reasonable amount for services

The principal also has an obligation to reimburse the agent for any reasonable expenses incurred in the performance of the agency function. If this obligation has not been expressly included in an agency contract, it will be implied. As long as the agent acts as specified in the contract and within the authority given, the agent is entitled to expenses such as phone bills and car expenses that come from the direct performance of the agency function. It should be noted that this point may be modified by specific contractual agreement or by industry traditions. For example, real estate agents normally do not receive reimbursement of expenses, but this can be modified by agreement.

> Principal must reimburse agent's expenses

A dispute will sometimes arise between the principal and the agent about the interpretation of the contract between them. When agency agreements are vague about the extent of the agent's authority, the courts will usually favour an interpretation that gives the agent the broadest possible power. Thus, if Jones hires Smith to be sales manager for her manufacturing business and gives Smith authority to enter into all sales related to the business, it is probable that a court would use the reasonable person test to find that the sales manager had the authority to sell large blocks of product but that his authority fell short of selling the plant itself. Although the courts tend to interpret vague agency agreements as granting the agent the broadest possible power, it is important to note that they do just the opposite when the power to borrow money is involved. Thus, if Klassen hired Johnson as a purchasing agent with "all the authority necessary to carry out that function" and Johnson found it necessary to borrow money from a third party to make such purchases, the authorization found in the agency agreement would not give Johnson sufficient authority to borrow money without Klassen's additional approval. It is necessary for an agent to be given specific authority to borrow money on the principal's behalf in order to proceed.

> Ambiguous authority will be interpreted broadly

> —except when power to borrow money is in question

Undisclosed Principals

The nature of the relationship between the principal and the third party is most often determined by the authority of the agent. As long as an agent acts within the actual or apparent authority, the contract between the principal and the third party will be binding. It is only when both the actual and apparent authority are exceeded that the agent may be found liable to the third party.

Third party can sue agent or principal if principal undisclosed

The only other situations in which the agent will be held directly liable to the third party are when he or she acts for an undisclosed principal. In some instances the principals may want to keep their identities secret in dealings with third parties. For example, agents may assemble land for a development without disclosing whom they are acting for. The agent can accomplish this wish in several ways. The agent may make it clear that he or she is functioning as an agent but withhold the identity of the principal. The third party can still elect to enter into the agreement in the face of this knowledge, but there will be no recourse against the agent. In the event of a breach, the third party must seek out the identity of the principal and look to that individual for redress. The second situation in which the agent can act for the principal without revealing the principal's identity is when the agent pretends to be the principal. For example, an agent sells property on behalf of a principal but signs the documents as if he or she was the actual owner. In such circumstances, the third party has been misled and can look to the agent for damages in the event of a breach. The third situation in which an agent can act for an undisclosed principal is when the agent deals with a third party in a way consistent with the agent either being an agent or the main contracting party, for example, when the agent signs a purchase order in a way consistent with being an agent for the purchaser or the actual person purchasing the goods. The third party may not be aware that the deal is through an agent with an undisclosed principal but still has not been misled. In these circumstances, the third party has the option of treating the agent as the contracting party and suing the agent in the event of breach or, if the identity of the principal is discovered, suing the principal for compensation in the event of a breach. The injured party cannot sue both; once the choice is made, the third party is bound by it.

To avoid the undisclosed principal problem, a person acting as an agent should be extremely careful to make it clear that they are acting in an agency capacity. This is normally done by writing "per" immediately before the signature of the agent. If Sam Jones were acting for Ace Finance Company he would sign:

Ace Finance Ltd. per Sam Jones:

Alternatively, the agency relationship could be specified:

Sam Jones acting for Ace Finance Ltd.

NO LIABILITY UNDER CONTRACT WHERE AGENT MAKES IT CLEAR HE IS ACTING AS AGENT

Chartwell provided stevedoring services for Q.N.S., which operated a chartered ship. Although Chartwell never mentioned specifically who they were acting for, at all times they made it clear they were acting as agents on behalf of others in their dealings with Q.N.S. The deal fell through. Q.N.S. sued Chartwell. The court had to decide whether this was an undisclosed principal situation where the agent could be successfully sued. The court held that because Chartwell had made it clear at all times that they were functioning as an agent, there was no personal liability for that agent on the contract. An agent cannot be held personally liable for a contract that he enters into with a third party if he makes it clear he is acting as an agent even though he doesn't disclose the identity of the principal.

Q.N.S. Paper Co. v. Chartwell Shipping Ltd., 62 D.L.R. (4th) 36 (Supreme Court of Canada)

As a general rule, the third party is bound to the principal by contracts entered into by an agent even when the principal is undisclosed, providing the agent is acting within the actual authority given. Note that apparent authority does not apply, since an undisclosed principal can make no representations. Not all contracts with undisclosed principals are binding on third parties. An exception is when the identity of the undisclosed principal is important to the third party. In a contract involving personal services, the third party would be able to repudiate upon discovering that the deal had been made with an agent rather than with the principal. In the case of *Nash v. Dix*,[4] a religious group acquired the services of an agent to purchase a church building from another religious organization. They felt that the church would not be sold to them if they disclosed who they really were. Their fear was justified in that the sale was challenged when the identity of the principal was discovered. The court held that this was not a situation in which the identities of the parties were important and the sale went through. In the case of *Said v. Butt*,[5] a theatre refused to sell a ticket to someone on opening night because he had caused a disturbance in the past. That person arranged for a friend to acquire the ticket on his behalf but was refused admittance even though he had a ticket. He sued for breach but the court held that, in this situation, the identity of the party was obviously important and the court did not enforce the contract.

> Third party can repudiate when identity of undisclosed principal important

Undisclosed principal relationships are often used when well-known companies are assembling land for new projects. Property owners in the area are approached by agents to obtain options on their properties. The options are only exercised if a sufficient number of property owners are willing to sell at a reasonable price. The undisclosed principal approach is used to discourage people from holding out for higher prices once they find out who is really buying the property.

A third party can choose to sue either the agent or the undisclosed principal but the third party is only bound by this choice once the identity of the principal has been determined. The principal can enforce the contract unless the identity of the parties is an important factor in the contractual relationship. Similarly, the

NO APPARENT AUTHORITY WITH UNDISCLOSED PRINCIPAL

Sign-O-Lite entered into an agreement with Calbex Properties Ltd., the owners of a Calgary shopping mall, to put up a large outdoor sign there. By the time this agreement expired, the actual ownership of the mall had changed hands, although Sign-O-Lite was not aware of it. In fact, a series of complex dealings had taken place which left another company controlled by the same principal as Calbex as the managing company of the mall but not the owner, and so Sign-O-Lite thought they were dealing with the same people when they entered into a renewal agreement with the mall management company. The mall management company didn't have the authority to renew, and the company owning the property, the defendant in this case, refused to go through with the deal. The court had to decide whether a contract entered into by an agent on behalf of an undisclosed principal is binding on that principal when the agent has gone beyond his or her authority. The court found that in such circumstances, the principal cannot be bound; the concepts of apparent authority or ostensible authority do not apply, as they are inconsistent.

Sign-O-Lite Plastics Ltd. v. Metropolitan Life Insurance Co., 73 D.L.R. (4th) 541 (British Columbia Court of Appeal)

---

4. *Nash v. Dix* (1898) 78 L.T. 445.

5. *Said v. Butt* (1923) K.B. 497.

agent may sue or be sued under the contract when the principal is undisclosed. The agent only loses the right to enforce the agreement when the principal chooses to act like a principal and takes steps to enforce the agreement. It is usually possible for a principal to ratify an agreement created by an agent who has exceeded both actual and apparent authority and make the agreement binding on the third party. But to do so, the agent must claim to be acting for a specifically identified principal. An undisclosed principal cannot ratify the acts of an agent.

Only identified principals can ratify

The Third Party

Westcom Radio Group Ltd. v. MacIsaac[6]

Through all these dealings, Mrs. MacIsaac was acting on behalf of a corporation which had not yet been incorporated. She entered into a contract with Westcom for advertising on the radio. At the time she did this she honestly thought that she was the director and signing officer of the corporation in question, and Westcom, on their part, thought as well that they were dealing not with Mrs. MacIsaac but a properly incorporated limited company. But because the corporation had not yet been incorporated it was nonexistent at the time the contract was entered into. The advertising was supplied and bills were sent to the business, but they remained unpaid. Both the business and Mrs. MacIsaac were sued by Westcom for the unpaid bills.

The question in this case was that because Mrs. MacIsaac was acting for a principal that didn't exist, was she responsible for the resulting debt? The court held that because it was clear that Mrs. MacIsaac never intended to be bound personally by the contract, and had made that clear to Westcom, she was not. Usually when promoters contract on behalf of businesses yet to be incorporated, they know they are doing so and quite often the other party does as well, hence personal liability. But in this case, Mrs. MacIsaac and the plaintiff were equally convinced that the corporation did exist at the time of the transactions and that she was acting on the corporation's behalf.

It should be noted there is a provision in the *Ontario Business Corporations Act* which reads, "Except as provided in this section, a person who enters into an oral or written contract in the name of or on behalf of a corporation, before it comes into existence, is personally bound by the contract and is entitled to the benefits thereof" [Section 21:1]. This section did not apply here because no contract was entered into on behalf of that corporation; Westcom intended that contract with the corporation, not Mrs. MacIsaac.

This case illustrates several important principles. Normally, when an agent acts on behalf of a purchaser without the authority to do so, she could be sued for breach of warranty of authority. In this case, however, there was no principal at all and both parties were ignorant of that fact. Had Mrs. MacIsaac known that the corporation had not been incorporated, she would likely have been liable. The language throughout this case seems to indicate that, in common law at least, the agent is not responsible because Westcom intended and thought that they were dealing with a corporation, but the corporation didn't exist. That language seems to be couched in terms of mistake, a principle dealt with in Chapter 5. Because of that mistake, there was no meeting of the minds, and hence no contract.

6. 63 D.L.R. (4th) 433 (Ontario High Court of Justice, Divisional Court).

This exception should be kept in mind during the discussion of the liability of an agent to a third party which is discussed below.

An agent owes an obligation to the third party to actually possess the authority he or she claims to have. If she has exceeded both her actual and apparent authority, she has breached that obligation and is subject to action for breach of "warranty of authority." This action is founded on contract law and is one of the few situations in which the agent can be sued directly by the third party. In addition to this remedy, an agent who intentionally misleads the third party into believing that she has authority she does not hold is liable to be sued for damages for the tort of deceit. Furthermore, agents who inadvertently exceed their authority can be sued for negligence. An action for breach of warranty of authority, however, is much more common in these circumstances.

Third party can sue agent for unauthorized acts

The *Westcom* case discussed above illustrates one of these rare instances where an agent was not liable to the third party for exceeding her authority. In that case all parties were under a misapprehension as to the existence of the corporation that was the principal. There was no intentional wrongdoing or negligence on her part and any contractual liability based on breach of warranty of authority was not present because of mistake, as discussed in Chapter 5.

It is important to distinguish between the tortious liability of the agent based on fraud or negligence and an action based on breach of warranty of authority. The damages available for breach of warranty of authority are limited to the type of damages available for breach of contract, such as injuries that are reasonably foreseeable to the parties at the time the contract is entered into or injuries which flow naturally from the breach. The types of damages available when fraud or negligence are involved are governed by tort law. The practical result is that an agent who has exceeded authority in dealings with the third party in such a way that the principal is not liable may escape paying full compensation if sued by a third party for breach of warranty of authority. If, for example, unknown to the agent, the third party planned to resell goods purchased from that agent at an unusually high profit but was unable to do so because of the breach of warranty of authority, the agent would not be liable for these unusual losses. They would not have been within the reasonable contemplation of the agent at the time the contract was entered into in the first place, and therefore not reasonably foreseeable. However, if the third party could establish the agent's fraud, the lost profits might be recovered from the agent because they are the direct consequence of the fraud.

Remedies in tort available for fraud or negligence

Liability for Agent's Tortious Conduct

As discussed in Chapters 2 and 10, an employer is vicariously liable for the acts an employee commits during the course of employment. When an agent is also an employee of the principal, the principal is vicariously liable for any tortious acts committed by the agent in the course of that employment. The difficulty arises when the agent is not an employee but acting independently. The Supreme Court of Canada has held that the principle of vicarious liability is restricted to those situations in which a master/servant relationship can be demonstrated.[7] Still, it is often argued that a principal can be held vicariously liable for the wrongful conduct of an independent agent. In this text, we have taken the more conservative position

Vicarious liability limited to employment

7. *T. G. Bright and Company v. Kerr* (1939) S.C.R. 63.

that employment must be present for vicarious liability to exist. It must be emphasized, however, that the courts have been expanding the definition of employment. Fleming pointed out that, "The employment of a servant may be limited to a single occasion, or extend over a long period; it may even be gratuitous."[8] Even if the relationship involves a person who is essentially an independent agent, that agent may be functioning as an employee in a given situation and thus impose vicarious liability on the principal. With such a broad definition of employment, judges will have little difficulty imposing vicarious liability on principals when the circumstances warrant. Of course, the principal can then look to the agent for compensation for any losses incurred by having to pay compensation to the person injured by the agent's wrongful conduct.

Vicarious liability where independent agent deceitful

There are some situations in which vicarious liability will apply even if the agent is acting independently. The courts are clearly willing to hold the principal responsible for the fraudulent misrepresentation of an agent even when no employment exists. The vendor can be held responsible for a fraud committed by a real estate agent in the process of selling a house on behalf of the vendor. In the example used to introduce the chapter, it made no difference whether Mr. Snarey was an employee or was acting as an independent agent; because fraud was involved, the principal was liable for the agent's wrongful conduct. In rare cases there may be other wrongful conduct such as negligence that gives rise to the imposition of vicarious liability on the principal even for the acts of such independent agents. But it is clear that these will be limited to those situations where the wrongful conduct takes place as the agent does the specific act they have been employed to do.

Direct liability if principal is origin of fraud

In addition to being vicariously responsible for the tortious conduct of an agent, the principal may be found directly liable. If the principal has requested the act complained of, told the agent to make a particular statement that turns out to be defamatory or misleading, or is negligent in allowing the agent to make the particular statements complained of, the principal may be directly liable. In the case of *Junkin v. Bedard*,[9] Junkin owned a motel that was sold to a third party through an agent. Junkin provided false information regarding the profitability of the motel to the agent, knowing that the agent would pass it on to the purchaser, Bedard. The agent did so and Bedard bought the property. Bedard later discovered the falsification and sued Junkin for fraud. Because the agent had innocently passed the information on to Bedard, Junkin alone had committed the fraud even though the agent had communicated the information. This is an example of direct liability rather than vicarious liability. If the agent had been the one to fabricate and communicate the misleading information, the principal's responsibility would have been based on vicarious liability. As was the case with employment law, the fact that the principal is found vicariously liable for tortious acts of the agent does not relieve the agent of direct liability for his or her own tortious conduct. Both can be sued, but the principal can then turn to the agent and demand compensation for any loss suffered.

Vicarious liability—both parties liable

Termination of Agency

Termination as per agreement

Since the right of an agent to act for a principal is based on the principal's consent, as soon as the agent is notified of the withdrawal of that consent, that authority ends. An agency relationship created through agreement is usually terminated in

8. John G. Fleming, *The Law of Torts*, 8th ed. (Sydney: The Law Book Co. Ltd., Australia, 1990), p. 371.

9. *Junkin v. Bedard* (1958) 11 D.L.R. (2d) 481.

the same way. If the authority to function as an agent is embodied in an employment contract, the principles discussed in Chapter 10 under "Termination" apply although termination is not always required since the agent employee may simply be reassigned or given a different job description. In situations where the agent functions outside of the employment relationship, either gratuitously or pursuant to some independent contract, different principles apply. The principal needs only to give notice to withdraw authority from an agent who is acting gratuitously. If the agency relationship is based on a separate contractual relationship, the terms of the agreement itself may provide for the termination of the agency. If the agency relationship was created for a specific length of time, the authority of the agent automatically terminates at the end of that period. Similarly, if the agency contract created the relationship for the duration of a particular project or event, for example, "for the duration of the 1998 Canadian National Exhibition," the authority ends when the project or event ends.

If one of the parties wishes to terminate an ongoing agency relationship, simple notice to this effect from either party is usually sufficient. Notice to terminate the agent's authority would take effect immediately upon receipt by the agent. There is no requirement that the notice be reasonable, only that it be communicated to the agent. This applies to the termination of authority to enter into new contracts on the principal's behalf, not necessarily to the right to continued payment which may be based on other contractual considerations. If the activities the agent is engaged to perform become impossible or essentially different from what the parties anticipated, then the contractual doctrine of frustration may apply and terminate the agent's authority. Similarly, an agent's authority to act on behalf of a principal is terminated when the actions the agent is engaged to perform become illegal. If Cantello had agreed to act as Jasper's agent to sell products in a pyramid sales scheme, Cantello's authority to represent Jasper would have been terminated automatically when the *Criminal Code* provision prohibiting such activities was passed.[10]

Requirement of notification for termination

Frustration may terminate agency

An agent's authority to act on behalf of a principal can be terminated in several other ways. The death or insanity of a principal will automatically end the authority of an agent. When the principal is a corporation, its dissolution will have a similar effect. An agent will lose authority when a principal becomes bankrupt, although other people may assume such authority under the direction of the trustee. The third party will normally not be affected in the same way. Certainly, as far as termination of authority on the basis of agreement is concerned, unless the principal notifies the third party of such termination, the actions of the agent may still be binding on the principal on the basis of apparent authority. Though it is not entirely clear, this may also be the case when the principal becomes insane. In the case of bankruptcy, death or dissolution of the company, the agent's actual and apparent authority ceases. Because of the principle of apparent authority, it is vitally important for a principal to take steps to notify current and potential customers as well as other people and businesses that they may have dealings with, of the termination of the agent's authority.

Death, insanity or bankruptcy will terminate agency

Enduring Powers of Attorney

As stated above, loss of sanity on the part of the principal will terminate an agency; consequently authority to act under a power of attorney terminates when the

---

10. *Criminal Code*, R.S.C. (1985) c. C-46 s. 206.

principal or grantor loses capacity. This is problematic, especially where society is aging and many individuals may desire to appoint someone as their agent or decision maker with power to act in the principal's stead after the principal loses capacity. In the past, it was necessary for family members (or others) to apply to the courts for an order appointing them as the **Trustee** of the person who had lost capacity. These applications, made pursuant to the *Dependent Adults Act*,[11] could be expensive and time consuming, especially if the family was divided as to who should act as trustee. The process could also be a humiliating one for the principal involved, whose loss of mental capacity would be openly examined in a public setting.

To remedy some of these difficulties, Alberta's government passed the *Powers of Attorney Act* in 1991.[12] The Act allows individuals to execute **enduring powers of attorney**, vesting powers similar to those given to Trustees, to the person chosen to act as one's attorney. These powers typically are exercisable after the principal or donor loses mental capacity. The attorney generally can make all financial decisions on behalf of the donor. Through use of an enduring power of attorney, a person can decide, in advance, who to entrust with the future handling of her financial affairs. (Note: it is now also possible for Albertans to exercise some control over who will make health care decisions and similar personal decisions for them. The *Personal Directives Act*[13] enables an adult to appoint a health care agent. The agent is authorized to make health care decisions on behalf of the donor once the donor is no longer able to give consent to treatment due to incapacity.)

Specialized Agency Relationships

Many examples of specialized services offered to businesses and the public are essentially agency in nature, such as those of travel agents, real estate agents, lawyers, accountants, stockbrokers and insurance representatives. Some of these agents do not enter into contracts on behalf of their clients but negotiate and act on their clients' behalf in other ways. For example, a real estate agent neither offers nor accepts on behalf of a client. In fact, the client is usually the vendor of property and the agent's job is to take care of the preliminary matters and bring the purchaser and vendor together so they can enter into a contract directly. Nonetheless, few would dispute that these real estate agents are carrying out an essentially agency function and thus have a fiduciary obligation to their clients. The important thing to remember is that the general provisions set out above also apply to these special agency relationships, although there may be some exceptions. For example, in most of these specialized service professions, the rule that an agent cannot delegate usually does not apply. But the very nature of these businesses requires that employees of the firm, not the firm itself, will act on behalf of the client.

It is important to note that most of these specialized agencies are fulfilling a service function and are governed by special statutes and professional organizations. For example, the real estate industry in each province has legislation in place that creates commissions or boards which govern the industry.[14] The commissions require that anyone acting for another in the sale of property be licensed or be in the employ of a licensed real estate agent. These bodies license their members and provide disciplinary action when required. It is beyond the scope of this text to

General principles apply to specialized agencies as well

Special statutes and professional organizations

11. *Dependent Adults Act,* R.S.A (1980) c. D-32.
12. *Powers of Attorney Act,* S.A. (1991) c. P-13.5.
13. *Personal Directives Act,* S.A. (1996) c. P-4.03.
14. *Real Estate Act,* S.A. (1995) c. R-4.5.

examine these professional bodies in detail; the student is encouraged to examine the controlling legislation as well as to seek information from the governing professional bodies in these areas directly. Most of these bodies are concerned about their public image and are happy to cooperate.

Often these agencies perform a service to their customers that involves not only representing those customers but giving them advice. Because of the specialized expertise provided, the customers are particularly vulnerable to abuse when such agencies try to take advantage of them. The governing bodies hear complaints and go a long way towards regulating the industry and preventing such abuses. But abuses still occur, and victims should know that they have recourse based on the fiduciary duty principles set out here as well as remedies in contract and tort discussed before. Such fiduciary duties in fact may be imposed on other professional advisers even when their duties do not extend to being agents.[15]

SUMMARY

An agent acts as a go-between when the principal enters into a contract with a third party. The agent's authority is usually defined in a contract but there might be further apparent authority when the principal has done something to lead the third party to believe that the agent has authority even when such authority has been specifically withheld. Even if the agent has exceeded both the actual and apparent authority, the principal may ratify the agreement. Such ratification works retroactively. Only when the agent acts beyond all authority can he or she be sued (breach of warranty of authority).

When the agent does not disclose that he or she is acting for a principal, the third party has a choice to sue the agent or the undisclosed principal to enforce the contract. In the absence of an employment relationship, the principal is not vicariously liable for the acts of the agent except when fraudulent misrepresentation is involved.

A fiduciary relationship exists between the agent and the principal, and the agent, as a result, has the obligation to act in the best interests of the principal. The agency relationship is typically terminated by simple notification or as agreed in the agency contract. Death or insanity of the principal, or, when the principal is a corporation, the dissolution of that corporation, will also terminate the agent's authority.

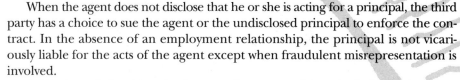

QUESTIONS

1. What is the agent's function? Why is it important to understand the law of agency in business?

2. Distinguish between agents, employees and independent contractors. Describe the relationship between them.

3. What is the significance of the agency agreement for the parties to it?

4. Explain what effect an agent's limited capacity will have on the contractual obligations created between a principal and a third party. What effect would the incapacity of the principal have on this relationship?

15. *Hodginson v. Simms* [1994] 3 S.C.R. 377.

5. Distinguish between an agent's actual, implied and apparent authority. Explain why this distinction can be important from the agent's point of view.

6. Distinguish between promissory, or equitable, estoppel and ordinary estoppel. Explain the role estoppel plays in agency law.

7. Explain what is meant by ratification. Why is the principal's right to ratify often considered unfair to the third party?

8. Describe the limitations on a principal's right to ratify the actions of his or her agent. How can the principle of ratification be as dangerous to the principal as it is to the third party?

9. What effect does it have on the relationship between the principal and the third party when an agent writes on an agreement "subject to ratification"?

10. Agents owe a fiduciary duty to their principals. What are the requirements of that duty?

11. What options are open to a third party who has been dealing with an undisclosed principal if the contract is breached?

12. Does an undisclosed principal have the right to ratify an agent's unauthorized act?

13. Explain how the doctrine of vicarious liability applies in a principal/agent relationship.

14. How does the function performed by a real estate agent differ significantly from that normally performed in a principal/agency relationship? What governs the real estate agent's conduct?

CASES

1. Kisil v. John S. Stevens Ltd.
Mr. and Mrs. Kisil bought a house through Buckley, an agent for the John S. Stevens firm. In the process of selling the house, Buckley assured the Kisils that there was no problem with the water in the well. They decided to buy the house, but Buckley kept them out of the house until after the deal's closing date. All this time, Buckley maintained that the condition of the well was good and that the water would clear up as soon as it was used a bit. In fact, the well had been improperly constructed and the water it produced was unfit for use. The Kisils sued Buckley and the real estate company. Describe the arguments which would form the basis of their complaint, their likelihood of success and the remedies available. Explain as well the legal position of the vendor.

2. Rockland Industries Inc. v. Amerada Minerals Corporation of Canada Limited
Curtz was a salesman in charge of bulk sales and the manager of marketing who reported to Devron, a senior vice-president of Amerada. Curtz negotiated and concluded a deal with Powers and Lederman, employees of Rockland Industries Inc., for the sale of 50 000 tons (45 360 tonnes) of sulphur. During the process of negotiation, Curtz gave no indication of any qualifications on

his authority. However, any sale of this magnitude had to be approved by an executive operating committee of Amerada and signed by the chairman of the board. After the deal was completed, Rockland's representative was informed of the limitations on Curtz's authority, but was also told that the operating committee had given approval and that the chairman of the board's signature was merely a rubber stamp. In fact, Amerada refused to deliver the sulphur and Rockland had to acquire it from other sources. They were able to acquire only 25 000 tons and sued Amerada for damages. Explain the arguments available to both sides and the likely outcome.

3. Alberta Housing Corporation v. Achten and Alberta Housing Corporation v. Orysiuk

The Alberta Housing Corporation was established to secretly create a landbank to stabilize residential prices as the city of Edmonton expanded. Orysiuk was the managing director of the Alberta Housing Corporation, who was given the task of making the acquisitions for the landbank. The Housing Corporation acquired the services of Achten, a lawyer, who was given a commission of 5 percent on the acquisition of lands. Other parties were also engaged to assemble the land, including a real estate company that was given a commission of 3 percent. Achten acquired a large amount of land on behalf of the Alberta Housing Corporation and earned over $200 000 in commissions. After a number of properties had already been acquired under the relationship between Achten and the Alberta Housing Corporation, Achten entered into a separate secret agreement with Orysiuk whereby he paid back one-half of his commission. When this deal was eventually discovered, the Alberta Housing Corporation sued both parties for the recovery of the Corporation's money.

Explain the arguments available on both sides and the likely outcome. Would it affect your answer if you learned that the Alberta Housing Corporation was not injured by Orysiuk and Achten's actions and had paid a fair price for the property including legal fees and commissions? The Alberta Housing Commission also insisted on the return of over $30 000 they had paid to Achten in legal fees. Explain the likely outcome.

4. Guertin v. Royal Bank of Canada

Mrs. Guertin worked at a snack bar. The owners of the snack bar owned another restaurant which was located in the same mall as a branch of the Royal Bank managed by Mr. Arcand. Mr. and Mrs. Guertin were good customers of the Royal Bank and went to talk to the bank manager about the possibilities of buying this snack bar. They told him that the price was $30 000 but they also told him they thought they could get it for $22 000 or $23 000. In fact, the Guertins were waiting to see if the price would come down. In the meantime, Mr. Arcand offered $23 000 for the snack bar which was accepted. The purchase was made through his wife because the bank rules prohibited him from buying it himself. Explain the liability of Mr. Arcand and the bank in these circumstances and any complaints the Guertins might have about his conduct.

5. Wakeford v. Yada Tompkins Huntingford & Humphries et al.

Mr. Humphries was a public accountant working for the Yada Tompkins accounting firm. He advised his client, Mr. Wakeford, to purchase a condominium in California as a tax shelter. Mr. Wakeford later sold the condominium at a considerable loss and then discovered that Mr. Humphries had obtained a $2000 payment from the developer. Mr. Humphries had since been dismissed from the firm because of this practice of accepting finder's fees and was also bankrupt. Mr. Wakeford sued Yada Tompkins, the firm Mr. Humphries had been working for.

Explain their liability in this circumstance and any defense that may be available to them. Would your answer be affected by the knowledge that when Mr. Wakeford purchased the condo it was at a very advantageous price and that it is quite likely that had he known about the finder's fee he still would have purchased the condo? It was eventually sold at a loss because of a serious downturn in the real estate market in California.

6. Raso v. Dionigi

Guerino Siranni was a real estate agent working for the firm of Joseph Lianagus. His sister-in-law Raffaela was looking for some income property and after some searching, Siranni entered into a deal with Mr. and Mrs. Dionigi, persuading them to list their property for sale with him and subsequently presented an offer to purchase from his sister-in-law, who used her maiden name Raso so the sellers wouldn't know that he was related to the purchaser. Before the deal was to close the Dionigi's discovered the relationship between the agent and the purchaser and refused to go through with the deal. Mr. Siranni sued for his commission and his brother and sister-in-law sued for specific performance.

Explain the arguments that are available to the sellers in response to these claims. How would your answer be affected by the knowledge that the brother and sister-in-law of Mr. Siranni had disclosed to him that they were willing to pay between $250 000 and $300 000 for the property, and in the negotiations that followed this was not disclosed to the sellers. In fact the first offer made by his brother and sister-in-law was only $270 000. The sellers eventually took $285 000 for the property not knowing that the purchasers were willing to go to $300 000. The actual fair market value of the property was determined to be $300 000.

LEGISLATION

Alberta

Factors Act, R.S.A. (1980) c. F-1
Land Agents Licensing Act, R.S.A. (1980) c. L-2
Powers of Attorney Act, S.A. (1991) c. P-13.5
Real Estate Act, S.A. (1985) c. R-4.5

WEBLINKS

Custom Brokers Association of Canada
www.cbac.ca/

New Brunswick Real Estate Agents Act
inter.gov.nb.ca/acts/acts/r-01.htm

Realtists Institute of North America
www.realtist.com/

Independent Real Estate Brokers Association of Canada
www.ireba.ca/

Canadian Institute of Chartered Accountants
www.cica.ca/

Canadian Association of Independent Accountants
www.caia.org/

Alberta Powers of Attorney Act
www.gov.ab.ca/qp/ascii/acts/P13P5.txt

Public Legal Education Society of Nova Scotia—Powers of Attorney
www.chebucto.ns.ca/Law/PLENS/power-at.html

REFERENCES FOR PART 4

Bell, Stacey Reginald, J. Braithwaite. *Canadian Employment Law*. Aurora, Ont. : Canada Law Book, 1996.

Bishop, Peter J. *Winning in the Workplace: ADR Strategies for Employment Disputes.* Scarborough: Carswell, 1994.

Corry, David J. *Collective Bargaining and Agreement.* Aurora, Ont.: Canada Law Book, 1997.

McArthur, Stephen A., Jules B. Bloch, Robert F. Salisbury. *Canadian Construction, Labour and Employment Law.* Markham, Ont.: Butterworths, 1997.

Saxe, Stewart D. *Ontario Employment Law Handbook: An Employer's Guide.* 4th ed. Markham, Ont.: Butterworths, 1997.

Smyth, J. E., D. A. Soberman, and A. J. Easson. *The Law and Business Administration in Canada.* 8th ed. Toronto: Prentice Hall Canada, 1998.

Labour Problems in Port Alberni

VIDEO CASE

CBC

Trade unionism has played an important role in the economic and social development of Canada in the past century. Labour relations legislation was originally designed to quell labour unrest and create a tolerable working environment. But there is great debate now as to whether trade unions impede business and industry and whether their demands create greater problems for workers than they solve.

In Port Alberni, a mill town on Vancouver Island, trade unions have become an important part of the town's culture. When the town's major employer, forest industry giant MacMillan Bloedel, employed a company with a "Rat Union" to do some construction work, all the might of the traditional unions was brought to bear to fight the management tactics. A Rat Union, in this case the Canadian Iron and Steel Workers Union, is, in effect, a company-dominated union. Their workers will work for less money, cross picket lines and cooperate with management. They also support an open shop, that is, they do not require their employees to be members of a union. Traditional unions run closed shops where all employees are required to be union members; workplaces are closely monitored by union representatives and bound by labour contracts.

The result was violence on the picket line, and intimidation of townspeople who offered any services to members of the Rat Union. MacMillan Bloedel was determined to make the Port Alberni mill a test site to challenge the power of the traditional union and the result was an extended and sometimes violent conflict that has badly hurt the town and divided its citizens. After protracted negotiations, MacMillan Bloedel announced massive layoffs at the Port Alberni mill, claiming that the loss of markets for their products and the expense of operations necessitated downsizing.

Source: "Port Alberni," *The National*; telecast date December 12, 1994. Running time: 15:44.

DISCUSSION QUESTIONS

1. What legislation applies in this situation and what is the goal of that legislation?
2. What should be the primary goal of such legislation: to quell violence or create a level playing field between employees and management?
3. Should Rat Unions be allowed and consider how they could be controlled?
4. Is it true that alternative unions provide "no dignity and no security"?
5. What does the legislation in your province do to try to resolve these problems?
6. What are or what should be the legal consequences of violence and intimidation during job action?
7. How effective is the legislation in your jurisdiction in balancing the conflicting objectives of an employer-dominated workforce and unfettered union power?
8. What interferes with the free market system more, allowing trade unions or prohibiting them?

Business Organizations

One important characteristic of our modern commercial world is the effort that has been made by the legal system to facilitate the involvement of large groups of people in various business projects and activities. Partnership is the historical method of people joining together to carry on such business activities and this along with an examination of the sole proprietorship is the subject matter of Chapter 12. Chapter 13 deals with the now-more-common method used where people come together to participate in business, the corporation. Corporations are artificial persons and their uniqueness results in a complex world of interaction between the corporation, shareholders, creditors, managers and workers and developing an understanding of these relationships is the objective of that chapter.

Photo Courtesy of
Crown Life Insurance.

Sole Proprietorship and Partnership

OBJECTIVES OF THE CHAPTER

- To describe a sole proprietorship and the government regulations that affect it
- To identify the rights and obligations of partners
- To outline the advantages of partnership as a form of business

One of the partners in a law firm was helping to administer an estate when he was asked to transfer the amount outstanding in the estate ($60 025) to a bank in California. These funds were on deposit at a local branch of the Royal Bank and a cheque was drawn up, signed by the executrix of the estate and made out to the California bank as payee. The lawyer, however, made another copy of that cheque with himself as payee, forged the signature of the executrix and destroyed the first cheque. He then cashed the cheque at his own bank. When this action was discovered, he was charged and convicted of fraud.

The bank on which the cheque was drawn was required to reimburse the estate and they turned to the convicted lawyer's partners to compensate them. There is no question but that the partners were honest and innocent of any wrongdoing. Yet in the subsequent court action, they were found liable to compensate the Royal Bank for their $60 000 loss even though that branch had had no direct dealings with the partnership at all.[1]

Although this case deals with lawyers, the principles apply to any situation in which partnership exists. Partners are responsible for the wrongful conduct of each other. The case also illustrates just how careful people going into business with others have to be. This chapter is primarily devoted to an examination of partnership law, how partnership is created and the obligations of the parties involved.

---

1. *Victoria & Grey Trust Company v. Crawford et al.*, Ont. Sup. Ct. 636-012.

A commercial enterprise, usually called a business, can be established on the basis of several different methods of ownership. It is vitally important that the parties participating in the commercial activity clearly understand the legal responsibilities and rights which apply to their choice of business organization. This information could be significant to the owners of the business, its employees or representatives, and outsiders involved in commercial transactions with it.

TYPES OF BUSINESS ORGANIZATION

There are essentially three major types of business organization. The first, the **sole proprietorship**, is an individual carrying on business alone. Employees may be hired and business may be carried on through the services of an agent, but the business is the sole responsibility of one person, the owner. A second method of carrying on business is called a **partnership**. In a partnership, ownership responsibilities and profits or losses are shared by two or more partners. As was the case with the sole proprietorship, the partnership may also employ others and act through agents. The third type of business organization is the incorporated company. Any type of business organization involving more than one person can be called a company; a **corporation**, however, is a legal entity. By statute it has been given an identity separate from the individual members who make it up. Thus, contracts with a corporation are dealings with the corporation itself as if it were a person in its own right.

Sole proprietorship is one person

In a partnership owners share responsibilities

Corporation is a separate legal entity

People in a community can carry on business in other ways. For example, it is possible to set up a **society** under the *Societies Act* [2] if the enterprise is not for profit. The result is also a separate legal entity, but the procedure of incorporation and the obligations of those involved are quite different.

Societies are separate legal entities but obligations differ

There are also several ways in which these various types of business organizations can be combined. For example, it is possible for the business of one corporation to be holding shares in another corporation. Or several different corporations can band together to form a special corporation or partnership to accomplish a major project by participating in what is known as a joint venture. The discussion in this text will be limited to an examination of the three main types of business organizations outlined above. This chapter will examine sole proprietorship and partnership, and Chapter 13 will deal with corporations.

THE SOLE PROPRIETORSHIP

The sole proprietorship is simply an individual carrying on a business activity in his or her own right. The sole proprietor makes all the decisions associated with the business and is the only one entitled to the benefits deriving from the business. A sole proprietor also bears full responsibility for all of the costs, losses and obligations incurred in the business activity. Thus, there is no distinction between the personal assets of the sole proprietor and those of the business. They are all the assets of the proprietor and are available to creditors if things go badly.

Sole proprietor carries on business in own right

Government Regulations

The sole proprietor, like all other types of business organizations, must satisfy many federal, provincial and municipal requirements in order to carry on business. A

Must adhere to licensing and governing regulations

2. *Societies Act,* R.S.A. (1980) c. S-18.

There are several organizational options available when starting a business.

Photo by Dick Hemingway.

sole proprietor is usually required to register the business name, if different from her personal name,[3] and buy a license from the municipality and, in some cases, the province. The provinces control certain types of business activity, such as door-to-door sales, credit information services and money-lenders, through this licensing process. The provinces discourage or restrict some types of business activities which are subject to abuse, including massage parlours, video outlets that deal in pornographic material, steam baths, hotels and cabarets. Sole proprietors who undertake business activities that handle food or dangerous commodities are subject to further controlling provincial and federal regulation. Sole proprietors must also satisfy local zoning bylaws which restrict the types of activities that can be carried out in a particular location. Sole proprietors with employees are subject to employment legislation such as workers' compensation, unemployment insurance and income tax regulations. These regulations apply to all types of business organizations, and fees are levied in proportion to the size and extent of the operation. As a general rule, sole proprietors are subject to

Sole proprietor relatively free of outside interference

fewer government regulations than partnerships and corporations. Only minimal records need be kept, and sole proprietors are usually not required to disclose information about the business to others. They must keep sufficient records to satisfy government agencies such as the tax department. In essence, the sole proprietor has complete control and complete responsibility for the business activity.

Sole proprietors have no accountability to others in the running of their businesses, but the responsibility for making important business decisions rests entirely on their own shoulders. Sole proprietors can only look to their own resources to finance the business operation; they cannot sell shares and are restricted to their own credit standing when borrowing money to finance the business. The sole proprietor owns all the assets, receives all the profits of the business and is responsible

Sole proprietor has unlimited liability

for all the debts and liabilities. This **unlimited liability** can be the most significant disadvantage of the sole proprietorship. When debts are incurred or the business faces some other sort of liability, such as tort claims or breach of contract, the whole burden falls on the sole proprietor. Under the principle of vicarious liability, the sole proprietor is responsible for any tort committed by an employee during the course of employment. Here again the sole proprietor's entire personal fortune is at risk.

Sole proprietor vicariously liable for employees' actions

It is important for people carrying on business by themselves to have sufficient insurance to cover such potentially devastating liability. Any profit derived from a sole proprietorship is subject to personal income tax, and some tax advantages available to partnerships and corporations are not available to sole proprietors. These factors alone are often enough to encourage the business person to incorporate.

Professionals bound by certain rules

It should be noted that some individuals cannot incorporate or derive little advantage from doing so. Professionals such as doctors, dentists, lawyers and accountants are usually prevented from incorporating, and in those jurisdictions where professional incorporations are permitted they normally derive little benefit from doing so.[4] Such professionals usually carry on business as sole proprietors or band together in a group as partners. A sole proprietor who is a professional is required to join the appropri-

3. In Alberta, see s. 85 of the *Partnership Act*, R.S.A. (1980) c. P-2.

4. See, for example, the *Chartered Accountants Act*, S.A. (1987) c. C-5.1 which, in s. 28, confirms that a shareholder of a professional corporation is liable as if the business were being carried on as a partnership or a sole proprietorship.

ate professional organization such as the law society or medical association of the province. Typically, these bodies are set up under legislation which gives them extensive power to regulate educational and professional qualifications and standards of behaviour, and to establish methods of disciplining members for wrongful conduct or incompetence. Note that it is only the practice of the professional service that cannot be incorporated and so these professionals obtain most of the advantages of incorporation by establishing companies that own the building, employ the office staff, and supply the management service and equipment to the professional.

PARTNERSHIP

From the earliest times, people have found it more efficient to pool their talents and resources by forming partnerships. **Partnerships** are essentially groups of people acting together for a business purpose with a view to making a profit. The primary relationship between the partners is one of contract, and thus basic contract law applies. However, the courts have developed special provisions to deal with this particular kind of legal relationship. It is important to realize that the group so formed does not take on a legal personality separate from the people who make it up as is the case with a corporation. It has become possible over the years, however, to enter into legal relationships with the partnership as such, thus eliminating the need to enter into a separate agreement with each partner individually. This allows the partnership the convenience of functioning in many situations as a single business unit. For instance, a partnership can own land, contract with others and sue or be sued in its own name.

Partnership—carrying on business together for profit

Partnerships governed by contract law

Legislation

Although partnership has always been an important method of carrying on business, the dramatic increase in commercial activity in England in the eighteenth and nineteenth centuries resulted in the development of a considerable body of case law. As part of the great effort to update the laws of England in the nineteenth century, the law of partnership was summarized in one well-drafted statute called the *Partnership Act* (enacted in 1890). This legislation was adopted in all of the common law provinces of Canada where it has remained in place to the present day with only a few alterations.

Partnership Act still used today

Although there have been some additions to the *Partnership Act*, most notably the parts related to limited partnerships (which in some provinces are contained in separate statutes), the legislation varies little from province to province; the principles discussed in this chapter need little qualification for provincial variation. For convenience, the Alberta version will be used whenever the *Partnership Act* is referred to and the sections discussed will refer to that statute.[5]

Creation of the Partnership

Olson v. Gullo[6]

Mr. Gullo had learned that the municipality was interested in having a 1000-acre (405-hectare) tract of land developed as an industrial park. He and Mr. Olson entered into a verbal agreement whereby each would contribute equal funding, and

---

5. *Partnership Act*, R.S.A. (1980) c. P-2.

6. 113 D.L.R. (4th) 42 (Ontario Court of Appeal). Leave to appeal to the Supreme Court of Canada was refused on October 13, 1994, 179 N.R. 400.

Mr. Gullo would provide his real estate speculation skills and Mr. Olson his marketing and promotion skills in the acquisition and development of that tract of land. The pair had difficulty purchasing the designated land from the owners and eventually abandoned the project.

However, Mr. Gullo was able to purchase one 90-acre (36-hectare) parcel in his own name and in his own behalf and quickly turn it around at a $2.5 million profit. When Olson found out about this, he left his job, which was in one of Gullo's companies, and commenced this action. It is interesting to note that before the trial Mr. Gullo died, but not before trying to have Mr. Olson murdered. The action was carried on by Mr. Gullo's son.

Several important questions are raised by this case. The court had first to deal with whether a partnership existed between the parties. The plaintiff claimed that an oral agreement to that effect had been entered into, a claim flatly denied by the defendant. The judge did, however, recognize an agreement whereby the parties were to be equal partners in the purchase of the 1000 acres in question. The court held that each was to contribute an equal share of money, and Gullo would negotiate the purchases and Olson find interested investors and prepare promotional material. Thus they were carrying on business together with a view to profits making their relationship one of partnership. As a result of that partnership, Mr. Gullo had a fiduciary obligation to act in the best interests of his partner. When he secretly dealt in the 90-acre parcel, he did so in breach of that obligation.

The court then had to find an appropriate remedy in the circumstances. At the trial level the court decided that the whole $2.5 million should be forfeited to Mr. Olson in order to discourage this kind of wrongful behaviour. If Mr. Gullo were allowed to keep half the profits, he'd only be in the position he would have been in had he not committed the fraud in the first place. When this decision was appealed the appellate court decided that because the nature of a partnership is the equal sharing of assets and profits, it wasn't possible to award Mr. Olson the whole profit. Mr. Gullo, despite his misconduct, was entitled to half of it.

The case illustrates not only what is necessary for a partnership to exist and the essential nature of that partnership, but also the fiduciary obligation or duty between the partners to act in the best interests of each other.

Essentially, the *Partnership Act* provides that, whenever two or more people **carry on business in common with a view towards profits**, a partnership exists.[7] This does not mean that a profit was made, only that profit was the object of the exercise. The *Act* goes on to set out a number of circumstances which by themselves will not give rise to a partnership. Owning property in common, even though the object is to make a profit, will not be enough to create a partnership. Two friends who purchase a house and rent it out, sharing the profits, will not be considered a partnership on the basis of this relationship alone. The *Act* also points out that the sharing of gross returns from a business activity does not in itself create a partnership. Only when the net receipts, the profits, from the investment are shared is the existence of a partnership presumed. Two real estate agents who split the commission for selling a vendor's house will not be partners; but if they first deduct the expenses associated with the sale and then share the profits, this will be evidence of partnership. The *Partnership Act* goes on to set out a number of other circumstances which, though they involve sharing, by themselves will *not* establish a partnership:[8]

Partnership Act lists
exceptions

7. *Partnership Act*, R.S.A. (1980) c. P-2 s. 1(d).

8. *Ibid.*, s. 4.

1. When a debt is repaid by the creditor's taking a share of the debtor's profits. For example, Pallas owes Clegg $10 000 and Clegg agrees to let Pallas pay it back by paying 20 percent of the profits of Pallas's furniture store per month until repaid.

2. When the payment of an employee is based on a share of sales or profits, such as commission selling or profit-sharing schemes.

3. When the beneficiary of a deceased partner receives the deceased partner's share of the profits.

4. When a loan is made in relation to a business and payment of interest varies with the profit. For example, Pallas loans Clegg $10 000 to start a furniture business and Clegg pays interest on that $10 000 principal by paying 10 percent of the store's profits per month.

5. When a business is sold and the payment of the goodwill portion varies with the profitability of the business. For example, Pallas sells Clegg a furniture business for $10 000 for the assets and 50 percent of the first year's profits for goodwill.

The question remains: What does constitute carrying on business together with a view towards profit? When evidence indicates that there has been a joint contribution of capital to establish a business, an intention to share expenses, profits or losses, or joint participation in the management of a business, then a partnership will be presumed. If two people operate a restaurant together by sharing the work and the expenses and jointly making decisions, the relationship is a partnership.

Partnership exists when profits shared

It should be further noted that the *Partnership Act* requires that the parties carry on a continuing business together. A single joint project—for example, a school dance put on by two university students who combine their resources—would probably not be classed as a partnership. (If the students put on several dances, they would be in the "business" of providing this type of entertainment and thus would be in legal partnership whether they looked at it that way or not.)

Partnership must carry on continuing business

Creation by Inadvertence.

It is important to realize that the partnership relationship can be implied from the conduct of the parties and therefore can be created inadvertently. The exis-

Partnership can be created by conduct

CO-OWNING PROPERTY DOES NOT CREATE PARTNERSHIP

In this case a number of people owned an apartment building together under the name of one of them, "M. Kalmykow in trust," that is, in trust with the other owners as well. A corporation was created to control the property called Kamex Developments Ltd. The co-owners met monthly to discuss the property and what should be done including the possibility of sale. One of these parties, March, took it upon himself to list the property for sale under an exclusive listing agreement. He was not authorized to do so by the others. The property was eventually sold by a differ-

ent agent and A. E. Lepage under this agreement claimed their commission of $45 000 on the basis that March was in partnership with the rest and therefore bound the partnership to the exclusive listing agreement. Looking at the nature of the agreement, the court found that although people all owned property together, this was not enough to constitute a partnership and so the others were not liable for the commission.

A. E. Lepage Ltd. v. Kamex Developments Ltd. et al., 78 D.L.R. (3d) 223 (Ontario Court of Appeal)

PARTNERSHIP EXISTS WHERE BUSINESS CARRIED ON TOGETHER

Two brothers, Peter and Michael Boychuk, operated a series of businesses in St. Paul, including a taxi service, bowling alleys, billiard rooms, school buses and the rental of buildings. Mike died intestate, and his wife brought an action for a declaration that the brothers were carrying on a business in partnership. The action was contested by Peter. Evidence showed that the brothers carried on their businesses together. There was also evidence that the taxis and buses were owned separately. The court looked at the licenses for the billiard rooms and the bowling alleys and saw that they were issued jointly to the Boychuk brothers. Also income tax returns were filed as partners. The returns showed that they split the profits fifty-fifty. Since partnership is defined as parties carrying on business together with a view towards profit, this qualified as a partnership.

Boychuk et al. v. Boychuk et al., 55 D.L.R. (3d) 751 (Alberta Supreme Court, Trial Division)

tence of a partnership relationship is a question of fact to be determined by the court. The establishment of such a relationship can have significant consequences because each partner must bear the responsibility for the misconduct of fellow partners, and any one partner has the authority to bind the other partners in contracts with outsiders. It is vital to consider the possibility that a partnership exists, with its inherent responsibilities and obligations, whenever a person is involved in any kind of business activity with another. Failure to appreciate this possibility can have disastrous financial consequences when one partner incurs liability to a third party.

Creation by Agreement.

• or by agreement

The partnership relationship is primarily one of contract, usually created by agreement, but this agreement often does not take a written form. The *Olson v. Gullo* case used to introduce this section is an example of where the court found that the partnership had been created by such an oral agreement.

In addition to setting out the responsibilities of partners to third parties, the *Partnership Act* also sets out the rights and obligations of the partners to each other insofar as the partners have not agreed otherwise. Although a partnership agreement will not modify the relationship between the partners and outsiders, it can significantly alter the rights and obligations of the partners between themselves. So it is important for the partners to enter into a written agreement setting out the exact nature of the relationship between them. A written document means there is less likelihood of disputes arising between the parties about the terms of the agreement.

Partnership contract must contain all elements of contract

A partnership agreement should set out the duties of each partner, what type of work or talent each is expected to contribute, the amount of time to be committed to the business, how the profits are to be shared and how the capital is to be distributed, and any limitations on the powers or authority of each partner. The partners can also set out methods of resolving any disputes between them and under what circumstances the partnership will be dissolved. It must be remembered that the rights of outsiders dealing with the partnership are unaffected by any agreement between the partners; outsiders' rights are determined by the provisions of the *Partnership Act* and partnership law generally.

Partnership can be imposed by the principle of estoppel

It should also be noted that, even when the provisions of the *Partnership Act* do not impose a partnership relationship on the parties, such a relationship can still exist because of estoppel. If one of the parties represents to a third party either by words or by conduct that another person is a partner and that representation is

HOLDING OUT AS PARTNER CREATES PARTNERSHIP

Mr. Lloyd owned and operated a truck that he purchased under a conditional sale agreement and that he used primarily to move mobile homes from one location to another, usually for dealers. But Mr. Lloyd lived in British Columbia and was not able to deliver mobile homes from point to point in Alberta, just from Alberta to other locations. He approached the principals of Caravelle Homes Ltd. with a scheme whereby they would purchase the truck. They declined this arrangement, but agreed to a sham transaction in which they completed a bill of sale stating that they had purchased the truck for one dollar. They advanced money to pay Lloyd's arrears. They changed insurance permits etc. which then showed the company's name as owner. Also they added signs to the truck that indicated Caravelle was its owner. Whenever the truck stopped at weigh stations, Lloyd produced documents showing the truck was owned by Caravelle. He did, however, continue his own independent trucking business separately from Caravelle. On one of these deliveries for Caravelle, to a business owned by Mrs. Poulos, he was careless in unhitching a mobile home whereupon it slipped and pinned Poulos' husband's arm causing him serious injury. She sued Caravelle, claiming Lloyd and Caravelle were partners. The courts decided that because this activity was carried on jointly for the purpose of making a profit, the two were in partnership and Lloyd was acting as an agent when he dropped off the mobile home. Therefore, Caravelle as a partner was liable for the injuries.

Poulos v. Caravelle Homes Ltd. [1995] 32 Alta. L.R. (3d) 76 (Q.B.).

relied on, the person holding out the other as a partner will not be able to deny it later, even if it can be clearly demonstrated that the two were not carrying on a business together. The principle of estoppel applies to partnership just as much as it does to agency because each partner acts as an agent for the partnership.

The Partner as an Agent

At the heart of partnership law lies the relationship of agency. When dealing with third parties, every partner is considered an agent of every other partner, at least for the purposes of the partnership business.[9] Every partner has the power to bind the other partners in contract as long as the contract involves the business of the partnership.[10] To properly understand the law of partnership, this chapter must be read in conjunction with Chapter 11 on agency. Even if the partners have specifically limited the authority of one of their members to make contracts on behalf of the business, if that partner exceeds the specific authority granted and creates a contract relative to the business with a third party who is unaware of the limitation, the contract is binding on all the other partners.[11]

Laws of agency apply to partnership

The following example demonstrates the apparent authority of a partner as agent and the principle of estoppel. A shoe store opened by Akbari and Carlson would qualify as a partnership if no incorporation had taken place. If Akbari were to take a trip to Toronto, and while visiting his regular supplier come across a great deal on 500 pairs of yellow patent-leather oxfords he was unable to resist buying for only $5000, that contract would be binding on Carlson as well because the two are partners. Even if the partnership agreement between Carlson and Akbari specifically

9. *Ibid.,* s. 6.
10. *Ibid.,* s. 7.
11. *Ibid.,* s. 7, s. 10.

set out that neither partner had the authority to enter into any contracts which committed the firm to pay over $1000 without the other's approval, the contract would be binding on both partners, unless the seller were aware of this particular limitation. However, if Akbari bought a new boat during his trip to Toronto, this purchase would not be binding on his partner, because the purchase could not be said to be made pursuant to the partnership business of selling shoes.

Vicarious Liability

Partners fully liable for each other's acts

Partners liable for wrongful acts of employees

Partners liable for breach of trust

The liability of a partner is not restricted to contractual obligations created on the basis of agency. All partners are also liable in tort for the wrongful conduct of partners as if they had committed the act themselves. This is an application of the principle of vicarious liability and applies to liabilities incurred in all business-related activities, including personal injury. If a partner carelessly makes a mistake and causes harm to a third party in the course of performing duties in the business, the other partners will also be liable for the damages. If Agostino and Paradis are in the business of selling firewood and Agostino negligently drops a load of wood on a passing pedestrian, both Agostino and Paradis would be liable to pay compensation for the injury. Partners are similarly liable when the wrong has been committed intentionally. For this reason, the partners of the lawyer who fraudulently acquired the $60 000 from his client in the example used to open this chapter were required to make good the loss even though they were completely innocent. Similarly, all partners are responsible for the tortious acts of any employee which are committed in the course of their employment. Partners can also be held responsible for the wrongful conduct of other partners that takes the form of breach of trust, such as the misuse of their clients' money. In such situations, all of the partners are responsible for compensating the victim's loss. It should be noted, however, that the *Partnership Act* states that in such circumstances the other partners will only be liable for the breach of trust if they have prior notice of the breach of trust.[12]

Since a partnership can employ individuals, the principles set out in Chapter 10 on employment law apply. A partnership with employees has an obligation to adhere to government regulations on workers' compensation, employment insurance and income tax.

Unlimited Liability

Partners share losses equally or proportionally by agreement

The sole proprietor's liability is unlimited in that his or her entire personal fortune is at risk to satisfy the claims of an injured party. However, the sole proprietor is responsible only for his or her own wrongful conduct and for those they employ. In a partnership, the partners' liability is unlimited and they are responsible for each other partner's conduct as well. Thus, if the assets of the partnership are not sufficient to satisfy the claims of the creditors, the partners must pay out of their own personal assets in the same proportion as they share profits. If a partnership agreement creates different classes of partners in which two senior partners are entitled to 30 percent of the profits and the two junior partners 20 percent of the profits, the senior partners will bear 30 percent of the loss each and the junior partners will bear 20 percent of the loss each. But this will not affect the right of the victim to collect the loss from whichever party has the ability to pay.

12. *Ibid.,* s. 15

In some cases, the partnership agreement will specify that one of the partners will bear all or a significant portion of the loss because that party is better able to do so. It must be remembered in all of these cases that such provisions will not affect the position of any creditors or third parties. An outsider is not affected by any term in the partnership agreement that limits the liability of one of the partners. He or she is able to sue any partner for full compensation. If one partner is particularly well off and the other partners have few personal assets, the injured party will look to the partner with significant assets for compensation once the assets of the partnership have been exhausted. The partner who pays then can seek contribution from the other partners on the basis of the partnership agreement if they have anything left to contribute.

Third party can collect from any partner regardless of agreement

In most provinces, partners are only **jointly liable** for the debts and obligations of the partnership as opposed to jointly and **severally liable**.[13] This means that, for someone to seek a remedy against all of the partners, they all must be included in the original action. Thus, if only two of the three partners are sued and it later turns out that they do not have enough assets to satisfy the judgment, it is then too late to sue the third. It must be emphasized, however, that when liability arises because of wrongful conduct (tort) or because of breach of trust, this liability is both joint and several. This means that it is possible for the injured party to sue one partner and still maintain the right to sue the other partners if the claim is not satisfied.[14] The result of this vicarious liability is that all the partners are personally responsible for the injuries incurred to the extent of their entire personal fortunes.

All personal assets at risk

When a partnership is dissolved or one partner retires from the business, the unlimited liability continues to apply to that ex-partner for any wrongs committed or liability incurred during the partnership period. This liability also continues for acts committed after the dissolution of the partnership or the retirement of the partner unless the third party has been given notice that the retiring party has left the firm. A new partner coming into the firm cannot be required to compensate a third party for any liabilities incurred by the firm before entering the partnership unless the new partner has agreed to take over such an obligation in the partnership agreement. This is why such care is taken when the membership of partnerships change to notify colleagues and customers of the change.

Registration

Most provinces require that a partnership be registered. Saskatchewan, Manitoba and Prince Edward Island require that a partnership be registered in all circumstances. Alberta requires registration only when the partnership involves trading, manufacturing, contracting or mining.[15] Registration may also be required when all of the partners are not listed or in limited partnerships as discussed below.

Registration usually required

Failure to register properly can result in the partnership having to pay a fine[16] and can cause a liability that was only joint to be expanded to joint and several liability.[17] Many provinces prohibit an unregistered partnership from maintaining any action against third parties, such as customers who have not paid.[18] And there is no

---

13. *Ibid.*, s. 11.

14. *Ibid.*, s. 14.

15. *Ibid.*, s. 85.

16. *Ibid.*, s. 87. In Alberta, the fine may not exceed $500.

17. *Ibid.*, s. 90.

18. In Alberta, see *ibid.*, s. 88.

protection of an unregistered partnership from being sued. Because of these factors, there are pressing reasons for obeying the legislation requiring registration of a partnership and no advantage in not doing so.

Rights and Obligations of the Parties

Fiduciary Duty.

Fiduciary duty exists between partners

Partners must account for any profits or use of property

The relationship between partners is primarily governed by an obligation of utmost good faith on the part of each partner to act in the best interests of the others. This is a fiduciary relationship, imposing on the partner an obligation to account for any profits that have been made or for any partnership funds or property that have been used. A partner who uses partnership property for personal benefit without the consent of the other partners must pay over any profit made to the partnership and reimburse the partnership for any deterioration of the property. Property brought into a partnership for the purposes of the partnership business becomes the property of the partnership even though the title documents might not reflect this ownership. The partner holding title is said to hold the property in trust for the other partners. This was the situation in *Olson v. Gullo*, discussed earlier, and why Olson had the right to one-half the profits from the sale of the property that Gullo had secretly purchased. It also underlines why the appeal court found it necessary to reverse the lower court's decision to award all of the profits to Olson. This was inconsistent with the true nature of the partnership where they all shared the ownership of the property and thus the rights to the profits.

Partners cannot compete with partnership

A partner is not permitted to operate a similar business without the consent of the other partners. If this occurs, the partner will be required to pay over to the partnership any profits made, which will then be distributed normally to all of the partners. However, if the separate business loses money, the other partners will not be required to reimburse those losses. If a partnership business was set up to operate a restaurant in Toronto and one of the partners, unknown to the others, independently sets up a restaurant in Vancouver, the other partners could require that partner to pay over any profits made from the Vancouver operation to the partnership to then be distributed equally among them. If the Vancouver operation lost money, the partner who set it up must bear the loss alone.

Partners have an obligation to use any information they discover in their position as partners which might be beneficial to the partnership for the benefit of the partnership and not for personal use. Noorami is in a mining partnership where he is likely to run across opportunities in the mining business. If an outsider offered to sell him some mining claims because of his position in the firm, upon purchasing them and the other partners finding out, he would be required to turn over to the firm any profits earned from the claims if they turned out to be valuable. In effect, the information he used was the property of the partnership. But if the claims turn out to be worthless, he could not ask the firm to participate in his loss.

Provisions of the Partnership Act.

Other rights and duties

Because a partnership is a special type of contract, the rights and obligations between the partners can be modified by agreement.[19] However, if there is no such agreement, the general provisions set out in the *Partnership Act* governing the relationship between partners will apply.[20] Some of these obligations and rights are as follows:

19. *Ibid.*, s. 21.
20. *Ibid.*, s. 27.

1. *The partners will share profits equally between them.* Similarly, any losses incurred are shared equally between the partners. In the absence of an agreement to the contrary, equal sharing holds true even when the partners have made unequal capital contributions. This provision is often modified by a partnership agreement, but an outside third party will not be affected by such provisions even when a partnership agreement exists. Outsiders can pursue any remedy available and collect the whole amount from all or any one of the partners. That partner will then have the right to seek a contribution from the other partners so that they eventually share the loss equally or in the proportion set out in the agreement.

   Profits and losses shared equally or as modified by agreement

2. *The partners are entitled to be paid for any expenses they incur in the process of the partnership business.* They are also entitled to be repaid for any money other than capital they have advanced to the partnership before the other partners can claim a share of the profits. In addition, the partner advancing such funds is entitled to the payment of interest on that money.

   Partners' expenses reimbursed

3. *All partners have the right to take part in management and to have a vote in the firm's affairs.* This provision is often modified by partnership agreements which create different classes of partners, particularly in firms with a large number of partners.

   Partners participate in management

4. *A partner has no right to payment for the work done in a partnership business but only to share in the profits.* A partner cannot be both a partner and an employee at the same time. Partners share the profits, they are not entitled to a salary or wages. If one partner is to be paid a salary, this must be clearly stated in the partnership agreement. Such remuneration normally takes the form of a monthly draw against the yet-to-be-calculated profits of the partnership.

   No salaries paid to partners

5. *No major changes can be made to the partnership without the unanimous agreement of all the partners.* No new partner can be brought into the partnership, nor can a partner be excluded from the firm without the unanimous consent of all the partners. However, for the normal operations of the firm, a simple majority vote is sufficient unless the partnership agreement states otherwise.

   Unanimous agreement needed for major changes

6. *Partners do not have the right to assign their partnership status to some other party without the consent of the other partners.* They can, however, assign the benefits they receive from the partnership. The assignees do not have the right to participate in the operation of the business or in the decisions relating to it in any way unless there has been unanimous approval by all the partners to this effect.

   Assignment requires consent of other partners

7. *The business records of the partnership must be kept at the partnership office and all of the partners have the right to inspect them.*

   Partners must have access to records

As can be seen from this summary, the general principle governing a partnership relationship is that the partners function as a unit and have a considerable responsibility to look after each other's interests.

Advantages of Partnership

At first glance, the problems associated with a partnership may appear overwhelming. These difficulties can be reduced considerably by having appropriate insurance coverage. It should also be noted that many features of a partnership that are often considered disadvantages are advantages from the point of view of some business people. For example, although the requirement of the unanimous consent of all partners for any changes in the nature of the partnership may be viewed as an encumbrance to effective management, such a requirement provides considerable

Insurance coverage important

Unanimous consent protection

protection to the individual partner. This requirement significantly increases the individual partner's security in the firm and the control he or she has over it as opposed to minority shareholders in corporations who may find themselves completely ineffectual. Similarly, the right of the individual partner to inspect all records of the business confers advantages not shared by minority shareholders in corporations to the same extent.

Partnership less costly to form

Another advantage is that the legal expenses of drawing up an agreement and of registering the partnership may be less than the expenses involved in incorporating a company. Unlike corporations, partnerships have few formal requirements once the business has been established. For example, a corporation must keep certain types of accounting records, and file reports with the appropriate government agency. A partnership, on the other hand, has only the needs of the partners to satisfy in this regard. But, as with sole proprietorships and corporations, there are other government regulatory bodies that require records, such as the taxation department, workers' compensation and employment insurance. Some of the tax advantages are available to a partnership.

Too many business people assume that incorporation is a better way to carry on business than partnership because of the unlimited liability and unwieldy management structure of partnerships. While it may be true that an incorporated company is the best vehicle for carrying on business in many situations, there are other situations in which a partnership is more appropriate. Some activities, such as the practice of law, medicine and dentistry, are not allowed by statute to be engaged in by corporations. A partnership is the only alternative when more than one of these professionals wishes to join together to carry on business. Before a decision is made to incorporate, consideration should also be given to the pros and cons of using a partnership to carry on the business instead.

Dissolution of a Partnership

One advantage of the partnership is its ease of dissolution. Typically, a partner need only give the other partners notice of intention to dissolve the partnership to bring the partnership relationship to an end. This ease may be an advantage to some but it can be a considerable disadvantage to the other partners, especially if a large partnership is involved, since the dissolution requires the sale of the assets for distribution to the partners. In these circumstances, provisions can be built into the partnership agreement controlling the dissolution process. These provisions usually provide for a mechanism whereby one partner can leave without causing the remainder of the partnership to dissolve.

Dissolution—by notice, death, bankruptcy or insolvency

Subject to the partnership agreement, the partnership is ended by the death of a partner, the assignment of a partner's property in trust for the benefit of his creditors, or the bankruptcy of any partner.[21] Dissolution can give rise to significant problems in ongoing, long-term partnerships of professional groups. Therefore, professionals will typically set out in partnership agreements that the death, assignment of property or bankruptcy of one partner will not dissolve the partnership; and that instead, the partner's share will be made available to the heir or creditor of the partners. Insurance coverage is often taken out to cover such a contingency.

British Columbia's partnership legislation is unique because it establishes that, when more than two partners are involved, the partnership will be dissolved only in relation to the partner who has died or becomes insolvent. This provision can be

21. *Ibid.*, s. 36.

modified by agreement, but its unique feature is that the death or bankruptcy of one partner will not bring to an end the whole partnership relationship in the absence of an agreement between the partners.[22]

A partnership that has been set up for a fixed term will end at the expiration of that term. Similarly, a partnership which is set up for a particular adventure or undertaking will end when that adventure or undertaking terminates. A partnership is automatically dissolved if the business engaged in by the partnership becomes illegal. Even if none of these factors is present, if one partner feels that the partnership should be dissolved, that partner has the right to apply to court for dissolution.

Partnership established for specified time will end at expiry

The court may dissolve the partnership if it is satisfied that any one of a number of factors are present.[23] For example, when the court is satisfied that the partnership business can only be carried on at a loss, it can order the partnership dissolved. If one of the partners is of permanently unsound mind or otherwise incapable of performing partnership responsibilities, the partnership can be ordered dissolved. Similarly, the court can end the relationship when the conduct of one partner is such that it is prejudicial to the partnership relationship or otherwise in breach of the partnership agreement. Finally, there is a catch-all provision empowering the court to dissolve the partnership whenever it considers that it is "just and equitable that the partnership be dissolved."[24]

Partnership can be dissolved by request to the court

The effect of dissolution is to end the partnership relationship, oblige the partners to wind up the business, liquidate the assets to pay off any obligations to creditors and then distribute any remaining assets and funds to the former partners. Individual partners should take care to give public notice of dissolution.[25] When a partnership is dissolved, any of the former partners may sign, and file with the registrar, a Declaration of Dissolution.[26] For further protection, such notice should be sent to all regular customers of the business. Failure to do so may render each partner liable for the acts of the other partners even after dissolution. Note that, although dissolution takes place, the partners still have the authority to act as partners and bind the other partners by their actions in doing whatever is necessary to wind up the business.[27]

Public notice may avoid liability

Distribution of Assets and Liabilities

The affairs of the partnership must be wound up when the partnership is dissolved. Subject to any partnership agreement, the debts of the firm are paid out of profits and, if there are not enough profits to pay all the debts, they are paid out of the partners' original capital investment.[28] If there is still not enough money to pay the debts, the creditors can then turn to the partners themselves who are liable to the extent of their personal fortunes. On the other hand, once all creditors have been paid and the other obligations of the partnership satisfied, any assets still remaining are applied first to pay back the partners for expenses they have incurred in the process of carrying out the partnership business. Once this has

Debts paid out of profits first, then capital, then personal assets of partners

22. *Partnership Act*, R.S.B.C. (1996) c. 348 s. 36(1)(b).

23. *Partnership Act*, R.S.A. (1980) c. P-2 s. 38.

24. *Ibid.*, s. 38(f).

25. See *ibid.*, s. 40, which says that any partner may publicly give notice of a dissolution of the partnership.

26. *Ibid.*, s. 91.

27. *Ibid.*, s. 41.

28. *Ibid.*, s. 49.

been done, any further funds are used to repay money the partners provided to the partnership in addition to their original capital investment. Any remaining funds are used to pay back the capital investment of the partners and, finally, any funds left after that are divided among the partners on the established basis for sharing profits.

The problem with dissolving a partnership is that all of the firm's assets must be sold to accomplish the division of assets, even when some of the partners want to form a new partnership and carry on the business. To avoid this problem, the parties often agree to a different process in the partnership agreement. It should be noted that, if one partner owes a debt to an outside creditor which has nothing to do with the partnership business, that creditor can claim against only the assets of that partner, including his or her share of the partnership assets left after all other claims against the partnership are settled.

Limited Partnerships

Additions to the legislation governing partnership in every province provide for the creation of limited partnerships.[29] This measure gives some of the advantages of incorporation to partnerships. To qualify as a limited partner, the partnership must closely adhere to all of the requirements of the governing legislation. If a limited partner fails in any way to follow the provisions set out in the statute, the usual outcome is that the limited partner is then deemed to be a general partner with all of the consequences inherent in that designation. The main advantage of a limited partnership is that it allows the partners so designated to invest money in a partnership but to avoid the unlimited liability that goes with being a general partner. The only loss a limited partner can incur is the original investment.[30]

Limited partners liable only to the extent of their investment

For example, if Pak is a limited partner who has invested $25 000 in a firm with two general partners, Kimmel and Ingram, Pak might conceivably lose the $25 000 but no more. If one of the partners caused injury to a customer through negligence and that customer suffered $250 000 in damage, the customer could sue the other partners for the loss and Kimmel and Ingram would be required to com-

---

LIMITED PARTNER LOSES STATUS BY PARTICIPATING IN MANAGEMENT

Zivot wanted to launch a magazine, but the corporate organization that he set up to do it was quite complex. He incorporated a company called Lifestyle Magazine Inc. with himself as an employee. He then had Lifestyle enter into a partnership, called Printcast, with him and several other partners. Zivot and the other partners were limited partners, whereas Lifestyle Magazine was a general partner. Houghton supplied printing services to Printcast in order to produce the magazine and was not paid. He sued Zivot and another limited partner, claiming that be-

cause they participated in the general management of the business, they ceased to be limited partners and became general partners. The court agreed, and declared Zivot and the other limited partner to be general partners and liable for the indebtedness of the partnership. Zivot had not only participated in management but also led people to believe he was an officer in Printcast; therefore, he was liable as a general partner.

Haughton Graphic Ltd. v. Zivot et al., Ontario Supreme Court, May 5, 1986, as reported in *Lawyers Weekly Consolidated Digest*, Vol. 6.

---

29. In Alberta, see *ibid.*, ss. 48-79.

30. *Ibid.*, s. 56.

pensate the victim, even if it meant sacrificing their own personal fortunes. Pak, on the other hand, would stand only to lose the initial investment of $25 000. Even if the combined assets of Kimmel and Ingram were insufficient to cover the claim of the injured customer and Pak did have sufficient assets to cover the $250 000 claim, Pak would not be required to pay, because a limited partner's liability is limited to the amount invested.

The problem with limited liability in a partnership is that it is relatively easy for the limited partner to lose that status and, when that happens, the limited partner becomes a general partner with unlimited liability. In the preceding example, if Pak had done something to become a general partner, such as allowing himself to be represented as a partner in the business, allowing his surname to be used in the name of the partnership, providing services to the partnership, or actively taking part in control of the partnership business, the injured customer could have sued Pak along with Kimmel and Ingram and all would have been required to pay with no limitation on liability.

To be a limited partner, the first thing one must do is register at the appropriate registry by filing a certificate.[31] This certificate must contain information such as the terms of the agreement, the amount of cash contributed and the way profits are to be shared. The name used by the partnership can contain the name of the general partners but the surname of a limited partner cannot be included in the firm name.[32] Limited partners will be deemed to be general partners if these requirements are not satisfied.

A limited partner can contribute money or property to the business but cannot take part in the control of the firm without becoming a general partner.[33] The limited partner is not prohibited from giving the other partners advice but, since it is often difficult to determine where advice stops and taking part in the control of the firm starts, there is a considerable risk in doing so. This restriction can create problems if the business begins to experience financial difficulty, because the natural inclination of the limited partner is to get involved to protect his or her investment. If he or she does so, the partner will probably be considered a general partner and hence subject to a much greater potential loss. It is not possible to form a partnership with only limited partners. The legislation requires that there be at least one general partner in the firm.[34] It should also be noted that limited partners don't have the power to bind the partnership in their dealings with outsiders. A limited partner is not an agent of the firm.

As was discussed above, the rights and duties between partners can be modified in a partnership agreement. This applies as well to the relationship between general and limited partnerships. Limited partnerships are attractive to people because of favourable tax implications. To obtain these tax benefits, one big advantage normally associated with limited partnership, limited liability, must be sacrificed to a considerable extent through modifications set out in the partnership agreement. Often these changes are not brought to the attention of prospective investors, and so great care should be taken before entering into such a limited partnership as an investment vehicle.

Registration required to become a limited partner

Limited partners cannot participate in management

---

31. *Ibid.*, s. 51.
32. *Ibid.*, s. 53.
33. *Ibid.*, s. 63.
34. *Ibid.*, s. 50.

SUMMARY

Business is usually carried on as a sole proprietorship, a partnership or a corporation. Sole proprietors carry on business by themselves and have unlimited liability for their debts and obligations. The partnership involves two or more partners carrying on business together with a view to profits. This is controlled by the *Partnership Act* and by specific agreement of the partners. The partnership can be created by agreement, but it often comes into existence by inadvertence when people work together in concert in a business activity. Each partner is an agent for the partnership and all partners are liable for the contracts and torts of the other partners and employees. That liability is unlimited and all of the assets of the partner, including personal assets, are at risk to satisfy such debts and obligations.

The partners have a fiduciary obligation to each other and must act in the best interests of the partnership. To make significant changes in the partnership, the partners must unanimously agree. The usual method of dissolving a partnership is for the partners to give notice to that effect. Death or bankruptcy of one of the partners will also usually dissolve the partnership unless the partners have agreed otherwise in their partnership agreement. A limited partner is liable only to the extent of the investment made in the business but, to protect that limited liability status, he or she must be registered as such and not participate in the management of the partnership business.

QUESTIONS

1. Distinguish between a sole proprietorship, a partnership and a corporation.

2. What risk does a business person face in a sole proprietorship or partnership that is avoided in a corporation?

3. What advantages and disadvantages are associated with carrying on business as a sole proprietorship?

4. What advantages and disadvantages are associated with carrying on business as a partnership?

5. What distinguishes a partnership from other types of joint activities?

6. Distinguish between sharing profits and sharing fees.

7. If two people enter into a business together with the object of making money but lose it instead, can the business still be a partnership?

8. Why is it impossible to understand the law of partnership without first understanding the law of agency?

9. What danger exists when a third party is led to believe that two people are partners who in fact are not? This situation is an application of what legal principle?

10. What is the significance of the existence of a partnership agreement for outsiders dealing with the partnership? What is the advantage of entering into a formal agreement?

11. Explain the different ways in which a person can become responsible for the acts of his or her partner and describe the limitations on this responsibility.

12. Describe the liability of retiring and new partners.

13. Partners have fiduciary obligations to each other. Explain what this means.

14. What will the consequences be if a partner operates a business similar to the partnership without the partners' consent or uses information acquired through the partnership to his or her own advantage?

15. What events may bring about the end of a partnership prematurely? Under what circumstances might it be necessary to get a court order to end a partnership?

16. What will the normal effect on a partnership be when a partner dies or becomes insolvent? How is the law of British Columbia significantly different?

17. When a partnership is being dissolved and does not have sufficient assets to pay its debts, how is the responsibility for these debts distributed? How are excess assets distributed?

18. Explain the significance of being a limited partner. How are a limited partner's activities registered? What happens when a limited partner violates one of these restrictions?

CASES

1. Hogar Estates Ltd. (in trust) v. Shebron Holdings Ltd. et al.

The defendant and plaintiff companies agreed to go into partnership to develop a certain parcel of land. Because the land was situated on a flood plain, it was difficult to get permission to build on it and the land lay dormant for some time. Mr. Klaiman, the principal of Shebron Holdings Ltd., proposed to Hogar Estates Ltd. that Shebron purchase Hogar's interest in the property. Shebron was the active partner dealing with the planning authorities who had blocked the development of property and Shebron was the partner who had informed Hogar of the problems with obtaining permission to build. After informing Hogar of this difficulty, Klaiman discovered that the planning authority was about to change its mind and that the prohibition on developing the property would be lifted. He failed to inform Hogar of the change and went through with the agreement to terminate the partnership. When Hogar Estates learned that the property had been built on, it sued Shebron and asked the court to set aside the termination agreement.

Explain the nature of the arguments for both sides and the likely outcome. It should be noted that before the change in attitude of the planning authority the principals of Hogar and Shebron had had a disagreement and were barely speaking to each other.

2. The Bank of Montreal v. Sprackman et al.

The members of a partnership had a falling-out and agreed between them that one of the partners (Sprackman) would retire from the partnership. A handwritten letter was drawn up and signed stating that Sprackman's interest in the partnership and responsibility for liability would be taken over by one of the other partners, Dinardo. Dinardo subsequently sold his interest in the partnership to a third partner, Gotzaminis, who subsequently became bankrupt. When the partnership was active, arrangements had been made for a $3000 loan and an overdraft arrangement with the Bank of Montreal. Sprackman verbally advised Martin, the bank manager, that he was retiring and that his obligation was being taken over by Dinardo. Martin agreed to release Sprackman from the loan if he paid $1500, which he did over some period of time. Unfortunately, neither side said anything about the overdraft, which amounted to $2899.66 at the time of Sprackman's retirement. This amount increased after Sprackman's retirement to $6029.82 including interest at 18 percent per annum. The bank then insisted on payment of this overdraft from Sprackman. One of the documents Sprackman had signed with the bank required that the overdraft arrangement would stay in force until "terminated by written notice." Explain the arguments available to both sides and the likely outcome of the case.

3. Fischbach and Moore of Canada Ltd. et al. v. Gulf Oil Canada Ltd. et al.

Two federally incorporated companies, Fischbach and Canadian International Comstock Company Ltd., entered into an agreement to supply materials to a third company, Gulf Oil Canada Ltd. They made a tender to Gulf Oil which was accepted, and Gulf sent a purchase order for the materials. There were some variations made to the resulting contract and the court concluded that all or part of the contract between Gulf Oil and these partners occurred in Nova Scotia. Subsequently, a dispute arose and this action was brought to enforce a mechanics' lien which had been filed against Gulf Oil. Gulf Oil challenged the right of the partners to bring this action on this basis that they were not registered as required under the Nova Scotia *Partnership Act*. Explain the arguments available to both parties and the likely outcome.

4. Lambert Plumbing (Danforth) Ltd. v. Agathos et al.

Magoulas was just starting up as the sole owner of Alpha Omega Construction Company when he signed a contract with Agathos, the owner of a Toronto radio station, for advertising over a period of time. Magoulas was unable to pay but Agathos continued to give him advertising in hopes that the business would get going to the point that he would be able to pay. Agathos also helped Magoulas out in his business, signed many contracts and performed other acts on behalf of Magoulas, including writing cheques on his personal account. In January, Kreizman, president of the plaintiff corporation, entered into a contract to supply the Alpha Omega Construction Company with certain plumbing and heating equipment. This contract was entered into at the construction company and the person Kreizman dealt with was Agathos. Kreizman thought he was dealing with the owner and Agathos did nothing to dissuade him of this notion. In all of the many subsequent dealings between these two parties, Kreizman continued to think that Agathos was the principal of the construction company and Agathos did nothing to correct it. It is clear that there was no partnership agreement or arrangement between Agathos and Magoulas and that Agathos was helping Magoulas out gratuitously, hoping for eventual payment under the advertising contract. Magoulas only partially paid for the plumbing and heating equipment with $500 outstanding. Lambert Plumbing sued

Agathos as a partner for the unpaid funds. Explain the arguments available to both sides and the likely outcome.

5. Klutz v. Klutz

The plaintiff and defendant had been married for 25 years when Mrs. Klutz left in 1958. During that period, two pieces of land had been obtained, both of which were in the husband's name. It was clear that Mrs. Klutz had done considerable work on the land, such as milking cows and feeding livestock, but she had made no financial contribution to the properties. She claimed that the property was held in partnership and demanded an accounting from the husband. Explain the likely outcome and arguments from both sides.

6. Barnes v. Consolidated Motors Co. Ltd. et al.

Hall was negligently driving a motor vehicle when he struck and injured Mrs. Barnes. Hall was an employee of Distributors Used Car branch which was a business established by Consolidated Motor Car Co. Ltd., Dan MacLean Motor Ltd. and J. M. Brown Motor Company Ltd. for the purpose of disposing of their used cars. The business had its own bank account, management, employees, etc., but the cars remained the property of the company that supplied them. Hall was driving one of the cars owned by Consolidated Motor Car Co. Ltd. to the Distributors Used Car Branch premises when the accident took place. Mrs. Barnes sued all three of the car companies claiming that they were a partnership. Explain the arguments for each side. Discuss the likely outcome.

7. Castellian v. Horodyski and Lynkowski

Horodyski and Lynkowski were partners in the operation of a hotel which they sold to Castellian in 1953. One of the assets sold in this transaction was a heater/boiler. Horodyski had made fraudulent misrepresentations about this boiler which induced Castellian to enter into a contract for its purchase. Although Horodyski knew that what he said was false, Lynkowski was not aware of what was said or that there was any problem with the boiler. Shortly after Castellian's purchase, the boiler broke down and had to be rebuilt. Castellian sued both Horodyski and Lynkowski for the cost of rebuilding the boiler. Explain the legal position of the parties and the likelihood of success.

8. Dockrill v. Coopers & Lybrand Chartered Accountants

Coopers & Lybrand are a national partnership of chartered accountants and they merged with a firm of chartered accountants carrying on business in Halifax. Subsequently to that, two managing partners in the Halifax office decided that as a result of the merger, there were too many partners in Halifax, and they terminated Mr. Dockrill. Before doing that, they had approached the partners in Toronto and obtained legal advice from an in-house counsel which they relied on in asking for Mr. Dockrill's resignation. Mr. Dockrill brought this action for wrongful termination of his partnership and in the process of the action brought an application to the court for a copy of the information supplied by the Toronto lawyers to the Halifax partnership. Mr. Dockrill hoped that this information might contain disclosures that would help his case for wrongful termination.

Explain whether Mr. Dockrill is entitled to the information supplied by the Toronto lawyers. Would your answer be different if Mr. Dockrill had been asked to resign and then the Halifax partners had sought this legal advice? (See *Akman & Son v. Chipman et al.*, 45 D.L.R. (4th) 481 [Manitoba Court of Appeal].)

LEGISLATION

Alberta
Partnership Act, R.S.A. (1980) c. P-2

WEBLINKS

Government of Alberta: Small Business Guide Series
www.edt.gov.ab.ca/guides/
Six "booklets" designed to help with various aspects of planning, setting up and running a small business: (1) Starting a Small Business, (2) Starting a Home-Based Business, (3) Marketing a Small Business, (4) Managing a Small Business, (5) Record Keeping for Small Business, and (6) Financial Planning for Small Business.

Alberta Partnership Act
www.gov.ab.ca/qp/ascii/acts/P02.txt

Alberta Partnership Fees Regulation
www.gov.ab.ca/qp/ascii/regs/92_288.txt

Alberta Societies Act
www.gov.ab.ca/qp/ascii/acts/s.18.txt

Alberta Registries: Information Page
www.gov.ab.ca/~ma/reg/cr/crmain.htm

In Alberta, as of February 1998, an innovative computerized system called CORES was implemented for registration of business organization documentation. Registration is done by computer via the Internet by "accredited persons" who are employed by registry offices and law firms.

Corporations

OBJECTIVES OF THE CHAPTER

- To describe the process of incorporation
- To consider how the fact that a corporation is a separate legal entity affects the operation of the business
- To examine the duties of corporate officers
- To consider the advantages and disadvantages of incorporation

Mr. Sinclair was a professional engineer who had worked for Dover Engineering Services Ltd. for a number of years, although he had been paid by Cyril Management Ltd. On January 31, 1985, he was discharged without notice and without cause. He initiated a wrongful dismissal action against Cyril Management Ltd. since Dover Engineering had no assets and was no longer in operation. Dover was owned 50 percent by Mr. Goudal, and he and his wife together owned 100 percent of Cyril Management Ltd.

The question the court had to answer was which company had employed Sinclair: Dover Engineering or the management company? The judge decided that the close relationship between the two companies made them both Mr. Sinclair's employers. Sinclair was, therefore, successful in his action against the management company.[1]

This case illustrates the significance of the myth that each corporation is a legal entity, separate and apart from the people who make it up. It also demonstrates the court's willingness in some circumstances to ignore that separate existence by "lifting the corporate veil." This chapter will discuss the concept of the corporate entity and the legal benefits and responsibilities that result from the creation of a corporation.

---

1. *Sinclair v. Dover Engineering Services Ltd. et al.*, B.C.S.C. (1987) 642-028.

The previous chapter dealt with the simpler methods of carrying on business: the sole proprietorship and the partnership. This chapter will examine the third method, the incorporated company. Since incorporation is by far the most common means of setting up a large business organization, exposure to the concepts and forms that regulate this important aspect of the commercial world is a vital part of the study of business law. In this chapter, we will examine the process and effect of incorporation, some features of incorporated bodies and the rights and responsibilities of various parties involved.

THE PROCESS OF INCORPORATION

The concept of an incorporated company developed in response to the need to finance large economic projects without the limitations associated with sole proprietorships and partnerships. The problem with sole proprietorships was that they did not allow for the acquisition of large amounts of capital through the participation of many entrepreneurs, and the difficulty with partnerships was that major decisions had to have the agreement of all the partners, making large partnerships impractical. What was needed was to have a large number of people participate in a venture without playing active roles in it. The incorporated company was the means to accomplish this end. The most significant feature of an incorporated company is that it has a separate legal personality from the people who own shares in it. The shares that represent an individual's interest in the incorporated company can be bought and sold; thus the shareholders can be continually changing while the company itself remains intact. This structure provides considerably more flexibility in meeting the needs of owners and directors and is a much more effective method of attracting capital.

Corporation is a separate legal entity

Even in early times it was not unusual for groups of people to be treated as one separate personality. It was common for a monarch to grant a charter to a city or town making it a separate legal entity capable of acting in its own right. This practice was extended to institutions such as universities and organizations such as craft guilds. It was a natural step to extend that practice to commercial ventures. The earliest of English commercial corporations were created by royal charter, including the Hudson's Bay Company. While the Crown held exclusive power to create corporations in the early stages, Parliament started to exercise some control over the incorporation process through "special act companies" in the nineteenth century. Certain ventures were considered important and unique enough to be incorporated by their own special legislation

Royal charters created early corporations

Special act companies were corporations

Ordinary citizens, however, were still precluded from incorporating companies for general business activities. Instead, they created their own unofficial companies through contracts called deeds of settlement. When Parliament decided to permit incorporation on a general scale, a considerable number of these contractual associations had to be accommodated. The resulting legislation gave these companies formal status and the advantages of incorporation by allowing them to simply register at the appropriate government office and pay a fee.

Canada adopted many of the features of the British approach to incorporation. Both the federal and provincial governments have created many corporations through their power to pass special statutes. For example, the Canadian Broadcasting Corporation (CBC) and the Canadian Pacific Railroad (CPR) were created by special acts of Parliament. Some Canadian jurisdictions adopted the British practice of incorporation through **registration**. Other jurisdictions developed their

Three general methods of incorporation in Canada

incorporation process from the royal charter approach and created incorporated bodies through the granting of **letters patent**. A third approach has been borrowed from the United States based on the filing of **articles of incorporation**. (This is the approach followed in Alberta.) Although there are technical differences between these three methods of incorporation, it is important to understand that the practical effect of each system is the same.

In Canada it is possible to incorporate a company at the federal level or in each province. The choice should be made on the basis of what the company will be doing and where it will be done. If the activity is to be confined to a local area, it is likely that incorporation under the provincial legislation would be appropriate. Thus, a restaurant would be provincially incorporated. When the activity involves something that will be carried on in several provinces such as a chain of restaurants, or generally across Canada as with some service provided on the Internet, the federal option might be preferable. Cost will be the major consideration. It is possible, even after choosing to incorporate provincially, to carry on business in other provinces as well, but the incorporated company will have to be registered in all of the provinces in which it does business, with corresponding fees paid in each jurisdiction. If a company has been federally incorporated, the governing legislation is the *Canada Business Corporations Act*,[2] and it can carry on business in any part of the country without the need of being registered in each province. The relevant statute in Alberta is the *Business Corporations Act*.[3] As both the federal and provincial legislation governing corporations in Alberta are based on the filing of articles of incorporation, this chapter will focus primarily on that particular process.

Articles of Incorporation.

In 1970, the Ontario government abandoned the letters patent system of incorporation and adopted a system similar to one used in the United States. It is based on the filing of **articles of incorporation** and the granting of a **certificate of incorporation**. It has features of both the letters patent and the registration methods and was adopted, with considerable modification, by the federal government when it abandoned its letters patent system in 1975. Ontario has since further modified its system to bring it more in line with the federal statute. Of the provinces which previously used the registration system, Alberta, Saskatchewan and Newfoundland have turned to the articles of incorporation method as have the previously letters patent provinces of Manitoba and New Brunswick. Appendix 13-1, at the end of this chapter, contains the forms used in Alberta to effect incorporation, including the Articles of Incorporation (form 1).

Articles of incorporation method borrows features from each

The articles of incorporation method has much in common with the letters patent method. Instead of being organizations based on contractual relationship between their members, articles of incorporation corporations are primarily the creations of government. The articles that are filed are more similar to a constitution or statute controlling the activities of the parties than a binding agreement between them. A corporation is granted a certificate of incorporation by filing the articles of incorporation and paying the appropriate fee. The articles of incorporation serve the same function and contain the same types of information as the memorandum of association and the letters patent in the other systems. The day-to-day operation is controlled through bylaws similar to those in a letters patent system, which also correspond to the articles of association used in the registration

Incorporation accomplished through granting certificate of incorporation

2. *Canada Business Corporations Act*, R.S.C. (1985) c. C-44.

3 *Business Corporations Act*, S.A. (1981) c. B-15.

system. It is not necessary to file these bylaws when applying for incorporation. Another important distinction between the letters patent method and this new approach is that the government body assigned to grant certificates of incorporation has no general discretion to refuse the request in an articles of incorporation system.

Other Incorporated Bodies

The concept of incorporation has been used for purposes other than business. Cities, universities and other public institutions are incorporated legal entities which can sue or be sued in their own right. A study of these bodies is beyond the scope of this text because their object is not business. However, they owe their existence to legislation and anyone dealing with them should be aware of the statutes which regulate such things as capacity and responsibilities of agents. It should also be noted that in Canada, under both federal and provincial legislation,[4] it is possible for private citizens to establish (incorporate) non-profit bodies, sometimes called "societies" or non-share capital corporations. These bodies are primarily cultural, social, charitable and religious organizations such as the Society for the Prevention of Cruelty to Animals (SPCA), the Red Cross and the Canadian National Institute for the Blind (CNIB). The one thing these bodies have in common is the non-profit nature of their activities. The legal obligations and technicalities associated with these bodies are much simpler and more straightforward than those associated with corporations generally. Since the subject of this text is business law and these bodies must by definition be non-profit organizations, no attempt will be made to deal with them here.

SEPARATE LEGAL ENTITY

Salomon v. Salomon and Co. Ltd.[5]

In this case, Salomon ran a successful shoe manufacturing business which he decided to incorporate. He set up a company in which he owned almost all of the shares. He then sold the business to that company. Since the company had no assets to pay for the business, he loaned the company enough money to purchase the business from himself, securing the loan with a debenture similar to a mortgage on the company's assets. In short, Salomon loaned the company which he "owned" enough money to purchase the business from him and had a mortgage on the assets of the business created to secure the loan.

Unfortunately, the business suffered financial reverses in the form of strikes and other problems, and the company became insolvent. When the creditors lined up to get what little was left in satisfaction of their debts, they found Mr. Salomon at the front of the line claiming first payment. The creditors were not happy with this state of affairs because they blamed Mr. Salomon for their problems. They had dealt with him; they had thought they were doing business with him, and that the company was merely a convenience. They claimed in court that not only should Mr. Salomon not get his money first but also that he should be responsible for paying them if the company's assets were not enough.

The court decided that, since the company was a separate legal entity, it had a separate legal existence apart from Salomon and so Salomon could indeed sell

4. *Societies Act,* R.S.A. (1980) c. S-18 is the relevant legislation in Alberta.

5. (1897) A.C. 22 (House of Lords).

his assets to the company and could take security back. The end result was that Salomon was a secured creditor who stood in line ahead of the other unsecured creditors and thus had first claim on the remaining assets of the company. For the same reason, the court held that Salomon was a person separate from the company and was in no way responsible for its debts.

This case illustrates as graphically as any not only what is meant by the characteristic that the corporation is a separate legal entity from the shareholders, but also the most significant result of that characteristic, that of limited liability on the part of the shareholder.

When a person goes through the process of incorporating a corporation with himself or herself as the sole shareholder, the important and difficult concept to grasp is that when the process is complete and the fees are paid, there are now two legal persons, that person and a corporation. Although the corporation does not exist except on paper and is only a "legal fiction," all of the forces of the law assume that it does exist as a separate entity from the shareholder and that it can function in the commercial world. The corporation as a separate legal person may be a difficult concept for the "owner" of a newly incorporated business to understand. Advisers may have a problem convincing the business person that he or she does not own the business but that it is owned by the corporation which has been created. The individual may own the shares in the corporation but not the corporation itself. Shares held in a corporation bestow the rights of control and only give the right to share in the liquidation of the assets (right to participate in capital) if the corporation is wound up.

Corporation a separate legal entity

A different problem is encountered when dealing with large corporations such as Sears Ltd. and Imperial Oil Ltd. When most people think of a corporation such as Sears Ltd., they identify the individual stores and warehouses as the corporation itself. But those are just assets of the corporation in the same way that Vandenberg's car is not Vandenberg but an asset owned and used by her. On the other hand, some people think that the shareholders are the corporation, the idea being that the legal personality of the corporation consists of the members that make it up. While this idea describes what happens in a partnership, it does not apply to a corporation since it would defeat the whole purpose of incorporation: to create a separate legal personality independent of its shareholders. It must be remembered that this distinct entity is created for the sake of convenience. It does not exist as a real tangible thing; it is a legal fiction or myth that forms the basis of corporate law.

Unfortunately, business people often act as if the corporation were a real person. Managers often make decisions they find repugnant and which they would not otherwise make because they think that the corporation they serve is real. They draw a distinction in their minds between the corporate entity and themselves as managers. While it is true that the legal duty of directors and managers is to the corporation it must also be remembered that the corporation itself is merely a fiction and does not excuse immoral conduct.

It is also important to recognize that the status of separate legal entity for a corporation is a flimsy one. What the law has created, the law can just as easily remove, and it often comes as quite a shock to the business person to see the separate legal entity aspect of a business operation cast aside by the court and government institutions. For example, when one shareholder has set up several corporations, the tax department will often deem these corporations to be one person for tax

Courts will sometimes ignore separate legal entity

purposes. Similarly, if the object of incorporation is to get around some government regulation or commit a fraud, the courts will usually be willing to "lift the corporate veil" and ignore the separate legal entity aspect of the corporation in order to gain access to the shareholders or managers who are attempting to commit the fraud or to avoid the operation of the government regulation. The example used to introduce this chapter illustrates a situation where the courts were willing to lift the corporate veil. Two recent Alberta cases also provide examples of courts ignoring the separate corporate entity and "piercing the corporate veil."[6]

Nevertheless, the separate legal entity aspect of a corporation is tremendously important for commercial activities. It is this aspect that has permitted the isolation of the shareholders from the business activity. Not only does it allow for the acquisition of capital without involving the shareholders in the operation of the corporation, it also provides significant flexibility for investors by allowing them to purchase and sell their shares without interfering with the ongoing operation of the business. As was the case with sole proprietorships and partnerships, a corporation is responsible not only for contracts made on its behalf, but also for torts committed by people acting for the corporation such as employees under the principle of vicarious liability. The corporation can even be convicted and fined for the commission of a crime. But it is the corporation itself that is liable, not the shareholders. Because of this separation of the shareholders from the corporation, only the corporation is responsible for its activities. This is known as **limited liability** since the shareholders are liable to lose only the money they have invested.

Limited liability derived from separate legal entity

The case of *Salomon v. Salomon and Company Ltd.,*[7] discussed above, graphically illustrates the significance of the principle of separate legal entity and limited liability. Because the company he incorporated was a separate legal entity from Salomon, he was free to be its creditor. Not only was he not responsible for the company's debts, even though he was the shareholder, he was also able to be a secured creditor claiming against the assets before the other creditors he had dealt with.

Creditors have since developed ways of protecting themselves in this type of situation. For example, they can insist that the person incurring the debt on behalf

COURT WILL LIFT CORPORATE VEIL IN EVENT OF FRAUD

Mr. Kehoe was the sole director, shareholder and person in charge of Terra Nova Auctioneers Inc., and in his auctioneering capacity sold a number of vehicles on behalf of Newfoundland Telephone Company. He operated one bank account and put all the funds in that account and used the money to pay off bills. When it came time to pay Newfoundland Telephone, he was about $42 000 short. Newfoundland Telephone sued Mr. Kehoe in his personal capacity for that money and the court was asked to hold the principal liable for the company's debts. The court said that it was the auctioneer's duty to hold the money in trust for the sale of the vehicles, and keep it separate from any of their own funds. This was not done. The money was commingled. The court found that Kehoe used the money for his own purposes in a fraudulent and improper manner. Therefore, it was appropriate to lift the corporate veil and hold him personally liable.

Newfoundland Telephone Co. Ltd. v. Terra Nova Auctioneers Inc., as reported in *The Lawyers Weekly,* Vol. 12, No. 30 (December 1992).

---

6. *Alwest Neon Signs Ltd. v. 464460 Alberta Ltd.* (1994) 24 Alta. L.R. (3d) 420 (Alta. Prov. Ct.); *Southern Transportation Ltd. v. Valgardson* (1995) 173 A.R. 299 (Alta. Q.B.).

7. *Salomon v. Salomon and Co. Ltd.* (1897) A.C. 22 (H. of C.).

of the corporation sign a personal guarantee and become a party to the debt. It must be emphasized, however, that the trend today is for the courts to lift the corporate veil as the situation warrants. This tendency makes the actuality of limited liability less and less certain for shareholders, directors and other officers of corporations. Thus in the *Sinclair v. Dover Engineering Services* Ltd. case used to introduce this chapter, the employee Sinclair was able to demand wages from Cyril Management Ltd. even though his employer was Dover Engineering Services Ltd. The court looked behind the corporate veil and discovered that the principles behind the two corporations were essentially the same and allowed Sinclair to seek compensation from Cyril Management Ltd.

Capacity

Once the concept of separate legal entity has been grasped, it is important to identify the extent of the powers or capacity of the separate legal personality. In the past, companies that were incorporated using the registration method had their capacity to contract limited. This was more of a nuisance than anything else and in those two provinces still using that method, legislation was passed giving these corporations all the capacity of a natural person. In Alberta, a corporation has the capacity and the rights, powers and privileges of a natural person, subject only to the provisions of the *Business Corporations Act*.[8]

Registration jurisdictions limit capacity

The only case in which corporations may have limited capacity today involves special act corporations; the legislation creating the corporation may limit its power to contract to certain specified activities. In these circumstances, a contract with a corporation that is beyond the capacity of that corporation will not be binding on either the corporation or the outsider who entered into the contract. In some jurisdictions, such as Alberta, it is possible to set down restrictions on what the corporation can do,[9] but outsiders dealing with that corporation would only be affected in the unlikely event that they had specific notice of that limitation.[10]

Capacity of natural person

The Role of Agents

Since the corporate entity is a legal fiction, it does not have the ability to act for itself. All its activities must be carried out through the services of real people acting as agents. The principles of agency law set out in Chapter 11 are therefore extremely important when dealing with corporations. The question of whether the agent was acting within the actual or apparent authority given must be determined. Not only the directors and managers of a corporation but also the individual employees right down to the clerks may have the capacity to bind that corporation, depending on the nature of their positions and the duties assigned to them. As is the case with other agents, these people undertake special obligations to act in the best interests of the corporation as they carry out their agency responsibilities. The specific nature of the responsibilities borne by selected people in the corporate organization will be discussed in detail below.

Corporations must act through agents

Historically, a principal's liability for the apparent authority of an agent could be severely limited when the principal was a corporation simply by filing with the incorporation documents a specific limitation on the actual authority of the agent.

8. *Business Corporations Act*, S.A. (1981) c. B-15 s. 15.

9. *Ibid.*, s. 16

10. *Ibid.*, s. 17.

Filed documents no longer notice of limited authority

Since these documents were filed publicly, everyone was deemed to have notice of them. This is referred to as constructive notice. Most provinces, including Alberta,[11] have abolished this practice, while others such as Nova Scotia have retained the practice.

FUNDING

Shareholders do not "own" corporations

Issued shares usually less than authorized share capital

One of the main reasons for creating a corporate entity is to establish an efficient means of providing capital to an enterprise from a large number of sources. The primary vehicle for accomplishing this end is the **share**. While the share gives the holder an interest in the corporation, that interest falls short of ownership. The corporation remains an independent personality separate and apart from the shareholders or members who make it up. The share gives the shareholder certain rights in relation to the corporation. These rights are primarily concerned with the control of that corporation and, under certain circumstances, a right to the assets of the corporation upon dissolution.

Generally, one of the restrictions placed on a corporation in the constitutional document in a letters patent or registration jurisdiction is the number of shares that can be sold. This authorized share capital sets an upper limit on the number of shares the corporation can sell. If it becomes necessary to go beyond this upper limit, the original incorporating documents must be amended. To avoid this problem, the authorized share capital is usually quite generous. In articles of incorporation jurisdictions, such as Alberta and federally, such a limitation on the authorized share capital is no longer required.[12] This change eliminates a feature with few redeeming benefits.

Shares of public companies are traded on the stock exchange.
Photo by David Abel/Canapress.

Par-Value Versus No-Par-Value Shares

A share about to be issued can be valued in two different ways. Either the corporation can place a **par value**, or face value, on those shares, such as one dollar, or the corporation can issue shares with no face value at all. The idea in this case is that the value of the share will reflect the worth of the business. For example, if Bandura owns 100 shares of a corporation with a net worth of $20 000 and only 200 shares were ever issued, it is not difficult to calculate the total value of her shares at $10 000, or $100 each. Issuing par-value shares can be misleading; if a par-value share is issued and each share is valued at one dollar, the actual value of the shares would still be $100 each in the above example. The $1 par value may indicate the price at which those shares were originally issued; but, once on the market, such value placed on the share itself would have no significance. The more common practice in Canada and the United States is to put no value on the share at all, making it a no-par-value

Common practice is to issue no-par-value shares

11. *Ibid.*

12. *Ibid.*, s. 6(1)(b) gives the incorporators discretion as to whether or not a maximum number of authorized shares is set.

share. With such a share, the only value associated with it is the value determined by the marketplace. Some jurisdictions, such as Alberta[13] and the federal government,[14] have abolished par-value shares altogether.

Special Rights and Restrictions

The shares issued by a corporation are normally divided into different classes, usually called common shares and special or preferred shares. Although the rights and restrictions associated with special shares can be designed or molded to fit the requirements of the corporation issuing them, special shares are usually designed to give the shareholder preference when dividends are declared, and are therefore called **preferred shares**. Once dividends are declared, the preferred shareholders will have the right to collect a specified dividend before any dividends can be distributed to the common shareholders. Shares usually carry with them voting rights to control the affairs of the corporation. One of the characteristics of preferred shares is that there is no right to vote in most matters (normally given to common shareholders) is denied to preferred shareholders, unless the corporation fails to pay a specific dividend in a given year. If Bandura has 100 preferred nonvoting shares in a corporation which committed to pay a dividend of $10 per share per year, she may receive $1000 in dividends from that corporation in any given year. However, Bandura has no right to force the corporation to pay this dividend, since no creditor/debtor relationship is created between a shareholder and the corporation, she does have the right to payment of such dividends before any dividends are paid to the common shareholder.

Preferred shares usually provide that this right is cumulative. This means that if the corporation does not pay the appropriate dividend for a number of years, the preferred shareholder will have the right to have the back payments paid before the corporation can pay dividends to its common shareholders. For example, if Bandura held a preferred share entitling her to a dividend of $5 per year but did not receive this dividend for five years, she would be able to insist that a back claim of $25 be paid before the common shareholders are paid a dividend.

As long as the dividends are properly paid, the preferred shareholder usually has no right to participate through voting in the affairs of the corporation. But if those dividends are not paid, the preferred share normally has a clause incorporated into it which converts it into a voting share. It must be emphasized, however, that whether these features are present or not depends on what has been designed into the share. It should also be noted that there are some situations in which such preferred shareholders have the right to vote regardless. Typically, when major changes are proposed which would materially affect the position of the preferred shareholder, they retain the right to vote. For example, a proposal to change the rights or nature of the preferred share or to sell the assets of the corporation could not be adopted without allowing the preferred shareholders to vote.[15] Also when a company is dissolved preferred shareholders usually have the right to have those shares repaid before any funds are paid out to the holders of common shares.

Since a variety of rights and restrictions can be incorporated into preferred shares depending on the interests of the parties, it is important that these matters be negotiated before preferred shares are issued. Commonly included in the shares

Different classes of shares can give some shareholders preference

Preferred right to dividend possible

---

13. *Ibid.*, s. 24(1) and (2).

14. *Canada Business Corporations Act*, R.S.C. (1985) c. C-44 s. 24(1).

15. See s. 170 and s. 183 of the *Business Corporations Act*, S.A. (1981) c. B-15, which deals with class votes, and extraordinary sales or leases of the corporation's assets, respectively.

of a non-distributing corporation is a restriction on the transfer or sale of the shares. An example of such a restriction would be to require the board of directors to approve the sale before it can take place. (Non-distributing and distributing corporations are discussed below under that heading.)

Special shares can be used to create shares with objectives other than giving creditors preference to receive dividends. For example, often for the purpose of estate planning, two classes of shares will be created: one with a right to vote and some control in the affairs of the corporation but no right to dividends or money upon dissolution; another with a right to such funds but no right to vote. In these circumstances, the holder of the voting shares will maintain control of the corporation and will give the non-voting special shares to his or her heirs. Such a division allows the holder of the voting shares to maintain control of the operations of the company but to surrender the income and the beneficial interests of the corporation to any heirs.

Borrowing

The second major method of acquiring funds for a corporation is to borrow them, much as individuals do. Whether the money is borrowed from a single large investor, such as a bank in the form of a bank loan, or from a number of individuals in the form of secured or unsecured bonds or debentures, the resulting relationship is a creditor/debtor relationship and not a simple investment as is the case with the issuing of shares. Shareholders, even preferred shareholders, do not have the right to demand a dividend, but creditors do have the right to demand payment of a debt. Even a profitable corporation can choose to plow those profits back into the business rather than declaring a dividend. Failure to repay a debt, however, constitutes a breach of the corporation's legal obligation. Although corporations can and often do borrow money in single large loan transactions, they often borrow money from many different sources in much the same way shares are sold. They do so by issuing debentures, usually called bonds in Canada and the United States.

Technically, a bond is an acknowledgement of an obligation or indebtedness in writing and under seal, whereas a debenture is simply an acknowledgement of debt. The bond is a particular type of debenture and although business people often use the terms interchangeably the term "bond" is usually used when some specific asset has been taken as security.

The corporation typically makes a debt commitment to a trustee who then issues bonds in the indebtedness to individual bondholders. These individual creditors are entitled to share in the proceeds of the corporation's obligation to pay a certain amount of money on a specific date and at a set rate of interest. This arrangement allows for the free transfer of these instruments from person to person and has resulted in a considerable and viable market for this form of "securities." Such bonds or debentures can be unsecured but are usually secured against specific assets or by a floating charge. If a corporation becomes insolvent, a secured creditor will have first claim against the assets used as security when that asset is sold. In jurisdictions with a personal property security act, the same effect can be accomplished without the use of a floating charge.

There is a significant difference between shares and bonds. A shareholder is a participant in the corporation, not a creditor. A bondholder, on the other hand, has loaned money to the corporation and thus a creditor/debtor relationship has been established. The corporation is in debt to the bondholder for the amount of the bond, but the corporation is not in debt to the shareholder for the price paid for the share. It is for this reason that the bondholder has the right to demand repayment of a loan with interest when it comes due and to enforce that right in court. The shareholder has no similar right to demand payment of a dividend or repayment of the cost of the share. This is true even for a preferred shareholder.

On the other hand, bondholders have no right to participate in the management of the corporation, although managerial rights may be acquired, depending on the terms of the agreement, if the company defaults on the loan. In the event of default, this right can extend to the right to appoint a receiver to take over the assets of the corporation and operate the business much as a trustee does in a bankruptcy. If the corporation remains solvent, however, the shareholders retain control through the voting power and the bondholders retain the right to be paid on a regular basis. From the investor's point of view, the choice between shares at one end, bonds at the other and preferred shares in the middle is likely to be simply a question of balancing risk and return. But in order to calculate the risks a clear understanding of the legal differences between these vehicles is essential, not to mention an understanding of their different tax implications.

Many business people prefer to use a combination of these methods of acquiring funds. Most large corporations usually maintain a balance between common and preferred shares on the one hand and various types of debt instruments such as large loans and secured and unsecured corporate bonds on the other. To illustrate, suppose Bowman wanted to incorporate a small manufacturing business which he owned. There are several ways to transfer the assets of the business to the corporation. Bowman might incorporate a corporation which would acquire the manufacturing business and any property associated with it in return for all the shares of the corporation. But a better alternative might be to have the corporation purchase the manufacturing business as well as any property associated with it from Bowman, giving him a bond secured by a mortgage on the property as security for the repayment of the debt.

Bowman has all the shares in the corporation in either case. However, in the second case, instead of simply having shares in a corporation with significant assets, Bowman is a creditor of that corporation. Because the debt will be secured, he will be in a better position to get his money back if the corporation eventually runs into financial difficulties. This is similar to the situation in which Salomon found himself in the case described above. There may be favourable tax implications to acquiring the property in this way as well.

Non-Distributing and Distributing Corporations

Traditionally, corporate law statutes in the various jurisdictions have recognized a distinction between distributing and non-distributing corporations, which were usually called, respectively, public and private corporations. In recent years, statutory provisions relating to these two classes of corporation have received considerable attention and have been significantly modified. In Alberta, corporations that offer shares to the public and that have more than 15 shareholders are called distributing corporations,[16] and such corporations have more stringent auditing and reporting requirements.

16. *Ibid.*, s. 1(l).

Bondholder has right to payment

• no right to participate in management

A **non-distributing corporation** is one in which there are relatively few shareholders, some restriction on the sale of shares, and the shares are not sold to the public openly on the stock market. These are usually small corporations, such as a family business, in which the management is performed by the shareholders. In those jurisdictions where the corporate law statute still distinguishes between non-distributing and distributing corporations (such as Alberta), the non-distributing corporation is much freer of government regulations and control. Some jurisdictions require the **distributing corporation** to have more directors than the non-distributing company. Some jurisdictions also require distributing corporations to have more structured shareholders' meetings, more complete and audited financial statements, and more public access to company records and reports. For Alberta, no fewer than three directors are required for a distributing corporation, at least two of whom are not officers or employees of the corporation or its affiliates. A non-distributing corporation only requires one or more directors. The special requirements for distributing corporations are found not only in the appropriate federal or provincial corporations acts, but also in the securities legislation of that jurisdiction.[17]

Distributing corporations more closely regulated

CORPORATE OFFICERS

Directors (Managers)

Within the Corporation.

While it is true that the shareholders have the ultimate control over a corporation, this control is achieved by the process of electing directors who are legally responsible for the management of the corporation. In large corporations, once these directors are elected, the shareholders normally have little real say in the operation of the business until the next election. It is only when the decision to be made involves a fundamental change in the very nature of the corporation, or when the incorporating documents place an obligation on the directors to do so, that the directors need to go back to the shareholders to ask for approval before implementing a decision. The directors' knowledge that they face another election theoretically encourages them to act in a way that is consistent with the wishes and interests of the shareholders. Smaller (non-distributing) corporations are more often run like an incorporated partnership. The shareholders are usually the managers as well as the directors and they participate in all important decisions.

For a person to serve as a director, he or she must not be a minor, nor mentally incompetent, nor an undischarged bankrupt.[18] The requirement that directors also be shareholders has been eliminated in Alberta, and in most jurisdictions.[19] Because many Canadian corporations are subsidiaries of foreign firms, most jurisdictions require that a significant portion of the directors be resident in Canada.[20]

Director owes duty not to be negligent

Under common law, a director owes a duty to the corporation to be careful, although it is clear that this obligation is restricted. To succeed against a director for negligence under common law, it was necessary to establish some blatant or

17. *Securities Act*, S.A. (1981) c. S-6.1.

18. *Business Corporations Act*, S.A. (1981) c. B-15 s. 100(1).

19. *Ibid.*, s. 100(2).

20. *Ibid.*, s. 100(3), which requires that at least half of the directors of a corporation be resident Canadians. But see s.100(4), which states that only one-third of the directors of a holding corporation need be resident Canadians if it earns less than 5 percent of its revenues in Canada.

gross carelessness on his or her part. Some jurisdictions have increased the standard of care required from a director by imposing an obligation to "exercise the care, diligence and skill of a reasonably prudent person."[21] Other jurisdictions, including Alberta, require a director to "exercise the care, diligence and skill that a reasonably prudent person would exercise in comparable circumstances."[22] Directors must show that in carrying out the affairs of the business, they did what a reasonably prudent person would have done.

In addition to this duty to be careful, directors also have a duty based on their fiduciary relationship with the corporation.[23] As discussed above, the fiduciary duty of a director is to act in the best interests of the corporation, to be loyal, to avoid conflict and to otherwise act honestly and in good faith towards the corporation. Directors are not permitted to take personal advantage of any opportunities which arise because of their positions as directors. These are considered the property of the corporation and to take advantage of such an opportunity would be a violation of the directors' fiduciary duty to the corporation. Any gains made by directors from such dealings must be paid over to the corporation. But the directors alone are responsible for any losses they may incur. When a director is personally involved in some transaction that the corporation then becomes involved in, the director must disclose that interest by making a declaration to the board of directors, avoid any involvement in the discussion of the matter and abstain from voting.[24] Similarly, because of a duty of loyalty, the director cannot enter or start any business which is in competition with the corporation.[25]

Director owes fiduciary duty

A significant problem that has always placed limitations on the responsibility of directors to answer for their actions is the question of to whom the director owes the duty. In common law, the answer was clearly established in the case of *Foss v. Harbottle*[26] and has subsequently been incorporated into many statutes. The director owes fiduciary duties to the corporation, not to the shareholders. Who can sue the director when this duty is violated? The answer is the corporation, which was the person injured. And since the corporation is really a myth and all decisions are made on behalf of the corporation by the director, we have come full circle. Under common law, in other words, it is clear that a decision to sue the directors must be made by the directors and they are not likely to decide to sue themselves.

Director owes duty to corporation, not to shareholders

To solve this problem, some jurisdictions have granted shareholders the right to bring action against the directors or others on behalf of the corporation.[27] In Alberta, this is called a derivative action (in some provinces it is called a representative action), which gives even minority shareholders the right to sue the directors on behalf of the injured corporation. This change, along with the change in the nature of the imposed duty to be careful, has significantly enhanced the peril associated with being a director. It has even been argued that the fiduciary duty of a director extends to the creditors of the corporation in some limited situations.

Representative action

21. British Columbia *Company Act*, R.S.B.C. (1996) c. 62 s. 118.

22. *Business Corporations Act*, S.A. (1981) c. B-15 s. 117(1)(b).

23. *Ibid.*, s. 117(1)(a).

24. *Ibid.*, s. 115.

25. In two recent cases in Alberta, the court found directors of corporations in breach of their fiduciary duties to the corporations. See *Maiklen v. Springbank Oil & Gas Ltd.* (1994) 27 Alta. L.R. (3d) 282 (Q.B.); and *Calmont Leasing Ltd. v. Kredl* (1993) 11 Alta. L.R. (3d) 232, affirmed (1995) 30 Alta. L.R. (3d) 16 (C.A.); additional reasons at (1995) 32 Alta. L.R. (3d) 345 (C.A.).

26. *Foss v. Harbottle* (1843) 2 Hare 461 (High Court of Chancery).

27. *Business Corporations Act*, R.S.A. (1981) c. B-15 s. 232.

DIRECTORS OWE A FIDUCIARY DUTY TO THE CORPORATION THEY DIRECT

PWA's subsidiary Canadian Airlines entered into a limited partnership agreement with Canada's other major airline in creating a computer reservation system called Gemini. This agreement was to last for some time, but PWA and Canadian Airlines were having a difficult time and entered into negotiations with American Airlines to bail them out. Part of this arrangement required PWA/Canadian to get out of the Gemini computer reservation system. They tried to have the limited partnership dissolved in this action. The court found that the directors who were nominated by PWA/Canadian to sit on Gemini had a duty to disclose to Gemini the negotiations that were going on concerning their leaving the Gemini partnership. Even where a director is nominated from another corporation, he or she has a fiduciary duty to the corporation or body for which he or she is a director to disclose all relevant information. The directors failed to do this, breaching their fiduciary duty, and as a result the application to have the limited partnership dissolved failed.

PWA Corp. v. Gemini Group Automated Distribution Systems Inc., 103 D.L.R. (4th) 609 (Ontario Court of Appeal)

In addition to these general duties, statutes in all jurisdictions set out many specific responsibilities and liabilities the directors are subject to when they make specific prohibited decisions. For example, directors become personally liable if they allow shares to be sold for consideration that is less than the fair equivalent of the money that the corporation would have received if the share had been issued for money.[28] Directors will also be personally liable if they allow transactions that are not permitted by the legislation, such as the purchase of shares by the corporation, the payment of dividends by the corporation, or the provision of financial assistance to shareholders or directors by the corporation, if there are reasonable grounds for believing that the corporation would, after carrying out the transaction, be unable to pay its liabilities as they become due.[29] Finally, directors may be liable if they contravene specific responsibilities set out in the legislation, such as the calling of annual shareholders' meetings.[30]

Directors are prohibited from using "insider knowledge" to their own advantage or to the advantage of their friends or family. That is, directors who are aware of something about to happen that will materially affect the value of shares, bonds or other assets in the corporation are prohibited from using that knowledge to their own advantage through dealing in these assets. This misuse of such insider information is prohibited by securities legislation and an offender is subject to fines and imprisonment. The *Business Corporations Act* also provides for personal civil liability of a director who commits insider trading.[31]

External Obligations.

Director's statutory duty for

Statutorily imposed duties on directors are found in many federal and provincial statutes.

Perhaps the areas of personal liability of most serious concern for directors fall into three categories. Today, legislation makes it clear that directors can be held

---

28. *Ibid.*, s. 113(1).
29. *Ibid.*, s. 113(3).
30. *Ibid.*, s. 127(1).
31. *Ibid.*, s. 125.

personally liable when a corporation fails while owing workers unpaid wages.[32] In British Columbia, the Westar Mines ran into difficulty and nine members of the board of directors resigned because of the potential personal liability for unpaid wages. The three remaining directors entered into an indemnification agreement with the corporation so that any liability they faced would be reimbursed to them by the corporation. While indemnification agreements may give the directors some reassurance, if the corporation fails, such agreements are worthless. Insurance is available, however, that can protect directors from this kind of liability. Directors can be held personally liable for other breaches by the corporation of the employment standards legislation as well as violations of the workers' compensation and occupational health and safety legislation in place in the particular jurisdiction.

• wages

A second area of personal liability for directors is for unpaid taxes. For example, under federal income tax legislation, the directors are personally responsible if back taxes are left unpaid when a corporation fails. In many jurisdictions in Canada, (including Alberta; see footnote 20), if foreign firms wish to operate, they must have local, resident directors. Business people are often approached to fill these positions in a token way but are not actually expected to participate in the decision-making process of the corporation. Whether they actually participate or not, many do not understand their personal exposure if the corporation fails, leaving unpaid taxes and other obligations. In some cases, the liability can be ruinous.

• taxes

The third area is perhaps the most frightening. Under present and contemplated environmental and waste disposal statutes the directors of corporations can be held personally responsible not only for the damages caused to the environment by the activities of the corporations but also for substantial fines for violations of the various statutes. Contamination of property, pollution of the air, unexpected spills and the cost of cleanup are examples of potential sources of a director's personal liability. In addition to potential fines and imprisonment, the directors face being personally responsible for the actual damages caused or costs of cleanup in a civil action.[33]

• environment

In a case involving Bata Industries, two directors were fined \$12 000 each for failing to ensure that a waste storage site was cleaned up. This fine was reduced to \$6000 on appeal.[34] Note that in this case the directors were found liable not for what they did, but for what they failed to do.

In many of these statutes the obligations imposed on the directors can only be escaped where the director can show that they acted with "due diligence." In effect they must show that they kept themselves informed of what was required of the corporation, of what the corporation was doing to comply, and did all that was reasonable to avoid any problems. What specific conduct is required to satisfy the due diligence requirement will vary with the situation.[35]

Individual liability has also been imposed on directors for offenses under consumer protection legislation such as the *Unfair Trade Practices Act*, the federal *Competition Act*, securities legislation and provincial human rights codes. It is important to note that many of these statutes not only contemplate fines but also

32. *Ibid.*, s. 114 makes directors of corporations in Alberta liable for up to six months' wages payable for each employee of the corporation.

33. For example, in s. 218 of the *Environmental Protection and Enhancement Act,* S.A. (1992) c. E-13.3, where a corporation has committed an offence, any officer, director or agent of the corporation who "directed, authorized, assented to, acquiesced in or participated in" the commission of the offence is also guilty of the offence, and liable to the punishment provided for the offence.

34. *R. v. Bata Industries Limited (1992),* 70 C.C.C. (3d) 394.

35. Section 215 of the *Environmental Protection and Enhancement Act, ibid.,* allows for a due diligence defence if the person "establishes on a balance of probabilities that he took all reasonable steps" to prevent the commission of certain offences.

DIRECTORS MAY BE LIABLE FOR UNPAID TAXES

Stuart was a director of an incorporated company with employees. But he was a director in name only: he received no documents, reports, financial statements, etc., invested no money, and paid no dividends. When the company failed to properly deduct and remit taxes with respect to wages and salaries pursuant to the *Income Tax Act*, the court held Mr. Stuart vicariously liable, since a director can be held liable for such a failure. To avoid liability he would have had to show that he had taken reasonable steps to ensure the deductions and payments were properly made, and of course because he played such a passive role he could not show this.

Stuart v. M.N.R., as reported in *The Lawyers Weekly*, Vol. 15 (1995–96)

provide for imprisonment in extreme situations. Usually both criminal and civil responsibility may be imposed on the corporation itself, its directors and officers.

Remember also that under common law, anyone in the corporation can be sued for torts such as negligent misrepresentation or deceit, if he or she has directly caused the loss or injury. The corporate structure is no protection to the person who actually commits the tort. Whether that person is a majority shareholder, a director or a manager, if they actually caused the injury they can be personally sued.

Officers and Senior Executives

Roper v. Murdoch et al.[36]

In this case Catalina Productions Inc. instituted negotiations with Richard Deacon, a well-known Hollywood personality, to produce a television program called *Micro Magic* that involved microwave cooking and celebrity guests. Catalina Productions was involved in several high-profile programs such as *Let's Make a Deal*, *The Tom Jones Show* and a game show called *Pitfall*.

But in 1981, because the rest of the companies that the owner Ian McLennan was associated with, referred to as the Catalina Group of Companies, were in financial difficulties, things were chaotic at Catalina. In fact, McLennan had handled the negotiations with the Hollywood celebrities, but once the tentative deal had been arranged, he handed these negotiations over to Bill Armstrong, the vice-president of program development at Catalina Productions. The other defendant, Murdoch, was the vice-president of marketing at Catalina. Both Murdoch and Armstrong resigned from Catalina Productions, eventually setting up their own company, Northstar Productions.

McLennan, acting for Catalina, experienced some problems in the negotiations with the Hollywood people, and on September 9 he received a letter from Robert Prete, the agent of Richard Deacon and the person McLennan had been dealing with, stating that "We now withdraw from entering any deal with you concerning *Micro Magic* and consider all dealings and commitments to be at an end. We deem ourselves now free to seek alternative avenues for our project.—J. Robert Prete and Richard Deacon." On that same day Northstar Productions Inc. was incorporated by Murdoch and Armstrong, who had resigned from Catalina Productions in late August. A new deal was struck by Northstar with the Hollywood people (Prete and Deacon) to produce *Micro Magic*. That agreement contained

36. 39 D.L.R. (4th) 684 (British Columbia Supreme Court).

virtually the same terms as the handshake agreement entered into August 17 with Catalina Productions. The project went ahead and during the year 1981/82 the show was produced by Northstar.

In this case Murdoch and Armstrong were executives of Catalina Productions and as such owed a fiduciary duty to Catalina Productions. Armstrong had been in the planning stages of *Micro Magic* while at Catalina Productions and Murdoch in his position at Catalina was certainly aware of the project. Subsequently Catalina went into bankruptcy and the trustee in bankruptcy assigned any rights they had arising out of television production to Roper, who brought this action against Armstrong and Murdoch.

The court held that Armstrong and Murdoch, because of their position with Catalina Productions, owed a fiduciary duty to Catalina. It was clear from the evidence that on the day they resigned Armstrong and Murdoch had it in mind to produce *Micro Magic*. This opportunity came to them because of their corporate position and thus they were prevented from taking personal advantage of it. The court required them to pay over any profits they made from the deal to Roper, the successor of Catalina Productions.

This case shows clearly the fiduciary duty imposed on officers and directors of a corporation and also how that duty continues after the officers' resignation. It is also interesting to note that the right to sue did not die with the bankrupt corporation but was subsequently exercised by a complete stranger to these dealings, the assignee Roper.

Although the directors are legally responsible for management, in a large corporation they usually appoint a managing director or CEO who is given overall responsibility along with a managing committee of the directors to run the affairs of the corporation. The day-to-day operation of the corporation is assigned to others who report to the CEO. These officers may include a president, a treasurer and a secretary, but the fiduciary duty discussed here is also extended to other senior executives such as vice-presidents and managers as deemed appropriate for the organization. In general, these officers and managers are in a fiduciary relationship to the corporation similar to that of the directors. They have the same types of general obligations and duties of care and competence to the corporaton as the directors. In the case of statutory obligations such as the disclosure of contracts; the payment of wages or taxes; or compliance with human rights, consumer or environmental protection legislation, officers must usually satisfy the same obligations as those imposed on directors. The *Roper* case set out above not only shows the nature of this fiduciary duty for directors, officers and managers but also shows how that duty can continue even after the employment relationship has ceased.

Similar duties owed by senior management

Promoters.

A promoter is someone who participates in the initial setting-up of the corporation or who assists the corporation in making a public share offering. Provincial securities statutes control the sale of shares to the public whether through the stock exchange or other means.[37] A securities commission is established to prevent fraud and encourage a free and efficient market in corporate shares and other securities. This requires the complete disclosure of as much information as possi-

Promoters also owe duties

37. In Alberta, the relevant legislation is the *Securities Act*, S.A. (1981) c. S-6.1.

ble. To accomplish this, a proper prospectus must be issued when shares are to be sold to the public. The purpose of the prospectus is to disclose all pertinent information of interest to investors about the corporation and its business operation. The corporation as well as the promoters are responsible to ensure full disclosure and no misrepresentation in the prospectus. In addition to any civil liability, significant fines and the possibility of jail sentences may also be imposed when such misrepresentations take place.

The securities commission is also charged with controlling other forms of abuse, including insider trading, wherein officers or people holding significant percentages of the shares of a corporation trade in those shares using their insider's knowledge to anticipate a rise or fall in prices. The securities commission also controls abuses by providing for the registration and regulation of all those involved in the selling and marketing of shares and other securities, including dealers, salespeople and the issuers of the shares (the corporations) themselves.

Promoters may not be officers of the corporation at all, but like directors and the officers of the corporation they are in a fiduciary relationship to that corporation and have similar responsibilities. A person will often acquire property in anticipation of promoting a corporation and the corporation will then purchase that property from the promoter. In these circumstances, the promoter has a duty to act in the best interests of the corporation he or she is going to incorporate. The promoter has an obligation not to take advantage of the corporation by selling the property to the corporation at an excessive profit. He or she must divulge the prices paid for the original purchase and not participate in the decision-making process when the corporation purchases the property from him or her. The promoter has a fiduciary duty to the corporation and a duty to disclose any personal interest in deals in which the corporation is involved.

Promoters will often purchase property on behalf of a corporation before it has been incorporated and then have the corporation ratify the agreement after incorporation. Under the common law, such ratification of pre-incorporation contracts is invalid, since the corporation did not exist at the time the promoters were claiming to act on its behalf. Although this approach may be sound legally, it causes some real difficulties from a business point of view and many jurisdictions (notably Alberta and the federal government) have included provisions in their legislation permitting the after-incorporated corporation to ratify a pre-incorporation contract.[38] The result is that the contract is valid and binding on the corporation once it is so ratified. Of course, if the corporation does not ratify or if a pre-incorporation contract is signed in a jurisdiction where the corporation cannot ratify, the promoter remains solely liable for any losses since there was no authority to act.

Shareholders

Richardson Greenshields of Canada Ltd. v. Kalmacoff[39]

In this case there were two companies involved, Security Home Mortgage Investment Inc., referred to as "Security Home," and Security Home Financing Ltd. referred to as the "advisor." Security Home was controlled by a small group of

---

38. In Alberta, see s. 14 of the *Business Corporations Act*, S.A. (1981) c. B-15.

39. 123 D.L.R. (4th) 628 (Ontario Court of Appeal).

individuals holding 85 percent of the common shares. In addition there was a large number of preferred shares which had been sold on the open market through the agent, Richardson Greenshields of Canada Ltd. These preferred shares had no voting rights except when it came to the role of the advisor. The shares of the advisor company were also largely owned by the same individuals who owned the common shares in Security Home. The role of the advisor was to manage and run the operations of Security Home. Problems arose when Security Home ran into financial difficulty and the contract for the advisor company came up for renewal. It was renewed and then Richardson Greenshields obtained enough proxies from the preferred shareholders to override that decision. Since the renewal of that management contract with the advisor required the approval of the preferred shareholders and this approval was not given, that contract was terminated.

It is at this point that the basis of the complaint arises. Instead of that being the end of the matter, the directors of Security Home, in order to thwart the spirit of the direction given them by the preferred shareholders, simply hired the people employed in the advisor company as managers for Security Homes. In effect they were doing exactly the same jobs they were doing before, but now they were employed by Security Homes instead of the management company. In response to this, Richardson Greenshields bought 100 shares of Security Home on the open market and brought a derivative action against Security Home and its directors.

The question in this case was whether Richardson Greenshields has the right to bring such a derivative action. At trial it was held that they didn't, because they had acquired the shares after the action complained of. But the appeal court decided that the issues involved were significant, that it didn't matter when they obtained the shares and as a shareholder they had the right to ask the court for permission to commence a derivative action against the directors of the company, which permission was granted.

The court's decision here did not decide the merits of the dispute; it simply authorized the action to proceed. But it does illustrate some very important points. First of all it shows how "preferred" shares can be set up with different rights and obligations than common shares and what the effects of those differences can be. It also illustrates how different corporate entities can be used and intermingled to accomplish different purposes, as was the case here with Security Home and the advisor company having essentially the same investors owning common shares in each. But for our purposes the most important thing is the right of a disgruntled shareholder to overcome the tyranny of the majority and bring an action against those who have, for their own ulterior purposes, made decisions not in the best interests of the company.

Few responsibilities are imposed on a shareholder, which is one of the main attractions of incorporation. Unlike the director, the shareholder usually has no duty to act in the best interests of the corporation, although obligations can be imposed on shareholders if they hold enough shares to be classified as insiders as discussed above. The number of shares required for one to be deemed an insider varies from one jurisdiction to another[40] but shareholders who have been classified as insiders have the same obligation as directors not to use insider information to their own benefit or to the benefit of friends or relatives.

Shareholder has few responsibilities

40. Section 121 of the *Business Corporations Act*, S.A. (1981) c. B-15 states that any beneficial owner of at least 10% of the voting shares of a corporation is considered an "insider."

Shareholder has right to see records and reports

Shareholders do have significant rights and remedies available to them. The statutes of the various jurisdictions require that specific records be kept at certain designated offices of the corporation. These records must include the documents of incorporation; lists of all the shareholders; lists of transactions or changes in relationship to the shares; lists of officers, directors and debenture holders; minutes of directors' and shareholders' meetings; audited financial statements; and so forth.[41] Not all corporate records are available to shareholders. The actual accounting records (the books), for example, are not available, only the financial reports; otherwise, such information could not be kept from competitors. Nonetheless, much important information is contained in documents that are accessible to anybody who holds a share in the corporation.[42]

Shareholders are also entitled to receive copies of the financial statements of the corporation. Whether the financial statements must be audited or not depends on the jurisdiction and status of the corporation (for example, whether it is distributing or non-distributing).[43] The audited financial statements are perhaps the most important of these documents to the shareholder. An auditor is an unbiased outsider whose responsibility is to ensure that the financial statements use generally accepted accounting principles and are accurate. The auditor's duty is to the shareholders, not to the directors, and the auditors do have access to the corporation's books to ensure the accuracy of their conclusions. In most jurisdictions, shareholders who have some doubts about the accuracy of these audited statements can have an inspector appointed to examine the auditing process.[44]

Shareholders have the right to vote

The shareholders also have some power to affect the decisions made by the corporation. Shareholders must be given notice of an annual general meeting of shareholders which must include the appropriate financial statements. At that meeting, the shareholders must be given an opportunity to vote for the directors of the corporation. The directors are thus directly answerable to the shareholders for their actions. Any major changes which will affect the nature of the corporation must be placed before the shareholders to vote on before the decisions are implemented. The incorporating documents or bylaws of the corporation may provide for the right of shareholders to vote in other situations as well. Any shareholder entitled to vote at an annual general meeting will also have the right to set out any matter for shareholder decision in the form of a proposal. The corporation need not comply if the proposal is self-serving or is in some way an abuse of the process.[45] Of course, it must be remembered that each vote is based on the number of shares held. Thus, someone holding a majority of the shares will always be able to outvote minority shareholders.

Proxy can be passed to someone else

Shareholders who are not going to be present at the annual general meeting can pass their right to vote on to someone else. Such a right is called a **proxy** and can be quite important when one group of people tries to collect enough proxies to

---

41. In Alberta, the list of documents that must be prepared and maintained at the records office is set out in s. 20(1) of the *Business Corporations Act*, ibid. Section 132(4) of the *Act* also states that the list of shareholders must be available for examination at the records office.

42. Ibid., s. 149.

43. In Alberta, the financial statements of distributing corporations must be audited; see s. 157 and s. 163(1) of the *Business Corporations Act*, ibid.

44. Part 18 of the *Business Corporations Act*, ibid., allows any security holder to apply to the court for an order directing that an investigation be made of the corporation.

45. Most of the requirements regarding annual general meetings are set out in Part 11 of the *Business Corporations Act*, ibid. But see also s. 101(3), requiring the election of directors by shareholders at the annual general meeting of the shareholders; and Part 14, dealing with Fundamental Changes, which must be approved by special resolution of the shareholders (i.e., by at least two-thirds of the votes cast).

affect the course of the elections at the annual general meeting. The rules for the creation and operation of proxies are quite strict, because of the potential for abuse.[46] For example, in some jurisdictions, a management group soliciting proxies is required to state this fact in bold print on the face of the information circulated to the members. The bylaws or articles set out how many votes each shareholder is entitled to but this may vary with the type of shares held. Holders of common shares are usually entitled to one vote per share.

In several situations a shareholder can insist on an extra meeting of the shareholders. A shareholder who holds a significant portion of the shares can usually demand a meeting as a matter of right. A shareholder with fewer shares may be able to convince a court that such a meeting would be appropriate. But such a right still only protects the majority shareholder, since a majority vote or greater is necessary to decide all matters once the meeting is held.

A significant risk faced by minority shareholders is the danger of dilution of their shares. A minority shareholder's proportion of the outstanding shares decreases if, when additional shares are sold, none are acquired by that minority shareholder. For example, if Pantazis holds 500 shares and the total number of shares issued by the company is only 1000, then Pantazis has 50 percent of the shares and 50 percent control. If the directors decided to issue another 500 shares and those shares were sold to anyone else, Pantazis would lose his 50 percent control. Even though he still has 500 shares, they now represent only 33.3 percent voting rights. This problem can be avoided if the shareholder insists in a shareholder agreement or in the incorporating documents that he or she be offered any new shares first and only after a failure to purchase them can they be sold to anybody else. Such a right is called a preemptive right. In jurisdictions such as the United States and Britain, preemptive rights are in place, but in most jurisdictions in Canada (including Alberta) they exist only where actually granted in the incorporating documents.[47]

Preemptive rights entitle shareholder to be offered any new shares first

These shareholder rights may seem to confer great power, but in fact the reverse is true. In large corporations so many shares are extant that any individual shareholder's rights are very diluted, and in most cases his or her only recourse is to sell the shares. In small, non-distributing corporations the situation may be worse. There is usually a restriction on the sale of shares and the shareholder may find him- or herself "locked in," unable to sell those shares and unable to influence the course of the corporation because of the overriding control exercised by the majority shareholder.

To protect the shareholder from abuse in these circumstances, the statutes have provided several safeguards, the most important of which is the shareholder's right to sue the directors on behalf of the corporation when the directors have done something actionable. The right to derivative action (discussed on p. 441) action exists in Alberta and other jurisdictions that use the articles of incorporation method of incorporation.[48]

Derivative or representative action

To succeed in these jurisdictions, a shareholder must show that the corporation was in some way injured by the directors' actions. This was the nature of the action brought by Richardson Greenshields in the case used to introduce this section. The directors had, in effect, used a technicality to thwart the rights of the preferred shareholders to their detriment and that of the company. Richardson

---

46. The rules relating to proxies are set out in Part 12 of the *Business Corporations Act,* ibid.

47. *Ibid.,* s. 28.

48. *Ibid.,* s. 232.

SHAREHOLDERS HAVE THE RIGHT TO BRING A DERIVATIVE ACTION

Northwest Sports owned the Canucks hockey team and created a wholly owned subsidiary, Arena Corp., for the purpose of building a stadium in downtown Vancouver. Northwest also explored the possibility of getting an NBA franchise for Vancouver. Eventually Mr. Griffiths, who was the president of Northwest Sports, pursued this opportunity on his own, and made arrangements to obtain an NBA franchise for Vancouver with the cooperation of the McCaw Group. This required that Northwest sell out their interest to the new organization. The directors of Northwest, with Griffiths abstaining, agreed to this new arrangement. A few of the minority shareholders, however, did not like the deal. One of them brought this action before the B.C. Supreme Court seeking permission to bring a derivative action against Mr. Griffiths and the other directors for violation of their fiduciary duty with respect to Northwest. The court granted leave for such a derivative action, noting that Mr. Griffiths had violated his fiduciary duty by taking advantage of a corporate opportunity. The other directors who were refusing to sue on behalf of Northwest were in no position to do so since they would be suing themselves. This is an appropriate situation for a derivative action.

Re Abraham and Inter Wide Investments Ltd. et al., 20 D.L.R. (4th) 267 (Ontario High Court of Justice); *Primex Investments Ltd. v. Northwest Sports Enterprises Ltd. 1995*, 4 W.W.R. 54

Greenshields as a shareholder was seeking permission of the court to bring an action on behalf of the company against those directors. This was necessary, as there is no way the directors would decide for the company to bring an action against themselves.[49]

Shareholders have rights to relief from oppression

A shareholder's complaint might not be that the corporation was hurt but that the shareholder was being oppressed in some way. For example, the directors might arrange for the sale of shares just to weaken the voting position of a particular shareholder or, if the shareholder is an employee, the directors might fire the shareholder to force sale of the shares. In some jurisdictions, both shareholders and creditors have the right to go to court and seek an order for relief from oppression if this type of abuse takes place. In Alberta, current (or past) shareholders, creditors, directors or officers, or "any other person who, in the discretion of the Court, is a proper person"[50] may seek relief from the Court on the basis of oppression or unfair prejudice. The Court then may make any order it thinks fit, including appointing a receiver or providing for the liquidation and dissolution of the corporation.[51]

Dissent provisions provide relief for shareholders

When the directors did something that adversely affected the position of a minority shareholder but was beneficial to the corporation as a whole, historically there was no recourse. In many jurisdictions, however, the injured minority shareholder now has the right to file a dissent.[52] Such dissent procedures are implemented

49. For a good discussion of the derivative action remedy, see *First Edmonton Place Limited v. 315888 Alberta Ltd. et al.* (1988) 60 Alta. L.R. (2d) 122(Q.B.).

50. *Ibid.*, s. 231(b).

51. *Ibid.*, s. 234. For a case where the Court found that there was oppression of, and unfair prejudice to, the interests of the shareholders, see *218125 Investments Ltd. v. Patel* (1995) 33 Alta. L.R. (3d) 245 (Q.B.).

52. *Ibid.*, s. 184. This is a very significant shareholder power, but it is only available in limited circumstances, such as when a decision is being made to amend the articles of incorporation in order to restrict the issue or transfer of shares, or to restrict the type of business the corporation can carry on. It is also available when amalgamation with another corporation is involved or when a significant portion of the assets of a corporation is going to be sold or leased.

when major changes to the corporation adversely affect the shareholder and require that his or her shares be purchased at a fair price.

Small, non-distributing corporations whose shareholders are also directors and
managers of the company are often essentially an incorporated partnership. Often
they will also be full-time employees of the corporation, and when they fall out
with each other the problems can go far beyond what can be remedied or even
what has been anticipated in the legislation. When a minority shareholder is forced
out in these circumstances, he or she may lose not only a job as director and manager but also full-time employment, and may still not be able to sell his or her
shares. One of the most useful ways of avoiding the problems associated with the minority position in a non-distributing corporation is to draw up an agreement between
the shareholders, which builds in protections against any of these eventualities. A
term will often be included whereby one shareholder must buy out the other if
these types of events or other forms of dissatisfaction occur. Provisions relating to
employment are often included in such agreements as well. Shareholder agreements are very important and can be used to set out many important obligations between the parties much as a partnership agreement does in a partnership
relationship.

Although they may often think otherwise, shareholders do not have the right to
claim any dividend or force the directors to declare one. Shareholders only have a
right to a dividend if one is declared by the directors. Of course, if the directors fail
to declare a dividend when the shareholders expect one, they might have a tendency to vote against them at the next shareholders' meeting, but the shareholders cannot go to court and sue for a dividend. This is true even if they hold preferred
shares declaring that they are entitled to a specified dividend each year. However,
in the case of such special shares, the shareholders may have a right to a cumulative
dividend which involves the payment of all prior dividends that have been missed
before any dividend can be paid to other shareholders. The rights associated with
the shareholders' position are rights of control, information and protection, but
there is no corresponding right to a specific return on the funds invested. Many provisions are in place to protect the position of shareholders, but it is important to balance these rights against some important drawbacks for shareholders.

Shareholders have no right to dividends

PROS AND CONS OF INCORPORATION

Advantages

There are several advantages associated with incorporation, most of which are derived from the concept of the separate legal personality of the corporation.

Limited Liability.

As illustrated in the *Salomon* case, shareholders are not liable for the debts and
other obligations of the corporation because of the separate legal entity aspect of
the corporation. The corporation, as a separate legal person, is responsible for its
own wrongful conduct. The shareholders' liability is limited to the amount they
have paid for their shares. If the total assets of the corporation are not sufficient to
satisfy the obligation, the creditor demanding payment cannot turn to its shareholders for the difference.

Liability of shareholder limited to investment

Limited liability is one of the most attractive features of the corporation, and
often the primary reason for choosing to incorporate, but such an advantage is

EVEN A SUBSIDIARY CORPORATION IS A SEPARATE PERSON

In 1981 two large oil companies, Sunmark Worldwide Services Inc. and Ocelot Industries, created two subsidiaries to explore for oil in the Sudan as a joint venture—Sun Sudan and Ocelot Sudan respectively. When, after considerable exploration, the point came that Ocelot Sudan was to put more funds into the project according to the agreement, they were unable to do so. Sun Sudan sued, not the subsidiary, but the parent company Ocelot Industries. The court had to determine whether the parent company was responsible for the debts of its subsidiary. The court determined from the evidence that there was no fraud on the part of Ocelot Sudan or any of the parties, and that a substantial effort had been made to

provide funding. Also there were good and valid reasons for creating the subsidiaries, not the least of which was to reduce risk and insulate the parent companies from liability. The judge found that because of the *Salomon v. Salomon* principle, each corporation had a separate legal personality and the parent Ocelot Industries was not responsible for the debts of Ocelot Sudan. He pointed out that these were sophisticated business people who knew they were dealing with limited liability companies, and concluded there was no wrongdoing and so the separate legal liability element was in effect.

Sun Sudan Oil Company, Inc. v. Methanex Corp., (1992) 5 Alta. L.R. (3d) 292 (Q.B.).

Limited liability lost when personal guarantee is given

often only an illusion. Any institution providing funds to a small, non-distributing corporation will insist that certain principals of the firm, such as the majority shareholder, the president or anyone else the bank feels will have funds, guarantee the indebtedness of the corporation. This effectively eliminates any advantage of limited liability for those asked to sign such a guarantee.

Nevertheless, the principle of limited liability is attractive when unexpected liability is incurred. Thus, if a corporation's employee negligently causes another injury or if the corporation fails to honour its contractual obligations, the injured party will not be able to seek compensation from the shareholders for any damages suffered. Similarly, suppliers of materials usually do not obtain any personal commitment from shareholders, so suppliers cannot turn to the shareholders for payment if the business becomes insolvent. For example, if a person operating a grocery business incorporates a corporation and borrows money from the bank for business purposes, that bank will probably insist on a personal guarantee from the shareholder, but a supplier of groceries would normally have no such personal commitment. If the business becomes insolvent, the shareholder will be obligated to pay back the loan to the bank but will not be obligated in any way to the supplier, because the contract for the goods supplied was with the corporation rather than with the shareholder. Similarly, if an employee of the grocery business negligently caused an injury while carrying out assigned activities, the corporation would be vicariously liable for that injury. The injured individual, however, would not be able to sue the shareholders.

Even this amount of limited liability is not certain. As the case used to introduce this chapter illustrates, the courts are now more willing to look behind the corporate veil and hold the principals liable for the obligations of that corporation. This is especially true when there is any taint of wrongdoing or avoidance of obligations that ought to be honoured.

Taxes.

Although tax reform was supposed to do away with the differences between the federal income taxes paid by sole proprietors, partners and corporations, because the system is so complex there still may be advantages available to the individual tax-payer through incorporation. At the least, the shareholder can leave the funds in the corporation and use it as a vehicle of investment, thus avoiding some taxes until a later date. In addition, as many provinces have not followed the federal lead, there may still be significant provincial tax advantages to be gained through incorporation.

Tax advantages gained through incorporation

However, federal and provincial income tax laws are extremely complicated. It is possible that incorporation will backfire and that the process will lead to more income taxes rather than fewer. When losses are experienced, as is normally the case with a new business, the taxpayer is better off if the business is not incorporated so that these losses can be applied directly against personal income. Great care must be exercised in the process of tax planning for any business and a prudent business person will seek expert advice in these circumstances.

Succession and Transferability.

Because a corporation is a separate legal entity and a mythical person, it does not suffer from the normal frailties of human beings. A corporation will not die unless some specific steps are taken to end its existence. When a partner dies, the partnership will usually come to an end. The death of a shareholder, even a shareholder who owns 100 percent of the shares, will not affect either the existence or the normal operation of the corporation, assuming the shareholder was not personally involved in that operation. The share is simply an asset in the hands of the shareholder and is treated like any other asset the deceased may have.

Corporation survives death of shareholders

For example, if two people formed a corporation in which each owned 50 percent of the shares and both were killed in an airplane crash, the corporation would still continue to exist, the shares would form part of the deceaseds' estates and the heirs would become the new shareholders. If the two people were carrying on business as a partnership, however, the corporation would automatically be dissolved.

Since partners are responsible for each other's actions and since they play such a significant role in the management of a partnership, the process of one partner divesting him- or herself of interest in the partnership is complex and involves negotiating with and obtaining the consent of the other partners. Since a shareholder does not have similar rights and responsibilities, shares usually can be transferred at will without reference either to the other shareholders or to the corporate body. This free transferability of shares was one of the attractive features that led to the creation of the corporate entity in the first place and it provides an effective method for the contributors of capital to restrict their relationship with the corporation. Because free transferability of shares is not always desirable, it is possible to introduce a measure of control on this right by a shareholders' agreement or by provisions contained in the bylaws and incorporating documents. Share transfer restrictions can take many forms and are usually required by law in non-distributing corporations.

This does not mean that a corporation cannot die. Several things can cause a corporation to be dissolved.[53] When a corporation goes through the process of bankruptcy and cannot repay its debts, it will be dissolved by operation of law. Similarly, the court can dissolve a corporation where it deems it proper to do so. This usually happens when a minority shareholder is being oppressed or otherwise injured by the actions of the other shareholders or directors. The shareholders themselves

---

53. See Part 17 of the *Business Corporations Act,* ibid., for the legislatative provisions relating to the liquidation and dissolution of corporations.

can vote to bring the corporation to an end when they feel it is appropriate and a declaration is filed to that effect at the appropriate government office. But the more common way is for the corporation simply to fail to file the required annual reports. Eventually the corporation will be considered inactive and removed from the registry. Such corporations can be restored by filing the missing reports after the fact.

Obligations of the Participants.

No duty on shareholder in a corporation

Another attractive feature of the corporation is that the shareholder is free of any obligation or duty to that corporation or other shareholders. Unlike a partnership where each partner is obligated to act in the best interests of the other partners, the shareholder has no such obligation. A shareholder is free to enter into business in competition with the corporation.

The extent of this freedom of action can be illustrated by the activities of several environmental groups. They have acquired a few shares in some of the large corporations they consider a threat to the environment with the express purpose of using the special privileges available to shareholders, such as rights to information and to attend shareholders' meetings, to acquire information which can be used in the battle against the polluting corporation. Even when the interests of the environmental group are diametrically opposed to, and interfere with, the profit-making ventures of the corporation and other shareholders, they are under no obligation to act otherwise. Only when people acquire sufficient shares to be classed as insiders or become directors or officers, or when an individual has a majority of the shares are certain restrictions placed on their activities. These restrictions usually take the form of rules which prevent the shareholders from abusing their positions of power within the corporation and causing injury to other investors.

Management.

Separate management can be maintained

In a sole proprietorship, the business is controlled by the proprietor; in a partnership, each partner is entitled to participate in the business decisions of the partnership; in a corporation, however, it is common to separate the managers from the owners. The shareholders elect a board of directors who control the business. They in turn can hire professional managers who have the expertise to make sound business decisions on behalf of the corporation. The shareholders do not have to devote time or attention to managing but they can change the management by electing different people to the board of directors if they are unhappy with the decisions being made.

Disadvantages

A corporation is not always the best method of carrying on business. Many of the characteristics outlined above as advantages can just as easily be seen as drawbacks from another person's perspective.

It is helpful to compare incorporation with partnership to illustrate some of the disadvantages of incorporation. Partners who wish to change important aspects of their partnership arrangement need only reach an agreement to that effect. In the case of a corporation, however, the incorporating documents themselves may have to be altered, which is an involved and expensive procedure. A partner may come to appreciate having the power associated with the partnership position when there is disagreement between colleagues. In a partnership, one partner can veto a proposal supported by ten others. A minority shareholder in a corporation can do little to alter unsatisfactory decisions and may not even be able to sell his or her shares. In some circumstances, mechanisms have been created to control the free transferability of shares, either through shareholder agreements or by limitations placed in the incorporating documents themselves. A shareholder in this type of corporation will often be required either to sell the shares to other shareholders or to acquire their consent before a share transaction can proceed. As with partnerships, the reason people organize themselves into a small, non-distributing corporation is often because of the individual skills each shareholder brings to the corporation. These shareholders are usually employees as well, and their contribution to the operation of the business is often vital to its success. Free transferability of shares in such circumstances might be a significant threat to the corporation, especially if the shareholder withdraws his or her services when the shares are sold.

Weak position of minority shareholders in corporations

A corporation is the most expensive way to operate a business. Not only is the process of incorporation costly but the ongoing operation involves more expense than either sole proprietorship or partnership. There are more formal record-keeping requirements associated with corporations, and generally there is more government control exercised with a corporation.

Corporations more expensive than other forms of business

It is important to note as well that there are many variations on the corporate approach to business. Often corporations are set up that merely hold shares in other corporations. Corporations may join others or individuals in joint ventures and partnerships. Corporations may license others to use their products, software, or other form of intellectual property such as patents or copyrighted materials.

It is also common to see small business enterprises that are part of a larger organization through franchising—a business arrangement based on contracts of service and the supply of products between the larger and the smaller unit. Fast food restaurants specializing in pizza and fried chicken, hamburgers, etc., are normally set up this way. Many difficulties can arise in such relationships, and the changing nature of contract law and corporate responsibility are softening the normally narrow approach to these businesses. For example, the good faith requirements that are now being read into business contracts put franchisees in a much more favourable position than they have formerly been.[54]

Termination of the Corporation

Corporations can be dissolved in several ways. Most jurisdictions include winding-up provisions in their corporate law statutes, but some provinces have retained a separate winding-up act. (In Alberta, as discussed above, liquidation and dissolution are dealt with in Part 17 of the *Business Corporations Act.*). If the corporation owns sufficient assets, it may be worthwhile to follow this process.

If something has happened to make a business unprofitable, however, usually it is not worth incurring the expense to go through the formal process of winding up the corporation. Dissolution can take place either voluntarily or involuntarily and the procedure can be induced internally by the directors or shareholders or externally by a creditor. On occasion, a court will order a corporation to be dissolved when a minority shareholder has been unfairly treated.[55] If there are more debts

---

54. Franchises in Alberta are governed by the *Franchises Act,* S.A. (1995) c. F-17.1.

55. For a case where the court ordered a court-supervised liquidation and dissolution of a corporation upon the application of the majority shareholder, see *Hurler v. M.L.E. Industries Ltd.* (1991) 122 A.R. 358 (Q.B.).

owing to the creditors than the corporation has assets to cover, the common procedure is bankruptcy and the end result is usually the dissolution of the corporation.

The process of distributing the assets upon winding up the corporation is set out in the various statutes and will not be dealt with here. It is important to note, however, that the directors have a considerable obligation not to allow any of the assets of the corporation to get into the hands of the shareholders until the creditors have been satisfied.

One of the commonest ways for corporations, especially small non-distributing corporations, to come to an end is for the principals simply to neglect to file their annual return. In Alberta, a corporation will be dissolved if it is in default for a period of one year in filing its annual return.[56] Some jurisdictions, notably Ontario and the federal government, have abolished the requirement that these annual reports be filed. In those jurisdictions, it is only necessary to report when changes are made in matters that were required to be filed in the original incorporating documents.

Often when a corporation is to go out of business a decision must be made whether to sell the shares of the corporation or sell the assets. If the shares are sold, the corporation continues as before. The debts and other obligations continue, but problems may arise if the purchaser decides to make changes in wages and contracts with suppliers. Because the corporation continues, the contracts stay in place and continue to bind the corporation even with new ownership. When the assets are sold, on the other hand, the purchaser is not affected by the contractual or other obligations of the corporation selling those assets except if those assets are encumbered. If the asset in question has been used to secure a debt, that creditor has first claim against the asset and the creditor would be well advised to search the title of the assets for such liens and charges before entering into the transaction.

As explained in Chapter 8, some provinces (not including Alberta) have bulk sale statutes in place to protect creditors from the sale of all or substantially all of the assets of the debtor. Any debts or other obligations that have been incurred by the selling corporation remain those of that corporation. After the assets are sold and the corporation no longer has a business, the corporation can be wound up.

SUMMARY

A corporation is a fiction or a myth that has a separate status as a legal person from the shareholders who make it up. Registration, letters patent and articles of incorporation are the processes used in the various jurisdictions in Canada to accomplish incorporation. At law, the corporation is a separate legal entity. Nor are the shareholders liable for its debts. The shareholder can only lose what they have invested (limited liability). Where special statute corporations are involved, the capacity of that corporation may be limited.

Financing for the corporation is derived from the selling of shares (which may be common shares or shares with special rights and restrictions) or through borrowing (which involves the sale of bonds and debentures, secured or unsecured). Distributing corporations have more stringent government controls and greater reporting requirements than do non-distributing corporations.

Directors and other officers of the corporation have a fiduciary duty and must act in the best interests of that corporation, avoiding conflicts of interest. The

56. *Business Corporations Act*, S.A. (1981) c. B-15 s. 205(c).

shareholders, on the other hand, have very few duties to the corporation or other shareholders unless they have sufficient shares to be classed as insiders. Since the duty of the director is owed to the corporation, a shareholder has no right to sue the director when he or she acts carelessly or wrongfully in carrying out his or her duties. In many jurisdictions, however, the shareholder can bring a derivative or representative action against the director on behalf of the corporation. A shareholder has no right to dividends.

The advantages of incorporation are limited liability, tax benefits, the ease of transferring shares, separate management and ownership, the fact that the corporation does not die and the fact that the shareholders are free of obligations to the company and other shareholders.

QUESTIONS

1. What is meant by a corporation having a separate legal identity?

2. Explain the significance of the articles of incorporation.

3. Explain how the liability of a shareholder is limited.

4. What is meant by a "preferred" share? Contrast this with the normal "common" share. Explain why the term "preferred shares" is misleading.

5. Explain why the concept of a par-value share is misleading and why such shares have declined in popularity.

6. Does a shareholder, whether preferred or common, have a right to a dividend? Explain.

7. What is the significant difference between a bondholder and a preferred shareholder, both of whom are entitled to a specified payment each year?

8. Distinguish between a non-distributing and a distributing corporation and explain these differences in terms of the provisions in place in your jurisdiction.

9. Set out the nature of the duties owed by a director of a corporation. To whom are these duties owed? Who else in the corporate organization owes a similar duty?

10. Explain why it is becoming increasingly difficult to get prominent individuals to serve as directors of Canadian companies.

11. Explain any duties shareholders assume. Summarize the rights of the shareholders in relationship to other shareholders, the management and directors of the corporation.

12. Explain what is meant by a proxy and why proxies can be so important at a corporation's annual general meeting.

13. Explain the advantages of free transferability of shares and how and why this right is often modified by shareholder agreement.

14. Set out and explain some of the disadvantages associated with the corporate method of carrying on business.

15. How can a corporation be terminated?

CASES

1. Re Graham and Technequit Limited

Graham was one of four shareholders in Technequit and, according to the shareholders' agreement, he was a director and an employee as well. At one directors' meeting, the other three directors fired Graham from his position as director and from his employment. He retained only his status as a minority shareholder. What courses of action are available to Graham in these circumstances? Explain the likely outcome. How would your answer be affected by the knowledge that Graham was not adequately performing his duties as either employee or director and that the shareholders' agreement had a buyout provision Graham could have implemented but chose not to?

2. W. J. Christie v. Greer et al.

Greer was a long-standing employee of the plaintiff company, W. J. Christie, and had held the position of director and executive officer for ten years. Greer left Christie and went on to establish his own company, Sussex Realty and Insurance Agency Limited. In the process, Greer approached several customers of Christie and persuaded them to transfer their business to the new firm. In this action, W. J. Christie sued Greer for his conduct. Explain the arguments available to both parties and the nature of the compensation Christie would probably obtain if successful.

3. Wedge et al. v. McNeill et al.

In this action, the appellants were directors and shareholders in the respondent company, Hillcrest Housing Limited, and as such had the right to vote at meetings of directors and shareholders. A bylaw of Hillcrest Housing Limited allowed the directors to vote in matters in which they had an interest after having made proper disclosure. The majority of the directors set up a company called Arcona Construction Limited which was fully owned by them. At various directors' meetings, after fully disclosing their various interests, they participated in the decision to direct considerable amounts of business to Arcona Construction Limited even though the directors representing minority shareholders, Richard and Mary Wedge, complained about this action and voted against it. Explain the nature of the complaint lodged by the Wedges, the arguments to be raised by both parties and the probable outcome.

4. Heinhuis v. Blacksheep Charters Ltd.

Mr. Hanson agreed to sell Mr. Heinhuis some property for $200 000 cash plus a yacht. To avoid paying sales tax, Mr. Heinhuis incorporated a company into which the boat would be transferred and then the shares in that company were to be transferred to Hanson. The shares were transferred to Hanson and as security the company was to register a chattel mortgage on the vessel back in favour of Mr. Heinhuis. The money was deposited, the keys were given to the new owner and several payments were made on the chattel mortgage. The company that was incorporated was called Blacksheep Charters Ltd. and eventually the payments stopped. Heinhuis made a demand for payment which was not satisfied and so took steps to seize the vessel. It should be noted that the arrangements to sell the property and the chattel mortgage were all done before the company was incorporated. It was only after the fact that the company was created and the shares transferred. Explain the legal position of the parties and give arguments.

5. Re Keho Holdings Ltd. et al. and Noble et al.

Twenty investors came together and incorporated Keho Holdings Ltd., taking 100 shares each at one dollar a share. One member of that group, Oliver, voluntarily directed the company's affairs and did so very successfully, bringing the company's value up to $6 million. Oliver bought out some of the other shareholders and eventually acquired a 66 percent or greater controlling interest in the company. He then exercised control over those voting shares to his own personal advantage. The first complaint is that he used his position to structure the directors in such as way as to give him complete control over the company and its assets. He appointed himself, his two sons, and an ally, A. S. Cameron, as directors; the people representing the minority shareholders were completely frozen out. The second complaint was that Oliver had the shareholders grant him stock options for 12 500 shares of common stock priced at $1 per share. These shares were selling at $72 a share. This was supposedly done in recognition of his voluntary service to the company over the prior 25 years. The third complaint was that Oliver and the directors under his control voted to borrow $258 000 from the bank and then loaned that money to Gyron Petroleum Ltd. at 12 percent interest without any security. Gyron was Oliver's personal company.

Explain whether these complaints are valid and what course of action is available to the minority shareholders in these circumstances.

6. B. G. Preeco I (Pacific Coast) Ltd. v. Bon Street Developments Ltd.

Preeco owned property and agreed to sell it to Bond Street Developments Ltd. for $4 220 000. The contract was firm and the day for closure was September 25. On September 5, however, the purchaser repudiated the agreement and subsequently offered $3 300 000 instead. The realtor involved pointed out that there was a firm contract and the purchasers would be liable for their repudiation. The representative of the purchasers said that he could "walk away from the deal because their lawyer had some angle." What had happened was that during the negotiations, unknown to the sellers, Bond, the company that they were dealing with, had changed its name to a numbered company, then eventually to Bond Street Holdings Ltd. Another company had been incorporated that was a shell company with no assets and had been given the name Bond Street Developments Ltd. In effect, the company that they were dealing with had been changed to a new company with the same name but no assets. The purchaser had been switched without their knowledge.

When the sellers sued Bond Street Developments Ltd. (the new company) for breach of contract, they were successful and were awarded $1.7 million, but were unable to collect because there were no assets. It is important to note in this case that the principals (the directors, shareholders, etc.) were the same for the old Bond Street Developments Ltd., which changed its name, and the new Bond Street Developments Ltd. Explain the options available to Preeco in these circumstances.

7. Mills-Hughes v. Raynor

Canadian Admiral Corporation Ltd. was a successful company until it was bought by York Lambdon Inc. from its previous parent company and brought under York's control. Admiral made significant loans against its assets to the point that when interest rates increased, they could not meet their obligations and went into receivership. They were forced into bankruptcy in 1981.

Section 114 of the *Canada Business Corporations Act* governing this corporation holds the director of the corporation personally "liable to employees of the corporation for all debts not exceeding six months' wages ... for services performed for the corporation" while they were directors. The former employees of Admiral claimed against the directors personally for vacation pay, severance pay and bonuses.

Discuss whether or not the directors are liable to pay these amounts. Would your answer be different if you understood that the bonus in question was a "guaranteed bonus of $3500 for the year 1981," and would it affect your answer to know that these parties appealing were all senior officers and managers of Admiral?

LEGISLATION

Alberta

Business Corporations Act, S.A. (1981) c. B-15
Companies Act, R.S.A. (1980) c. C-20
Co-operative Associations Act, R.S.A. (1980) c. C-24
Franchises Act, S.A. (1995) c. F-17.1
Securities Act, S.A. (1981) c. S-6.1
Societies Act, R.S.A. (1980) c. S-18

Federal

Canada Business Corporations Act, R.S.C. (1985) c. C-44
Canada Co-operative Associations Act, R.S.C. (1985) c. C-40
Winding Up and Restructuring Act, R.S.C. (1985) c. W-11

WEBLINKS

Corporations Directorate
strategis.ic.gc.ca/sc_mrksv/corpdir/engdoc/homepage.html
Administers several federal laws governing federal companies; involved in incorporation and related services, dissolution of corporations, ruling on use of corporate names, collection and dissemination of information on federal companies, etc.

Canada Business Corporations Act
canada.justice.gc.ca/FTP/EN/Laws/Chap/C/C-44

TSE—The Toronto Stock Exchange
www.tse.com/

Montreal Exchange
www.me.org/

Vancouver Stock Exchange
www.vse.com/

Alberta Business Corporations Act
www.gov.ab.ca/qp/ascii/acts/B15.txt

Alberta Business Corporations Regulation
www.gov.ab.ca/qp/ascii/regs/82_027.txt

Alberta Municipal Affairs: Corporate Registry
www.gov.ab.ca/~ma/reg/cr/crmain.htm

In February, 1998, an innovative computerized system was implemented in Alberta for the purpose of registering incorporations in Alberta. This system is now used to file the Articles of Incorporation, annual reports and other corporate documents. Registration is done by computer via the Internet by specially trained individuals (called "accredited persons") who are employed not by the government necessarily but by law firms and registry offices.

REFERENCES FOR PART 5

Campbell, Andrew N. *Merger Law and Practice.* Scarborough, Ont.: Carswell, 1996.

Insight Information Inc. *Hostile Takeovers and Shareholder Rights.* Toronto: Insight Press, 1994.

Manzer, Alison R. *A Practical Guide to Canadian Partnership Law.* Aurora, Ont.: Canada Law Book, 1994.

Smyth, J. E., D. A. Soberman, and A. J. Easson. *The Law and Business Administration in Canada.* 8th ed. Toronto: Prentice Hall Canada, 1998.

Welling, Bruce. *Corporate Law in Canada: The Governing Principles.* Toronto: Butterworths, 1984.

APPENDIX 13-1   Forms Used to Incorporate a Business under the *Business Corporations Act* of Alberta

Articles Of Incorporation

BUSINESS CORPORATIONS ACT
FORM 1

INSTRUCTIONS

Documents required to be sent to the Registrar pursuant to the Business Corporations Act must conform to Section 1 of the Regulations made under the Act.

Item 1.   Give the proposed corporate name that complies with Sections 10 and 12 of the Business Corporations Act.

Item 2.   Give details of the:
- rights,
- privileges,
- restrictions, and
- conditions

attached to each class of shares, along with the other details required by paragraph 6(1) (b) of the Act. All shares **must**:
- be without nominal or par value, and
- comply with Part 5 of the Act.

Item 3.   If you want to restrict the right to transfer shares, give the restriction. If transfer will NOT be restricted, please write "NONE" on the form.

Item 4.   Give the following:
- the number of directors, or
- the minimum AND maximum number of directors that the corporation is allowed to have.

Item 5.   If you want to restrict the business that the corporation may carry on:
- name the restrictions, and
- make clear whether the corporation is to be restricted TO carry on the business you have named or restricted FROM carrying it on.

Item 6.   Give any rules or provisions that are:
- permitted by the Act or Regulations,
- to be set out in the corporation's by-laws, and
- to form part of the Articles.

If there are no other provisions, please write "NONE" on the form.

Item 7.   Give the date on which the incorporators sign the form.
Each incorporator must:
- sign the form
- give his or her home address.

If the incorporator is a corporation, give the corporation's name and the address of its registered office, and have a person authorized by the corporation sign the form.

Other Documents:
Please include the following with this form:
- Notice of Address (Form 3)
- Notice of Directors (Form 6)
- an Alberta Search Report, dated not more than 90 days from the date the documents are received by Corporate Registry.

Form 3 and Form 6 must be sent to the Registrar within 15 days of any change of address of directors.

Note: Due to limited space, an appropriate attachment adhering to Section 1 of the Regulations will be accepted.

Complete this form and return both copies along with the $300.00 incorporation fee. Make cheque payable to the Provincial Treasurer and mail to:		
	Walk-in Service	**For information call:**
	Corporate Registry	
Alberta Registries	John E. Brownlee Bldg.	Edmonton: (403) 427-2311
PO BOX 1007 STN MAIN	10365 - 97 Street	
EDMONTON AB T5J 4W6	Edmonton, Alberta	Calgary: (403) 297-3442

REG 3047 (96/08) FORM 1

Form 1

Articles of Incorporation

Business Corporations Act
Section 6

1. Name of Corporation

2. The classes of shares, and any maximum number of shares that the corporation is authorized to issue:

3. Restrictions on share transfers *(if any)*:

4. Number, or minimum and maximum number, of directors that the corporation may have:

5. If the corporation is restricted FROM carrying on a certain business, or restricted TO carrying on a certain business, specify the restriction(s):

6. Other rules or provisions *(if any)*:

7. Date signed by Incorporators: _____.

Incorporators

	Address: (including postal code)
Signature: _____ Print Name:	
Signature: _____ Print Name:	Address: (including postal code)
Signature: _____ Print Name:	Address: (including postal code)
Signature: _____ Print Name:	Address: (including postal code)

This information is being collected for the purposes of corporate registry records in accordance with the Business Corporations Act. Questions about the collection of this information can be directed to Alberta Registries, Research and Program Development, 9th Floor, John E. Brownlee Building, 10365 - 97 Street, Edmonton, Alberta   T5J 3W7, (403) 422-7838

REG 3047 (96/12) MS Word 6.0

Business Corporations Act
Articles of Incorporation

Form 1
Instructions

Documents required to be sent to the Registrar pursuant to the Business Corporations Act must conform to Section 1 of the Business Corporations Regulations made under the Act.

Item 1
- Give the proposed corporate name that complies with Sections 10 and 12 of the Business Corporations Act.
- The name must be identical to the name on the Alberta Name Search Report (NUANS report) and must be uniform throughout the incorporating documents.

Item 2
- Give details of the:
  - rights
  - privileges
  - restrictions
  - conditions

  Each class of shares, along with the other details required by paragraph 6(1) (b) of the act, must:
  - be without nominal or par value
  - comply with Part 5 of the Act
- Only no par value shares can be issued under the Business Corporations Act. However, the incorporator may authorize different classes of shares. If different classes of shares are authorized, the privileges, rights, restrictions, and conditions attached to each class of shares must be stated. Further, the right to vote, the right to receive dividends, and the right to share the remaining property of the company on winding up, must be attached to one or more classes or shares, although they need not be attached to the same class. If only one class of shares is authorized and no rights are stated, then it is assumed these shares carry all the above rights.

Item 3
Any restrictions on the transfer of shares must be stated. If you want to restrict the right to transfer shares, give the restriction. If transfer will **NOT** be restricted, please write "NONE" on the form.

Item 4
Give the following:
- the number of directors
- the minimum **AND** maximum number of directors that the corporation is allowed to have

A corporation may choose to have a specific number of directors (e.g. two directors) **OR** it may choose to have a range of directors (e.g. not less than one and not more than seven). If a range of directors is designated, ensure that both the minimum and the maximum number of directors are stated. A corporation which distributes shares to the public, and has more than 15 shareholders must have at least three directors.

Item 5

If you want to restrict the business that the corporation may carry on:
- name the restrictions
- make clear whether the corporation is to be restricted **TO** carry on the business you have named or restricted **FROM** carrying it on

Item 6

Give any rules or provisions that are:
- permitted by the Act or Regulations
- to be set out in the corporation's bylaws
- to form part of the Articles

If there are no other provisions, please write "NONE" on the form.

The Business Corporations Act does not define "Private Company" as do the Securities Act and Companies Act. As a result, some small corporations under the Business Corporations Act must also file under the Securities Act. You can avoid potential problems by including in the "Other Provisions" section of this form the "Private Company" provisions that are defined under the Securities Act. If the following three provisions apply to the corporation, write them in:
- the right to transfer the corporation's shares is restricted. When including this provision, make it clear in Item 3 of the form, how the transfer will be restricted
- The number of shareholders is to be no more than 50. This maximum number does not include persons employed by the corporation or persons
  - who were once employed by the corporation
  - who held shares in it when they were employed by it
  - who still hold shares in the corporation even though they are no longer employed by it
  - two or more persons who are joint registered owners of any number of shares are counted as one shareholder
- the public cannot be invited to subscribe to the corporation's securities

Item 7

Incorporators are to:
- sign the form
- give his or her home address including the postal code
- give the date on which they signed the form

If the incorporator is a corporation, give the corporation's name and the address of its registered office, and have a person authorized by the corporation sign the form.

Other Documents

To incorporate an Alberta corporation please include the following with the Form 1:
- Notice of Address or Notice of Change of Address - (Form 3)
- Notice of Directors or Notice of Change of Directors - (Form 6)
- An Alberta Name Search Report - (NUANS Report), dated not more than 90 days from the date the documents are received by Corporate Registry.
- Transaction Fees

Notes

- Documents required to be sent to the Registrar pursuant to the Business Corporations Act must conform to Section 1 of the Regulations made under the Act.
- Due to limited space, an attachment adhering to Section 1 of the Regulations will be accepted.
- Attachments or schedules should clearly indicate to which item they pertain.
- Form 1 and any attachments should be submitted in duplicate with the other necessary forms to the Corporate Registry office.
- This form will be rejected if not properly completed.

Form 3

Notice of Address Or Notice of Change of Address

Business Corporations Act
Section 19

1. Name of Corporation   **2. Corporate Access Number**

3. Address of Registered Office (P.O. Box number can **only** be used by a Society)

Street	City/Town	Province	Postal Code

OR

Legal Land Description	Section	Township	Range	Meridian

4. Records Address (P.O. Box number **cannot** be used)

Street	City/Town	Province	Postal Code

OR

Legal Land Description	Section	Township	Range	Meridian

5. Address for Service by Mail (if different from Item 3)
   Note: If this is a change, please read the instructions carefully.

Post Office Box Only	City/Town	Province	Postal Code

_____   _____ .
Signature   Date

_____   _____ .
Title *(please print)*   Telephone Number

REG 3016 (96/12) MS Word 6.0

Business Corporations Act
Sections 101, 108 and 276

Form 6

Notice Of Directors Or
Notice of Change of Directors

1. Name of Corporation:	2. Alberta Corporate Access Number (CAN):

3. On the _____ day of _____ , 19_____ , the following person(s) were **appointed** director(s):

Name	Mailing Address (including postal code)	Resident Canadian?
		Yes ☐ No ☐
		Yes ☐ No ☐
		Yes ☐ No ☐

4.   On the _____ day of _____ , 19_____ , the following person(s) **ceased** to hold office as director(s):

Name	Mailing Address (including postal code)

5. As of this date, the director(s) of the corporation are:

Name	Mailing Address (including postal code)	Resident Canadian?
		Yes ☐ No ☐
		Yes ☐ No ☐
		Yes ☐ No ☐
		Yes ☐ No ☐

6. To be completed only by Alberta corporations:
   Are at least half of the members of the board of directors resident Canadians?
   Yes ☐　　　　No ☐

Date:	Signature	Title
		Telephone Number
For Department Use Only		Filed

This information is being collected for the purposes of corporate registry records in accordance with the Business Corporations Act. Questions about the collection of this information can be directed to Alberta Registries, Research and Program Development, 9th Floor, John E. Brownlee Building, 10365 - 97 Street, Edmonton, Alberta　T5J 3W7, (403) 422-7838

REG 3017 (96/12) MS Word 6.0

Cooperatives and the Changing Nature of Business Organizations

VIDEO CASE

CBC

Cooperatives are a distinctively Canadian form of business first developed in the Prairie provinces as a means of keeping ownership, money and control in the community and as a way farmers could keep control of the of the marketing and distribution of their produce. Since the creation of the first Wheat Pools, other cooperative enterprises, including credit unions, gas stations and retail stores have been developed in Canada.

As those businesses have grown and spread beyond their original community, administration problems have begun to plague the cooperatives, forcing them to change their ways of doing business. Some co-ops have more than 3000 members, and that makes decision making cumbersome and inefficient, since the tradition is that every member has a vote on every decision affecting the company. In a sense, a co-op is a huge partnership and thus carries with it all the disadvantages of trying to obtain member approval for its business decisions. Most co-ops have boards of directors, but the boards' power is limited by the necessity to consult members before they act. They can't spend the profits for growth or to modernize equipment, since the profits must be divided and distributed to the members. The co-ops are unable to compete with the big publicly owned companies that move into their territory.

The trend now is to look for ways for cooperatives to redefine themselves. "More and more it means acting like any other big business." Saskatchewan's biggest company is a cooperative, and it is on the verge of a revolution that will take it away from the control of the farmers who own it. They plan to sell shares on the stock market to bring in new income and protect it from the big American companies that are competing for market share. The reality is that co-op businesses will have "to adapt or die."

Source: "Co-ops," Venture, Show Number 577; telecast date February 11, 1996. Running time: 5:59.

DISCUSSION QUESTIONS

1. What is the difference between a co-op and a corporation?
2. What problems in a co-op are solved by incorporation?
3. Compare the advantages and disadvantages of co-ops and corporations.
4. If you were a member of a co-op, what would be your reaction to these suggested changes?
5. Would it be possible to include the advantages of a co-op in a corporation structure?

6

Property

Our legal system is often criticized for its historical preoccupation with property rights over other matters that might have been a greater concern of the law. Such property rights are normally a vital concern of business. Property is traditionally divided into personal property and real property. Chapter 14 is an examination of personal property including chattels (or moveables) and intangibles or claims that one person may have against another. A significant part of the chapter is devoted to a discussion of intellectual property, which in modern times has become a very important example of such intangible personal property. The final part of Chapter 14 is devoted to an examination of insurance, which is often of vital importance where property considerations are involved. Chapter 15 introduces real property, which concerns the rights of people in relation to land and things affixed to the land. Real property rights are examined generally and the landlord and tenant relationship as well as mortgages are the concern of the rest of the chapter.

Photo by Al Harvey/
The Slide Farm.

Personal and Intellectual Property and Insurance

OBJECTIVES OF THE CHAPTER

- To define and distinguish between personal and real property
- To discuss bailment and its consequences
- To illustrate the different forms of intellectual property
- To discuss the statutory and common law protection provided for intellectual property
- To consider the purposes and various types of insurance

A young artist made two sketches of tall ships that he intended to have mechanically reproduced to sell to sightseers when two tall ships visited a neighbouring community. The job of reproducing the prints was given to a print shop where two employees ran off the requested 50 copies and then 60 more for themselves. The artist received his prints but decided not to sell them. The two print shop employees sold their copies of the prints and kept the profits. When the artist discovered this violation, he took the necessary steps to have them prosecuted.

The court decided that the artist owned the copyright in the two sketches and that the actions of the print shop employees went beyond mere copyright infringement and amounted to theft under the *Criminal Code*. They were convicted.[1]

It is important to note that, although the artist retained the original sketches, reproduction of them without his permission not only was a violation of copyright but also amounted to theft. Art work, photographs, computer programs, compact discs and videotapes are often improperly copied without authorization and without affecting the original. The protection afforded to the owners of intellectual property is an important topic discussed in this chapter.

---

1. *R. v. Wolfe and Campbell*, 633-016. *The Lawyers Weekly*, December 19, 1986.

INTRODUCTION

Most people think of property as a physical object, such as a boat, car or land, but the term "property" more correctly refers to the relationship existing between the item and the individual who owns it. When a person owns a boat, it is said to be his or her property. Thus, the term is more descriptive of the nature of the interest a person has in a particular item than descriptive of the item itself. It is helpful to keep this distinction in mind when trying to understand the nature of the different interests in property. The highest form of property rights is generally called ownership or the possession of title to a particular item. In our legal system, it is possible to separate ownership or title from possession. Thus, one person might be in possession of something that belongs to someone else. The rights that may be held in relationship to a particular item, such as land or a vehicle, can be restricted either by law or by simple contractual agreement.

Ownership and possession separated

Property interests can be divided into different categories. Traditionally, these categories have been real property and personal property. A third, called intellectual property, has been added recently and, in reality, is a particular kind of personal property. The term "real property" means land and anything affixed to or constructed on the land including chattels (for example, lumber) that have become attached to the land in a permanent way. Real property is immoveable.

Things fixed to the land become real property

Personal property, on the other hand, is moveable and can be divided into two categories. Tangible property, also called **chattels**, consists of things which can be measured, weighed or otherwise identified as items. Intangible rights one person has in relationship to another, such as a claim of debt or compensation for performance of a service, are called a **chose in action**. (A chose in action arises when one person has a claim against another which is of some value.) A chose in action is a form of personal property and, in effect, is the right to sue. A claim may be based on debt or another type of contract. Bonds, share certificates, and negotiable instruments are examples of choses in action.

Chattel—tangible property

Chose in action—intangible property

A special category of chose in action is now called intellectual property. Intellectual property includes copyrights that give authors the right to prohibit the unauthorized copying of their work; patents that give inventors the right to control the use, manufacture and sale of their inventions; trademarks that protect logos and other forms of names and designs identifying products or businesses; and certain industrial designs and other private information that can be categorized as trade secrets.

Intellectual property deals with ideas and creative work

The first section of this chapter is devoted to tangible personal property, the second to intellectual property. A discussion of insurance concludes this chapter. The topic of real property is discussed in Chapter 15.

A TAXI LICENCE IS PERSONAL PROPERTY

Foster had a taxi licence which he used as security in financial arrangements with several different people. These four creditors all claimed priority with respect to that licence. The court held that although the licence was subject to regulation it still represented a valuable asset, and therefore it was a form of intangible personal property known as a chose in action.

Re Foster, 89 D.L.R. (4th) 555 (Ontario Court, General Division)

PERSONAL PROPERTY

Chattels.

Chattels are moveable things

Personal property in the form of chattels consists of moveables and personal possessions, such as baggage, clothes, radios, animals and boats. Even construction cranes and locomotives are examples of chattels. Real property, on the other hand, is land and things fixed or attached to the land. These **fixtures** may be affixed to the land by the owner, a tenant or some other third party, and concern about who is the rightful owner may arise. When a person buys and installs an item, such as a furnace or a hot water heater, in a house he or she owns, the item is a chattel that becomes part of the house and thus part of the real property.

Chattels attached become part of the real property

Who has installed the item and the degree to which it has been affixed to the real property can be important factors in determining who has the rights to the affixed item. If Gauthier, who owns a house with a mortgage owing to Cembier, buys a new hot water tank, and if Gauthier loses the house because of his failure to pay the mortgage, the secured creditor would have no special claim on the water heater if it has not yet been installed. If Gauthier had installed the water heater before the default took place and the mortgagee took action against him, then that water heater is a fixture or part of the real property covered by the security of the mortgage. Whether a chattel is a fixture or not usually depends on the degree of attachment to the land and the use to which the object is to be put. Of course, the owner of the land is free to remove a chattel that has become a fixture (severance) just as he or she was able to fix the chattel to the land in the first place. Difficulty arises when third parties become involved. For example, when property is sold or a mortgage has been defaulted, whether or not something has become a fixture can be vital in determining who is entitled to it. Similarly, when a tenant brings a chattel onto a rented property, it is important to know whether the chattel has become a fixture and what rights the tenant has relative to it.

Trade fixtures can be removed by tenant

Generally, when a chattel has been affixed to real property, it becomes part of that real property, but there are two situations in which it may be removed again. The tenant of a commercial property who has brought chattels onto the land and affixed them in such a way as to enhance trade or carry on business has the right to remove those trade fixtures when leaving unless they have been incorporated into the real property in such a way that they clearly are intended to stay, for example, reinforcing timbers set into the framework of the building to support heavy machinery.

In residential or commercial tenancies, non-trade fixtures attached for the comfort, convenience or taste of the tenant, can be removed, provided they have not been incorporated into the structure of the building in such a way that they cannot be removed without causing damage to the real property. Trade fixtures and domestic fixtures can only be removed during the term of the tenancy. When the tenant moves out at the end of the tenancy and takes mirrors, light fixtures, rugs and display cases installed by the tenant, the landlord has no complaint. If those items are left, and the tenant seeks their return only after the tenancy is surrendered and the landlord has retaken possession, the tenant is too late. Those fixtures have become part of the property of the landowner. Of course, any provisions in the lease to the contrary override these general provisions.

Finders Keepers.

A finder gets good title against all but original owner

The rights of a person who finds some item are subject only to the prior claim and title of the original owner. If Cruz were to find a watch in a park and show it to his friend, O'Neil, who took it and then refused to return it, Cruz would be successful in regaining possession of the watch if he took legal action. The true owner, Gan, is entitled to demand its return from either Cruz or O'Neil. "Finders keepers" applies only against subsequent claimants to the property, that is, a third party who acquires the item. As far as all subsequent claimants are concerned, Cruz, the finder, is the owner. Only Gan, the original owner, has a better claim to the watch.

More importantly from a business point of view, a person's entitlement to "found" property sometimes depends on where the chattel is found. Who owns a chattel found on private property—the person finding it or the person who owns the property? If it is found on a part of the property frequented by the public, such as the sales floor of a department store or the lounge of a hotel, then the finder is entitled to it. If the goods are found in an area where the public does not go, such as the kitchen of a restaurant or the storage area of the department store, the owner of the store is entitled to it. If the item is found by an employee, the employer is entitled to the chattel whether it is found in a public or private part of the establishment. But the finder also has an obligation, however slight, to return those goods in good condition to the proper owner. This obligation is based on the law of bailment.

BAILMENT

Amo Containers Ltd. v. Mobil Oil Canada, Ltd.[2]

In this case Amo supplied containers to Mobil which used them to transport goods to the oil rigs off the east coast of Canada. The particular containers in question were being transported when the vessel sank with the loss of all on board. In this action Amo as bailor is suing Mobil as bailee for the loss of their containers.

The court found as a matter of law that Mobil would be liable if it could be shown they were negligent. However, the court also found that as a general rule, such negligence is presumed and it is up to the bailee to show that there was no negligence. The reason for this is because the goods are in their care and keeping, and they are the only ones that have the information to be able to establish whether there was negligence or not. The one exception to this is when the bailee no longer exists and the goods are lost. The court in this case held that the bailee still existed, and in fact an inquiry was going on, so there was information available at the bailee's behest to establish whether they were negligent or not; therefore, the onus was still on Mobil to prove that they were not negligent.

This case is illustrative of bailment in several ways. First of all, it shows that bailment applies when personal property is used, even on a large scale such as containers; and second, it shows that the principles can be quite significant in commercial relationships. Here the bailment was one for value and the obligation was on the bailee (the person holding the goods) to establish they were not negligent. This they could not do, and Mobil was liable for the loss.

When a person acquires possession of personal property through a voluntary arrangement with the owner, the relationship is called a bailment. The person giving

Bailment created by giving goods to bailee

2. 62 D.L.R. (4th) 104 (Newfoundland Court of Appeal).

up possession is called the bailor and the person acquiring possession is called the bailee. The personal property involved is usually chattels but intangible personal property (a chose in action) such as bonds, share certificates, or negotiable instruments, can also be the subject of a bailment. One feature of bailment is that the bailee must be given possession of the chattel in such a way that it is clear that the possession is intended to be temporary and that the chattel is to be returned at the end of the bailment period to the bailor. Another requirement for bailment to exist is that the goods be delivered to the bailee from the bailor.

Determining whether the goods have been delivered is not as easy as it may first appear. When a car is left in a parking lot, has a bailment taken place or not? If the keys are left with an attendant or the car is handed over to a valet, a bailment has been created, because those persons have been given control and possession of the car. But when a person drives onto a lot, parks the car and takes the keys, there is no bailment. Rather, the driver has acquired a license to use the parking space and has not relinquished control and possession of the car. During this period of bailment, the title to the goods remains with the bailor and only the possession goes to the bailee. As a general rule subbailment (where the bailee in turn gives the goods to someone else) is prohibited unless it is done with the knowledge and permission of the bailor or is the custom of the industry as might be the case where automobile repairs are involved requiring the services of different specialists.

With fungibles the same goods need not be returned

Goods such as timber, oil and wheat are often placed in the care of another for the purpose of storage. They may be mixed with similar items being stored for others and become indistinguishable. Such goods are called **fungibles**. When they are returned to the owners, there is no obligation to return the exact goods deposited. The only requirement is that goods of a similar quality and quantity be delivered. This situation is still a bailment and is treated under bailment law.

Bailee has a duty to care for the goods

The primary concern of bailment law is the liability of the bailee (the person in possession of, but not the owner of, the goods) for damage done to the goods in his or her care. Bailees are responsible for any willful, negligent or fraudulent acts by themselves or their employees which cause injury or damage to the goods in their care. The standard of care imposed on bailees in determining whether they have been negligent will vary with the type of bailment created.

For Value.

Bailment for value—both parties receive benefit

Bailments are either gratuitous or for value. Bailment **for value** involves a mutual benefit or consideration flowing between the parties. It may be based on a business arrangement, such as a repairperson repairing the goods, a warehouse storing them, or a carrier transporting them, or the relationship might be merely domestic. When a friend stores goods for another in exchange for the right to use them, the standard of care imposed in such circumstances is simply the ordinary standard for negligence—that is, the amount of care that would be expected from a prudent person looking after his or her own goods in similar circumstances.

Duty—reasonable person caring for own goods

Thus, the amount of care that should be exercised will vary with both the value of the goods and their nature. When delicate items are involved, such as china or an insect collection, more careful handling is expected from the bailee than is the case if a heavy-duty machine were being stored. Similarly, if a bailee were storing or handling diamonds, more care would be expected to keep them safe than if the stored items were rhinestones.

Duty may be determined by contract or common practice

If the bailment is created on the basis of a business relationship, the provisions of the contract, as well as the customs and traditions of the industry, will be taken into consideration when establishing the degree of care the bailee must exercise in the circumstances. In the Amo Containers case used at the start of this discussion the court needed to determine whether Mobil was negligent. Just how careful Mobil had to be would likely be determined by the customs and traditions of the industry, but there was a complication. The Amo case is a good illustration of how the court reverses the onus onto defendants to show that they were not negligent. Reversing the onus of proof in this way is rarely done in our legal system but it is necessary in this type of action because only the defendant, the person in possession of the goods, is in a position to know what happened to them.

The standard imposed can vary with the contract created between the parties. Contracts of bailment may contain exculpatory or exemption clauses which limit the liability of the bailee. An example of such a clause is, "Any goods left on the premises are entirely at risk of the owner. The proprietor assumes no responsibility for any loss whether caused by damage, loss or theft of those goods." As was discussed in Chapter 6, courts are reluctant to give effect to these exemption clauses and as a result, they are narrowly interpreted by the courts. To be enforceable, such clauses must be brought to the attention of the customer at the time the contract is entered into.

Exculpatory clauses may limit liability

Two situations in which the standard imposed on the bailee is particularly onerous involve innkeepers and "common carriers" (trucking and bus companies, railroads and airlines, even pipelines). Common carriers must be distinguished from private companies or individuals providing transportation services only to a particular bailor. Such a private carrier is merely a bailee for a reward and has the obligation of a reasonably prudent person in the circumstances. A common carrier, on the other hand, undertakes the standard of an insurer. That is, if the goods are damaged or destroyed while in its custody, it is liable even when faultless, unless the damage is caused by an act beyond its control. If the goods deteriorate because of some inherent problem or because the packaging provided by the shipper is inadequate, then the common carrier is not liable. If an animal dies in transit because of a previously contracted disease or goods are destroyed by spontaneous combustion, there is no liability. A common carrier is also not liable where the damage is caused by an act of war or some condition of nature ("act of God") such as flood or earthquake. A common carrier can limit its liability by contract and may include such a term as "Not responsible for lost or stolen goods or damage over $500." Again, to be valid and binding on both parties, such a provision must be clearly brought to the attention of the shipper at the time the contract is entered into. Common carriers are usually controlled by statutory provisions regulating their industry.

Common carrier has duty of an insurer

According to the common law, an innkeeper is responsible for the lost or stolen goods of a guest unless it can be shown that they were lost because of some act of God or negligence on the part of the guest. For liability to lie with the innkeeper, it must be established that the accommodation was an inn and the plaintiff was a guest of that inn. Only those establishments providing both food and temporary lodging for their patrons (transient-type accommodation) are classified as inns and the innkeeper assumes the obligation of an insurer.

Innkeeper has duty of an insurer

Because this obligation is quite onerous and the historical justification is no longer relevant, most jurisdictions have passed legislation limiting the liability of innkeepers and hotel keepers.[3] This protection reduces innkeepers' liability from that of an insurer to that of a reasonable business person or limits that liability to a specified amount ($40 in Ontario. Note: no similar cap on liability exists in

Liability may be reduced by statute

3. *Innkeepers' Act*, R.S.A. (1980) c. I-4.

Alberta.) Otherwise, they are only liable when it can be proven that they or their servants have been negligent or acted willfully. This protection is only available to the innkeeper when the *Act* is properly complied with. Compliance usually requires the posting of copies of selected sections of the *Act* in every bedroom and public room and the office of the inn or hotel. When this is not done, the common law liability of the innkeeper (that of an insurer) prevails, and the innkeeper is liable for lost, stolen or damaged goods whether or not there has been negligence on his or her part. (See the excerpts from the *Innkeepers Act* in Chapter 2 herein.)

Gratuitous.

The second major situation that creates a bailment occurs when one of the parties receives a benefit and the other does not.

This is known as a **gratuitous** bailment. When the bailee is receiving the benefit of the bailment, as is the case when a neighbour borrows a lawnmower or a friend borrows a car, the standard of care imposed on the bailee is very high. The bailee is expected to show great diligence in the care of the goods and, therefore, is liable if the goods are damaged or stolen even when the bailee has been only slightly careless. Where the bailment is for the benefit of the bailor, however, the bailee is only liable if there has been gross negligence.

An example of the latter situation would be when a person asks a friend to look after her violin while she is away on vacation. The provision of this service is without benefit to the bailee and so only imposes an obligation to be slightly careful in relation to the goods. At least this has been the traditional approach to such a situation; it must be emphasized, however, that the courts have been moving towards imposing the normal definitions and tests for negligence and standards of care, requiring a higher standard of care for the bailee even when the benefit of the bailment is for the bailor.

Finally, it should be noted that the onus of proof has shifted to the bailee. Normally, the person bringing the action is required to prove that the other person was negligent. In these cases, once the bailment has been established and damage to the goods has been shown, the bailee is obligated to show that he or she was not negligent towards the goods belonging to the bailor.

Involuntary Bailment.

Bailment can be established involuntarily. When goods are left at a home or place of business without the approval of the homeowner or business person, the care of such goods has been imposed and, therefore, the relationship is involuntary. Theoretically, for bailment to exist, the bailee must consent. Whether an involuntary relationship is bailment or not, there is no duty imposed unless custody has been accepted. A person who sees a watch lying on the sidewalk has no obligation to pick it up. But if he does pick it up, he assumes the obligations associated with a gratuitous bailee for the benefit of the bailor. Thus, when a person exercises any control, even simply moving the item from one location to another, that person becomes the bailee of the goods and has a duty to take care of them. If a canvasser were to stop and chat with a person working in his garden and leave her coat on the fence, no bailment would be created until the resident moved the coat. By picking it up, the resident exercises control over it and thereby assumes the responsibility to look after the coat. One of the basic obligations of the bailee is to return the goods to the bailor. Generally speaking, if the goods are returned to the wrong person, the bailee is responsible.

Gratuitous bailment

• when bailee benefits, duty high

• when bailor benefits, duty less

Involuntary bailment—duty low

The Position of the Bailee.

Whenever the bailment is for value the parties are entitled to the payment agreed upon by operation of contract law. All of the terms of any contract in place must be complied with. Often such contracts have terms requiring one of the parties to insure the goods. These provisions will be binding if they have been properly brought to the attention of the other party to the agreement. Where the bailee is not paid, at common law that bailee had a right of lien if he had repaired or otherwise worked on the goods. Where the goods were just stored as with a warehouse or transported, there was no common law right of lien. And even where there was a right of lien there was no right to resell the goods. All jurisdictions have passed legislation giving common carriers, repairpersons, warehousemen and other bailees for value the right of a lien against the goods (usually this is a possessory lien and the right to impose it is lost if possession is given back to the bailor). This statutory right to a lien now includes a right to resell the goods after giving the bailor appropriate notice and an opportunity to reclaim the goods. In Alberta, for example, garagemen who store or repair motor vehicles have a lien for the storage and repairs rendered as well as for the price of accessories or parts furnished. If the vehicle is eventually sold, the proceeds are applied first to cover the expenses of sale, next in payment of the lienholder's debt.[4] Similarly, warehousemen who store goods as bailees for hire are entitled to sell the goods and recover their fee from the proceeds.[5] *The Possessory Liens Act*[6] recognizes a lien in favour of those who have stored goods (gratuitously or for a fee) or who have enhanced goods. All three pieces of legislation require that notice be given the owner as a precondition to the sale.

Where the bailor is the one to be paid, as in situations where goods are leased or rented to others, since they still have title they have the right to retake their goods and seek normal contractual remedies. Where no price is agreed on, the bailor or bailee for reward is usually entitled to recover a reasonable payment based on the principle of *quantum meruit* discussed in Chapter 6. Where the transactions involve consumers such as automobile repair services, the special consumer protection statutes must be kept in mind when determining the rights of both parties to the transaction. (Refer to the discussion in Chapter 7.)

INTELLECTUAL PROPERTY

Intellectual property law has as its purpose the balancing of two opposing interests. On one side is the protection of the product of a person's mental effort and, on the other, the free flow of new and innovative ideas which stimulate the advancement of the commercial environment. The law is intended to make ideas and information as freely available as possible while giving the creator the rights to develop, distribute and sell the results of his or her effort. Its primary focus is on the rights and responsibilities which exist between individuals in relation to ideas and information.

Intellectual property law acts to protect results

Although this topic has been included in a chapter devoted to property law, there are significant differences between the forms of intellectual property discussed in this section—copyright, patents, trademarks and industrial designs—and the other forms of property law discussed in this chapter. When a chattel is stolen

4. *Garagemen's Lien Act,* R.S.A. (1980) c. G-1.

5. *Warehousemen's Lien Act,* R.S.A. (1980) c. W-3.

6. *Possessory Liens Act,* R.S.A. (1980) c. P-13.

or destroyed it is no longer available for the use of the original owner. When an idea is taken and used by somebody else, or confidential information is wrongfully communicated to another, the idea or information does not change. It is still available to the original holder but its value to the owner might be considerably diminished by the fact that others have free access to it.

Because of the explosion in the amount of data and information available and the tremendous advances in methods of storing and transmitting information, intellectual property law has grown significantly in importance. Most legislation protecting intellectual property is federal, copyright and patent legislation being exclusively granted to the federal government in the *Constitution Act (1867)*[7] Areas such as confidential information, trade secrets and passing off are not considered property rights and are protected by common law principles. Some provincial statutes such as privacy acts can have an important impact in the intellectual property area.

Copyright

The term "copyright" refers to the right to copy or reproduce a created work. The federal legislation in place is intended to give the author or owner of the copyright a monopoly over the use of the created work. Such rights extend only to the work itself and are not meant to limit the ideas or thoughts which led to the creation of the work. A person may copyright the manuscript for a book but not the ideas expressed in it. To avoid a violation of copyright law, those ideas must be expressed in a different way and not be simply a reproduction of the original work.

The work is protected, not the idea

In recent years because of great advances in technology, and the ease of reproducing written, musical, visual, and computer works, huge changes have taken place. Massive copying of books, records, tapes, CDs, videos and computer programs is not only possible but now common. The power to make copyright law has been given to the federal government exclusively and the *Copyright Act* was significantly amended for the first time in over 50 years in 1988.[8]

Matters Covered.

It is not possible to copyright everything that results from creative or intellectual effort. To be copyrightable, the work need not be good, but must be original, that is, it must be the product of the artist's or author's own work or skill. The work must also be preserved in some permanent, material, written or recorded form. This includes electronic and computer data storage methods.

To be copyrightable, work must be original and preserved in some permanent form

Four categories of copyrightable material are set out in the legislation. **Literary works** include tables, poems, stories, articles (books), and computer programs. **Dramatic works** include shows (movies, television and theatre) and mime performances, including the choreography and scenery. **Musical works** include written melody and harmony and recordings. Finally, **artistic works** include paintings, drawings, charts, maps, plans, photos, engravings, sculptures, works of artistic craftsmanship and architecture.

One of the most significant changes in the 1988 amendments is that they provide copyright protection for computer software and hardware. Prior to this there was considerable debate and confusion as to whether unique computer software and

7. *Constitution Act (1867)*, Section 91, ss. 22, 23.

8. *Copyright Act*, R.S.C. (1985) c. 42, as amended by R.S.C. (1985) (4th Supp.) c. 10 and subsequent amendments.

hardware was protected under patent or copyright law and how extensive that protection was. The 1988 amendment made considerable progress in clarifying the problem and was greeted with considerable enthusiasm in the industry. With a computer program it is sometimes difficult to distinguish between what constitutes the idea behind the software and its expression. The courts have concluded, however, that where the one product has the same look and feel in its operation as the other an infringement of copyright has taken place.

Creation.

A copyright comes into existence in Canada automatically with the creation of the work itself and nothing more is necessary. In Canada, it is not even necessary that the work be published. However, a work can be registered if one chooses, and registration is an advantage, since it proves when the copyright came into existence and also creates a presumption that the person named in the registration is the owner of the copyright. Although not specified in the Canadian legislation, a notification of copyright generally takes the form of the symbol "©" with the word "Copyright" beside it, followed by the year the copyright was first published and the name of the owner of the copyright. Other countries, including the United States, that are signatories to the copyright conventions discussed below recognize valid Canadian copyright and so registration is not necessary for copyright protection to be extended to those jurisdictions. In the United States, however, notification as set out above is required and where the copyright is not registered the remedies available for infringement may be significantly restricted.

Copyright comes with creation of work

For a person to obtain copyright protection in Canada, he or she must be a Canadian citizen, a British subject, or a resident of one of the countries that adhere to the Berne Copyright Convention or the Universal Copyright Convention—international agreements that set out common rules of conduct in matters concerning copyright. Canada will also provide copyright protection to foreign nationals when the country of origin of that national would provide the same kind of protection to a Canadian citizen as it would to one of its own citizens.

Many countries, for example the People's Republic of China, do not have the same traditions of protection of artistic and literary works that we have in the West, and the disregard for intellectual property protection in such countries has been a major stumbling-block in the further development of trade relations.

Ownership.

In general, copyright resides in the creator, but when a work is created as part of the author's employment, the employer owns the copyright unless there is an agreement between the parties stating otherwise. Once the copyright has been created, its owner can assign or license it all or in part to someone else. Even when copyright is assigned, the author or creator maintains the right to be listed as such. Despite any assignment, the author will continue to have **moral rights** in the work. That is, when the copyright is assigned, the new owner cannot change the work in such a way as to degrade it and bring harm to the reputation of the author. In any form of dispute or litigation, in the absence of evidence to the contrary, the court will presume copyright is held by the creator of the work.

Copyright can be assigned but moral rights retained

Rights Granted.

The copyright gives the owner of the work the right to publish it and receive any benefits from it. This right can be assigned, but whoever has copyright has complete

Anti-Copying War Is Escalating

The battle to protect authors' and publishers' rights to their books is heating up. Last month, the RCMP laid seven charges related to copyright violations against Laurier Office Mart, a copy shop near the University of Ottawa, where professors had been photocopying material for their courses without prior permission. Then, on Nov. 8, Ontario Court judge Madam Justice Marie Corbett granted CANCOPY, the Canadian reprography collective established to protect the rights of authors and publishers, its first-ever search-and-seizure order. This was unusual, because it is rare for a court to award a search order for a civil as opposed to a criminal offence. The order was granted against a copy shop near the University of Toronto, Copy Ink (its legal name is Ink Copy Inc.). Although copyright infringements against several titles were investigated, the application against the copy shop specified one text, *Computer Organization*, Third Edition, published by McGraw-Hill Ryerson, written by three University of Toronto faculty members. The text cost $88 at the University of Toronto Bookstore. Students were buying photocopied versions at the outlet for about $20. Toronto police conducted the raid on Nov. 12 with officials from CANCOPY. The police and CANCOPY officials carried off evidence which will enable them to file a civil application against Copy Ink. The case has not yet come to court.

Source: Val Ross, "Anti-Copying War Is Escalating," *The Globe and Mail*, November 27, 1993, p. C1.

---

control over the work except for the moral rights mentioned above. No one else can perform, copy, publish, broadcast, translate or otherwise produce the work without the permission of the owner of the copyright (see In Practice box).

Generally, the period of copyright protection equals the life of the author plus 50 years. There are exceptions, however, such as photographs, for which the protection is 50 years from the creation of the negative. The period of protection is also limited to 50 years when the copyright is held by the government.

A copyright infringement can take place when anyone tries to obtain a benefit from the sale, distribution, performance, broadcast or other commercial use of the work. It is an infringement of the moral rights of the author if someone else claims authorship or if the work is mutilated or modified in such a way that the reputation of the author is harmed. When the author's moral rights have been violated, he or she has the right to compensation even when the copyright has been sold to someone else, provided the author has not waived these moral rights.

> Copyright holder has complete control over work for author's life plus 50 years

COPYRIGHT PROTECTS VIDEOTAPES

The managers of Wall & Redekop were impressed with a set of videotapes titled "How to Master the Art of Listing and Selling Real Estate" that had been prepared by the plaintiff. In 1981 they obtained a used copy of the tapes, made ten copies and distributed them to their various offices. When the plaintiff was informed of this, they wrote to Wall & Redekop complaining about the infringement. Wall & Redekop immediately called in the ten tapes and erased them. This action was successfully brought claiming a violation of copyright and the tort of "conversion," wherein ownership in something is wrongfully taken over by another. Damages were awarded.

Tom Hopkins International, Inc. v. Wall & Redekop Realty Ltd., 20 D.L.R. (4th) 407 (British Columbia Court of Appeal)

There are, however, exceptions to this copyright protection. Quotations that are not extensive and are attributed to the author do not amount to an infringement. The *Copyright Act* specifically states that "Any fair dealing with any work for the purposes of private study, research, criticism, review or newspaper summary"[9] is not an infringement of copyright. There is considerable debate as to just what these words mean, but it seems clear that where the reproduction even for classroom or study purposes is so extensive as to deprive the author of the market for the product it would be an infringement of the copyright. Copying whole chapters of texts meant to be sold to students, for instance, would likely be an infringement, as would the showing without permission of videos or other single- or multimedia materials intended to be used in the classroom for a fee. Photocopying a few pages of a work for study purposes, however, would not likely be an infringement. An important aspect of the 1988 amendment to the *Copyright Act* makes it clear that anyone who is in lawful possession of a computer program can make a backup copy of it as long as only one of the copies is being used by that authorized person at any one time.[10]

Exceptions

Remedies.

When a copyright is violated, the standard remedies available in a civil action are available to the copyright holder although they may take on a special significance in this kind of action. These remedies may be interim in nature, in the sense that they take place before the trial of the issue and are not intended to have permanent effect but just to prevent further damage to the victim before the final disposition of the dispute; or they may be final remedies. It is important to note that where a complainant is successful in obtaining an interim remedy the effect may be so devastating to the offender that no further action need be taken.

One of the most important remedies available is the **interlocutory injunction**. This form of injunction is obtained before the actual trial of the issue if the plaintiff can demonstrate to the court that there is a *prima facie* case supporting his or her claim of infringement and damage would be suffered if it were not granted. This means that the evidence presented must show that a copyrighted work has been infringed upon and that if the injunction is not granted, irreparable harm will be suffered that could not properly be compensated for by damages after the trial has been concluded. To be successful in such an application, it must also be established that the balance of convenience is in the plaintiff's favour. (Is the harm caused by issuing the interim injunction more than the good realized?) This means that an injunction will probably not be granted if a small business is asking the courts to issue an order to stop the production and sales of a much larger operation. Because of recent decisions in the Federal Court, interlocutory injunctions for violation of intellectual property rights, especially in the area of trademark infringement will be much harder to obtain.[11]

Another somewhat unusual remedy that may be available before the trial is an **Anton Piller** order, an order by the court that the offending works actually be seized from the manufacturer or distributor. This is an *ex parte* procedure in which the evidence must be seized by surprise before the goods or relevant documentation can be hidden or destroyed. The court will not make such an order lightly, and before it can be obtained there must be clear and compelling evidence of the

Interlocutory injunctions granted before trial

Anton Piller order provides for seizure of goods

9. *Copyright Act*, s. 27(2)(a).

10. *Copyright Act*, R.S.C. (1985) c. 42 s. 17(2)(1), as amended by R.S.C. (1985) (4th Supp.) c. 10.

11. *Sci-Tech Education Inc. v. The Nature Company* [1992] F.C.A.D. 3344-01.

infringement of copyright, the danger of significant damage to the plaintiff and some indication that surprise is needed to protect the evidence.

Once the trial has taken place and the plaintiff has obtained a favourable judgment, one of the most important remedies available is that of the **permanent injunction**. By court order, a permanent injunction prohibits the defendant from the production, sale or distribution of any of the infringing products. If the defendant is not aware that the product being produced is in violation of copyright, the only permanent remedy available under the act is an injunction. Otherwise, damages or an accounting may be obtained. **Damages** are an attempt by the court to have the wrongdoer compensate the victim of the infringement for the losses suffered, including the lost profits he or she would have earned had the copyright not been violated. An **accounting for profits** requires the defendant to pay over to the plaintiff any profits made from the sale or rental of the offending product even if this amount exceeds the damages suffered by the plaintiff. Such an accounting may be granted because of the difficulty encountered in assessing the actual damages suffered as a result of the infringement. In some very blatant infringement cases, the court may even award **punitive damages** to punish the offender rather than simply to compensate the victim of the infringement. In any case, it must be noted that the limitation period in which an action should be commenced is three years.

In addition to these civil remedies, the *Copyright Act* provides for penalties. It is generally conceded that before the 1988 amendments these penalties were so slight as to provide little deterrent (for a summary offense the fine was up to $10 per copy and a maximum of two months in jail). The 1988 amendments, however, expand these penalties so that they are significant indeed (up to $1 000 000 in fines and five years in jail for an indictable offense), making them a much more effective deterrent. The provisions set out in the *Criminal Code*, such as those sections prohibiting theft and fraud, may also apply to the infringement of copyright cases.[12] The *Code* was used to impose the penalties in the example used to introduce this chapter.

Changes.

The most significant changes included in the 1988 amendments to the *Copyright Act* are those related to computer programs, moral rights and increased penalties. Another important change is a provision for the creation of a Copyright Board having broad powers. The Board is entitled to handle disputes between individuals and otherwise regulate the industry. It is common for associations or corporations to be created to represent the owners of copyright in their dealings with those who would like to use their materials. These bodies usually enter into agreements (licensing arrangements) with the users, who pay royalties to reproduce or perform the copyrighted material. SOCAN (Society of Composers, Authors, and Music Publishers of Canada) performs this service in the music industry and CANCOPY (Canadian Reprography Collective) serves a similar function in the literary field entering into general licensing agreements for works to be photocopied and paying royalties to the authors. Under the new legislation, these bodies must file with the Board copies of the copyrighted material and information regarding any agreements entered into as well as statements of royalties that have been paid. Summaries of these lists and the royalties are to be published regularly in the *Canada Gazette* (a federal government publication). These associations have the exclusive right to collect the agreed-upon royalties (or sue if they are not paid) if adequate statements of royalties have been properly filed with the board. The amendments to

Permanent injunction granted at trial

Damages compensate for loss

Accounting requires handing over profits

Punitive damages may be available to punish wrongdoer

Fine and imprisonment available for infringement

Criminal Code may apply

Changes broaden protection, increases penalty and creates Board

12. *Criminal Code*, R.S.C. (1985) c. C-46.

the *Copyright Act* made in 1988 were only the first stage and while some subsequent changes have been made, more significant amendments are anticipated in the near future.

Patents

A patent is a government-granted monopoly to produce, sell or otherwise profit from a specific invention. Once a patent is granted, no one else can use or sell the invention without the permission of the patent holder. For something to be patentable, it must be both new and an invention. If a patent has already been granted to someone else, or the invention has been in the public domain for some period or has been the subject of a publication over one year before the application, a patent will not be granted. The subject of the patent must also be original and come from the inventor, and not be the product of the skill and labour of others. Thus a person could not take an invention found in another country and patent it in Canada as his own. It must be novel in that it has unique qualities which separate it from other products. It must have utility, meaning that it must be capable of being constructed and used on the basis of the information supplied to the patent agent upon application and have some useful function.

> Patent creates monopoly

> Must be original invention to be patentable

Under the federal *Patent Act*, a patent cannot be issued for a scientific principle or abstract theorem.[13] Newton would not have been granted a patent for his development of the concept of gravity. Other things which cannot be patented include improvements to objects that would be obvious to someone skilled in the area, objects designed for an illegal purpose, something that cannot work, and, generally, those things covered by copyright law. New varieties of plants, trees and crops are also not patentable but with the tremendous new strides taking place in genetic research there is some question as to whether new forms of microorganisms and other significant developments in the field will be patentable. In Canada, as a general rule, computer programs cannot be patented and are now covered by copyright legislation, but such patents have been granted in the United States.

> Theories, concepts or obvious improvements are not patentable

In contrast to copyright law, patent law is intended to protect an invention, that is, ideas and concepts, rather than the expression of the work itself, which is the objective of copyright law. In this sense, the protection granted is all-encompassing once the patent has been obtained.

> The idea is protected rather than the work

Creation.

While a copyright exists from the point of creation of the work, a patent only comes into existence when registered. The inventor must take care to apply for the patent as soon as possible. Any delay increases the risk that someone else will invent and patent the same item, causing the original inventor not only to lose the right to patent but also preventing him or her from producing or otherwise using or profiting from the invention. As was the case with copyright law, if the invention is developed by an employee, the employer has the right to obtain the patent. Similarly, if the inventor assigns his or her right, the purchaser has the right to obtain the patent. Joint patents can be obtained when two people have worked on the same invention.

> Patent must be applied for and registered

The process of obtaining a patent is complex and some lawyers have specialized in this area, becoming patent agents. To obtain a patent, the inventor acquires the services of such an agent who searches the patent records usually in both Canada

13. *Patent Act,* R.S.C. (1985) c. P-4 s. 27 ss. 8.

COMPLETE DISCLOSURE NEEDED FOR PATENT

Through a process of artificial cross-breeding the appellant developed a new soybean having very significant advantages, and applied for a patent. There were two problems the court had to deal with: whether this was a patentable invention and whether there was sufficient disclosure. The court decided this case on the second question, not wanting to consider whether a new plant form created by genetic engineering was patentable. Because the particulars disclosed in the application failed to describe the genetic engineering process, and even suggested that a certain amount of luck was involved, there was not sufficient disclosure and the patent application was refused. Disclosure must be sufficient for someone to be able duplicate the results. One of the main purposes of the patent process is to make the information associated with the invention available to others so they can duplicate it and knowledge can advance. This was not done in this case.

Pioneer Hybrid Ltd. v. Commissioner of Patents, 60 D.L.R. (4th) 223 (Supreme Court of Canada)

and the U.S., to determine whether a patent already exists for the invention, or one similar to it, and then submits documents along with a petition applying for a patent. These documents include specifications and claims statements which set out not only what the invention is supposed to do, but also enough information so that someone looking at these specifications could build the invention. An appropriate drawing is also submitted along with an abstract summarizing the nature of the invention. A fee to cover the issue of the patent is also required.

The patent office will assign an examiner to look at the application. He or she may have some objections which can then be satisfied by further submissions from the applicant. When all the conditions have been met, a patent will be granted. It is not uncommon for the process to take two or three years.

If opposing applications have been made for the patent, the patent office will grant it to the person who first made an application. This is a recent change; prior to 1987 the patent went to the applicant who first invented the subject matter of the application.

Difficulties can arise if an inventor outside Canada registers a similar invention independently. Pursuant to international agreement, once a Canadian patent has been granted, application can be made for patents in other jurisdictions. Even though there can be considerable delay in the granting of patents in countries where protection is needed, the application will be taken to have been made on the same day as the Canadian patent was applied for, thus establishing a prior right to a patent in those jurisdictions as of that date. Of course, the reverse is also true and the Canadian patent office will grant a patent to a foreign applicant who applies in his or her own country before the Canadian applicant applies here. There is a limited period of time after obtaining the Canadian patent to make an application for a foreign patent and so this should be done without delay.

Once the patent has been issued, the patent number should be put onto the manufactured item to which it applies. Often prior to the grant of the patent the label "Patent Pending" is put on the goods, but this has no legal effect other than warning other manufacturers that in the future, a patent may be issued in relation to the product. A patent gives its holder a monopoly in relationship to the product for a period of 20 years, provided the appropriate fees are paid to maintain it. In exchange for that protection, the inventor must publicly disclose the invention in its entirety so that someone inspecting the file documents, which are open to the

Date of application in own country determines priority

Patent grants monopoly for 20 years but requires disclosure

public, could create a working model of the invention. Thus, patent law does not protect information; rather, it provides for its disclosure. The inventor gives up any secrecy associated with the invention in exchange for the 20-year protection. After that time, anyone can produce the product. It is thought that this disclosure of information creates a stimulating environment for further invention and development while still protecting the position of the inventor and encouraging that inventor to develop and produce the product and engage in further invention. The granting of the patent gives the patent holder exclusive rights to manufacture, sell and profit from the invention, and it even protects someone who merely develops a variation of the product.

Unlike copyright law, which protects the specific way an idea is stated, patent law is intended to protect the idea or principle behind the product. Another person would not be able to produce a simple variation of the product without breaching the patent. When an infringement of a patent has taken place (through some unauthorized person manufacturing, importing, selling or otherwise dealing with or using the invention), the patent holder is entitled to the same remedies that would be available in any civil action, including injunction, damages and accounting, which have been discussed under the heading of copyright.

Remedies same as copyright

It should be noted that an important amendment to the *Patent Act* was enacted in 1987 whereby drug manufacturers were given more exclusive control over the production and sale of their products, preventing competitors from producing much-lower-cost "generic drugs" by capitalizing on the research and development of the manufacturer. At the same time, to keep prices reasonable, a Patent Medicine Prices Review Board was established with broad powers, including the power to reduce the sale price of medicines covered by this legislation.[14] This period of exclusive control has been extended to 20 years. Often where there are inadequate resources to manufacture or otherwise exploit the invention, the inventor will license its manufacture to another company. Where it is an important invention and the inventor does not or cannot exploit it, there is provision for **compulsory licenses** to be granted with the payment of royalties even over the objections of the inventor.

Trademarks

Another type of intellectual property given protection is any term, symbol, design or combination of these that identifies a business service or product. These are called **trademarks** and are protected by the federal *Trademarks Act*.[15] Words such as "Kodak" and "Xerox," symbols such as that used on Arm and Hammer baking soda, and combinations of words and symbols, such as the Apple logo on computers, are examples of protected trademarks. Even the distinctive design of a product's container, such as the Coca-Cola bottle, may be the object of such protection. Trademarks also include the special marks used by some organizations such as Canadian Standards Association to indicate quality or certification.

Symbols or designs of business protected as trademarks

The purpose of the legislation is to prevent people from deceiving others by using trademark words or symbols for their own purposes, thereby profiting from the goodwill or reputation developed by others. As well, the value of the trademark might be diminished if consumers are led to believe that inferior products or services are produced by the owner of the trademark when, in fact, they are not.

Purpose to prevent consumer deception

A trademark must be registered to be protected under the statute. As part of the process, the trademark is published in the *Trademark Journal* and if someone feels

Registration protects trademark

14. *Patent Act Amendments,* R.S.C. (1985) (3d Supp.) c. 33.

15. *Trademarks Act,* R.S.C. (1985) c. T-13.

that it does not qualify they can "oppose" the registration. Once registered, the trademark gives its owner exclusive rights to use it throughout Canada. This protection is granted for 15 years and is renewable. The registration also establishes a presumption that the person so registered is the owner of that trademark, thus requiring a defendant in an action claiming infringement to produce strong evidence that the owner was not entitled to the trademark.

Restrictions

In general, any mark, word, design, symbol or packaging that distinctively identifies a business or product can be registered as a trademark. A sound or colour by itself cannot be registered as a trademark, nor can something obscene or scandalous. There is also a general prohibition against anything that resembles the insignia, crests or other symbols of royalty, the government or government agencies, such as the RCMP, service organizations such as the Red Cross, or even names, portraits or signatures of individuals, without their consent. There is also a prohibition against using any marks, symbols or designs that have become well known and would lead people to believe that the registrant was associated with that body or with the products or services of that body. As a general rule, ordinary surnames will not be registered as trademarks unless it can be shown that they have become connected to a product or service through use. As a result people can use their own surnames in their business without fear of violation unless that name has become associated with another product such as McDonald's hamburgers or Campbell's soup. It is possible for trademarks to lose their status through common use. In effect, the trademark becomes a generic term to describe the type of product itself. "Aspirin" is such a generic term and can be used by any manufacturer to describe that type of painkiller. This is also the case with the terms "trampoline" and "linoleum." "Xerox" has become so connected with the photocopying process that the term is also in danger of losing its trademark status.

Applying for trademark registration is a complicated process, and anyone doing so should acquire the services of a lawyer specializing in that field. It should be noted that after registration has taken place, there is an obligation to use the trademark. Failure to do so can result in the loss of the trademark through abandonment. In addition, every item on which the trademark is used should also be marked with the symbol "®" indicating that the trademark has been registered.

Essentially, the purpose of trademark legislation is to prevent others from using distinctive marks that will confuse people into thinking they are dealing with the owner of the trademark when they are not and thus prevent one party profiting from the goodwill developed by another. To enforce that right, the owner must convince the court not only that he or she is the registered owner of the trademark but also that it is likely the public has been or will be confused by the wrongful use of the trademark causing damage to the owner.

Remedies same as copyright infringement

If the action to protect a trademark is successful, the types of civil remedies available are the standard ones discussed under copyrights and patents. It should be mentioned, however, that one of the more effective remedies possible (when circumstances warrant it) is an order giving the owner of the trademark custody of the goods that are infringing on the trademark. Although it is possible to bring an action for infringement of a trademark before the Federal Court when the trademark has been properly registered under the *Act*, it is also possible, and sometimes a more practical course of action, to bring the matter before the appropriate provincial court. Such courts are not limited to enforcing the statute (as is the Federal Court) but may rely on common law principles as well.

Common law passing-off action gives similar protection

Although trademarks are covered by federal legislation, this is one area in which there are overlapping common law provisions. When a business or product comes

Disney's No Mickey Mouse

What's in a name? Plenty, if that name is Fantasyland. Walt Disney Productions did not take kindly to the use of that name by Triple Five Corp., the owners of a shopping mall and tourist attraction known as West Edmonton Mall. Disney brought a passing-off action against the mall owners and succeeded in securing a permanent injunction prohibiting the use of the name Fantasyland as the name of the amusement park in Edmonton.

Since 1955, the plaintiff, Disney, has used the name Fantasyland in connection with its amusement parks. Disney coined the name Fantasyland, and used it in its operations and advertising for Disneyland and Disneyworld. In 1983 Disney engaged in extensive worldwide advertising and promotions concentrating on the rebuilding of Fantasyland in California and its scheduled reopening in June 1983. Coincidentally, West Edmonton Mall opened its Phase II in 1983, containing an amusement area called Fantasyland. They described Fantasyland in their advertising as an "indoor Disneyland."

This advertisement prompted an immediate response from Disney, which claimed exclusive rights to use of the names Disneyland and Fantasyland. The owners of West Edmonton Mall discontinued reference to Disneyland in their advertising but continued to use Fantasyland as the name of the amusement park.

At the trial, evidence of public association of the name Fantasyland with Disney was adduced. A goodwill or reputation, linking Disney with Fantasyland in the mind of the public, was established. Disney also established misrepresentation by the mall owners likely to lead the public to believe that the mall amusement park was that of Disney or authorized by Disney. The court then proceeded to presume damages.

The mall owners appealed. They argued that the tort of passing-off involved deliberate misrepresentation and the appellants did not intend to mislead. They challenged whether the public was actually misled. The appellants also argued that the trial judge erred in presuming damage had been or was likely to be sustained.

Surveys conducted in malls across Canada suggested that in Alberta at least, the majority of the public did associate Fantasyland with West Edmonton Mall. Elsewhere, the majority associated Fantasyland with Disney.

The appellate court held that the law of passing-off does not require proof of actual confusion which leads to specific pecuniary damages; likelihood of confusion or deception resulting from misrepresentation is sufficient. Also, passing-off does not require proof of any intent to deceive or misrepresent.

The foundation of the action of passing-off is the protection of the plaintiff's property right in the goodwill and reputation which has come to be associated with its name. The essence of the action is described as a misrepresentation or deception of the public, which demonstrates that the plaintiff has suffered harm for which it should be compensated. In simple terms, the three necessary components in passing-off actions are

1. the existence of goodwill,
2. the deception of the public due to a misrepresentation, and
3. actual or potential damage to the plaintiff.

The fact that some Albertans linked the name Fantasyland with West Edmonton Mall was enough evidence of some actual damage to the goodwill of Disney. Accordingly, the appeal was dismissed.

The amusement park at West Edmonton Mall is now named Galaxyland.

Walt Disney Productions v. Triple Five Corp. (1992) 93 D.L.R. (4th) 739 (Alta. Q.B.) upheld on appeal (1994) 113 D.L.R. (4th) (Alta. C.A.).

on to the market and people confuse it with another product, it is possible to bring an action called a **passing-off action**. A passing-off action is founded in tort and prevents a person from misleading the public into thinking it is dealing with some other business or person when it is not. (See In Practice box.) The person being harmed can request the court to order compensation or that the offending conduct stop. This remedy is also available when a trademark is involved even if it is unregistered.

For a passing-off action to succeed, it is necessary to establish that the public was likely to be misled. Therefore, the person who brings the action must be able to show not only that the mark, name or other feature of the business was associated with his or her business, but also that the offending party used that mark in such a way that it became associated with its own operation, thus causing confusion in the mind of the public. It would be an actionable passing-off for an independent hamburger stand operator to put golden arches in front of his place of business or use the same colour scheme as McDonald's in such a way that people would assume his operation was part of the chain. But if a business person were to see an attractive logo which had been developed by another person but not yet registered or used and use it in her own business, the originator of the design could not sue on the basis of a passing-off action because the logo had not become associated with any business.

Industrial Designs

Industrial Design Act—reproduced artistic designs must be registered

A design or pattern that distinguishes a manufactured article is not covered by copyright law. Protection is provided by registering a unique shape, pattern or ornament under the federal *Industrial Design Act*.[16] A Coca-Cola bottle with its distinctive shape would appropriately be registered under the *Act*. In addition to registration, every item should be marked with the letter D enclosed in a circle, the name of the registered owner and the date of registration. Failure to do so will limit the remedies to an injunction in the event of an infringement. Registration must take place within one year of the design being published. Any product, with a few specified exceptions, with a distinctive shape or pattern, can be registered and will receive protection for a period of five years, providing all the requirements of the *Act* are met. This period is renewable for a further five years if desired.

The *Act* is intended to protect attractive and distinctive patterns or shapes as opposed to useful ones. As with copyrights, patents and trademarks, the product involved must be original and not a copy of some product already on the market. In a case before the Exchequer Court in 1964, a uniquely designed sofa was deemed to be protected by an industrial design registration.[17]

Confidential Information

Cadbury Schweppes Inc. v. FBI Foods Ltd.[18]

Duffy-Mott produced Clamato Juice in the United States. They entered into an agreement with Caesar Canning to produce the product in Canada. FBI Foods was further engaged by Caesar Canning to produce Clamato Juice for other parts of Canada. One of the terms of the agreement with Caesar Canning was that they as licensee would agree not to produce a similar product for a period of five years after the agreement was terminated. Duffy-Mott provided a recipe to Caesar Canning and FBI Foods for the production of the juice; however, the special herbs and spices that were used to create its unique flavour were prepackaged

16. *Industrial Design Act*, R.S.C. (1985) c. I-9.

17. *Cimon Ltd. v. Benchmade Furniture Corp.* (1964) 1 Ex. C.R. 811.

18. *Cadbury Schweppes Inc. v. FBI Foods Ltd.*, 138 D.L.R. (4th) 708 (British Columbia Court of Appeal).

and sent as a dry product to the licensees and so they didn't have access to that part of the specific recipe.

Eventually Duffy-Mott's shares were bought out by Cadbury Schweppes and shortly after that Duffy-Mott notified Caesar Canning that they were cancelling the agreement. In fact Caesar Canning and FBI Foods had invested a fair amount in their plant and equipment to produce Clamato Juice and with the cancellation of their license, they sought out another product. Lorne Nicholson, an employee of Caesar Canning, developed a new product called Caesar Cocktail to replace the Clamato Juice.

The court found that except for some minor variations, the Caesar Cocktail product copied the recipe of Clamato Juice. "It is beyond doubt that without the formula and process information about Clamato, Mr. Nicholson could not have developed Caesar Cocktail personally. He did not have the necessary skills. The evidence is equally persuasive that Caesar Canning could have developed a product as much like Clamato as Caesar Cocktail without using the Clamato recipe by hiring the appropriate skills. It could have done this within the twelve-month notice period at a modest cost." The judge found that the recipe was copied, but the product could have been developed without copying the recipe within the time frame. The judge also found that anyone who saw the recipe for Caesar Cocktail would have known that it was derived solely from the Clamato formulation, it being essentially the same recipe without the clams. "The other variations were minor."

There was some delay in bringing any action because Cadbury Schweppes at first did not think their rights had been infringed. The first problem was to find out whether a breach of confidence had taken place. The answer was yes. The court found that three elements were necessary to establish breach of confidence. First, that the information in question was confidential; second, that it had been communicated in confidence; and third, that it had been misused by the party to whom it was communicated. In this case all three of these requirements were clearly established.

The next problem is to determine the appropriate remedy. Although Caesar Canning could have produced a product like Clamato Juice without using the Clamato recipe, they did copy the recipe and this gave them a head start in coming to market with the product. This head start was calculated to be approximately 12 months. The defendant asked for damages equal to the profits during that time period.

The judge at the trial level decided that they should be entitled to damages in the amount of what it would have cost Caesar Canning and FBI foods to hire somebody to develop an independent recipe—which was determined to be almost $30 000.

This amount was considered to be a nominal award and it was that award that was questioned by the Court of Appeal, for it did not take into consideration any deterrents for breach of confidence; the Court of Appeal suggested that such a nominal award would encourage breaches of confidence. After consideration of the authorities, the judges decided that damages ought to be awarded on the basis of what Cadbury Schweppes may have earned had they made the unauthorized sales of Caesar Cocktail in Canada over that 12-month period (the head start). The judges also thought it was appropriate in these circumstances to issue an injunction to prohibit the confidential information (the recipe) from being used. This did not prohibit the defendants or anybody else from developing a competing tomato juice product. They simply could not use the recipe to do it or any product developed by copying that recipe.

For our purposes this case is important for several reasons. First, it illustrates what constitutes a breach of confidential information; it does not require a copyright, patent, or other form of government-provided protection. The information was given in a manner that indicated it was intended to remain confidential, so there is an obligation to keep it so. The case also provides an interesting insight into the way the court determines appropriate remedies.

Confidential information is information given to a person in circumstances in which it is clear that the information is intended to remain confidential and not be disclosed. In business, confidences may be required to be kept by managers, partners, shareholders and other investors, employees, outside contractors, consultants, suppliers of goods and services, and customers. While such confidential information may not technically qualify as property, disclosure may prove devastating to the company and so the protection of this kind of information is a vital concern of business. Information cannot be classified as confidential unless it is not generally known and the holder of the information has not already disclosed it to others. Over the years, a common law duty has been imposed on different kinds of trust or fiduciary relationships making it unlawful for individuals in such relationships to use confidential information in a way that will harm the confider or personally benefit the confidant or the third party to whom the information was given. The duty not to disclose confidential information arises primarily from the relationship between the confidant and the owner of the information, such as between principal and agent, between partners, between employer and employee, or between officers and their corporation, or can be the result of other express or implied contracts between the parties as was the situation in the *Cadbury* case used at the beginning of this discussion.

Confidential information protected by common law

The largest settlement to that time in Canadian court history arose when LAC Minerals Ltd. and Corona Resources Ltd. found themselves in such a situation. The case is very complicated but, to simplify, Corona had obtained land claims in the Hemlo District of northwestern Ontario. Representatives of LAC entered into discussions with the representatives of Corona with the prospect of entering into a joint venture or partnership. In the process of these discussions, information was given to LAC in confidence to the effect that Corona did not own the surrounding gold claims but was in the process of negotiating for them. When negotiations broke down between LAC and Corona, LAC independently purchased the surrounding claims and made huge profits from the resulting mines. The court held that this was a violation of a duty imposed on LAC not to disclose or use the information, as a result of the special circumstances in which it was obtained. Although the court did not go so far as to find a fiduciary duty, a trust relationship had been established and the information gained because of it was intended to remain confidential. When the representatives of LAC used that information for LAC's gain at the expense of Corona, it was a violation of that duty of confidentiality.[19]

In both this case and the *Cadbury* case the courts found that the duty to keep information confidential arose when the information was in fact confidential in the first place, and when it had been communicated in a way to show it was to remain confidential. They found that a breach took place when there was an unauthorized use of that information.

Trade Secrets.

A trade secret is a particular kind of confidential information that gives a business person a competitive advantage. Customer lists, formulas or processes, patterns, jigs and other unique features unknown to competitors are trade secrets. Successful

---

19. *LAC Minerals Ltd. v. Corona Resources,* as reported in *The Globe and Mail,* November 19, 1986.

actions for the wrongful disclosure of trade secrets have been brought in such varied matters as recipes for fried chicken and soft drinks, formulas for rat poison, methods to flavour mouthwash, processes for making orchestral cymbals and even the techniques prescribed in a seminar to help people quit smoking. A trade secret has the additional requirement that it be valuable to the business and not readily available to any other user or manufacturer. Customer lists available through government publication cannot be classed as trade secrets, nor can a process involved in the manufacturing of a product that is plainly discoverable simply by examining or disassembling the product.

Duty of confidentiality covers trade secrets as well

It should be noted that it is the conveying of the private information that is wrongful. There is no proprietary right in the idea or information itself. If Deng operated a company manufacturing tiddlywinks and had a secret process by which they could be produced more cost-effectively, which he failed to patent, and one of Deng's employees were to give that information to a competitor, it would be a wrongful disclosure of a trade secret. But if the competitor were to develop the same or a similar procedure independently, Deng would have no complaint since he has no proprietary right in the idea or process.

While an employee may be required either expressly or by implication in the employment contract not to disclose trade secrets and confidential information that he or she acquires in the process of employment, the employee can use the general skills and knowledge he or she gains on the job in another employment situation. An employee working in a guitar manufacturing factory who acquires the skills of a luthier would not be expected to refrain from using any of those skills if she were to work for another manufacturer. However, specific processes or jigs used to make guitars might qualify as a trade secret. It is sometimes difficult to draw the line, and in such circumstances it would be wise for the first guitar manufacturer to include a restrictive covenant in the employment contract (a non-competition clause).

Employees must not disclose trade secrets or confidential information

Although the courts are reluctant to enforce such covenants against employees, if the covenant is reasonable, and limited to an appropriate time and area, it may be enforceable. It will likely at least encourage the employee to seek subsequent employment with a non-competitor. In any case it is good policy to specifically include prohibitions and consequences in an employment contract dealing with the disclosure of confidential information and other forms of intellectual property of the employer.

From a practical point of view, the owner of secret information can best maintain its confidentiality by informing the employee or other confidant that he or she is in a position of confidence and is expected to keep the information private. It is good policy to require them to sign a specific non-disclosure agreement with respect to that information. As mentioned above, with employees this agreement can be incorporated into the contract of employment. It is now normal practice for businesses using co-op students on special projects in conjunction with their college to sign such agreements.

Confidant should be advised of confidentiality

It is important to specify what information is confidential and what is not. Even the most honest employee can disclose such information if he or she does not know it is confidential. No liability will be imposed for the disclosure of information if a person could not have been expected to know it was intended to be confidential. Steps should also be taken to minimize the number of people to whom the information is given or who have access to it, and the copies that are distributed should be marked "Confidential."

Care should be taken not to take this too far. If too much is marked confidential, the notification loses its effect. In addition, a person cannot be accused of wrongful disclosure of information if it has been widely distributed and is no longer confidential. It should also be noted that while in Canada the law related to trade secrets is founded on common law and equity, in some parts of the United States statutes have been passed to govern this area (*Trade Secrets Act*). Whenever those jurisdictions are involved, care should be taken to be aware of and comply with the statutes.

Remedies.

Disclosure must harm confider

To succeed in an action for wrongful disclosure, it is necessary for the plaintiff to show that the disclosure of the confidential information has caused harm. Whether the confidant used the information personally or passed it on to someone else who used it to the detriment of the first party, both offending parties can be sued.

Remedies similar to copyright infringement

When trade secrets have been wrongfully disclosed or confidential information passed on, the remedies of injunction, damages and accounting discussed above may be available. If it is clear that there is a real likelihood the information will be disclosed because of some new relationship the confidant is in, then an injunction may be obtained to prohibit the disclosure. The court, however, is very reluctant to grant an injunction that will prevent an employee from earning a living in his or her field. Damages or an accounting are also available when confidences have been breached in this way. Even punitive damages have been awarded.

Other protection for intellectual property— contract

Contract and tort law may be used to give increased protection to the various forms of intellectual property. There are often contractual provisions in service or employment contracts which prohibit the misuse of position or the misappropriation or disclosure of confidential information or trade secrets. When an employee or other contracting party breaches one of the terms, it is a breach of contract which is grounds for dismissal. The offender can be restrained from further disclosure and can be required to compensate the employer for damages suffered. Because the employee will probably not be in a position to pay such damages, the victim will often turn to others for compensation. When the information holder has been enticed away and persuaded to breach the contract by a rival business, it is possible to sue the competitor for the tort of inducing breach of contract. Although this tort was first developed to prevent one employer from hiring away the employee of another, it has been expanded to many different kinds of contractual relationships and even to some relationships not based on contract. To succeed in such an action, the plaintiff is not required to establish malice on the part of the defendant but it must be clear that the interference was intentional.

Tort
• inducing breach of contract

• breach of privacy

Another remedy that may be available when someone uses another's name or photograph without permission is founded on breach of privacy. The courts in Britain and Canada have not recognized the right generally for a person to have his or her privacy protected, but the British courts have established such a right to a limited extent by indirect means. When a manufacturer of a chocolate product promoted it by using a cartoon of a famous golfer with the package of the product in his pocket, an English court held this action to be defamation because it communicated the idea that the golfer had lent his name to the promotion of the product which would have been a serious violation of his amateur status.[20] Such indirect protection, while interesting, is not likely to prove effective, and several provinces have passed privacy acts intended to supply remedies for this kind of improper invasion of privacy. The British Columbia *Privacy Act*, for instance, specifically makes such wrongful use of another's name or portrait to promote a product or service without permission an actionable tort.[21] Alberta does not have such legislation.

20. *Tolley v. Fry* [1931] A.C. 333.
21. *Privacy Act*, R.S.B.C. (1996) c. 373 s. 3.

Another example of an effective tort in these situations is injurious falsehood, often called trade slander. When a rival misleads a customer of another company about the nature or suitability of its product, an injurious falsehood has been committed and that person can be held accountable for the damage suffered. For example, if a person in the business of selling widgets were to approach a competitor's customer and suggest falsely that the competitor was going out of business or that its product was inferior or made with inferior materials, that competitor could bring a tort action demanding compensation for the damages done. Such damages might be calculated on the lost sales which would have been made had the false information not been communicated. The courts have also resorted to the provisions of the *Criminal Code* relating to theft and fraud to deal with people who have wrongfully disclosed information or personally profited from its use. Even a civil action for conversion has been used to discourage such conduct.

> • injurious falsehood

> Crime—fraud

With the advancement of technology there are many new and clever ways that people can be abused by others, especially as we become dependent on that technology. An increasing problem related to privacy is developing over the use of the Internet. Many who use the World Wide Web think of it as reasonably confidential, like a telephone line. In fact, however, email and other information transferred over the Internet typically goes through several computers and it is very easy for others with the necessary technical knowledge to intercept and access it.

In addition to the problems related to the use of the Internet, we must contend with computer viruses that interfere with the operation of programs and corrupt or destroy data. Hackers can steal telephone services and access confidential or secret information through misuse of the phone system and the computers of other businesses. Outright piracy of computer programs, tapes and videos is already a huge problem.

Currently the *Criminal Code* has several provisions designed to deal with these kinds of abuses. There are provisions against offenses such as theft, fraud, mischief, and unauthorized use of computers. Where there is a will to prosecute, these provisions can be used effectively by the authorities and criminal prosecution can be an embarrassment to the wrongdoer. But criminal prosecution is not always a good answer; the victim must rely on the prosecutors and police to stop these violations and punish the wrongdoers and these institutions are often underfunded, do not have enough resources or expertise, and may have other priorities. Also, the standard of proof that has to be met is much higher in a criminal prosecution than in a civil action.

For these reasons business people often prefer the civil process over criminal prosecution. In fact, businesses often try to find business solutions rather than legal ones. The Internet is an example of how the development of technology has outstripped that of the law, and we can expect important legal developments in this area. In the meantime businesses are turning to more practical means to deal with the problem. For example methods for the encryption of data are being developed so that dealings on the Internet can be kept private.

INSURANCE

When property in any of its forms is the topic of discussion, insurance is an important consideration. Insurance was designed to provide compensation for damaged, lost or stolen property. Insurance coverage has been expanded, however, to include non-tangibles such as liability and life insurance, as well as business interruption insurance.

Insurance spreads risk

Industry regulated by statutes

Standard form contracts are used and must be carefully examined

The purpose of insurance is to reduce the cost of loss by spreading the risk among many people. Premiums—the amount paid to the insurance company or the **insurer** by the person wishing coverage (called the **insured**)—are based on a prediction of the total cost of losses that might be suffered by a particular group, plus an amount to cover administrative and operation costs as well as a profit for the insurance company. Vast sums of money are involved in this business and, because of the potential for abuse, the industry is closely regulated. In 1991 the federal *Insurance Companies Act* [22] was passed, replacing the *Canada and British Insurance Companies Act* and the *Foreign Insurance Companies Act*. This legislation requires that all non-provincial insurance companies be registered and sets out matters such as the amount of reserves that must be retained to cover eventual claims. All provincial jurisdictions have similar insurance legislation. These provincial and federal statutes can be viewed as a type of consumer protection legislation in the field of insurance.

Contracts for insurance are covered by general contract law, and although insurance companies use standard form contracts the actual wording used will vary considerably between companies. Government controls ensure that the terms do not give unfair advantage to the insurance companies although, as in most contracting situations, the parties are generally considered free to bargain as they wish. Many different types of standard form policies cover the specific kinds of losses that can be anticipated. When modifications are made to these standard form contracts, **riders** are attached setting out the changes. When a contract already exists between insurer and insured and changes need to be made, an **endorsement** to that effect is attached to the policy.

It is vital for businesses to acquire adequate coverage. Fire insurance, for example, will not normally cover damages caused by nuclear contamination, war or insurrection, and for such events to be covered under a fire insurance policy special provisions in the form of a rider must be included. Similarly, burglary insurance would not cover shoplifting or theft by employees. Natural disasters, such as earthquakes or floods, are excluded from most standard form policies, at least in relation to some types of property loss. Most insurance contracts require insured parties to maintain certain safety and security standards to protect themselves against the risk of fire and theft.

Property Insurance

The predominant form of property insurance covers losses to buildings and their contents due to fire. Most fire insurance policies contain a co-insurance clause with reference to certain specific types of risks which require that the insured be covered to a minimum percentage of the value of the property involved (usually 80 percent). A person who fails to maintain the minimum insurance will be considered a co-insurer for the difference and will bear the responsibility of that portion of any loss suffered that corresponds to the amount he or she underinsured. If insured persons have too little coverage, they will be co-insurers for the difference

2777 KIPLING AVE. **FOR RENT** Spacious **2 & 3 BEDROOM SUITES** 746-0041

Photo by Dick Hemingway.

22. *Insurance Companies Act*, S.C. (1991) c. I-11.8.

and receive only partial compensation. If they have too much coverage, they will be overinsured and therefore paying for coverage they cannot collect. It becomes important, then, for the insured to have coverage that is at least close to the maximum potential loss. This is especially true when the coverage refers to one of those areas in which a co-insurance clause applies.

Co-insurance clause may reduce coverage

Overinsurance wasteful

Business Interruption Insurance

An increasingly common and important form of insurance is business interruption insurance. Often, an ongoing business will find itself unable to function because of some unforeseen eventuality, sometimes caused by events covered by other forms of insurance. For example, if Rampal operated a plant manufacturing widgets and due to no fault of his own the plant burned down, fire insurance and other forms of property insurance would normally cover the loss. Such insurance would not, however, cover the loss of profits suffered because of the business ceasing operation while the plant was being rebuilt. Business interruption insurance will normally cover not only lost profits but also any added expenses incurred to bring the business back into production.

Business interruption insurance covers lost profits

Essentially, these two forms of insurance, physical damage and business interruption insurance, are designed to put the insured in the position he or she would have been in financially had the fire or other damage never taken place.

Life and Health Insurance

Life insurance is usually purchased as a method of providing security for dependants after the death of the insured. Life insurance is also taken out on key personnel in a business or on partners in a partnership to provide compensation for losses incurred from any disruption that may result from the death or illness of an executive or partner.

Life insurance in business used to cover key personnel

Death is inevitable and so the likelihood of the insurance company having to pay out eventually during the coverage period is considerable. This is not a difficulty, however, because premiums are calculated on the basis of a prediction of how long a person of a certain age and health can be expected to live.

There are various forms of life insurance to meet the needs of different individuals. Premiums paid for term insurance provide a simple cash settlement for the **beneficiary** of the policy at the death of the insured, while whole life insurance provides coverage in the event of death as well as investment potential and retirement income. These are just two of several different variations of life insurance available.

Other forms of insurance quite common today are medical and disability insurance, which is designed to pay health care expenses and provide an income for a person who is unable to earn a living because of illness or accident. Medical insurance can be arranged individually or as part of group coverage. Health care services in Canada are funded through the government-sponsored medicare system which is simply a large group insurance scheme. In the United States, however, such coverage is not universally available and must be negotiated with insurance companies as either group or individual coverage. In most Canadian jurisdictions, disability insurance can be obtained on an individual basis with an insurance company, but it is more often acquired by large organizations as part of an employee compensation package.

Health and disability insurance usually part of group coverage

Liability Insurance

There are many situations in which people may incur liability for their wrongful or careless conduct. Visitors to the homes or businesses of others can be hurt because of some condition on the property. When people carry on their professional or business activities, they often run the risk of causing injury to other people or their property. Driving an automobile is a risk-taking endeavour. Personal liability insurance and motor vehicle insurance go a long way towards protecting individuals from potentially devastating claims against them.

Liability insurance covers negligence by self or employees

Another source of liability in business is when an employee causes injury to some third party. Vicarious liability will impose responsibility on the employer for such conduct. Many people think that when they have insurance coverage for a personal liability, they are no longer responsible for their conduct. Liability insurance does not prevent the injured party from suing the insured directly. Once liability has been established and judgment has been obtained, the insurance company, according to the contract, is obligated to reimburse the insured for the loss. This kind of insurance contract normally will provide for the insurance company to conduct the insured's legal defense as one of the terms of coverage. The insurance company is interested in keeping insurance losses as low as possible, and so has an interest in providing a good legal defense for the insured. It also has the right to settle the matter if it considers that the best course of action.

Coverage only when insured is at fault

It is important to realize that the insurance company is only obligated to pay where it can be shown that the insured was at fault. If there was no negligence or other wrongful conduct on the part of the insured, he or she is not liable for the losses suffered and neither is the insurance company. Many people are under the false impression that, if there is insurance coverage, the injured party is entitled to payment whether fault is established or not. Many argue for no-fault coverage in these circumstances. No-fault insurance is similar to workers' compensation, in that the injured party is entitled to compensation no matter who was responsible.

Only to extent of coverage

Similarly, if the insured has not purchased sufficient insurance coverage, he or she will be responsible for any shortfall. If Jones has liability insurance for only $500 000 and causes a $750 000 loss, he will be required to pay the $250 000 not covered by insurance.

Liability coverage has become so important in the operation of automobiles that several provinces have instituted compulsory automobile coverage, and some have or are considering going to no-fault schemes. A mimimum of $200 000 liability coverage is required for motor vehicle policies in Alberta.

Insurable Interest

Upon consideration, it becomes clear that insurance has many of the characteristics of a wager. An insured pays a premium (the wager) and if the insured-against event then takes place (if, for example, the house burns down), he or she wins a prize in the form of a payment from the insurance company. Of course, this example also illustrates the essential difference between insurance and a wager. That is, to win, the insured comes out even at best. Insurance is only intended to put the person who suffers a loss back in the original position he or she was in had the event not taken place. The contract for insurance is a contract of indemnity; consequently, except in the case of life insurance, the insured can recover only what he or she has actually lost up to the limit set out in the policy. When the payout becomes a windfall, the insurance agreement is void as an illegal contract.

To realize on a claim for insurance, the insured must demonstrate that he or she has an insurable interest in whatever has been insured. The insured will only be able to collect on the claim to the extent of the value of that interest. The insurable interest, then, is the amount he or she stands to lose if the insured-against event takes place. If Nahanee owned a half-interest in a house worth $150 000, Nahanee would have an insurable interest of $75 000. If Nahanee carried an insurance policy of $150 000 on the house and it was destroyed by fire, Nahanee would only be able to collect $75 000 even though he had insured it for the higher amount. Any other result would give Nahanee a windfall instead of merely indemnifying or compensating the insured for losses suffered, and this is prohibited.

Must be insurable interest to avoid illegality

The *Insurance Act* [23] of Alberta codifies the requirement that an insurable interest exist, otherwise the insurance contract is just a wager and is therefore void.

247 (1) Subject to subsection (2), if at the time a contract would otherwise take effect the insured has no insurable interest, the contract is void.

The following subsections specify exceptions to the above rule, and then Section 248 determines in whose life one has an insurable interest.

247 (2) A contract is not void for lack of insurable interest

    (a) if it is contract of group insurance, or

    (b) if the person whose life is insured has consented in writing to the insurance being placed on his life.

    (3) If the person whose life is insured is under the age of 16 years, consent to insurance being placed on his life may be given by one of his parents or by a person standing in loco parentis to him.

248 Without restricting the meaning of the expression "insurable interest", a person has an insurable interest in his own life and in the life of

    (a) his child or grandchild,

    (b) his spouse,

    (c) any person on whom he is wholly or in part dependent for or from whom he is receiving, support or education,

    (d) his employee, and

    (e) any person in the duration of whose life he has a pecuniary interest.

A problem arises when property owned by a corporation is insured by an individual shareholder. Technically, the property is not owned by the shareholder but by the corporation, and it can be argued that the shareholder has no insurable interest. The Supreme Court of Canada has dealt with this issue and decided that it was not necessary for the insurer to actually have a legally enforceable interest in the property to insure it. It is enough that a relationship to the subject matter or a concern in it exists such that the organization would suffer a loss if the insured-against event took place.[24]

Other Features

Wellington Insurance Co. Ltd. v. Armac Diving Services Ltd.[25]

In 1978 a boat owned by Armac Diving Services Ltd. and insured by Wellington Insurance Co. Ltd. capsized. Armac made a claim against Wellington. The

23. *Insurance Act,* R.S.A. (1980) c. I-5.

24. *Kosmopoulos et al. v. Construction Insurance Company of Canada Ltd.* [1987] 1 S.C.R. 2 (S.C.C.).

25. 37 D.L.R. (4th) 462 (British Columbia Court of Appeal).

insurance company denied the claim, saying that the boat was not covered by the policy. Armac sued. Wellington settled the action and paid Armac half the claim, making it clear that they were doing so not pursuant to the policy, but rather to bring an early end to the legal proceedings and as a public relations gesture. Armac then successfully sued the third party that had caused the capsize of their vessel, obtaining judgment. Wellington in this action takes the position that since they paid out on the policy they were subrogated to the rights of the policyholder and had the right to collect the proceeds of any judgment taken against the person who caused the loss in the first place. But the Court of Appeal found that subrogation did not apply.

In marine insurance policies, as in most insurance policies, when an insurer pays out a policy, they assume the rights (subrogation) to any actions against anyone causing the loss. In this case, however, they disputed the claim and when they settled the matter for half the amount claimed, they made it clear that they were settling a disputed action, not paying out on their policy. In fact they specifically stated that they were not admitting liability; therefore, the settlement between Armac was exhaustive of the rights between the two parties and Armac was then free to carry on in their action against the third party.

This case illustrates the nature of subrogation and the right that the insurance company has once it pays out on a policy to step into the shoes of the insured in any actions that they may have against the party causing their loss. It also points out the limitations on that right.

Contract of utmost good faith

One important feature of insurance that must be mentioned is the considerable duty of disclosure imposed on the insured. Since an insurance agreement is an "utmost good faith" contract, a relationship of trust exists between the insured and the insurer and there is an obligation to disclose any pertinent information. Even after the contract for insurance comes into existence, the insured may have an obligation to disclose information to the insurance company. If material changes take place which will increase the risk of loss, those changes must be communicated. For example, when an occupied building is insured and after creation of the policy becomes vacant for an extended period of time, or when the use of the building is changed so that the risk to the insurance company is materially affected, the insured must inform the company of the changes.

Certain types of information must be disclosed when applying for property insurance, such as whether the property is to be used for business purposes or whether it will be vacant for any period. When there has been an injury, disease or other health problems in a person applying for life, disability or medical insurance, these facts must be disclosed. The insurer depends on the insured to inform it of any pertinent factors that might affect eligibility or the rates charged for insurance. The insurer has no way of determining such important information by itself and must depend on the honesty of the insured to disclose it. Failure to disclose such information, if it is relevant to the loss, may result in the loss being unrecoverable because of misrepresentation. Even where it is not relevant to the loss, if it is a material misrepresentation it may cause the entire policy to be void. Some provinces by legislation uphold the insurance where the misrepresentation was innocent, but even in those jurisdictions, if the misrepresentation or failure to disclose was done knowingly, the insurance policy cannot be enforced.

In Alberta, for example, section 298(1) of the *Insurance Act*[26] addresses misrepresentation in applications for automobile insurance. It provides:

26. *Insurance Act*, R.S.A. (1980) c. I-5.

298(1) If

(a) an applicant for a contract
   (i) gives false particulars of the described automobile to be insured to the prejudice of the insurer, or
   (ii) knowingly misrepresents or fails to disclose in the application any fact required to be stated therein,

(b) the insured contravenes a term of the contract or commits a fraud, or

(c) the insured wilfully makes a false statement in respect of a claim under the contract,

a claim by the insured is invalid and the right of the insured to recover indemnity is forfeited.

Some drivers who experience difficulty in securing insurance or who wish to avoid high premiums may succumb to the temptation to mislead the insurer as to who really owns the car. This has proven disastrous in the past. For example, in the *Morrow* case[27] the insurer refused to pay claims made under the policy following a motor vehicle accident. The insurer was able to prove that the insured, the parents of the driver, had no insurable interest in the vehicle. Further, they had misrepresented material facts by saying they owned the vehicle and that their son was an occasional driver, whereas the son owned the vehicle and was the exclusive driver. Similarly, in *Virani v. Edwards*,[28] the driver didn't have a licence to drive due to a suspension of his licence following an impaired driving conviction. He insured the vehicle using his mother's name as the registered owner. Following a traffic accident in which another party was injured, the insurer avoided payment on the policy. The Court declared the policy void due to misrepresentation. It doesn't pay to try to fool your insurer.

Another important feature of insurance law is the **right of subrogation** mentioned earlier. After making a payment on a claim, an insurance company acquires all the rights of the insured in relation to that claim. In other words, the insurance company steps into the shoes of the insured. Thus, if the loss has been caused by the interference of some third party and that outside interference is actionable, the insurance company assumes the right to sue the third party. If this were not so and the insured could still sue, the existence of the insurance would create a windfall instead of indemnifying against the loss. Thus, if Kostachues has an insurance policy on her house against fire and a neighbour carelessly allows a fire to get out of control causing Kostachues' home to burn down, Kostachues can turn to her insurance company for compensation. Her insurance company will then turn to the neighbour and sue him for negligence as if the insurance company were Kostachues. This important feature of insurance law is another reason why people should not assume that just because someone they are involved with in an accident has insurance coverage they are protected as well.

Insurer steps into shoes of insured upon payment

The principle of subrogation is nicely illustrated in the *Wellington Insurance* case used at the beginning of this discussion but that case also graphically brings home how important it is for an insurance company to preserve that right. In that case the right to subrogate was lost because in the settlement it was made clear by the parties that that settlement was exhaustive of their rights. It was clearly stated that the money was paid as a matter of goodwill and not because they admitted any liability on the claim by the insurance company.

27. *Morrow et al. v. Royal Insurance Co. of Canada* (1990) 8 C.C.L.I. (2d) 135 (upheld on appeal) (1992) 11 C.C.L.I. (2D) 86 (Alta. C.A.).

28. *Virani v. Edwards* (1997) CanRepAlta 806 (Alta. Q.B.).

People quite often misunderstand the nature of an insurance contract when they acquire two or more policies on the same property. When they have a claim for $2000, they think they can claim against both polices and collect a total of $4000. This is not possible because of a principle called **contribution**, according to which each insurance company will merely pay a share of the loss so that the insured will collect no more than the total amount of loss suffered. This is illustrative of the indemnification nature of insurance.

Right of salvage

Insurance contracts will also usually permit the insurer to minimize its loss in other ways. For example, if a house or boat is damaged, the agreement will usually give the insurance company the right to rebuild, repair or replace it. If the company is in the position of having to replace the lost property, the agreement will give the insurance company the right of salvage, meaning that if anything of value is to be recovered from the damaged item, the insurance company is entitled to sell it and keep the proceeds.

Depreciated rather than replacement value

When personal property is destroyed, the insured is entitled to claim for whatever is lost. However, the claim is usually for the depreciated value of the goods, not the replacement value. Most personal household insurance policies today provide for the replacement of destroyed or stolen goods at their full retail value. When a loss does take place, there is a general requirement on the part of the insured to report that loss to the insurance company right away so that the insurance company can take steps to minimize the damage. There might also be an obligation to report the matter to the police if a crime is involved or if the loss resulted from an auto accident. It should also be pointed out that an insured is not permitted to profit from his or her own willful misconduct. In addition to the prohibition against insuring against your own willful misdeeds, such as theft and assault, even where coverage is in place, if the insured deliberately causes the loss, he or she will not be able to collect. Thus if Floaen burns down his own house killing his wife in the process, he will not be able to collect on the fire insurance and he will not be able to collect on his wife's life insurance even where he is named as beneficiary.

It also follows that if one drives a motor vehicle while impaired by alcohol or drugs in violation of the insurance policy, the insurer will not be required to pay for any damage caused to the insured's vehicle or for any bodily injuries the driver sustains. Alberta's *Insurance Act* requires insurers to use certain prescribed forms for automobile insurance; those forms stipulate that driving while impaired invalidates

WRONGDOING OF PARTNER DOES NOT AFFECT INSURANCE

Higgins and Wood operated a sporting goods business as a partnership. They took out a fire insurance policy for their building and contents, naming themselves as the beneficiaries. Wood, without the knowledge of Higgins, conspired with a third party to intentionally burn the store in order to defraud the insurers. He got caught. It was clear that Higgins was perfectly innocent and had no knowledge of the conspiracy or the attempt to defraud the insurance company. However, his claim under the policy was refused. The court had to decide whether as an innocent partner of a wrongdoer, he was entitled to collect on the policy. The court held that the wrongdoing of Wood, while forfeiting any claim he had under the policy, did not automatically deprive his innocent partner of the policy protection. He did have the right to claim and was successful.

Higgins v. Orion Insurance Co. Ltd. et al., 17 D.L.R. (4th) 90 (Ontario Court of Appeal)

the contract of insurance. The consequences of drunk driving must thus largely be borne by the driver alone.

Most insurance is purchased through the services of an agent. An insurance agent acts on behalf of the insurance company, not the insured purchasing the insurance coverage. A discussion of agency law and the responsibilities of such agents is set out in Chapter 11. Insurance agents owe an important obligation to their principals (the insurance companies) but they also owe an important duty to the customer and will be responsible if they fail to provide the insurance coverage asked for or otherwise fail to honour the instructions given. Customers are finding themselves increasingly successful in suing agents for negligence when mistakes such as these are made.

People will also often find themselves dealing with insurance adjusters—employees or representatives of the insurance company charged with investigating and settling insurance claims against the company after the insured-against event takes place. It is important to remember when dealing with adjusters that they are not normally looking after the interests of the person making the claim, but the insurance company.

There are also many independent people working in the industry available to assist both parties, to arbitrate disputes, to mediate, and otherwise ensure that the interests of whoever they represent are protected.

Finally, when there is a situation of considerable risk to an insurance company, such as a large project that needs to be insured (for example, a new chemical plant), the company will often turn to other insurance companies so that the risk is spread among them all. This pooling of risk is called **re-insurance** and is an important aspect of the industry.

Bonding

While insurance coverage is not generally available for intentionally wrongful acts such as assault, many business people insist on some protection against the people they deal with who act wrongfully in a more willful sense. Bonding is available in these circumstances, and it takes two forms. Usually an employer will pay a fee to have an employee bonded against that employee's own wrongful conduct (**fidelity bond**). If the employee steals from the employer or a customer, the bonding company will be required to compensate the employer for that loss. It must be emphasized, however, that this does not relieve the bonded employee of responsibility. The bonding company can turn to the employee and collect from him or her, which is what distinguishes bonding from normal insurance arrangements.

Bonded parties still liable

The second form of bonding (**surety bond**) occurs when the bonding is designed to provide assurance that a party to a contract will perform its side of the contract. For example, in a large construction project, the company doing the drywalling may be required to put up a performance bond that it will finish the job by a certain time. If it fails to complete or does not complete on time, the bonding company will be required to pay compensation. A standby letter of credit as discussed in Chapter 9 can also be used for the same purpose.

SUMMARY

Personal property involves tangible, moveable property in the form of chattels and intangible property called a chose in action. Chattels can become fixed to real property but where they are trade or tenant fixtures they can be removed when the tenant leaves if this can be done without damage. A bailment involves property owned by one person which is temporarily in the possession of another. The obligation imposed to look after that property depends on contractual terms or on who benefits from the bailment when there is no contract.

Both federal legislation and common law protect intellectual property. A copyright protects literary, artistic and dramatic works from being copied or used by unauthorized parties for the author's life plus 50 years. Producing the work creates the copyright, but registration ensures international protection. Remedies can include injunctions, Anton Piller orders, damages and an accounting of profits. The registered patent gives international monopoly protection on the use of an invention for 20 years. The registered trademark protects certain terms, symbols and designs associated with a business or product, preventing consumer deception and protecting goodwill. Where there is no trademark protection, the common law remedy of a passing-off action may provide similar protection. Industrial designs are also protected by federal legislation. At common law, an employee or associate under a fiduciary obligation is prohibited from disclosing confidential information including trade secrets; damages or an injunction may be awarded when such confidences are breached.

Insurance is designed to spread the risk of loss. To be valid, the insured must have an insurable interest in the subject matter and, except in the case of life insurance, the recovery will be limited to the extent of that insurable interest. Property, business interruption, life and health, and liability are the primary forms of insurance available. With liability insurance, payment will only be made where the insured was at fault. When a claim is paid, the company is subrogated to the rights of the insured and can salvage the property or take over the insured's right to sue a third party.

QUESTIONS

1. Indicate the difference between personal, intellectual and real property. In your answer, give the different categories of personal property and discuss the nature of intellectual property.

2. Indicate how personal property can become real property and discuss why a determination of why and when this has happened may be significant.

3. What is a fixture, and under what circumstances can someone other than the owner of real property remove those fixtures?

4. Explain what is meant by the saying "Finders keepers" in terms of who is entitled to property that has been found.

5. Discuss the different ways in which a bailment may be created and the nature of the duty imposed on the bailee in each circumstance.

6. Distinguish between the obligation placed on a bailee for value and that imposed on a common carrier or innkeeper.

7. What two principles does the law of intellectual property try to balance?

8. Explain how a copyright is obtained and the qualifications that must be met to obtain such protection.

9. What is the significance of the 1988 amendments to the *Copyright Act*?

10. Summarize the nature of the protection given to the holder of a copyright and indicate what remedies are available to enforce such rights.

11. Discuss under what circumstances an Anton Piller order would be given and indicate how this remedy might be more valuable than other remedies which might be available.

12. What is the purpose of patent law and why is registration required for protection?

13. What kinds of things are protected by the trademark legislation and how is that protection obtained or lost?

14. Industrial design is intended to protect what kinds of material? How is this protection obtained?

15. How does the duty of confidentiality arise and what protection or remedies are available to the confider?

16. Indicate how criminal law, tort law and contract law can be used to protect intellectual property. How effective are such alternatives?

17. Explain conceptually the purpose of insurance and why it is not void as an illegal contract. (See also Chapter 5.)

18. Distinguish between business interruption insurance and fire insurance. Why might a business person want to have both forms of coverage?

19. What kinds of things cannot be covered under a liability insurance policy? Indicate any other methods a person or business might use to ensure that the people they are working with perform their jobs properly.

20. Discuss the similarities and differences between insurance and a wager.

21. What is meant by an insurable interest and how does it apply to the various types of insurance discussed in the chapter?

22. Explain what is meant by the right of subrogation and how this may affect not only the insured but the person who has caused the injury or damage. Also indicate what other means the insurance companies have to keep their damages as low as possible.

23. What is meant by bonding? In your answer, distinguish between bonding and insurance coverage.

CASES

1. Hammill v. Gerling Global Life Insurance Company

Mrs. Hammill obtained a life insurance policy in which she stated that she had been a non-smoker for the past 12 months. In fact, this information was incorrect. It was clearly established that she had smoked considerably during this period. She had taken out the policy in 1985 and was killed in an auto accident on February 2, 1986. Although her smoking in no way contributed to the accident, the insurer refused to pay the beneficiary under the policy. Explain the legal obligations of the insurer in these circumstances.

2. Punch v. Savoys Jewellers Limited et al.

Mrs. Punch owned a very valuable antique ring which was in need of repair. She took it to Savoys Jewellers who then sent it by registered mail to Walkers, a Toronto jeweler. By the time Walkers had repaired the ring, there was a postal strike in progress so they used Rapidex, a branch of the Canadian National Railway, to transport the ring back to Savoys with their agreement. There was a provision on the bill of lading limiting Rapidex's liability for "negligence or otherwise" to $50. Walker put a $100 value on the bill of lading when in fact the ring was worth about $11 000. The ring was never delivered and Mrs. Punch sued Savoys, Walkers and CN for the loss. CN had no record of what happened and was not able to show whether the ring had been lost or stolen.

Explain the nature of the duty owed by Walker, Savoys and CN to Mrs. Punch and the likely outcome of her action against them for the recovery of the value of the ring.

3. Bell v. Tinmouth

In this case Bell owned a series of paintings which he normally kept in his apartment. Several of them were on display for sale at an art shop owned by Sopina. Bell had arranged for insurance on these paintings through Sopina's insurance company and had dealt with Adheads, an employee of that company. Sometime later Bell arranged to have the paintings that were kept at Sopina's art shop displayed at a gallery owned and run by Buschlen and Mowett. The gallery was part of a suburban residence where they lived. They were both professionals who worked during the day. As part of this arrangement to have the paintings shown at the gallery, Bell arranged insurance for while they were there. This he did through Adheads. Adheads in turn talked to the proprietor about the security of the gallery. Mowett told him that there was always somebody there, that the police often attended and that the place was secure. None of this was true. Mowett advertised the show, and afterwards while the paintings were still there he and Buschlen left the premises vacant overnight. During that night there was a burglary and the paintings were stolen. The insurance company refused to pay for the loss.

Explain Bell's options in these circumstances. Explain the arguments available to the insurance company and the position of Buschlen and Mowett.

4. Spiroflex Industries v. Progressive Sealing Inc.

Mr. MacDonald designed a new pump coupler (a device used in a circulating water pump) which he intended to produce and sell. But he could not produce a special spring used in the device and so had to turn to others. He produced freehand sketches of the product as well as directions and specifications, and went to different manufacturers to have it made. He entered into an agreement to have the product marketed and provided a photograph of the device to illustrate a brochure. Once the device was on the market, several companies made copies of the coupler, including the people he originally asked to produce the device and some of those involved in the production of the brochure.

Explain MacDonald's rights against those parties.

5. Thurston Hayes Devs. v. Horn Abbott

The plaintiff was the developer of the board game Trivial Pursuit, which had been on the market successfully for several years. The defendants brought out a new board game with the same approach but which involved a different sub-ject matter, and called it Sexual Pursuit. The board used was essentially the same, the box the game came in was similar, and the games were even played in the same way. Explain the nature of the complaint the plaintiff has, any legal action that can be taken to protect his rights and the likely outcome.

6. Ciba-Geigy Canada Ltd. v. Apotex Inc.

Ciba-Geigy had the right to manufacture in Canada the product Metoprolol, a drug used for treating hypertension and angina. Under the patent act then in place, other manufacturers could acquire a license and manufacture and sell the product in Canada. These versions are known as generic drugs. Apotex and Novopharm both obtained licenses and in the process produced a drug with the same appearance as that produced by Ciba-Geigy. They used the same shape, size and colour. Even the dosages were the same. In fact, these drugs were interchangeable with the original product. Given that these companies have the right to produce generic drugs that are similar and useable for the same purpose, is there any complaint Ciba-Geigy can use against these imita-tors? Would your answer be affected by the fact that only doctors and phar-macists are aware of the differences and the ultimate consumer would not notice the difference?

7. Allen v. Toronto Star Newspapers Ltd.

Jim Allen, a photographer, took a photograph of Sheila Copps, M.P. wearing leather and sitting on a motorcycle. It was used on the cover of *Saturday Night* magazine, who had employed Allen to take the picture. Allen sold the picture on two other occasions. It became a matter of some controversy. The *Toronto Star*, without permission, published the picture, including the cover, in their newspaper as part of a news story. What options are available to Jim Allen and what defenses are available to the *Toronto Star*?

8. Aldrich et al. v. One Stop Video Ltd. et al.

A video was produced in the United States and Jartech Inc. held the registered copyright in both the U.S. and Canada. The defendant, 251440 B.C. Ltd., re-produced it without permission from Jartech and distributed it for sale and rental at One Stop Video Ltd. and Shannon Marketing Ltd. In effect, it was a pirated video. In these circumstances, what is Jartech's claim and what reme-dies are available? How would it effect your answer to know that the video in question was clearly pornographic and illegal for sale and distribution in Canada?

LEGISLATION

Alberta

Alberta Health Care Insurance Act, R.S.A. (1980) c. A-24
Health Insurance Premiums Act, R.S.A. (1980) c. H-5
Innkeepers Act, R.S.A. (1980) c. I-4
Insurance Act, R.S.A. (1980) c. I-5
Motor Vehicle Accident Claims Act, R.S.A. (1980) c. M-21
Workers' Compensation Act, S.A. (1981) c. W-16

Federal

Copyright Act, R.S.C. (1985) c. C-42 (note 1988 amendments)

Industrial Design Act, R.S.C. (1985) c. I-9 (note 1992 amendments S.C. (1992) c. 1)
Insurance Companies Act, S.C. (1991) c. 47
Patent Act, R.S.C. (1985) c. P-4 (note 1987 amendment S.C. 1987 c. 32 and 1993 amendment S.C. c. 15)
Trademarks Act, R.S.C. (1985) c. T-13

WEBLINKS

Canadian Intellectual Property Office
xinfo.ic.gc.ca/CIPO/welcome/intro_e.html

World Intellectual Property Organization
www.wipo.org/

Canada: *Copyright Act*
canada.justice.gc.ca/FTP/EN/Laws/Chap/C/C-42

SOCAN—Society of Composers, Authors and Music Publishers of Canada
www.socan.ca/

CANCOPY's Home Page
cancopy.com/

Canada: *Patent Act*
canada.justice.gc.ca/FTP/EN/Laws/Chap/P/P-4

Canadian Patents Database
www.cbsc.org/english/fedbis/bis/2030.html

Electronic Frontier Foundation "Intellectual Property Online: Patent, Trademark, Copyright" Archive
www.eff.org/pub/Intellectual_property/

Electronic Frontier Canada
insight.mcmaster.ca/org/efc/efc.html

Canada: *Trademark Act*
canada.justice.gc.ca/FTP/EN/Laws/Chap/T/T-13

Insurance Canada
www.insurance-canada.ca/

Insurance Bureau of Canada
www.ibc.ca/

Electronic Privacy Information Center
www.epic.org

Risk and Insurance Management Society, Inc.
www.rims.org/

Intellectual Property Magazine
www.ipmag.com

Alberta: *Insurance Act*
www.gov.ab.ca/qp/ascii/acts/IOS.txt

Real Property

OBJECTIVES OF THE CHAPTER

- To consider the nature of real property and ownership of land
- To discuss landlord and tenant relationships
- To examine mortgages and their effect on real property

Mr. Hill was a bad credit risk who had been turned down by Paramount Life Insurance Company when he tried to obtain a loan through a mortgage on the house he and his wife owned. He then sold the property to his business partner and had his partner arrange for a loan with Paramount Life Insurance Company on the basis of a mortgage on the property. This mortgage was granted. The problem was that he had not obtained his wife's consent for the sale but had forged her signature on the documents. Neither the business partner nor the life insurance company knew this fact.

Shortly after this transaction Hill died. Because Paramount was not receiving mortgage payments, it foreclosed. It was then that Mrs. Hill found out what her husband had done. She fought the foreclosure action on the basis of her late husband's fraud, claiming she was entitled to the property. Because the court action took place in a land titles jurisdiction where the Torrens System (see later in this chapter) of land registry was in place, and because the partner and Paramount were innocent of any wrongdoing, the court found that the business partner had obtained good title to the property and that the mortgage granted was good. The government, through the local Land Titles Office, had granted a certificate of title to the land to the partner. This certificate determines ownership against all other parties. Mrs. Hill was the victim of her husband's fraud and lost the property.[1]

---

1. *Paramount Life Insurance Co. v. Hill et al.* (1987) 34 D.L.R. (4th) 150 (Alta. C.A.).

This case illustrates the significance of the difference between the land titles system of registration used in some parts of Canada and the system of land registry used in the rest of the country. In the land titles system, a certificate of title is granted which establishes ownership of the property. Such a certificate had been issued to the business partner in this case. This chapter explores real property interests which are created under these two systems as well as landlord/tenant and mortgage law.

The need to understand the law of real property (land and buildings) extends beyond business relationships because accommodation is one of life's essentials. Whether shelter is obtained through ownership, rental or even squatting, the relationships created are governed by real property law. The premises used to carry out a business activity must be owned or rented and a thorough understanding of the legal relationships involved is fundamental for anyone studying business law. A significant industry has developed to serve the property needs of business, that is, the provision and management of space and the purchase and sale of property. Many private individuals and corporate entities acquire property purely for investment purposes with the objective of making profits, either by renting or by reselling the premises. There are several ways a business person can become involved with the use, possession and ownership of real property. The material in this chapter is necessarily abbreviated but it will serve as an introduction to the most significant aspects of the law of real property: interests in land and their transfer, landlord and tenant relationship, and mortgages.

LEGAL INTERESTS IN LAND

Real Property

Real property is land or anything affixed to land

The term **real property** means land and anything affixed to or constructed on it, including buildings and chattels that have become attached to it in a permanent way. It used to be thought that such interest in land included an unlimited area above and below the land. Today, a right to the air space above privately owned land is limited, extending only to the area the owner can permanently use or occupy, and even this space will probably be restricted by local zoning regulations. A landowner has no right to sue for trespass when an airplane flies over the property, but a permanent incursion into this air space, such as power lines or overhanging portions of an adjoining building, would give the owner the right to take action against those responsible for such an incursion. Although property owners in Canada still have rights to the area under their land, most Crown grants have reserved the mineral rights, oil and gas rights, and in some cases timber rights for the Crown so that the sub-surface rights, beyond those normally occupied by foundations or wells, are no longer intact. The Crown can grant these rights to others and the surface owner will have no claim to sub-surface mineral, oil and gas rights and no complaint about a mine tunnel under the property. Where oil, gas or minerals are discovered under the land, the surface owner is entitled to a licensing fee or lease payment to compensate for surface disturbance in the form of access roads, shafts, etc., but he or she is not entitled to a share of the profits coming from the minerals, oil or gas.

An Historical Glimpse at Land Ownership in Alberta

In 1670, the Hudson's Bay Company secured a charter from King Charles II of England, granting it extensive rights to ownership, trading and government in Rupert's Land. Rupert's Land extended from east of Winnipeg to the Rockies. In 1870, the company surrendered its land to the new Dominion of Canada. In exchange, it received one-twentieth of the "fertile belt" (areas south of the North Saskatchewan River) in the newly named Northwest Territories. The Dominion Government had these lands surveyed into townships, square plots six miles by six miles in size. Townships contain 36 "sections," each being one square mile (approximately 640 acres). The Hudson's Bay Company generally selected Section 8 and the SE, SW, and NW quarters of section 26 from every township in the fertile belt as its one-twentieth share. The Dominion Crown also gave land to settlers and railway companies and up until 1887 it would grant mineral rights with surface rights to land.

In 1905, Alberta became a province. In 1930, the power to grant both surface and mineral rights was transferred by the Dominion Government to the Government of Alberta pursuant to the Natural Resources Transfer Agreement Act. Alberta now leases, but does not sell, any of the mineral rights that it owns. It is estimated that approximately 10 percent of the titles issued in Alberta contain some rights to mines and minerals.

Land that has not been subdivided is legally described according to its geographical location, by its meridian, range, township, section and quarter-section. (There are some exceptions, including Settlement Plans fronting onto a river or lake. An example is the Edmonton Settlement Plan.) Meridians are lines of longitude, running north-south through Alberta. The 4th meridian forms the Alberta-Saskatchewan border, the 5th meridian runs through Calgary, the 6th meridian through Jasper. Legal descriptions designate land as being west of the 4th (or 5th or 6th) meridians. Between the meridians are vertical lines called ranges. Townships are stacked in rows lying north of the U.S. border, the row next to the border being township 1, the next row northward being township 2, and so on. Alberta is thus surveyed in a grid-like fashion. One can locate a plot of land on the map of Alberta by knowing its legal description.

Alberta uses the Torrens Land Titles system. This system is based on three principles: the Mirror Principle, the Curtain Principle, and the Insurance Principle. The Mirror Principle means that the title to property will reflect completely and accurately all the current facts of the title so that it is free of adverse claims or burdens unless they are mentioned. "What you see, is what you get," except for certain public rights or burdens (such as zoning requirements). The title shows the registered owner and all outstanding registered interests and encumbrances. The Curtain Principle means one need not search through history to be sure the registered owner has good title. The current certificate of title contains all the information about the title. The

Insurance Principle means that an insurance fund exists to compensate those who suffer as a result of a mistake being made concerning the validity or accuracy of a title.

Interest in Land

The current law of real property is rooted in the legal system introduced in England after the Norman invasion by William the Conqueror in 1066. The feudalism of that time was a rigid and complex system in which people held rather than owned their land. All land was actually owned by the king who granted the privilege of use to his favourites. The right to the exclusive possession and use of the land was called an **estate in the land** and the nature of that estate or interest in the land depended on the type of relationship and obligation imposed on the land holder. This tradition has had a great influence on our present law of real property. The original estates in land have been reduced to a few significant types known today as estates in fee simple, life estates and leasehold estates.

Fee Simple.

All land owned by Crown

Fee simple comparable to ownership

The greatest interest a person can have in land today is **an estate in fee simple**. Although the Crown (the provincial or federal government) theoretically still owns the land and the person claiming it only has an estate in the land, the fee simple estate is the closest thing we have to ownership today. A fee simple estate gives the holder of that estate the right to use the land subject only to any local restrictions which have been imposed by agreement or legislation. An important aspect of an estate in fee simple is the right of the holder to freely sell an estate, thus transferring all rights of use and control. This free transferability is what brings an estate in fee simple closest to our idea of ownership. In Canada, a person who is said to own land really holds an estate in fee simple in that land.

It should be noted that even when a fee simple interest in land is present, the "owner" of the property is not free from any interference in relationship to it. Several different levels of government may regulate what the property can be used for, the nature and description of the buildings that can be erected on it, and the health, sanitary and appearance levels to be maintained. The "owner" may not even be able to keep the property if a governing body decides to expropriate it. Although these factors are significant limitations on the value of ownership of property, it may be best to view them as one of the costs of living in a social environment rather than as an aspect unique to property law.

Life Estate.

Life estate divides fee simple

Another type of estate in land more restrictive than a fee simple is a life estate.

Fee simple estates can be inherited but a person who has an estate in land for a lifetime cannot will the property to his or her heirs. Upon the death of the life tenant, the property reverts back to the original owner of the fee simple or that owner's heirs. The original grantor of the life estate retains a **reversionary interest** in the property. If this right of reversion is transferred to a third party, that person is called a **remainderman** and has a right to the remainder of the fee simple after the life estate expires. Life estates are not particularly common in Canada but they are an important method of establishing interest in land and are usually used to ensure that some member of the family such as a spouse is cared for to the end of his or her life. It should be noted that a grantor of a life estate could decide to establish the duration of the life estate not on the lifetime of the person obtaining possession (the normal practice) but upon the longevity of some other person. This introduces several complications, however, and so it is very unusual. The holder of a life estate in land has significant responsibilities that a normal landowner does not. That life tenant must pay for normal upkeep, pay fees and taxes and not commit "waste"—that is, not do anything to harm the value of the reversionary interest such as cut down trees or damage the house.

Life estates are generally avoided today because of the difficulties they create in dealing freely with property, but interests close in concept to life estates are created through the operation of law. Historically, a woman's right to act in relationship to property was submerged when she married and her husband obtained full use and control of all family property. The **right of dower** was created to protect the wife in these circumstances. This right allowed the wife to claim a one-third interest in the husband's land as a matter of right. There are many difficulties associated with dower rights, not the least of which is the fact that they establish significant impediments to the free transferability of property. Another difficulty is that a divorce eliminates any dower claim since dower rights are founded on the marriage relationship. Dower rights have been modified by statute in Alberta (note that some provinces have abolished these rights). The Dower Act[2] extends to married persons a life estate in the entire **homestead**, if that homestead is owned by the other spouse alone. A homestead is defined as the property on which the dwelling house, occupied as a residence, is located. It's the property where the spouses have cohabited. A couple may have more than one homestead, but the size of the homestead is restricted to the quarter section of land on which the residence is situated (if farm land) and a parcel consisting of no more than four lots (if urban land). No disposition (sale, mortgage or other transfer of rights) of this property can proceed unless the spouse consents thereto. If disposed of contrary to one's dower rights, the injured spouse may have recourse against the other married person or against the Assurance Fund. The fund is contributed to whenever land is transferred. It provides a pool of money available to those injured by the operation of the land titles system. Land ceases to be a homestead when transferred with consent of the spouse, when a release of dower rights is registered at Land Titles or when a judgment is obtained against the married person who disposed of the property contrary to the spouse's dower rights. A further right given by this *Act* is the right of the surviving spouse to a life estate in the personal property of the deceased married person to that which is exempt from seizure.

Dower and homestead right protect spouse

Leasehold Estates.

Fee simples and life estates are described as **freehold estates** because a person has exclusive possession of the property for an indeterminate time. **Leasehold estates** are significantly different because, when a person grants a lease on land to another, it is for a definite period and the landowner reclaims the land at the expiration of that time. Although a definite time period must be involved, it is possible to convey an almost unlimited right to possess the land by granting a long-term (99-year) lease. It is also possible to create a periodic tenancy. This means that there is no definite termination date; rather, the term is an automatically renewable monthly or yearly tenancy. An example of periodic tenancy is when a person rents an apartment or house by the month without a specified lease period. If neither land-

Leasehold estates determined by time

• but may also be periodic

2. *Dower Act*, R.S.A. (1980) c. D-38.

lord nor tenant do anything to alter the periodic monthly tenancy relationship, the lease period will automatically be extended from period to period. To end such a relationship, one of the parties simply serves notice that the next period will be the last month of the landlord/tenant relationship. Legislation or agreement between the parties may impose a longer period of notice or other restriction on the tenancy.[3] This topic of leasehold interests is generally called landlord and tenant law and will be discussed in a separate section of this chapter.

Lesser Interests in Land

Wells v. Wells[4]

The defendant and his brother, the plaintiff's father, obtained adjacent tracts of land under the *Veterans Land Act* in 1950 and 1957 respectively. The plaintiff inherited his property from his father in 1983. While the properties were side by side, only the plaintiff's property had access to Cows Bay Road and then only 60 feet (18.3 metres) of frontage of a 6.5-acre (2.6-hectare) property. The defendant's property had no access to any road. The closest point of access to Cows Bay Road was 150 feet and that necessitated crossing the plaintiff's property. The defendant walked and drove across this property to gain access to his property from the time he first acquired the land in 1950, which was seven years before the plaintiff's father had obtained the other piece of land. The access continued after this land was acquired by the plaintiff's father and continued unabated for 40 years. Unfortunately, the road across the plaintiff's property goes diagonally across the 60 feet of frontage so that the narrow front section is useless for anything else. In fact the plaintiff's father had at one point wanted to sell the front portion of the property, but could not do so because the access road to the defendant's property blocked off any potential building sites.

The plaintiff now has an offer for the property, but it is conditional upon being able to relocate the defendant's access road, so rather than crossing the property diagonally, it would go down one side allowing the narrow frontage areas to be used to construct a house. The defendant has refused to give permission for the change and this action has been brought to ask the court to order such a change to be made. The court refused, finding that since the defendant had been using that access to property openly for 40 years and in a way adverse to the plaintiff, he had gained a right of way across that land by prescription. The court went so far as to agree with the defendant that the plaintiff's actions amounted to a trespass and awarded $2000 in damages.

This case illustrates the nature of a right of way. A right of way is an interest one person has against another's property to cross it to get access to his own. The property that has the advantage of the right of way is called the dominant property and the property over which the right of way extends is called the servient property. This is a form of easement and is an important interest in land. This case also illustrates that it is possible to obtain such a right of way in many jurisdictions by prescription, which means by continuous usage over a significant period of time. An understanding of rights of way, easements and prescriptions is an important aspect of real property.

---

3. *Residential Tenancies Act*, R.S.A. (1980) c. R-15.3.

4. 116 D.L.R. (4th) 524 (Nova Scotia Supreme Court).

Freehold and leasehold estates are called estates in land because they give the person holding the estate a certain status in relationship to the land, that is, the right to exclusive possession of that land while the estate is in place. However, there are several different types of interest a person can have in land that do not convey the right to exclusive possession of the property. The most important of these lesser interests in land is an **easement** which gives a person the right to use a portion of another's land, usually for a particular purpose. **The right of way** is one of the most common forms of easement. This entitles the holder of the right of way to cross another person's land, usually to get to his or her own property or to reach another point of interest such as a lake or the sea. The dispute in the *Wells v. Wells* case discussed above was over such a right of way used to gain access to the property. Once the right of way has been established, the owner of the property must honour the holder's rights to cross the property, but this right of way does not extend to allowing that person to stop and picnic or build some permanent structure on the property. Another form of easement might involve a permanent incursion onto the property where, for example, a property owner is given permission to have part of a building hang over onto his neighbour's property. For an easement to exist, there must be a property upon which the easement is imposed (servient tenement) and another property whose owner is deriving a benefit (dominant tenement). In most instances, these properties are side by side or in reasonable proximity.

Easement gives right to use of land—not possession

Must be dominant and servient tenement

There are many situations in which people must surrender the use of a portion of their property to facilitate power lines, sewer lines and other public utilities. In these cases, there is usually no dominant tenement because no identifiable, specific, public land benefits by the power lines or sewer lines. These restrictions on the use of land are not easements in a true sense because there is no dominant tenement. They are created by statutes and impose similar rights and responsibilities, and are sometimes called **public easements** or utility rights of way.

There are several other types of interests or rights a person can have in another's land in addition to easements. A **licence** which can be revoked at any time gives a person permission to use another's land. This use of land by permission over a period of time, under common law in some provinces, can acquire the attributes of an enforceable right. For example, an individual who, without interference, habitually crosses the corner of a person's property with the permission of the owner of that property, either express or implied over a number of years, will acquire a right to cross that property as a matter of right (a right of way) even though no actual grant of an easement has been given.

In the *Wells v. Wells* case used to open this section, the use of the right of way had gone on openly for a period of some 40 years and in the process the owner of the adjacent land had acquired a right of way over that land. Acquiring such a right over property through use is called an easement acquired by **prescription**. The effect of such an easement is as significant to the landowner as any other form of easement. The landowner must periodically exercise some control over the portion of land in question to avoid the creation of an easement by prescription. For this reason, the owners of private property with public access will periodically block it off. A period of 20 years is usually sufficient to establish a right by prescription under the *Statute of Limitations* of most jurisdictions. Alberta, however, has abolished the acquisition of interests by prescription by virtue of the *Law of Property Act.*[5]

Property rights may be obtained by prescription

5. *Law of Property Act*, R.S.A. (1980) c. L-15 s. 50.

MINERAL CLAIM RIGHT IN PROPERTY

Tener's predecessors in title obtained a right to the mineral claims on certain lands in British Columbia in 1937. These lands were later incorporated into a park—at first a Class B park and then a Class A park. The park's designation prohibited the development of lands within it except where it would benefit the park. Tener, with others, applied for a permit to operate the mineral claims and was refused. They then applied for compensation for expropriation. This required the court to determine the nature of the min-

eral rights that were owned. The court found that they were a *profit à prendre*. The Supreme Court decided that this was an interest in land giving them rights to minerals below the land and a right to interfere with the surface of the land as much as needed to extract the minerals. When the permit was denied, this was a form of expropriation for which they were entitled to compensation.

The Queen in Right of British Columbia v. Tener et al., 17 D.L.R. (4th) 1
(Supreme Court of Canada)

A right to actual possession of land can be acquired in the same way. When a person has had possession of land for a number of years in an open and notorious fashion and possession has been tolerated by the actual owner, that owner may lose the right to reclaim possession of the land. This process is called acquiring a right to possession of the property through **adverse possession**. Several Canadian jurisdictions, specifically those using a land titles system, have abolished both the right to an easement by prescription and the right to acquire land by adverse possession.[6] Oddly enough, one can still acquire title to land through adverse possession in Alberta.[7] One must be in continuous open possession of the land for 10 years to secure these "squatters' rights" and the land in question cannot belong to the Crown or any municipality. It is strange that adverse possession has not been abolished as it is inconsistent with indefeasibility of title, a concept central to the Torrens Land Titles system in place in Alberta.

—or by adverse possession

Another interest in land may be created when a contract is struck between the owner of land and another person to come onto the land and use some aspect of the land for personal profit, such as the taking of trees, gravel, soil, peat or sand from a property. Such rights convey an interest in land that is quite different from an easement or a license and are referred to as a *profit à prendre.*

Restrictive covenant may
bind future owners

Finally, a person can acquire a right in relation to another's property through the vehicle of a **restrictive covenant**. It is possible for a person granting an estate in land to another to place restrictions on the use of that land that will bind all subsequent holders. These are called restrictive covenants. These restrictions can take many forms but they are typically the following: restrictions as to the type of buildings that can be put on the property—their height, shape and style; restrictions as to how the property may be used—residential, commercial or light industrial; and restrictions as to who can own the property—adult-only facilities and even restrictions on the grounds of racial, religious or ethnic origin. Many of these last types of restrictive covenants are invalid because they are discriminatory in their nature and thus are prohibited by provincial or federal human rights law.

These and other interests in land run with the land, meaning that they are tied to the property itself rather than to the owner of it. They are binding not only on the original purchasers of the property who granted the restriction, easement, or

6. *Land Titles Act,* R.S.B.C. (1996) c. 406 s. 24.

7. *Land Titles Act,* R.S.A. (1980) c. L-5 s. 42.

profit à prendre but are also on any subsequent owner. They are better viewed as an interest in land rather than as a simple contractual relationship and so the rule of privity of contract does not apply.

However, when a person covenants to do or not do something in relationship to the land, the covenant must be negative in its nature for the restrictive covenant to be binding on a subsequent purchaser of the land. For example, a requirement that an owner not place a building over three storeys high on a particular property is a negative covenant and thus binds subsequent purchasers. But a requirement stating that a building be built within a specific period would be positive in nature and only binding on the initial purchaser. It should also be noted that when a large development has the same restrictive covenants in place on all of the properties, this is called a **building scheme**. Building schemes take on many of the attributes of zoning bylaws because the developers have imposed basic rules governing the construction and use of property in the development just as a municipality would normally do through zoning bylaws.

Tenancy in Common and Joint Tenancy

It is possible for two or more people to hold property together in either of two ways, and it is important to distinguish between the two different methods. A **tenancy in common** is when two people share an estate in the same property with each owning a percentage and having an undivided interest in it. This means that each can enjoy the whole property. If one of the parties dies, his or her share in the property goes to that person's heirs and either party can sell his or her interest to someone else without changing the interest in the land. It is also possible for two people to hold a joint interest in property so that if one dies the other will be left with the whole property. This is called a **joint tenancy**. In effect, both individuals own the entire property outright. When one dies, the essential nature of the other's interest does not change. He or she continues to own the entire property through right of survivorship. Joint tenancy avoids many of the problems associated with inheritance and estate taxes, and so couples often hold property this way.

Owning property together may be joint or in common

Only joint ownership creates right of survivorship

There may be instances, however, when people who hold property in joint tenancy do not want the other party to acquire the entire property upon their death. In such circumstances, it is possible to "sever" the joint tenancy. Severance of the joint tenancy must take place before the death of the party wishing to sever and is accomplished by that party acting towards the property in some way that is inconsistent with the joint tenancy continuing. If a joint tenant sold his or her half interest in a property to a third party or in some provinces to him or herself, this would sever the joint tenancy. The relationship formed between the other joint owner and the new third party is a tenancy in common rather than a joint tenancy. Creditors can also bring applications to the court to partition or sever a joint tenancy so that the debtor's half of the property can be sold to pay the debt.

When people hold property together and wish to avoid joint ownership, they should not use such words as "held jointly" or "joint ownership" in the title document since the use of these terms will create a joint tenancy. When such words do not appear, the creation of a tenancy in common is presumed.

Other Interests in Land

Several other types of interest in land are of significance to landowners. When a person makes an offer to sell property, the offer can be revoked by the offeror any time before the point of acceptance, unless some added consideration is given by the offeree that imposes on the offeror an obligation to hold that offer open for a specific period of time. When such added consideration is given, it is called an **option agreement** and when the property involved is land, it conveys with it significant rights. The offeree has acquired the right to purchase the property at a given price, and this right in and of itself can be of significant value and can be sold. Often, when a person leases land and makes improvements, the lease will contain an option to purchase, but this option agreement must be registered to be effective against outsiders who may subsequently purchase the property.

An **agreement for sale** illustrates another kind of interest in land. When the person selling the land is providing the financing for the transaction, the conveyance of the title will be delayed until the last payment is made. In the interim, between the time the agreement is entered into and the title is conveyed, the agreement for sale bestows a significant interest in the property on the purchaser, including the right of possession. Upon final payment, the purchaser has the right to force the completion of the transfer of the freehold interest in the property.

A more common way of financing the purchase of property is through a **mortgage**. Typically, a mortgage transaction involves some outside third party lending the purchaser enough money to buy property from a vendor. The title of the property is conveyed (transferred) to the purchaser and the moneylender (mortgagee) registers the mortgage against the title as an encumbrance. This occurs in Alberta and other jurisdictions using a land titles system. In other jurisdictions, the title is conveyed to the moneylender as security to be reconveyed upon receipt of the last payment. The use of the mortgage as security is not restricted to the process of purchasing property but can be used at any time by the owner of property as a method of raising needed funds. Because the use of mortgages is so common and important, special rules have been developed which will be examined in more detail in a separate section of this chapter.

Transfer and Registration of Interest in Land

In the past in Britain, the most common method of transferring real property during the lifetime of the owner was by grant. The **grant** involved the act of the grantor (the person selling) giving the grantee title to the property. The document used to accomplish this transfer had to be under seal and was called a deed of conveyance, now shortened simply to **deed**. A major difficulty developed with this method of transferring property. Because the passage of time and the possibility of many different deeds or other documents affecting the title to the property, it was impossible to be certain that good title to the property had been transferred by the most current deed, without inspection of all of the past documents. Two different solutions to this problem were developed and either one or the other has been adopted in different jurisdictions in Canada.

In both cases, the solution required that the transfer of land be registered at a registry office. The distinction between the two systems is in the effect of that registration. In most jurisdictions in Canada, the registration process does not affect the rights of the parties under the documents registered but simply provides assurance that the parties dealing with the property will not be affected by any unregistered documents. The registry is merely a repository of the documents that may affect the title of the property. It is still necessary for the parties to examine the title documents and establish a chain of valid deeds to determine whether the seller has good title. This usually means going back over the documents for a set pe-

Option gives right to purchase

Security given through mortgage or agreement for sale

Grants gave title to property

Registration imposed to assist ascertaining title

riod of time (40 years in Ontario) to make sure no mistakes have been made. Anything before that period is presumed to be correct.

The western provinces, New Brunswick, and some areas of Ontario, Nova Scotia and Manitoba have taken the registry system one step further and adopted a system based on the **Torrens System** of land registry, today more commonly referred to as the **land titles system**. Although both systems require registration, the essential difference between the normal land registry system and the land titles system is that, in the latter, once registration has taken place in a central registry, a certificate of title is created and registered which is binding on all parties. The government guarantees that the information on that certificate of title is correct. This information includes the declared, registered owner of the property as well as any mortgages, easements or other interests which might be held by others in that property. The key to understanding this system is that the certificate of title determines the interest of the parties listed on it to the land specified. For example, in Alberta, the *Land Titles Act*[8] states that the certificate of title is conclusive evidence in any court that the person named on the certificate is the holder in fee simple of that property and that is an end to the matter. For this reason, in the example used to introduce this chapter, Mrs. Hill was not able to retain the property. Even though she was innocent and her signature had been forged, a certificate of title was issued to Mr. Hill's partner and this certificate extinguished any claim she had to the property. In both systems, parties claiming an interest in land must register that interest to be protected from some innocent third party buying the property. However, in the normal land registry system, it is up to the parties to sort out the legal relationships derived from those registered documents, whereas in the land titles system, the certificate of title determines the interests.

In both registry and land titles systems, great strides are taking place to modernize the process using modern computer data compilation techniques. This has already introduced significant changes and more changes can be expected in the future.

> Some provinces guarantee title

Condominium Legislation

Because traditional real property law did not recognize the difference between the land and the buildings affixed to it, it was incapable of handling the modern practice of creating ownership in suites stacked vertically in an apartment building. All of the Canadian provinces have passed legislation allowing fee simple interest in individual apartments in a condominium structure. But because condominium ownership also involves a form of common ownership, many unique rights and responsibilities apply. Although individuals may own their separate apartments, all common areas such as the halls, reception areas and laundry facilities are owned in common.

> Condominium legislation allows vertical title
>
> Condominium interest involves some shared property

The condominium association is a corporate body and functions in a way similar to a municipality, company or society, holding regular meetings with each member (those owning apartments in the development) having a vote. Bylaws are passed and put in place that outline the rights and duties of members. The condominium association will also levy a fee on each member to pay for such things as repairs, the cost of management and other services. If these fees are not paid, the condominium corporation has a right to place a lien on the title of the member and

---

8. *Ibid.*, s. 66.

force sale, if necessary, to recover the funds. Each member of the condominium owns his or her own suite and the normal rules of real property apply; the suites can be sold, mortgaged or rented, but the interest the member has in the common area goes with that conveyance and so do the responsibilities associated with it.

Apartments can be owned through cooperatives

A cooperative is another method of owning apartment buildings and other forms of accommodation in common. A cooperative is quite similar to a condominium in that the members of the cooperative all have shares in the apartment building. However, their rights to their individual suites are based on the terms of the contract and the bylaws of the cooperative as opposed to a specific real property interest in the suite itself. In this case, the real property interest in all of the suites and the common areas is held by the cooperative which is a company composed of the members holding shares in it. There are some disadvantages to condominium and cooperative ownership, such as submission to the bylaws and the monthly fee, but there are also significant advantages. This form of ownership is the only viable alternative to renting an apartment. Condominium or cooperative ownership ensures a constant monthly cost, since the property is purchased rather than rented. Rents can change, whereas a purchase price is fixed. However, it must be noted that the monthly service fee can increase over the years and be a significant cost in the ownership of the suite. In condominiums or cooperatives, residents can be required to leave if they violate the bylaws. For example, some of these organizations stipulate that residents be adults only. Couples who have children cannot buy in, and if children are born after the couple move in the couple is required to sell their property. (This particular provision may violate human rights legislation.)

THE LANDLORD/TENANT RELATIONSHIP

Leasehold Estates

A leasehold estate in land is different from a freehold estate in that it is limited in its duration to a specific or determinable time. The lease for real property will usually be for a specific period or end on a specified date. The leasehold interest is similar to a freehold estate in that it bestows on the tenant the right to exclusive possession of the land and buildings during the period of the lease while the landlord retains a reversionary interest in the property. This right to exclusive possession is a hallmark of an estate in land and must be distinguished from a mere license in which the licensee may be only one of several people allowed to use the property. Such a license can be based on contract or given gratuitously. There is no exclusive right conveyed with the right to come on the property in question when a license has been granted. For example, if Jones were to take a room in a hotel for a week, the relationship established would normally be one of license. The hotelkeeper would still have the right to come in the room, make the beds, clean the room, do any repairs and even move Jones to another location if it is deemed appropriate. On the other hand, if Jones were to rent an apartment on a lease arrangement for a week, Jones would have the exclusive right to use the premises and the landlord could not come in without Jones' permission. A lease is created by contract and the rights and responsibilities can be modified by the parties to the agreement. Thus, in the lease, Jones could give the landlord the right to enter the premises under certain circumstances. However, in the absence of such agreement and in the

Tenant has right to exclusive possession during period of lease

Terms of lease can modify obligations

absence of a statutory provision permitting entry by the landlord, that apartment is the property of Jones for the duration of the lease and Jones is entitled to possess it exclusively. When the agreement calls for occupancy at some future time it is an **agreement for lease** rather than a lease. The distinction may be important, since the remedies available to the parties may be considerably different.

Because a lease is created by contract, the general requirements of contract law apply to leasehold estates. As with any form of contract, it is a good idea for contracting parties to put their agreement in writing. The *Statute of Frauds* requires agreements dealing with interest in land to be evidenced in writing to be enforceable.[9] When there is no written evidence of a lease, part performance, such as the occupation of the premises by the tenant, may satisfy the requirements of the *Statute of Frauds* and the lease may be enforceable as against the parties to the lease. But the *Land Titles Act* requires longer leases (three years or longer) to be registered to protect the tenant's interests against third parties, such as subsequent purchasers of the property.[10]

Registration and writing requirements for leases

A leasehold estate is as much an interest in land as a freehold estate and when a landlord sells property, any lease arrangements that were entered into before the new owner took over the property are binding on the new owner. Similarly, when the landlord mortgages the property after a lease arrangement with a tenant has been entered into, the creditor is subject to the lease arrangement. If the landlord fails to make payments and the mortgagee is forced to take action against the property to protect his or her investment, either by seizing the property or by having it sold, the tenant has the right to remain on the premises until the lease expires. If a lease arrangement were based solely on contract law, the principle of privity of contract would prohibit this result, but since a leasehold interest is said to "run with the land," the tenant is able to insist on the right to exclusive possession of the property for the duration of the lease, even against strangers who have acquired the property after the creation of the lease. Because of this, Alberta and many other jurisdictions require long-term leases to be registered along with other claims affecting the title of the property.

Leasehold interests run with the land

Other provisions of the law of contract also apply to the contracts that create leasehold estates. A landlord who contracts with an infant, a drunk or a mentally incompetent person runs into all the problems associated with incapacity discussed in Chapter 4 and the resulting contract may not be binding. Historically, the principle allowing a contract to be discharged because of some frustrating event that makes the performance of the contract impossible did not apply to land.[11] Many jurisdictions have introduced legislation changing this; if residential premises are destroyed or otherwise rendered unusable, the contract will be discharged by frustration and the tenant's obligation to pay rent will cease.[12] There are many other examples of legislation which significantly modifies the common law relationship of landlord and tenant. This is especially true when the premises involved are used for residential purposes. Most jurisdictions have introduced special legislative provisions determining the rights and obligations of landlords and tenants in residential relationships. This legislation varies from province to province, so no attempt will be made to make a comprehensive summary of these statutory provisions except to indicate some of the more interesting provisions in place.

Statutes apply frustration to some tenancies

9. *The Statute of Frauds,* 1677 (29 Car. 2) c. 3 s. 4.

10. *Land Titles Act,* R.S.A. (1980) c. L-5 s. 98.

11. *Paradine v. Jane* (1647) Aleyn 26 (K.B. Div.).

12. *Residential Tenancies Act,* R.S.A. (1980) c. R-15.3 s. 32.

Types of Tenancies

There are two main methods of holding a leasehold estate in property. The first is by having an agreement establishing a leasehold estate for a specific period of time such as "one year" or "ending September 5." When such an agreement has a set duration, it is a **term lease**, often called simply a lease. In the absence of a breach on the part of either party, the lease entitles the tenant to exclusive possession of the property for the specified period. During that period, the tenant may have the right to assign or sublet the lease to another party depending on the terms of the lease. If the lease is assigned, the tenant gives up all rights and claims in relationship to the property. However, if the property is sublet, the tenant retains a reversionary interest. Just as the landlord who holds the fee simple estate in the property has the right to retake possession of the property at the expiration of the lease, a tenant also has the right to retake possession of the property at the expiration of the designated period when a sublet is involved. Usually leases contain provisions allowing for such assignment or subletting with the permission of the landlord, "which shall not be unreasonably withheld." This gives the landlord some say in who takes possession of the property, but does not allow him or her to unreasonably interfere.

The second common method of creating a leasehold estate is with a **periodic tenancy** which is a period-to-period rental with no specific time duration. The rental period is specific, but the parties have agreed that the lease period will be automatically renewed in the absence of notice to the contrary. The period involved can be weekly, monthly or yearly, but the most common is the month-to-month tenancy. The feature of a periodic tenancy which distinguishes it from a normal lease arrangement is that there is no specific identified time when the relationship between landlord and tenant will terminate. The dominating aspect of a periodic tenancy is the requirement of notice necessary for any modifications in the status of the relationship between landlord and tenant. If the lease period in the periodic tenancy is one month, no notice can be given to take effect during that period. It must be given before the commencement of one period to be effective at the end of the next. This has caused considerable problems; tenants wishing to terminate monthly apartment tenancies who served notice when paying rent on the first of the month would be surprised to learn that the notice was not effective until the end of the next month. This is an area that has been modified by statute in many jurisdictions. The *Residential Tenancies Act* of Alberta, for example, now permits the tenant to give notice on the first day of the month, effectively terminating the lease on the last day of that same month.[13] The landlord may also serve notice on the first day of the "notice period," but that notice period is generally three consecutive months.

There are two other, less important types of tenancies. A landlord creates a **tenancy at will** when he or she allows a purchaser to take possession of a property before the date specified for the exchange of title. Under such an arrangement, either party retains the right to end the relationship at any time and no notice is required. While the requirement of rent by the landlord may give rise to a periodic tenancy, it is possible to specify that the relationship remains a tenancy at will regardless of the rent. A **tenancy at sufferance** is created when a landlord has given the appropriate notice but the tenant fails to vacate, or when the set term of a lease has expired and the tenant remains in possession. While this is called a tenancy, it is simply an over-holding tenant who may have rights of possession in relationship to outsiders but can be ejected at any time by the landlord. If the landlord accepts

Lease sets out rights of parties

Property may be sublet

Periodic tenancy usually month to month

Notice period is one clear rental period

13. *Ibid.*, s. 6.

a further rental payment from an over-holding tenant, there is the danger that a periodic tenancy will result. It is better to view tenancy at will and tenancy at sufferance as special situations rather than examples of leasehold estates.

Rights and Obligations of the Parties

No distinction is made in common law between tenancies dealing with commercial property and residential property. Most provinces have created legislation that significantly alters the common law provisions relating to residential, and to a lesser extent, commercial tenancies. Some provinces have several different statutes dealing with landlord and tenant law.[14] Others have incorporated all of their landlord and tenant legislation into one general landlord and tenant act meant to cover all leasehold tenancies.[15] The following comments are directed to the landlord and tenant law in place generally and apply primarily to commercial tenancies. The unique provisions which have been introduced in Alberta to deal with residential tenancies will be discussed under a separate heading. It is recommended that the reader refer to the specific legislative provisions in effect in his or her jurisdiction.

Obligations may be modified by statute

Since the primary relationship between landlord and tenant is based on contract, the terms in that contract can modify the traditional obligations of the parties. As the rights and responsibilities of the parties are discussed below, it is important to remember that these provisions should be regarded as binding on the party *unless they have agreed otherwise* in their lease agreement. In addition to the rent to be paid and a description of the property, provisions often included in commercial leases relate to what use the property can be put to and who is responsible for the payment of utilities, taxes, repairs and insurance. In special situations such as services or retail stores in shopping malls, provisions may relate to the kind of businesses that can be located in the same mall. In the shopping mall situation, rent is sometimes fixed as a percentage of sales. Long-term commercial leases often include an option for the review of the rent at set periods or for its renewal.

Vacant Possession.

The landowner has an obligation to ensure that the premises are vacant and ready for occupancy at the time agreed for the lease period to start. A failure on the part of the landlord to deliver vacant possession to a new tenant may be caused by several factors, such as failure to eject an over-holding tenant, an error in calculating the prior tenant's rights to stay on the premises, or construction or renovation. The landlord's liability and the compensation due the tenant in these situations will be calculated on how much it costs the tenant to find other accommodation in the interim.

Landowner must provide vacant premises

Quiet Enjoyment.

A landlord is obligated to give a tenant quiet enjoyment of the premises. This term is somewhat misleading because it does not mean that the tenant has to be happy or like the premises, only that the landlord must ensure that nothing happens to interfere with the tenant's use of the property. Suppose Cho negotiates the purchase of an office building from Rankin and, in anticipation of the completion of the deal, rents accommodation in that building to Coghlan. Then the deal falls through.

Landlord must not interfere with tenant's use of property

---

14. *Rent Review Act,* R.S.N.S. (1989) c. 398; *Residential Tenancies Act,* R.S.N.S. (1989) c. 401.

15. *Residential Tenancies Act,* R.S.A. (1980) c. R-15.3.

Coghlan will not be able to occupy the office space, since Rankin is still the owner of the property. Because this interferes with Coghlan's quiet enjoyment of the lease, Coghlan can take action against Cho for failure to provide quiet enjoyment. It is also possible for a landlord to fail to provide quiet enjoyment of the property by allowing something to physically interfere with the use of the premises. For example, if Coghlan rents office space in a building owned by Cho and one day discovers that the only entrance to his office is blocked because of construction or that blasting next door makes it impossible to stay on the premises, this would interfere with his quiet enjoyment of the premises and Coghlan could sue Cho for breach of the lease agreement.

Repair of Premises.

No general obligation to repair

The landlord has no general obligation to deliver premises that are clean or in good repair. The tenant takes the property the way it comes and if he or she wants it in better condition, the cost is the responsibility of the tenant. Only when the premises are in such disrepair that it amounts to a breach of quiet enjoyment can the landlord be held responsible. In the example above Coghlan would have no complaint if the premises are not painted or the carpet is threadbare when he moves in. If Coghlan is dissatisfied with the condition of the office, he should put a term in the lease agreement which requires the landlord to correct these problems. If the structure of the building is in such poor repair that it is no longer capable of supporting a wall or a floor and a resulting cave-in would make the office unusable, that would be a breach of the covenant of quiet enjoyment. Because the lease is contractual in nature, it is possible for the parties to modify the commonly accepted terms and care should be taken to do so. There are many situations in which the courts will imply into the contract obligations on the parties because of the circumstances. For example, when a tenant rents only part of a building, the court will assume that the landlord has an obligation to provide heat unless otherwise stated in the lease. But when the tenant leases the entire building, the obligation may be that of the tenant.

Frustration usually applies to both commercial and residential tenancies.
Photo by David Young-Wolff/PhotoEdit.

Termination.

If a lease for a specific period of time is involved, the lease is terminated at the expiration of the specified period. Of course, the parties can enter into a new agreement extending the lease or for that matter shortening it. If the rental arrangement is ongoing (for example, month-to-month) the tenancy is terminated by either party giving proper notice. If the tenant fails to leave after the lease has expired or after being given the appropriate notice, a tenancy at sufferance relationship is established. In these circumstances, the landlord is generally entitled to compensation from the tenant in the form of payment. However, if a normal rent payment is made for this period and accepted by the landlord, there is a danger of creating a periodic tenancy which would require the landlord to give additional notice before the tenant could be ejected. The length of notice required to vacate the premises when a periodic tenancy is involved is generally equal to the length of the tenancy period.

TENANT RESPONSIBLE FOR INJURY TO CUSTOMER

Mr. Silad leased a laudromat where a customer was injured by a falling fluorescent light fixture. She sought damages from Mr. Silad, who paid $27 000, and in this action he was seeking contribution from the landlord. The problem for the court to decide was whether the tenant or the landlord was responsible for keeping the premises in repair and also who was responsible for the injury to the customer. Under the *Occupiers' Liability Act*, it is clear the tenant occupier is responsible to the person using the premises and because there was no provision in the lease making the landlord responsible for repairs, the occupier had no claim against the landlord for the condition of the premises, which were entirely within the control of Mr. Silad. This case shows how important it is to specify in a lease agreement who is responsible for repairs.

Barnett-Black v. Silad Investments Inc., 74 D.L.R. (4th) 734 (Ontario Court, General Division)

Periodic tenancies may be week to week, month to month or year to year, but one clear rental period must be given for notice. In most jurisdictions, the notice period has been extended when residential tenancies are involved.

Frustration.

Historically, the doctrine of frustration did not apply to real property but many jurisdictions have modified this in their landlord and tenant statutes. The effect of this modification is that the obligation of the parties to a lease may be ended by the destruction of the property or other conditions that make the performance of the lease agreement impossible. In Alberta, the *Residential Tenancies Act* states that the doctrine of frustration will apply to residential tenancies and as a result the province's *Frustrated Contracts Act* will apply.[16]

Frustration may apply to residential tenancies by statute

Tenants' Obligations.

The most obvious obligation on the tenant in a leasehold agreement is to pay the agreed-upon rent for the premises at the appropriate time. This obligation is independent of any special obligations that the landlord may have agreed to in the lease contract, such as a duty to make repairs. If the lease requires that the landlord repair the premises and the landlord fails to do so, the tenant cannot withhold rent until the repairs are made. The tenant must still pay rent and the landlord can use the courts to enforce the payment if there is a failure to pay. Failure to pay rent, although it may appear justified in these circumstances, would give the landlord grounds to evict the tenant. On the other hand the tenant would have the right to seek other compensation. The tenant has no obligation to repair normal wear and tear or even to make serious repairs when they occur, unless they are caused by waste (his or her own action). The landlord should be notified of any serious problems, but at common law the landlord has no obligation to make these repairs unless failure to do so would interfere with the quiet enjoyment of the tenancy. If Coghlan rents an office from Cho and the rug on the floor wears out over the years, Coghlan would be under no obligation to replace it. But neither would Cho be obligated to replace it since the landlord is not required to provide premises of any standard of fitness for the tenant. Of course, the landlord and tenant can

Tenant must pay rent

Tenants not responsible for normal wear and tear

16. *Residential Tenancies Act*, R.S.A. (1980) c. R-15.3 s. 32; *Frustrated Contracts Act*, R.S.A. (1980) c. F-20.

BOWLING LANES FIXTURES

Although this case does not deal with a landlord and tenant relationship, it does illustrate the nature of a fixture. The debtor in this case built a bowling alley in White Rock and acquired equipment from Florida including 20 bowling alleys complete with setters, lanes, gutters, ball returns, ball racks, score sheets, bowling seats, masking units, divisions, capping and foundations. This equipment was installed in the building and the dispute in this case is between the mortgagee and another creditor who has a chattel mortgage agreement in relation to the equipment. The court had to decide whether the equipment had become part of the realty, thus giving the mortgagee priority. The court decided that although it was possible to remove the equipment, including the lanes which had been securely attached by screws, their purpose was to remain attached. The mortgagee as a result had priority. Today, with the new personal *Property Security Act*, the same challenge with respect to priorities would have a different result, but we can still appreciate the decision, which shows that affixed bowling alley equipment becomes part of the realty.

North West Trust Co. v. Rezyn Developments Inc., 81 D.L.R. (4th) 751 (British Columbia Court of Appeal)

agree otherwise and in many lease agreements, the landlord assumes the responsibility for keeping the property in good repair.

A tenant who uses property for a purpose other than that for which it was originally rented will assume the responsibility for any undue wear and tear, and the landlord can require the premises to be vacated. For example, if Coghlan rents premises from Cho to be used as an office and instead uses it for manufacturing furniture, Cho would have the right to require Coghlan to leave regardless of the terms of the lease. Cho could also sue for any damage that might have been caused by inappropriate use.

Tenant can remove some of his or her fixtures before termination of lease

A problem that often arises with rental premises is when tenants attach some item to the building and then wish to take it away when leaving. The attached item is called a **fixture**, and tenants are not permitted to remove fixtures which have been attached in such a way that suggests they were intended to remain a permanent part of the building. If Coghlan installed modern wiring and added a staircase to the second floor in his rented office, these fixtures would become permanent and he could not remove them when he left. Fixtures attached to the premises which are really meant to stand by themselves but are attached merely to facilitate their usefulness and can be detached without damaging the premises can be taken away by the tenant. Shelving, display counters, machinery, decorative artwork and signs go with the tenant who attached them. However, where the removal of the item will cause significant damage to the premises, it has become a fixture and cannot be removed. If the tenant neglects to take fixtures and tries to regain possession only after leaving, it is too late since the fixtures have become part of the real property. A more detailed discussion of fixtures and personal property generally is found in Chapter 14.

Remedies

Breach of Lease.

Landlord can sue for compensation when lease breached

If the tenant breaches the lease agreement in some way, such as by failing to pay rent, the landlord can sue for the overdue rent. The landlord also has the right to require the tenant to vacate the premises and can evict tenants who fail to do so. This is called **forfeiture** and when unpaid rent in a commercial lease is involved, no court order is needed and may be accomplished by the landlord simply changing the locks. When the tenant is in breach of some other term of the lease such as the use of the premises or repair, the landlord must first give the tenant notice to end the breach and time to do so. When residential premises are involved, legislation often limits the availability of this remedy.

In any case, the services of a civil enforcement agency, must be obtained to carry out the eviction if the tenant resists. This process can be costly and time-consuming. In these circumstances, and for other, lesser breaches of the lease agreement, several other remedies may be available to the landlord.

When the landlord does retake the property for failure to pay rent prior to the end of the lease term, the tenant can apply to the court to have the lease reinstated. This **relief against forfeiture** is an equitable principle similar to a right to redeem an interest in real property after a mortgage has been foreclosed, which will be discussed below.

When the tenant abandons the premises, the landlord retains the right to payment of rent for the duration of the lease period. It should be noted that the landlord is not obligated to mitigate this loss, at least in commercial tenancies, by finding a new tenant until the expiration of the lease period.

The landlord also has the right to seize any property left by the tenant and hold it until the rent is paid or to sell the tenant's property to pay the rent owing. By so doing the rent is paid and the lease continues. This power to seize the tenant's property, called **distress**, is usually significantly limited or eliminated in residential tenancy legislation.

Because the lease arrangement is primarily contractual, the landlord also has the right to sue for monetary compensation whenever the lease is breached. In most circumstances, compensation amounts to the rent due. However, if damage has been done to the premises, the landlord can seek compensation for the cost of repairs.

Injunction is another important remedy available for both landlord and tenant when the terms of the lease are breached. When either party is acting in a way inconsistent with the terms of the lease, the courts will not tolerate a refusal to honour lease obligations and will issue an order that such activity stop. Thus, when a tenant is misusing the premises and causing damage to them, the landlord can get an injunction to prevent the misuse of the property.

The remedies available to the tenant for the landlord's breach of the lease are more limited. The tenant is generally entitled either to sue the landlord for compensation for any injury suffered because of the breach or to seek an injunction. The tenant is not entitled to withhold rent to force the landlord's compliance with the lease obligations. But if the landlord's breach is significant enough to qualify as a breach of a major contractual term, the tenant may be entitled to treat the lease agreement as discharged and vacate the premises voluntarily, thus terminating the lease. For example, if the lease agreement requires the landlord to provide heat and water and those services are turned off, this would probably be a significant enough breach for the tenant to terminate the agreement. In any case, the tenant always retains the right to seek a court order that the lease be declared as ended or the tenant's obligation to pay rent be reduced because of the landlord's breach.

It is a principle of tort law that the occupier of property, including a tenant, is responsible for any injury caused to people using the property. The landlord may also be liable if the landlord is responsible for repairs under the lease and the tenant has notified the landlord but the repairs are not made. The landlord will be responsible for injuries to the tenant or the tenant's family in these circumstances.

Landlord can seize tenant's property when lease breached

Monetary compensation available for breach of lease

Occupiers' liability applies

Residential Tenancies

Applewood Lane West Ltd. v. Scott et al.[17]

Thomas Scott and Dave Hines were tenants and Applewood Lane West Ltd. was their landlord. They had a one-year lease running from the end of July 1985 to end of July 1986. Their rent was almost $600 a month and they had paid just under $300 as a security deposit. In the fall of 1985 they decided they didn't want to live there any more and informed their neighbours and friends that they were going to have a series of "lease-breaking parties" which they proceeded to do. Several noisy parties lasting well into the morning were held. Neighbours complained, police attended and finally the landlord was driven to give them notice to vacate within five days. They didn't leave until a month later and did not pay that month's rent. The landlord retook possession of the premises, made necessary repairs incurring expenses of $231 in the process and was unable to rent it before April 1. The landlord brought this action to recover the damages from the two tenants. The tenants, on the other hand, applied to have their security deposit returned. The question was whether landlords in evicting their tenants give up any claims to rights they had under the lease.

The judge in this case made it clear that the conduct of the tenants in deliberately provoking the landlord to terminate the lease, constituted abandonment of the lease on their part. The tenants had breached the lease, not the landlord; therefore, the landlord was entitled to lost rent as well as the cost of repairs and was successful in his action.

This case illustrates the nature of the landlord/tenant relationship and the obligations existing between them. "Lease-breaking parties" held by young people have gained notoriety, but such inappropriate behaviour on the part of tenants can make them liable for significant damages if landlords decide to pursue their legal rights. While there are many modifications to the rights of tenants contained in residential tenancy acts, such behaviour will not be tolerated in any jurisdiction. The Applewood case shows how the interests of the parties in a residential tenancy relationship can be quite different from those in a commercial tenancy; it also underscores the need for the introduction of special legislation to deal with those relationships.

In a residential tenancy, a tenant rents or leases premises for the purposes of acquiring living accommodation. The common law provisions are the same whether the tenancy is commercial or residential, but most jurisdictions have passed legislation putting in place unique provisions dealing with residential tenancies. The *Residential Tenancies Act* of Alberta is an example.[18] It applies only to tenancies of residential premises, but not all residential premises qualify. The *Act* does not apply to mobile home sites, premises that form part of the landlord's living quarters, hotels, bed-and-breakfast inns, resorts (except for stays of more than six months), premises with mixed commercial and residential use, student residence units (unless self-contained), nursing and senior citizen homes, correctional institutions, and hospitals.

The *Act* enables municipalities to establish local Landlord and Tenant Advisory Boards that function to advise landlords and tenants on tenancy matters, to receive

---

17. 35 D.L.R. (4th) 287 (Manitoba Court of Appeal).

18. *Residential Tenancies Act,* R.S.A. (1980) c. R-15.3 s. 2.

and investigate complaints, and to mediate disputes.[19] However, parties must still go before the courts to secure damages, and landlords still need court orders to secure possession from tenants refusing to vacate.

This residential tenancy legislation restricts the number of rent increases to two per year and requires the landlord to give the tenant three months' written notice of any rent increase (in the case of a monthly tenancy).[20] If the lease itself provides for a longer notice period, then that longer notice must be given before increasing the rent payable.

The *Residential Tenancies Act* increases the amount of notice to be given when the landlord wants the tenant to vacate the premises. For a monthly tenancy, the notice period is generally three consecutive months.[21] The landlord must serve a signed written notice that sets out the reasons for which the tenancy is being terminated.[22] If the tenant is also an employee of the landlord and that employment is being terminated, the notice period will depend on factors such as the length of the employment.[23] If the landlord is seeking possession so as to convert the premises and sell them as a condominium, the notice is increased to 180 days.[24] On the other hand, if the tenant wishes to terminate the tenancy, only one month's notice is necessary and no reasons for termination are required.

The general obligations of landlords and tenants are significantly altered by the *Residential Tenancies Act*. An obligation is imposed on the landlord to provide "habitable" premises.[25] The privacy of the tenant is protected by restricting the landlord's right to enter the premises. Unless there is an emergency or the tenant has abandoned the premises, the landlord must serve 24 hours' notice of its intent to enter (to inspect the state of repairs, make repairs or show the premises to prospective tenants, etc.). The landlord may only then enter between 8 a.m. and 8 p.m. on a day that's not a holiday or day of worship.[26] The statute also requires that, if the tenancy agreement is in writing, the tenant be given a signed copy of the written lease; payment of rent can be withheld until the tenant is served with a copy.[27]

Landlords generally require security deposits from tenants to ensure that rent is paid and that funds are available to repair damage done to property. The return of the security deposit was one of the questions facing the judge in the *Applewood* case discussed above. This practice can easily be abused. Alberta has thus restricted the amount of the security deposit to the equivalent of one month's rent or less.[28] These security deposits must be deposited in interest-bearing trust accounts, at a bank or other financial institution, and thus kept separate from the landlord's other funds (and protected from the claims of the landlord's creditors).[29] The interest earned on these deposits shall be paid, annually, to the tenant unless the tenant specifically agrees to allow interest to be compounded and the entire sum to be paid to him on termination of the lease. The security deposit is to

19. *Ibid.*, s. 49.
20. *Ibid.*, s. 13.
21. *Ibid.*, s. 6.
22. *Ibid.*, s. 8.
23. *Ibid.*, s. 9.
24. *Ibid.*, s. 10.
25. *Ibid.*, s. 14(c).
26. *Ibid.*, s. 17.
27. *Ibid.*, s. 15.
28. *Ibid.*, s. 37.
29. *Ibid.*, s. 37.1.

be returned to the tenant within 10 days of the tenant vacating the premises. No deductions can be made for normal wear and tear; no deductions can be made to cover damage to the premises unless the landlord and tenant have completed both an incoming and outgoing inspection report.[30]

Alberta also imposes on landlords a duty to mitigate their losses following a tenant's abandonment of the premises. After abandonment, the landlord may continue the tenancy; the landlord is free to let the lease period run out and then try to retain the security deposit or seek out the tenant for further payment. But the *Act* also provides that the landlord must make reasonable efforts to rent the premises so that losses are kept to a minimum.[31] Any goods abandoned by the tenant may be promptly sold if the costs of storage would exceed the proceeds, or if their value is below the amount prescribed by regulation (below $1000). If the goods have a higher value, the landlord may have to store them for the prescribed period (30 days) and thereafter sell them. From the proceeds of sale, the landlord is entitled to keep sums to cover the costs of removal, storage and sale and any other established liabilities of the tenant to the landlord.[32]

Under the *Act*, it is possible for the tenant to assign or sublet the lease, but landlords are given the right to veto this course of action. A landlord's consent to the assignment or subletting cannot be unreasonably withheld; reasons for any refusal must be provided in writing to the tenant.[33] Neither the landlord nor the tenant is allowed to change the locks to the premises without the other party's consent.[34]

There have been significant statutory changes to the common law in the field of residential tenancies. These changes seem to favour the tenant, but they should be viewed as a form of consumer protection legislation designed to prevent the serious abuses that have occurred in the past in landlord and tenant relationships.

STATUTE OVERRULES LEASE

This case involves a lease entered into between a landlord and tenant for residential premises. The lease contained a provision indicating that in the event of termination, 30 days' notice would be given. The tenant stayed until the lease expired and then continued to stay from month to month. In 1993 the tenant served one month's notice on the landlord pursuant to the provisions of the lease for termination. This was rejected by the landlord, who insisted on two months' notice as set out in the *Landlord and Tenant Act* in force in the province. The court had to decide whether the provisions of the *Act* would apply or whether they would be overridden by the terms of the lease. The *Act* specifically stated that its provisions applied despite any agreement or waiver to the contrary and so the court decided that the 60-day notice required by the *Act* applied. The tenant was required to pay the landlord one month more rent. Such legislation usually favours the tenant, but note that in this instance it was the landlord that benefited.

Pinheiro v. Bowes, 109 D.L.R. (4th) 315 (Ontario Court, General Division)

30. *Ibid.*, s. 39.
31. *Ibid.*, s. 21.
32. *Ibid.*, s. 24.
33. *Ibid.*, s. 16.1.
34. *Ibid.*, s. 18.

MORTGAGES

The purchase of real property usually involves significant funds which the purchaser often has to borrow to finance the purchase. To secure such a loan, the borrower will normally mortgage the property, which in some jurisdictions involves temporarily transferring title in the property to the creditor as security for the funds advanced. Upon proper repayment, the creditor will reconvey the title. However, if there is a default, the creditor's title in the real property gives the creditor first claim on that property above other creditors.

The terminology used to designate the parties to such transactions can be confusing. The person who grants the mortgage is the one borrowing the money and is called the **mortgagor**. The creditor is called the **mortgagee**.

Debtor is the mortgagor, creditor is the mortgagee

In Alberta, however, mortgages do not involve transferring title of the secured property to the creditor or mortgagee. Because Alberta adopted a Torrens Land Titles System, mortgages simply appear as encumbrances or charges registered against the borrower's title. The *Land Titles Act* stipulates that no mortgage or encumbrance operates as a transfer of land, but is merely security over the land charged.[35] This provision has been in the *Act* since its original enactment in 1906 (SA 1906, c. 24).

Alberta's mortgage law differs significantly from that of other jurisdictions in many respects. Accordingly, we shall briefly look at the historical development of mortgage law. Then we shall examine Alberta's law in some detail.

Mortgages at Common Law

Originally, the mortgagee took the title and possession of the land. This was inconvenient for both the lender and the borrower, and the practice soon developed by which the creditor held title to the property used to secure the loan but the debtor retained possession of the property used as security for the loan. In the event of default, the creditor had the right, because of title, to take possession of the property as well. Still, problems were associated with the process. Since the mortgagees had title, they could take the land upon default, but the debtors still had to pay back the loan even though they had lost their land. Subsequent developments of the law of mortgages, especially in the courts of chancery, were intended to overcome these problems and have resulted in a unique body of law.

Mortgage involves transfer of title as security

Equity of Redemption.

The law relating to mortgages is a significant example of how the courts of chancery stepped in to relieve the harshness or unfairness of the common law. At common law, a mortgagor's rights in relation to the property were completely extinguished by a failure to make a payment. The courts of chancery recognized that the nature of the relationship was primarily creditor/debtor with the property only intended to be security for that debt. The chancery recognized that the mortgagor had a continuing claim or right in relationship to the property. This right consisted of a right to redeem the property by paying the money owed plus any expenses involved. This right to redeem became known as the **equity of redemption** and it bestows on the mortgagor an interest in the land which goes beyond the basic contractual responsibility established between the parties. Assume Nagai has property valued at $100 000 and a mortgage from Dhillon for $60 000, and Nagai fails to

Mortgagor retains right to redeem after default

35. *Land Titles Act,* R.S.A. (1980) c. L-5 s. 106.

make the appropriate payments. Although Dhillon will have the right to obtain the title to the property, Nagai will have the right to redeem that property by making the $60 000 payment plus any expenses and interest. Since the value of the property is $100 000 and the cost of redeeming it is $60 000, the value of this right to redeem or equity of redemption is $40 000. Today, business people often use the shortened term "equity" to refer the value left in any asset they own after they subtract what they owe. Thus if I own a car worth $12 000 and I owe $5000 I will have $7000 equity in that vehicle.

Foreclosure.

The mortgagor's right to reclaim the land by making the appropriate payment even after default was unfair because no time limit was established in which the mortgagor had to exercise the right of redemption. Therefore, as long as the mortgagee held the property after taking possession, the mortgagor had the right to redeem the property by making the appropriate payments. This could be very disruptive to the mortgagee, since theoretically it could be exercised 20 or 30 years later, leaving the mortgagee in an uncertain position.

Mortgagee can foreclose the right to redeem

The courts of chancery devised a simple solution to this problem. The mortgagee simply went to the courts and asked them to establish a time limit within which the mortgagor's right to redeem had to be exercised. If the mortgagor failed to pay within that time, an order could be obtained from the court which forever foreclosed the mortgagor from exercising that right to redeem. The process of **foreclosure** involves the courts imposing a time limit on the defaulting mortgagor within which action must be taken to pay off the debt and reclaim the property. Failure to do so within that time period forecloses the mortgagor from exercising a right to redeem. This combination—a right to redeem on the part of the mortgagor and a right to obtain foreclosure on the part of the mortgagee—has worked well and is the system in place in Canada today.

Foreclosure is a two-stage process

The process of obtaining foreclosure has two stages. Upon default, the mortgagee goes to the court and asks for an order establishing the time limit within which the mortgagor can redeem (called an *order nisi* in some provinces). This time limit will vary with the circumstances and from jurisdiction to jurisdiction. (In Alberta, the redemption period is six months for urban land and one year for farm land, but these periods can be varied by the court depending on the circumstances.) If the property is not redeemed within the designated period, the mortgagee returns to court and asks the court for a final order of foreclosure (called an *order absolute*). This order, once obtained, prevents any further exercise of the equity of redemption on the part of the mortgagor. It should be mentioned that even then, in most jurisdictions, the court retains the discretionary right to reopen the redemption period if the circumstances warrant. Once the property has been resold to a third party and a new certificate of title has been issued in a land titles system, the original owner no longer has a right to redeem the property.

As discussed above, the registration of mortgages and other interests in land is necessary to preserve those rights against innocent third parties. It is important to note that the form of registration of mortgages is quite distinct in the registration system and the land titles system. In a registration system, under the common law rules, the actual title transfers from mortgagor to the mortgagee when a mortgage takes place. In a land titles system jurisdiction, the registration process does not show this transfer; in fact, the Alberta *Land Titles Act* specifically states that the mortgage does not operate as a transfer. The certificate of title establishing the fee simple interest in the property remains in the name of the mortgagor. The interest of the mortgagee is merely noted as a charge against the property, as an easement or a leasehold interest would be. But since the nature of the charge indicated on the title document is a mortgage, the rights bestowed by such a charge in the event of default are those of a mortgage as established by the common law and the parties are still generally referred to as the mortgagor and mortgagee. Thus, the mortgagee (chargeholder) has the right in the event of default to start the foreclosure process. In the event of the property not being redeemed before the time limit specified, the mortgagee has the right to apply to the courts to have a new certificate of title created with the mortgagee identified as the new holder of the fee simple on a certificate of title. In other words, while the method of recording the relationship in the provinces using the land titles system might be different, the effect is in many respects similar.

In land titles system jurisdictions, a mortgage is registered as charge on title

The Second Mortgage.

Nothing prevents a mortgagor of property, even after a mortgage has been granted on it to another person, from granting a second mortgage to someone else. After all, the mortgagor still has something of value, the "equity" left in the asset, to sell, transfer or further encumber. It should be obvious that the more mortgages involved, the weaker the security, so anything beyond first, second and third mortgages is rare.

Of course, there is considerably greater risk associated with a second or third mortgage, since the first mortgage has the right to foreclose the equity of redemption upon default by the mortgagor. If the first mortgagee is successful in obtaining foreclosure, the second and third mortgagees will be stripped of any interest or claim they have against the property. The second and third mortgagees must be prepared to buy out any mortgagee whose mortgage comes before them in this process. In other words, if Redekop gave Johal a $75 000 first mortgage on the property and Nelson a $30 000 second mortgage, Nelson must be prepared to pay out the $75 000 owing on the first mortgage to protect his interest if Redekop defaults. This puts any subsequent mortgagees in a very vulnerable position. As a result, higher rates of interest are charged for second and third mortgages.

In a land titles jurisdiction, the first, second and subsequent mortgages are listed on the certificate of title as charges against the property and the order of priority is established by the order in which they have been registered. This priority between mortgage holders is established by the date of registration rather than by the date of creation of the mortgage. In other jurisdictions in Canada which require interest in land to be registered, the rights of mortgagees will also be determined by the time of registration of their interest at the appropriate land registry office. The prompt registration of mortgages is vital in both systems. The whole purpose of a registration system is to notify people who are acquiring interest in land of other claims against the property. Those other interests must be registered to be effective and a person who fails to properly register an interest in a property will lose priority to any person who acquires an interest in that property afterwards and does register it.

Types of Mortgages.

In fact there are several different types of mortgages in common use today. If the mortgage is used to finance some business activity, rather than the purchase of the property in conjunction with a promissory note, it is called a **collateral mortgage**. Mortgages are also available in some situations where the payments are actual guaranteed by some third party. This is an **insured mortgage**.

There is some confusion about the term of a mortgage. People often refer to a 30- or 40-year mortgage and think that this is the term of the mortgage. In fact this is the **amortization period**, meaning that this is the period calculated for repayment. At a given interest rate and a given monthly payment, it would take that long to repay the loan. But the term of the loan, called the **mortgage term**, is much less, usually only for periods such as one, two, or five years. The mortgage agreement expires at the end of that term and the entire amount left owing on the mortgage becomes due. The mortgagor must negotiate a renewal of the mortgage, usually at a different interest rate. This can work to the advantage of either party depending on whether the interest rates have gone up or down. Some people use open-ended mortgages, wherein the mortgage continues and a varying rate of interest is charged fluctuating with changes in the banks' prime rate.

Remedies Upon Default

Regional Trust Co. v. Avco Financial Services Realty Ltd.[36]

Mr. and Mrs. Foster owned property on which they had a first and second mortgage. The first mortgage was to Regional Trust and the second was to Avco. They ran into financial difficulties and made arrangements with Avco to transfer their title to Avco in the form of a quitclaim deed. Avco made payments to Regional Trust for about a year and then defaulted. Regional Trust exercised their right to sell the property under the power of sale and then sought payment of the deficiency of $6500 from Avco.

This action was brought to determine whether the second mortgagee, Avco, was required to pay a deficiency in these circumstances. The court held that they were. When they had assumed title to the property, they had also assumed the obligations. They stepped into the shoes of the Fosters and when the property was sold for less than what was owing, Avco was required to pay the difference.

This case illustrates the nature of first and second mortgages. The Fosters mortgaged their property; it became security for the loan from Regional. They retained the right to redeem the property. This they mortgaged to Avco. But Avco's position as second mortgagee is precarious, and they have to be prepared in the event of default to pay out the first mortgage. Unfortunately for all parties, the market fell at this time and the value of the property wasn't enough to cover the amounts owing. Likely this wasn't apparent to Avco when they obtained the quitclaim deed and attempted to continue making payments. Had the market rebounded and the value of the property increased, Avco would have taken advantage of any such increase making a windfall profit, but since it continued to decline, it became apparent to Avco that it wasn't worth it to hold onto the property, and they allowed Regional Trust Company to exercise their power of sale. Because they had obtained title from the Fosters, however, they were now responsible for any shortfall, because rather than foreclosing and taking title to the property Regional exercised their power of sale under the mortgage contract, retaining the right to demand any deficiency from the sale from the title holder, which was now Avco.

Had the Fosters retained title and Avco remained in their position as second mortgagee, Avco would still have received nothing when Regional exercised their power of sale, but as a creditor they also would not have owed anything. Only the

36. *Regional Trust Co. v. Avco Financial Services Realty Ltd.* (1984) 45 O.R. (2d) 89 (Ont. H. Ct.).

Fosters would have been liable to pay any deficit. But by taking title from the Fosters, Avco also assumed their obligations.

Bank of Montreal v. J.R. Lakusta Holdings Ltd.[37]

A similar result was reached in Alberta in the case against J.R. Lakusta Holdings Ltd. Lakusta was the mortgagee under a second mortgage registered against lands owned by Potter. Potter defaulted on both the first mortgage (granted to the Bank of Montreal) and the second mortgage held by Lakusta. Potter then went into bankruptcy. The plaintiff bank sued Potter upon its mortgage. Lakusta initially decided to protect its investment by taking title to the property, which it bought from the Trustee in Bankruptcy for $500.

Lakusta signed the transfer documents, but never attended to registering them. Someone else did so without its knowledge. When Lakusta was told it would cost another $3000 to bring the first mortgage into good standing, Lakusta refused to pay. It "walked away from the deal." Later the plaintiff bank secured a **Rice Order** in the mortgage foreclosure action on the first mortgage. Now the bank was seeking a deficiency judgment against Lakusta as transferee of the title and registered owner.

The court held that the contract between Lakusta and the Trustee in Bankruptcy was a "done-deal" and Lakusta was the owner regardless of whether it registered the transfer or not. As transferee it could not evade the obligations created by section 62(1) of the Alberta *Land Titles Act*: "That the transferee will pay the principal money, interest, annuity or rent charge secured by the mortgage or encumbrance. . . ."

Accordingly, a deficiency judgment was awarded against Lakusta.

These cases not only illustrate the nature and distinctions between first and second mortgages and the rights associated with exercising a power of sale, but also graphically illustrate the danger associated with someone in the second or third mortgagee position.

The process of foreclosure is just one of the remedies available to the mortgagee when the mortgagor has failed to live up to the terms of the mortgage agreement. A mortgage is a form of **security**, and as such the lender is entitled to become the owner of the secured property following default. But mortgages are also contracts that contain covenants or **promises to pay**. These contractual obligations, if defaulted on, enable the lender to sue. It is this dual nature of mortgages that makes legal actions following their breach so unique and interesting.

Suing on the Covenant in Alberta.

As with other types of contracts involving security, a mortgage agreement contains a covenant to repay the amount borrowed; the creditor has the option to ignore the security and simply sue on that promise of repayment. This right to sue on the personal covenant is available in most common law jurisdictions, but the Social Credit government set Alberta apart by amending the *Judicature Act* in 1939.[38] These changes prevented any action on the covenant to pay contained in a

---

37. *Bank of Montreal v. J.R. Lakusta Holdings Ltd.* (1995) 35 Alta. L.R. (3d) 161 (Q.B.).

38. *Judicature Act Amendment Act*, S.A. (1939) c. 85 s. 2.

mortgage. Through this controversial and bold move, the government restricted mortgagee's rights to recovery of the land itself. The amendments also required the land to be advertised for sale by the court and only if not so sold could a final order of foreclosure be granted.

These 1939 protections enabled mortgagors, who could no longer afford their regular mortgage payments, to simply walk away from those properties. Deficiency judgments (judgments for the difference between the amount owing under the mortgage and the value of the property) can be substantial, especially when property prices are falling. After 1939, such deficiency judgments could no longer be obtained in Alberta.

This changed when, in 1964, the government further amended the *Judicature Act*,[39] allowing actions on the covenant where the mortgagor was a corporation. Further, the section prescribing the redemption periods was declared not to apply to corporations. Redemption periods had been set at one year for farm land and six months for other lands (but these periods could be extended on application by the mortgagor, or decreased if, for example, the lands had been abandoned). If a corporation was the mortgagor, the mortgagee could seek a final order of foreclosure or order for sale without having to give the mortgagor time to attempt to redeem the mortgage. This expedited foreclosure actions against corporate mortgagors significantly.

In the 1980s, Alberta's economy slid into a recession. Property values declined dramatically. Mortgagors started to abandon their properties in unheard-of numbers because in Alberta mortgagees were "restricted to the land." Since judgments on the covenants were unavailable against individuals, many whose property values dropped below the amount owing on their mortgages simply abandoned their properties. "Dollar dealers" then arrived on the scene. These dealers would offer to assume the mortgages and take title to the property for a nominal sum. By selling to a dollar dealer, a mortgagor could "walk away" from his property and avoid the damage to his credit rating that a foreclosure action might create. The dollar dealers would assume ownership but make no payments on the mortgages, for the only remedies available to the mortgagees was to foreclose and take the property. The dealers knew this process would take months, and in the interim they profited, generally by renting out the property.

Over the years, the federal government had enacted several versions of the *National Housing Act*,[40] which enabled financial institutions to extend more credit to potential mortgagors. To facilitate home ownership and residential construction, high-ratio mortgages, insured by the Canada Mortgage and Housing Corporation (C.M.H.C.), were made available to the public.

The combination of these factors—actions on covenants being prohibited except against corporate mortgagors, the granting of high-ratio mortgages with as little as a 5% or 10% initial investment, and the collapse of Alberta's real estate market—all contributed to a flurry of foreclosures in the province in the 1980s. Throughout it all, Alberta continued to prohibit actions on the personal covenant to pay. But the provincial legislation could not limit the rights of mortgagees under mortgages created pursuant to the *National Housing Act*. Accordingly, deficiency judgments could be obtained if the mortgage was an N.H.A. mortgage or the mortgagor was a corporation.

---

39. *An Act to Amend the Judicature Act*, S.A. (1964) c. 40 s. 4.

40. *National Housing Act*, S.C. 1944 c. 46; *National Housing Act*, R.S.C. 1952 c. 188; *National Housing Act*, R.S.C. 1985 c. N-11.

Later amendments to the *Law of Property Act* [41] clarified that if a person assumed a mortgage initially granted by a corporation, the protection against actions on the covenant to pay could still be available. Persons who assumed corporate mortgages could still benefit from this protection if the subject lands were being used as a residence by the mortgagor or a member of his family. If the lands were farm lands, and they were being used for bona fide farming operations by the mortgagor or member of his family, the protection likewise applied.[42] Amendments to the *Law of Property Act* were also made to enable mortgagees to proceed quickly against "dollar dealers" and others who assumed mortgages that were in default (or went into default shortly after assumption).

As a result, actions on the covenant to pay and deficiency judgments are only available against corporate mortgagors, against those who assume corporation mortgages and do not qualify for protection (because the land is not residential/farm land being used for residential/farming operations by the mortgagor or by his family) and against mortgages made under the *National Housing Act*, R.S.C. 1952 c. 188 or the *National Housing Act*, R.S.C. 1970 c. N-10.

The Foreclosure Process in Alberta.

Foreclosure actions are time consuming. If there is no equity and the mortgagor is a corporation (or the redemption period is otherwise waived), the action may take half a year to resolve. With residential property owned by an individual, foreclosures may take over one year to conclude; farm land takes even longer to foreclose upon.

Following default, the mortgagee commences the action by Statement of Claim. Time to defend is allowed, but generally no defence is filed. The next step is to apply for an Order Nisi/Order for Sale. At this application, the redemption period is set. Applications to extend the redemption period may further delay the process.

At the end of the redemption period, the property is advertised for sale. Tenders are received and reviewed by the Court. If no tenders exceed the amount owing under the mortgage, the mortgagee may ask for an order accepting its proposal to buy the land at market value. (This is commonly called a Rice Order, so named after the *Trusts & Guar. Co. v. Rice* case [43] where the process was approved.) The mortgagee may still be able to sue on the covenant to pay, for the land has been "sold" and not foreclosed. A deficiency judgment may be available.

If the property's value exceeds the indebtedness, a Final Order for Foreclosure may be sought. Alternatively, if tenders are received that exceed the indebtedness, an Order Confirming Sale to the highest bidder may be made.

As is evident, there is no sense in incurring the legal expense of court action if the defaulting mortgagor can be persuaded to surrender the property, participate in a joint sale, or otherwise rehabilitate her position by, for example, accepting a different repayment schedule. The adversarial process described above is time consuming, especially with an uncooperative mortgagor, and when payments are not being made, the amount owing, including interest, can quickly grow. When this happens, most creditors will only partially recover what they are owed and the mortgagor will get nothing. Where default does take place, an acceleration clause (usually included in mortgages) provides that the entire indebtedness becomes

---

41. *Real Property Statutes Amendment Act*, 1983 (No.2), S.A. 1983 c. 97; *Law of Property Amendment Act*, S.A (1984) c. 24.

42. *Law of Property Act*, R.S.A. (1980) c. L-8 ss. 43 (1.1)(3), 43.1 and 43.3.

43. *Trusts & Guar. Co. v. Rice*, 20 Alta. L.R. 444 (Alta. A.D).

immediately due and payable. If the mortgagor fails to promptly repay any arrears and costs and reinstate the mortgage, the mortgagee can proceed with the foreclosure action.

Default by the Mortgagor.

In addition to the requirement that the mortgagee make the specified payments, including principal and interest as set out in the agreement, the mortgagor has other obligations. Mortgage contracts usually include an obligation on the mortgagor to insure the property. A considerable amount of the value on any property is often tied up in the buildings attached to it which are susceptible to damage or destruction. To protect the value of the security for the mortgagee, the mortgagor must take out insurance so that there is adequate compensation to ensure repayment of the mortgage if the property is damaged.

Similarly, the mortgagor usually has an obligation in the mortgage agreement to pay property taxes. Legislation gives municipal governments the right to seize property and sell it to pay back taxes when taxes are not paid. This would defeat the security of the mortgagee, so the mortgagee can insist that such tax payments be made, by requiring either that the mortgagor make the payments to the mortgagee and the mortgagee pay the taxes, or that the mortgagor produce proof that the taxes have been paid. Similar provisions require the mortgagor to keep any buildings on the property in good repair as well as refraining from committing waste (doing anything to the land or buildings to reduce their value). When second or third mortgages are involved, a provision will also be included making the failure to pay a prior mortgage a default as well. Although the most common method of breaching a mortgage agreement is failure to make the appropriate payments to the mortgagee, a breach of any of these terms will constitute default and entitle the mortgagee to seek a remedy.

Possession.

The mortgagee also has the right to ask the court for an order giving him possession of the property upon default of payment. The problem with this course of action is that any profits earned through the property must be accounted for and given to the mortgagor upon redemption. Nor is the mortgagee entitled to compensation for any expenses incurred in looking after the property, such as the cost of a caretaker. If any damage is done to the property while the mortgagee is in possession, the mortgagee is responsible to compensate the mortgagor upon redemption. The mortgagee will generally not seek an order of possession of the property if it appears that redemption is likely because of the responsibilities involved. Only where the property has been abandoned or is in danger of deterioration for some other reason, will this course of action be used.

Discharge of Mortgage.

Where all payments have been properly made and no default has taken place, the mortgagor is entitled to have that mortgage discharged. A discharge transferring the property to the mortgagor is filed at the appropriate land registry providing notice that the legal title has been reconveyed and the mortgagee no longer has any interest in the property. In a land titles system, a notice of discharge is filed at the land registry and the mortgage charge is removed. Depending on the terms of the mortgage agreement, the mortgagor may have the right to pay off the mortgage or a portion of it prior the expiration of the mortgage term. Such payments can reduce the payment period, significantly reducing the amount paid. In many cases, under the terms of the agreement the mortgagor will have to pay an additional amount to compensate the mortgagee for the interest that will not be earned because of the early payment. This is particularly true if the interest rates have gone down and the mortgagee will have to reinvest that money at a rate lower than would have been earned had the mortgage continued. This may be an important consideration when the propery is to be sold and the purchaser will not be assuming the mortgage.

SUMMARY

Real property is land and things attached to it. The right to exclusive use of the land is called an estate and the fee simple estate is comparable to complete ownership of the land. The right to use the land for life is a life estate and, for a specific period, a leasehold estate. Easements, restrictive covenants and, in some cases, licenses, constitute lesser interests in land. When property is held jointly and one of the parties dies, the other takes the whole property by right of survivorship. In a tenancy in common, however, the separate interests remain apart even with death. The land registry systems provide a depository of documents that may affect the title and interested parties must search those documents to determine the state of the title. The land titles system of registration goes further. Where in use, the government provides a certificate of title that is conclusive proof of the interests affecting the title of the land.

Leasehold estates involve landlord and tenant relationships. Commercial tenancies, although provincial statutes are usually in place, are governed primarily by the common law with the rights of the parties set out in the lease. Residential tenancies, however, have been significantly modified by statute. Changes include the notice that must be given by the landlord to increase rent or terminate a lease as well as the obligations of the parties to repair or pay security deposits. Rent controls are in place in some jurisdictions.

In some jurisdictions, a mortgage involves the title to the property being transferred to a creditor/mortgagee as security for a loan. In Alberta, a mortgage does not transfer title; it is simply an encumbrance registerable against title. The debtor/mortgagor retains a right to redeem the property. In the event of default, the creditor seeks a foreclosure order which forecloses or ends the mortgagor's right to redeem. Foreclosure actions are time consuming and costly. In Alberta, the mortgagee may be restricted "to the land," as judgments on the covenant to pay may not be available.

QUESTIONS

1. What does the purchaser get when he or she buys a house?

2. Distinguish between personal and real property.

3. What is meant by a fee simple estate in land?

4. Explain the rights and obligations of reversion and remainder when discussing a life estate.

5. Explain and contrast life estates and leasehold estates.

6. What is meant by an easement? Give examples and explain why an easement is called a lesser interest in land.

7. Explain the significance of a dominant and servient tenement when dealing with easements.

8. What is meant by a restrictive covenant? Under what circumstances will such a covenant be binding on subsequent landowners? How does this relate to a building scheme?

9. Contrast a tenancy in common with a joint tenancy and indicate how one can be changed to another. Why is the distinction important?

10. How can failure to properly register a mortgage or deed affect the initial parties to an instrument in a land titles jurisdiction? What happens when an innocent third party becomes involved?

11. How is a leasehold right different from the rights of a resident created under a license agreement?

12. Under what circumstances must a leasehold interest be evidenced in writing? Why?

13. What is a periodic tenancy? How does it compare to an ordinary lease arrangement? What special problems come into play with periodic tenancies which are not present with term leases?

14. Explain what is meant by a landlord's obligation to ensure a tenant's "quiet enjoyment."

15. What is meant by mortgage, equity of redemption and foreclosure? Distinguish between the mortgagor and mortgagee.

16. Compare the terms "equity of redemption" and "equity in property."

17. What is mortgaged when a second or third mortgage is created? Explain how the risk of a second or third mortgagee is greater than that of the first mortgagee.

18. How is the registration of mortgages handled differently under a land titles system of land registry as opposed to the registration system in place in the rest of Canada? Why is the time of registration of a mortgage significant in all jurisdictions in Canada?

CASES

1. National Trust Co. v. Chriskim Holdings Inc.

A bank and a restaurant were located on adjoining properties. The company operating the restaurant wanted to expand by extending the restaurant into a lane that it thought it owned but which in fact was owned by the bank. The restaurant only had a right of way across it. Unwittingly, the owners of the restaurant started the expansion but soon discovered their mistake. They sent a letter to the bank offering to pay an annual rental of $1 per foot. When the bank did not accept this offer, instead of stopping, they continued with the construction. The bank sued. The restaurant countersued; it seems a mistake had been made when the bank was built and it encroached slightly onto the property owned by the restaurant. The restaurant had been leasing the property since 1983 and had purchased it in 1987. Before this time, however, the former owner had used that right of way since 1952. The bank building had been at its location since 1967.

Explain the obligations and rights of the parties to each other in these circumstances and the arguments available to each in defending their positions. Would your answer be any different if this had taken place in a land titles jurisdiction?

2. Re Ramsay and Heselmann

The appellant was the owner of a property consisting of 12 furnished rooms, one of which was rented to the respondent. Rent was paid weekly. The respondent failed to make proper payments and the appellant seized her clothing and personal effects as security for the non-payment of rent. (The *Innkeepers' Act*, R.S.A. (1980) c. I-4 allows an innkeeper or boardinghouse-keeper to seize goods in this way. The *Residential Tenancies Act*, R.S.A. (1980) c. R-15.3 does not allow a landlord a similar right.)

The respondent has brought this action, applying for a declaration that her goods and personal effects have been wrongfully seized. Explain the arguments on both sides and the likely outcome of the case.

3. North Bay TV & Audio Ltd. v. Nova Electronics Ltd. et al.

North Bay TV is the landlord and Nova is the tenant operating a store selling audio and electronic equipment. They entered into a five-year lease agreement in 1981. In 1982 business started to go bad for Nova. They were late paying their rent in April and only paid partial rent in May and June. They failed to pay their rent in July altogether or make even partial payment for their share of the utility services supplied to the building. This caused North Bay's representative, Mr. Stanfall, to call Nova about these lapses. Mr. Smith and Mr. Becock were the principals involved in Nova. Becock informed Smith that he understood the landlord was intending to close the premises down and he suggested to Smith that they remove as much inventory as possible that evening, which they proceeded to do. They removed three station wagon loads of electronic goods from the store. While they were doing this Mr. Stanfall arrived, confronted them and asked what they were doing. The tenants told him they were moving out of the premises. When the tenants had left, Mr. Stanfall closed the shop door with a sign saying that the store had been closed by landlord, and anyone taking anything from the premises without permission of the landlord would be prosecuted. The next morning they changed the locks.

Explain the rights and remedies available to each party. Who has terminated the lease? Who is entitled to any goods still on the premises? How would your answer be affected if you understood that several months later the landlord re-let the premises at a higher rent than they were receiving from Nova?

4. The Toronto-Dominion Bank v. Faulkner et al.

Mr. Faulkner, a lawyer, owned property in the town of Goldbourn which he mortgaged to the Toronto-Dominion Bank as security for a loan of $50 000. Two years later Faulkner physically moved the house from this location to a piece of property in another town (West Carlton) which was owned by his wife.

Faulkner and his wife mortgaged the second property with its relocated house to Crown Trust Company for $55 000. The problem here is to determine which of the two mortgagees is entitled to priority in relation to the house. Explain the legal position of the parties and the arguments to support the parties' claims.

5. Hermanson v. Martin et al.

The plaintiff and her husband jointly owned the matrimonial home. The plaintiff moved away after their divorce and her husband sold the house to the defendant, Martin. To do this, he used a female accomplice to forge his former wife's signature on the transfer. Martin had no knowledge of this forgery. The transfer was appropriately registered and only then did the ex-wife find out about the fraud. Explain the courses of action available to her and any arguments that can be raised on either side. Where might she turn for compensation for any loss she incurs? These events happened in a land titles jurisdiction. Would your answer be different if this problem had arisen in a standard registration jurisdiction?

6. Sterne v. Victoria & Grey Trust Co.

Mr. Sterne owned a hobby farm with a first mortgage held by Victoria & Gray Trust. Sterne was unable to make payments when they came due. The mortgagee commenced sale proceedings under their power of sale as set out in the mortgage. They obtained two appraisals, one for $190 000 and the other for $195 000. The mortgagee advertised the property, received an offer of $185 000 and sold it for that price. During this time Mr. Sterne had listed the property and had received an offer for $210 000, but the offer had conditions and the closing date was several months away, so the mortgagee went ahead with their deal for $185 000.

Explain the rights of the parties in this circumstance. Would your answer be any different if you learned that at the time of the sale the mortgagee was aware of other appraisals which placed the value of the property as high as $240 000 and also that the property was listed only as "work" property not as a hobby farm and then only in the local newspapers?

LEGISLATION

Alberta

Condominium Property Act, R.S.A. (1980) c. C-22
Dower Act, R.S.A. (1980) c. D-38
Family Relief Act, R.S.A. (1980) c. F-2
Land Titles Act, R.S.A. (1980) c. L-5
Landlord's Rights on Bankruptcy Act, R.S.A. (1980) c. L-7
Law of Property Act, R.S.A. (1980) c. L-8
Mobile Home Sites Tenancies Act, S.A. (1982) c. M-18.5
Real Estate Act, S.A. (1995) c. R-4.5
Residential Tenancies Act, R.S.A. (1980) c. R-15.3
Statute of Frauds, 1677 (29 Car. 2) c. 3

WEBLINKS

Real Estate Institute of Canada
www.reic.ca/

Canadian Real Estate Association
realtors.mls.ca/crea/

Alberta *Condominium Property Act*
www.gov.ab.ca/qp/ascii/acts/C22.txt

Alberta *Condominium Property Act Amendment 1996* (awaiting proclamation)
www.gov.ab.ca/qp/ascii/acts/96/CH12.txt

Canada Mortgage and Housing Corporation
www.cmhc-schl.gc.ca/

Alberta Municipal Affairs: Land Titles Services
www.gov.ab.ca/~ma/reg/lt/ltmain.htm

Alberta Municipal Affairs: The *Residential Tenancy Act* - Information for Landlords and Tenants
www.gov.ab.ca/~ma/hca/html/rta.htm

Alberta Real Estate Foundation
www.extension.ualberta.ca/~sthomas/aref/

REFERENCES FOR PART 6

DiCastri, Victor. *The Law of Vendor and Purchaser: The Law and Practice Relating to Contracts for Sale of Land.* 3rd ed. Toronto: Carswell, 1988.

McGill University Faculty of Law. *Making Business Sense of Intellectual Property.* Montreal: Faculty of Law, McGill University, 1996.

NGL Nordicity Group Ltd. Canada, for Industry Canada. *Study on New Media and Copyright: Final Report Prepared for Industry Canada.* New Media, 1994.

Price, Francis C.R. and Trussler, Marguerite. *Mortgage Actions in Alberta.* Calgary: Carswell, 1985.

Racicet, Michael. "The Cyberspace Is Not a 'No Law Land': A Study of the Issues of Liability for Content Circulating on the Internet." Ottawa: Industry Canada, 1997.

Copyright and Trademarks

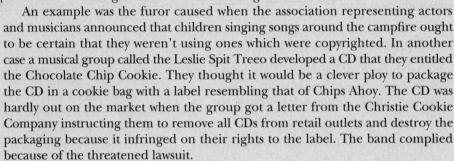

"Some products have become so familiar, they are more like pop culture than merchandise." The names, logos, sounds and colours associated with such products are often worth more than the products themselves and so companies are going to great lengths to protect their trademarks. The first step after identifying a unique feature or image of a product is to register it, and in the past few decades the office of trademarks has seen an incredible increase in business. Companies are impelled to discover and take action against anyone who in any way infringes on their trademark rights.

An example was the furor caused when the association representing actors and musicians announced that children singing songs around the campfire ought to be certain that they weren't using ones which were copyrighted. In another case a musical group called the Leslie Spit Treeo developed a CD that they entitled the Chocolate Chip Cookie. They thought it would be a clever ploy to package the CD in a cookie bag with a label resembling that of Chips Ahoy. The CD was hardly out on the market when the group got a letter from the Christie Cookie Company instructing them to remove all CDs from retail outlets and destroy the packaging because it infringed on their rights to the label. The band complied because of the threatened lawsuit.

Another artist decided to challenge the trademark principle when he was accused of infringing on the rights of the owners of the Rock and Roll Hall of Fame. He had taken a photograph of the Hall of Fame's pyramid-shaped glass building and published it as a poster. He thinks that such restrictions infringe on his rights as an artist. A unique tree on the famous Pebble Beach Golf Course in California has also been protected by copyright, preventing people using their photographs of it for commercial purposes.

Source: "Copyright," *Undercurrents*, Show Number 7; telecast date November 15, 1996. Running time: 7:40.

DISCUSSION QUESTIONS

1. Should Harley-Davidson be entitled to copyright the sound of its engine? Or should Pepsi have the right to copyright the shade of blue it uses on its labels?

2. Should the companies in question 1 be required to show that they will suffer some special loss in order to stop another from using the same sound or colour?

3. What impact does this have on artists, and are such restrictions fair?

4. Has this protection been extended too far?

Dealing with Government

One of the characteristics of our modern society is the ever-expanding role of government within it. This involvement is even more extensive where business activities are concerned. The first part of the chapter examines laws relating to the environment and the relatively recent statutes that have imposed very stringent controls and requirements on businesses engaged in activities that affect it. The environmental statutes, government departments and enforcement bodies that businesses have to deal with are used primarily as an example of the expanding regulatory environment that businesses must function within.

  The increasing interference of government in our affairs and the legal rights and recourses available to business and non-business people alike when government in the form of bureaucrats, lawmakers or enforcement bodies such as the police and others overstep their authority or otherwise abuse their positions is the focus of this chapter. The rest of Chapter 16 sets out limitations on government power and the avenues of recourse that may be available when individuals. find themselves the victims of such improper use of governmental power.

Photo by Grant Black/
First Light.

Environmental Law and the Regulation of Canadian Business

OBJECTIVES OF THE CHAPTER

- To describe the source and nature of government powers
- To examine environmental law in place at the provincial and federal levels
- To identify the issues associated with the protection of the environment
- To outline the nature of the competing interests of the economy and the protection of the environment
- To outline the role of the courts in interpreting statutes
- To examine the government regulatory activities of taxation and licensing, securities and environmental control
- To explain the remedies available when administrative bodies abuse their powers
- To discuss methods used by legislatures to restrict judicial interpretation

The Bata shoe organization is a large company operating several different factories and facilities in southern Ontario. At one of these locations, inspectors from the Ministry of the Environment discovered metal drums leaking industrial waste into the soil. Tests were performed and it was discovered that the ground water had been contaminated. Despite the fact that Bata had shown a willingness to cooperate on environmental matters and that members of the family had made significant contributions to cleaning up the environment, charges were laid against the company and also against the individual directors who were in charge of the sites where the contamination was discovered. The Ministry disposed of the offending material with the cooperation of the company and at company expense. Fines were imposed on the company as well as on the individual directors. These fines were reduced somewhat on appeal but the fines remained significant and had to be individually paid by the directors in question. In fact, when the company tried to reimburse the directors for the cost of the fines and legal expenses, the courts prohibited it from doing so.[1] On appeal the court held that the company did have the right to indemnify their directors for the fines they had to pay and what was expected to be an effective deterrent has become considerably less so.

1. *R. v. Bata Industries Limited* (1992) 70 C.C.C. (3d) 394.

Laws to protect the environment are significant and an important consideration in calculating the cost of doing business. As can be seen from this example, directors and officers of a corporation must carefully consider the risks and the potential costs associated with their positions. Some directors are extremely reluctant to serve on boards of corporations where they may experience such exposure. This chapter will discuss the power of government, its regulatory agencies and the rights of people who deal with them.

Environmental concerns have great impact on business

REGULATORY ROLE OF GOVERNMENT

The commercial and industrial progress of this century has been matched by the growth of government agencies to regulate it. In the last few decades the size of government has expanded at an astonishing rate, intruding into the lives of its citizens, especially in their business activities, in an unprecedented way. Businesses face increasingly stringent government restrictions and regulations, and while many of those intrusions are beneficial and justified, sometimes in the process government officials abuse their position or go beyond their authority. This chapter will begin with an examination of one of the areas in which government regulation has increased dramatically in recent years and then outline the recourses available to people when government or its agents have infringed on their rights.

As outlined in Chapter 1, government can be divided into three different functions: the judicial, the legislative and the executive branches. In the United States, care has been taken to keep these three branches separate and the lawmaking capacity of government is balanced between them. Canada followed the British example of parliamentary supremacy and so, except for the division of powers between the federal parliament and the provincial legislatures, parliamentary bodies are supreme in their assigned areas. Parliamentary supremacy has been modified to some extent by the *Charter of Rights and Freedoms* which limits what Parliament, the provincial legislatures and their representatives can do.

Government consists of executive branch, legislative branch and judicial branch

There is little difficulty in distinguishing the judicial branch of government (the courts) from the rest of government activity. However, the legislative branch and the executive branch have become somewhat blurred in Canada. Parliament is the principal lawmaking body, that is, it represents the legislative branch. From that assembly is drawn the prime minister (or premiers at the provincial level) and cabinet ministers. They are the executive branch—the managers of the country. They are responsible for the various ministries and departments, the employees of which perform the work of government. When people have dealings with government, it is almost always with the executive branch of government and the civil servants who make up its bureaucracy.

The executive branch is divided into categories on the basis of primary functions: for example, service agencies such as law enforcement, education, health and welfare; administrative departments which include revenue, taxation and the internal management of government systems; and regulatory bodies concerned with such matters as the environment, product safety, employment and human rights.

There are many areas in which governments exert control over business, but regulations designed to protect the environment are typical of governmental involvement and an important and growing area of concern for business people. We will begin our look at government regulation from that perspective.

THE PROTECTION OF THE ENVIRONMENT

Environmental concerns vast problem

Our society and the natural world are interdependent in a way that historically has not been recognized in either our economic system or our laws. The production of wealth is the underlying objective of the business world (which the economic system facilitates) and wealth is produced to a large extent through the consumption of natural resources. In the wake of economic progress, forests are stripped, fish stocks are depleted, minerals, oil and gas reserves are exhausted, and great scars are left on the earth in the process. Species of animal life are decimated as they are either directly consumed or their environment is destroyed around them. The byproducts of this production in the form of waste materials are discharged into the atmosphere, into the seas and onto the lands, further degrading the environment. Industries such as mining, fishing, forestry, farming, construction, transportation and manufacturing have all greatly contributed to Canada's environmental problems.

The economic structures that form the basis of business and industry have traditionally not factored in these environmental costs. The range of problems contributing to the environmental crises is vast. From nuclear disasters to automobile emissions, from the disposal of chemical wastes to domestic sewage and from the depletion of the ozone layer to the depletion of the soil—all have serious consequences for the environment. Only recently have we been forced to consider the depletion of the environment as one of the important factors in the economic equation.

The law has been even slower to react to these modern realities; it has only been in the last few years that our legislators have considered it necessary to create statutes which introduce some balance into the system. Such statutes have been enacted as the result of public pressure and the urgency of the problems, and sometimes fail to ensure the necessary balance between the production of wealth and the preservation of the environment. Most of the statutes are remedial in nature and are becoming increasingly stringent as the extent of the damage that has already been done to the environment is realized.

Common Law

Common law protection

The rights of individuals to have property and person protected from pollution and destruction have been recognized for centuries in common law. Through such judge-made law, people who live near rivers are entitled to have the water come to them in undiminished quantity and quality, except for limited domestic usage such as washing, drinking and normal sewage disposal. Such entitlements are called

• riparian rights

riparian rights. These rights, however, can be overridden by a government permit that allows for the withdrawal of large quantities of water from the system for irrigation or industrial use and also for the discharge of other waste materials into a stream or river.

• nuisance

Under tort law and specifically the tort of "private nuisance," people who have adjoining properties have the right not to have their enjoyment and use of their property unreasonably interfered with by their neighbours. Thus, if a person or industry carries on a polluting activity such as burning or operating a smelter which pumps toxic chemicals into the atmosphere or effluent into the land or waterways, the injured neighbour can bring an action for private nuisance against the polluting party. "Public nuisance" has occasionally been used to support actions against those who pollute public waterways and the air. Normally, only the government is able to bring an action for public nuisance but if an individual can show that she was

COMMON LAW RIGHTS TO WATER

Mr. Steadman had a spring on his property feeding a small reservoir from which he took mainly domestic water. The Erickson Gold Mining Company built a road on adjacent property and in the process silted the water supply. Even after some corrective action was taken, the water remained unusable and Steadman had to truck water in. He sued for nuisance. The court said that although the Crown owned the water, Steadman had a right to the use of it, that Erickson's conduct amounted to a nuisance and that they were liable for their interference. This is an example of common law control of environmental interference. Steadman's right to use the water is said to be a riparian right and his remedy in nuisance illustrates the effectiveness of this common law tort action.

Steadman v. Erickson Gold Mining Corp., 43 D.L.R. (4th) 712 (British Columbia Supreme Court)

harmed to a greater extent than other members of the general public, she may be able to bring a personal action and seek a remedy such as monetary compensation or an injunction to stop the activity. While private nuisance can be effective in protecting individual rights, public nuisance is largely ineffectual as a method of protecting either community or individuals from environmental contamination.

The torts of negligence and trespass can also be used to enforce a person's right not to be interfered with in this way by others, including municipal, provincial and federal government agencies which are to some extent liable for their wrongful conduct in tort law. One of the requirements of tort law generally is that some blameworthy conduct must be involved. That is, either the activity must be intentional or the person doing it must be careless or negligent. *Rylands v. Fletcher* established that in some special situations people who bring dangerous substances onto their property that escape are responsible for any damages that ensue, whether or not it is their fault that the substance escaped. Such dangerous substances include stored water and chemicals. These torts are an important source of legal rights for people wanting to take action against those interfering with their property or person through pollution. Chapter 2 is devoted to a more in-depth discussion of tort liability. Some modern statutes that are designed to control damage to the environment give individuals the right to sue privately for compensation for personal injuries suffered because of a violation of the statute. In effect, these statutes create a statutory tort, but this is only the case when the statute makes clear that it creates a personal right to seek a remedy. (See, for example, the Canadian *Environmental Protection Act*.)

Strict liability under *Rylands v. Fletcher*

Statutory Law

There are substantial limitations to the common law protection discussed above. An individual rather than the Crown must sue and in doing so, he or she must be able to show some personal damage that others have not suffered and must bear the costs in the process. Quebec's civil law contains similar rights to those embodied in our common law, with the same problems of costs and the difficulties associated with enforcement. Because of these inadequacies, the great bulk of the law intended to protect the environment is found in statutes of the federal and provincial governments. One of the main features of these statutes is that polluting activities are generally prohibited. Other provisions allow government to enforce the statutes whether or not individuals have been harmed.

R. v. Consolidated Maybrun Mines Ltd.[2]

Consolidated Maybrun operated a copper-gold mine in northwestern Ontario. Employees of the Ministry of Environment inspected the site about ten years after its shutdown and discovered the mine site had been completely abandoned. It had been vandalized, windows were broken, chemicals were strewn around, the mine shaft had filled with water, and oils contaminated with PCBs had leaked from several electrical transformers located in a generator building in a fenced-off area.

The Ministry officials wrote to the owners of the mine asking them to correct the situation, but they did nothing. They then served notice on the mine owners that they would be issuing an order in 15 days requiring them to take specific steps to clean up the property. The owners were given 15 days to make written submissions to the Ministry before the orders were made. The mine owners responded that the order was ridiculous and blamed the government for their problems. The Ministry then made the order on June 2, 1987. They also informed Consolidated Maybrun that they had the right to appeal the order by making written submissions, again within 15 days.

No appeal was made and the order was generally ignored. The Ministry stepped in, took the necessary steps to clean up the site, and laid charges against Consolidated Maybrun for failing to comply with the order which in the *Environmental Protection Act* is identified as an offense.

The case was quite complex, but for our purposes it is sufficient to note that the accused responded to the charges by saying that the order of the Director was unreasonable and that was the reason they didn't comply. At the trial level they were allowed to argue on the merits of whether it was a reasonable order or not. On appeal the court held that whether the order was reasonable didn't really matter, and they were required to respond to the order given by the Director under the *Act.* They had had other methods to deal with the merits of the charge. They could have appealed and challenged the decision, in effect gaining a new hearing. They didn't take advantage of this option but simply ignored the order. It was their failure to respond to the order that resulted in the charge and they were convicted.

This case is instructive because it illustrates not only the statutory liability of business people for long-forgotten operations, such as this old mine, but also the power of the Ministry officials given by the *Environmental Protection Act.* Such orders should not be ignored or lightly treated for the impact can be profound. From the point of view of dealing with these kinds of government agencies, it is important to understand that prompt action must be taken in response to such orders. It is important to take advantage of all remedies within the structure of the regulatory body involved—in this case the original right to make written submissions in response and once the order was given the right to make an appeal. It was failure to take advantage of those options and the accuseds' lack of willingness to treat these matters seriously that got them into trouble.

---

2. 133 D.L.R. (4th) 513 (Ontario Court of Appeal).

Jurisdiction.

A discussion of statutory law must be preceded by an examination of the level of government which has the constitutional jurisdiction to pass environmental laws. Essentially, forests, minerals and fresh water are all local matters and under the jurisdiction of provincial governments. The federal government has power only when the activity becomes international or interprovincial in scope, takes place on federal lands or coastal waters, or when an area specifically assigned to the federal government is involved, such as the military. Of course, the federal government can exercise a considerable amount of control by requiring that provincial environmental projects satisfy federal standards to qualify for federal funding. Furthermore, if the activity becomes a threat to society generally, the federal government can use its power under the *Criminal Code* to declare the activity a criminal offense.

Businesses may face federal and provincial regulation

Both federal and provincial regulatory authorities become involved when businesses initiate projects and activities that have environmental implications. Corporations must receive permits and licenses from various levels of government and must submit to environmental regulation. Federally incorporated corporations may face regulations in both jurisdictions. Provincial corporations engaged in activities that are local in nature deal only with provincial and to some extent municipal regulations. In fact, today there is movement towards considerable cooperation between the federal and provincial levels of government in environmental regulation. Hopefully in the future the various statutes having environmental impact will be consolidated and similar legislation will be put in place at both the federal and provincial levels so that one consistent system will prevail in Canada. Because this is not yet the case, we will now look at some of the environmental legislation that is characteristic of each jurisdiction.

Provincial Legislation.

All provinces have some form of environmental legislation. The standard type of legislation is a statute creating a ministry or government department designed to grant permits and establish standardized codes for the use of natural resources and the elimination of waste products. These departments have inspectors who enforce the standards and assess penalties for violations. In some cases, the rules and regulations are found in general environmental statutes such as the federal *Environmental Protection Act*, or Alberta's *Environmental Protection and Enhancement Act*. Other provinces have opted to control specific activities under specific statutes, such as by monitoring air pollution under a *Clean Air Act*.

Alberta's *Environmental Protection and Enhancement Act*[3] replaced eight acts (including the *Clean Air Act*, *Clean Water Act* and *Hazardous Chemicals Act*), amended the *Department of the Environment Act*, and streamlined environmental regulation under one framework. Project proponents no longer have to seek numerous separate approvals under different acts. One comprehensive application is now submitted to Alberta Environmental Protection. A designated director then coordinates the preparation of a single integrated approval for the project.

The *Act* establishes a legislated **environmental assessment process** for Alberta. This process ensures that economic development occurs in an environmentally responsible manner. Furthermore, the public is given notice of projects and opportunities for participation in the approval process. Mandatory projects, such as

3. *Environmental Protection and Enhancement Act*, S.A. (1992) c. E-13.3.

pulp mills and oil refineries, are always subject to the environmental assessment process. Other projects may be exempt from the process, as prescribed by the regulations accompanying the *Act*.

Projects. For mandatory projects, an **Environmental Impact Assessment** (EIA) report is automatically required. For other projects, the proposal is screened and the public is notified that the project is being screened. The screening report is made available to the public and the Director later decides if an EIA report is required.

The EIA report generally must include such things as a description of the potential positive and negative impacts to the environment and to the community's social, economic and cultural well-being. Plans for responding to potential emergencies are to be spelled out. Human health issues are to be identified. The EIA report is submitted before the Energy Resources Conservation Board or Natural Resources Conservation Board depending on which board reviews the project.

Activities. The *Act* also lists a broad schedule of activities that could adversely impact the environment, ranging from processing natural gas to drilling a water well. The regulations define which activities require an **approval**. To secure an approval, the proponent files a detailed application with Alberta Environmental Protection. Where an EIA report is also required for the project, the Director reviewing the application must be satisfied that the environmental assessment process has been completed and the results of any related public hearings are taken into consideration. The Director ultimately decides whether to issue an approval. If approval is refused, an appeal to the Environmental Appeal Board is available. Public involvement is a part of the approval process as well. The public is notified when proposals are submitted. Anyone affected by a proposed project may submit a written statement of concern to the Director. If the Director still grants approval, those who submitted statements of concern may appeal to the Environmental Appeal Board.

Approvals include any requirements or conditions that must be followed. A certificate of variance should be obtained by the approval holder if any conditions cannot be satisfied. To ensure compliance with the terms of an approval, the approval holder may be required to provide financial security, which can later be used to remedy any problems that arise.

Part 4 of the *Act* deals specifically with **controlled releases of substances** into the environment, be it through a spill, discharge, leak or other method of release. If an unauthorized release occurs or is suspected, an Environmental Protection Order (EPO) may be issued by the Director. Such orders allow investigation of the situation, monitoring the release or ensuring action is taken to clean up the problem. The *Act* now imposes a duty to report releases of substances so as to ensure prompt control and clean up. Enforcement action may be taken if the *Act* is contravened.

A thorny issue is who should be responsible for cleaning up abandoned sites or sites that have been foreclosed upon. The broad definition of who may be responsible gives the Director flexibility in dealing with the specifics of each site. The potential liability for cleaning up contaminated sites has caused several lenders to reconsider foreclosure as a remedy. Now environmental audits are done by lenders before taking land as security for a loan.

Those responsible for contaminated sites can voluntarily prepare remedial action plans and enter an agreement with the Director for carrying them out. In this manner, individuals may avoid having an EPO imposed. Such orders may be burdensome and may require the party responsible for the site to bear all or part of the costs of the clean up, as in the *Consolidated Maybrun Mines* case described above.

Conservation and reclamation of land are the focus of Part 5. Operators are required to undertake conservation measures during construction and operation of projects and to reclaim the land when the project is finished. Conservation and reclamation are not considered complete until an inspector examines the site and issues a **reclamation certificate**. Larger scale projects (such as a coal mine or gravel pit) require both approval and reclamation certificates; smaller scale activities (like an oil well site) do not require approvals. Nonetheless, a reclamation certificate at the conclusion of the project is required, thus ensuring that operating requirements are met. If there are deficiencies, then an EPO, requiring further work to be done, may be issued. Once again, provision of financial security may be required so that the costs of reclamation are paid up front should there be any failure to meet the requirements.

Protecting and conserving Alberta's groundwater by ensuring that water wells are drilled properly and safely is the aim of Part 6. Qualifications for drillers are set, as are standards for drilling, so as to protect the water supply from contamination. Part 7 deals with protecting the quality of drinking water by ensuring that water distribution systems and water treatment plants are operated properly. Concentrations of substances in drinking water are regulated. An EPO can be issued if the water is unfit for human use. These orders can direct the parties responsible to make adjustments to the waterworks system.

The *Act* (Part 8) also outlines measures to ensure that **pesticides and hazardous substances** are handled, used and disposed of safely. Part 9 focuses on **waste**, its minimization and management, and on recycling. The *Act* allows for regulations aimed at reducing and controlling packaging and encouraging reuse and recycling. As to waste management, there are prohibitions against improper disposal of waste (garbage, paper, even old vehicles) and sites deemed unsightly may have to be cleaned up under EPOs. The *Act* also requires that hazardous wastes be tracked from their origins to their final destinations by a party who has obtained an identification number.

Enforcement is the subject matter of Part 10. Reports from the public may cause an investigation to be launched. If contraventions of the *Act*, an EPO or approval are discovered, an Enforcement Order may be issued. These orders can require a shutdown, require the activity to be stopped and the problem fixed, or may require remedial action. Failure to comply with an Enforcement Order is likewise a contravention that may lead to prosecution. The Minister may apply for a court order directing compliance with the Enforcement Order. If necessary, the government may undertake the required work and recover the costs from the party responsible.

Injunctions are available under the *Act*. Either the Director or someone who fears damage from a contravention can apply for such a court order stopping a particular activity. The *Act* also creates a statutory cause of action for any person suffering loss or damage as a consequence of a contravention. The plaintiff can sue for and recover an amount equaling the loss or damage.

The penalty provisions vary. A maximum penalty of $1 million and two years in jail is imposed for the most serious offences such as where a party knowingly commits an environmental offence. Less serious offences, such as littering, carry maximum fines of $250 for individuals or $1000 for corporations. Corporate directors and officers may be charged with offences committed by the corporation, and so they cannot hide behind the corporate veil.

COMPANY COMMITS OFFENCE

The parties concerned were in the business of collecting, transporting and re-refining waste oil. This business is closely regulated including the requirement of a number of manifests which must be filled out by the generator of the waste, by the transporter of it, and by the receiver of it. Mr. Cochrane picked up oily waste from a Petro-Canada facility with the proper manifest. On the way his truck broke down and he contacted Mr. Howitt, a representative of Safety-Kleen, who brought his truck and transferred the oil from one truck to the other. This required verbal permission from the Ministry as well as the completion of a new manifest. Although an attempt had been made, neither the appropriate documentation nor the necessary authorization was present and false information was filled in on the original manifest. Mr. Howard's truck was pulled over by a Ministry official as soon as it got out on the highway and the violations that had taken place became apparent. There were two offences here: failing to comply with the regulations and providing false information. The question the court had to determine was whether the corporate personality of Safety-Kleen could be responsible in its own capacity for the offences committed by its employee. The court held that the failure to comply with the completion of the manifests was a strict liability offence. The only way the corporation could avoid liability would be to show due diligence, that is, show that they had taken reasonable steps to set up a system to avoid this sort of thing. The court looked at the complete independence allowed employees and decided that no such system had been in place, and that therefore the offence had been committed by the company. The second offence of providing false information was a mens rea offence: it required intent to do the wrongful deed. This intent was not possible in the "mind" of the corporation and therefore it was not liable for the second offence of making a false declaration.

R. v. Safety-Kleen Canada Inc., 145 D.L.R. (4th) 276 (Ontario Court of Appeal)

These enforcement provisions, if exercised vigorously, can have considerable effect. The imposition of personal liability upon directors and officers has prompted many corporations to pay greater attention to environmental concerns, and to at least put a due diligence plan into effect.

The appropriateness of a criminal prosecution model for protection of the environment has been questioned by some. Is it necessary to impose fines and even imprisonment for violations where many offenders have not acted maliciously or intentionally? Would models that emphasize settlement, and utilize mediation to resolve environmental disputes, foster a greater sense of responsibility for the environment amongst businesses? The current philosophy seems to be more concerned with making polluters pay for the damage they cause. The Alberta *Act* focuses on who has the right to sue, who has to pay, and how much, reflecting an adversarial rather than remedial approach.

Federal Legislation.

Federal regulations control provincial areas through funding

The federal government has jurisdiction only in certain areas as set out in the *Constitution Act (1867)* but it has become involved through financing in environmental programs that primarily fall under the jurisdiction of the provinces. One of the purposes of the federal legislation is to help the provinces pay for their environmental programs. With such funding comes control; the federal government can stipulate how the funds will be used and, to some degree, control the extent of the environmental legislation in place in the provinces.

The federal *Environmental Protection Act* controls the manufacturing, import and use of many hazardous materials such as PCBs and asbestos, sets standards for and regulates the use of these substances, and establishes a reporting process that must be followed. The *Act* also makes it an offense to fail to adhere to the regulations to intentionally damage the environment and to fail to cooperate with the officials. It goes further in that it imposes personal liability on directors and officers of corporations for a number of failures to comply with the act or regulations. This *Act*, a comprehensive one meant to prevent pollution, provide for research and development, investigate and measure pollution levels, and monitor industry, has become a model for other levels of government to follow.

Another area of federal attention is the handling and disposal of hazardous wastes and material. The *Transportation of Dangerous Goods Act* controls the transport of dangerous chemicals and goods. The *Act* applies when goods are transferred between provinces or internationally, including between Canada and the United States. Again at the federal level, the *Fisheries Act* with its 1970 amendments is very important because of its provision prohibiting the discharge of any dangerous substances into waterways, lakes and oceans. This *Act* has been used effectively to control the discharge of sewage from municipalities as well as effluent from pulp mills.

Federal and provincial environment statutes grant considerable power for enforcement to the government officials charged with the application of the various statutes, including the power to enter premises, to inspect, to seize documents, to take samples and in some circumstances to order certain activities stopped. But in most cases their power stops short of the right to use force. In fact, except in the most blatant cases of intentional dumping of waste, the enforcement branches find it much more productive to work with the offending business to help it live up to the standards rather than to punish it for failing to do so.

Corporations may be required not only to refrain from future activities that threaten the environment but may also face prosecution for past uncontrolled dumping and the costs of cleanup. It is not only the corporations that face these responsibilities, since the statutes often lift the corporate veil, making the directors personally responsible for the offenses committed by the corporations they direct. Even secured creditors, such as mortgagees, landlords and receivers, can be held responsible for the cost of such cleanup. Note that recent amendments to the *Bankruptcy and Insolvency Act* provide additional protection to receivers in such circumstances. It is uncertain just how far this responsibility will or should go but it is clear that if such secured creditors realize their security by taking possession of the property, the responsibility to clean it up goes with it. Because of this responsibility, many lenders choose not to exercise their security in the face of default. It is now incumbent on lenders, investors and potential purchasers of property or business, to make a careful examination to determine any risks before they become involved.

Such an environmental audit, fast becoming an essential aspect of modern business practice, can take one of two forms: the **site audit**, used to determine contamination problems associated with a business or site before a transaction is made, and the **compliance audit**, used by an ongoing business to examine its own practices to determine whether they are in compliance with the legislation. The latter form is a necessary part of establishing due diligence where the director or officer of a corporation must show that he or she has taken all reasonable steps to do everything necessary to live up to his or her personal responsibilities under the act and regulations. This is taking place at both the federal and the provincial level.

Although the approach used in these statutes is primarily regulatory, controlling rather than prohibiting environmentally sensitive activities, the penalties involved

Extensive enforcement power

in environmental offenses have been greatly increased. Under the federal act, fines range up to a million dollars and sentences can be imposed for up to five years in prison. The directors of the responsible government departments (or in some cases the ministers responsible) also have the power, under these statutes, to issue stop orders for any activity that violates the standards established in the regulation. In other circumstances, less drastic control orders can be issued that direct compliance with the standards. In some cases, orders can be issued that require an offender to repair any damage caused by the activity. These penalties involve criminal or quasi-criminal prosecution. One alternative being used in some jurisdictions is the use of the "administrative monetary penalty," a non-criminal alternative to the criminal prosecution model and is intended to create a less adversarial and more cooperative administrative environment. The "administrative monetary penalty" is also being introduced in other areas and is one of the recommended inclusions in soon-to-be-made changes to the *Competition Act.*

A New Direction.

Environmental assessment reviews required

Following the American example of the *National Environmental Policy Act (1969)*, the trend in Canadian legislation is to impose an environmental assessment review process on those wishing to undertake some new, potentially hazardous project. The objective is to require the parties proposing the project to file a report with a designated government agency which highlights its potential impact on the environment including any health risks. The government authority studies this report, seeks public input and holds a public hearing to air all of the various points of view. The authority then decides whether to give its permission for the activity, to withhold it or to grant the permit with conditions. Environmental assessment reviews were initially limited to public activities, but the trend is for environmental impact studies to be required for private industrial and resource-based projects as well. As this trend continues, producing such reports will mean a significant increase in the cost of doing business. Such reports are now required not only for large projects such as steel plants, pulp mills, hydroelectric dams and the like but also for smaller types of business activities that use specific types of chemicals or otherwise threaten the environment.

The federal *Environmental Assessment Act*, proclaimed in September 1993, replaced non-legislated Cabinet guidelines and imposed significant obligations of reporting on businesses dealing with the federal government. The proclaimed purposes of the *Act* are the following:

1. to ensure that the environmental effects of projects receive careful consideration before any action is taken;

2. to promote sustainable development and thus a healthy environment;

3. to ensure that projects on federal lands do not cause adverse environmental effects to other lands;

4. to ensure an opportunity for public participation.

The *Act* requires an environmental assessment for any project done on federal lands, any project the federal government finances, or any project for which it provides a permit or license. The environmental review process consists of a comprehensive study of the environmental impact of the project, evaluation by a review panel and the implementation of a followup program where necessary. The panel also considers the purpose of the project, any alternative means that could be used and their environmental effect, and how renewable resources might be affected. Once approval has been given by the review panel, it issues a certificate and the project can proceed. To ensure public access and involvement, a registry is established to make available all information collected or submitted relative to the environmental review process for the various projects. The *Act* also establishes a federal environmental review agency which advises and assists the Minister by administering and promoting the environmental assessment process, encouraging research, promoting uniformity throughout Canada and ensuring an opportunity for public input. In the process, the agency provides administrative support, training and information. This new *Act* is an important step towards establishing a comprehensive process for protecting the environment.

Other jurisdictions have followed the federal example and now require similar environmental review processes. The Alberta *Environmental Protection and Enhancement Act* is designed to increase public input into the decision process and requires that hearings take place before either the Energy Resources Conservation Board or the Natural Resources Conservation Board before certain types of projects can proceed.

Economy Versus Environment.

The tendency by government towards increasing interference into business activities in relation to the environment may appear to be an unwarranted and unfair intrusion, but there is considerable justification for it. As our economy worsens and costs increase, businesses sometimes have difficulty surviving as profitable enterprises. Pressing bottom-line concerns are bound to affect the attention given to environmental issues. This creates a dilemma in that as the environment is threatened, businesses become less economically viable and can less afford to take the steps necessary to preserve it. The increased attention that government is paying to the environment may be justified, but it is understandable that the imposition of more government regulation is not popular in business circles. It is usually in this regulatory arena that the clash between government bureaucrats, businesses and private individuals takes place.

The ongoing dispute between the environmental movement and various industries is forcing a reassessment of how government should deal with these matters; business people must not only concern themselves with a costly and interfering regulatory environment but also must contend with uncertainty and flux. Government regulatory officials impose standards, establish environmental screening processes and require reports when any new project is undertaken. An involved process of public hearings and submissions may be required before a license or permit is granted. Once the project is under way, inspectors may measure compliance and, for industries that are considered dangerous, such inspections become routine.

Industries must consider the costs of complying with environmental standards and the costs of prosecution when offenses do take place. Even if a site was previously contaminated, modern statutes may require that it be cleaned by or at the expense of the polluter or current owner and that compensation be paid to those injured. These statutes may apply even when no regulations were in place at the time the pollution occurred or if the standards in place were lower than they should have been.

Regulations only part of environmental costs

It is enough to say that the trend is for government departments to become more and more powerfully involved in industrial and other forms of business

Reducing pollution is a significant cost of doing business.　Photo by Al Harvey/The Slide Farm.

Environmental costs threaten business

activity. Almost any business decision taken today must consider the environmental factors and the procedures that are laid down by the government agencies established to protect it, and must recognize the fact that all businesses are subject to inspection and prosecution when their day-to-day activities pose a risk to the environment. It is crucial that any business plan contain provisions for compliance to current and projected regulations. In order to protect directors, officers and the company itself, strategies must be developed so that the reasonable conduct required to establish due diligence is built into the business operation.

The controversy extends to whether development ought to take place at all—whether the forests ought to be cut down; rivers ought to be dammed; plants ought to be built. The recurring examples of environmental activists risking jail terms to stop logging in sensitive areas or strapping themselves to oil drilling rigs, illustrates that the problem is more fundamental than waste disposal and pollution. The impact of these disputes can have a profound effect on businesses to the point of raising the question of whether they will be able to carry on business at all.

For example, when a company applied to develop a considerable ore deposit in the Tatsensheny Wilderness area, the outcry and pressure were so great that in 1992 the British Columbia government stepped in, declared the area a national park and put an end to the project. The Old Man River hydroelectric project in Alberta ran into many obstacles, most hinging on environmental concerns. The fixed-link bridge between Prince Edward Island and the mainland ran into similar difficulties. The Kamano completion project in British Columbia was stopped completely because of concerns about the fish habitat in the Fraser and Nechako river systems.

Even when a government has given approval for a project, protesters may continue their activities. On the west coast of Vancouver Island, the provincial government gave permission to MacMillan Bloedel to log in the Clayoquot Sound area, but the protests of environmentalists in the area (the arrests were in the hundreds) put great pressure on the government to backtrack from its decision.

As our population continues to grow and production grows, the pressure on the environment will increase. These conflicting interests will place greater pressure on businesses in the form of costs and restrictions. Government is the only body that can try to find a balance between these interests, and it is hoped that our elected officials will be able to find some compromise or common ground.

Sometimes government officials through ignorance or because the law is uncertain will go beyond the power they have been given or will exercise it improperly. People affected by such actions can enforce their rights, and the methods available to them are outlined in the rest of this chapter.

ADMINISTRATIVE LAW

The relationship between business and the environment is just one of many areas of government regulation that businesses have to contend with. Consumer rights, taxation, competition, labour relations, securities and human rights legislation are some of the other areas in which businesses must deal with government agencies. The resulting paper burden is another of the high costs of doing business. Government officials can and do make decisions that have far-reaching consequences. Not surprisingly, they sometimes make incorrect decisions or otherwise abuse or go beyond their power.

Challenging Government Regulations

As the executive branch of government has grown in recent years, the power of government departments and agencies such as Canada Employment and Immigration Commission, the Workers' Compensation Board and the RCMP have been increasing at a significant rate. The officers and employees of government bodies are given the authority to administer their programs. In the process, they make decisions which affect people's lives. Generally, when a bureaucrat is simply making or implementing government policy, an individual's right to challenge the decision is limited unless it can be shown that his or her rights are directly affected. When the decision maker is functioning as a referee or judge, or acts in a quasi-judicial manner, the decision, or the process by which it was arrived at, may be challenged in the courts. A typical example in business is a labour relations board deciding whether a particular union should be certified as the bargaining agent at a factory.

Governments function through administrative bodies

When government officials are called upon to make decisions on how to implement legislation or government policy, they act as **administrative tribunals**. The area of law that describes individuals' rights before them is administrative law. To determine whether the decision of a civil servant or administrative tribunal can be challenged, one should refer to the two basic principles that govern the actions of decision makers: (1) the decision must be made within the authority of the government official or board and (2) the process involved and the conduct of the decision maker must have been proper.

Clearly the intention is that these administrative tribunals have a positive role to play in bringing their special expertise to bear on the matters in question, and that their decisions should not lightly be interfered with by the courts. The Supreme Court of Canada has recognized the legitimate role played by administrative tribunals in a recent decision that established a standard to determine when a decision of a tribunal can be challenged. They determined that when courts are asked to review the decision of an administrative tribunal they should recognize that those tribunals have special expertise and that decision should not be overruled unless it is "unreasonable."[3] All of what is discussed below should be examined in the light of the general reluctance to interfere with that standard.

The Authority of the Decision Maker

A fundamental aspect of the constitutional tradition we took from Britain is the **rule of law**. The rule of law holds that, even given the supremacy of parliament, neither parliament nor any government official representing parliament can act arbitrarily. Professor R. M. Dawson, in *The Government of Canada*, defines the rule of law as "the restriction of arbitrary authority in government, and the necessity for all

Government agents must act within existing law

---

3. *Canada (Director of Investigation and Research) v. Southam Inc.* 144 D.L.R. (4th) 1 (Supreme Court of Canada).

acts of government to be authorized by reasonably precise laws as applied and interpreted by the courts."[4] This principle is effectively illustrated by J. A. Corry and J. E. Hodgetts in *Democratic Government and Politics*. The authors point out that government officials cannot rely on their status to interfere with the rights of a person but must rely on some empowering legislation to authorize the action. This proposition is summarized in these words: "This state can throw away the conscript's life but it cannot conscript him [or her] in the first instance on the plea of high policy or public expedience except as supported by law sanctioned by parliament."[5] A government official or board must be able to point to some valid statute that authorizes the conduct, including any decision reached. If the decision maker has gone beyond this authority, the decision can be challenged as *ultra vires* and set aside.

Does administrative tribunal have authority?

The first step in the process of challenging an administrative tribunal, then, is to examine the statutory authority and determine if the tribunal's conduct or actions were authorized under it. This statutory authority may be found not only in the statute itself but also in the regulations passed under that statute. While Parliament and the provincial legislative assemblies create law primarily through legislation, the resulting statutes often give government institutions such as the Workers' Compensation Board the power to make further rules or regulations under that legislation. These regulations have the same force as the statute under which they were created. When the source of authority for the conduct complained of is in the regulations, it is important to determine not only whether the section relied on does authorize the conduct but also whether the regulations themselves have been made within the statutory authority given to the body creating them. If the regulations have been properly passed as authorized under the statute, they are valid because that body has acted within its power (*intra vires*). But if the regulations exceed the authority granted by the enabling statute, those regulations are invalid and the government body has acted beyond its powers (*ultra vires*). When the conduct complained of is not authorized under the statute or when the regulation itself is invalid, that conduct can be challenged, and the courts will have no hesitation in overturning the decision.

Statutory Interpretation

Rules of statutory interpretation

When determining whether a regulation has been properly imposed under the statute in question or whether any other aspect of the statute is being properly enforced, the courts will apply accepted rules of **statutory interpretation**. These rules have developed from three basic principles. First, if a provision of the statute is clear and unambiguous, and conveys a certain meaning that is not inconsistent with other sections of the statute, the court is obligated to apply the **plain** or literal meaning. If the statute is ambiguous, either because the provisions are inconsistent with other sections of the legislation or because the wording is capable of more than one meaning, the courts may apply either the golden rule or the mischief rule. The **golden rule** means a reasonable interpretation based on common sense will be used and that the literal meaning of the statute will be departed from only as far as necessary to overcome the ambiguity or inconsistency. The **mischief rule** means that the courts will try to give effect to the specific purpose for which the statute was enacted. Many statutes are passed to cure some defect or injustice in the

• plain meaning

• golden rule

• mischief rule

4. R. MacGregor Dawson, *The Government of Canada*, 4th ed. (University of Toronto Press, 1966), p. 77.

5. J. A. Corry and J. E. Hodgetts, *Democratic Government and Politics*, 3rd ed. (University of Toronto Press, 1959), p. 96.

common law or in some other statute. In applying the mischief rule, the courts look first at the original common law or statute with its defect and how the legislation in question was intended to overcome it. The court then imposes the interpretation that gives best effect to the original intent of the legislation. Thus, if there was a problem of interpretation with the federal *Young Offenders Act*, the application of the mischief rule would require that any ambiguity be interpreted to give effect to the intention of the *Act*, that is, to give the youth involved the same kind of rights and protection given to adults.

Another rule of statutory interpretation available to the courts is that a judge is not obligated to follow a statute unless it clearly and unambiguously overrules the common law provision. This is referred to as **strict interpretation of the statute**. Other specific rules have been developed to assist the courts to interpret statutes. These rules may range from principles of grammatical construction to rules favouring one interpretation over another in different situations. The courts may also turn to similar statutes, both within and outside the legislative jurisdiction involved, and to the official translations of statutes and other publications such as dictionaries and academic articles. Each jurisdiction in Canada has passed legislation setting out general principles and specific rules judges must follow when determining the meaning of statutes or regulations. In Alberta, these rules are found in the *Interpretation Act*.[6] This statute contains a lengthy definitions section, setting out specific meanings that must be applied to words used in enactments. It also contains rules for computation of time, so as to clarify when certain actions must be taken (e.g., If filing the Statement of Defence within "15 days," does that mean clear days? What if the 15th day is a Sunday?). Other statutes often contain a definition section that sets out specific meanings that must be applied to words used throughout that statute.

It is beyond the scope of this chapter to discuss statutory interpretation in any greater detail. However, it should be apparent that when faced with disputes over the meaning of statutory provisions, the courts have a cohesive framework of rules and guidelines to help them determine the appropriate interpretation. The interpretation eventually settled on by the court may affect whether the particular regulation in question was valid, whether the conduct complained of has violated a particular statute or whether the particular regulatory body or government agency had the power to make the decision or impose the control it did. Once this has been determined, the question remains whether or not the legislation itself was validly passed pursuant to the division of powers as set out in the *Constitution Act (1867)*.

As mentioned in Chapter 1, the powers of government are divided between the provincial and the federal level of government as set out primarily in Sections 91 and 92 respectively of the *Constitution Act (1867)*. When a level of government that does not have the authority to do so under this division of powers passes the statute that authorizes the conduct complained of, the courts will have no hesitation in declaring the statute *ultra vires* and the action of the decision maker improper. If a city council were to pass a bylaw prohibiting the sale of adult videos within the city boundaries, and the council, on the strength of that bylaw, were to deny such a business a license to operate, the business could challenge that decision. Neither the province nor a city deriving its authority from the province can pass such a bylaw because it encroaches on the federal government's criminal law powers. Since the bylaw was invalid, any decision made under its authority is also invalid and the

Statutes strictly interpreted

Division of powers and constitutional authority

6. *Interpretation Act*, R.S.A. (1980) c. I-7.

courts would, upon application, declare the decision *ultra vires* and void. In the same way, the statute or regulation must be consistent with the provisions of the *Charter of Rights and Freedoms*, also discussed in Chapter 1. A statute which had the effect of discriminating on the basis of gender, religion or ethnic origin, or one which denied a person the right to a hearing, or restricted freedom of the press or religion, could be challenged and a decision made under such a statute would be invalid.

Proper Process.

Administrator must act fairly

Once it has been established that the decision maker has acted within the authority given under a valid statute or regulation, the question remains whether that authority was exercised in a proper way. Historically, the obligation of the administrator to act in a procedurally fair manner varied to a great extent depending on the function performed. The decision maker might at one extreme be acting like a judge adjudicating disputes or at the other simply acting as an administrator, implementing government policy. The distinction is less important today. Even when the decision maker is acting as an administrator there is an obligation to maintain at least a minimum standard of procedural fairness. If the issues being dealt with are important, the decision maker's function is to decide between competing parties or interests, or the remedies or penalties which can be imposed can have a significant impact on the parties, the courts are much more likely to find an obligation on the decision maker to act fairly. These minimum standards of fairness have been imposed on the Cabinet and ministers of the Crown as well, although it should be noted that such obligations may be modified by statute. What constitutes fairness in these situations is determined by the rules of natural justice, and what constitutes the minimum requirements of justice or procedural fairness is set out below.

Rules of Natural Justice

Sinkovich v. Strathroy (Town) Commissioners of Police[7]

An inquiry involving the Ontario Police Commission was instigated into the operations of the police in the town of Strathroy after complaints had been made including allegations of criminal conduct against some of the police officers. That Ontario Police Commission report showed some serious problems in the Strathroy police force. It was after this report, which included a number of recommendations, that it became necessary for a new police chief to be hired by the town, and Mr. Sinkovich was hired.

Shortly afterwards the relationship between the mayor and Chief Sinkovich deteriorated. Over the years a number of reports were given to the Strathroy Police Board from different sources about the management of the police, its morale, the style of the police chief, etc. A number of these reports were negative and some came from the Ontario Police Commission. Finally the Commission was asked to hold an inquiry, which it did.

Chief Sinkovich was told that the inquiry was looking at the management and administration of the force, and he came to the hearing prepared to discuss the matter. It turned out, however, that it was the competence and personal conduct

7. 51 D.L.R. (4th) 750 (Ontario High Court of Justice, Divisional Court).

of the police chief himself that were being reviewed. His performance was found to be unsatisfactory and the Commission recommended that he be dismissed.

He complained and brought an application to the court that the decision of the Ontario Police Commission and the resulting report be quashed. The court agreed, saying that the only time a police chief could be terminated was after a proper hearing of the Board or after an inquiry of the Ontario Police Commission, and since Sinkovich wasn't given proper notice of the inquiry or told his position was in jeopardy, that inquiry was not proper.

This case illustrates that in order for a proper hearing to take place, a person must be notified of that hearing, and a significant aspect of such notification is for him or her to be told the nature of the charges to be dealt with so that he or she will have an opportunity to respond. In this case, although Sinkovich was notified of the hearing, he wasn't told the nature of the hearing or that his own position was in jeopardy. Notice and a fair hearing are central to the rules of natural justice.

To determine what constitutes procedural fairness, one must first look to any governing statute and determine what obligations it imposes. Even if the obligations imposed by the statute are lower than the requirements of procedural fairness and natural justice, the statute will prevail if its provisions are intended to set out all of the procedural requirements. Today, the process may be significantly affected by the *Charter of Rights and Freedoms* which requires that interference with one's life, liberty or security of person can only be done in accordance with "the principles of fundamental justice." The principles of fundamental justice have been taken to mean the same thing as procedural fairness.

Statute may impose or modify duty

Fair Hearing.

The most fundamental requirement of the rules of natural justice is that the party being affected by the decision of an administrator have an opportunity to a fair hearing. What constitutes a fair hearing will vary from situation to situation, but, essentially, the person being affected by the decision must have been notified that a decision is to be made and must have been given an opportunity to put his or her side forward. The courts have held that a fair hearing has not taken place when

All information must be disclosed at a fair hearing

FAIR HEARING REQUIRES OPPORTUNITY TO BE HEARD

Ladney and others wished to propose an amendment to the official plan for the Township of Moore. They appeared before a session of the Ontario Municipal Board to make this application. The Board called one expert witness and then recessed for 20 minutes. When they returned they proceeded to turn down the Ladney application without hearing evidence from the other side and without hearing submissions from the lawyers. The question for the court was whether the Board had the power to make a decision without having given Ladney or his council an opportunity to make their arguments. The court held that it had exceeded its jurisdiction; the decision was set aside and a new hearing scheduled. To be given a fair hearing on a decision, a person must have the opportunity to call evidence and submit his or her arguments before the decision is rendered.

Re Ladney et al. and Township of Moore, 10 D.L.R. (4th) 612 (Ontario High Court of Justice, Divisional Court)

DECISION MAKER MUST HEAR ALL EVIDENCE

Pursuant to the *Canada Corporations Act*, the Restrictive Trades Practices Commission had an investigator examine the affairs of Javelin International Ltd. Once such an investigation takes place, the Commission holds a hearing in which the inspector presents evidence of what he or she has found and the other party is given an opportunity to respond. During the Javelin hearing, three members of the commission sat and listened to the proceedings. At various stages one of them stepped out, always leaving two members present which was required for a quorum. The Commission found evidence of fraud and made recommendations to the Minister. Mr. Doyle, a principal of Javelin, brought this application to have the findings of the Commission set aside. The court agreed. People who had not heard all the evidence had participated in the decision, resulting in an unfair hearing.

Re Doyle and Restrictive Trade Practices Commission et al., 21 D.L.R. (4th) 366 (Federal Court of Appeal)

no notice of the hearing was given, or when the person was not informed of the nature of the complaint. This was the basis of Chief Sinkovich's complaint in the case used to open this discussion. The failure to notify him that his position was the subject of the hearing he was to attend denied him the opportunity to properly defend himself. There can be no fair hearing without notice and an opportunity to prepare a defense.

Part of the requirement of a fair hearing is that all of the evidence that forms the basis of the decision be disclosed to the individual being affected by it. An individual must be given the opportunity to cross-examine witnesses who present material testimony or to refute any written declarations. Similarly, it is essential to a fair hearing that the individual be given an opportunity to present arguments and evidence to support those arguments.

No obligation to allow counsel or follow rules of evidence

A fair hearing may extend to the right to demand an adjournment in certain circumstances. But there is no requirement that the decision maker follow the strict rules of evidence or even that the person affected have a right to counsel, although legal representation is a right if the proceedings might result in criminal charges. There is no general obligation on the decision maker to give reasons for the judgment, but many statutes do impose a duty on the decision maker to give reasons and often require that these reasons be put in writing. The test is reasonableness and an unreasonable imposition on the time of an administrator will not be tolerated. In some situations, the opportunity to present a case by letter is enough to satisfy the rule. This illustrates that the applications of the rules of natural justice or procedural fairness involve a considerable degree of flexibility, depending on the circumstances.

Heard by Decision Maker.

Decision must be made by person hearing evidence

Another requirement of the rules of natural justice is that the decision must be made by the person hearing the evidence. If a board of inquiry is convened requiring five people to participate in the decision and something happens to one of them, that person cannot be replaced by another because the new person would not have heard all of the evidence presented. Similarly, the board of inquiry cannot proceed and make the decision with only four people because the statute requires five. It is permissible for the decision maker to use staff services to gather and summarize the evidence but the person making the decision must be the one who hears the evidence.

Impartiality.

Bailey v. Saskatchewan Registered Nurses' Assn.[8]

This case deals with the rights of the members of professional associations against disciplinary actions of that association—in this case the Registered Nurses Association. A resident at the Sherbrook Community Centre died and an investigation commenced against three nurses working at the centre. Karen Klassen was the director of Nurses Services at the Sherbrook Centre and she filed a complaint against the three nurses. An investigation was launched to determine what happened and it was chaired by another nurse, the unit manager, at the centre. One problem here was that Klassen was the president-elect of the Saskatchewan Nurses Association. She was a member of the executive body and the chairperson of the Legislation and Bylaws Committee.

A number of complaints were raised with regard to the investigation and the subsequent hearing before the disciplinary committee which resulted in the three nurses' employment being terminated. First, the investigation committee failed to interview a number of individuals whose statements might have been in favour of the nurses. When the lawyer for the nurses asked for information which had been gathered by the investigation team, some documents were never disclosed, some were only partially disclosed and others were disclosed in the middle of the hearing. The investigation file itself wasn't disclosed until they were four days into the hearing. Even the physical structure of the hearing was set up in a way that wasn't fair. The hearing room was set up so that the lawyer for the nurses was unable to see the witnesses who were testifying and the disciplinary committee at the same time. No room was provided for the nurses to meet with their lawyers during the hearing and there was a sense of urgency to get on with the matter whenever the nurses were presenting their defenses. A complaint was made also that Karen Klassen was on the council, creating possible bias. There was no response.

Even the lawyer acting for the Nurses Association was in a difficult position. He had been the general lawyer for the Association, then the lawyer for the investigating body, and now was acting as prosecutor against the three nurses. He had also been involved in the orientation of the members of the disciplinary committee itself and had conducted education days for them. The firm for which he worked had made financial donations to the Association's building fund and there was a general air of familiarity between him and the members of the committee, giving the nurses the feeling that this was just a one-sided process out to get them.

All of these factors created an atmosphere where there was a reasonable apprehension of bias on the part of the investigation committee. The court held that a proper hearing had not taken place, which was a breach of natural justice, and therefore the decision of the committee was quashed.

This case illustrates very well the problems that can arise when there is a conflict of interest or bias on the part of decision makers. The court said the investigation committee should have looked at the evidence of all the witnesses with more diligence, and given proper hearing and interview facilities to the nurses. They should not have conducted the hearing in an atmosphere of haste. The nurses should have been given an opportunity to give full answers in defense to the charges that were laid against them. It was extremely important that full disclosure be made in a timely manner so that the nurses could have known what they were

8. 137 D.L.R. (4th) 224 (Saskatchewan Court of Queen's Bench).

responding to. Disclosing information in the middle of a meeting was not sufficient. This was not a fair hearing as required under the rules of natural justice, the main problem being a lack of impartiality on the part of the decision makers.

Decision maker must be free of bias

A significant requirement of the rules of natural justice is that the decision be made in good faith and impartially. If it can be shown that the decision maker is biased, the decision can be overturned. Because it is so difficult to establish a condition of bias, the courts have developed the principle that a reasonable likelihood of bias is enough to invalidate the decision. Bias is assumed when the matter being decided involves a relative, friend or business acquaintance of the decision maker. Similarly, if there has been an exhibition of bad feelings or hostility between the decision maker and the individual being affected by the decision, there is a real likelihood of bias and the decision can be challenged. Where it can be shown that the decision maker has an interest in the matter being decided or has already decided the matter, he or she will be disqualified from the decision-making process. A monetary interest in the subject matter affected by the decision will be grounds for challenge and the size of such an interest should not be relevant. If Mueller participated on a rent review panel and was given the responsibility of deciding whether rents ought to be increased in a particular apartment building, the decision of the board could be challenged if it could be established by the landlord that Mueller had a brother living in one of the apartments. The decision could also be challenged if one of the tenants discovered that Mueller had a part-interest in the property. Even if Mueller was merely one of several people on the decision-making panel, the presence of a bias on the part of one of the decision makers can disqualify them all.

Bias may be permitted by statute

Decision-making bodies are sometimes structured to incorporate a bias. For example, the statutes for labour arbitration cases require that each side appoint one of the arbitrators who together then choose a third. The two parties will probably appoint people who are clearly favourable to their position and thus are biased. The principle involved is that the bias represented by one side will be balanced by the bias of the other and the third arbitrator chosen by both will mediate between them. This emphasizes the point that the rules of natural justice are guidelines only. The courts retain a considerable amount of flexibility in the exercise of their supervisory jurisdiction as they ensure that the procedures involved are fair to all parties.

JUDICIAL REVIEW

Most statutes establishing decision-making boards or commissions provide for an appeal to another level of decision maker. This may be another board, a commissioner, director or even the minister in charge and in many instances the appeal can go eventually to the courts. **Judicial review** must be distinguished from this appeal process. Appeal is the process whereby the decision of an inferior court or tribunal is reviewed at a higher level. Judicial review involves the superior court's inherent right to supervise the judicial process. Whether or not an appeal is allowed, whether or not there are other courses of action open to the person affected by the decision, the courts retain the right to supervise and oversee the administration of justice. They have to correct the action of a decision maker who acts improperly, and so it is the process itself that is of more concern in a judicial review.

Judicial review—inherent right of courts

As a rule, the courts require that all other remedies be exhausted before they exercise their supervisory capacity in the form of judicial review. If an appeal is available under the statute or regulations, that appeal process must be finished before turning to the courts. Generally, judicial review is available "where an administrative body has acted without authority, or has stepped outside the limits of its authority, or has failed to perform its duties."[9]

The following is a summary of the situations in which a person affected by the decision of an administrator or administrative tribunal can go to the courts for relief.

1. When the decision maker has no authority to make the decision or has stepped outside of his or her authority in some way, that decision can be challenged in the courts. In determining whether or not the decision maker has the required authority, the courts must look not only to the contents of the statute to determine if the decision or act was authorized, but also to the validity of the statute itself under the *Charter of Rights and Freedoms* and the *Constitution Act (1867)*. If the statute is valid, the decision can still be challenged on the grounds that the administrator was not functioning within the authority granted under the statute. For example, if a school board is required to review a dismissal application but appoints a committee of the board to hear the complaint because of the inconvenience of meeting over the summer, the decision of that committee is reviewable if the school board does not have the power to delegate its authority to a committee.

   Another such error can be made if the decision maker makes an initial, incorrect decision which brings the matter in dispute under his or her jurisdiction. For example, if a labour relations board is given the authority to hear disputes between employees and employers and decides that a dispute between independent fishers and the fish-packing companies they do business with falls within its jurisdiction, this primary jurisdictional determination can be challenged in the courts. Another type of jurisdictional error occurs when a decision-making body takes it upon itself to re-hear a matter after it has made a final decision. Usually, statutes will empower such a body to decide in the first place but not authorize them to re-hear the matter. Therefore, the second hearing is outside the jurisdiction of the decision maker. Although it is possible for such a body to cure a procedural defect in the original hearing by holding another hearing to overcome that defect, this is not a re-hearing since the first hearing was not valid.

   Authority of decision maker may be reviewed

2. The decision-making process itself is subject to the scrutiny of the court. There is a requirement of procedural fairness, as discussed above, that must be followed whenever a decision is made that has an adverse impact on an individual.

   Process must be fair

3. If the decision maker is functioning within the proper jurisdiction and the process is procedurally fair, the courts are generally reluctant to interfere with the decision. But if the decision incorporates a remedy beyond the decision maker's power to grant, it will be reviewable on the grounds of jurisdiction. For example, under labour legislation, an arbitrator is given the authority to determine whether an employee was properly dismissed. If that arbitrator were to impose some other kind of consequence, such as a suspension from employment for a number of weeks, rather than simply deciding whether the dismissal was justified or not, the arbitrator would be assuming authority he or she does not have and that decision would then be invalid.

   In some cases, the decision itself may be reviewed

9. *Judicial Review Procedure Act,* R.S.O. (1990) c. J.1.

Under rare circumstances, the court may find that there was not sufficient legal evidence for the administrator to reach a particular decision. The legal standard requires that there be at least some evidence to justify the conclusion reached by the decision maker.

Abuse of discretionary power

The courts have been willing to overturn a decision when the decision maker has committed an abuse of power. If a decision maker acts dishonestly, out of malice or with fraudulent intent in the exercise of his or her discretionary power, even though the decision may be within his or her power to reach, that decision is reviewable on the basis of abuse of power. The case of *Roncarelli v. Duplessis*[10] is a classic example of the abuse of power by a minister of the Crown which was reviewable by the courts. In that case, a restaurant owner in Montreal supported Jehovah's Witnesses facing charges by paying their legal expenses. The premier of the province exerted his influence to have the plaintiff's liquor license cancelled. This act was clearly outside the jurisdiction he had as premier and an abuse of his power. The court ordered the premier to pay compensation to the plaintiff.

The decision maker must consider all relevant matters and must not make a decision for an improper purpose. The exercise of the decision must be a genuine exercise. For example, if a decision maker with discretionary power merely follows the direction of a superior, that is an abuse of such power and reviewable in the courts.

Error of law on record

4. Finally, the courts are willing to interfere with any decision that involves an error of law which is incorporated into the record of the hearing. The record consists of the decision, the reasons for it and any documents involved in the process of reaching the decision. A transcript of the proceedings can also be included as part of the record. Such an error of law on the record cannot be tolerated by the supervising judicial body and the decision will be overturned whenever such an error is substantial enough to affect the decision. Of course, an error of law must be distinguished from an error of fact. The decision maker is generally empowered to decide questions of fact and those decisions will not be interfered with. But when there is an incorrect declaration as to the law, this is of concern to the superior court and will not be tolerated. The error of law may be in misconstruing common law or statutes or a procedural error such as the refusal to hear evidence or hearing evidence that ought to have been excluded. The courts will not usually interfere with the decision merely because they do not like the decision or would have come to a different one themselves.

Methods of Judicial Review

Prerogative Writs.

The courts have traditionally used the method of prerogative writs as opposed to the appellate process in exercising their supervisory power over administrative tribunals. These are ancient remedies traceable to the prerogative power of the Crown. Four main prerogative writs are in use today, the best known of which is the writ of *habeas corpus*, a court order to the custodial authority to present a person being kept in custody before the court. *Habeas corpus* is used whenever there is con-

---

10. *Roncarelli v. Duplessis* [1959] S.C.R. 121 (Supreme Court of Canada).

cern over whether a person is being improperly detained. While this remedy is primarily used in criminal matters, it is also used in immigration and child custody cases and when people have been institutionalized for mental health reasons. Many jurisdictions have passed legislation modifying the application of this judicial remedy, such as Ontario's *Habeas Corpus Act*.[11] Alberta has not followed this lead.

The other three prerogative writs, *certiorari*, prohibition, and *mandamus*, play a significant role as the courts exercise their supervisory jurisdiction over administrative tribunals. A writ of **certiorari** renders the decision of the inferior body as having no legal effect, and thus null and void. The granting of an application for *certiorari* nullifies an administrator's decision and eliminates any impact that decision might have on an individual. Prohibition is similar to *certiorari*, but *certiorari* overturns and voids a particular decision whereas prohibition prevents the decision from being made in the first place. For *certiorari* to apply, a decision must have been made that can be challenged. **Prohibition**, on the other hand, is used to prevent administrators or decision makers from using their power to make a decision in an unfair or otherwise inappropriate procedure. Prohibition is obtained before any decision and can be extremely effective in stopping an unfair or abusive process at an early stage.

Certiorari overrules a decision

Prohibition prevents decision from being made

Mandamus has quite a different application. When an individual is dealing with an administrator, delay in reaching a decision can be every bit as devastating as an improper decision or an abuse of procedure. A writ of *mandamus* can force the administrator to perform his or her duty and make the decision. It should be noted that administrators sometimes have the discretion to act or not; in such circumstances, *mandamus* cannot be used. But where the administrator has a duty, usually imposed by statute, to decide, *mandamus* can be used to force a decision.

Mandamus forces decision

There is a danger that after being forced to reach a decision through the operation of *mandamus*, an administrator might be predisposed to decide in a way that is not in the best interests of the individual who invoked *mandamus*. If it is suspected that this has occurred, other prerogative writs can be used to challenge the decision.

In the rare case in which there is only one decision the decision maker can legally reach, *mandamus* can be used to compel that decision.

Declaratory Judgment.

Although the use of prerogative writs is the backbone of judicial review today, there are many situations in which this type of remedy is ineffective. They are available only when a duty to act fairly is not met; they do not provide remedies when the impact of the decision has already been felt. For example, if Yamada owns property and builds a home on it that Adolfo, the city engineer, feels does not comply with the zoning regulations, and Adolfo then orders and supervises the demolition of the house, it would be little comfort to Yamada to go to the court, obtain a writ of *certiorari* and have Adolfo's decision quashed. The damage has already been done and a court declaration nullifying the decision will not undo it.

To deal with situations in which there is no other appropriate action, the court has developed the concept of **declaratory judgment**. The court reserves the right to declare the law, assess damages and grant compensation in almost all situations. Declaratory judgments are available in situations in which prerogative writs are not, and are often more effective in application. They have become an effective tool to assist the courts' exercise of their supervisory jurisdiction over administrators.

Court can make declaratory judgment

11. *Habeas Corpus Act*, R.S.O. (1990) c. H.1.

The eminent English jurist Lord Denning went so far as to say, "I know of no limitations to the power of the courts to grant a declaration except such limit as it may in its discretion impose upon itself. ..."[12]

Injunction.

Injunction stops illegal conduct

Another remedy available to the courts to help them in their supervisory jurisdiction is the **injunction**. An injunction is simply an order by the court to an individual or body to stop breaking the law or otherwise interfering with another's rights. In the example above, an appropriate remedy for Yamada after the decision was made but before it was put in place would have been to obtain an injunction to prevent the implementation of the decision. If the decision involved is merely the application for a license, however, since no private rights of Yamada are being interfered with, an injunction would not be available. An injunction is somewhat limited in its application. In fact, there are many situations in which an injunction is completely inappropriate, such as when the damage has already taken place. In addition, there are limitations concerning against whom an injunction can be obtained. In many cases, the Crown and servants of the Crown are immune from the effect of an injunction.

Modification by Statute.

Complex requirements modified by statute

While the declaratory judgment and the injunction are more straightforward than prerogative writs in their application, they are inappropriate in some circumstances and in some jurisdictions may not be available where *certiorari*, prohibition, or *mandamus* are available. And the procedure to obtain a declaratory judgment or an injunction is quite different from that to obtain one of the prerogative writs.

Judicial review is often not achieved in administrative law proceedings because of the failure to meet technical requirements. Because of this, many jurisdictions have passed statutes incorporating these methods of judicial review into a consolidated and simplified procedure (for example, the Ontario *Judicial Review Procedure Act*[13] and the British Columbia *Judicial Review Procedure Act*[14]). The statutes go so far as to say that whenever an application for *certiorari*, prohibition, *mandamus*, declaratory judgment and injunction are applied for, the application will be deemed to be one for judicial review under the statutes. The court then has the power to grant any relief available under statute or common law. Alberta's government has dealt with judicial review differently. Through Part 56.1 of the Rules of Court, it simply provides that any application for judicial review shall be commenced by originating notice and the court may grant one or more orders in the nature of *mandamus certiorari*, prohibition, *quo warranto*, or *habeas corpus*, or grant a declaration or injunction.

Alberta has also provided for statutory review in the *Municipal Government Act*,[15] under the heading "Challenging Bylaws and Resolutions." A person may apply by originating notice to the Court of Queen's Bench for a declaration that a bylaw or resolution is invalid. If the applicant establishes that the manner of passing the bylaw was improper or that proceedings held prior to passage of the bylaw were unfair or flawed, the court may declare the bylaw or resolution invalid.

12. *Barnard v. National Dock Labour Board* [1953] 2 Q.B. 18 at 41 (C.A.).

13. *Judicial Review Procedure Act*, R.S.O. (1980) c. 224.

14. *Judicial Review Procedure Act*, R.S.B.C. (1996) c. 241.

15. *Municipal Government Act*, S.A. (1994) c. M-26.1.

It should be pointed out that the process of judicial review as outlined in this section and contained in the modern statutes is available only when the decision maker is exercising a statutory power. When an individual is being subjected to the decision of an administrator exercising a non-statutory power, such as a trade union, professional association, club or religious group, statutory judicial review will probably not be available and the individual will have to resort to the more traditional remedies such as breach of contract, tort or human rights legislation.

It must be emphasized that one of the dominant elements present in the common law provisions has been carried over into statutory judicial review, that is, the discretionary power of the judges. The courts always reserve the right to refuse to grant a prerogative writ or declaratory judgment when it would be inappropriate to do so. This is an exercise of pure discretionary power and under the *Judicial Review Procedures Acts* of Ontario and British Columbia, this power has been retained.

NO BINGO HALL IN YOUR MALL

What constitutes bad faith?

The applicants, owners of a shopping mall, wanted to develop a bingo hall in their shopping mall; but when they broached the matter with the mayor of the town, they met resistance. According to the applicant, the mayor threatened to do everything in his power to prevent this bingo hall from being opened. A new bingo hall would compete with the two existing bingo operations in town. One of those bingo facilities was owned by the town and leased to an association that actually ran the bingos. The president of the association also sat on Town Council. The Town thus benefited from the rent paid by one of the existing bingo facilities. Under the existing arrangement, bingo revenues benefited those community groups that ran the bingos. The mayor admitted being sympathetic to those community groups, thus he resisted any change that would put community dollars into the private sector.

Days after the applicant submitted its application for a development permit, Town Council proposed an amendment to its land use bylaw. Even though the town administration and the Regional Planning Commission recommended against passing the amendment, it was passed.

The applicant sought to have this amending bylaw quashed on the basis that the mayor acted in bad faith, that one of the Council members was in a conflict of interest position, and further that Council acted outside its powers by amending the bylaw.

The Court held that although Council had no prior intent to amend the bylaw, the following actions, individually, were not conclusive of bad faith: Council deciding to amend the bylaw; Council's moving in haste to implement the amendment; Council acting against the advice of their advisors.

The Court declared that the test for bad faith is not the presence of corrupt motive. Council acted honestly and frankly throughout. Rather, good faith requires more than honesty. Good faith requires those exercising statutory power to do so within the objectives of the legislation. The *Planning Act* (pursuant to which the land use bylaw was made and amended) did not authorize Council to design a bylaw so as to protect community funds and limit competition; but this is what Council was trying to do. Accordingly, the Court found Council had acted outside its powers and the amendment was quashed.[16]

Privative Clauses

Because the courts have always been protective of their role, they have been reluctant to give up any of their power to oversee administrative tribunals. For this

Privative clauses attempt to prevent judicial review

16. *Parks West Mall Ltd. v. Hinton (Town)* (1994) 15 Alta. L.R. (3d) 400 (Q.B.).

reason, many of the statutes contain provisions called **privative clauses** which attempt to make it clear to the courts that they are not to interfere with the decisions of tribunals. The principle of supremacy of parliament would lead one to believe that such a direction would be effective. However, the courts have resisted the operation of such clauses and often find ways to avoid them, causing legislators to develop better and more specific privative clauses.

A typical example of a privative clause taken from the Alberta *Labour Relations Code* is

> 18(1) Subject to subsection (2), no decision, order, directive, declaration, ruling or proceeding of the Board shall be questioned or reviewed in any court by application for judicial review or otherwise, and no order shall be made or process entered or proceedings taken in any court, whether by way of injunction, declaratory judgment, prohibition, quo warranto or otherwise, to question, review, prohibit or restrain the Board or any of its proceedings.

> (2) A decision, order, directive, declaration, ruling or proceeding of the Board may be questioned or reviewed by way of an application for judicial review seeking an order in the nature of certiorari or mandamus if the originating notice is filed with the Court and served on the Board no later than 30 days after the date of the decision, order, directive, declaration, ruling or proceeding, or reasons in respect thereof, whichever is later.

> (3) The Court may, in respect of any application under subsection (2),

> > (a) determine the issues to be resolved on the application,

> > (b) limit the contents of the return from the Board to those materials necessary for the disposition of those issues, and

> > (c) give directions to protect the confidentiality of the matters referred to in section 13(6).[17]

The intent of this legislation is obvious, but the courts have simply assumed that the legislature intended this to apply only when the board is acting within its jurisdiction. Thus, the original question as to whether or not the administrator has jurisdiction is still open to review. In fact, the way the courts have interpreted this type of privative clause varies with circumstances. It seems that if the courts wish to review a decision, they will find a way to do so despite the presence of a privative clause.

In addition to privative clauses which directly prohibit judicial review, the legislators have embodied in statutes other clauses which indirectly have the same effect. Legislative provisions which assign the right to review specific questions of law or other matters to a minister or other administrator can exclude the courts from this function. Other clauses try to define the nature of the power exercised as discretionary by using subjective wording: "the director may," "Where the administrator is satisfied," "Where it appears to be," "Where in the opinion of." It is difficult to tell when discretionary power is being abused when it is assigned in a subjective way. Subjective assignments of power are, therefore, quite effective in keeping the courts from reviewing a decision.

There are as many different types of privative clauses as there are drafters of legislation, but they are often not as effective as they might seem on first reading.

---

17. *Labour Relations Code*, S.A. (1988) c. L-1.2 s. 18.

It should not be assumed that judicial review has been excluded because a privative clause is present. The only way to be certain of the interpretation of a specific privative clause would be to find a case where a superior court has interpreted and applied it. The courts' right to interpret statutory provisions gives them the power of supervision over these administrative bodies. The result has been a contest between the courts and the legislature, and this must be kept in mind when examining clauses which attempt to oust the jurisdiction of the court. The effect of such privative clauses must also be viewed as subject to the operation of the *Charter of Rights and Freedoms* which guarantees and enshrines the right to fundamental justice when a person's life, liberty or security is at stake. If these rights are interfered with by an administrative tribunal, the decision can be reviewed in the courts regardless of a privative clause.

Courts resist operation of privative clauses

Even when there is no privative clause present, the courts must be very cautious when intervening in the area given to an administrative tribunal. Usually there is good reason to give this decision-making function to such a body rather than a court. The tribunal may be more efficient and quicker in dealing with a particular kind of problem. It may be possible to tailor the procedures involved to the types of disputes and parties involved. And the decision maker may have particular expertise not found in a court. For these and other reasons shifting the decision-making power from the courts to such administrative bodies may be both prudent and efficient. When Parliament or the legislators have shifted such authority away from the courts, those courts must be very cautious in interfering even without a privative clause.[18]

Other Remedies

The powers and rights discussed in this chapter are largely extraordinary rights present when administrators or bureaucrats abuse their power or act incorrectly when making a decision that affects the position of an individual. In addition to the unique and special remedies discussed, the normal rights that arise when one individual has been injured by the act of another may be available. For example, if a contract is breached, all of the rights relating to breach of contract are applicable, even when one of the parties is the government or a Crown corporation. Similarly, if the actions of the decision maker involve the commission of a tort such as negligence, defamation, trespass or even assault and false imprisonment, the injured individual has the right to pursue tort remedies against the administrator.

Contract and tort remedies may be available

However, there are some limitations to the availability of remedies under these headings. Until recently, an individual had no power to sue the Crown, on the premise that since the government was the source of the law it was not subject to it and therefore could not be sued in its own courts. All jurisdictions in Canada have passed legislation making it possible to take the government to court. The *Proceedings Against the Crown Act*[19] of Alberta, for example, enables parties to sue the Crown and obtain judgment for breach of contract, tort, and so on. However, most jurisdictions have retained some of the Crown's former immunity, so it is difficult, if not impossible, to execute a judgment against the Crown. For example, it is almost impossible to get an injunction against the Crown; an order declaratory of the rights of the parties may be the prescribed alternative remedy.[20] Similarly, property of

Enforcement of judgment may be difficult

18. *Pezim v. British Columbia (Superintendent of Brokers)* 114 D.L.R. (4th) 385 (S.C.C.).

19. *Proceedings Against the Crown Act,* R.S.A. (1980) c. P-18.

20. Ibid., s. 17.

the Crown will not generally be available to satisfy judgment. Once a judgment is obtained, the good faith of the government agency has to be relied on to satisfy that judgment. No force can be used to ensure payment.

It should also be noted as a matter of common law that when an administrator exercises a statutory power properly, it will not give rise to tort action even if damage to an individual results from it. Some jurisdictions have extended this protection by statute. New Brunswick's *Protection of Persons Acting Under Statute Act*[21] is an example. The effect of such legislative protections may be to exclude a right of action in any given case and the student should be aware of any such local legislation.

A discussion of tort and contract law as well as many special rights and obligations created by statute are discussed in depth in previous chapters.

SUMMARY

Environmental law is one important example of government regulation of Canadian business. In common law, individuals have the right to sue others who damage the environment under riparian rights as well as the torts of nuisance and negligence. But these are inadequate to protect the general contamination of the environment and so controls have been enacted by federal and provincial statute. These statutes prohibit waste disposal except under prescribed standards and provide an enforcement body to investigate and prosecute violations. New projects which potentially threaten the environment are required to go through an environmental assessment process, sometimes requiring public hearings before permits are granted. The two objectives of government involvement are to penalize violation of environmental laws and to encourage good environmental practices.

When government bureaucrats make decisions affecting the lives of Canadians, they must act fairly, following the rules of natural justice. These rules require that there be a fair hearing including adequate notice, that the decision be made by the hearer of the evidence, and that it be made free of bias. When the rules are followed but the decision maker acts beyond the authority given under the statute or regulation, or when the statute or regulation is invalid because it violates the *Charter* or other constitutional provisions, that decision can be challenged in the courts and historical remedies applied. Governments often include provisions in legislation to restrict the power of courts to review the decisions of bureaucrats but such privative clauses are often ineffective.

---

21. *Protection of Persons Acting Under Statute Act*, R.S.N.B. (1973) c. P-20.

QUESTIONS

1. Identify and describe the three different functions of government. Explain how the concept of supremacy of parliament affects how the three functions interrelate.

2. What common law provisions protect the environment? Why was it necessary to pass new federal and provincial legislation?

3. Is all pollution prohibited under modern environmental legislation? Explain.

4. What is the negative impact of these environmental statutes on business?

5. What is the extent of the power of the government officials who enforce these environmental laws?

6. Describe the principle of the rule of law. Explain how it affects the exercise of government power.

7. What is meant by the terms *ultra vires* and *intra vires* and how do they relate to federal and provincial legislation?

8. What is meant by the golden rule and the mischief rule? Under what circumstances can the courts apply these rules of statutory interpretation?

9. What is an administrative tribunal?

10. What obligations are placed on an adjudicative decision maker, even if not included in the legislation under which he or she is acting?

11. What three main elements constitute the rules of natural justice? Under what circumstances must a decision maker follow these rules of natural justice?

12. What requirements must be met for a person to receive a fair hearing?

13. Under what circumstances will judicial review be available?

14. Distinguish between *certiorari*, prohibition, *mandamus*, and declaratory judgment.

15. What is a privative clause? How do courts usually react to them?

16. Give examples of three different types of privative clauses.

CASES

1. Re Eastern Provincial Airways Ltd. and Canada Labour Relations Board et al.

During a labour dispute between the employer and the union, a series of events took place which led to charges by both sides of unfair labour practices. The Canada Labour Relations Board heard these complaints. The union's complaint was that the employer had failed to bargain in good faith, had interfered in the administration of a trade union, and had discriminated against, intimidated and threatened striking employees. The employer's complaint was that the union had failed to bargain in good faith, and intimidation and coercion were used to get people to join or quit the union. After the union had put its case and after the employer had presented some of its evidence, the board declared that it had heard enough evidence and decided in favour of the union. The employer brought this action to have the decision of the board overturned.

Explain the nature of its complaint and the likely outcome. How would your answer be affected if the board gave the employer an opportunity to complete the presentation of evidence with the possibility that it might change its decision after the decision had been rendered?

2. Re Young and Board of School Trustees of School District #47

A parent wrote a letter to the district superintendent complaining about the conduct of a teacher. The conduct in question occurred when the teacher chastised the letter writer's son for bullying a classmate. The teacher made several remarks to the boy and the letter complained about them. When confronted with the accusation, the teacher said his comments were taken entirely out of context.

According to the *Public Schools Act* (R.S.B.C. 1960 Chapter 319) the Board of School Trustees was required to schedule a day in which a board or a committee appointed by the Board would interview the teacher and the district superintendent. This date was scheduled and the teacher was notified.

The teacher asked permission to bring a witness to testify and the request was denied. The teacher was suspended and brought a request to the court to have the decision overturned. Explain the nature of the teacher's complaint and explain the probable outcome.

3. Bennett v. British Columbia (Superintendent of Brokers)

Bill Bennett, former Premier of British Columbia, was charged with insider trading, a violation of the *Securities Act* of the province. One of the people accused with him, Herb Doman, was the president of a large forestry company. Under the legislation Mr. Bennett and Mr. Doman had the right to a hearing before a panel of commissioners. During the hearing an objection was heard that Mr. David Divine should not be sitting on the panel. He also was a director of a forestry company. Explain the argument on both sides. Would your answer be affected by the determination that the two companies were or were not in competition with each other?

4. Re Saskatchewan Oil and Gas Corporation and Leach et al.

Mr. and Mrs. Leach, the owners of a property on which Saskatchewan Oil and Gas Corporation operated an oil well, had a dispute with the gas company over what Mrs. and Mrs. Leach ought to be paid as compensation for a well site and access roadway on their property. In Saskatchewan, the owner of surface rights to property does not own the mineral and gas rights. Saskatchewan Oil and Gas Corporation had the right to develop the subsurface minerals and oil and was only required to pay suitable compensation for the disruption of the surface rights.

When such a disagreement takes place, the *Surface Rights Acquisition and Compensation Act* (R.S.S. (1978) provides for arbitration. This legislation gives broad powers to the arbitrator and great flexibility as far as what evidence can be heard. A hearing was held and evidence presented, but after the hearing was finished, the chairperson of the arbitration board wrote to a professional evaluator, Racine, for his opinion. Racine responded in the form of a letter.

Neither the owners nor the operators were aware of the request to Racine nor of his use of the information in his response.

The owner challenged the arbitration award. What is the nature of the complaint? Explain the probable outcome.

5. Re Workers' Compensation Board of Nova Scotia and Cape Breton Development Corp.

Mr. Slade, an employee of Devco, allegedly fell down the stairs and suffered an incapacitating injury. When he made a claim to the Workers' Compensation Board, Devco objected, as permitted under the legislation. At the hearing, the tribunal said that it was going to follow its policy and common practice of not allowing the employer's lawyer to cross-examine Mr. Slade. They also refused to give the employer access to the medical examination reports that formed the basis of the decision. The employer refused to proceed and challenged the Board in court.

Explain the arguments on both sides, and the appropriate remedy. Would your answer relating to the disclosure of the confidential medical information be any different if you realized that the tribunal was relying on the following section? "No officer of the board and no person authorized to make an inquiry under this part shall divulge or allow to be divulged except in the performance of his duties under the authority of the board any information obtained by him or which has come to his knowledge in making or in connection with inspection or inquiry under this part."

6. Bailey v. Local Board of Health for Corporation of Township of Langley, McDonald and Attorney-General for British Columbia

Mr. McDonald owned property in the Township of Langley on which he wanted to build. He brought an application before the medical health officer of the township (the petitioner in this action) for permission to build a conventional septic tank system. This request was turned down because of the disposal regulations passed under the *Health Act*. In October 1978, the council of the Township of Langley issued a building permit for the construction of a house on that property, providing McDonald obtained approval for the septic tank system from the medical health officer.

He proceeded to build, but instead of obtaining approval McDonald sought an appeal of the medical health officer's refusal before the local board of health, which then held a hearing in several sessions. An election took place and the makeup of the council changed after the first session. In subsequent sessions, some members were absent for part of the hearings, but all members of the council participated in the decision at the end. The decision was to permit the septic tank system over the medical health officer's objections.

The medical health officer appealed this decision to the court. What is the nature of his complaint and the likely outcome of the action?

7. Regina v. Canadian Pacific Limited

The Canadian Pacific Railway Company is a transcontinental railway that falls under the legislative jurisdiction of Parliament. Under the *Railway Act* the railway is obligated to keep its right of way clear of dead grass and other unnecessary combustible matter.

To do so, on several occasions the railway instituted what is called a full burn. This procedure produced a considerable amount of smoke, including obnoxious odours which were offensive and caused discomfort to the people in the various towns along the tracks. The Ontario *Environmental Protection Act* prohibits such activities and the railway was charged with violating the *Act*.

Explain some of the arguments available to the railway in its defense and the likely outcome.

8. Bank of Montreal v. Lundrigans Ltd.

Lundrigans operated a series of businesses in Newfoundland including interests in "road construction, civil engineering, buildings construction, building supply sales, mixed and pre-cast concrete production, gypsum and wallboard production and sales in residential, commercial and industrial real estate development." They were having financial difficulties and could not meet their obligations to the Bank of Montreal. The Bank wished to appoint a receiver, but the receiver insisted that a clause be included in the court order stating that the receivers would not be personally liable for any environmental liability incurred.

Discuss whether the creditors and receivers appointed by them should be responsible for environmental damage and cleanup costs. Discuss the extent of this liability. In your answer consider whether the receiver ought to be responsible for continuing environmental problems that arise while they operate the business as a going concern in order to preserve its value.

LEGISLATION

Alberta

Administrative Procedures Act, R.S.A. (1980) c. A-2
Arbitration Act, S.A. (1991) c. A-43.1
Environmental Protection and Enhancement Act, S.A. (1992) c. E-13.3
Interpretation Act, R.S.A. (1980) c. I-7
Proceedings Against the Crown Act, R.S.A. (1980) c. P-18

Federal

Canadian Bill of Rights Act, R.S.C. (1985) Appendix III
Canadian Environmental Assessment Act, S.C. (1992) c. 37
Canadian Environmental Protection Act, R.S.C. (1985) (4th Supp.) c. 16
Constitution Act (1982) as enacted by the *Canada Act (1982)* (U.K.) c. 11,
   including the *Canadian Charter of Rights and Freedoms and Constitution Act
   (1867)*, formerly the *British North America Act*, R.S.C. (1985) Appendix II

WEBLINKS

Environment Canada
www.ec.gc.ca/

Canadian Environmental Assessment Agency
www.ceaa.gc.ca/

Alberta Environmental Protection and Enhancement Act
www.gov.ab.ca/qp/ascii/acts/E13P3.txt

Canadian Environmental Protection Act
canada.justice.gc.ca/FTP/EN/Laws/Chap/C/C-15.3

Canadian Environmental Assessment Act
canada.justice.gc.ca/FTP/EN/Laws/Chap/C/C-15.2

International Institute for Sustainable Development
iisd1.iisd.ca/

National Round Table on the Environment and the Economy
www.nrtee-trnee.ca/english/index.htm

Canadian Institute of Resources Law Home Page
www.acs.ucalgary.ca/~cirl/

World Resources Institute (WRI)
www.wri.org/wri/

United Nations Environment Programme (UNEP)
unep.unep.no/

Supreme Court of Canada: Friends of the Oldman River Society v. Canada (Minister of Transport)
**www.droit.umontreal.ca/doc/csc-scc/en/pub/1992/vol1/html/
1992scr1_0003.html**

Industry Canada Regulatory Affairs Information
strategis.ic.gc.ca/sc/mrksv/regaffengdoc/welcome.html

Canadian Competition Bureau
strategis.ic.gc.ca/sc_muksv/competit/engdoc/homepage.html

Canadian Council of Ministers of the Environment
www.ccme.ca/ccme/

REFERENCES FOR PART 7

Klimek, Jennifer. *Insolvency and Environmental Liability.* Scarborough: Carswell, 1995.

Law Society of Upper Canada. *Administrative Law: Principles, Practice and Pluralism.* Scarborough: Carswell, 1993.

The Regulators and Confederation Life

VIDEO CASE

CBC

When a big corporation goes down, the investors are usually the last to hear about it. This is particularly true when it is an insurance company where the investors are the policyholders or hold deposits in retirement savings plans. When Confederation Life failed recently, many of the policyholders wondered why they hadn't been warned or why the company continued to sell policies even after they knew there was a good chance it would fail.

Insurance regulators—in this case the Office of the Superintendent of Financial Institutions and the Canadian Deposit Insurance Fund—had been investigating the financial state of Confederation Life several years before its demise and knew of it precarious state. In 1993 the regulating bodies stopped them from lending any more money but allowed them to continue selling insurance polices. In 1994, in an eleventh-hour attempt to rescue the company, they announced a merger, but it failed to take place and the company went into receivership.

There is much debate as to whether the regulators were on the scene soon enough and whether they offered sufficient warning to creditors of the financial state of the company. Perhaps the most important issue raised here is the dilemma of choosing between the goal of regulating a company in trouble in order to rehabilitate it, and the responsibility of warning the public, creditors, customers and shareholders of the impending collapse with the associated danger of creating a self-fulfilling prophesy.

Source: "Confederation Life Collapse," *Venture*, Show Number 504; telecast date September 4, 1994. Running time: 8:21.

DISCUSSION QUESTIONS

1. Who do the regulators serve and to what purpose?
2. What should be the nature of their job?
3. Is the cost spent on such regulation justified by the results?
4. When does the public have the right to know?
5. Should the regulators have acted sooner, and should they have the power to decide when to intervene?

CASE STUDIES

An effective way of learning business law is to participate in activities designed to simulate the business environment. Being involved in the resolution of hypothetical legal problems can provide invaluable experience in applying the principles discussed in this text. We provide here a series of case studies designed to raise legal issues from a business point of view. They can be used in a variety of ways in a business law course, and they are made available here in the hope that they may be of some assistance in the educational process.

Solving Legal Problems in the Business Environment

These are not primarily business cases with a legal twist; rather, they are law cases with a focus on legal issues which can be approached from a business point of view. The focus is on the legal issues. One recommended way of using them is to assign students to role-play members of management teams from opposing sides of the hypothetical situation and undertake the task of solving the problem presented. An essential part of this process is for that management team to determine the nature and significance of the problem and in the process, to assess the legal issues involved. It is only with a good understanding of the legalities surrounding the problem that the team can recommend a business solution.

Each team should first get a clear grasp of the facts, determining precisely what has happened and then perhaps predict the likely outcome. Next, on the basis of that examination of the facts, the team determines the legal issues involved. The law surrounding the facts may be clear or ambiguous (where a court's decision could go either way) and determining this should form part of the objective of assessing the risks to each of the parties in any potential resolution to the problems.

The next stage is to assess the impact or likely impact on the firm. This means to look at what would likely happen if the matter were to go to court; what decision would likely take place and what the damages or other remedy might be. Risk must be assessed. For example, it is unlikely that when the Loewen Group entered into their agreement with the Mississippi funeral business, they imagined a court awarding punitive damages of $500 000 000 for their dealings over an $8 000 000 dispute. Ford, on the other hand, likely did anticipate that even if a jury was to award a huge judgment in a Pinto disaster, it would be reduced on appeal to something they could manage, as it was. This case involved a design defect where the tailpipe was pushed into the gas tank in a rear-end collision, causing the car to burst into flames. The team should consider the business risk involved, not just in terms of this one case, but also what the decision and attendant publicity would mean to the rest of the business. Ford failed to anticipate this in the Pinto case.

Setting Up a Simulation Activity

In order to present a simulation activity in the classroom, students should divide themselves into teams of three and select one of the case studies. After reading the case and deciding on the division of roles and responsibilities, team members should review and discuss the following general questions and any other specific questions which may appear in the individual cases.

- What are the legal issues that arise in this problem?
- Why are they important?
- What are the applicable legal rules?
- Is there a clear answer as to the operation of the law?
- If not what are the potential legal outcomes and which is most likely?
- What is the objective or purpose behind the rules being applied?
- Will the purpose or objective behind the rule being applied likely affect the outcome of a court action?
- What effect can these outcomes have on the business involved?
- What is the best course of action for the business? (Why?)
- Discuss the potential impact on the business of the various possible courses of action that can be taken.
- What should have been done (if anything) to avoid this problem in the first place (risk analysis)?
- What steps (if any) should be taken to avoid similar problems in the future (risk avoidance)?

The opposing teams for each case study should then devise an interesting and informative means of presenting the facts, the problems and the proposed resolution to the rest of the class. Students should expect to be evaluated on their individual and team presentation performance, the extent to which they deal with the problems, and the means by which they solve them. Teams might conclude with the questions for class discussion and then present the class with a quiz question to be answered by class members and graded by the team as a means of evaluating student learning as a result of the presentation of the case study.

1. Adams v. The Royal Vancouver Hospital (Part 2, Part 4)

The Royal Vancouver Hospital (RVH), needed a givings officer—a person who seeks donations on behalf of the hospital from private donors. Their old givings officer was retiring on June 1. RVH, like all such federal and provincial institutions, was facing huge cutbacks in government funding and so private donations promised to be much more important in the future. A perfect candidate was brought to their attention, a Mr. Adams, who had worked very successfully for ten years at a large American hospital, a private institution largely dependent on donations from business.

Mr. Adams had come to Canada two years ago, when the federal government was encouraging research and development projects by giving substantial tax credits for funds spent on those projects. Mr. Adams and several other people from the U.S. had come to take advantage of this favourable research climate. He was involved for the past two years in developing a successful containment system for fighting oil spills. That project came to an end because changes in the Canadian tax laws ended the tax credits for such projects and because there had been no oil spills where the newly developed technology could be put to use.

In February it came to the attention of one of the assistants in the personnel office at RVH that at the end of March Mr. Adams' job would end and that he intended to return to the U.S. to find employment. The assistant told the personnel manager, who contacted the director of the hospital. With the approval of the Board of Governors, they decided to explore the possibility of hiring Mr. Adams. After several interviews it was agreed that Mr. Adams should come to work for RVH on a contract basis for the months of April and May and that on June 1 he would take over the permanent position of Givings Officer.

Mr. Adams agreed to this and had been working for the hospital quite competently in his position for a month and a half when in mid-April an article appeared in the *Chronicle*, a very influential national paper directed primarily at the business community, on the shameful abuse by some parts of the business community of the special tax advantages given for research and development in Canada. Not only did the article point out that the reason the program was stopped was because of the abuses outlined and cases of outright fraud; it referred to several people by name as having come to Canada from the U.S. and set up phony research projects but failed to do any research and on the basis of falsified claims still obtained the tax credits. The article speculated on the likelihood that these people would be prosecuted. Mr. Adams was named and described, along with five others, as one of these "carpetbaggers from the US, fraudulently taking advantage of the Canadian tax system." Because the article was published and distributed across Canada and was specifically directed at the business people Mr. Adams would have to approach for donations in his new job, it was clearly very damaging to him.

Shortly after the article appeared, Mr. Adams made it clear to the vice-president of Finance of the Hospital that the allegations referring to him in the article were false, that he had proof, and that he intended to sue the *Chronicle* for defamation. The VP Finance conveyed this to the President, Chairman and Board of Governors. The matter was then handed back to the personnel office to make recommendations.

Under these circumstances what should the hospital do with Mr. Adams and the full-time position that he had been promised which comes available in two weeks?

From the point of view of the *Chronicle*, after Mr. Adams complained and threatened to sue, the reporter who did the article was questioned about it. She made further inquiries, and concluded that the basic facts were correct and there was no doubt about the accuracy of the allegations as far as the other five men were concerned, and that if they were prosecuted there was every likelihood they would be convicted of fraud. It was also clear that Mr. Adams had been associated with them in the U.S. and came to Canada as part of that group intending to take advantage of the friendly Canadian tax environment for research and development.

However, Mr. Adams in fact did do the research and development and had obtained from the appropriate government department a letter stating they were entirely satisfied with the validity of the project with which he was associated, that Mr. Adams was in no difficulties whatever with them, and that there were no outstanding complaints against him. Such letters are only rarely given out.

In a meeting with the editor of the paper, the reporter, submitting copies of this letter and documents detailing the nature of the oil containment system developed by Mr. Adams, acknowledged her mistake. What should the *Chronicle* do in these circumstances?

From Mr. Adams' point of view, he presented proof to RVH of the inaccuracy of the report and they still fired him. He presented proof to the *Chronicle* of the falsehoods in the article, and the untold loss suffered (the loss of his job and ultimate damage to his career). He has requested a retraction and an apology and none has come. What courses of action are available and what should be taken into consideration before choosing what course of action to take?

2. Valley Homes v. Ace Minerals Corp. (Part 2, Part 4)

Jones is a young, recently hired female salesperson working for Valley Homes, a small company manufacturing and selling prefabricated dwellings. They sell primarily to people wanting to build their own cabins and summer homes. Jones' job consists in working out the designs with the customers, pricing that design, and then working out the specifics with the engineering section, which develops plans and sets out the exact specifications for the production of the dwelling. She then follows up with the customer, even providing a contractor to build the dwelling if needed.

A large mining company, Ace Minerals Corporation, as part of the development of a huge mineral deposit in northern Manitoba had to build a townsite for the miners and their families consisting of some 50 dwellings as well as a sports and recreation complex. Under the supervision of the vice-president of finance, Li, Ace Minerals published a request for tenders for the supply and erection of these 50 homes and recreation centre. Upon request Ace provided the specifications and the other details of the tendering process, including a statement that (1) once submitted the bid could not be withdrawn before the formal opening of all the bids and (2) that the lowest bid would be accepted, following the standard practice in the industry. Jones obtained these details and brought them to the attention of the Valley Homes executive arguing that the company had to change their method of doing business from just servicing the residential retail market and get more into the growing industrial sector. This was consistent with conversations that had recently taken place between the president of the company and major shareholders and so it was decided to submit a bid on the Ace Minerals project.

Jones and Brundel, the sales manager, were designated as the team to develop Valley Homes' bid. They worked for several days, enlisting the help of the engineering department completing and submitting the bid on the day specified by Ace.

That evening Jones was reviewing the bid and to her horror discovered a significant error in the calculations prepared by Brundel, the sales manager. Jones quickly redid the calculations and found to her added horror that instead of making a 15 percent profit on the deal they would suffer a 20 percent loss. On such a huge order this could be enough to bankrupt the company. On further examination it became clear that Brundel had intentionally structured the error and cleverly hid it in a way that made it very difficult to find. It was only by chance that Jones had discovered the error at all. It was later learned that Brundel as sales manager felt threatened by this business brought in by the upstart Jones and set out to sabotage the project to make sure things stayed the way they were. He felt that when the deal lost money, Jones would be blamed and he could then get rid of Jones with the blessing of the president.

Jones brought the miscalculations and conduct of Brundel to the attention of the president of the company. The president called Brundel into the office, confronted him with what he had done and it was at this point that Brundel broke down, confessed his misconduct and explained that because of his age he felt threatened by Jones and worried that he would lose his position to her. The president fired Brundel outright, and then went to the offices of the mining company. He met with the vice-president of finance, Li, and presented him with a letter explaining the mistake and in a formal way revoking the bid that had been submitted the day before. Although the bids had not yet been opened, Li declared that even though he was very sympathetic to the problems of Valley Homes, he could not interfere with the integrity of the bidding process once the bid had been accepted by the company for consideration. He said that they would simply have to wait until that afternoon when the bids would be opened to determine their fate. When the bids were opened, not surprisingly, Valley Homes was the lowest bidder and their bid was then automatically accepted by Ace.

The next day the president of Valley Homes and Jones met a management team of Ace headed by Li, where the problem was discussed. The Ace group confirmed their position but did indicate an understanding of the difficult position that Valley Homes found themselves in. They also pointed out that they realized that it was not in their interests to see Valley Homes fail and not be able to finish the job. They therefore agreed that if the project was satisfactorily completed on time, a bonus of would be paid to Valley Homes of half the difference between their price and the next lowest bid. This would allow Valley Homes to do just a little better than break even on the job, thus avoiding bankruptcy. It was also understood that there would likely be future dealings between these two companies and because of the good relations created in this meeting Valley Homes would give Ace Minerals an especially good deal on the next project.

As the project proceeded, a series of payments were made to Valley Homes, all 59 days after the date specified in the contract. As is normally the case with these kinds of projects, there was a clause in the contract whereby Ace would not have to pay interest on any late payments so long as payment was received by Valley within 60 days of the day payable.

Eventually the project was finished on time to the satisfaction of all parties, but the bonus was not paid. Valley Homes waited the specified 60 days and when the bonus was still not paid, they went to Li's office for an explanation. They learned at this time that Li had been replaced and they were invited to meet with the new vice-president of finance, Mr. Grey. He explained that over the months Ace had carefully monitored the project and the health of Valley Homes and had decided that they were in better financial shape than either party had anticipated. Bankruptcy was not a threat and therefore the mining company had decided not to pay the bonus. Mr. Grey went on to explain that they were entirely satisfied with the work that had been done and that Valley Homes should in no way take this failure to pay the bonus as an indication of dissatisfaction on their part with the company, the personnel, or the quality or timeliness of the work performed. In fact Grey's final comment was that he hoped that the two companies would have many years of cooperative ventures in the future.

Discuss the options available to Valley Homes in these circumstances.

3. Busy Bee v. Stefan et al. (Part 3)

Part 1

After graduation as a business student at SFU and taking a year off to travel, Stefan decided that he wanted to go into business for himself. He was attracted to the franchise business and chose one that required very little initial outlay. This involved the opening of a hot dog stand to be set up in front of a major sports retailing outlet recently opened in Burnaby. The franchising company, Ace, arranged for the site and supplied the cart itself, with a cooler, stove and storage area. It also supplied jumbo and regular wieners, buns, and condiments as well as soft drinks for a fee only slightly higher than would be available through normal wholesale outlets. Although Stefan had no choice but to get his supplies from Ace, he considered this slightly higher cost to be well compensated for by the convenience of getting them all from the same source with a consistent and known quality, and because of the other services supplied by Ace. Ace insisted on supplying the food inventory as a matter of quality control and to ensure product consistency between all of their franchised carts at various locations around the lower mainland. The franchise fee to be paid by Stefan to start the business was $20 000 and for this in addition to the cart and an initial supply of buns and wieners, Ace would supply a limited amount of advertising and other services such as bookkeeping and tax preparation. Ace also was entitled to a set percentage of Stefan's sales to pay for this service.

Stefan's initial problem was to raise the $20 000. He had no money himself, having just finished his business program and travels, and in fact owed about $15 000 in government student loans. He did, however, have a relatively new sports car worth, in his estimation, about $13 000. He also had an older cabin cruiser given to him by his grandparents which he estimated to be worth about $10 000. His mother had recently passed away and his father was a teacher in the Vancouver area. Although his father was encouraging in the business venture, he was not in a position to lend Stefan any money. He did suggest, however, that Stefan use a sound business approach to the problem and arrange financing through a company recommended by a friend, the Busy Bee Trust Company.

Stefan took this advice and made an appointment to see Gabrielle, a recently hired loans officer working for Busy Bee. When Stefan showed up for his appointment she recognized him as one of her fellow students in the business program at SFU. She remembered him as an adequate student if not particularly a bright light. Stefan did think to prepare a business plan and after some pleasantries presented it to Gabrielle with a request for the loan. Gabrielle could see that the business plan was quite optimistic, but recognized that there was a clear potential for success and leaned towards making the loan if she could be satisfied that the risk to Busy Bee was minimized. It was clear that the assets of the hot dog stand itself including the cart was of little value and that the $20 000 being paid by Stefan was for the franchising services provided by Ace.

What steps should Gabrielle take in these circumstances to make the loan and also minimize the risk of loss to Busy Bee?

Part 2

Gabrielle made the loan to Stefan, taking a chattel mortgage against the car and boat and getting Stefan's father to guarantee the $20 000 loan. Unfortunately, when the chattel mortgage against the boat was registered (using the financial statement under the PPSA) two numbers were inadvertently reversed and the security was registered under the wrong serial number.

Stefan continued in the business for some six months and by that time it became clear that the business was not as profitable as he hoped it would be. He needed more money to operate, and wanted to sell the boat to generate more working capital. He approached his friend Gabrielle at Busy Bee to get permission to do so and after reviewing the file she determined that the guarantee and the remaining chattel mortgage against the car satisfied Busy Bee's minimum requirements for security, and gave permission for the boat to be sold and the funds to be used by Stefan in his business.

About four months later, with the business still not doing as well as he had hoped, Stefan got bored and decided to go back to school and get a master's degree. He had also heard a rumour that the health departments in the various municipalities were planing a coordinated crackdown on roadside food vendors. Without informing Busy Bee, he sold the car to Kendra for $10 000, abandoned the cart in front of the sports complex, and caught a plane for Ireland where he had been admitted to a university to pursue his further education.

Kendra quickly resold the car to her friend Hakeem for $10 500, who used it for the three summer months and resold it to Lorenzo for $9500. By this time Gabrielle at Busy Bee found Stefan in arrears, checked and upon some investigation found that he had abandoned his business and left the country. When they took steps to repossess the car, they discovered their error, corrected it and reregistered the loan. This reregistration took place while the car was in the hands of Hakeem. After the correction and changes to the registration were made, Hakeem resold the car to Lorenzo for $9500. Neither Hakeem nor Lorenzo knew of the claim against the car by Busy Bee at the time of the sale, but had Lorenzo checked with the registry the corrected information would have made it clear that Busy Bee claimed a charge or lien against the car. Busy Bee repossessed the car from Lorenzo and demanded payment of the remainder of the $20 000 loan from Stefan's father on the guaranty.

Discuss the legal position of the various parties.

4. O. Mann v. The Builder's Friend et al. (Part 2, Part 4)

Sanjay had recently been promoted to the position of manager at one of the Lower Mainland outlets of a retail sales business selling home and garden supplies called The Builder's Friend. This business had 20 retail outlets in western Canada concentrating on supplying the needs of the homeowner and amateur builder.

There had always been a considerable problem with shoplifting and this was particularly true at Sanjay's location. Matters had been made worse in recent months with a serious downturn in the economy which showed a related increase in theft from the store. All normal steps had been taken to reduce this problem including hiring floorwalkers, inspecting customers' packages and requiring all vehicles to submit to a vehicle inspection as they left the premises.

When Sanjay became manager he was told that one of the major problems he had to deal with was the excessive shoplifting taking place at his store. Sanjay was also told that the old manager had lost his job because of his inability to reduce such thefts, so he knew his success in his new job would depend to a large extent on the way he dealt with this problem.

Sanjay decided to enlist all of his staff in this struggle, and devoted a significant part of his regular weekly sales meetings to a program encouraging all the employees to get involved in theft prevention—"to have a go," as he put it. He also made sure any new person hired not only looked like he or she could "take care of him- or herself" but actually could. He encouraged everyone to be watchful for any sign of shoplifting and a large part of the weekly training sessions were spent on how to spot theft.

Within six months of taking over as manager, Sanjay was satisfied that all of the employees were excited about the program. They seemed not only vigilant but eager to catch shoplifters, and indeed in that time several had been apprehended. Sanjay took a zero-tolerance approach and made sure all were prosecuted fully, even kids. He further rewarded employees involved in apprehensions by recognizing their contributions on the staff bulletin boards and also in a more tangible way by giving them a day off with pay. He noticed that the other employees appreciated this and were further encouraged to participate in the program.

One Saturday afternoon Sanjay was walking around the floor of the store when he saw a well-dressed customer (Oliver Mann) carrying an obviously full large brown paper bag in both hands, looking at merchandise in the store. Sanjay had noticed him because on another occasion one of the employees had pointed him out as a person who had been acting suspiciously but they had never caught him taking anything in the past. This time Sanjay saw him pick up a small but expensive power tool and put it into the bag he was carrying. Sanjay called over two of his new employees, both young, vigorous, athletic-looking young men. He gave Leo the keys to his car and his cellular phone, telling him to drive around the block and call into the customer service desk to coordinate so that he could cut the customer off if he tried to get away. Sanjay and Henrik, the other young man, looked around and found the customer in the building supplies section, which was near the supply entrance where there was no cashier located, and sure enough the customer left the store through that open side door. Sanjay sent Henrik off to follow and as he went out the front way to intercept the fleeing customer he told the customer service clerk to alert Leo in the car that the customer was fleeing and was heading across the intersection at the front of the store.

When Mr. Mann saw that he was being followed, he started to run. Henrik ran after him. Sanjay also ran after him, cutting across at an angle from the front door. Henrik caught up to him first in the intersection, grabbing him, but Mann dropped his package, shrugged off Henrik and, leaping away, made a run for it. Just then Leo drove into the intersection, jumped out of the car and made a flying tackle, sending both himself and Mr. Mann in a heap onto the street. Leo sat on Mann, and proceeded to hit him several times in the head. Henrik joined the action at this time and added several of his own blows, all before Sanjay the manager caught up and arrived at the scene. All three then picked up Mr. Mann, who was severely dazed, and half-dragged and half-carried him back into the store.

When Sanjay returned to the store he immediately called the police. About the same time the police arrived at the store, a man named Richard also presented himself at the store, identified himself to the police, and explained that while stopped at the intersection waiting for a red light immediately beside where Leo had parked his vehicle, he had witnessed the whole thing from when the customer had left the store. His attention was first drawn to the well-dressed man carrying a large parcel and hurrying across a right-turn segment of the intersection just ahead of a right-turning car. He had witnessed one person come after the man from around the side of the store and another out of the front door. He had witnessed Henrik's initial attempt to subdue the customer, and said he had had a "grandstand seat" for what he had described as a perfect "flying tackle" made by the driver beside him who had jumped out of his car and brought the man down. He had also described the blows that Henrik and Leo had administered to the man and had seen him being dragged into the store. Richard left his name and address with the police and they said he would likely be called on later.

Mr. Mann at this time wasn't making much sense and so the police arrested him and called an ambulance. The next day at the hospital Mr. Mann, who had suffered a concussion in the fray, explained to the police that he had simply been looking at what was in the store, and although he had at first intended to buy a small tool he had decided it was too expensive and had changed his mind. Because he was not purchasing anything, he had left by the most convenient exit. When asked why he ran, Mann replied "Wouldn't you run if you saw several big men chasing you?" The police went back to the store and asked to look in the bag that Mann had been carrying. Sanjay realized that in the excitement they had not brought it back to the store with them. They went out into the street looking for it but by that time of course it was gone.

Discuss the position of The Builder's Friend, Sanjay and the other employees. What options are available to Mr. Mann?

5. *Chan v. Everybody* (Part 2, Part 3, Part 4, Part 5)

Part 1

Chan, a recent business graduate, decided to start his own business. After attending a franchising and small business opportunity conference he was attracted to a franchising opportunity involving a pot and pan repair and refurbishing business. After the conference he researched the business, getting all the information he could from Tinker's Damn Inc., the people selling the franchise. He talked to Theo, the salesperson trainer and area representative for Tinker's Damn and found that the services offered involved the company providing training in the repair of pots, pans, and other such utensils as well as training in a new technique of refurbishing such items to almost-new condition. The company would also provide the specialized equipment necessary, a designated area in which Chan was entitled to carry on the business involving both residential and commercial customers and a commitment to provide a certain amount of advertising in the local paper, on billboards and the like. Theo also promised that they would solicit sufficient appointments in the first two months so that the business would not only break even (including a salary for Chan) but also generate a modest profit. After these three months, Tinker's Damn would provide a list of 500 potential clients but other than that, some advertising, and an ongoing bookkeeping service that would be supplied by the head office, Chan would be on his own. Part of Chan's training involved where to look for customers and how to solicit business. The fee to be paid to Tinker's Damn was $20 000 and 15 percent of all revenue earned by Chan. These provisions were clearly stated in a written contract between Chan and Tinker's Damn Inc., which Theo signed on behalf of the company.

In addition Chan had to purchase a truck in which to house the equipment and from which he would do his business. This was a further $25 000 investment. He borrowed enough money from his father to pay the franchise fee and to make a $3000 down payment on the truck. They agreed that this should be done in a businesslike way and so Chan incorporated a company and on its behalf agreed by promissory note to repay at a rate of $500 per month with 9 percent annual interest. Without consulting Chan, his father gave the note to Chan's recently married sister to use as a down payment on a house.

Chan also felt that he needed to establish a small office in his home. For this he needed a computer, printer, fax machine, a telephone answering machine and photocopier. He felt that he would like a scanner as well. On the basis of the projected sales and income figures supplied by the franchise company and his own needs, he calculated that he had enough income to be able to carry the extra debt and went to Tomorrow Town, a retail electronics store, to see what kind of deal he could get on these items. When he entered the store, he was approached by the salesperson Michel, who after listening to him for a few minutes told him he had just what he needed. He showed him a computer, monitor, hard drive and printer which were on sale for $2500. Michel explained that this was the most up-to-date technology available anywhere; the computer was not only on the leading edge of development and would be current for years to come, but also upgradeable when advances beyond its capabilities finally were developed, "not that Chan would ever need anything better." Michel also pointed out that the computer would run all current software, even the most advanced, and would run any software that might be developed in the foreseeable future. He also pointed out that the printer was the most recent high-impact 24-pin design and that nothing was better. For the other equipment, Michel showed Chan a Concord 100, which was a special combination fax, scanner, and photocopier that was available for only a further $1700. Michel said that this was what everyone was using nowadays and that they were extremely fortunate to find one in the store that had not yet been sold. Chan was told that he had better decide to take it right away as it would not likely be available later in the day as they were going so fast. Michel said he would throw in one of the new Brother answering machines they had on sale that day for no extra charge.

Chan, impressed, agreed to buy the computer, the printer and the combination fax/scanner/photocopier. He also agreed to purchase an extended warranty as well as a management contract for a further $500 which provided that any repairs and servicing necessary would be done by the provider of the service for only a "small fee" at Chan's office. He also agreed to purchase a packaged "office" software bundle. All together the price came to $5800 including provincial sales tax and GST.

Chan paid his last $500 as a down payment and agreed to repay the loan at a rate of $150 per month for five years. He was not worried, as the sales projections and costings he and the advertising company had done assured him of a monthly income high enough to not only pay a substantial salary to him but also cover the franchise payments, the payments on the truck and this further debt to Tomorrow Town. Because Chan had incorporated his business, and wanted to put the purchase in the company's name for tax purposes, he had to sign a promissory note in his own name for the money owed as well as a conditional sale agreement in the name of the company secured against the computer equipment purchased.

Chan took the computer home, hooked it up, and, when he tried to run the standard software, found the hard drive was not big enough to install it. He also found that while the computer was able to run some of the software it did so very slowly. He further discovered that he didn't really need some of the software purchased (a presentation program). He asked a friend knowledgeable in computers to come over and have a look. The friend pointed out that the computer was an older model (a "386") that had been sold as a special package (CPU, monitor, drives, etc.), and while it could be upgraded to run some of this newer software, the upgrade would require replacement of the motherboard, in effect a replacement of the whole heart of the computer. Even then the monitor (and video card) and other internal components packaged with it were really designed for this outdated technology and would not operate with the new CPU that efficiently. Chan was further disappointed that some video games that he had hoped to use on the computer were incompatible with such an obsolete system. He was also disappointed to find out from his friend that although the combination fax/scanner/photocopier worked, it required special paper and ink that made any kind of volume work prohibitively expensive compared to the alternative. For this reason the Concord 100 was no longer being sold in other stores and was being sold off at Tomorrow Town at a sale price in order to get rid of them. The main difficulty with this was that the special paper and ink were used only with this unit and it would be extremely difficult to get them in the future. The printer itself was completely compatible with the computer because it too was obsolete. He found that he should have purchased a laser or inkjet printer which would have provided better resolution, much greater speed with modern software, and less noisy operation. His friend also noticed that the telephone answering machine he had been "given" was a used model.

Chan went back to Tomorrow Town in an irate mood to demand return of his money. He looked for Michel, but he was not there. He demanded to talk to the manager. The manager, Ruth, was sympathetic. She explained that Michel was only a sales trainee who had been on the floor that day only to get exposure to the "real world" of sales. Michel had not been authorized to make any sales without the direct involvement of one of the regular sales staff. Despite that, when the sales manager realized what Michel had done he had decided to honour the sale even though they didn't have to, and Ruth had supported that decision.

Ruth explained that she could not help Chan now, because earlier that day they had assigned the conditional sales agreement along with the promissory note to Ready Cash, an independent finance company that handled all Tomorrow Town's installment sales. Thus, Tomorrow Town Electronics was no longer involved, and any problems Chan had ("except warranty problems of course"), would have to be taken up with Ready Cash.

The manager also pointed out the small print in the contract which stated that all sales were final, and that unless the product was actually defective, in which case it would be repaired or replaced, there was no other warranty express or implied. The contract also said that any statements made by salespersons or otherwise that were not specifically included within the written contract were void and of no effect. The manager did offer, however, to upgrade the motherboard of the computer for another $1000, which would solve "many" of Chan's problems, but otherwise since there was nothing actually wrong with the computer he was out of luck.

Chan, by now very angry, said he would not make any further payments and demanded his down payment back. The manager, feeling that she had been more than generous and that Chan was not only ungrateful but insulting, managed to hold her temper and simply told him he would have to take that up with Ready Cash as she ushered him out of her office.

Later that week Chan received a letter from Ready Cash, informing him of the assignment of the conditional sale agreement along with the promissory note and requesting him to make any further payments to Ready Cash at a specified address. Chan wrote a letter back stating what had happened, demanding that the computer be replaced or that his down payment be returned. He also clearly stated that he would be making no further payments until the matter was rectified to his satisfaction.

Part 2

Chan made no payments. Ready Cash did not return any money paid by Chan. Tomorrow Town Electronics refused to have anything more to do with the matter or with Chan. A bailiff attended at Chan's house to repossess the computer but Chan refused to let him take it until he "at least got my down payment back."

Ready Cash sued Chan and Tomorrow Town. Chan sued Tomorrow Town and Ready Cash.

To make matters worse for Chan, he was in no financial position to carry on these court actions. It turned out that the business he had started was not anywhere near as profitable as he had anticipated and been led to believe by Tinker's Damn Inc. If it hadn't been for the help of his father he would have lost the truck, to say nothing of the electronic equipment he had purchased from Tomorrow Town Electronics. He had considered just not making any further payments on the promissory note he had given to his father, but when he learned that it had been used as part payment on a house for his sister, he was unsure what effect not paying would have on his sister and father.

Upon further investigation he discovered that Theo, the salesperson and trainer for Tinker's Damn, had misled him. When Chan went to the appointments made by Theo, he found that half of them had never been contacted and about half of those that had, said no to the appointment. Only about 25 percent of the appointments he had been given by Theo were in fact valid and he was now scrambling to drum up enough business to keep afloat. As a result he had to immediately turn to the list provided of potential customers, and to his dismay he discovered this list was simply the restaurant section extracted from the Yellow Pages and consisted of only 200 names, each listed twice. He could see that with a lot of hard work over several months he could build up a sufficient clientele to "do okay" in the business, but it would be touch and go for quite awhile. It was clear that he had not received anywhere near the value he had expected from Tinker's Damn Inc.

What should Chan do in these circumstances?

How would the situation have been different if Chan had signed a personal guarantee instead of a promissory note?

Comment on the appropriateness of the conduct and legal position of the other parties involved.

6. I'm a Lumberjack and I'm Okay (Part 2, Part 3)

Jack owned and operated one of a multitude of small logging operations in western Canada called Lumberjack Inc. A few of these small operators had their own allocations of timber (as licensed by the provincial government) but most, including Jack, were "contractors" working for larger companies (the "Majors"); this meant that for a negotiated contract price they would go into the areas licensed to the Majors and harvest that timber for them. They also occasionally harvested timber for private landowners who had stands of timber on their own land. They would contract to purchase the standing timber, cut these logs and sell them to one of the Majors to be made into pulp or sawed and sorted for lumber depending on the type of timber and the quality and size of the log. There were only a few of these major companies, and the small loggers usually had no choice but to sell their logs to the one operating nearest to them because of the prohibitive cost of transporting the logs.

The value of working together was clear very early, and years ago a Small Loggers' Association (SLA) was formed to handle the problems of Jack and other small loggers like him. A great problem they all had was that they could usually sell their logs to only one buyer, the one nearest their operation. Because of this and the fact that there were only one or two Majors interested in purchasing their logs, the market was very restricted and the majors could dictate the price. Jack and the other small loggers didn't really have much choice.

As a result a big concern of the SLA was to ensure they got the best price for their timber, and one of the main purposes of the SLA was to provide a monthly forum for Jack and his friends to get together and discuss the prices they should get for their logs. They invited the purchasers from the major logging companies and together they would all set prices for the timber to be sold in the following month. The members of the SLA agreed that they would sell exclusively to the Majors and the representatives of the Majors in turn agreed on behalf of their companies to purchase a set amount of timber from those small loggers at a specified price. The Majors agreed to this because they were not happy about the control they had over the pricing in the past, feeling that they had too much power to control the market and as a result were vulnerable to prosecution. Also this kind of arrangement created a certain security of supply that they had never had before.

The Majors had another problem that this arrangement solved. They were all divided into different divisions, and the divisions that purchased logs and chips from the small logger often found themselves selling the same logs and chips along with others they had produced themselves to other divisions of their own company or they were purchasing from those other divisions, and it was required that this be done at fair market price or they would again be vulnerable to prosecution. Because of this arrangement with the SLA they had set a price they could use in their internal dealings. Thus the representatives who attended these monthly meeting of the SLA were both the customers and the competitors of Jack and the other small loggers.

The chips purchased were either used locally in the pulp and paper division of the Major, or, if there was an excess, sold offshore. The logs also might be sawn up by the timber division of the Major for export or be exported offshore in their raw state. But often these logs were also sold to private specialized sawmills for use in the local building industry. One of these private mills, Busy Bee Enterprises, learned of the arrangement with the SLA and was irate at what it saw as price fixing. Busy Bee approached three of the smaller loggers, including Jack, and demanded logs be sold directly to Busy Bee for the same price at which they sold logs to the Majors.

Jack didn't know what to do and took the matter to the next SLA meeting.

He had another significant problem to deal with as well. In one of his deals he had agreed to log a stand of timber covering one-third of Otto's ranch. This was a nice property located on the wall of a small valley near a lake which Otto intended to convert into a guest ranch in the near future, although he never told this to Jack. The ranch covered 150 acres (60.7 hectares) and was worth about $200 000 on the open market. This was a little higher than normal because of the nice location of the ranch. In fact this was what Otto had paid for the property six months earlier. One of the reasons Otto bought the ranch was because he knew he could sell the timber. Otto's deal with Jack required Jack to pay Otto $100 000 for the standing timber. Jack then would come onto the property with his men and equipment and remove the trees "with as little disruption to the rest of the property as possible." In addition to this provision the agreement required that after the trees were harvested the property be "restored" within two years of the harvest.

Jack's workers cut down the trees in June 1993 using clearcut methods and Jack resold the timber for $200 000, which left a profit to the company of $25 000. Unfortunately, the property was left in very bad condition. Roads had been made crossing other parts of the ranch, stream beds were destroyed in the process, and the clearcutting itself left that part of the property not only dug up by the equipment but covered with all sorts of unsightly debris. No attempt was made by Jack's company to "restore" the property after the removal of the trees. Jack explained to Otto that there was "just not enough money in it." Otto had expected this part of the ranch to be cleared and then to be landscaped giving a dramatic view of the valley and lake, making it ideal for use as a guest ranch. Instead he was left with a blasted landscape extending beyond the original tree stand and making it impossible to develop the property as he intended. Otto determined that it would cost him $150 000 to clean up the property and put it into the shape he had envisioned when he started.

Otto complained and threatened to sue. He demanded that the property be restored as agreed or that he receive compensation so that he could have the work done by someone else. Jack was surprised when Otto told him he intended to develop the property as a guest ranch. Jack had assumed he would be using it as a cattle ranch like all of the others in the areas and that the esthetics were "no big deal." He investigated and found that if the property were used as a cattle ranch, as he had thought it would be, the increased market value had it been landscaped as Otto wanted would only go from $200 000 to $215 000. On the other hand if the property were developed as a guest ranch the restoration and landscaping would be a vital part of the project and would have increased the value dramatically.

Explain the legal position of the parties in these situations and explain what should be done by them.

7. *Something Fishy* (Part 2, Part 3, Part 4)

Liam had operated a very successful chandlering business supplying the needs of the fishing industry on the west coast of British Columbia for 20 years. Unfortunately, because of overfishing, drastic cutbacks had to be made to the west coast fishing fleet and to the overall fishing industry there, and his business suffered. In an effort to save his business, Liam set his mind to other, related fields but realized he knew very little about other types of businesses. Liam's operation consisted of about 20 employees. Five employees worked in the store ordering supplies, doing the paperwork and servicing the customers. The rest manned the dock and the fuelling facilities, or worked in the machine shop.

Liam's particular talents were in obtaining supplies at reasonable rates and in operating the machine shop. When Liam understood that the impending cutbacks would severely affect his business, he realized he needed expert help to survive. He decided to hire a sales and marketing manager who would run the sales and generally market the business while finding them something else to do. He interviewed Maia, a recent graduate of Simon Fraser University who had graduated at the top of her class and had concentrated in small business entrepreneurship with a specialty in sales and marketing and was just what Liam needed. Maia had also worked on fishing boats before going to university and during the summers and knew the industry. He offered Maia a job and this offer was accepted.

The terms of the employment were that Maia would agree to work for four years in this position at a generous and increasing yearly salary. At the end of that period both parties would review the situation and if they agreed would negotiate a new and continuing contract. As with most contracts of this type, a three-month probation period was included whereby Maia could be let go if Liam was not satisfied with her performance. Maia had a similar right to leave during this period.

Maia knew her stuff, and after a few weeks working with Liam and getting to know what they had to offer, Maia suggested that they turn to the offshore fleet who were taking great amounts of fish off the west coast of B.C. "We might as well try to get something back from them since they likely caused this problem in the first place." Maia explained that when fishing they often would see many ships of other nations working the fishing grounds and that these ships would have to go home or to distant ports for supplies or to make repairs. "Why not offer the service of supplying and making minor repairs to those ships right here? We have the equipment, the talent and the facilities. It would not be much different from what you have been doing all along with our own boats." Liam liked the idea, but had no idea of how to go about starting the business. Maia did, and under Liam's signature sent a series of letters to companies operating the offshore fleets offering their services. They received several serious replies and after some further negotiating by mail, three viable potential agreements looked certain. Of these one of the companies was Japanese, and another was from Algeria owned and operated by Arab/Muslim interests.

The next stage was to do in-person negotiations to clinch the contracts. Maia was eager to go, but Liam spoke to several friends in the lumber industry who had done business with the Japanese and they explained that the Japanese were extremely conscious of the status of the people they dealt with and might consider dealing with Maia an affront, for besides being female Maia was of African-American heritage. Liam made inquires and discovered that the problem might be even more serious in dealing with the Algerian company. Because of the size of Liam's operation, he couldn't afford to hire another person to do the negotiations, especially since he realized that an ongoing relationship would result and the person he originally sent would have to be kept on to service the contract.

After serious soul-searching Liam called Maia into his office and explained that because she couldn't do this part of her job he would have to let her go. He explained that even though he was not required to (because her probation period wasn't up), he would pay her three months' wages if she would stay and help her replacement get started. Liam then hired James, another Simon Fraser graduate, second in his class and Caucasian but without the specialization in small business and sales that had made Maia so suitable. Liam felt that with Maia's help James's limitations could be overcome. Maia reluctantly agreed to help and, while angry, said she understood Liam's dilemma.

James did successfully carry on the negotiations with the Japanese and Algerian companies and agreements were signed giving Liam's business exclusive rights to do minor repairs and supply these ships. The only difficulty that James had was when dealing with the Algerian Company. He was in fact dealing with an agent of that company and that agent insisted on a payment of 15 percent of the value of the contract to cover "advanced promotional expenses." Liam and James did some further investigation and found that this was nothing more than a kickback or bribe. They also found out that it was a common and expected aspect of doing business in that part of the world. If they wanted the business Liam felt that he had no choice and so reluctantly made the payment.

Liam's only potential rival in this new business was another person in the same town who had also supplied the west coast fleet. Nathan was an old friend of Liam's, and he had struck up a great friendship with Maia as well. He had faced similar problems when the west coast fishing industry went down the tubes, but had taken another way out. Instead of looking to the offshore fleet, he had turned his interest to the still-viable recreational fishery. Nathan went into the business of providing supplies for the recreational fishers as well as the many resorts and boat rental facilities catering to them. Nathan and Liam had been rivals in the past and each feared the other would go after his new business.

After some conversation the two men agreed that there was only enough business in the two areas for one. They prepared and signed an agreement to the effect that Nathan would not carry on the business of supplying or offering services to any foreign commercial fish boats and Liam agreed to stay out of the recreational fishery business in any form. Each retained the right to continue to supply and service any B.C. fishing boats as they had in the past. They agreed that if either violated this agreement the victim would be entitled to liquidated damages in the amount of $500 per day for each day the breach continued.

All went well for another season and then the recreational fishing business also began to go sour. At about this time, several other companies operating offshore fleets who now saw the advantage of the arrangement their rivals had with Liam came to town and approached Nathan eager to obtain access to the same kind of services. Nathan could not pass up the opportunity and made arrangements to provide similar services for them. Although this did not directly hurt Liam's business since he had all he could handle just servicing the needs of the three companies that he had contracted with, he still felt that was in breach of this agreement even though Nathan had not solicited the business.

Liam had a falling-out with Nathan and threatened to sue. When Maia discovered how well Liam's business was going and how he was treating Nathan she also decided to sue. Discuss the legal position of the parties and the appropriateness of their conduct.

8. *Software the Hard Way* (Part 4, Part 5, Part 6)

Noah is a software developer working for New Ware Development Company for the past ten years. While he has no management position with the company, he is one of the five directors because he is key to its operation and one of the original founders of the company. He and two other friends (Kyoshi and Catrina) originally set up New Ware to develop some software they had created at the beginning of the personal computer boom.

They had all been employed by a major computer company, but they had found the atmosphere, the suits, the eight-to-five schedule, etc., stifling and decided to take the ideas they were working on and set up their own company. Originally 1 000 000 shares were issued in New Ware Development Corp. Noah, Kyoshi and Catrina each own 30 percent of the shares (300 000); the remaining 10 percent are divided equally between Amir, the President and Production Manager, and Rasheeda, the Marketing Manager, who also hold director positions.

Noah, Kyoshi and Catrina all knew that their skills were in the software development aspect of the business, not in management, and so from the beginning they planned to hire the needed management skills so they could get on with the research and development. This worked out to be a very successful strategy, and over the years New Ware developed into one of the most influential companies in their field with 30 employees and annual sales in the millions. New Ware specialized in the development of communications software, particularly networking, and more recently the company had directed its attention towards exploiting the exploding interest in the Internet.

The next part of the strategic plan developed by Amir and Rasheeda was to go public and sell shares on the stock market. This would require a further expansion of the business with an infusion of borrowed funds of about $1.5 million from the bank. It is important to note that although Kyoshi and Catrina made important contributions, it was Noah that was considered the software genius. He was key to the whole operation and had a great reputation in the industry. There was no question but that the success and reputation of New Ware was largely dependent on Noah's role. It is clear that the bank's willingness to provide the additional capital needed was on the assumption that Noah would continue with the company.

Noah was not interested in the business aspects of New Ware. He had a lab at home and a couch at work, and he would wander in and out whenever he felt like it, often not distinguishing between his personal and his work life. Certainly he was just as likely to be working or sleeping at his home as at the office. Everyone was tolerant of his eccentric lifestyle because of what he produced. But Noah was finding New Ware in its new successful corporate status as stifling and restrictive as the company he had left, and he felt the resentment of the other employees towards his "privileged position." He couldn't deny how successful the company had become, however; so he just kept plodding along in what he considered a rut.

On the morning of June 18, Noah and his assistant Sang were summoned along with the other employees to a general meeting where it was announced that everything was now in place: the funding had been obtained and the public share offering was to go ahead over the summer. Every employee of the company was to have the right of first refusal of the additional 1 000 000 shares to be offered to the public. Amir, the president, explained that they had borrowed $1.5 million from the bank and they intended to use this money to diversify.

Noah had known vaguely about the intention to go public but he now realized that they had borrowed a considerable amount of money, affecting the value of his shares, and that with the sale of the new shares his percentage of New Ware would also be severely diluted as well as any say he had in its operation. The fact that New Ware was being diverted from its original purpose and now would be just another business completed his disillusionment. Of course he would have known all this had he bothered to attend the directors' meetings.

The champagne was broken out and everyone began to celebrate, congratulating Noah and commenting on the role his expertise, skill, and genius had played. Amir toasted Noah and his great accomplishments. Left unsaid was the fact that the reason the management of New Ware wanted to diversify was to make the company fortunes less dependent on such an unstable character as Noah.

Noah's son, Josh, had a lot of his father's characteristics. There was that same flash of genius, and also much of the same instability. He had followed in his father's footsteps and taken computer programming at university, but become bored and found the regime of university study stifling. He dropped out after his third year, saying they weren't teaching him anything he couldn't learn on his own anyway. He and two friends who had graduated decided to set up their own development company just as Noah and his friends had done 20 years ago.

One of the projects Josh had been working on at university was a revolutionary interface that promised to up the speed and convenience of using the Internet. The idea had come from his father. Josh had been out with Noah on his boat one day and had complained about needing a major project to work on as part of his studies. Noah remembered a conversation he had had with one of his clients, who had expressed a need for a faster and better Internet interface and outlined some basic ideas about how it could be accomplished. Noah had been too busy to follow up on it and had never told anyone at New Ware about the idea.

Josh took the idea back to the university and got the permission and support of his supervisors to proceed. In fact, the university thought so highly of the idea that they provided a lab and several other personnel to work with Josh. They told him that if things worked out this could be the basis for a major part of the new product development and marketing strategy of the university.

Josh and his two graduate friends proved the workability of the new software. They were the only three people who had any detailed knowledge of the project. When they decided to leave the university their main concern was not to leave anything behind that would give away their ideas and work. They went to Noah who advised them that although it was they who had acquired the equipment, it was done with university grant money so the equipment belonged to the university. Instead, Noah said, they should erase all copies of their data that remained on those computers.

It was clear to Noah that a new business should be set up and that capital would have to be raised to recreate the lab. Other funds would be needed for marketing. Noah also suggested they could enter into an arrangement with New Ware to co-develop the software. They already had the market developed, the marketing expertise, and the production facilities, and there was no question but that they could successfully market the new product.

Although Noah was enthusiastic about the new enterprise, his years of experience in the industry had taught him to be cautious. Many new ideas ran into snags and never got anywhere. He mentioned this to Josh and his friends, but they didn't care; they knew it would work, and anyway they had nothing to lose. They were just concerned about how best to complete the development of the product and how best to exploit it and get it out on the market.

Noah said he would help as much as he could. After a considerable amount of thinking and after checking his finances, he decided that he could take some personal risk and told the boys to count him in. It was clear they would need at least $900 000 to set up the lab and get the business going. He decided that he could risk $300 000. Since Josh and his friends had no money, the rest would have to come from other sources.

Noah wanted to make sure the rest of his fortune was protected and not at risk. He couldn't start all over again. He also didn't want to do anything to put New Ware in danger, as most of his wealth was tied up in shares in that company. He had to consider whether to stay working for New Ware and remain as a director or to sell his shares, quit and go into business with Josh and his friends even with all of the negative impact that would have on New Ware. One thing was sure: if he left New Ware he would take with him his sidekick Sang, who was a technician and an absolute miracle worker with software and this would further damage New Ware.

Remembering his own experience with his own friends and New Ware, he wanted to not only limit his liability to the $300 000 but also make sure he had more say in management and a share of the profits. He didn't want to discourage or control the enthusiasm of the young people he was helping out, but he knew there had to be some guiding hand and with his experience and age it might as well be his.

A major difficulty was just what kind of business arrangement would be appropriate. Noah decided he needed advice, and although it was against everything he stood for he decided he had to talk to his lawyer. The lawyer went on and on about companies, limited liability, limited and general partnerships, shareholder agreements, share structures, security arrangements, collateral, directors' duties, personal liability, fiduciary duties and so on. By the time he left his head was reeling.

Examine this situation and discuss it from the point of view of New Ware, the university, Noah, the bankers, and Josh and his friends. In your answer look at the different methods of carrying on business that Noah, Josh, Amir and Rasheeda might consider.

TABLE OF STATUTES

Note: The page numbers given in parentheses at the end of each entry refer to pages in this book.

Age of Majority Act, R.S.A. (1980) c. A-4 (p. 151)

Alberta Business Corporation Act, S.A. (1981) c. B-15 s. 14 (p. 386, 446-48, 456)

An Act to Amend the Judicature Act, S.A. (1964) c. 40 s. 4 (p. 538)

An Act to Repeal the Statute of Frauds, L.M. (1982-83-84) c. 29 (p. 167)

Bank Act R.S.C. (1991) c.46 (p. 282)

Bankruptcy and Insolvency Act R.S.C. (1992) c.27 (p. 279, 292-93)

Bankruptcy and Insolvency Act, R.S.C. (1995) c. B-3 s. 81.1 (p. 248)

Bills of Exchange Act R.S.C. (1985) c.B-4 (p. 264, 308, 310-14, 319, 321-24, 327-28)

British Columbia Company Act, R.S.B.C. (1996) c. 62 s. 118 (p. 441)

Builder's Lien Act, R.S.A. (1980) c. B-12 (p. 288, 297)

Business Corporations Act R.S.O. (1990) c.C.16 (p. 297, 309); c.B.16 (p. 431, 455)

Business Corporations Act, S.A. (1981) c. B-15 s. 15 (p. 157)

Canada Act, 1987, (U.K.), 1982, c. 11 (p. 22)

Canada Business Corporations Act, R.S.C. (1985) c. C-44 (p. 431, 437)

Canada Health Act, R.S.C. 1985 c. C-6 (p.14)

Canada Labour Code R.S.C. (1985) c.L-2 (p. 364); s.95e (p. 374)

Canadian Bill of Rights, S.C. 1960 c. 44 (p. 18)

Canadian Charter of Rights and Freedoms, Sections 15, 16 and 28 (p. 345)

Canadian Human Rights Act, R.S.C. 1985 c. H-6 (p. 19)

Chartered Accountants Act, S.A. (1987) c. C-5.1 (p. 410)

Civil Enforcement Act, S.A. (1994) c. C-10.5 (p. 43, 44, 279, 292) Collection Practices Act, R.S.A. (1980) c. C-17 (p. 251, 259)

Competition Act R.S.C. (1984-85-86) c.91 (p. 161, 261)

Constitution Act (1867) s.91 ss.22 (p. 308)

Constitution Act, 1982, being Schedule B to the Canada Act, 1987, (U.K.), 1982, c. 11 (p. 22)

Constitution Act (1982) Part 1 Canadian Charter of Rights and Freedoms (p. 345)

Consumer Credit Transactions Act, S.A. (1985) c. C-22.5 (p. 137, 251, 257, 258)

Consumer Packaging and Labelling Act R.S.C. (1985) c.C-38 (p. 264)

Consumer Product and Warranties Act R.S.S. (1978) c.C-30 s.14(1) (p.252)

Consumer Protection Act R.S.O. (1990) c.C-31 s. 34 ss. 2 (p. 251)

Controlled Drugs and Substances Act, S.C. (1996) c. 19 (p. 263)

Copyright Act, R.S.C. (1985) c. 42 as amended by R.S.C. (1985) (4th Suppl.) c. 10 and subsequent amendments (p. 482-83); s. 27 (2) (a) (p. 485)

Criminal Code R.S.C. (1985) c.C-46 (p. 486); s.206 (p. 258, 399)

Currency Act R.S.C. (1985) c.C-52 (p. 206)

Defamation Act, R.S.A. (1980) c. D-6 (p. 94)

Dependent Adults Act, R.S.A. (1980) c. D-32 (p. 400)

Department of Consumer and Corporate Affairs Act R.S.C. (1985) c.C-37 (p. 261)

Direct Sales Cancellation Act, R.S.A. (1980) c. D-35 (p. 183, 186, 251, 256)

Divorce Act, R.S.C. 1985 (2nd Supp) c. 3, as amended (p. 32)

Dower Act, R.S.A. (1980) c. D-38 (p. 515)

Emergency Medical Aid Act, R.S.A. (1980) c. E-9 (p. 101)

Employment Insurance Act R.S.C. (1996) c.23 (p. 362)

Employment Standards Code, S.A. (1996) c. E-10.3 s. 56 (p. 346-47, 352-56, 360)

Environmental Protection and Enhancement Act, S.A. (1992) c. E-13.3 (p. 443)

Explosives Act R.S.C. (1985) c.E-17 (p. 264)

Food and Drug Act R.S.C. (1985) c.F-27 (p. 263)

Franchises Act, S.A. (1995) c. F-17.1 (p.455)

Fraudulent Preferences Act R.S.S. (1985) c.F-213.2 (p. 284)

Frustrated Conracts Act, R.S.A. (1980) c. F-19 (p. 220) Highway Traffic Act, R.S.A. (1980) c. H-7 (p. 84, 352)

Garbagemen's Lien Act, R.S.A. (1980) c. G-1 (p. 277, 481)

Guarantees Acknowledgment Act, R.S.A. (1980) c. G-12 (p. 168, 285)

Habeas Corpus Act R.S.O. (1990) c.4.1 (p. 571)

Hazardous Products Act R.S.C. (1985) c.H-3 (and amendments 3 Supp.) c.24 (p. 263)

Human Rights, Citizenship and Multiculturalism Act, R.S.A. (1980) c. H-11.7 (p. 19, 345, 358, 360)

Indian Act R.S.C. (1985) c.1-5 (p. 157)

Industrial Design Act R.S.C. (1985) c.1-9 (p. 492)

Industrial Relations Act R.S.N.B. (1973) c.I-4 s.104 (p. 372)

Innkeepers Act R.S.0. (1990) c.I.7 (p. 105, 479)

Insurance Act, R.S.A. (1980) c. I-5 (p. 195)

Insurance Companies Act R.S.C. (1991) c.1-11.8 (p. 494, 501)

Interest Act, R.S.C. (1985) c. I-15 (p. 258)

International Conventions Implementation Act, S.A. (1990) c. I-6.8 (p. 249)

Interpretation Act, R.S.A. (1980) c. I-7 (p. 563)

Judicature Act Amendment Act, S.A. (1939) c. 85 s. 2 (p. 537)

Judicature Acts (1873-75) 31 Geo. III (p. 9, 143, 196)

Judicial Review Procedure Act, R.S.B.C. (1996) c. 241 (p. 572)

Judicial Review Procedure Act, R.S.O. (1980) c. 224 (p. 572)

Judicial Review Procedure Act R.S.O. (1990) c.J.1 (p. 535): c.241 (p. 569)

Labour Relations Act R.S.O. (1995) c.1 ss.43 (p. 341) c.232 s.97 (p. 574)

Labour Relations Code R.S.B.C. (1996) c.244 s.55 (p. 374)

Labour Relations Code, S.A. (1988) c. L-1.2 (p. 158)

Land Titles Act, R.S.A. (1980) c. L-5 s. (p. 166, 194)

Land Titles Act, R.S.A. (1980) c. L-5 s. 152.3 (p. 166)

Land Titles Act, R.S.B.C. (1996) c. 406 s. 241 (p. 518)

Law of Property Act, R.S.A. (1980) c. L-8 (p. 280)

Law Reform Act [1943] 6 and 7 Geo. 6, c.40 (p. 219)

Licensing of Trades and Businesses Act, R.S.A. (1980) c. L-13 (p. 256)

Limitation of Actions Act, R.S.A. (1980) c. L-15 (p. 36, 47)

Limitations Act, S.A. (1996) c. L-15.10 (p. 47)

Matrimonial Property Act, R.S.A. (1980) c. M-9 (p. 168)

Motor Vehicle Accident Claims Act, R.S.A. (1980) c. M-21 (p. 107)

Motor Vehicle Safety Act R.S.C. (1985) c.B-10 (p. 264)

Municipal Government Act, S.A. (1994) c. M-26.1 (p. 572)

National Housing Act., R.S.C. 1985 c. N-11 (p. 538)

National Housing Act, S.C. 1944 c. 46; National Housing Act, R.S.C. 1952 c. 188

National Labour Relations Act (1935) 49 Stat.449 (p. 363)

Negligence Act R.S.O. (1980) c.315 (p. 114)

Occupational Health and Safety Act R.S.O. (1990) c.0.0 (p. 361)

Occupiers Liability Act R.S.O. (1980) c.322 (p. 104, 115)

Partnership Act, R.S.A. (1980) c. P-2 (p. 410-12, 415-18, 421-23)

Patent Act Amendments R.S.C. (1985) (3rd supp.) c.33 (p. 489)

Patent Act R.S.C. (1985) c.P-4 s.27 ss.8 (p. 487)

Personal Directives Act, S.A. (1996) c. P-4.03 (p. 400)

Personal Property Security Act R.S.B.C. (1996) c.359 (p. 275, 277, 279-80)

Personal Property Security Act, S.A. (1988) c. P-4.05, s. 41 (p. 198, 237)

Pest Control Products Act R.S.C. (1985) c.P-9 (p. 264)

Police Officers' Collective Bargaining Act, S.A. (1983) c. P-12.05 (p. 373)

Possessory Liens Act, R.S.A. (1980) c. P-13 (p. 481)

Possessory Liens Act, R.S.A. (1980) c. P-13 s. 4 (p. 277)

Powers of Attorney Act, S.A. (1991) c. P-13.5 (p. 400)

Privacy Act R.S.B.C. (1996) c.373 s.1 (p. 82) s.3 (p. 107, 416)

Proceedings Against the Crown Act, R.S.A. (1980) c. P-18 (p. 575)

Protection of Persons Acting Under Statute Act R.S.N.B. (1973) c.P-20 (p. 576)

Provincial Court Act, R.S.A. (1980) c. P-20 s. 36 (p.32)

Provinical Court Act, R.S.A. (1980) c. P-20 (p. 37)

Provincial Court Act, R.S.A. (1980) c. P-20 s. 37 (p. 33)

Public Service Employee Relations Act, R.S.A. (1980) c. P-33 (p. 364, 373)

Real Estate Act, S.A. (1995) c. R-4.5 (p. 400)

Real Property Statutes Amendment Act, 1983 (No. 2) 1983 c. 97; Law of Property Amendment Act, S.A. (1984) c. 24 (p. 539)

Rent Review Act R.S.N.S. (1989) c.401 (p. 525)

Residential Tenancies Act, R.S.A. (1980) c. R-15.3 (p. 207) c. S-2 (p. 220)

Sale of Goods Act, R.S.A. (1980) c. S-2 s. 3 (1) (p. 237); s. 4 (p. 152); s. 9 (p. 177); s. 10 (p. 220); s. 11 (p. 129, 144, 235); s. 14 (p. 209, 243); s. 15-18 (p. 183); s. 18 (p. 246, 253); s. 41 (p. 277); s. 49 (p. 248), s. 55 (p. 251)

Sales of Goods Act, R.S.A. (1996) c. 410 s. 20 ss. 2 (p. 251)

Securities Act, S.A. (1981) c. S-6.1 (p. 440, 445) Sterilization Act, R.S.A. (1970) c. 341 (repealed) (p. 24)

Societies Act, R.S.A. (1980) c. S-18 (p. 409, 432)

State Immunity Act R.S.O. (1985) c.S-18 (p. 158)

Textile Labelling Act R.S.C. (1985) c.T-10 (p. 264)

Trademarks Act R.S.C. (1985) c.T-13 (p. 489)

Unconscionable Transactions Act, R.S.A. (1980) c. U-2 (p. 193, 255); U-3 (p. 255)

Unfair Trade Practices Act, R.S.A. (1980) c. U-3 (p. 251, 253, 258); s.7 (p. 258)

Warehousemen's Lien Act, R.S.A. (1980) c. W-3 (p. 481)

Wartime Labour Relations Regulations of 1944 P.C.1003 (p. 363)

Weights and Measures Act R.S.C. (1985) c.W-6 (p. 264)

Winding-up and Restructuring Act, R.S.C. (1985) c. W-11 (p. 297)

Workers' Compensation Act, S.A. (1981) c. W-16 s. 126, as amended (p. 44, 197)

Young Offenders Act R.S.C. (1985) c.Y-1 (p. 32)

TABLE OF CASES

Note: The page numbers given in parentheses at the end of each entry refer to pages in this book.

A. E. Lepage Ltd. v. Kamex Developments Ltd. et. al. 78 D.L.R. (3d) 223 (Ont. C.A.) (p. 413)

Abbott v. Kasza (1977) 71 D.L.R. (3d) 581, 588 (p. 112)

Adams-Eden Furniture Ltd. v. Kansa General Insurance Co., 141 D.L.R. (4th) 288 (Manitoba Court of Appeal) (p. 391)

Alberta (Director of Trade Practices) v. Edanver Consulting Ltd. (1993) 6 W.W.R. 719 (Alta. Q. B.) (p. 254)

Allcard v. Skinner (1887) 36 Ch.D. 145 (p. 190)

Alwest Neon Signs Ltd. v. 464460 Alberta Ltd. (1994) 24 Alta. L.R. (3d) 420 (Alta. Prov. Ct.) (p.434)

Amo Containers Ltd. v. Mobil Oil Canada, Ltd., 62 D.L.R. (4th) 104 (Newfoundland Court of Appeal) (p. 477)

Anns v. Merton, London Borough Council [1977] 2 All E.R. 492 (p. 99)

Applewood Lane West Ltd. v. Scott et al., 35 D.L.R. (4th) 287 (Man. C.A.) (p. 530)

Athey v. Leonati (1996) 140 D.L.R. (4th) 235 (p. 113)

Avery v. Bowden (1855) 5 E. & B. 714: (1856) 6 E. & B. 953 (p. 213)

Bahner V. Marwest Hotel Company Ltd., Muir et al. (1969) 6 D.L.R. (3d) 322 (p. 66); 325 (p. 89-90)

Bailey v. Saskatchewan Registered Nurses' Assn., 137 D.L.R. (4th) 224 (Sask. Court of Queen's Bench) (p. 567)

Baillie v. Charman 94 D.L.R. (4th) 403 (B.C.C.A.) (p. 391)

Bains v. Hill, 93 D.L.R. (4th) 117 (British Columbia Court of Appeal) (p. 103)

Baldry v. Marshall [1925] 1 K.B. 260 (p. 245)

Banfai et al. v. Formula Fun Centre Inc. et al. 19 D.L.R. (4th) 683 (Ont. High Court of Justice) (p. 91)

Bank of British Columbia v. Coopers & Lybrand Ltd. et al., 15 D.L.R. (4th) 714 (British Columbia Supreme Court) (p. 315)

Bank of British Columbia v. Shank Investments et al. (1985) 34 Alta. L.R. 379 (Q.B.) (p. 285)

Bank of Montreal v. J.R. Lakusta Holdings Ltd. (1995) 35 Alta. L.R. (3d) 161 (Q.B.) (p. 537)

Bank of Nova Scotia v. Hallgarth et al. 32 D.L.R. (4th) 158 (B.C.C.A.) (p. 140)

Bardal v. The Globe and Mail Ltd. 24 D.L.R. (2d) 140 (H.C.) (p. 346)

Barnard v. National Dock Labour Board [1953] 2 Q.B. 18 p, 41 (p. 572)

Barnett-Black v. Silad Investments Inc., 74 D.L.R. (4th) 734 (Ontario Court, General Division) (p. 527)

Bayview Credit Union Ltd. v. Daigle, 3 D.L.R. (4th) 95 (N.B. Court of Queen's Bench) (p. 153)

Beaufort Realties v. Chomedey Aluminum Co. (1981) 116 D.L.R. (3d) 193 (p. 188)

Blainey and Ontario Hockey Association et al., 26 D.L.R. (4th) 728 (Ont. C.A.) (p. 25)

Blyth v. Birmingham Water Works Co. (1856) 156 E.R. 1047, 1049 (p. 102)

Borek v. Hooper, 114 D.L.R. (4th) 570 (Ont. Court [General Division] Divisional Court) (p. 236)

Bourne v. Otis Elevator Co. Ltd. 6 D.L.R. (4th) (Ont. High Court of Justice) (p. 370)

Boychuk et al. v. Boychuk et al. 55 D.L.R. (3d) 751 (Alberta S.C. Trial Div.) (p. 414)

British Columbia (Minister of Crown Lands) v. Cressey Development Corp. 97 D.L.R. (4th) 380 (p. 216)

Brownscombe v. Public Trustee (1969) S.C.R. 658 (p. 170)

Burkitt, L.J., Yeoman Credit Ltd. v. Apps [1961] 2 All E.R, 281 (p. 210)

Byle v. Byle, 65 D.L.R. (4th) 641 (B.C.C.A.) (p. 189)

Cadbury Schweppes Inc. v. FBI Foods Ltd., 128 D.L.R. (45h) 708 (B.C.C.A.) (p. 492)

Calmont Leasing Ltd. v. Kredl (1993) 11 Alta. L.R. (3d) 345 (C.A.) (p. 441)

Canada (Director of Investigation and Research) v. Southam Inc., 144 D.L.R. (4th) 1 (Supreme Court of Canada) (p. 561)

Canadian Broadcasting Corp. v. Canada (Labour Relations Board) 121 D.L.R. (4th) 385 (S.C.C.) (p. 365)

Canadian National Railway Co. v. Norsk Pacific Steamship Co. (1992) 91 D.L.R. (4th) 289 (p. 111)

Caners v. Eli Lilly Canada Inc. 134 D.L.R. (4th) 730 (Man. C.A.) (p. 245)

Capital City Savings and Credit Union Ltd. v. Milligan (1989) 94 A.R. 47 (Q.B.) (p. 324)

Carlill v. Carbolic Smoke Ball Co. [1892] 2 Q.B. 484 [1893] 1 Q.B. 256 (p. 165)

Central London Property Trust, Ltd. v. High Trees House, Ltd. [1947] K.B. 130 (p. 144)

Central Okanagan School District #23 v. Renaud 56 (B.C.L.R.) (2d) (p. 18)

Central Trust Co. v. Rafuse et al. (1986) 31 D.L.R. (4th) 481 (p. 188)

Cimon Ltd. v. Benchmade Furniture Corp. (1964) 1 Ex. C.R. 81 (p. 492)

Cole v. Turner (1705) 87 E.R. 907 (p. 86)

Colour Your World v. Canadian Broadcasting Corp. (Ont. General Division) 17 O.R. (3d) 308 (p. 93)

Combe v. Combe [1951] 1 All E.R. 767, 769, 772 (p. 144)

Consumer Glass Co. Ltd. v. Foundation Company of Canada Ltd. 20 D.L.R. (4th) 126 (Ont. C.A.) (p. 34)

Cooper v. Phibbs [1867] L.R. 2 H.L. 149 (pp. 177, 183)

Cooperators Insurance Association v. Kearney (1965) 48 D.L.R. (2d) 1 (p. 343)

Coote v. Hudson's Bay Company and Swift Canadian Con. Ltd. (1977) 6 A.R. 59 (Alta. District Ct.) (p. 246, 252)

Cottreau v. Rodgerson (1965) 53 D.L.R. (2d) 549 (p. 87-88)

Coull v. Kolbuc (1969) 68 W.W.R. 76 (Atla. Dis. Ct.) (p. 154)

Couturier v. Hastie (1852) 8 Ex. 40 (p. 177)

Crocker v. Sundance Northwest Resort (1988) 51 D.L.R. (4th) 321 (S.C.C.) (p. 96)

Cundy v. Lindsay (1878) A.C. 459 (p. 180)

DeFrancesco v. Barnam (1890) 45 Ch.D. 430 (p. 152)

Derrickson v. Derrickson, 9 D.L.R. (4th) 204 (British Columbia Court of Appeal) (p. 13)

Derry v. Peek (1889) 14 App. Cas. 337 (p. 187)

Dickinson v. Dodds (1876) 2 Ch. 463 (p.127)

Dominion Home Improvements Ltd. v. Knuude, 605-029, *The Lawyers Weekly*, May 30, 1986 (p. 234)

Donoghue v. Stevenson [1932] A.C. 562 (pp. 98-99) 580 (p. 193)

E. Hulton & Co. v. Jones [1910] 26 T.L.R. 128 (p. 94)

Elcano Acceptance Ltd. v. Richmond, Richmond, Stambler & Mills, 79 D.L.R. (4th) 154 (Ontario Court of Appeal) (p. 258)

Elliott v. Freison et al. (1984) 6 D.L.R. (4th) 338 (p. 93)

Eng v. Evans (1991) 83 Alta. L.R. (2d) 107 (Q.B.) (p. 165)

Entores Ltd. v. Miles Fareast Corp. [1955] 2 All E.R. 493 (p. 134)

Fayant v. Campbell's Maple Village, 3 W.W.R. 171 (Alta. Q.B.) (p. 357)

Fibrosa Spolka Akeyjna v. Fairbairn, Lawson, Combe, Barbouk Ltd. [1942] (A.C.) 32 (p. 219)

Fisher v. Bell [1960] 3 All E.R. 731 (p. 130)

Fletton Ltd. v. Peat Marwick Ltd. 50 D.L.R. (4th) 729 (B.C.C.A.) (p. 212)

Foakes v. Beer (1884) 9 App. Cas. 605 (pp. 142, 215)

Folley v. Classique Coaches (1934) 2 K.B. 1 (p. 141)

Foss v. Harbottle (1843) 3 HARE 461 (p. 441)

Freeth v. Burr (1874) L.R. 9 C.P. 213 (Court of Common Pleas) (p. 212)

Gadd v. London Drugs Ltd. et al. (1991) 123 A.R. 335 (Alta. Prov. Ct.) (p. 246)

Gee v. White Spot (1986) 32 D.L.R. (4th) 238 (p. 252)

Gilbert Steel Ltd. v. University Construction Ltd. (1976) 67 D.L.R. (30) 606 (p. 139)

Gregorio v. Intans-Corp. 115 D.L.R. (4th) 200 (Ont. C.A.) (p. 213)

Gross v. Wright [1923] 2 D.L.R. 171 (p. 89)

Hadley v. Baxendale (1894) 156 E.R. 145 (pp. 223, 249)

Haig v. Bamford (1976) 72 D.L.R. (3d) 68 (pp. 108, 188)

Haig v. Canada [1993] 2 S.C.R. 995 (p. 20 357)

Hamilton & Olsen Surveys Ltd. v. Otto, 12 Alta. L.R. (3d) 431 (Alta. C.A.) (p. 350)

Hardman v. Falk [1955] 1 D.L.R. 432 (p. 155)

Harrison v. University of British Columbia, 77 D.L.R. (4th) 55 (S.C.C.) (p. 359)

Hedley Byrne v. Heller [1963] 2 All E.R. 575 (pp. 107, 188)

Henthorne v. Fraser [1892] 2 Ch. 27 (p. 137)

Hercules Management Ltd. v. Ernst & Young (1997) 146 D.L.R. (4th) 577 (S.C.C.) (pp. 100, 108)

Higgins v. Orion Insurance Co. Ltd. et al. 17 D.L.R. (4th) 90 (Ont. C.A.) (p. 504)

Hill v. Church of Scientology of Toronto (1995) 126 D.L.R. (4th) 129 (S.C.C.) (p. 96)

Hodginson v. Simms [1994] 3 S.C.R. 377 (p. 401)

Hoy v. Lozanovski as reported in The Lawyers Weekly, April 3, 1987 (p. 176)

Hunter Engineering Co. v. Syncrude Canada Ltd., 57 D.L.R. (4th) 321 (pp. 211, 242)

Hunter v. Southam Inc. (1984) 2 S.C.R. 145 @ 169 (p. 21)

H.W. Liebig & Co. Ltd. v. Leading Investments Ltd. 25 D.L.R. (4th) 161 (S.C.C.) (p. 178)

Industrial Acceptance Corp. v. Lalond [1952] 3 D.L.R. 348 (S.C.C.) (p. 297)

Island Properties Ltd. v. Entertainment Enterprises Ltd. et al. 26 D.L.R. (4th) 347 (Nfld. C.A.) (p. 224)

Jacobsen v. Nike Canada Ltd. 133 D.L.R. (4th) 377 (B.C.S.C.) (pp. 106, 121)

Jaremko v. A.E. LePage Real Estate Services Ltd. 39 D.L.R. (4th) 252 affirmed 60 D.L.R. (4th) 762 (Ont. High Court of Justice) (p. 341)

Junkin v. Bedard (1958) 11 D.L.R. (2d) 481 (p. 398)

Kauffman v. Toronto Transit Commission (12959) 18 D.L.R. (2d) 204 (p. 111)

King v. Mayne Nickless Transport Inc. 114 D.L.R. (4th) 12 (B.C.C.A.) (p. 348)

Kosmoupoulos et al. v. Construction Insurance Company of Canada Ltd. [1987] 1 S.C.R. 1 (p. 501)

Krell v. Henry [1903] 2 K.B. 740 (p. 217)

Kripps v. Touche Ross & Co. et al., CA019919 B.C.C.A., April 25, 1997 (p. 110)

Krocker et al. v. Midtown Mortgage Loans Ltd. et al., 52 D.L.R. (3d) 286 (Alta. S.C.T.D.) (p. 255)

LAC Minerals Ltd. v. Corona Resources as reported in *The Globe and Mail*, Toronto, November 19, 1986 (p. 494)

Lambert v. Lastoplex Chemicals Ltd. (1972) 25 D.L.R. (2d) 204 (p. 253)

Lanca Contracting Ltd. v. Brant County Board of Education, 26 D.L.R. (4th) 708 (Ont. C.A.) (p. 136)

London Drugs Ltd. v. Kuehne & Nagel International Ltd. [1993] 1 W.W.R. 1 (pp. 195, 253)

Machtinger v. HOJ Industries Ltd. 91 D.L.R. (4th) 491 (S.C.C.) (p. 352)

Maiklen v. Springbank Oil & Gas Ltd. (1994) 27 Alta. L.R. (3d) 282 Q.B. (p. 441)

Mallette v. Shulman 67 D.L.R. (4th) (p. 85)

Marvco Colour Research Ltd. v. Harris et al. (1983) 141 D.L.R. (3d) 577 (p. 181)

McIntyre v. Pietrobon (1987) 15 B.C.L.R. (2d) 350 (p. 124)

McRae v. Commonwealth Disposals Commission (1951) 84 C.L.R. 377 (High Court of Australia) (p. 177)

McWilliam v. Morris [1942] O.W.N. 449 High Court Justice (p. 7)

MDS Health Group Limited v. King Street Medical Arts Centre Limited, reported in *The Lawyers Weekly*, Vol. 14 No. 7 (p. 211)

Meditek Laboratory Services Ltd. v. Purolator Courier Ltd. 125 D.L.R. (4th) 738 (Man. C.A.) (p. 209)

Megill-Stephenson Co. v. Woo 59 D.L.R. (4th) 146 (Man. C.A.) (p. 166)

Metropolitan Stores of Canada Ltd. v. Nova Construction Co. 50 D.L.R. (4th) 508 (N.S. Supreme Court Appeal Division) (p. 183)

Milani v. Banks, 98 D.L.R. (4th) 104 Ontario Court (General Division) (p. 259)

Mitchell v. Thompson 33 D.L.R. (4th) (B.C.S.C.) (p. 131)

Morrow et al. v. Royal Insurance Co. of Canada (1990) 8 C.L.I. (2d) (upheld on appeal) (1992) 11 C.C.L.I. (2D) 86 (Alta. C.A.) (p. 503)

Moss v. Chin 120 D.L.R. (4th) 406 (B.C.S.C.) (p. 179)

Motherwell v. Motherwell (1977) 73 D.L.R. (3d) (p. 91)

Mulloy v. Hop Sang (1935) 1 W.W.R. 714 (p. 86)

Murray v. Bitango 135 D.L.R. (4th) 442 (A.C.A.) (p. 115)

Murray v. Sperry Rand Corp. (1970) 23 O.R. (2d) 456 (p. 253)

Nash v. Dix (1898) 78 L.T. 445 (p. 395)

Newfoundland Telephone Co. Ltd. v. Terra Nova Auctioneers Inc. as reported in *The Lawyers Weekly*, Vol. 12 No. 30 (p. 434)

North West Trust Co. v. Rezyn Developments Inc. 81 D.L.R. (4th) 751(B.C.C.A.) (p. 528)

Ocean City Realty Ltd. v. A & M Holdings Ltd. et al. 36 D.L.R. (4th) 94 (B.C.C.A.) (p. 389)

Olson v. Gullo 113 D.L.R. (4th) 42 (Ont. C.A.) (p. 411)

Ontario v. Ron Engineering (1981) 119 D.L.R. (3rd) 267 (p. 134)

O.P.S.E.U. v. Air-Dale Ltd., 111 D.L.R. (4th) 163 (Ont. Court, General Division) (p. 12)

Osorio et al. v. Cardona 15 D.L.R. (4th) 619 (B.C.S.C.) (p. 163)

Palsgraf v. Long Island Railroad Co. (1928) 248 N.Y. 339 (p. 98)

Paradine v. Jane (91647) Aleyn 26 (K.B. Div.) (p. 523)

Paramount Life Insurance Co. v. Hill et al. (1987) 34 D.L.R. (4th) 150 (p. 511)

Parks West Mall Ltd. v. Hinton (Town) (1994) 15 Alta. L.R. (3d) 400 (Q.B.) (p. 573)

Parris v. Reber (1994) 168 A.R. 79 (Prov. Ct.) (p. 34)

Pennefather v. Zanet B.C. County Court, Oct. 7, 1988 as reported in *The Lawyers Weekly*, Vol. 8. (p. 316)

Peterborough v. Ramsden 106 D.L.R. (4th) 233 (p. 22)

Peters v. Fleming (1840) 6 M. & W. 42 (p. 152)

Pezim v. British Columbia (Superintendent of Brokers) 114 D.L.R. (4th) 385 (S.C.C.) (p. 575)

Pharmaceutical Society of Great Britain v. Boots Cash Chemists (Southern) Ltd. [1952] 2 All E.R. 456 (p. 130)

Pinheiro v. Bowes 109 D.L.R. (4th) 315 (Ont. Court, General Division) (p. 532)

Pioneer Hybrid Ltd. v. Commissioner of Patents 60 D.L.R. (4th) (S.C.C.) (p. 488)

Poulos v. Caravelle Homes Ltd. [1995] 9 W.W.R. 262 (p. 415)

Polemis, in Re [1921] 3 K.B. 560 (p. 112)

Q.N.S. Paper Co. v. Chartwell Shipping Ltd. 62 D.L.R. (4th) 36 (S.C.C.) (p. 394)

Queen (The) in Right of British Columbia v. Tenera et al. 17 D.L.R. (4th) 1 (S.C.C.) (p. 518)

Queen, The v. Cote (1974) 51 D.L.R. (3d) 252 (p. 113)

R. v. Bata Industries Limited (1992) 70 C.C.C. (3d) 394 (pp. 443, 548)

R. v. Consolidated Maybrun Mines Ltd., 133 D.L.R. (4th) 513 (Ont. C.A.) (p. 552)

R. v. Keegstra (1990) 3 S.C.R. 697 (S.C.C.)

R. v. Safety-Kleen Canada Inc. 145 D.L.R. (4th) 276 (Ont. C.A.) (p. 556)

R. v. 3M Drug Mart Ltd. [1985] 3 W.W.R. 481 (S.C.C.) (p. 26)

R. v. Westendorp [1983] 1 S.C.R. 43 (Supreme Court of Canada) (p. 13)

R. v. Wolfe and Campbell 633-016 *Lawyers' Weekly*, December 19, 1986 (p. 474)

Raffels v. Wichelhaus (1864) 2 H. & C. 906 (p. 181)

Rapatax (a987) Inc. v. Cantax Corp. 145 D.L.R. (4th) 419 (Al.C.A.) (p. 182)

Rasanen v. Rosemount Investments Ltd., 17 O.R. (3rd) 267 (Ont. C.A.) (p. 357)

Regional Trust Co. v. Avco Financial Services Realty Ltd. 5 D.L.R. (4th) 670 (p. 536)

Reid et al. v. Royal Trust Corporation of Canada 20 D.L.R. (4th) 23 (P.E.I. S.C. Appeal Division) (p. 286)

Re Doyle and Restrictive Trade Practices Commission et al. 21 D.L.R. (4th) 366 (Federal Court of Appeal) (p. 566)

Re Fancy 8 D.L.R. (4th) 418 (Ont. S.C. in Bankruptcy) (p. 296)

Re Foster 89 D.L.R. (4th) 555 (Ont. Court, General Division) (pp. 276, 475)

Re Ladney et al. and Township of Moore 10 D.L.R. (4th) 612 (Ont. High Court of Justice, Divisional Court) (p. 565)

Re McAfee 49 D.L.R. (4th) 401 (B.C.C.A.) (p. 297)

Re Speedy Roofing Ltd. 45 D.L.R. (4th) 142 (Ont. S.C. in Bankruptcy) (p. 295)

Richardson Greenshields of Canada Ltd. v. Kalmacoff 123 D.L.R. (4th) (Ont. C.A.) (p. 446)

Ripplinger v. Ryan, 131 D.L.R. (4th) 697 (Saskatchewan Court of Appeal) (p. 14)

Roberts v. Gray [1913] 1 K.B. 520 (p. 152)

Rochdale Credit Union Ltd. v. Barney, 14 D.L.R. (4th) 116 (Ont. C.A.) (p. 190)

Roncarelli v. Duplessis [1959] S.C.R. 121 (p. 570)

Roper v. Murdoch et al. 39 D.L.R. (4th) 684 (B.C.S.C.) (p. 444)

Rose and Frank v. Crompton [1923] 3 K.B. 261 (p. 164)

Rosseway v. Canadian Kenworth Ltd. 6 Alta. L.R. (2d) 177 (Alta. District Ct.) (p. 246)

Rossdale v. Denny [1921] 1 Ch.57 (p. 128)

Royal Bank of Canada v. Bauman (1986) 46 Alta. L.R. (2d) 68 (Q.B.) (p. 317)

Royal Bank of Canada v. J. Segreto Construction Ltd. 47 D.L.R. (4th) 761 (Ont. C.A.) (p. 278)

Royal Oak Mines Inc. v. Canada (Labour Relations Board) 133 D.L.R. (4th) 129 (S.C.C.) (p. 368)

Rushak v. Henneken 84 D.L.R. (4th) 87 (B.C.C.A.) (p. 249)

Rylands v. Fletcher (1868) L.R. 3H.L. 330, 339 (p. 115-16)

Said v. Butt (1923) K.B. 497 (p. 395)

Salomon v. Salomon and Co. Ltd. (1897) A.C. 22 (p. 432, 434)

Scammel v. Ouston [1941] A.C. 251, 269 (p. 135)

Sci-Tech Education Inc. v. The Nature Company [1992] F.C.A.D. 3344-01 (p. 485)

Sign-O-Lite Plastics Ltd. v. Metropolitan Life Insurance Co. 73 D.L.R. (4th) 541 (B.C.C.A.) (p. 395)

Sinclair v. Dover Engineering Services Ltd. et al. (B.C.S.C.) (1987) 642028 (Unreported case) (p. 429)

Sinkovich v. Strathroy (Town) Commissioners of Police, 51 D.L.R. (4th) 750 Ont. High Court of Justice, Divisional Court (p. 564)

Smith Brothers and Wilson v. B.C. Hydro Authority, (B.C.S.C.) February 24, 1997 reported in *The Lawyers Weekly*, Vol. 16, No. 42 (p. 207)

Smith v. Hostess Frito-Lay Co. 116 D.L.R. (4th) 378 (Alberta C.A.) (p. 354)

Smith v. Leech Brain [1961] 3 All E.R. 1159 (p. 113)

Smith v. Stone (1647) 82 E.R. 533 (p. 88)

Southern Transportation Ltd. v. Valgardson (1995) 173 A.R. 299 (Alta. Q.B.) (p. 434)

Standard Precast Ltd. v. Dywidag Fab Con Products Ltd., 56 D.L.R. (4th) 385 (B.C.C.A.) (p. 204)

Steadman v. Erickson Gold Mining Corp. 43 D.L.R. (4th) 712 (B.C.S.C.) (p. 551)

Stevenson v. Hilty (Canada Ltd.) R.S.N.S. (1989) c. 258 (p. 192)

Stuart v. M.N.R. as reported in *The Lawyers Weekly* Vol. 15 (1995) (p. 444)

Sumner Sports Inc. v. Pavillon Chasse & Peche (440) Inc. 72 D.L.R. (4th) 317 (Que. C.A.) (p. 261)

T.G. Bright and Company v. Kerr (1939) S.C.R. 63 (p. 397)

Taylor v. Caldwell (1863) 3 B. & S. 826 (p. 218)

Thornton v. Prince George [1978] 2 S.C.R. 167 (p. 84)

Tolley v. Fry [1931] A.C. 333 (p. 496)

Tom Hopkins International, Inc. v. Wall & Redekop Realty Ltd. 20 D.L.R. (4th) 407 (B.C.C.A.) (p. 484)

Toronto Dominion Bank v. Jordan [1985] 61 B.C.L.R. 105 (p. 306)

Toronto Dominion Bank v. Rooke et al. (1984) 3 D.L.R. (4th) 716 (p. 274)

Tree Savers International Ltd. et al. v. Savoy et al. 87 D.L.R. (4th) (Alberta C.A.) (p. 349)

Trusts & Guar. Co. v. Rice, 20 Alta. L.R. 444 (Alta. A.D.) (p. 539)

Tsakiroglou and Co. Ltd. v. Noblee and Thorl G.M.B.H. [1962] A.C. 93 (p. 218)

Tutinka v. Mainland Sand and Gravel Ltd. 110 D.L.R. (4th) 182 (B.C.C.A.) (p. 115)

U.T.U. v. Central Western Railway 76 D.L.R. (4th) 1 (S.C.C.) (p. 11)

Vachon et al. v. Roy et al. (Ont. District Court) Jan. 1987 642-009 (unreported case) (p. 82)

Victoria & Grey Trust Company v. Crawford et al. (Ont. S.C.) 636-012 (p. 408)

Videan v. British Transport Commission [1963] 2 All E.R. 860 (p. 115)

Virani v. Edwards (1997) CanRepAlta 806 (Alta. Q.B.) (p. 503)

Vriend v. Alberta (1994) 152 A.R. 1 (Alta., Q.B.), (1996) 181 A.R. 16 (Alta. C.A.), (2 April 1998), 25285 (S.C.C.) (p. 20)

Wagon Mound (No. 1) [1961] A.C. 388 (p. 112)

Waldick v. Malcolm 83 D.L.R. (4th) 125 S.C.C. (pp. 110, 115)

Walt Disney Productions v. Triple Five Corp. (1992) 93 D.L.R. (4th) (Alta. Q.B.) upheld on appeal (1994) 113 D.L.R. (4th) (Alta. C.A.) (p. 491)

Wellington Insurance Co. Ltd. v. Armac Diving Services Ltd. 37 D.L.R. (4th) 462 (B.C.C.A.) (p. 501)

Wells v. Wells 16 D.L.R. (4th) 524 (N.S.S.C.) (p. 516)

Westcom Radio Group Ltd. v. MacIsaac 63 D.L.R. (4th) (Ont. High Court of Justice Divisional Court) (p. 396)

White v. Bluett (1853) 23 L.J. Ex. 36 (p. 141)

Wickberg v. Patterson (1997) 145 D.L.R. (4th) 263 (Alta. C.A.) (p. 114)

Wong v. Shell Canada Ltd., 35 Alta. L.R. (3d) 1 (Alta. C.A.) (p. 357)

Youssoupoff v. Metro-Goldwyn Mayer Pictures Limited (1934) 50 T.L.R. 581, 584 (p. 93)

69971 Manitoba Ltd. v. National Bank of Canada 122 D.L.R. (4th) 609 (Man. C.A.) (p. 329)

INDEX

Note: The page numbers in boldface type indicate where to find key term definitions.

A

Absolute privilege 94 *See also* Defamation
Acceleration clause 221
Acceptance
  by conduct 136
  communication of 134-135, 136-138
  defective offer 135-136
  Entores Ltd. v. Miles Far East Corp.
    134-135
  postbox rule 135, 137-138
  specified means of 138
  unconditional 135
  unilateral contract 136
  unsolicited goods 137
Accounting 225-226
Adams-Eden Furniture Ltd. v. Kansa General
  Insurance Co. 391
Administrative law
  authority of government officials
    561-562
  Bailey v. Saskatchewan Registered
    Nurses' Assn. 567-568
  challenge of government decisions
    561
  Crown immunity 575
  division of powers 563
  fair hearing 565-566
  golden rule **562**
  Interpretation Act 563
  impartiality 567-568
  mischief rule **562-563**
  natural justice 564-568
  opportunity to be heard 565
  proper process 564
  rule of law 561-562
  Sinkovich v. Strathroy (Town)
    Commissioners of Police 564-565
  statutory interpretation **562**-564
  ultra vires legislation 562, 563-564
  see also Administrative tribunals;
    Judicial review
Administrative tribunals **561**
  Copyright Board 486
  intra vires decisions 562
  labour relations boards, 364, 366, 374
  ultra vires decisions 562
  see also Administrative law; Judicial
    review
Affirmative action 359
Age of Majority Act 151
Agency
  by necessity **387**-388
  consent to relationship 383
  contract, 382-383, 388, 393
  defined 382
  and estoppel principle 384-386

and partners 415-416
power of attorney **383**
principal **382**, 386
duties of principals 393
  direct liability of 398
  liability. *See* Agents
  undisclosed 393-396
privity of contract 194
ratification by principal 386-387, 396
reasonable person test 385
relationship 382-383
specialized relationships 400-401
termination of 398-399
and third party, **382**, 390-391,
  393-396, 396-397
unauthorized agreement 386
utmost good faith **390**
vicarious liability. *See* Vicarious
  liability
Westcom Radio Group Ltd. v. MacIsaac
  396-397
see also Agents
Agents **343**
  acceptance of actions of 385
  accounting 389
  actual authority **384**, 435
  ambiguous authority 393
  apparent authority 384-386, 395-396
  competition with principal 392-393
  and corporations 435-436
  deceit of 398
  duties of 388-393
  duty of reasonable care 388
  express authority **384**
  fiduciary duties 389-393. *See also*
    Fiduciary duties
  full disclosure by 391
  function of 382
  implied authority **384**
  insurance 505
  and interests of principal 390-393
  liability of, 394, 397, 397-398
  non-delegation of responsibility
    388-389
  power to borrow 393
  reimbursement of expenses 393
  see also Agency
Alberta Act (1905) 10
Alberta Business Corporation Act 386,
  446-448, 456
Alberta (Director of Trade Practices) v.
  Edanver Consulting Ltd. 254
Alberta Registries agent 36
Alternative dispute resolution 47-48
Alwest Neon Signs Ltd. v. 464460 Alberta
  Ltd. 434

An Act to Amend the Judicative Act 538
An Act to Repeal the Statute of Frauds 167
Anticipatory breach. *See* Breach of
  Contract
Arbitration 47-48 **369**-370
Assault and battery **86**
Assignment 195-198
  chose in action 195
  consent 197
  of contractual rights **195**-196
  equitable **196**-197
  involuntary 198
  notice of 196
  prohibited 197
  and subsequent claims 198
  vicarious performance **197**
Assignment of Book Debts Act 275, 277
Assignment and Preferences Act 284
Attachment 277-278. *See also Personal*
  Property Security Act (PPSA)

B

Bailment **209**
  bailor 478
  common carriers 478
  duty of bailee 478-481
  exculpatory clauses 479
  gratuitous 480
  involuntary 480
  payment for 481
  for value 478-480
Bains v. Hill 103
The Bank Act 282
Bank of British Columbia v. Coopers &
  Lybrand Ltd. et al. 315
Bank of British Columbia v. Shank
  Investments et al. 285
Bank of Montreal v. J.R. Lakusta Holdings
  Ltd. 537
Bankruptcy, 292, **293**-297, 298, 337
  act of **293**
  agricultural 294
  assignment in **293**
  discharge 296
  discharged bankrupt 296-297
  effect on agency 399
  fraudulent transfers and prefer-
    ences, **295-296**, *see also* Creditors
  insolvency **293**
  involuntary 293, 298
  offences 296-297
  partnership 420
  priority 295-298
  proposals under the *Bankruptcy and*
    Insolvency Act 248, 293-294
  Re Speedy Roofing Ltd. 295

receivership **297**
receiving order **293**
and supplier of goods 294
trustee's duties 294
undischarged bankrupt **296**
Bankruptcy Act 295, 296, 297
Bankruptcy and Insolvency Act 248, 284, 292-298, 557
Barnard v. National Dock Labour Board 572
Barnett-Black v. Silad Investments Inc. 527
Barter transactions 237
Bets and wagers 161-162
Better Business Bureau 260
Bill of lading **239**
bill of sale **274**
Bill of Rights (Canada) 17-18
Bill of Rights (UK) 10
Bills of exchange 308, 309-311
acceptance 310
consumer bills 328-329
draft **310**
maturity 309
Bills of Exchange Act 264, 308-314, 316, 318-321, 322, 324, 327, 328-329, 332, 383
Bills of Sale Act 275, 297
Bona fide purchaser 284
Bonding 505
Breach of contract **208, 325**
anticipatory breach **212**-213
breach of condition 208, 243
breach of warranty 208, 243
by government agency 575
collateral contract **253**
conditions 208, 209
construction approach 211
defined 208
exemption clause 209-211. *See also* Exemption clause
fundamental breach **210**, 211, 242
mortgages 537
performance 205-208. *See also* Performance of contract
personal service contracts 225
and product liability **100**, 251-252
remedies
acceleration clause **221**
accounting 225-226
damages 222
see also Damages
deposits **222**
down payments **222**
equitable 224-227
injunction 225
liquidated damages **221**-222
quantum meruit 226-227
rectification. *See* Rectification
rescission. *See* Rescission
specific performance 224-225
repudiation, **212**, 213
Fletton Ltd. v. Peat Marwick Ltd. 212
vs. tort liability 84, 252

warranties 208-209
British Columbia Company Act 441
British North America Act (BNA Act). *See Constitution Act* (1867)
Brownscombe v. Public Trustee 170
Builders' Lien Act 288-291, 297
Builders' liens 287-291, 298
execution of 291
holdbacks 288-289
payment into court 291
priority 291
registration of 288
rights of parties 289-291
secured creditors 290
and unjust enrichment 291
see also Mechanics' liens
Bulk sales **283**-284
Bulk Sales Act 284
Business Corporations Act 157, 297, 309, 386, 431, 435-462
Business organizations. *See* Corporations; Partnership; Societies; Sole proprietorship
Business Practices Act 251

C
Calmont Leasing Ltd. v. Kredl 441
Canada Act 22
Canada and British Insurance Companies Act 498
Canada Business Corporations Act 431, 437
Canada Gazette 486
Canada Labour Code 11, 364
Canadian Broadcasting Corp. v. Canada (Labour Relations Board) 365-366
Canada (Director of Investigation and Research) v. Southam Inc. 561
Canada Health Act 14
Canadian Bill of Rights 18
Canadian Charter of Rights and Freedoms 345
Canadian Human Rights Act 19, 20, 357
Canadian Labour Code 352, 361
CANCOPY 484, 486
Canon law 7
Capacity to contract
aliens 158
bankrupts 159
corporations 157-158, 435
drunkenness 155-157
Hardman v. Falk 155-156
infants 151-155
See also Infants
insanity 155-157
married women 158
Native Indians 157
trade unions 158
Capital City Savings and Credit Union Ltd. v. Milligan 324
Caveat emptor, 179, 245-246
Central London Property Trust, Ltd. v. High Trees House, Ltd. 144

Champerty **197**
Charlottetown Accord 30
Charter of Rights and Freedoms, 10, 11, 20-21, 22-30, 49, 58-63, 564
aboriginal rights 63, 157
collective bargaining 364
democratic rights 26-27, 58
and employment law 357-359
entrenchment of rights 23
equality rights 28, 60
language rights 28-29, 60-61
legal rights 27-28, 59-60
limitations 23-25
mobility rights 27, 59
personal freedoms 26, 58
Peterborough (City) v. Ramsden 22
picketing 364
pornography 23
right to strike 364
Section 1 23-24, 25
Section 33 24-25
Steralization Act 24
termination of employment 345
and union membership 364
Chartered Accounts Act 410
Chattels. *See* Personal property
Cheques 309, **311**-313
certification 312-313
countermand of payment 311, 312
death of drawer 312
postdated 311
stop payment 311-312
Child labour 360
Choses in action **195, 236, 272, 475**
C.I.F. contracts 238
Civil Code (Quebec) 5
Civil Enforcement Act 43, 44, 45, 279, 292
Civil Enforcement Agency 44, 45
Civil Enforcement Regulations 44
Civil law **5**
Civil litigation 30-33, 34-47
alternatives to 47-48
Clean Air Act 553
Clean Water Act 553
Consumer Glass Co. Ltd. v. Foundation Company of Canada Ltd. 34-35
enforcement 42-43. *See also* Enforcement
judgment 41-45
limitation periods 46-47. *See also* Limitation periods
remedies 42. *See also* Remedies
trial process 41
Class action lawsuits 80
Clean Air Act 553
Clean hands doctrine 226
Clean Water Act 553
C.O.D. contracts 238-239
Collection Practices Act 251, 259
Collective agreement 367
arbitration **369**-370
checkoff provision **370**

closed shop clause **370**
minimum period of 369
Rand Formula **370**
retroactivity of 369
union shop **370**, **374**
see also Collective bargaining; Trade
unions
Collective bargaining 362-374
bargaining agents **365**
bargaining unit **365**
collective agreements. *See* Collective
agreement
conciliation 368
disputes 363-364
essential services 373-374
good faith bargaining 367, 368
legislation. *See* Labour relations legislation
lockouts **370**-371
mediation **368**-369
organization of employees 364-367
picketing 371-373
public sector 373-374
ratification 367-368
strikes **370**-371
working to rule **371**
see also Trade unions
Colourable legislation 12-13
Combines Investigation Act 261
Common law 5, **6**, 7
environmental protection 550-552
Company Creditors' Arrangement Act 297
Competition 161
Competition Act 161, 260-261, 261-263,
443, 558
Competition Tribunal Act 262-263
Conditional Sales Act 275, 277
Conditional sales agreements. *See* Sale of
goods
Conditions 208-209
breach of. *See* Breach of contract
Sale of Goods Act. See Sale of Goods Act
see also Contractual terms
Condominiums
condominium associations 521-522
cooperatives 522
shared property 521
vertical title 521
Confederation 10
Confidential information
*Cadbury Schweppes Inc. v. FBI Foods
Ltd.* 492-494
common law duty 494
defined 494
e-mail 497
fiduciary duties. *See* Fiduciary
duties
fraud 497
remedies 496-497
theft 497
trade secrets 494-496
Consideration 125, 139-145

adequacy of 141
defined 140
existing duty 141-142
*Gilbert Steel Ltd. v. University
Construction Ltd.* 139
gratuitous promise **141**, 42
for guarantees 285-286
illegal 143
nature of 140-141
obligation to pay 143-144
out-of-court settlements 143
past 142
payment of lesser amount of debt
142-143
request for services 143-144
sealed documents 145
Constitution Act (1867) 10, 22
administrative law 563
environmental law 556
intellectual property 482
labour law 364
and negotiable instruments 308
Sections 91 and 92 55-57
Sections 91 and 92 11-15
unemployed workers 362
U.T.U. v. Central Western Railway 11
Constitution Act (1982) 10, 22-23
Section 29
Construction Lien Act 282
Construction liens. See Builders' liens
Constructive dismissal. *See* Termination
of employment
Consumer Credit Transactions Act 137, 251,
257, 258
Consumer Packaging and Labeling Act 264
Consumer Protection Act 257
Consumer protection legislation 186, 210
anti-competitive trade practices 262
Competition Act. See Competition Act
control of specific businesses 257-
258
credit-reporting practices 258-259
debt collection processes 259-260
door-to-door sales 256
enforcement of 263
federal legislation 260-264
government agencies 260
government investigation 258
implied terms 250
limitation of exemption clauses 251
misleading statements 254
moneylending transactions 254-255,
258-259
purpose of 261
referral selling 256-257, 263
responsibility for goods sold 251-253
Rushak v. Henneken 249-250
*Sumner Sports Inc., v. Pavillon Chasse
& Peche (440) Inc.* 261
unacceptable business practices
253-257
unconscionable transactions 254-255

see also Sale of Goods Act
Consumer transactions **250**
Contract
acceptance. *See* Acceptance
against public policy 160-163
assignment of 195-198. *See also*
Assignment
of bailment **209**
bilateral 126
breach of. *See* Breach of contract
capacity to. *See* Capacity to contract
C.I.F. 238
C.O.D. 238-239
collateral **253**
consensus 125, 127-128, 176, 236
Dickinson v. Dodds 127
consideration for. *See* Consideration
defined 125
employment 344-345
enforceability of 126, 159-162, 169,
see also Statute of Frauds
essential nature of 217
executed **153**
executory **153**
F.O.B. 238
form of 165-166
formal 126, 169
illegal 159-160
imposition of 250
inducement to. *See*
Misrepresentation
inducing breach of **117**
infants. *See* Capacity to contract;
Infants
insurance. *See* Insurance
intention 125, 163-165
Osorio et al. v. Cardona 163-164
interpretation. *See* Contractual terms
legality of 125, 159-163
offer. *See* Offer
one-sided. *See* Consideration,
gratuitous promise
option agreement 133
partially executed **153**
performance of. *See* Performance of
contract
personal services 225
privity of **100**, 193-199, 252
remedies for breach. *See* Breach of
contract; Remedies
requirements of 125
restraint of marriage 162
restraint of trade 160-161
standard form 134
Statute of Frauds. See Statute of Frauds
subsidiary **133**
termination of. *See* Termination of
contract
terms of. *See* Contractual terms
under seal 126, 145
unilateral 126
validity of 126

verbal 126
void 126, 159, 160, 176, 177, 178,
    180, 188, *see also* Mistake
voidable 153-154, 189, 190
written 126, *see also* Statute of Frauds
see also Contractual relationships
Contractual breach. *See* Breach of
    contract
Contractual relationships
    duress. *See* Duress
    infants. *See* Infants
    mistake. 176-181
    mistake. *See* Mistake
    quasi-contracts 129
    service contracts 129
    unconscionable transactions. *See*
        Unconscionable transactions
    undue influence. *See* Undue
        influence
    see also Contract
Contractual terms
    acceleration clause **221**
    ambiguous wording 182
    clear and unambiguous 128
    conditions precedent **216**
    conditions subsequent **216**
    construction approach 211
    exclusionary clauses. *See* Exemption
        clause
    exculpatory clauses. *See* Exemption
        clause
    exemption clause. *See* Exemption
        clause
    implied 182-183, 226
    and law of equity 226-227
    literal meaning 181
    misrepresentation. *See*
        Misrepresentation
    mistake. *See* Mistake
    parol evidence rule. *See* Parol
        evidence rule
    specified risk 238-239
    termination of agreement 215-216
Contributory negligence 114
    last clear chance doctrine 114
Contributory Negligence Act 114
Controlled Drugs and Substances Act 263
*Coote v. Hudson's Bay Company and Swift
    Canadian Con. Ltd.* 246, 252
Copyright 482-487, 546
    artistic works **482**
    computer software and hardware
        482-483
Copyright Board 486
    creation of 483
    creator 483
    dramatic works **482**
    fair dealing 485
    imprisonment for infringement 486
    infringement 483-487
    literary works **482**
    moral rights **483**

musical works **482**
ownership of 483
photocopying 484, 485
protection of 484-485
remedies for infringement. *See*
    Remedies
videotapes 484
Copyright Act 482-487
Corporate officers
    board of directors 454
    directors 440-444
    consumer protection legislation
        443-444
    environmental fines 443
    liability for wages 442-443
    payment of taxes 443, 444
    fiduciary duties. *See* Fiduciary
        duties
    managers 440-444
    officers 444-446
    promoters 445-446
    Roper v. Murdoch et al 444-445
    senior executives 444-446
Corporations **409**
    and agents 435-436
    annual reports 454
    assets of 433, 455-456
    and bankruptcy 297
    bonds 438-439
    borrowing by 438-439
    bylaws of 431-432
    capacity of 435
    capacity to contract 157
    corporate officers. *See* Corporate
        officers
Crown 157-158
    debentures **283**, 438
    discharge for bankruptcy 297
    dissolution of 453-454, 455-456
    distributing 439-**440**, 456
    employment law 350-351
    lifting corporate veil 434, 435
    limited liability **434**, 451-452
    management 454
    non-distributing 439-**440**, 451, 453,
        455, 456
    Salomon v. Salomon and Co. Ltd.
        432-433
    as separate legal entity 432-436
    shareholder liability 434-435
    societies. *See* Societies
    special act companies 430
    subsidiary 452
    succession 453-454
    taxes 452-453
    termination of 453, 455-456
    transferability of 453-454
    see also Incorporation
Coull v. Kolbuc 154
Courts 30-34
    appeal courts 31, 32
    Court of Appeal 33

Court of Appeal (Alberta) 34, 349,
    350
Court of Chancery **8**
Court of common pleas **7**
Court of king's bench **7**
Court of Queen's Bench (Alberta)
    32, 33, 34, 39-41, 43, 45, 48, 324,
    572
    forms: Counterclaim 39
        Statement of Claim 39
        Statement of Defence 39, 563
    criminal 30, 31-33
    federal 33-34
    Federal Court 33-34
    payment into 40
    provincial 31-33
    Supreme Court of Canada. *See*
        Supreme Court of Canada
    Tax Court 33-34
    trial court 31
Credit Counselling Services of Alberta
    Ltd. 298
Creditors
    of corporations 432-435, 438-439
    frauds against 284, 295-297
    protection of 284, *see also Personal
        Property Security Act* (PPSA)
    secured. *See Personal Property Security
        Act* (PPSA)
    unsecured 283-284, 292-294
Criminal Code, 32, 83, 553

D
Damages **42**
    accounting for profits **486**
    copyright infringement 486
    for deceit 188
    defamation. *See* Defamation
    economic loss 107
    fraudulent misrepresentation 188
    general **90**
    liquidated **221**-222
    material loss 111
    mitigation 223-224
    mitigation of 532
    punitive **42**, **90**-91, **486**
    remoteness 223
    special **90**
    when contract breached 222-224
    wrongful dismissal 346, 350-351
    see also Remedies
Dangerous substances. *See* Strict
    liability
Dawson, R.M. 561
Debenture **283**
Debt
    collection 259-260
    of corporations 438-439
    orderly payment of 298
    partial payment of 215
    payment of 206
    security for 271-285

Debtor
consumer proposals 293
discharge for bankruptcy 296-297
imprisonment 43
see also Bankruptcy
Deceit **117**
Defamation **92**-96
absolute privilege **94**-95
damages 92, 96
dead person 93
defenses 94-96
fair comment 92, 95-96
freedom of expression 95
(Identity of parties withheld - case) 92
justification 94
libel **94**
qualified privilege 92, **95**
slander **94**
and truth **94**
Defamation Act 94-95
Defenses
against holder in due course 321-323
against remote holder 323-324
consent 86
defect of title 323-324
defense of fair comment. *See* Defamation
defense of qualified privilege. *See* Defamation
mere personal 325
negligence. *See* Negligence
non est factum 180-181
promissory estoppel. *See* promissory estoppel
real 321-323
self-defense 87
Democratic Government and Politics 562
Department of Consumer and Corporate Affairs 261
Department of Consumer and Corporate Affairs Act 261
Department of the Environment Act 553
Dependent Adults Act 400
Deposits **222**
and frustration 219, 220
Derrickson v. Derrickson 13
Direct Sales Cancellation Act 183, 186, 251, 256-258
Directors. *See* Corporate officers
Discharge
accord and satisfaction **215**
bilateral **214**
by agreement 213-216
Gregorio v. Intrans-Corp. 213-214, 215
unilateral **214**
Discovery process 39-40
Dismissal. *See* Termination of employment
Display of goods 129-130
Division of powers 11-15
Divorce Act 32
Dower Act 515
Down payment **222**

Duress 189-190
Duty 98-101
and consideration
existence of 98-101
innkeepers 105-106, 479-480
of occupier 103-105
to act in good faith 189

E
Economic loss 107-108
Emergency Medical Aid Act 101
Employees 494
confidential information 195
exculpatory clause
fiduciary duties. *See* Fiduciary duties
notice by 345, 349, 355
obligations of 344
organization of. *See* Collective bargaining
and secondary picketing 372-373
trade secrets 495
Employers
fidelity bond **505**
liability of 351-352, 410, 416
obligations of 344
notice by 345-351, 355
Employment
and agency 343
broad definition 343
contracts 344-345
dangerous working conditions 347
employees. *See* Employees
employer. *See* Employers
health and safety conditions 361-362
and human rights. *See* Human rights
independent contractor 341, 342, 343
Jaremko v. A.E. LePage Real Estate Services Ltd. 341-342
law of master and servant 344-362
reinstatement 351
restrictive covenant 345, 160-161
standards. *See* Employment standards
termination. *See* Termination of employment
wrongful hiring 348
Employment Equity Act 359
Employment insurance 362
Employment Insurance Act 362
Employment relationship 343
broad definition 343
control test 342
organization test 342-343
Employment standards 352-353
child labour and persons with disabilities 355-356, 360
complaints 356
employment insurance 362
health and safety 361-362
hours of work and overtime 354
human rights 357-360

Machtinger v. HOJ Industries Ltd. 352-353
maternity and adoption benefits 355
minimum standards 353, 354
minimum wage 353
notice of termination 355
payment of earnings 353-354
rcovery provisions 356-357
termination 355
vacation and holiday entitlements 354-355
workers' compensation 360-361
Employment Standards Act 352, 354-357
Employment Standards Code 346, 347, 352-357, 360
Employment Standards Regulation AR 14/97 353, 354, 360
Eng v. Evans 165
Enforcement 42-43
attachment of debt **45**
attachment order 45-46
garnishment 45
seizure of property 44-45. *See also* Seizure
Environmental Assessment Act 558-559
Environmental law
at common law 550-551
audits 557
criminal prosecution of offences 556, 558
economic concerns 559-560
enforcement of **555**
envirmental assessment process 553-554
federal legislation 556-558
government jurisdiction 553
National Environmental Policy Act (1969) 558
provincial legislation 553-556
R. v. Consolidated Maybrun Mines Ltd. 552, 555
regulatory role of government 549
riparian rights 550, 551
strict liability 551, 556
Environmental Protection Act, 551, 552, 553, 556-558
Environmental Protection and Enhancement Act 443, 553-556, 559
Equitable
contractual terms 183
estoppel. *See* Promissory estoppel
remedies 224-227
Equity, law of **8**-9
Estoppel. *See* Agency; Partnership; Promissory estoppel
Exchequer court **7**
Exclusionary clause. *See* Exemption clause
Exculpatory clause. *See* Exemption clause
Exemption clause, 195, 209-210, 211, 242, 246, 479
Explosives Act 264

F

Factoring of accounts receivable 196-197
Failure to act 101
Fair Trading Act 137, 210, 251, 255, 256, 257, 258, 259, 263, 265
Fairness. *See* Equity
False imprisonment **89**-91
　false arrest 89
Family Relations Act 13
Fayant v. Campbell's Maple Village 357
Fidelity bond **505**
Fiduciary duties
　　agents **390**, 389-393
　　confidential information 494
　　corporate officers 445
　　directors 441
　　employees 349
　　Ocean City Realty Ltd. v. A & M Holdings Ltd. et al 389-390
　　partnership 412, 418
Fisheries Act 557
Floating charges 282-**283**
F.O.B. contracts 238
The Food and Drug Act 263
Foreign Insurance Companies Act 498
Franchise Act 455
Fraudulent Conveyances Act 284, 296
Fraudulent Creditors Act 284
Fraudulent misrepresentation. *See* Misrepresentation
Fraudulent preference 284, 296-297, *see also* Fraudulent transfers
Fraudulent Preferences Act 284
Fraudulent transfers 284, **295**-296
Freedom of expression 22, 23-24, 26, 58, 69
　　see also Defamation
French Civil Code 5
Frustration
　　British Columbia (Minister of Crown Lands) v. Cressey Development Corp. 216-217
　　circumstances constituting 218
　　circumstances not constituting 218-219
　　and deposits 219, 220
　　effect of 219
Frustrated Contracts Act 217, 220, 527
　　Law Reform Act 219
　　and legislation 219-220
　　not shared mistake 217-218
　　reimbursement for expenses 220
　　self-induced 216, **218**
　　and strict liability 217
　　termination of agency 398-399
　　termination of contract 217
Fundamental breach. *See* Breach of contract

G

Garagemen's Lien Act 277, 481
Garnishment. *See* Enforcement
Good faith, *see also* Collective bargaining

Goods

　　chose in action **236**, **272**
　　defined **236**
　　effect of bankruptcy 295
　　exaggerated claims 175
　　fungibles **478**
　　Sale of Goods Act. See Sale of Goods Act
　　sale of. *See* Sale of goods
　　seizure of 279-281
　　see also Sale of goods; Sale of Goods Act
Government
　　protection of environment 550-560
　　regulatory role 549
Government agencies 4
The Government of Canada 561
Guarantees, 271, **285**-287, 298
　　continuing **287**
　　contractual requirements 285
　　duties of creditor 286
　　duties of guarantor 286-287
Guarantees Acknowledgment Act 168, 285
　　guarantor's defences 287
　　indemnity **285**
　　release of guarantor 286

H

Habeas Corpus Act 571
Haig v. Bamford 108
Hamilton & Olsen Surveys Ltd. v. Otto 350
Hazardous Chemicals Act 553
Hazardous Products Act 263
Hazardous Products Marketing Act 264
Hazardous products. *See* Sale of goods
Highway Traffic Act 84, 352
Hedley Byrne v. Heller 107
Hodgetts, J.E. 562
Holdbacks 288-**289**
Holmes, Oliver Wendell 3
Hoy v. Lozanovski 176
Human rights 18-22
　　Central Okanagan School District No. v. Renaud 18-19
　　disability 19
　　in employment law 357-360
　　harassment of employee 358
　　legislation 18-22
　　mandatory retirement 359
　　pay equity 359
　　religious beliefs 19
　　sexual discrimination 19
　　sexual orientation 19, 20-21
Human Rights, Citizenship and Multiculturalism Act 19, 345, 347, 357-360
Hunter v. Southam Inc. 21

I

Inadvertent conduct. *See* Negligence
Incorporation
　　advantages of 451-454
　　articles of **431**-432, 462-467

　　by letters patent 430-**431**
　　certificate of **431**
　　cost of 455
　　disadvantages of 454-455
　　forms: Articles of Incorporation 462-467
　　　　Notice of Directors 470-471
　　　　Notice of Address 468-469
　　letters patent **431**
　　limited liability 451-452
　　memorandum of association 431
　　pre-incorporation contracts 446
　　registration of 430-431
　　royal charter 430
　　see also Corporations
Indemnity 285
Indian Act 13, 157
Individual's Rights Protection Act 19, 20-21
Industrial Design Act 492
Infancy law. *See* Infants
Infants 151-155
　　Age of Majority Act 151
　　beneficial contracts of service 152
　　breach of contract 153-154
　　necessaries **151**-152, 154
　　parents' liability 154
　　ratification of contracts 153
　　tort liability 154-155
　　voidable contracts 153-154
Infants Relief Act 154
Injunction **225**
Injurious falsehood 117-**118**, 497
Innkeepers. 105 *See also* Duty
Innkeeper's Act 105-106, 479-480
Insanity. *See* Capacity to contract
Insolvency. *See* Bankruptcy
Insurance
　　adjusters 505
　　agents 505
　　beneficiary **499**
　　business interruption 499
　　co-insurance clause 498-499
　　as compensation 497
　　contribution principle **504**
　　depreciation value 504
　　disability 499
　　duty to disclose 502-503
　　insurable interest **162**, 500-501
　　insured **498**
　　insurer **498**
　　knowledge of fraud 504
　　liability 500
　　life and health 499
　　policy endorsement **498**
　　premiums 498
　　property 498-499
　　replacement value 504
　　right of salvage 504
　　subrogation 502, 503
　　utmost good faith 502-503
　　Wellington Insurance Co. Ltd. v. Armac Diving Services Ltd. 501-502

Insurance Act 195, 501, 502-503, 504
Insurance Companies Act 498
Intellectual property 475, 481-497
    confidential information. *See*
        Confidential information
    contract protection 495
    copyright. *See* Copyright
    industrial designs 492
    patents. *See* Patents
    purpose of 481
    tort law 496-497
    trademarks 489-492
Intentional torts
    assault and battery 85-87
Cole v. Turner 86
    defamation. *See* Defamation
    false imprisonment. *See* False
        imprisonment
Malette v. Shulman 85
    private nuisance. *See* Private nuisance
    trespass. *See* Trespass
Interest Act 258
Interest rates 255
International Conventions Implementation Act 249
International Sale of Goods Act 249
Internet 497
Interpretation Act 563

J
Job action. *See* Collective bargaining
Judicature Act 143, 196, 537, 538
Judicature Amendment Act 537, 538
Judicial review 568-576
    availability of 569-570
    declaratory judgment **571**-572, 573, 575
    injunction **572**
    prerogative writs 570-571
    certiorari **571**, 572
    habeas corpus **570**-571
    mandamus **571**, 572
    Municipal Government Act 572
    Planning Act 573
    prohibition **571**, 572
    privative clauses 573-575, **574**
    procedure 572-573
    supervisory capacity 569
Judicial Review Procedure Act 569, 572
Just cause. *See* Termination of employment

K
Kripps v. Touche Ross & Co. et al. 14
Kroker et al. v. Midtown Mortgage Loans Ltd. et al. 255

L
Labour Relations Act 364
Labour relations boards. *See*
    Administrative tribunals
Labour Relations Code 158, 366, 367-370, 373, 374, 574

Labour relations legislation
    jurisdictional disputes **364**
    labour relations boards. *See*
        Administrative tribunals
    Port Alberni 406
    recognition disputes **363**
    rights disputes **364**
Laches **226**
Land. *See* Real property; Sale of land; Title
Land Titles Act 166, 167, 194, 518, 521, 523, 533, 534, 537
Land titles system
    Curtain Principle 513
    Insurance Principle 513-514
    Mirror Principle 513
    Torrens Land title system 513, 521, 533
Landlord and Tenant Act 532
Landlord and tenant. *See* Leases
Law 2-6
Law and Equity Act 166
Law of equity. *See* Equity
Law of Property Act 280, 517, 539
Law of Property Amendment Act 539
Law merchant 7
Leases
    agreement for lease **523**
Applewood Lane West Ltd. v. Scott et al. 530
    commercial tenancies 525-529
    distress **529**
    exclusive possession 522, 523
    forfeiture **529**
    frustration 523, 527
    leasehold estates 522-523
    mitigation of losses 532
    notice of increased rent 531
    notice period 531
    periodic tenancy **524**
    quiet enjoyment 525
    registration 523
    remedies for breach 528-529
    repair of premises 526
    requirement for writing 523
    residential tenancies 530-532
    security deposit 531-532
    sublet of 524
    tenancy at sufferance **524**-525
    tenancy at will **524**
    tenants' obligations 527-528
    term lease **524**
    termination of 526-527
    vacant possession 525
Legal philosophy 2-3
Legal positivism **3**
Legal realism **3**
Legislation. *See* Statutes
Letters of credit 329-332
    in export/import 330-331
    international trade 330-331
    69971 Manitoba Ltd. v. National Bank of Canada 329-330

Letters patent. *See* Incorporation
Liability
    of employer. *See* Employer
    insurance 500
    limited. *See* Corporations;
        Exemption clause
    occupiers' 103-105, 115, 529
    strict. *See* Environmental law; Strict liability
    of tenant 528, 529
    tort. *See* Tort liability
    vicarious. *See* Vicarious liability
Libel. *See* Defamation
Licensing of Trades and Business Act 256
Liens 44, **244**, 277, 288
see also Builders' liens; Mechanics' liens
Limitations Act 47
Limitation of Actions Act 36, 47, 226
Limitation periods 46-47
Lockouts **370**-371
Loewen Group 232
Lord's Day Act 26

M
Magna Carta 10
Maiklen v. Springbank Oil & Gas Ltd. 441
Matrimonial Property Act 168
McWilliam v. Morris 7
Mechanics' Lien Act 288
Mechanics' liens 288
    see also Builders' liens
Mediation 57, 58, **368**-369
Meech Lake Accord 29
Mergers 262
Misfeasance **101**
Misrepresentation 107-109, 183, 188
    allegation of fact 184-185
    by non-disclosure 185
    by silence 185
    defined 184
    duty of care 107-109
    false statement 185-186
    fraudulent 187-188, 382
    inducement to contract 186
    innocent 186-187
Metropolitan Stores of Canada Ltd. v. Nova Construction Co. 183-184
    negligent 107-109, 188
    recession. *See* Remedies
    of salespeople 185
    as term of contract 186
Mistake 176-183, **323**
    ambiguous term 181-182
    caveat emptor. *See* Caveat emptor
    literal meaning 181
    misunderstanding 178
    Moss v. Chin 179
    negotiable instruments 323
    non est factum 180-181
    one-sided 179-180
    parol evidence rule. *See* Parol evidence rule

reasonable person test 181
rectification. *See* Rectification
Sale of goods 236
serious 176
shared **177**, 217-218
void contract 176
Morrow et al. v. Royal Insurance Co. of Canada 503
Mortgages **520**, 533-541
   amortization period **536**
   breach of contract 537, 540
   collateral **535**
   deficiency judgment 538, 539
   equity of redemption **533**-534
   foreclosure **534**-535, 536-541
   Final Order for Foreclosure 539
   insured **535**
   judicial sale 537-541
   mortgagee **533**
   mortgagor **533**
   Order Confirming Sale 539
   Order Nisi/Order for Sale 539
   possession by mortgagee 540
   power of sale 539
   redemption period 539
   Regional Trust Co. v. Avco Financial Services Realty Ltd. 536-537
   remedies on default 536-541
   Rice Order 537, 539
   second 535, 536, 537
   term of **536**
Motor Vehicle Accident Claims Act 107
Motor Vehicle Safety Act 264
Municipal Government Act 572

N
National Environmental Policy Act (1969) 558
National Housing Act 538, 410-12, 415-18, 421-23
National Labor Relations Act 363
Natural law theory **2**-3
Natural Resources Transfer Agreement Act 513
Necessaries. *See* Capacity to contract, infants
Negligence
   Crocker v. Sundance Northwest Resorts Ltd. 96-97
   defenses 112-115
   contributory negligence. *See* Contributory negligence
   crumbling skull rule **113**
   remoteness **112**-113
   thin skull rule **113**
   voluntarily assumed risk 114-115
   duty. *See* Duty
   economic loss 107
   legislated changes 104-105, 106, 252
   misfeasance **101**
   misrepresentation 188
   nonfeasance **101**

product liability **100**-101, 252
reasonable foreseeability test **98**, 108, 109, 112
reasonable person test **97**-98, 101-102, 103, 109-110
res ipsa loquitur. See Res ipsa loquitur
and risk 102
standard of care 101-102
strict liability. *See* Strict liability
Negligence Act 114
Negligent misstatement 107-109
Negligent words. *See* Negligent misstatement
Negotiability 315-318
   Bank of British Columbia v. Coopers & Lybrand Ltd. et al. 315
   characteristics of 315-318
Negotiable instruments **199**, **306**, 309-314
   bearer instrument **314**
   bills of exchange. *See* Bills of exchange
   characteristics of 307-308
   cheques. *See* Cheques
   defenses
      defect of title **323**-324
      discharged **321**-322
      forgery 321
      incapacity **322**-323
      lack of delivery of incomplete instrument 322
      material alteration **323**
      mere personal 325
      mistake **323**
      partial failure of consideration **325**
      real **321**-323
      right of setoff **325**
   defined 306
   drawee **309**, 310, 327-328
   drawer **309**, 310, 311, 321
   endorsements 314-315, 325-327
   endorsers 325-327
   holder in due course **307**, 318-323, 328
   instrument of credit 308
   IOU 314
   letters of credit. *See* Letters of credit
   negotiability 315-318
   order or direction to pay **309**
   order instrument **314**
   payee 309-310, 311, 312, 325
   promises **309**, 313
   promissory notes. *See* Promissory notes
   remote holder **323**-324
   transferability of 307
   unconditional 316
No-fault system 107
Non est factum 180-181
Non-competition covenant 150, 160-161
Non-profit organizations 432
Nonfeasance **101**
"Notwithstanding clause". *See Charter of Rights and Freedoms,* Section 33

O
Occupational Health and Safety Act 361-362
Occupiers' Liability Act 82, 104-105, 115, 527
Offer 128-134
   by conduct 130
   communication of 130-131
   counteroffer 132-133, 135
   death of offeror 132
   defective 135-136
   end of 131-133
   invitation to treat 129-130
   irrevocable 133-134
   reasonable time limit on 131
   rejection of 132
   revocation of 132, 138-139
Offer to settle 40
Ontario v. Ron Engineering (1981) 119 D.L.R. (3rd) 267 (p. 134)
O.P.S.E.V. v. Air-Dale Ltd. 11
Order bills of lading **239**
Orderly Payment of Debts Program 298

P
Paramountcy **13**
   see also Division of powers
Parks West Mall Ltd. v. Hinton (Town) 573
Parliamentary supremacy. *See* Paramountcy
Parol evidence rule **182**, 184
Parris v. Reber 34
Partnership **409**, **411**-423
   advantages of 419-420
   and agency law 415-416
   agreement 414-415
   assets and liabilities 421-422
   by inadvertence 413-414, 415
   co-ownership of property 412, 413
   cost of 420
   creation of 411-415
   defined 411
   dissolution of 420-421
   and estoppel 414-415
   fiduciary duties. *See* Fiduciary duties
   legislation 411
   liability 416-417
      joint **417**
      joint and several **417**
      unlimited 416-417
      vicarious 416
   limited 422-423
   notice of dissolution 420-421
   Olson v. Gullo 411-412
   registration of 417-418
   rights and obligations 418-419
   transferability 453-454
   unanimous consent 419
Partnership Act, 410-423
Passage of Bills 15-16
Passing off **118**
Patent Act 487, 489
Patents
   claims statements 488

creation of 487-489
disclosure required for 488
generic drugs 489
government-granted monopoly 487
of ideas 489
infringement 489
pending 488
priority of 488
protection of 487
registration of 487-489
remedies 489
specifications 488
Pawnbroker 272
Payment into court 40
Peace, order and good government 12
Perfection. *See Personal Property Security Act* (PPSA)
Performance of contract
by installments 207-208
conditions **208**-209
independent obligations 207-208
part performance 226
reasonable time and place 206-**207**
refusal of 205
substantial 205
tender of 205-207
Personal Directives Act 400
Personal property **272**-274, 475, 476-477
Amo Containers Ltd. v. Mobil Oil Canada, Ltd. 477
bailment 477-481
chattels **272**, **475**, 476, 478
finder 476-477
fixtures **476**
Personal Property Security Act. See Personal Property Security Act (PPSA)
taxi licenses 475
trade fixtures 476
see also Security
Personal Propety Registry 43, 44, 45
Personal Property Security Act (PPSA), 198, 237, 273, 274-282, 283, 298
applicability of 277
attachment 277-278
enforcement of court order 279-280
flexibility of 276-277
perfection 277-278
and possessory liens 277
possession taken 279-280
Re Foster 276-277
remedies under 278-282
repayment of deficit 281-282
repossession 280
retention of collateral 281
rights on default 278-282
Royal Bank of Canada v. J. Segreto Construction Ltd. 278-279
searches under 275
seizure of goods 279-280
Philosophy. *See* Legal philosophy
Picketing 371-373

POGG. *See* Peace, order and good government
Police Officers Collective Bargaining Act 373
Possessory Liens Act 277,481
Postbox rule. *See* Acceptance
Power of attorney 383
Powers of Attorney Act 400
Power of attorney 6-7
Precedent 6-7
see also Stare decisis
Prepayment. *See* Deposits; Down payment
Pre-trial conferences 40
Prerogative writs. *See* Judicial review
Priority 290-291
attachment of security 277-278
builders' liens. *See* Builders' liens
perfection of security 277-278
registration under PPSA 275
Privacy Act 496
Private law **4**
Private nuisance **91**-92
noise and fumes 91
Privity of contract. *See* Contract
Proceedings Against the Crown Act 575
Procedural fairness, rules of 27, 564-568
Procedural law **4**
Product liability
Donoghue v. Stevenson 98-100, 252
negligence. *See* Negligence
Sale of Goods Act 246
Professional liability
negligent misstatement. *See* Negligent misstatement
reasonable person 109-110
Promissory estoppel, 139-140, **144**-145
Promissory notes, 308, 309, 310, 313-314, 316
conditional sale agreements 328
consumer notes 328-329
Promoters 445-446
Property 473, 475
chose in action. *See* Choses in action
"found" 477
intellectual property. *See* Intellectual property
personal property. *See* Personal property
real property. *See* Real property
Protection of Persons Acting Under Statute Act 576
Provincial Court Act 32, 37
Provincial Court of Alberta 32, 34, 38
Civil Division 32-33, 34, 35, 36-39, 324
forms:
Affidavit of Service 37, 74
Certificate of Judgment 38
Civil Claim 36-38, 72
Dispute Note 37-38, 73
Notice of Appeal 38-39
Notice of Withdrawal 37

Notice to Attend 38
- Criminal Division 32, 34
Traffic Division 32, 33
Family Division 32, 34
Youth Division 32, 34
Prudence 97-98
Public law **4**
Public Service Employee Relations Act 364-373

Q
Qualified privilege. *See* Defamation
Quantum meruit 226-227
Quebec Civil Code 5

R
Racial Discrimination Act 18
Rasanen v. Rosemount Investments Ltd. 357
Real Estate Act 400
Real property **272**, 473, 475, 511-522
adverse possession **518**
building scheme **519**
dominant tenement 517
estate in free simple **514**
fee simple 514
fixtures **528**
freehold estates **515**
homestead rights **515**
interest in land 514-516
joint tenancy **519**
leasehold estates **515**-516, 522-523
lesser interests in land 516-519
life estate 514-515
meaning of "sale" 178
mineral rights 518
privity of contract 194
remainderman **514**
restrictive covenants **518**
reversionary interest **514**
right of dower **515**
Dower Act 515
right to use of
easement **517**
easement by prescription **517**
license **517**
profit a prendre **518**
public easements **517**
right of way **517**
and *Sale of Goods Act* 236
servient tenement 517
tenancy in common **519**
Wells v. Wells 516, 517
see also Condominiums; Sale of land
Real Property Statutes Amendment Act 539
Reasonable foreseeability test. *See* Negligence
Reasonable person test 165
see also Agency; Contract; Mistake; Negligence
Receivership. *See* Bankruptcy
Rectification 177-178, 220-221
Regulations **10**

Remedies
    accounting **42**
    breach of lease. *See* Leases
    breach of privacy 496
    clean hands doctrine 226
    confidential information 496-497
    copyright infringement
    Anton Piller order **485**-496
    damages **486**
    interlocutory injunction **485**
    permanent injunction **486**
    damages. *See* Damages
    declaration **42**
    equitable 224-227
    and hardship 226
    injunctions **42**, 89
    laches **226**
    pre-judgment 45-46
    rectification. *See* Rectification
    repossession 279
    rescission. *See* Rescission
    specific performance **42**
    under PPSA 278-282
Repudiation. *See* Breach of contract
Res ipsa loquitur 101, **102**-103
Rescission 186-187, 188, 220-221
Residential Tenancies Act 207, 220, 516,
    523, 524, 525, 527, 530-532
Restraint of trade 160-161
Revised Statutes 15
Revised Statutes of Alberta (1980) 15
Revised Statutes of Canada 15
Riparian rights 550, 551
Ripplinger v. Gadd v. London Drugs Ltd.
    et al. 246
Roman law 7
Rosseway v. Canadian Kenworth Ltd. 246
Royal Bank of Canada v. Bauman 317
Rules of Court 39, 572
Rule of law **10**, **561**-562
R. v. Keegstra 13

S
Safety boards 361-362
Said v. Butt 395
Sale of goods
    and bankruptcy of purchaser 248
    bill of lading **239**
    bona fide purchaser 284
    bulk sales 283-284
    by description 244
    conditional sale **237**, 273-274, 328
    contributory negligence 245
    damages on default 249
    effect of bankruptcy 294
    hazardous products 253, 263-264,
        see also Environmental law
    order bill of lading **239**
    remedies on default 247-249
    rights and obligations of parties
        242-243
    sale defined **238**

Sale of Goods Act. See Sale of Goods Act
    seller's lien **247**
    specified risk 238-239
Statute of Frauds 237-238
    stoppage *in transitu* **247**-248
    transfer of title 238, 239-241
Sale of Goods Act 134, 144, 152, 168, 177,
    183, 208-209, 210, 214, 220, 235-253,
    277
    agreement to sell **238**
    application of 242
    and barter transactions 237
    caveat emptor 245-246
    and commercial transactions 242
    conditional sale 237
    conditions and warranties 243
    and consumer protection
        legislation 248-249, 249-253
    contracting out of, 235, 243, 246,
        247
    damages 249
    delivery 247
    excluded transactions 236
    exemption clauses 242, 246
    fitness of goods 244-246
    food poisoning 252-253
    goods free from charge or
        encumbrance 244
    Hunter Engineering Co. v. Syncrude
        Canada Ltd 242
    implied contractual terms 235, 243,
        247
    merchantable quality **245**-246
    monetary consideration 237
    product liability 245
    quiet possession of goods **243**-244
    reasonable price 247
    requirement of writing 237-238
    risk **238**
    risk follows title 238
    sale **238**
    sale by description 244
    samples 246
    and service contracts 236
    specified risk 238-239
    and title. *See* Title
    transfer of goods 238
Sale of land
    agreement for sale **520**
    deed **520**
    grant of title **520**
    land titles system **521**
    mortgages. *See* Mortgages
    option agreement **520**
    registration of 520-521
    registry system 521
    Torrens System **521**
    transfer of 520-521
    see also Real property
Salomon v. Salomon and Co. Ltd. 434
Saskatchewan Act (1905) 10
Sealed documents. *See* Contract

Secured creditors 44
Security 298
    anticipated crops 282
    assignment 273-274
    assignment of book accounts 274,
        277
    attachment. *See Personal Property*
        Security Act (PPSA)
    chattel mortgages **274**, 277
    collateral 280
    conditional sales 273-274, 275, 277
    floating charges 282-**283**
    intangibles as 274
    perfection. *See Personal Property*
        Security Act (PPSA)
    personal property. *see also Personal*
        Property Security Act (PPSA)
        272-274
    pledge 277
    priority of. *See* Priority
    unsecured. *See* Bulk sales
Securities Act 440, 445
Seizure 44-45
    forms:
        Affidavit in Support of
            Garnishee Summons 45
        Bailee's Undertaking 44
        Garnishee summons 45, 46,
            78-79
        Notice of objection to seizure
            44, 77
        Notice of seizure 44,76
Sexual harassment 358-359
Shareholders
    agreements 451, 455
    board of directors 454
    non-distributing corporations 448,
        449, 451, 452, 453, 456
    corporate statements 448
    derivative action 441, 449-450
    duty to 440-441
    meetings 448-449, 454
    minority, 448, 449, 450, 455
    obligations of 447, 454
    ownership of corporation 433
    preferred 437
    proxy **448**-449
    relief from oppression 450
    representative action 441, 449
    Richardson Greenshields of Canada
        Ltd. v. Kalmacoff 446-447, 449
    right to dividend 451
    right to view records 448
    right to vote 448
    see also Corporations; Shares
Shares 436
    dividends 437, 451
    par value **436**-437
    preferred **437**-438, 447
    special 437
    transferability 453-454
    see also Corporations; Shareholders

Slander. *See* Defamation
SOCAN 4
Societies **409**, 432
Societies Act 409, 432
Sole proprietorship **409**-411
    government regulations 409-411
    professionals 410-411
    unlimited liability **410**
Southern Transportation Ltd. v. Valgardson
    434
Specific performance **224**-225
Stare decisis **6**-7
    see also Precedent
Statement of claim **39**
Statement of defense **39**, 563
Status Report 44
Statutes of Alberta 15
Statute of Frauds 126, 285
    agency contract 382-383
    discharge by agreement 214
    effect of 170
    evidence in writing 168-170, 345
    goods in excess of minimum value
        168
    guarantees 167-168
    lease 523
    part performance 170
    performance in one year 167
    promise of executor 168
    promises in consideration of
        marriage 168
    Matrimonial Property Act 168
    requirement of writing 166-167
    and sale of goods 237-238
    title to land 167
Statute of Limitations 517
Statute of Westminster (1931) 10
Statutes 9-10, 15-17
Statutes of Canada 15
Stevenson v. Hilty (Canada Ltd.) 192
Strict liability, 100, 115-116, 551, 556
Strikes **370**-371
Subrogation. *See* Insurance
Substantive law **4**, 35
Successor rights 11
"Sunset" clause 25
Supreme Court of Canada 7, 33, 34
    division of powers 11-15
Surety bond **505**
Surrogate Court (Alberta) 33, 34

T
Technical Institutes Act 362
Termination of contract
    discharge by agreement 213-216
    frustration. *See* Frustration
    ongoing contractual relationship
        215-216
    Statute of Frauds 214
Termination of employment 345-351
    compensation for 345-346
    constructive dismissal 349-**350**

disabled workers 347
failure to perform 347
human rights legislation 347
just cause **346**-347, 348
pay in lieu of notice **345**
probationary period 346
proper notice 345-346, 347, 349,
    350
reasonable notice **345**-346, 349-350
voluntary 345
wrongful dismissal 346, **348**, 349-
    350, 351
Textile Labeling Act 264
T.G. Bright and Company v. Kerr 397
Title
    defect of title defenses **323**-324
    guarantee of 521
    knowledge of defect in 320
    and risk 238-241
    rules for determining 239-241
    transfer of 239-241
    under *Sale of Goods Act* 243-244
Tort liability
    of agents 397-398
    "but for" test **111**
    of children, *see also* Infants 109-111
    of employer 351-352
    general principles of 83-85
    of parents 110
    vicarious liability. *See* Vicarious
        liability
Tortfeasors and Contributory Negligence Act
    245
Torts
    breach of privacy 496
    causation 111-112
    committed by government 575
    conversion **117**-118
    deceit. *See* Deceit
    defamation. *See* Defamation
    false imprisonment. *See* False
        imprisonment
    inducing breach of contract. *See*
        Contract
    injurious falsehood. *See* Injurious
        falsehood
    intentional. *See* Intentional torts
    material loss 111
    negligence. *See* Negligence
    negligent misstatement. *See*
        Negligent misstatement
    nuisance 550-551
    passing off. *See* Passing off
    private nuisance. *See* Private
        nuisance
    trespass to land. *See* Trespass
Trade Practices Act, 251
Trade unions
    bargaining agent **365**
    certification 364-365
    certification of 364-367
    employer organizations **367**

organization of 374
picketing 371-374
ratification of collective agreement
    367-368
unfair labour practices 365-367
see also Capacity to contract;
    Collective agreement; Collective
    bargaining
Trademark Journal 489
Trademarks **489**-492, 546
    infringement 490
    passing-off action **491**-492
    registration of 489-490
    remedies 490
Transportation of Dangerous Goods Act 557
Trespass 87-89
    continuing **89**
    indirect 88
    to land **87**-89
    to person 86-87
    see also False imprisonment
Trusts, privity of contract **194**-195
Trusts & Guar. Co. v. Rice 539

U
Ultra vires 13
Unconscionable transactions 191-**192**-
    193, 254-255
Unconscionable Transactions Act 193, 255,
    258
    Woods v. Hubley 191-192
Undue influence 190-191
Unfair Trade Practices Act 251, 253, 254,
    255, 258, 443
Unions. *See* Collective bargaining; Trade
    unions
Unjust enrichment, *see also* Equitable;
    Equity 291
Unsolicited goods 136-137
U.T.U. v. Central Western Railway 11

V
Vicarious liability **84**-85
    and agency 381, 397-398
    of partner 416
    sole proprietor 410
Vicarious performance **197**
Virani v. Edwards 503
Volenti non fit injuria 114-115
Vriend v. Alberta 19, 20-21

W
Wagner Act 363, 364
Walt Disney Productionis v. Triple Five Corp.
    491
War crimes tribunals 3
Warehouseman's Lien Act 481
Warranty **208**-209
    breach of. *See* Breach of contract
Wartime Labour Relations Regulations
    363
Weights and Measures Act 264

Wickberg v. Patterson 114
Winding Up and Restructuring Act 298
Wong v. Shell Canada Ltd. 357
Workers' compensation 360-361
Workers' Compensation Act 44, 197, 347

Writ of enforcement 43, 44, 45, 75
Wrongful conduct. *See* Tort liability
Wrongful dismissal. *See* Termination of
  employment

Y
Young Offenders Act 32